FEDERAL INCOME, ESTATE, AND GIFT TAX ASPECTS FOR SEPARATION AND DIVORCE

ROBERT A. ROMBRO

AMERICAN BAR ASSOCIATION
Family Law Section

Cover design by Sara Wadford/ABA Design

Printed in the United States of America.

28 27 26 25 24   5 4 3 2 1

ISBN 978-1-63905-363-6

A catalog record for this book is available from the Library of Congress.

For my wife, Lisa, and my son, Lance

Contents

2 Child Support 59

3 Dependency Exemption for Child 77

Introduction and Overview

This book discusses the federal income estate and gift tax consequences of marital separation and divorce. It covers the federal income tax aspects of alimony and child support; the dependency exemption and its application to other tax matters; tax credits; property settlements (with special emphasis on the marital residence); the tax treatment of certain expenses, such as medical expenses, attorney's fees, and life insurance premiums; filing status; and innocent spouse treatment. The book concludes with a discussion of the federal gift and estate tax aspects of marital separation and divorce.

This book has been written to reach the largest possible audience. It is written primarily for the domestic relations practitioner who should have at least a basic understanding of the federal income, gift, and estate tax aspects of separation and divorce. It is also written for tax attorneys and accountants who are oftentimes called upon to give tax advice in this area, and for beginning, intermediate, and advance domestic relations and tax practitioners.

The material that follows first discusses the law enacted by Tax Cuts and Jobs Act of 2017, and then discusses the law prior to the Tax Cuts and Jobs Act of 2017. The discussion of prior law has been included because it remains relevant for many taxpayers and will remain applicable to those taxpayers into the foreseeable future.

A. Tax Reform Act of 2017

On December 22, 2017, President Trump signed into law the Tax Cuts and Jobs Act of 2017 (TCJA 2017). The TCJA 2017 contained the most sweeping changes to the alimony provisions since the Tax Reform Act of 1984 (1984 TRA). Among the provisions affected are those pertaining to alimony, child support, the dependency exemption, the child tax credit, as well as changes to the deductibility of legal expenses. As will be noted, TCJA 2017 shifts the tax burden from the payee spouse to the payor spouse, eliminates the distinction between alimony and child support for federal income tax purposes, assigns a value of zero to the dependency exemption, and increases the child tax credit, among many other changes.

The provisions of the TCJA 2017 apply to post-2018 divorce or separation instruments, and pre-2019 divorce and separation instruments that are modified after 2018 where the modification expressly provides that the amendments made by TCJA 2017 apply to the modification.

Caution is advised in relying solely upon this book for an in-depth understanding of the tax consequences of divorce or for tax planning purposes. Thus, anyone seeking further knowledge and understanding should consult the statutes themselves, as well as the Committee Reports issued by the Committee on Ways and Means of the U.S. House of Representatives, the Committee on Finance of the U.S. Senate, and the Conference Committee composed of selected members of those committees. In addition, the regulations and rulings issued by the Internal Revenue Service (IRS) and the court cases interpreting these statutory provisions should be reviewed.

1 Income Tax Aspects of Alimony and Separate Maintenance Payments

A. Law as a Result of Tax Cuts and Jobs Act of 2017

The primary income tax issue to be considered by separated or divorced parties is the tax treatment of alimony payments made by one spouse to the other.

The Tax Cuts and Jobs Act of 2017 (TCJA 2017) turned the tax aspects of alimony payments upside down from the law in effect prior to TCJA 2017. Prior to January 1, 2019, alimony payments made by the payor spouse to the payee spouse were deductible by the payor spouse and includible in the gross income of the payee spouse if the nine tests set forth in prior Section 71 were met (discussed in Chapter 2, Section B in this book).

As a result of TCJA 2017, payments made by the payor spouse to the payee spouse pursuant to divorce or separation instrument that is (i) executed after December 31, 2018, or (ii) executed on or after December 31, 2018, and modified after December 31, 2018, if the modification expressly provides that the amendments made by the TCJA 2017 are no longer deductible by the payor spouse or includible in the gross income of the payee spouse. Thus, TCJA 2017 reversed the rules for the tax treatment of alimony by disallowing an alimony deduction to the payor spouse for the payment of alimony and excluding the receipt of alimony from the gross income of the payee spouse. In effect, the TCJA 2017 did a 180 degree turn by moving the tax burden on the payment of alimony from the payee spouse to the payor spouse. It accomplished this by disallowing the payor spouse a deduction for the payment of alimony and excluding the payment from the gross income of the payee spouse. This is similar to what the Tax Reform Act of 1984 did to property settlements when it shifted the tax burden from the transferor spouse to the transferee spouse, as discussed in Chapter 7 of this book.

Under the law prior to TCJA 2017, if the payor spouse was in a higher income tax bracket than the payee spouse, the payor spouse could afford to pay more alimony to the payee spouse than the payor spouse might otherwise have desired as a result of the alimony deduction afforded to the payor spouse. Now, with the loss of the alimony deduction to the payor spouse because of TCJA 2017, the payor spouse will likely argue for a smaller alimony payment than previous. This may not be necessarily detrimental to the payee spouse since the payee spouse will no longer be required to include the alimony payment in gross income. The result remains the same, however, to maximize the after-tax payments and receipts to the payor and payee spouses in which both can share, while minimizing the tax payments made to the holy fisc.

In effect, TCJA 2017 overruled 75 years of congressional precedent when the precursor of pre-TCJA 2017 Sections 71 (alimony is included in the gross income of the payee spouse) and 215 (alimony is deductible by the payor spouse) were first enacted by Congress. The reason for the change, though not specified, is clear—Congress needed to raise revenues to balance the budget to offset major tax cuts in order to pass TCJA 2017 as a continuing resolution. One of the places it turned to was the reversal of the alimony provisions under the Code, arguing that Congress should not subsidize divorces and hence alimony payments where the payor spouse is in a higher income tax bracket than the payee spouse. The effect of the change is that the payor spouse is now paying alimony with after-tax dollars, whereas under pre-TCJA 2017 the payor spouse was paying alimony with deductible dollars.

It is important to emphasize that the rules in effect as of December 31, 2018 (the pre-TCJA 2017 rules) continue to apply to divorce or separation instruments executed before January 1, 2019. In addition, if the taxpayers have a pre-2019 divorce or separation instrument and they have that instrument legally modified, then the rules of the TCJA 2017 will not apply to the modified divorce or separation instrument unless the modification expressly provides that the rules of the TCJA 2017 are to apply. Thus, the pre-TCJA 2017 rules continue to be important, and will be important for some time into the future because such rules apply to pre-TCJA 2017 divorce and separation instruments.

The TCJA 2017 requires the tax practitioner to alter his or her planning methods. Under pre-2019 divorce or separation instruments, if the payor spouse were in a higher income tax bracket than the payee spouse, the payor spouse may have been willing to pay more alimony than required or necessary because the payor spouse received an income tax deduction for the payment. Now that such payments are no longer deductible under post-2018 divorce or separation instruments, nor includible as the gross income of the payee spouse, the payor spouse will no longer pay more than what may be required or is necessary but will use all available means to pay less than what the payor spouse would have been willing to pay under the pre-2017 act. But if the parties modify a pre-2019 divorce or separation instrument, the practitioner must be careful to decide whether pre-TCJA 2017 law will continue to apply, or if the law as amended by TCJA 2017 should apply.

Example 1. Assume pursuant to a divorce or separation instrument the payor spouse agrees to pay the payee spouse alimony of $10,000.00 per month, or $120,000.00 per year. Assume the payor spouse is in the forty (40) percent Federal income tax bracket and the payee spouse is in the twenty (20) percent Federal income tax bracket. Under the law in effect prior to TCJA 2017, the payor spouse received an alimony deduction for the alimony payment, and the payee spouse had to include the alimony payment in gross income. Thus, the payor spouse was entitled to an above-the-line alimony deduction of $120,000.00 which resulted in a tax savings of $48,000.00, whereas the payee spouse had income of $120,000.00 and incurred a Federal income tax liability of $24,000.00. Under the law in effect prior to TCJA 2017, the payor spouse was out-of-pocket only $72,000.00, and the payee spouse netted $96,000.00 after tax. Hence, the tax benefit fell upon the payor spouse and the tax burden upon the payee spouse.

Example 2. Assume a decree of divorce was executed in 2012 and required alimony to be paid for ten years beginning January 1, 2013. In February 2022, the Court modified the decree to increase the monthly alimony payment beginning March 2022. The modification did not expressly provide that the post-2018 alimony rules would apply to alimony payments made after the February 2022 date of modification. Thus, alimony payments made after the February 2022 date fall under the pre-TCJA 2017 rules and are treated as alimony, deductible by the payor spouse and includible in the gross income of the payee spouse. This example highlights the importance of not only the parties being educated about the effects of modifying pre-2017 TCJA divorce or separation instruments but also the judiciary being educated (sometimes by counsel) of the effects of modifying a pre-2017 TCJA divorce or separation instrument.

Now look at the law as a result of TCJA 2017, which provides that alimony is not deductible by the payor spouse and is not includible in the gross income of the payee spouse. The tax burden has been shifted from the payee spouse to the payor spouse. As a result of this change in the law, the payor spouse must earn $200,000.00 pre-tax dollars in order to pay the payee spouse alimony of $120,000.00 per year. On the other hand, the payee spouse now nets $120,000.00. Thus, the payor spouse is out of pocket $200,000.00 (see example 1 in Table 1.1).

To substantially equalize the pre-tax and post-tax payment under TCJA 2017 with the law in effect prior to the TCJA 2017, the payor spouse will have to pay the payee spouse less than under the law in effect prior to TCJA 2017, but the combined alimony payment and tax bill to the payor spouse will be more than under pre-TCJA 2017. In the preceding example, this would mean that if the payee spouse wanted to net $96,000.00 to coincide with the amount received under pre-TCJA 2017, the payor spouse would have to earn $160,000.00, which is less than if the full $120,000.00 were paid (at a cost of $200,000.00), but more than under prior law (see example 2 in Table 1.1). Therefore, to more nearly equalize the pain to both parties, the payee spouse may be required to take less than $96,000.00 after tax, whereas the payor spouse will be required to pay more than $120,000.00 on a pre-tax basis (see examples 3 and 4 in Table 1.1). This then becomes a point of negotiation between the spouses, with the payor spouse playing limbo to see how low he/she can go, and the payee playing pole vaulter to see how high he/she can go.

As Table 1.1 summarizes, the payor spouse will have to pay $160,000 in order for the payee spouse to net $96,000.00. This will come at a tax cost to the payor spouse of $64,000.00. To reduce this cost to the payor spouse it will require the payee spouse to accept less than he/she needs to live, yet it may still cost the payor spouse more than he/she can afford. Let the wars begin.

Table 1.1

	Pre-TCJA 2017	
	Payor	Payee
Payment	120,000	120,000
Tax Savings	48,000	-0-
Tax		24,000
Net of Tax	72,000	96,000

	TCJA 2017 (Example 1)		TCJA 2017 (Example 2)		TCJA 2017 (Example 3)		TCJA 2017 (Example 4)	
	Payor	Payee	Payor	Payee	Payor	Payee	Payor	Payee
Payment	120,000	120,000	96,000	96,000	75,000	75,000	50,000	50,000
Tax Savings	-0-	-0-	-0-	-0-	-0-	-0-	-0-	-0-
Tax	80,000	-0-	64,000	-0-	50,000	-0-	33,333	-0-
Net of Tax	200,000	120,000	160,000	96,000	125,000	75,000	83,333	50,000

B. Law Prior to Tax Cuts and Jobs Act of 2017

The following applies to divorce or separation instruments entered into before January 1, 2019, that have not been modified after December 31, 2018.

If payments made by the payor spouse are included in the gross income of the payee spouse under I.R.C. § 71, they are deductible by the payor spouse under I.R.C. § 215.[1] The deduction is available without regard to whether the payor spouse elects to itemize deductions.[2] Thus, alimony payments are deductible whether the payor spouse itemizes deductions or uses the standard deduction.

The payor spouse cannot deduct, and the payee spouse does not include in gross income, property settlement payments or income from property settlement.[3]

For purposes of Federal income taxation, "alimony" is determined by reference to Federal tax law and not state law.[4] Thus, the label placed on the payment is not controlling.[5] See *East v. Commissioner*,[6] where the Court looked to the following four factors to determine whether a payment was in the nature of alimony or a property settlement: (i) whether the recipient surrenders property rights in exchange for the payments; (ii) whether the payments are fixed in amount and not subject to a contingency; (iii) whether the payments approximate one-half of the marital property acquired during the marriage; and (iv, c) whether there is a separate support agreement, and whether the payments are geared to the financial needs of the recipient.[7]

---

1. Temp. Prop. Treas. Reg. § 1.71-1T(A-1). All Section references are to the Internal Revenue Code of 1986, as amended, except as otherwise indicated.

2. I.R.C. § 62(a)(13); Tax Reform Act of 1976, I.R.C. § 502.

3. I.R.C. § 71(b)(1)(B).

4. Mills v. Comm'r, 54 T.C. 608 (1970), *aff'd*, 442 F.2d 1149 (10th Cir. 1971).

5. *See, e.g.*, Beard v. Comm'r, 77 T.C. 1275 (1981) (whether payments are in the nature of support or part of a property settlement does not turn on the labels assigned to the payments by the Court in the divorce decree or by the parties in their agreement); Schottenstein v. Comm'r, 75 T.C. 451 (1980) (payments designated as "property settlement" were held to be alimony); Henry v. Comm'r, 76 T.C. 455 (1981) (payments designated as "alimony" were held to be child support); and Widmer v. Comm'r, 75 T.C. 405 (1980) (payments designated as "alimony" were held to be in the nature of property settlements). Rojas v. Comm'r, T.C. Memo 2022-77 ("our holding today does not turn upon the labels used either in the divorce instrument or by the LA Superior Court to describe the payments in question, but rather upon the express terms of Section 71(a) and (c).").

6. T.C. Memo. 1989-658.

7. In Rangos v. Comm'r, T.C. Memo. 1998-130, the Court set forth seven factors which indicate that the payments are in the nature of a property settlement. Those factors are: (i) the parties in their agreement (or the Court in its decree) intended the payments to effect a division of their

For payments made under pre-2019 divorce or separation instruments to be characterized as gross income under I.R.C. § 71(a), *payments must be received (directly or indirectly) by the payee spouse.* In *Tyrer v. Commissioner*,[8] the payee spouse was indebted to the payor spouse and the written separation agreement provided that the payor spouse could offset his monthly alimony obligation by $1,000 per month until the debt was satisfied. The amounts offset by the credit constituted "payments received," even though the amount of the credit never actually exchanged hands. The Court then held that such payments constituted alimony and not a property settlement.[9] The Court reasoned that the payee spouse receives a reduction of his or her liability to the payor spouse. For every dollar the payor spouse is excused from making as a direct payment to the payee spouse, the payee spouse receives an equivalent dollar benefit in the form of reduced liability.

Credit offsets are not payments in settlement of property rights because the credit offset constitutes consideration moving to the payee spouse from the payor spouse to satisfy the payor spouse's alimony obligation, which the payee spouse then returns to satisfy his or her debt obligation. In other words, the payee spouse is "deemed" to have received the payments as alimony, which must be included in gross income, and the payee spouse is then deemed to have used the proceeds to satisfy his or her debt obligation.

Payments received by payee spouse's attorney on behalf of the payee spouse under pre-219 divorce or separation instruments are includable in the gross income of the payee spouse in the year received by the attorney, even if not paid by the attorney to the payee spouse until the following year. The doctrine of constructive receipt applies.[10] Payments of alimony to a nonresident payee spouse may be deductible by the payor spouse. In Priv. Ltr. Rul. 200251004,[11] the IRS held that the payor spouse may deduct payments as alimony even if

assets; (ii) the recipient surrendered valuable property rights in exchange for the payments; (iii) the payments are fixed in amount and not subject to contingencies, such as the remarriage or death of the recipient; (iv) the payments are secured; (v) the amount of the payments plus the other property awarded to the recipient equals approximately one half of the property accumulated by the parties during marriage; (vi) the needs of the recipient were not taken into consideration in determining the amount of the payments; and (vii) a separate provision for support was provided elsewhere in the decree or agreement.

8. 77 T.C. 577 (1981).

9. *See also* Pierce v. Comm'r, 66 T.C. 840 (1976) ($20,000 alimony payment offset by $20,000 debt held to be a "payment") and Smith v. Comm'r, 51 T.C. 1 (1968) ($5,000 credit to payor spouse for conversion of his personal property held to be a "payment" to the wife).

10. Burkes v. Comm'r, T.C. Memo. 1998–61. "Constructive receipt" means the taxpayer is treated as having received an item of income even if the taxpayer has not actually received the item of income or is not in possession of the income. Treas. Reg. §1.451-2(a).

11. Hereinafter Priv. Ltr. Rul. or PLR.

the payee spouse does not have to report the payment in income because of a treaty with the country in which the payee spouse resided, despite language apparently to the contrary under I.R.C. § 215. Thus, according to the IRS, there is no absolute requirement that the recipient be subject to U.S. tax on the alimony or separate maintenance payments for the payments to be deductible by the payor spouse under I.R.C. § 215, even though I.R.C. §§ 71 and 215 are intended to be reciprocal when the payor and payee spouses are subject to U.S. income tax. Rather, referring to Rev. Rul. 56585,[12] the IRS concluded that when there is an express statutory exclusion of otherwise includable payments from the recipient's income, this does not bar the payor's deduction. This exemption applies equally when the exemption from income for the alimony comes by treaty instead of by statute.

Court-ordered repayment of alimony, previously included in the gross income of the payee spouse, is deductible by the payee spouse in the year of repayment.[13] On the other hand, the payee spouse may not deduct unpaid alimony, even if evidenced by a promissory note of the payor spouse, unless the payee spouse had previously included the unpaid alimony in gross income.[14]

1. Alimony and Separate Maintenance Defined

As defined by I.R.C. § 71(b),[15] alimony or separate maintenance means any payment that meets the following nine tests.

(i) The payments are in *cash*.[16]

(ii) The cash payment may be paid directly to the payee spouse or on behalf of the payee spouse.

(iii) The cash payment is received by or on behalf of a spouse or a former spouse under a divorce or separation instrument.[17]

(iv) The divorce or separation instrument does not designate such payment as a payment that is not includable in gross income under I.R.C. § 71(a) and not allowable as a deduction under I.R.C. § 215.[18]

---

12. 1956-2 C.B. 166.

13. Feldman v. Comm'r, T.C. Memo. 1991-153.

14. Beshear v. Comm'r, T.C. Memo. 1990-544. *See also* Perry v. Comm'r, 92 T.C. 470 (1989), *aff'd*, 912 F.2d 1466 (5th Cir. 1990) where the Court held that the taxpayer was not entitled to a bad debt deduction for alimony arrearages because she had no basis in the debt.

15. All Section references are to the Internal Revenue Code of 1986, as amended, except as otherwise indicated.

16. I.R.C. § 71(b)(1); Temp. Prop. Treas. Reg. § 1.71-1T (A-2).

17. I.R.C. § 71(b)(1)(A); Temp. Prop. Treas. Reg. § 1.71-1T(A-2).

18. I.R.C. § 71(b)(1)(B); Temp. Prop. Treas. Reg. § 1.71-1T(A-2(b)).

(v) In the case of an individual legally separated from his spouse under a decree of divorce or separate maintenance, the payee spouse and the payor spouse are not members of the same household at the time such payment is made.[19]

(vi) There is no liability to make any such payment after the death of the payee spouse or to make any payment in cash or property as a substitute for such payments after the death of the payee spouse.[20] Although the regulations require this statement to be made in the divorce or separation instrument, such language is not required if state law provides that payments cease on the death of the payee spouse (see alimony test 4 in Chapter 2, B.2.f).

(vii) The parties do not file a joint return.[21]

(viii) The payment does not constitute child support under I.R.C. § 71(c).

(ix) The special rules to prevent excess front-end loading of alimony payments must be met.[22]

As noted earlier, a payment that qualifies as alimony is deductible by the payor spouse and includible in the gross income of the payee spouse,[23] whereas a payment that does not qualify as alimony is treated as a property settlement that is neither deductible by the payor spouse nor includible in the gross income of the payee spouse.[24]

Each of these requirements is discussed in detail next.

2. Nine Tests for Qualification as Alimony

For a payment to qualify as alimony under pre-TCJA 2017 law (and hence pre-2019 divorce and separation instruments), the *nine tests* that must be met are discussed in detail at a–i following.

a. Cash Payments (Alimony Test no. 1)

The first test requires that the payments must be *in cash*.[25] Cash includes checks and money orders payable on demand.[26]

---

19. I.R.C. § 71(b)(1)(C). Temp. Prop. Treas. Reg. § 1.71-1T(A-2(c)).
20. I.R.C. § 71(b)(1)(D). Temp. Prop. Treas. Reg. § 1.71-1T(A-2(d)).
21. I.R.C. § 71(e).
22. I.R.C. § 71(f).
23. I.R.C. §§ 215 and 71, respectively.
24. Johnson v. Comm'r, 541 F.3d 973 (C.A. 9, 2008) *aff'g* T.C. Memo. 2006-105.
25. I.R.C. § 71(b)(l); Temp. Prop. Treas. Reg. § 1.711T(A2) and (b)(A5). Medlin v. Comm'r, T.C. Memo. 1998-378 (payments for lease insurance and maintenance of automobile for wife's benefit constitute a cash payment).
26. Temp. Prop. Treas. Reg. § 1.71-1T(A-2).

This test eliminates the need to determine whether a transfer of property constitutes alimony or a property settlement.[27] A cash payment will always be treated as alimony (if all the other tests are met) and not as a property settlement, unless the decree or agreement provides otherwise. In other words, a cash payment may constitute alimony or property settlement depending on the application of the alimony tests, but a property settlement can only constitute a property settlement and never alimony.[28]

For example, in *Mehriary v. Commission*,[29] the husband transferred his interest in a piece of real estate to his wife. The wife agreed to pay the husband alimony of $4,000 per month for 60 months. Within the month the parties modified their agreement and agreed that the wife could re-convey the real estate to the husband in lieu of $80,000 of the alimony obligation. At trial the wife argued that the transfer of the property to the husband in lieu of some of her alimony obligation was a deductible alimony payment. The Court denied the deduction, because it was not a payment in cash. According to the Court, although the intent of the parties was that the transfer of the property would replace some of the wife's alimony obligation, the intent of the parties does not determine the deductibility of a payment as alimony under Section 71. Rather, whether a payment is deductible as alimony is a straightforward, objective test that results entirely on the fulfillment of the tests set forth in Section 71, including that payments be made in cash or a cash equivalent.

Transfers of services or property (including a debt instrument of a third party or an annuity contract), execution of a debt instrument by the payor, or the use of property of the payor *do not qualify* as alimony or separate maintenance.[30]

A third-party debt instrument does not constitute cash. In *Lofstrom v. Commissioner*,[31] the taxpayer was in arrears in his payment of alimony. In exchange for the alimony arrearage, the wife agreed to accept $4,000 cash and the husband's interest in a contract for a deed valued at $29,000. On his tax return, the husband claimed the entire $29,000 value of the contract for the deed as an alimony deduction. The IRS denied the deduction. The Court agreed with the IRS and held that the husband could not deduct as alimony the value of the contract because it did not constitute a payment of cash or cash equivalent as required by I.R.C. § 71(b)(1) and Treas. Reg. § 1.71-1T(A2). The Court found that the contract for the deed was a third-party debt instrument, a financing

27. *See* Martin v. Comm'r, 73 T.C. 255 (1979).

28. Preston v. Comm'r, T.C. Memo. 1999-49; Temp. Prop. Treas. Reg. § 1.71-1T(A-5).

29. T.C. Memo. 2015-126.

30. Temp. Prop. Treas. Reg. § 1.71-1T(A5). Agreement to pay "in the future" is not a cash payment. Preston v. Comm'r, T.C. Memo. 1999-49.

31. 125 T.C. 13 (2005).

arrangement that allows a buyer (or vendee) to purchase property by borrowing the money for the purchase from the seller (or vendor). The Court held that because the contract for the deed transferred to the wife is a debt instrument of a third party, it does not qualify as a cash payment and is not deductible as alimony. Accordingly, the Court disallowed the husband's alimony deduction for the value of the contract for the deed.

b. Direct or Indirect Payment (Alimony Test no. 2)

The second test provides that the payments must be *received by (or on behalf of) a spouse* under a divorce or separation instrument.[32] The payments may be direct or indirect. This requirement opens new planning opportunities, for no longer must payments be made directly to the payee spouse to qualify as alimony.[33]

Payments of cash to a third party on behalf of a spouse qualify as alimony if the payments are made to the third party pursuant to the decree of divorce or written separation agreement, or at the written request, consent, or ratification of the payee spouse.[34] For example, instead of making an alimony or separate maintenance payment directly to the payee spouse, the payor spouse may make a cash payment to a charitable organization if such payment is pursuant to the written request, consent, or ratification of the payee spouse. Such request, consent, or ratification must state that both parties intend the payment to be treated as an alimony or separate maintenance payment to the payee spouse subject to the rules of I.R.C. § 71, and the request, consent, or ratification of the payee spouse must be received by the payor spouse prior to the date of filing of the payor's first tax return for the taxable year in which the payment was made.[35] Thus, the payee spouse may direct the payor spouse to make a payment to a charity on behalf of the payee spouse. Although the payment would be deductible by the payor spouse as alimony and includable in the gross income of the payee spouse as alimony, the payee spouse should then be entitled to a charitable contribution deduction. Thus, the indirect payment rule can be made either pursuant to the terms of the divorce or separation instrument or pursuant to a written request, consent, or ratification of the payee spouse.[36]

32. I.R.C. § 71(b)(1)(A).

33. Cash payments made by automobile dealership owned by the husband for the lease, insurance, and maintenance of an automobile for the wife's benefit are deductible by the husband, since the husband included those amounts in income as constructive dividends. Medlin v. Comm'r, T.C. Memo. 1998-378. *See also* Preston v. Comm'r, *supra*, where payments for clothes, dentist, medical bills, car insurance, automobile expenses, and drug expenses, made directly to the provider were deductible as alimony.

34. Temp. Prop. Treas. Reg. § 1.71-1T(A-7).

35. *Id.*

36. *See* Medlin v. Comm'r, T.C. Memo. 1998-378, where the Court held that indirect payments were made pursuant to the terms of a written separation agreement.

As a result of this test, the payor spouse can pay the payee spouse's attorney directly for the payee spouse's legal fees and deduct them as alimony if all the tests of I.R.C. § 71 are met.[37] But see *Smith v. Commissioner*,[38] discussed later in the chapter at the end of test six, where the Court held that the taxpayer's liability to make payments to his former wife's attorneys would not have been extinguished if, prior to payment, the former wife had died. Therefore, since the sixth test was violated, the payment of the fees did not constitute alimony. On the other hand, see *Burkes v. Commissioner*,[39] where on an identical issue the Court held that the payments were alimony, since under Ohio law there is no obligation to make alimony support payments for any period after the death of the payee spouse. Thus, although payments may be indirect, they must meet all the tests of alimony to qualify as alimony.[40]

Cash payments to a third party of rent, mortgage, tax, or tuition liabilities of the payee spouse made under the terms of the divorce or separation instrument also qualify as alimony.[41] On the other hand, payments to maintain property owned by the payor spouse and used by the payee spouse (including mortgage principal, real estate taxes, and insurance premiums) are not payments on behalf of a spouse even if those payments are made pursuant to the terms of the divorce or separation instrument.[42] If, however, the payor spouse does not own the house, payments of mortgage principal, interest, property taxes, insurance, utilities, and repairs directly to a third party are payments "on behalf of" the payee spouse, and, therefore, such payments may be deductible

---

37. *See* Zinsmeister v. Comm'r, T.C. Memo. 2000-364; Hopkinson v. Comm'r, T.C. Memo. 1999-54 (1999); *see* Attorney Fees at Chapter 9, D.

38. T.C. Memo. 1998-166.

39. T.C. Memo. 1998-61.

40. *See* Moore v. Comm'r, T.C. Memo. 2011-200 (obligation of payor spouse to pay off mortgage obligation of payee spouse upon sale of house was not deductible as alimony because test no. 6 payment obligation of payor to reimburse payee the amount of the mortgage would not have terminated on death of payee spouse.).

41. Temp. Prop. Treas. Reg. § 1.71-1T(A-6); *see* Israel v. Comm'r, T.C. Memo. 1995-500 (rental payments paid by payor spouse pursuant to written separation agreement designated as "additional maintenance" constitute taxable income); Hopkins v. Comm'r, T.C. Memo. 1999-54 (tuition payments paid by former husband to a University met all the tests of I.R.C. § 71 for inclusion of the tuition payments in the wife's gross income as did payments made to the wife to reimburse her for her attorney's fees). *See* Zinsmeister v. Comm'r, T.C. Memo. 2000-364 where the Court held that mortgage payments for which the spouses are jointly liable are includable in the gross income of the payee spouse as payments in discharge of indebtedness, and deductible by the payor spouse as alimony (if the tests of alimony are met). Thus, the payor can deduct as alimony one-half of the mortgage payments, real estate taxes and home insurance premiums as alimony. Where, however, only the payor spouse is liable on the mortgage, payment of mortgage principal is not deductible as alimony.

42. Temp. Prop. Treas. Reg. § 1.71-1T(A-6). *See also* Tseng v. Comm'r, T.C. Memo. 1994-126 (alimony deduction denied where taxpayer makes payments to mortgagee on residence occupied by payee and owned by payor spouse).

as alimony by the payor spouse, and includable in the gross income of the payee spouse, if all the other alimony tests of I.R.C. § 71 are met.

To clarify, if the house is jointly owned, the payor spouse may deduct half the payments of mortgage principal, and interest may be deductible by the payor spouse as alimony but must be includable in the gross income of the payee spouse as alimony. The payee spouse may deduct the other half of the interest payments as an itemized deduction if the residence is a qualified residence for purposes of the interest deduction under Section 163. The real estate taxes are not deductible as alimony but are deductible by the payor spouse as an itemized deduction.

Premiums paid by the payor spouse for term or whole life insurance on the payor's life made under the terms of the divorce or separation instrument qualify as payments on behalf of the payee spouse to the extent the payee spouse is the owner of the policy.[43] If the policy is transferred by the payor spouse to the payee spouse, the payor must surrender all "incidents of ownership in the policy."[44]

Payments deposited by husband into a joint checking account with his wife from whom he was separated, or payments husband made by issuing checks to his wife that were then deposited into their joint checking account, or payments made on her behalf to the probation department where the wife had unfettered access to the funds to maintain herself, her children, and the household satisfy the requirements of alimony test no. 2 found in I.R.C. § 71(b)(1)(A).[45]

c. Divorce or Separation Instrument (Alimony Test no. 3)

The third test requires that the payments must be received by (or on behalf of) a spouse or former spouse under a *divorce or separation instrument*.[46] A divorce or separation instrument means:

- a decree of divorce or separate maintenance or a written instrument incident to such divorce;[47]
- a written separation agreement;[48] or
- a decree that requires a spouse to make payments for the support or maintenance of the other spouse and that is not a decree of divorce or separate maintenance or a written instrument incident to such divorce.[49]

43. Temp. Prop. Treas. Reg. § 1.71-1T(A-6). *See also Life Insurance*, at Chapter 9, C.
44. *See* I.R.C. § 2042 for a definition of "incidents of ownership."
45. Kean v. Comm'r, T.C. Memo. 2003-163, *aff'd*, 407 F.3d 186 (3d Cir. 2005).
46. I.R.C. § 71(b)(1)(A).
47. I.R.C. § 71(b)(2)(A).
48. I.R.C. § 71(b)(2)(B).
49. I.R.C. § 71(b)(2)(C).

These are the same divorce or separation instruments described in the marital division test under "prior law."[50] Each of these instruments is discussed in turn next.

(1) *Decree of Divorce or Separate Maintenance*

(a) Local Law

Whether a decree qualifies as a decree of divorce or separate maintenance is determined under local law. Payments made under a decree of divorce *a mensa et thoro* or *a vinculo matrimonii*, as well as payments made under a decree for permanent alimony, will be characterized as alimony.[51] In addition, payments made under a decree of *annulment* may also be treated as alimony for purposes of Federal income taxation.[52] But payments made under an *interlocutory decree* or decree for *alimony pendente lite* fall within the provisions of I.R.C. § 71(b)(2)(C)[53] and not I.R.C. § 71(b)(2)(A).[54]

(b) Invalid Decrees

The status of payments made under a divorce decree that is later declared invalid by a Court having proper jurisdiction is equivocal. The IRS takes the position that payments made under an invalidated decree are not alimony for purposes of Federal income taxation. The Second Circuit Court of Appeals in *Estate of Borax v. Commissioner*,[55] however, has held that payments under an invalidated decree retain their character as alimony for purposes of Federal tax law. The IRS will not follow *Estate of Borax v. Commissioner*.[56]

In *Ryan v. Commissioner*,[57] the payee spouse asked for alimony for eight years. The trial court granted the payee spouse alimony until the death of the payee spouse or a substantial change in circumstance. The Court of Appeals of Michigan rendered a per curiam opinion finding that the trial court's alimony

---

50. Temp. Prop. Treas. Reg. § 1.71-1T(A-4).

51. *See* Rev. Rul. 67442, 19672 C.B. 65; Deininger v. Comm'r, 313 F.2d 221 (4th Cir. 1963).

52. Newburger v. Comm'r, 61 T.C. 457 (1974); Reisman v. Comm'r, 49 T.C. 570 (1968).

53. Discussed at Chapter 1, B.2.c.

54. Rev. Rul. 57368, 19572 C.B. 896.

55. 349 F. 2d. 666 (C.A. 2, 1965). (State Court declaration of invalidity of Mexican divorce disregarded for Federal tax purposes). *See also* Feinberg v. Comm'r, 198 F.2d 260 (3d Cir. 1952) (Payments under Florida decree, later invalidated by New York Court, deemed alimony.).

56. Rev. Rul. 67-442,1967-2 C.B. 65 (The Internal Revenue Service generally will not question for Federal income tax purposes the validity of any divorce decree until a Court of competent jurisdiction declares the divorce to be invalid. Where a State Court declares the prior divorce to be invalid, the Service will usually follow the later Court decision rather than the divorce decree for Federal income tax purposes for such years as may not be barred by the statute of limitations.).

57. T.C. Memo. 1998-331.

award was improper and remanding the matter to the trial court "for modification of the divorce judgment to reflect an alimony award of $250 a week for eight years." The Tax Court held that the modification did not constitute a revocation of the alimony awarded by the trial court. The Tax Court concluded that the issue raised in the Court of Appeals was the length of the alimony payments. Thus, the original nature of the payments was not changed; instead, the payments were limited to no more than eight years. Accordingly, the Court held that the Court of Appeals decision did not modify the termination on death provision contained in the judgment of divorce.

In *Richardson v. Commissioner*,[58] the Court held that payments made pursuant to a written separation agreement later invalidated on the grounds of unconscionability nevertheless constituted alimony to the payee spouse. In so holding the Tax Court looked to Treas. Reg. § 1.71-1(b)(2)(i), which provides that payments are includible in the gross income of the payee spouse whether or not the agreement is a legally enforceable instrument.

(c) Voluntary Payments

Only those payments received after the decree of divorce or separate maintenance qualify as alimony under I.R.C. § 71(b)(2)(A).[59] Thus, payments voluntarily made before the decree of divorce or separate maintenance are entered are not treated as alimony made pursuant to a decree of divorce or separate maintenance, though the payments may qualify as alimony under the written separation agreement or decree of support marital division tests.[60] Payments made by the husband to the wife before the date of a court order, where there was no separation agreement, are voluntary in nature, not made pursuant to a divorce or separation instrument, and are therefore not deductible by the payor spouse as alimony.[61] But payments made in error and corrected nunc

58. 125 F.3d 551 (7th Cir. 1997), *aff'g* T.C. Memo. 1995-554.

59. Semel v. Comm'r, T.C. Memo. 1965-232 ("Advice" of judge or informal "order" not pursuant to decree). In *Anderson v. Comm'r*, T.C. Memo. 1999-53 (1999), the Judgment of Dissolution of Marriage provided that: "The issue of spousal support is reserved for both parties." The Court held that a total of $33,000 paid in 1994 and 1995 was not deductible as alimony since the payments were not required under a decree of divorce or decree of support.

60. *See, e.g.*, Grant v. Comm'r, 84 T.C. 809 (1985), *aff'd without op.*, 800 F.2d 260 (4th Cir. 1986) and Jachym v. Comm'r, T.C. Memo. 1984-181.

61. Meyer v. Comm'r, T.C. Memo. 2003-12. Mumtaz A. Ali v. Comm'r, T.C. Memo. 2004-284 (discussed in notes 65 and 97).

pro tunc apply retroactively.[62] But see *Hayes v. Commissioner*,[63] in which the U.S. Tax Court refused to give a nunc pro tunc order validity for tax purposes. The Court's reasoning was that the nunc pro tunc order was contrary to Ohio law because it changed retroactively the rights of the parties to the action, rather than simply correcting an error in the original judgment.[64] Thus, the general rule regarding retroactive adjudications appears to be that if the adjudication retroactively redesignates a divorce-related payment as alimony and not child support, or as child support and not alimony, such retroactive designation is generally disregarded for purposes of Federal income taxation if the State Court order retroactively changes the rights of the parties or the legal status of the payments.[65] An exception to this general rule applies when a retroactive judgment corrects a decree of divorce that mistakenly failed to reflect the true intention of the Court at the time the decree was entered.[66]

(d) Multiple Decrees

Where there is more than one decree, the earlier decree will govern until entry of the latter decree, and thereafter the latter decree will govern the character of the payments.[67]

---

62. Gordon v. Comm'r 70 T.C. 525 (1978); Newman v. Comm'r, 68 T.C. 494 (1977) (Nunc pro tunc order retroactively changing a State Court order to make the payments in question taxable to the payee spouse and deductible by the payor spouse as alimony was given retroactive effect because there was ample evidence that it was the intention of the State Court to characterize the payments as alimony for purposes of Federal income taxation.); Johnson v. Comm'r, 45 T.C. 530 (1966) (Nunc pro tunc order entered eight years after original divorce decree had retroactive effect for purposes of § 71. The original decree did not correctly reflect the State Court's intention at the time of its entry); Rev. Rul. 71-416, 1971-2 C.B. 83.

63. 101 T.C. 593 (1993).

64. See Chapter 6, I.C.4.e(2)(b)(iii) for a discussion of the *Hayes* case. *See also* Graham v. Comm'r, 79 T.C. 415 (1982). In Anderson v. Comm'r, T.C. Memo. 1999-53, the judgment of Dissolution of Marriage provided that: "The issue of spousal support is reserved for both parties." The Court held that $33,000 paid in 1993 and 1994 was not deductible as alimony since they were not required under a decree of divorce or decree of support. *See also* Mumtaz A. Ali v. Comm'r, T.C. Memo. 2004-284, where the Court held that retroactive treatment by a State Court of payments as unallocated family support does not meet the requirement of I.R.C. § 71(b)(1)(A) that the payments be received under a divorce or separation instrument. The Court's reasoning was twofold: First, payments made before the existence of a written divorce or separation instrument are not deductible by the payor spouse and, second, retroactive imposition of support by a State Court does not have retroactive effect for Federal tax purposes.

65. Turkoglu v. Comm'r, 36 T.C. 552 (1961); Segal v. Comm'r, 36 T.C. 148 (1961); Daine v. Comm'r, 9 T.C. 525 (1978).

66. Gordon v. Comm'r, 70 T.C. 525 (1978); Newman v. Comm'r, 68 T.C. 494 (1977)

67. De Wailly v. Comm'r, T.C. Memo. 1976-71 (1976).

(e) Civil Court

"Decree" means a civil court decree. A church decree is not acceptable.[68]

(2) *Written Separation Agreement*[69]

(a) Controlling Law

State law is not controlling to determine what constitutes a written separation agreement. Rather, the parties should look to Federal tax law.[70] Unfortunately, neither the Code nor the Regulations defines what constitutes a written separation agreement.[71] According to the Committee Reports and the income tax regulations, the agreement does not have to be an instrument that is enforceable in a court of law.[72]

(b) Must Be in Writing

The separation agreement must be in writing, although it may be informally structured, and must contemplate or deal with the separation of the parties. It need not actually employ the term "separation" so long as it is in contemplation of separation status.[73] An oral separation agreement does not qualify.[74] Moreover, an oral modification of a written separation agreement is not part of the written separation agreement for purposes of I.R.C. § 71(b)(2)(B),[75] nor is a unilateral statement by one party promising to pay support to the other.[76] Furthermore, correspondence between attorneys for divorcing spouses referring to an oral agreement between the spouses does not constitute a separation agreement.[77]

---

68. Clark v. Comm'r, 40 T.C. 57 (1963).

69. I.R.C. § 71(b)(2)(B).

70. Bogard v. Comm'r, 59 T.C. 97, 100–01 (1972), *acq.*, 1973-2 C.B. 1,

71. Faylor v. Comm'r, T.C. Memo 2013-143; Leventhal v. Comm'r, T.C. Memo 2000-92; Keegan v. Comm'r, T.C. Memo 1997-359; Jacklin v. Comm'r, 79 T.C. 340(1982).

72. S. Rep. No. 1622, 83d Cong., 2d Sess., p. 171 (1954); Prop. Treas. Reg. §1.71-1(b)(2); Richardson v. Comm'r, T.C. Memo 1995-554, *aff'd*, 125 F.3d 551 (C.A. 7, 1997); Dato-Nodurft v. Comm'r, T.C. Memo 2004-119.

73. Bogard v. Comm'r, 59 T.C. 97 (1972), *acq.*, 1973-2 C.B. 1, 1 (Express statement in the agreement that the parties are "separated" is "supererogatory").

74. I.R.C. § 71(b)(2)(A); Gordon v. Comm'r, 70 T.C. 525 (1978); Herring v. Comm'r, 66 T.C. 308 (1976), *acq.*, 1976-2 C.B. 2, 2; Clark v. Comm'r, 40 T.C. 57 (1963); Austin v. Comm'r, T.C. Memo. 1996-253; Wells v. Comm'r, T.C. Memo. 1998-2.

75. Bishop v. Comm'r, T.C. Memo. 1983-240; Blanchard v. United States, 424 F. Supp. 916 (D. Md. 1976).

76. Harlow v. Comm'r, T.C. Memo. 1984-393.

77. Rev. Rul. 59-397, 1959-2 C.B. 32. Bogard v. Comm'r *supra But see* Leventhal v. Comm'r, T.C. Memo. 2000-92 (written agreement between spouses' attorneys deemed a written agreement); *see* Azenaro v. Comm'r, T.C. Memo. 1989-224, where a letter from the husband's attorney containing financial terms which was signed by the wife and returned to the attorney was found to be a written agreement. *But see* Nemeth v. Comm'r, T.C. Memo 1982-646 and Keegan v.

A Memorandum of Understanding between the parties that was incorporated into the decree of divorce that states that the Memorandum "constitutes a full and complete settlement of this case" qualifies as a written separation agreement or as a written instrument incident to a divorce decree.[78] And a letter signed by one spouse offering to pay alimony to the other spouse that was accepted in writing by the other spouse has been held to constitute a written instrument.[79] The reasoning of the Court was that a written offer signed by one party and accepted by the other, in writing, constitutes a written agreement under contract law.

Interestingly, Temp. Prop. Treas. Reg. § 1.71-1(b)(2) states that the agreement does not have to be a "legally enforceable instrument." In *Dato-Nodurft v. Commissioner*,[80] the Court held that payments by the husband to the wife under a separation agreement constituted alimony for Federal income tax purposes, even though the agreement was not legally enforceable under state law. The payments in issue were made pursuant to a separation agreement entered into between the husband and the wife. The wife did not treat the payments as alimony includable in income. The wife argued that the separation agreement was not legally binding under state law, and therefore the payments she received from her husband did not constitute alimony. The Court first noted that payments made pursuant to a written separation agreement are includable in income as alimony, even if the agreement is not enforceable under state law. The Court determined that the agreement in issue was sufficiently explicit for it to be a written separation agreement. Moreover, the agreement did not contain a non-alimony statement. Therefore, the Court held that the payments were includable in the wife's income.

(c) Prenuptial Agreement

A prenuptial agreement is not a divorce or separation agreement under Section 71(b)(2) even if it contains provisions anticipating the separation of the parties. Rather, a prenuptial agreement is a contractual arrangement that is entered into by the parties prior to the marriage describing the actions and enforcement of marital rights of the parties toward each other both during and after the marriage. A separation agreement, on the other hand, is entered into as the marriage is ending. According to the statute, a separation agreement is a written instrument incident to a decree of divorce or separate maintenance. It describes the actions of the parties toward each other after the termination of the marriage.

Comm'r, T.C. Memo 1997-359, where the Court found that written exchanges between the attorneys for the spouses constituted proposals or suggestions and not agreements.

78. Sroufe v. Comm'r, T.C. Memo. 1995-256.

79. Campbell v. Comm'r, 15 T.C. 355 (1950).

80. T.C. Memo. 2004-119.

(d) Subsequent Decree

If the payee spouse is divorced or legally separated from the payor spouse under a decree of divorce or separate maintenance entered subsequent to the execution of the written separation agreement, payments made under such agreement may continue to fall within the provisions of I.R.C. § 71(b)(2)(B).[81] This, of course, depends upon whether the agreement is merged or incorporated into the decree, as discussed in (g) below.[82]

(e) Placement in the Agreement

Labels in a separation agreement are not controlling.[83] Thus, merely referring to payments as alimony is not determinative of whether payments are alimony.[84] Also, merely referring to payments as alimony in the section of an agreement entitled "Property Settlement," with nothing more, is not a sufficient expression to qualify the payments as property settlement and not alimony.

Where both support and property rights are involved, it would appear to be advisable to segregate the support payments from any property payments. When drafting the separation agreement, it is recommended that all payment plans for alimony be placed together in one portion of the agreement and all payment plans for property settlement be placed together in a separate portion of the agreement. As *Martin v. Commissioner*[85] states, "When the parties themselves differentiate among payments to be made under a divorce settlement by placing them in different portions of the agreement and making them subject to different terms, it is proper for a Court to accord them different tax treatment." Do not rely, however, on the place in the agreement to determine the character of a payment.[86]

(f) Remarriage

Payments after the remarriage of the payee spouse can still qualify as alimony. There is no requirement under Federal law that the payments must terminate when the payee spouse remarries—even if, for purposes of local law, alimony ceases on the remarriage of the payee.[87]

81. Miller v. Comm'r, T.C. Memo. 1972-9.
82. *See* Chapter 1, B.2.c(2)(f), B.2.c(2)(f).
83. Bishop v. Comm'r, 55 T.C. 720 (1971) and cases cited therein; Hammond v. Comm'r, T.C. Memo. 1998-53 (payments constitute child support even though labeled as "alimony").
84. *See* Hammond v. Comm'r, T.C. Memo. 1998-53 where payments were held to constitute child support even though they were labeled as "alimony."
85. 73 T.C. 255, 264 (1979).
86. *See* Schottenstein v. Comm'r, 75 T.C. 451 (1980) (payment "by way of settlement" held to be alimony). *See* Springer v. Comm'r, T.C. Memo. 2003-221 (discussed at Chapter 1, B.2.f(2)).
87. *See* Spector v. Comm'r, T.C. Memo. 1994-147.

(g) Merger or Incorporation

Caution is advised in drafting the separation agreement when deciding whether to have it incorporated or merged into the decree. If the agreement is merged into the decree, the decree controls. If the agreement is incorporated (but not merged) into the decree, the agreement controls and retains its identity as a contract and does not become a court order.[88] Generally, if the agreement is incorporated, but not merged, into the decree, the agreement can be modified by agreement of the parties without Court approval, whereas if the agreement is merged into the decree, modification can be accomplished only by a court order and not by agreement of the parties. But see *Mass v. Commissioner*,[89] which discusses the "dual remedy theory of incorporation without merger." The difference can affect whether the agreement is enforceable or modifiable.

In *Mass v. Commissioner*,[90] the Tax Court held that where spouses executed a separation agreement under which the payor spouse agreed to pay the payee spouse a specified sum for her support and maintenance over a 20-year period, and prior to the termination of the 20-year period the payee spouse remarried, but the payor spouse continued to make payments as required by the agreement, the payments made by the payor spouse to the payee spouse constituted gross income received by the payee spouse and were deductible by the payor spouse under prior I.R.C. §§ 71(a) and 215, respectively.

In so holding, the Court first determined that the payments were made "under a decree" within the meaning of prior I.R.C. § 71(a)(1) (current I.R.C. § 71(b)(2)(A)) because the decree, through incorporation of the agreement as "incident" thereto, required that the payments be made pursuant to the agreement, as the decree specifically ordered compliance with all terms of the agreement.

The Court then faced the "more troublesome question" of whether payments were made *under an agreement* for purposes of prior I.R.C. § 71(a)(2) (current I.R.C. § 71(b)(2)(B)). The issue was whether the agreement retained independent legal significance after its incorporation into the decree. The payor spouse argued that the payments were made pursuant to the agreement, whereas the payee spouse argued that the agreement became unenforceable when incorporated into the decree. To find for the wife, the Court concluded that the doctrine of merger must apply. Applying Illinois law, it found the doctrine of merger did not apply, thus siding with the husband. The Court held that the payments were made under both prior I.R.C. § 71(a)(1) (current I.R.C. § 71(b)(2)(A)) (decree) and I.R.C. § 71(a)(2) (current I.R.C. § 71(b)(2)(B)) (agreement) because merger had not occurred.

88. Sugarman v. Comm'r, T.C. Memo. 1996-410.
89. 81 T.C. 112 (1983).
90. *Id.*

The application of the doctrine of merger is thus a question of state law. In *Johnston v. Johnston*,[91] the Court of Appeals of Maryland held that where the parties intend a separation agreement to be incorporated but not merged into the decree of divorce, the agreement remains a separate, independent, and enforceable contract and is not superseded by the decree. According to the Court, the purpose of incorporation is to identify the agreement, establish its validity, and render it res judicata.

See *Platt v. Commissioner*,[92] holding that under Maryland law, if the parties intend to incorporate rather than merge the agreement into the decree, the agreement survives as a separate, independent contractual relationship between the parties, but if it does not contain a non-merger clause, it is then merged into the decree, and the decree controls for purposes of Federal income taxation. Thus, where the separation agreement does not contain a non-merger clause, it will be merged into the decree, and superseded by the decree.

As noted earlier in *Bogard v. Commissioner*,[93] Federal law and not state law controls to determine whether payments are alimony or child support. Moreover, the choice of law rules are not applicable to determine the character of the payments. Thus, where the state of divorce treats the payment as alimony, and the payee spouse moves to another state that treats the payments as child support, the payments are treated as alimony for purposes of Federal income taxation, because the payments are characterized as alimony under I.R.C. § 71.[94]

(h) Time of Payment

The payments must be made after the agreement has been executed. Payments made before the agreement is executed are not deductible, regardless of the effective date of the agreement, since the payments must be pursuant to a written agreement.[95] The written agreement must be in place at the time the payments are made.[96] Thus, voluntary payments made before there is a written

91. 297 Md. 48, 465 A.2d 436 (1983).

92. T.C. Memo. 1985-592.

93. 59 T.C. 97 (1972). See text at Chapter 1, B.2(c)(2)(a).

94. Cain v. Comm'r, T.C. Memo. 1976-175.

95. Newman v. Comm'r, 68 T.C. 494 (1977). *See also* Ali v. Comm'r, T.C. Memo. 2004-284 (2004) (payments made to payee spouse before the existence of a written separation agreement, that were retroactively deemed to be unallocated family support payments by a State Court order, are not alimony for purposes of I.R.C. § 71(b)(1)).

96. Mercurio v. Comm'r, T.C. Memo. 1995-312. Keegan v. Comm'r, T.C. Memo. 1997-359; Jones v. Comm'r, T.C. Memo. 2013-143; Mumtaz A. Ali v. Comm'r, T.C. Memo. 2004-284 (Payments made to payee before the existence of a written divorce or separation agreement that were retroactively deemed to be unallocated family support payments by a State Court order are not alimony because the payments were not made under a qualifying divorce or separation instrument when made and the retroactive imposition of support by a State Court does not have

separation agreement are not treated as alimony. This is similar to the preceding rule that payments made pursuant to a decree of divorce or separate maintenance must be made after the decree has been entered.

(3) Decree of Support

A decree of support is a decree that requires a spouse to make payments for the support or maintenance of the other spouse and that is not a decree of divorce or separate maintenance or a written instrument incident to such divorce.[97] A docket sheet entry that describes the results of a hearing for temporary support is a valid judgment or order under Missouri law and therefore constitutes a decree for purposes of Section 71.[98] The issue is whether a court order constitutes an enforceable order under state law requiring the payor spouse to make support payments to the payee spouse.[99] Any type of court order or decree, including payments made under an *interlocutory decree of divorce* or a decree of *alimony pendente lite,* would appear to come within this provision.[100]

d. No Non-alimony Statement (Alimony Test no. 4)

The fourth test provides that the divorce or separation instrument must not state that the payment is *not* alimony.[101] Thus, the divorce or separation instrument must *not* designate the payment as a payment that is excludable from the gross income of the payee and not deductible by the payor. On the other hand, the spouses may designate that payments otherwise qualifying as alimony or separate maintenance are nondeductible by the payor and excludable from gross income of the payee by so providing in a divorce or separation instrument as defined in alimony test 3 found in I.R.C. § 71(b)(2).[102] Thus, this provision allows the parties to decide whether to treat a payment as taxable alimony (taxable to the payee spouse and deductible by the payor spouse) or as nontaxable alimony (excludible from the gross income of the payee spouse and nondeductible the payor spouse).

---

retroactive effect for Federal tax purposes.) Payments made prior to the execution of a written separation agreement or divorce decree are not deductible as alimony. Rafferty v. United States, (2008-2USTC ¶ 50,470) (D.C. Col, July 8, 2008) (Civil Action No. 07-CV00903).

97. I.R.C. § 71(b)(2)(C).

98. Landreth v. Comm'r, T.C. Memo. 1997-169.

99. Peterson v. Comm'r, T.C. Memo. 1998-27. (Minute Order and Tentative Decision under California law constitutes a decree of support within the meaning of I.R.C. § 71(b)(2)(C)).

100. Prop. Treas. Reg. § 1.71-1(b)(3); Temp. Prop. Treas. Reg. § 1.71-1T(A-4); Korman v. Comm'r, 36 T.C. 654 (1961), *aff'd*, 298 F.2d 444 (2d Cir. 1962). Rev. Rul. 57368, 19572 C.B. 896, Heller v. Comm'r, T.C. Memo. 1994-463; Muracca v. Comm'r, T.C. Memo 1984-234.

101. I.R.C. § 71(b)(1)(B).

102. Temp. Prop. Treas. Reg. § 1.71-1T(A-8); Priv. Ltr. Rul. 9610019 (payment "not includable in gross income of wife as payee spouse" is not alimony).

If the spouses have executed a written separation agreement as described in I.R.C. § 71(b)(2)(B), any writing signed by both spouses that designates otherwise qualifying alimony or separate maintenance payments as nondeductible by the payor spouse and excludable from the gross income of the payee spouse and which refers to the written separation agreement will be treated as a written separation agreement (and thus a divorce or separation instrument).[103]

If the spouses are subject to temporary support orders as described in I.R.C. § 71(b)(2)(C), the designation of otherwise qualifying alimony or separate maintenance payments as nondeductible by the payor spouse and excludable from the gross income of the payee spouse must be made in the original or a subsequent temporary support order.[104]

A copy of the instrument containing the designation of payments as not alimony or separate maintenance payments must be attached to the payee's first filed income tax return (Form 1040) for each year in which the designation applies.[105] As a result of the filing deadline, it would appear that the parties do not have to make the election out until April 15th of the year following the year they desire to elect out. The better practice, however, would seem to be to execute an election out before the end of the year in which the election out is desired.

Although one cannot state with certainty, the provision should be revocable, so that if the parties designate a payment as not an alimony payment they can later decide to have the payment treated as alimony or vice versa. Based on the language in the regulations requiring the non-alimony statement to be attached to each return for which the designation applies, the election would appear to be an annual one, so that the parties can change their positions each year.[106]

This non-alimony statement must be clear and unambiguous. It cannot be designated by implication.[107] The divorce or separation instrument need not, however, mimic the statutory language of I.R.C. § 71(b)(1)(B) or refer to I.R.C. §§ 71 and 215 in order to constitute a non-alimony designation. Rather, the key factor is whether the substance of the designation is reflected in the instrument.[108] According to the Court in *Goldman*, the instrument must contain a

103. Temp. Prop. Treas. Reg. § 1.71-1T(A-8). Payments made pursuant to a modified agreement in which the husband agreed to make lump sum payments to his former spouse in lieu of periodic payments were not deductible as alimony because the modified agreement provided for the payments to be nondeductible by the payor spouse and excludible from the gross income of the payee spouse. PLR 200827030.

104. Temp. Prop. Treas. Reg. § 1.71-1T(A-8).

105. *Id.*

106. *Id.*

107. Medlin v. Comm'r, T.C. Memo. 1998-378.

108. Goldman v. Comm'r, 112 T.C. 317 (1999), *aff'd*, 242 F.3d 390 (10th Cir. 2000). (Agreement provided that *H* would pay *W* $20,000 per month for 240 months. The monthly payment would

"clear, explicit and express direction" that the payments are not to be includable in the gross income of the payee spouse.

In *Baker v. Commissioner*,[109] the Court found that labeling of payments as a "property settlement," with nothing more, was not a "clear, explicit and express" direction that the payments were not includable in the gross income of the payee spouse, and therefore the payments were deductible by the payor spouse. Such language did not constitute a valid nonalimony statement.

In Priv. Ltr. Rul. 200141036, payments made by the payor spouse to the payee spouse were held to be alimony because there was no "clear, explicit and express direction" that the payments not constitute alimony. The agreement provided that the wife would deliver a deed of the farm to the husband, and in exchange therefor the husband would provide the wife with a monthly income for as long as she lived, and that the income was not to be considered joint or marital property. The issue presented to the IRS was whether the payments were designated as nonalimony under I.R.C. § 71(b)(1)(B). The IRS concluded that the agreement contemplated the making of monthly payments by the husband to the wife in exchange for the farm, that there was no mention of the Federal income tax consequences of the payments, and the agreement did not contain a "clear, express and explicit direction" that the monthly payments are not intended to be includable in the former spouse's income. Thus, the IRS held that the monthly payments constituted alimony, deductible by the payor spouse and includable in the gross income of the payee spouse. Had the parties desired the payments to be nondeductible by the payor spouse and excludible from the gross income of the payee spouse, they could have done so by making such a statement, or by providing that the payments are intended to qualify as a property settlement under Section 1041.

In *Dato-Nodurft v. Commissioner*,[110] the Court held that payments by the husband to the wife under a separation agreement constituted alimony for Federal income tax purposes, even if the agreement was not legally enforceable under state law. The payments in issue were made pursuant to a separation agreement entered into between the husband and the wife. The wife did not include the payments as alimony in income. The wife argued that the separation agreement was not legally binding under state law, and therefore the payments she received from her husband did not constitute alimony. The Court

---

terminate on *W*'s death. The Agreement further provided that all transfers of property are to be subject to § 1041 and are to be reported by *H* and *W* as a "nontaxable event." Both spouses waived spousal support. Held: The monthly payments are nondeductible. According to the Court, the agreement clearly made known that the monthly payments constitute a division of marital assets and not spousal support. Thus, the agreement contains a non-alimony statement if the substance of the designation is reflected in the agreement.)

109. T.C. Memo. 2000-164.

110. T.C. Memo. 2004-119.

first noted that payments made pursuant to a written separation agreement were includable in income as alimony, even if the agreement was not enforceable under state law. The Court then determined that the agreement in issue contained support provisions that were sufficiently explicit for it to be considered a written separation agreement. Moreover, the agreement did not contain a nonalimony statement. Therefore, the Court held that the payments were includable in the wife's income.

In *Simpson v. Commissioner*,[111] the decree awarded the wife a monetary judgment of $17,900. The decree further provided that the monetary judgment "is part of a division of a community state between the parties and does not constitute, nor shall it be interpreted to be, any form of spousal support, alimony or child support." On his Federal income tax return, the payor spouse claimed an adjustment to income of $17,900 for alimony paid. In its notice of deficiency, the IRS disallowed this deduction. The Court held that the payment was a property settlement and not deductible alimony. The Court found that the language contained in the decree was a non-alimony statement within the meaning of I.R.C. § 71(b)(1)(B), that the payment was designated in the divorce decree as part of the division of community property between the spouses, and the decree specifically stated that the payment did not constitute alimony, and thus disallowed the alimony deduction.

In *DeLong v. Commissioner*,[112] the payor spouse was ordered to pay the payee spouse $3,000 per month. The order further provided that the family support payments were for both spousal support and child support. The Service argued that the family support payments were designated as non-alimony because the support orders indicated that the family support payments were partly for child support. The order did not, however, allocate any specific portion of the family support payments as spousal support or child support. The Court found that the support orders did not "fix" any portion of the family support payments as payable for child support. Thus, the Court found that the family support payments qualified as alimony and therefore rejected the Service's argument that the family support payments were designated as non-alimony.

Although the parties can designate that a payment otherwise qualifying as alimony is a nondeductible alimony payment, the reverse is not true. Thus, a payment not qualifying as alimony will not be treated as alimony for tax purposes merely because the parties designate the payment as alimony. For example, a noncash payment will not qualify as deductible alimony by calling it deductible alimony in the divorce or separation instrument.

This election gives the spouses great flexibility in determining their income, since alimony is includable in the gross income of the payee spouse and is

111. T.C. Memo. 2003-294.
112. T.C. Memo. 2013-70.

deductible by the payor spouse. Such variances could be used by a spouse to reduce his or her adjusted gross income in order to maximize his or her miscellaneous itemized deductions (which are subject to a floor of two percent of the adjusted gross income) or his or her medical expense deduction (which is subject to a floor of ten percent of adjusted gross income, 7.5 percent of adjusted gross income if the taxpayer or his or her spouse is age 65 or older).

Although the Tax Court in *Goldman v. Commissioner* held that the instrument need not mimic the statute or refer to the statute to constitute a non-alimony treatment, it is recommended that if your client desires non-alimony treatment, you should mimic the statute and refer to the statute.

e. Not Members of the Same Household (Alimony Test no. 5)

(1) General Rule

The fifth test provides that if the spouses are legally separated from each other under a decree of divorce or separate maintenance, the spouses cannot be members of the same household at the time a payment is made.[113] Thus, a payment made at the time the payor and payee spouses are members of the same household cannot qualify as an alimony or separate maintenance payment if the spouses are legally separated under a decree of divorce or separate maintenance.[114] A dwelling unit formerly shared by both spouses is not considered two separate households even if the spouses physically separate themselves within the dwelling unit.[115] The spouses are not treated as members of the same household if one spouse is preparing to depart from the household of the other spouse, and does in fact depart not more than one month after the date the payment is made.[116]

(2) Exception

The foregoing does not apply to spouses who are not legally separated under a written separation agreement pursuant to I.R.C. § 71(b)(2)(B) or a decree for support pursuant to I.R.C. § 71(b)(2)(C).[117] Thus, if the spouses are not legally separated under a decree of divorce or separate maintenance, a payment under a written separation agreement or a decree of support described in I.R.C. § 71(b)(2)(C) may qualify as an alimony or separate maintenance payment notwithstanding that the payor spouse and payee spouse are members of the same household at the time the payment is made.[118]

113. I.R.C. § 71(b)(1)(C).

114. Temp. Prop. Treas. Reg. § 1.71-1T(A-9).

115. *Id.*

116. *Id.*

117. I.R.C. § 71(b)(1)(C).

118. Temp. Prop. Treas. Reg. § 1.711T(A9); *see* Benham v. Comm'r, T.C. Memo 2000-165 (Payments made under written separation agreement. Thus, parties could reside in same residence

f. Terminating Liability on Death of Payee Spouse (Alimony Test no. 6)

(1) In General

The liability of the payor spouse must terminate on death of the payee spouse.[119] This test has fostered the most litigation in determining whether payments constitute taxable alimony. As originally enacted by the 1984 TRA, the divorce or separation instrument had to state this specifically.[120] This requirement was repealed by the 1986 TRA, so that payments will not be disqualified from treatment as alimony or separate maintenance solely because the divorce or separation instrument does not specifically state that the payments will terminate upon the death of the payee spouse. Nonetheless, as noted herein, a termination on death provision should be included in the divorce or separation instrument.

(2) Planning and Cases

According to Notice 87-9, IRB 1987-2, p. 12, the termination on death provision need not be stated in the divorce or separation instrument if the "termination would occur by operation of state law."[121] This quoted phrase is not found in the statute or the Committee Reports. It is therefore recommended that unless the draftsman is absolutely certain of state law, the termination on death provision should be included in the divorce or separation instrument. See Maryland Code Annotated, Family Law § 11108 inter alia, which provides that alimony automatically terminates upon the death of either party, unless they agree otherwise. Although Family Law § 11-108(1) appears to meet the requirements of I.R.C. § 71(b)(1)(D), it would still appear to be advisable for the agreement to state that payments terminate on the date of the death of the payee, not only to avoid reliance on state law, which could be changed by the legislature or the judiciary, but also to make this point clearly known to the parties, rather than leaving it to them to discover this after one of them dies.

To determine whether the tests of Section 71(b)(1)(D) have been met, the Courts generally apply a three-step approach. First, they look to the terms of the divorce decree to see if it contains an unambiguous termination provision. If it does not, the Courts next look to State law to determine whether the payments would terminate on the death of the payee spouse by operation of law. Finally, if the decree or agreement is silent on this point, and if State law is silent or ambiguous on this point, the Courts will independently review the decree or agreement to determine if this test is met.[122] To avoid this occurrence,

---

and payments were deemed alimony since all the other tests of alimony were met.)

119. I.R.C. § 71(b)(1)(D).

120. *Id.*

121. *See also* Priv. Ltr. Rul. 9326010.

122. Kean v. Comm'r, 407 F.3d 186 (C.A. 3, 2005) *aff'g* T.C. Memo. 2003-163; Lovejoy v. Comm'r, 293 F.3d 1208 (C.A. 10, 2002), *aff'g* T.C. Memo 1999-273; Hoover v. Comm'r, T.C. Memo.

and to avoid relying on State law, it is again recommended that the divorce or separation instrument contain a termination on death provision. Because of the substantial amount of litigation fostered by the failure to meet this test, this recommendation cannot be stressed enough.

The failure of the parties to include this provision in an agreement, or of the Courts to include this provision in any decree or order, has fostered a substantial amount of litigation, some of which is discussed in the following cases. See, for example, *Stokes v. Commissioner*,[123] where the settlement agreement did not provide for payments to cease upon death of payee spouse and Georgia law allowed for alimony to be paid after the death of the payee spouse. Thus, the tests of I.R.C. § 71(b)(1)(D) were not met and an alimony deduction was denied.[124] In *Heller v. Commissioner*,[125] the Tax Court had to look to California law to determine if payments ceased on the death of the payee spouse, since the Court order did not so indicate. See also *Baxter v. Commissioner*,[126] where the parties could have provided for this provision in their agreement, but for whatever reason, they did not. Thus, they left it to the Court to determine whether the husband's obligation "to continue to make house payments which terminate should the wife and the parties' children move from the residence" were intended to terminate on the death of the wife. The Court, after much anguish, concluded that the parties did not intend for the husband to make the payments after the wife's death.

1995-118, *aff'g* 102 F.3d 842 (C.A. 6, 1996); Moore v. Comm'r, T.C. Memo. 2011-200; Wingall v. Comm'r, T.C. Memo. 2014-22; DeLong v. Comm'r, T.C. Memo. 2013-70.

123. T.C. Memo. 1994-456.

124. *See also* Cunningham v. Comm'r, T.C. Memo. 1994-474 (1994); Ryan v. Comm'r, T.C. Memo. 1998-331 (Alimony award of $250 per week for eight years did not violate the "termination on death" clause, because Michigan law provides that alimony terminates on death of payee spouse in absence of written provision to the contrary. The limit to eight years did not violate Michigan law since the payments were limited to "no more" than eight years rather than continued indefinitely until death or a change in circumstances. Thus, payments would still terminate on the death of the payee spouse pursuant to state law.)

125. T.C. Memo. 1994-463, *aff'd* in part and remanded in part in 103 F.3d 138. (C.A. 9, 1996) [78 AFTR 2d 96-7610]. (California law, in effect at the time, provided that "except as otherwise provided by the parties in writing, the obligation of a party under order for the support of the other party terminates upon the death of either party or the remarriage of the other party." Thus, even though the agreement or decree did not state that the payments would not terminate on the death of the payee spouse, this test was met because the husband's obligation to pay support would terminate upon the wife's death under California law.).

126. T.C. Memo. 1999-190. In *Baxter*, the agreement provided for the cessation of payments only as long as the wife and the children continued to reside in the marital home. Because of the conjunction "and" the Court found the agreement to be of different interpretations. The Court determined that the agreement did not expressly address the husband's liability to include the payments in the event of the wife's death and so looked to Arkansas law to determine that the husband's liability to make payments terminated on the death of the wife.

And in *Gonzales v. Commissioner*,[127] a temporary support order for both spousal and child support was held to constitute child support since the order did not provide for termination of payments on the death of the payee spouse and the Court held that it was reasonable to assume that, under New Jersey law, the support payments would not cease on the death of the payee spouse. To the same effect, see *Miller v. Commissioner*,[128] decided by Judge Marvel applying Colorado law.

In *Barrett v. United States*,[129] the Chancery Court of Homes County, Mississippi, ordered the husband to pay the wife alimony for two years. The order did not state that the payments terminated on the death of the payee spouse. Because of this, the IRS disallowed the claimed alimony deduction. The Fifth Circuit Court of Appeals looked to Mississippi law, which provided that alimony terminates on the remarriage of the payee spouse, or the death of either the payor or payee spouse, and held that this test to determine whether the payments constituted deductible alimony had been met. Note: Had the parties provided in the original separation agreement, or had the Court provided in its order, that the payments terminated on the death of the payee spouse, the litigation could have been avoided.

In *Hoover v. Commissioner*,[130] the Tax Court ordered the husband to pay the wife $30,000 within 30 days of the final decree. The Court ordered the balance of said alimony in the amount of $380,000.00 shall accrue interest at the rate of six percent (6%) computed annually. The payee spouse was granted a lien on shares of stock owned by the payor spouse, and the payor spouse was to provide the payee spouse with a letter of credit guaranteeing payment of the alimony, the lien to remain in effect until all the alimony was paid in full. A preliminary draft of the decree of divorce provided that "all payments of alimony shall cease upon [the wife's] death [or] remarriage." This language was removed from the final decree of divorce. Because the final decree did not contain termination on death language, the Court was forced to look to Ohio law. Before 1991, Ohio law provided that alimony referred to both a division of property and support payments. Under Ohio law, payments made pursuant to a property settlement in a divorce decree did not terminate upon the death of the payee spouse. Based on the language in the decree and Ohio law, the Court concluded that the payments were in the nature of a property settlement and not alimony. Thus, the removal of the "termination on death" language from

127. T.C. Memo. 1999-332.

128. T.C. Memo. 1999-273. (Unallocated child support and maintenance payments under a temporary court order which could only be terminated by "further order of the court" or upon a final entry of decree did not terminate on death of payee spouse and therefore the test of I.R.C. § 71(a)(1)(D) was not met).

129. 74 F.2d. 661 (C.A. 5, 1996).

130. T.C. Memo. 1995-183, *aff'd*, 102 F.3d 842 (C.A. 6, 1996).

the decree resulted in the loss of an alimony deduction to the payor spouse. Again, this result could have been avoided by including "termination on death of payee spouse" language in the decree. And the case further illustrates that counsel should not rely upon the vagaries of State law to achieve the desired result, especially when it can be provided for in the agreement or decree.

In *Zinsmeister v. Commissioner*,[131] the Tax Court noted that under Minnesota law, an award of attorney's fees survives the underlying action for divorce. Thus, such payments do not end with the death of the payee spouse. Therefore, such payments cannot constitute alimony. Again, if the parties desire such indirect payments to constitute alimony, a termination on death provision should be included in the divorce or separation instrument.

In *Lovejoy v. Commissioner*,[132] the Court ordered the husband to make unallocated payments of alimony and child support. The payments did not specify that they would terminate on the death of the payee spouse. The Court looked to Colorado law to determine whether the payor spouse's legal obligation to pay unallocated family support would terminate upon the death of the payee spouse. The Colorado Uniform Dissolutions of Marriage Act provided that payments of alimony terminated on the death or remarriage of the either spouse, unless they otherwise agreed in writing, whereas the obligation to make payments of child support did not terminate on the death of the payee spouse. The Court, however, was unable to find any statute that addressed whether an obligation to pay unallocated family support terminated on the death of the payee spouse. Accordingly, the Court held that the termination on death requirement of Section 71(b)(1)(D) was not met with respect to unallocated family support payments. Again, reliance on State law resulted in a conclusion different from what the parties intended and caused the loss of an alimony deduction to the payor spouse. Again, a termination on death provision should have been included in the divorce or separation instrument if the parties desired alimony tax treatment.

In *Fithian v. United States*,[133] the Ninth Circuit Court of Appeals, in an unpublished opinion, upheld the district Court and held that bonus payments by a taxpayer to his ex-wife in exchange for stock did not constitute deductible alimony because the payments would not have terminated on the death of the payee spouse. The decree of divorce contained two support provisions. The first section, pertaining to spousal support, contained a termination-on-death provision. The second section, pertaining to the bonus payments, although described as additional spousal support, did not contain a termination-on-death

131. T.C. Memo. 2000-364. *See also* J.R. Stedman v. Comm'r, T.C. Memo. 2008-239 (Payment of ex-spouse's legal fees not deductible as alimony since payments did not cease on ex-wife's death).

132. T.C. Memo. 1999-273, *aff'd*, 293 F.3d 1208 (C.A. 10, 2002).

133. 45 Fed. Appx. 700 (9th Cir. 2002).

provision. The Court held that because the two provisions were in conflict, the divorce decree as a whole was ambiguous as to whether a termination-on-death condition applied to the bonus-sharing payments set forth in the second section of the agreement. The Court then looked to Oregon law to determine whether state law contained a termination-on-death provision and concluded it did not.

Where the parties desire different payments described in different sections of the agreement or decree to constitute deductible alimony, it would appear to be advisable to insert the termination-on-death provision in both sections, or to make sure the termination-on-death provision clearly applies to both sections.

In *Wignall v. Commissioner*,[134] the U.S. Tax Court did not follow *Fithian*, on the grounds that it was an unpublished decision that, according to the Rules of the Ninth Circuit Court of Appeals, could not be cited as precedent.[135] In *Wignall*, the decree of divorce did not contain a termination on death provision. This forced the Court to look to Oregon law to determine if the payments terminated on the death of the payee spouse. The Court found that Oregon did not have a statute that addressed the issue. The Court was thus forced to look to Oregon common law, which it found to hold that payments terminated on the death of either spouse. Thus, the Court concluded that the payments made by the payor spouse constituted alimony. Again, time and money could have been saved by the parties if they had inserted a termination on death provision in the agreement or decree, if that is what they intended, or a non-alimony statement if they intended that result.

In *Berry v. Commissioner*[136] the Tenth Circuit Court of Appeals upheld the Tax Court and held that the payment of attorney's fees incurred by the taxpayer's former spouse in the divorce proceeding was not deductible alimony because the decree that ordered the husband to pay his former wife's attorney did not contain a termination-on-death provision, nor did State law.

A case that supports including a statement in the agreement designating the parties wishes (i.e., that the payments will or will not terminate on the death

134. T.C. Memo. 2014-22.

135. The Tax Court declined to follow *Fithian* for the reason stated, despite its acknowledgment of the application of the *Golsen* rule. *See* Golsen v. Comm'r, 54 T.C. 742 (1970), *aff'd*, 445 F.2d 985 (C.A. 10, 1971) (For better judicial administration, the United State Tax Court will follow a Court of Appeals decision which is squarely on point where appeal from its decision lies to that Court of Appeals and to that court alone.) It should be noted that under the *Golsen* Rule, the Tax Court will follow the decision of the Court of Appeals to which an appeal lies even if the Tax Court disagrees with the decision of the Court of Appeals. In such a case, the Tax Court will generally state why it disagrees with the decision of the Court of Appeals; but will still follow the decision of the Court of Appeals. Under its Golsen Rule, the Tax Court may render different decisions based on identical facts for taxpayers in different judicial circuits to which an appeal lies. *Compare* Fausner v. Comm'r, 55 T.C. 620 (1971), *with* Hitt v. Comm'r, 55 T.C. 620 (1971).

136. 36 Fed. Appx. 400 (10th Cir. 2000), *aff'g* T.C. Memo. 2000-373. *See also* Delong v. Comm'r, T.C. Memo. 2013-70.

of the payee spouse) is *Moore v. Jacobsen*.[137] In *Moore*, the separation agreement, which was incorporated into the decree, provided that

> The husband shall pay to the wife non-modifiable alimony in the amount of $833.33 per month commencing on April 1, 2000 and payable on the 1st day of each month thereafter for eighty-four consecutive months or until the payment due on April 1, 2007.[138]

Six months after the divorce, the wife remarried and the husband ceased making alimony payments. The issue before the Court was whether, under the agreement and Section 11-108 of the Family Law Article of the Annotated Code of Maryland, the husband's obligation to pay alimony terminated when the wife remarried. The husband argued that the statute requires that alimony terminate on the wife's remarriage unless the parties agree otherwise; that his obligation to pay alimony terminated because the separation agreement was silent on the issue. The wife, on the other hand, argued that the definite termination date of alimony in the agreement indicated that the parties agreed "otherwise" per Family Law § 11-108. The Court held for the husband stating that the agreement must contain express and clear language evidencing the parties' intent that alimony will continue after remarriage of the recipient spouse; otherwise, pursuant to the language of the statute, remarriage terminates the obligation.

The case can be extended to payments continuing after, or terminating on, the death of the recipient spouse, since Family Law § 11-108, Annotated Code of Maryland, applies to death as well as remarriage. Thus, it would appear that if the Court were faced with a termination on death issue, it would hold that the agreement must contain express and clear language evidencing the parties' intent that alimony will continue after the death of the payor or recipient spouse; otherwise, pursuant to the statute, death terminates the obligation. Thus, even if alimony is payable for a specific term, that is, 84 months, it will terminate on the death of either spouse unless the agreement or decree provides for it to continue. Absent such language, alimony terminates on death of the payee spouse. As noted earlier, the prudent draftsman would state explicitly in the agreement the intent of the parties and not leave it to the vagaries of the statute.

If the payor spouse guarantees the payment to the payee spouse and secures the payments for a period of years, the termination on death requirement will not be met because the payments will not cease on the death of the payee spouse. Instead, the payor spouse would be required to continue to make

137. 373 Md. 185, 817 A.2d 212 (2003).
138. *Id.* at 187.

payments to the estate of the payee spouse.[139] In *Springer v. Commissioner*,[140] the Court was called upon to interpret two conflicting paragraphs in a separation agreement. In the first paragraph of Article 6 entitled "Alimony," the agreement provided for monthly payments of $1,500 continuing for 120 months or until the death of either party or the remarriage of the recipient. The second paragraph of Article 6, provided for an annual payment of $50,000 per year for a period of five years: "This portion of the alimony to be paid by the husband shall not terminate upon either the death of the husband or the remarriage of the wife." The IRS determined that the $50,000 payment was not deductible as alimony. The taxpayer claimed the payment was deductible as alimony. The Court held that in analyzing questions regarding termination of payments on the death of the payee, it must first look to the language in the divorce instrument to determine whether the liability survives the death of the payee spouse, and if the instrument is not clear, then determine whether such liability terminates at death by operation of State law. The Court held that although the marital settlement agreement attached to the divorce decree was not as clearly worded as it might be, the liability in question would have terminated at the death of the payee spouse pursuant to the divorce documents. Furthermore, the Court held the liability would have terminated at death pursuant to Nebraska law if the marital settlement agreement failed to address the issue of termination. The Court, in reaching its conclusion, determined that different types of payments made pursuant to a divorce decree are not treated as part of a single stream of payments, but rather each type of payment is analyzed separately to determine its proper characterization.

In *Kean v. Commissioner*,[141] the Court held that payments that the husband made to the wife would have terminated on the death of the wife pursuant to state law. Consequently, the payments constituted alimony for Federal income tax purposes and were deductible by the husband and includable in the gross income of the wife. In *Kean*, the Court looked to New Jersey law, which it found would require that the pendente lite payments terminate on the death of the payee spouse, even if the decree did not so provide. The Court in *Kean* distinguished the case from *Gonzales*[142] because in *Gonzales* the child was in the custody of the wife and the Court found that under a New Jersey statute custody did not automatically revert to the noncustodial parent when the custodial parent died. In *Kean*, on the other hand, the Court found that the parties had joint custody and that upon the death of the payee spouse, custody of the child would have reverted to the husband-noncustodial parent. The Court

139. Sroufe v. Comm'r, T.C. Memo. 1995-256.

140. T.C. Memo. 2003-221. *See also* Hoover v. Comm'r, T.C. Memo. 1995-183, *aff'd*, 102 F.3d 842 (C.A. 6, 1996), discussed earlier.

141. T.C. Memo. 2003-163, *aff'd*, 407 F.3d 186 (3d Cir. 2005).

142. T.C. Memo. 1999-332.

concluded that in New Jersey the Court would not require the husband to continue to make payments for the benefit of the children upon the death of the payee spouse when the children were placed in his custody. Neither the Tax Court nor the Third Circuit examined the substitute payment rule of Temp. Prop. Treas. Reg. § 1.711T(A14).[143]

In *Nukherjee v. Commissioner*,[144] the husband was ordered to pay his former wife as alimony a $55,000 "lump sum." The IRS disallowed the deduction on the basis that the taxpayer's obligation to make the payment would have survived his former wife's death in the event she died prior to the taxpayer's paying her the lump sum. The Court looked to Georgia law, which provides that the obligation of a payor spouse to make "lump sum alimony" to the payee spouse does not cease upon the death of the payee spouse, because the Georgia Courts have held that "lump sum alimony" is in the nature of a property settlement. In contrast to "lump sum alimony" under Georgia law, the obligation of periodic alimony terminates upon the death of either the payor spouse or the payee spouse. Because the award of the Court required the payor to pay the payee $55,000 alimony "lump sum," under Georgia law the taxpayer's obligation to pay the $55,000 would not have terminated upon his former wife's death prior to his making the actual payments. Thus, the Court held that the $55,000 lump sum payment that the husband made to his former wife did not qualify as deductible alimony under I.R.C. § 71(b)(1)(D). See *Rogers v. Commissioner, infra*, which applies Tennessee law that appears to be consistent with Georgia law.

Compare *Nukherjee* with PLR 200329003. In PLR 200329003 the parties entered into a marital settlement agreement pursuant to which the husband was required to pay spousal support to his wife each year in equal monthly installments. The payments were defined in the agreement as alimony, to be deductible by the husband and includable in the gross income of the wife. The agreement also provided that all obligations and payments by the husband were to terminate upon the death of the wife. The agreement also provided that in lieu of paying specified monthly alimony, the husband, at his sole discretion, could elect to pay the wife a lump sum as a payment in lieu of spousal support. The IRS held that a lump sum payment under the support agreement made in satisfaction of the husband's monthly alimony obligation qualified as an alimony payment because all of the tests of I.R.C. § 71 were met.

In *Muniz v. Commissioner*,[145] the Court held that a lump sum payment of alimony was not deductible because the payment would not have terminated on the death of the payee spouse. In *Muniz*, the Court-ordered payment did not

143. This rule is discussed at Chapter 1, B.3.f(5).
144. T.C. Memo. 2004-98.
145. T.C. Memo. 2015-125, *aff'd, per curiam* 661 F. App'x 1027 (C.A.11,2016).

specify whether the payor spouse would have been liable to make the lump sum payment to the payee spouse if the payee spouse had died before the payment was made. Therefore, the Court was forced to look to Florida law. Under Florida law, a lump sum payment created a vested right in the payee spouse that did not terminate upon the death of the payee spouse. Thus, according to the Court, under Florida law a lump sum payment of alimony constitutes a property settlement for Federal income tax purposes.

Muniz presents the difficult question of whether a lump sum payment of alimony can ever be deductible alimony because such a required payment creates a vested right in the payee spouse that survives the payee spouse's death. Therefore, it is recommended that if the parties desire a lump sum payment, the agreement or order should provide for two or more payments, and the agreement or order should provide that the payments are terminable upon the death of the payee spouse. If the payments are framed as such, the payor spouse should be careful to avoid the front end loading rules discussed in Chapter 1, B.3.i, which would cause the payor spouse to have phantom income in a subsequent tax year.

In *Rogers v. Commissioner*,[146] the Court disallowed an alimony deduction because the payments would not terminate on the death of the payee spouse. In *Rogers*, the decree ordered the husband to pay the wife $225 per week for 11 years. The decree did not contain a condition that the payments terminate on the death of the payee spouse. The Court analyzed Tennessee law, which was applicable to the case, and concluded that because of the language in the decree, under Tennessee law the weekly payments would be considered as "lump sum alimony" that, under Tennessee law, could be considered alimony that did not terminate on the death of the payee spouse. As a result, the payments were not deemed alimony for purposes of Federal income taxation. Thus, Tennessee law and Georgia law (see *Nukherjee* earlier in the chapter) appear to be identical on this issue.

Another case in which the Tax Court disallowed a payment as alimony is *Nye v. Commissioner*[147] In *Nye*, the payor spouse made a lump sum payment to the payee spouse in lieu of further alimony obligations pursuant to a Court-approved modification of agreement. The decree did not provide that the payment would terminate on the death of the payee spouse. The Court looked to Florida law, which was applicable in the absence of a provision in the modified agreement, and held that under Florida law the obligation to pay the lump sum would have survived the payee spouse's death prior to payment and would have been payable to her estate. *Nye* is another example where the parties failed to stipulate in the agreement that the payment would terminate on the

146. T.C. Memo. 2005-50.
147. T.C. Memo. 2013-166.

death of the payee spouse and left it to the vagaries of state law to determine the outcome.

In *Johanson v. Commissioner*,[148] the marital settlement agreement provided that the husband would make monthly spousal support payments from August 1996 through October 31, 2010. The agreement contained no provision regarding continuation or termination of payments if the husband died before November 1, 2010. The California Family Law Code, however, provides that in the absence of a written agreement, support payments terminate upon the death of the payee spouse.[149] The Court held that since the payor spouse has no liability to make payments after the death of the payee spouse, the spousal payments to the payee spouse constitute alimony, taxable to the payee spouse and deductible by the payor spouse. The Court noted that:

> This case is another chapter in the long saga of cases decided by this Court involving the failure of parties to divorce settlement agreements to specify what happens to payments should the payee spouse die. . . . By failing to so specify, the divorce litigants simply abdicate making a serious financial decision that others may then make for them, as here.[150]

Not only is it important to include a termination-on-death clause in the agreement if the parties want the payment to constitute deductible alimony, but also it is important to make sure such a provision is included in the decree of divorce, especially where there is no written agreement that is merged or incorporated into the decree.

The saga continued recently in *Delong v. Commissioner*.[151] There, the support order provided that the payor spouse was to pay the payee spouse $3,000 per month. The order provided that the family support payments were for both spousal support and child support. The Court order did not allocate any specific portion of the family support payments as spousal support or child support, nor did the Court order properly state that the support payments would terminate on the death of the payee spouse. The payor spouse claimed an alimony deduction for the family support payments. The Service disallowed the claimed alimony deduction. Because the order did not specify that the family support payment terminated on the death of the payee spouse, the Court was forced to consider whether such termination occurred by operation of California law.

---

148. T.C. Memo. 2006-105 (2006), *aff'd*. 541 F.3d 976 (9th Cir. 2008).
149. Cal. Fam. Code § 4337 (West 2004).
150. *Id*. at 6.
151. T.C. Memo. 2013-70.

The Court applied the three-step approach enunciated in *Kean, et al.*[152] to determine whether Section 71(b)(1)(D) applied. Following this approach, the Court found that the court orders did not expressly state that the taxpayer's liability for making payments would terminate on the death of the payee spouse. Therefore, the Court looked to California law.

The Court noted that California law provides that a spousal support obligation terminates upon the death of the payee spouse. In contrast, California law provides that a child support obligation survives the death of the payee spouse.[153] But the California Family Code did not specifically address whether a family support obligation terminates on the death of the payee spouse. The Court relied upon its decision in *Berry v. Commissioner*[154] and held that there is no continuing payment liability past the death of the payee spouse with respect to a family support obligation. Thus, the Court's interpretation of California law comported with Federal tax law that unallocated support payments are treated as spousal support/alimony. Thus, the Court held that the test of Section 71(b)(1)(6) had been met.

In *Logue v. Commissioner*[155] the marital separation agreement did not contain an unambiguous provision terminating the payor's obligation to pay the payee in the event of her death. This forced the Court to determine whether the payor's obligation would have terminated by operation of law. The Court applied Texas law, which it found did not terminate the payments on the death of the payee spouse absent a contract to the contrary. Thus, the Court held that the obligation of the payor to pay the payee would have not terminated on the death of the payee spouse and therefore denied the payor an alimony deduction.

(3) Required Payments

If the payor spouse is required to continue to make the payments after the death of the payee spouse as a substitute for continuing pre-death payments, *none* of the payments before (or after) the death of the payee spouse qualify as alimony or separate maintenance payments.[156] See PLR 9010051, where the IRS held that payments to a trust for the benefit of the minor children of the payee spouse, if the payee spouse predeceases the payor spouse, are not alimony, because the payments to the trust will be made only upon the death of the payee spouse and will not terminate upon the death of the payee spouse.

---

152. *See* Kean, Lovejoy, Hoover, Moore, Wignall, and DeLong, cited at note 123 (Chapter 1, B.3.f(2)).

153. *In re* Marriage of McCann, 32 Cal. Rptr. 2d 639 (Ct. App. 1994).

154. T.C. Memo. 2005-91. See Chapter 1, B.3.f(5) (text at note 169) for a further discussion of this case.

155. T.C. Memo. 2017-234.

156. Temp. Prop. Treas. Reg. § 1.71-1T(A-10).

Where a decree provided that payments must be "paid in full" and the decree required that security for the payments be maintained until the payments were made in full, the requirements of I.R.C. § 71(b)(1)(D) were not met and none of the payments was deemed to be alimony.[157] Clearly, if the decree or agreement creates a liability that is enforceable by the payee's estate, this test will not be met and the payments will not be alimony.[158]

(4) 1986 TRA

As noted earlier, the 1986 TRA repealed the provision that required the divorce or separation instrument to specifically state that the liability of the payor spouse must terminate on the death of the payee spouse. Temp. Prop. Treas. Reg. § 1.71-1T(A-12) still contain this requirement, but it has obviously been overridden by the 1986 amendment. As a matter of nontax law, however, the inclusion of such a provision in a decree of divorce or written separation instrument should not be overlooked. Accordingly, it is highly recommended that such language be used for tax purposes even though not required so that there can be no mistakes as to what the parties intended.[159]

(5) Substitute for Continuation Pre-death Payments

If the payor spouse is required to make one or more payments (in cash or property) after the death of the payee spouse as a substitute for the continuation of predeath payments that would otherwise qualify as alimony or separate maintenance payments, *none* of the otherwise qualifying payments made during the lifetime of the payor will qualify as alimony or separate maintenance payments.[160] The divorce or separation instrument need not state, however, that there is no liability to make any such substitute payment (though for the reasons stated earlier such a provision should be included in the divorce or

---

157. Hoover v. Comm'r, T.C. Memo. 1995-183 (1995), *aff'd*, 102 F.3d 842, 845 (6th Cir. 1996).

158. Priv. Ltr. Rul. 9542001.

159. The change made by the 1986 TRA was "technical" in nature. Thus, it is effective, retroactively, for divorce or separation instruments executed after 1984 or pre 1985 instruments modified to include the 1984 TRA rules, i.e., it is effective as if it were part of the 1984 TRA. Therefore, if the parties failed to include this provision in a divorce or separation instrument and desired the payments to be alimony, the 1986 TRA amendment has "saved" them. On the other hand, this provision was often intentionally omitted so that the payments would not qualify as alimony. With the "relation back" provision, however, the intent of the parties is changed. Thus, it may be advisable for the parties to seek modification of the divorce or separation instrument to bring the instrument in conformity with their intent. If the spouses did not treat the payment as alimony because they failed to include the termination at death language, and if the parties intended the payment as alimony, the payee spouse should file an amended return and the payor spouse should file a claim for refund. Note that the payee spouse may be subject to interest and penalty.

160. Temp. Prop. Treas. Reg. § 1.71-1T(A-13).

separation instrument).[161] See Priv. Ltr. Rul. 9010051, where the IRS held that payments to a trust for the benefit of the minor children of the payee spouse, if the payee spouse predeceases the payor spouse, are not alimony because the payments to the trust will be made only upon the death of the payee spouse.

To the extent that one or more payments are to begin, increase in amount, or become accelerated in time as a result of the death of the payee spouse, such payments may be treated as a substitute for the continuation of payments terminating on the death of the payee spouse, which would otherwise qualify as alimony or separate maintenance payments. The determination of whether or not such payments are a substitute for the continuation of payments that would otherwise qualify as alimony or separate maintenance payments, and of the amount of the otherwise qualifying alimony or separate maintenance payments for which any such payments are a substitute, depends upon all of the facts and circumstances.[162] The following two examples illustrate the foregoing rules:

Example. Under the terms of a divorce decree, *A* is obligated to make annual alimony payments to *B* of $30,000, terminating on the earlier of the expiration of three years or the death of *B*. *B* has custody of the minor children of *A* and *B*. The decree provides that at the death of *B*, if there are minor children of *A* and *B* remaining, *A* will be obligated to make annual payments of $10,000 to a trust, the income and corpus of which are to be used for the benefit of the children until the youngest child attains the age of majority. These facts indicate that *A*'s liability to make annual $10,000 payments in trust for the benefit of the minor children upon the death of *B* is a substitute for $10,000 of the $30,000 annual payments to *B*. Accordingly, $10,000 of each of the $30,000 annual payments to *B* will not qualify as alimony or separate maintenance payments.[163]

Example. Under the terms of a divorce decree, *A* is obligated to make annual alimony payments to *B* of $30,000, terminating on the earlier of the expiration of 15 years or the death of *B*. The divorce decree provides that if *B* dies before the expiration of the 15-year period, *A* will pay to *B*'s estate the difference between the total amount that *A* would have paid had *B* survived, minus the amount actually paid. For example, if *B* dies at the end of the 10th year in which payments are made, *A* will pay to *B*'s estate $150,000 ($450,000–$300,000). These facts indicate that *A*'s liability to make a lump sum payment to *B*'s estate upon the death of *B* is a substitute for the full amount of each of the annual $30,000 payments to *B*. Accordingly, none of the annual $30,000 payments to *B* will qualify as alimony or separate maintenance payments. The

---

161. *Id.*

162. Temp. Prop. Treas. Reg. § 1.711T(A14), *See* Berry v. Comm'r, T.C. Memo. 2005-91, and Wells v. Comm'r, T.C. Memo. 1998-2 both of which are discussed in the text at fn.169 and 170 below.

163. Temp. Prop. Treas. Reg. § 1.711T(A14) (Example (1)).

result would be the same if the lump sum payable at *B*'s death were discounted by an appropriate interest factor to account for the prepayment.[164]

In *Hawley v. Commissioner*,[165] the Third Circuit Court of Appeals upheld the decision of the Tax Court that unallocated payments of support set forth in a support agreement were not alimony under Pennsylvania law. In *Hawley*, the husband was ordered to make biweekly payments toward the support of his wife and the couples' three minor children. The Court did not allocate the amount of those payments between the wife and the children. The husband made the weekly payments and deducted them as alimony. The IRS, in order to avoid being whipsawed, determined that the payments were not deductible, but that the wife must, nevertheless, include them in income. The Tax Court held that under Pennsylvania law, the unallocated support payments were not deductible alimony. The Third Circuit agreed. The reasoning of the Court was that under Pennsylvania law, even if the husband's obligation to make payments to the wife would have ended upon her death, the husband would still have to make additional payments to support his children. Thus, the Court concluded that the payments were not deductible as alimony.

In *Okerson v. Commissioner*,[166] a State Court decree ordered the husband to pay alimony to the wife. The decree stated that the alimony payments would terminate if the wife died before all the payments were made, but that the husband would then be required to make the monthly payments toward the education of their children until the children completed four years of college. Two years later the Court issued another decree and ordered the husband to make additional monthly payments to the wife's attorney as additional alimony to the wife. This decree also stated that this additional alimony would terminate if the wife died before the payments were made in full, but that the husband would then be required to continue making the monthly payments to the wife's attorney until the payments were made in full. Both decrees stated that payments were to constitute alimony in order to be deductible by husband on his return and includable in the gross income of the wife on her return.

The issue before the Court was whether the husband's liability for the payments and for any substitute payments ceased as of the date of death of the payee spouse. The husband argued that the payments constituted alimony because they terminated upon the death of the payee spouse. The Court held that the taxpayer did not meet this test because both decrees stated specifically and unequivocally that the [taxpayer's] obligation to pay alimony [terminated] upon the death of [the wife], but that the [taxpayer would] then be liable to start making corresponding payments in substitute of the alimony

164. Temp. Prop. Treas. Reg. § 1.711T(A14) (Example (2)).
165. 94 Fed. Appx. 126 (3d Cir. 2004) *aff'd sub nom* Gilbert v. Comm'r, T.C. Memo. 2003-92.
166. 123 T.C. 258 (2004).

payments.[167] Thus, the Court in its conclusion looked to the plain meaning of the statutory test and not the intent of the parties.

The Court then turned its attention to decide whether the post-death payments described in the decree were substitute payments under the regulations. The Court concluded that all the postdeath payments described in the decrees would be made after the wife's death, and that they would be made only if the wife died before the husband satisfied his alimony obligations under the decrees. The postdeath payments would also be made in substitute of the alimony payments under the decrees, which would terminate on account of the wife's death. The husband then argued that he never actually made any of those post-death payments. The Court found this fact to be unimportant. According to the Court, the standard established by Congress for substitute payments is not whether a payor spouse actually makes a substitute payment, but rather whether the payor spouse would have to make a substitute payment upon the death of the payee spouse. Looking to the plain meaning of the decree, the Court concluded that all the postdeath payments described in the decrees were substitute payments for purposes of I.R.C. § 71(b)(1)(D). As a result, since the obligation would have terminated upon the wife's death, the husband would then have been required to pay the unpaid alimony toward the education of their children, and under the second decree the husband was required to make additional monthly alimony payments to the wife's attorney. Therefore, although these obligations would have terminated upon the death of the wife, the husband would have been required to continue paying the unpaid amounts to the children and attorney. Because under both decrees the substitute payments would have been the same amount as the amounts payable as alimony under the decrees, the Court concluded that the taxpayer was not entitled to deduct any of the alimony payments for Federal income tax purposes. In sum, when the terms of the applicable divorce documents state, as here, that the payor spouse upon the death of the payee spouse must continue to make payments in substitute of payments that are required to be paid as alimony, the post-death payments fail to qualify as alimony for Federal income tax purposes. In addition, a corresponding amount of any payment that is to be made before the payee's spouse's death, and which otherwise would be deductible as alimony, fails to qualify as well.[168]

In *Berry v. Commissioner*,[169] the parties were divorced in California. The divorce documents did not address whether the husband would have to continue to make payments to the estate of the wife after her death. The Court

167. *Id.* at 264.
168. *Id.* at 268.
169. T.C. Memo. 2005-91. See Chapter 1, B.3.f(2) for another discussion of this case.

examined California statutory law and concluded that the husband's family support obligation did not entail continuing payment liability to the estate of the wife upon her death.

The Court then looked beyond the issue of continuing enforceability upon the death of a payee spouse in search of any payment obligation after the death of the payee spouse that would, in effect, represent the continuation of the husband's family support payments.

The Court first reviewed its recent opinion in *Okerson v. Commissioner*. Unlike *Okerson*, this case did not involve language in a divorce decree that could be construed as imposing a substitute obligation with respect to the payments at issue. Rather, the issue in this case was whether a court could infer a substitute payment obligation with respect to the taxpayer's family support payments on the basis of their undesignated child support component. According to the Court, the taxpayer's potential liability for child support payments in the event of the payee spouse's death represents a substitute payment obligation with respect to a corresponding portion of the payor spouse's family support payments.

The Court rejected its position in *Wells v. Commissioner*,[170] wherein it assumed a "worst case scenario" under which someone other than the noncustodial spouse would be awarded custody of the children upon the death of the custodial spouse in determining the applicability of the substitute payment clause. Prior to *Berry*, the Court had never squarely addressed the tension between I.R.C. § 71(b)(1)(D) and I.R.C. § 71(c)(1) in the context of unallocated support obligations. It resolved the tension by rejecting the interpretation of I.R.C. § 71(b)(1)(D) inherent in the "worst case scenario" approach of *Wells*. The Court believed that the "worst case scenario" test made I.R.C. § 71(b)(1)(D) superfluous. Accordingly, the Court held that a payor spouse's general State obligation to support his or her children, without more, did not cause any or all of that spouse's unallocated support obligation to fail to qualify as alimony by reason of the substitute payment clause in I.R.C. § 71(b)(1)(D). The Court rejected the notion that the applicability of I.R.C. § 71(b)(1)(D) to an unallocated support obligation is to be determined by assuming that a third-party would take custody of the children upon the death of the payee spouse, thereby ensuring the existence of a substitute payment obligation. Accordingly, the Court held that there was no substitute payment liability attributed to the unallocated child support obligation. The case presents an excellent analysis and discussion of the historical context of I.R.C. § 71 and in particular the continuing payment liability obligation under I.R.C. § 71(b)(1)(D).

170. T.C. Memo. 1998-2.

In *Wells v. Commissioner*,[171] again the marital termination agreement between the husband and wife did not state whether the payments were to terminate upon the death of the payee spouse. The Court, therefore, looked to California law to determine whether a post-death legal obligation existed. The payments under the marital termination agreement were unallocated between the payee spouse and the children.

The Court concluded that California law did not support the payor spouse's position that the payments were to terminate on the death of the payee spouse. Rather, looking at the agreement as a whole, the Court was convinced that the parties intended the payments to terminate, on a pro rata basis, as each child married, died, was emancipated, or reached a certain age, if the payee spouse had deceased. Thus, the unallocated family support payments were to terminate at some point in time other than the death of the payee spouse. Accordingly, the Court held that the payments did not terminate on the death of the payee spouse and were not deductible as alimony.

The Court then discussed a "worst case scenario" (i.e., the custodial parent dies and custody is awarded to someone other than the surviving, noncustodial spouse). The Court felt that in that situation, California law would not permit the surviving parent to avoid any further support obligation.

(6) Bad Debt Deduction

A former spouse may not claim a bad debt deduction for unpaid alimony resulting from the death of the payor, even if the obligation to pay alimony is evidenced by a promissory note of the payor spouse, since the promissory note is presumed to have a zero basis.[172]

(7) Death of Payor Spouse or Remarriage of Either Party

Note that I.R.C. § 71(b)(1)(D) does not require the payments to cease on the death of the payor spouse or the remarriage of either party. It merely requires that the payments cease on the death of the payee spouse. As noted earlier in (2) where it is recommended that the termination on death requirement be placed in the decree or written instrument, the same is true with respect to termination on the death of the payor spouse or the remarriage of either spouse. If this is what the parties want, they should so provide in the decree or written instrument. See *Campitelli v. Johnston*,[173] where the Court of Special Appeals of Maryland (now known as the Appellate Court of Maryland) held that an agreement to pay alimony until the death of the payee spouse is not void as against public policy.

---

171. T.C. Memo. 1998-2.
172. Beshear v. Comm'r, T.C. Memo. 1990-544.
173. 134 Md. App. 689, 761 A.2d 369 (2000).

(8) Court Modification

If the required termination on death statement is contained in a judgment of divorce, but on appeal the appeals Court removes the termination upon death language from the judgment of divorce, payments made by the payor spouse may still qualify as alimony, where State law provides that alimony under Section 71(b) terminates upon the death of the payee spouse, and the use of the word "alimony" by the appellate Court shows an intent by the Court to have the payments qualify as alimony under Michigan law.[174] In *Gonzales v. Commissioner*,[175] the Court held that under New Jersey law, when a separation agreement is modifiable, the payor spouse could have remained liable to pay support under the separation agreement after the death of the payee spouse. Thus, the advisor should be careful that an opinion of an appeals Court does not revoke an "alimony-qualifying" revision in the decree of divorce.[176]

(9) Attorney's Fees

In *Smith v. Commissioner*,[177] the payor spouse was obligated to pay the attorney's fees of the payee spouse. The IRS argued that the payment of the fees did not constitute alimony since they were payable even if the payee spouse died before the payment was made, thus violating this test. The Tax Court agreed with the IRS, finding that the liability for payment of the fees would not be extinguished by the death of the payee spouse. Thus, if the payor spouse is required to make an indirect payment on behalf of the payee spouse, such as the payment of legal fees, rent, education, and so on, it is recommended that a termination on death of payee provision be added to the indirect payment provision.[178]

g. No Joint Tax Return (Alimony Test no. 7)

The seventh test provides that the parties may not file a joint Federal income tax return for the taxable year.[179]

h. Not Child Support (Alimony Test no. 8)

The eighth test requires that the payments must not constitute child support.[180] See the discussion at Chapter 2, Child Support, to determine what constitutes child support.

---

174. Ryan v. Comm'r, T.C. Memo. 1998-331 discussed in Chapter 1, B.3(1)(b).
175. T.C. Memo. 1999-332.
176. *See also* Nelson v. Comm'r, T.C. Memo. 1998-268.
177. T.C. Memo. 1998-166; *see also* Stedman v. Comm'r, T.C. Memo. 2008-239.
178. *See also* Zinsmeister v. Comm'r, T.C. Memo. 2004-364, and J.R. Stedman v. Comm'r, T.C. Memo. 2008-239.
179. I.R.C. § 71(e).
180. Temp. Prop. Treas. Reg. § 1.711T(A2), (A15).

i. Excess Front-end Loading Rules (Alimony Test no. 9)

The excess frontend loading rules are designed to prevent disguised property settlements from qualifying as alimony. The excess front-end loading rules were two special rules that applied to the extent that payments in any calendar year exceeded $15,000.[181]

The first rule, known as the *minimum term rule*, had to be met in order for any annual payment in excess of $15,000 to qualify as alimony or separate maintenance.[182] This rule requires that alimony or separate maintenance payments be called for, at a minimum, during the three post-separation years. If the alimony payments cease or decrease by more than a certain amount, this rule may apply, which will then subject the payor spouse to the second rule.

The second rule, known as the *recapture rule*, characterized payments retrospectively by requiring a recalculation and inclusion in income by the payor and a deduction by the payee of previously paid alimony or separate maintenance payments to the extent that the amount of such payments during any of the three postseparation years[183] falls short of the amount of payments during a prior year by more than $15,000.[184]

Thus, the excess front-end loading rules provide that if the total alimony paid in the first postseparation year exceeds the average alimony paid in the second and third postseparation years by more than $15,000, the excess amounts are recaptured in the third year. In addition, the recapture period is three years. The rule may apply because the payor spouse fails to make timely payments, or the payor spouse is unable to continue to make alimony payments, or the needs of the payee spouse decreases. Thus, the excess front-end loading rules may be invoked intentionally (not likely) or inadvertently (more likely).

(1) General Rule

(a) Minimum Term Rule

The minimum term rule operates in the following manner: To the extent payments are made in excess of $15,000, a payment will qualify as an alimony or separate maintenance payment only if alimony or separate maintenance payments are to be made in each of the three post-separation years. For example, pursuant to a divorce decree, *A* is to make alimony payments to *B* of $20,000 in each of the two calendar years 2000 through 2001. *A* is to make no payment in 2002. Under the minimum term rule, only $15,000 will qualify as an alimony payment in each of the calendar years 2000 through 2001. If the divorce decree

181. Temp. Prop. Treas. Reg. § 1.711T(A19).
182. *Id*. The $10,000 level was increased to $15,000 by the 1986 TRA.
183. *See* Arrearages at Chapter 1, I.B.4.
184. *Id*.

also required *A* to make a $1 payment in 2002, the minimum term rule would be satisfied and $20,000 would be treated as an alimony payment in each of the calendar years 2000 through 2001. The recapture rule would, however, apply for 2002. For purposes of determining whether alimony or separate maintenance payments are to be made in any year, the possible termination of such payments upon the happening of a contingency (other than the passage of time) that has not yet occurred is ignored (unless such contingency may cause all or a portion of the payment to be treated as a child support payment).[185]

(b) Recapture Rule

The recapture rule operates in the following manner: If the amount of alimony or separate maintenance payments paid in any post-separation year (referred to as the "computation year") falls short of the amount of alimony or separate maintenance payments paid in any prior post-separation year by more than $15,000, the payor must compute an "excess amount" for the computation year. The excess amount for any computation year is the sum of excess amounts determined with respect to each prior post-separation year. The excess amount determined with respect to a prior post-separation year is the excess of (i) the amount of alimony or separate maintenance payments paid by the payor spouse during such prior post-separation year, over (ii) the amount of the alimony or separate maintenance payments paid by the payor spouse during the computation year plus $15,000. For purposes of this calculation, the amount of alimony or separate maintenance payments made by the payor spouse during any post-separation year preceding the computation year is reduced by any excess amount previously determined with respect to such year. The rules just set forth may be illustrated by the following example.

A makes alimony payments to *B* of $25,000 in 2000 and $7,000 in 2001. The excess amount with respect to 2000 that is recaptured in 2001 is $3,000 ($25,000 – ($7,000 + $15,000)). For purposes of subsequent computation years, the amount deemed paid in 2000 is $22,000. If *A* makes alimony payments to *B* of $1,000 in 2002, the excess amount that is recaptured in 2002 will be $11,000. This is the sum of an $11,000 excess amount with respect to 2000 ($22,000 – $1,000 + $10,000)) and no excess amount with respect to 2001 ($12,000 – ($1,000 + $15,000)). If, prior to the end of 2003, payments decline further, additional recapture will occur. The payor spouse must include the excess amount in gross income for his or her taxable year beginning with or in the computation year. The payee spouse is allowed a deduction for the excess amount in computing adjusted gross income for his or her taxable year beginning with or in the computation year. However, the payee spouse must compute the excess amount by reference to the date when payments were made and not when

185. Temp. Prop. Treas. Reg. § 1.71-1T(A-23).

payments were received.[186] Alimony payments in excess of $15,000 per year are deductible only if required to be made for three consecutive calendar years beginning with the first calendar year in which the payor spouse pays to the payee spouse alimony or separate maintenance payments under I.R.C. § 71.[187] Thus, the recapture rule does not apply to payments to the extent the annual payments never exceed $15,000. For example, assume the payor spouse is to make a single payment to the payee spouse of $15,000. If all the other tests of alimony are met, the payment will qualify as an alimony payment. If, however, the payor makes a single payment of $20,000, $15,000 of the payment would qualify as alimony and $5,000 of the payment would be disqualified under the minimum term rule.[188]

If the alimony payments in the first postseparation year exceed the average payments in the second and third postseparation years by more than $15,000, the excess amounts are recaptured in the third postseparation year by requiring the payor spouse to include the excess in income and allowing the payee spouse who previously included the alimony in income a deduction for that amount in computing the payee spouse adjusted gross income. A similar rule applies to the extent the payments in the second postseparation year exceed the payments in the third postseparation year by more than $15,000.[189]

The reason for this rule is to prevent persons whose divorce occurs near the end of the year from making a deductible property settlement at the beginning of the next year. Only payments made in the first and second post-separation years are subject to recapture. Payments in the third postseparation year and thereafter are not subject to recapture. Thus, there is a $15,000 annual floor, and the excess for the second postseparation year is computed before the excess for the first post-separation year.

(c) Three Post-separation Years

The three postseparation years are the three consecutive calendar years beginning with the first calendar year in which the payor spouse pays to the payee spouse alimony or separate maintenance payments (except a payment made under a decree for support under I.R.C. § 71(b)(2)(C)). Each calendar year (or part of a year) within this period is referred to as a "postseparation year."[190] Thus, the term "first postseparation year" means the first calendar year in which the payor spouse pays alimony or separate maintenance to the payee spouse; the term "second postseparation year" means the second calendar year in which alimony or separate maintenance is paid; and the term "third

186. Temp. Prop. Treas. Reg. § 1.71-1T(A-24).
187. I.R.C. § 71(f).
188. *Id.*
189. Temp. Prop. Treas. Reg. § 1.71-1T(A-20).
190. Temp. Prop. Treas. Reg. § 1.71-1T(A-22).

postseparation year" means the third calendar year in which alimony or separate maintenance is paid.[191] The three-year period need not commence with the year in which the spouses separate or divorce, or with the year in which payments under the divorce or separation instrument are made, if no payments during such year qualify as alimony or separate maintenance payments.[192]

Example. For example, a decree for divorce of *H* and *W* is entered in October 1988. The decree requires *H* to make monthly payments to *W* commencing November 1, 1988, but *H* and *W* are members of the same household until February 15, 1989 (and, as a result, the payments prior to January 16, 1989, do not qualify as alimony). For purposes of applying the excess frontend loading rules to payments from *H* to *W*, the three-year postseparation years are the calendar years 1989, 1990, and 1991.[193] If the payor spouse had been making payments pursuant to a decree of divorce or separate maintenance or a written separation agreement under I.R.C. § 71(b)(2)(A) and (B), a modification of the instrument or the substitution of a new instrument (for example, the substitution of a divorce decree for a written separation agreement where the agreement is merged into the decree) will not result in the creation of additional postseparation years. If, however, the payor spouse has been making payments pursuant to a decree of support described in I.R.C. § 71(b)(2)(C), the three-year rule does not begin until the first calendar year in which alimony payments are made under a decree of divorce or separate maintenance or written separation agreement under Section 71(b)(2)(A) and (B).[194]

(2) Exceptions

There are four exceptions to the income recapture rule.

(a) Death or Remarriage

The first exception provides that recapture is not required if either party dies, or if the payee spouse remarries, by the end of the third postseparation year and payments cease because of such death of the payor or payee spouse or remarriage of the payee spouse.[195] For example, pursuant to a decree of divorce, *H* is to make cash payments to *W* of $30,000 in each of the calendar years 1990 through 1995. *H* made cash payments of $30,000 in 1990 and $15,000 in 1991, in which year *W* remarries and alimony payments cease. The recapture rule does not apply for 1991 or any subsequent year. If alimony payments made by *H*

191. I.R.C. § 71(f)(6), Temp. Prop. Treas. Reg. § 1.71-1T(A-22).

192. Temp. Prop. Treas. Reg. § 1.71-1T(A-22). The regulation refers to six post-separation years, but this is not correct because this was changed to three post-separation years by the 1986 TRA.

193. *Id.*

194. *Id.*

195. I.R.C. § 71(f)(5)(A); Temp. Prop. Treas. Reg. § 1.71-1T(A-25).

decline or cease during a post-separation year for any other reason (including a failure by the payor spouse to make timely payments, a modification of the decree of divorce or written separation agreement, a reduction in the support needs of the payee spouse, or a reduction in the ability of the payor spouse to provide support), excess amounts with respect to prior post-separation years will be subject to recapture.[196]

(b) Decree of Support

The second exception pertains to payments made under a decree of support under I.R.C. § 71(b)(2)(C), which is not a decree of divorce or separate maintenance.[197] Payments made under a decree for support are to be disregarded entirely for purposes of applying the excess front end loading rules.[198]

(c) Fluctuating Payment

The third exception provides that payments made under a continuing liability over a period of not less than three post-separation years to pay a fixed portion of the payor's income from a business or property or from compensation for employment or self-employment are not subject to recapture.[199] This exception is known as the fluctuating payment exception because it applies when the payment is not a fixed amount, but is a fixed percentage of the payor spouse's income from the sources named. For this exception to apply, the payments must cover at least 36 full months.[200]

According to the Joint Committee of Taxation, in its Explanation of the Deficit Reduction Act of 1984,[201] the fluctuating payment exception applies when the obligation is to pay different portions of income at different income levels. For example, the payor may be obligated to pay 25 percent of income up to $25,000, 20 percent of income from $25,001 to $50,000, and 15 percent of income above $50,000.

Example. The payor spouse agrees to pay the payee spouse 25 percent of his gross employment compensation for the next four years. The payor spouse's employment compensation is $100,000 in year one, $110,000 in year two, $150,000 in year three, and $140,000 in year four. Even though the payee spouse receives $25,000 in year one, $27,500 in year two, $37,500 in year three, and $35,000 in year four, which are frontend loaded payments, recapture is not

196. Temp. Prop. Treas. Reg. § 1.71-1T(A-25).

197. I.R.C. § 71(f)(5)(B); Prop. Treas. Reg. § 1.71-1T(A-21) and (A-25). *See* Chapter 1, B.3(C)(3) for a discussion of decree support. Payments made under decrees of support are disregard entirely for purposes of applying the excess front end loading rules.

198. Prop. Treas. Reg. *§ 1.71-1T(A-21).*

199. I.R.C. § 71(f)(5)(C); Temp. Prop. Treas. Reg. § 1.71-1T(A-25).

200. Temp. Prop. Treas. Reg. § 1.71-1T(A-25).

201. General Explanation of the Revenue Provisions of the Deficit Reduction Act of 1984, HR 4710, 98th Cong., Pub. Law 98-369, Joint Committee of Taxation, Page 716, December 31, 1984.

required because the payments are fluctuating and are not within the control of the payor spouse.

(d) $15,000 Ceiling

The fourth exception provides that the annual payments may never exceed $15,000. Some front-end loading is permissible without creating recapture where payments are substantially (though not identically) level. For example, assume the payor pays the payee $60,000 in year one, $55,000 in year two, and $50,000 in year three. Payments in year one ($60,000) do not exceed the average of payments in years two and three ($52,500) plus $15,000. Also, payments in year two ($55,000) do not exceed payments in year three ($50,000) plus $15,000.

(3) Two Calculations

Only two calculations are required.

First, payments in year two are compared to payments in year three. If the payments in year three, plus $15,000, are less than the amounts paid in year two, the difference is recaptured.

Second, payments in the first year are compared to the average of payments in years two and three. If this average, plus $15,000, is less than the payments in year one, the difference is recaptured. Thus, if the recapture rule applies, the payor spouse picks up income in year three and the payee spouse receives a deduction in year three.[202]

(4) Examples

Example 1. If the payor spouse makes alimony payments of $50,000 in the first postseparation year and no payments in the second or third postseparation years, $35,000 will be recaptured in the third postseparation year. (Payment in first postseparation year ($50,000) less sum of average of payments in second and third postseparation years (0) less $15,000 floor equals $35,000). Thus, the payor spouse will receive a $50,000 alimony deduction in the first year, and the payee spouse will include $50,000 in gross income in the first year; but because $35,000 is treated as excess alimony, that amount must be recaptured and included in income by the payor spouse in year three, and the payee spouse will receive a $35,000 deduction in year three. Not considered, however, is the time use of money, for here the payor spouse receives an interest-free loan from the payee spouse for two years. It should be noted that although in the third post-separation year the payor spouse has recapture income of $35,000 and the payee spouse receives a deduction of $35,000, this is

---

202. For a worksheet on calculating the recapture, see IRS Publication 504, Divorced or Separated Individuals, Worksheet 1, pages 17 and 18 (2021).

phantom income and a phantom deduction because the payee spouse *does not* repay $35,000 to the payor spouse.

Line		
1	Alimony Paid Second Year	-0-
2	Alimony Paid Third Year	-0-
3	Floor	15,000
4	Add Lines 2 & 3	15,000
5	Subtract Line 4 from Line 1 (but not less than -0-)	-0-
6	Alimony Paid First Year	50,000
7	Adjusted Alimony Paid Second Year	-0-
	Subtract Line 5 from Line 1	
8	Alimony Paid in Third Year	0
9	Add Lines 7 & 8	-0-
10	Divide Line 9 by 2	7,500
11	Floor	15,000
12	Add Lines 10 & 11	15,000
13	Subtract Line 12 from Line 6	35,000
14	Recaptured Alimony:	35,000
	Add Lines 5 & 13	

Example 2. Assume the payor spouse makes alimony payments of $50,000 in the first postseparation year, $20,000 in the second postseparation year, and no payments are made in the third postseparation year. The recapture amount is $42,500, determined as follows:

(a) Excess payments for the first postseparation year are the excess (if any) of:

(i) The amount of the alimony or separate maintenance payments paid by the payor during the first postseparation year ($50,000), over

(ii) The sum of:

(A) The average of:

(1) The alimony or separate maintenance payments paid by the payor during the second postseparation year ($20,000), reduced by the excess payments for the second postseparation year ($5,000), and

(2) The alimony or separate maintenance payments made by the payor during the third postseparation year (0), plus

(3) Which is $7,500, plus

(B) $15,000

(iii) Equals $27,500.

(b) Excess payments for the second postseparation year are the excess (if any) of

(i) The amount of the alimony or separate maintenance payments paid by the payor during the second postseparation year ($20,000), over

(ii) The sum of:

(A) The amount of alimony or separate maintenance payments paid by the payor during the third postseparation (0) plus

(B) $15,000

(iii) Equals $5,000.

Line		
1	**Alimony Paid Second Year**	**20,000**
2	**Alimony Paid Third Year**	**-0-**
3	Floor	15,000
4	Add Lines 2 & 3	15,000
5	Subtract Line 4 from Line 1	5,000
6	**Alimony Paid First Year**	**50,000**
7	Adjusted Alimony Paid Second Year	15,000
	Subtract Line 5 from Line 1	
8	Alimony Paid in Third Year	-0-
9	Add Lines 7 & 8	15,000
10	Divide Line 9 by 2	7,500
11	Floor	15,000
12	Add Lines 10 & 11	22,500
13	Subtract Line 12 from Line 6	37,500
14	**Recaptured Alimony:**	**42,500**
	Add Lines 5 & 13	

By spreading the property settlements evenly over three years, rather than in a lump sum in year one, the property settlement may be characterized as alimony and the recapture rule avoided. Thus, by spreading the $50,000 over three years, the recapture rules may be avoided.

Example 3. Assume that *H* and *W*, by written separation agreement, agree that *H* will pay *W* alimony of $75,000 in year one, $50,000 in year two, and $10,000 per year in each of years three through ten. The agreement provides that the payments will cease on the death or remarriage of *W*. All the other alimony tests are met.

(i) The excess alimony for year two is $25,000. This is the excess of $50,000 (the year-two payment) over the sum of (a) $10,000 (the year three payment) and (b) $15,000 (the threshold amount). Thus, the excess alimony of $25,000 in year two is recaptured in year three. In determining the recapture amount for year one, only $25,000, or the excess of the year two alimony payment ($50,000) over the excess alimony payment for year two ($25,000), is treated as alimony paid in year two.

(ii) The excess alimony amount for year one is $17,500, the excess of $50,000 (the year one alimony payment) over the sum of (a) $25,000 (the recomputed year two alimony payment), and (b) $10,000 (the year three alimony payment), which sum is then divided by two, and less (c) $15,000 (the threshold amount).

$$50{,}000 - \frac{(25{,}000 + 10{,}000)}{2} - 15{,}000 = 17{,}500$$

Thus, of the $50,000 alimony payment in year one, $17,500 is treated as excess alimony and is recaptured in year three.

Line		
1	**Alimony Paid Second Year**	**50,000**
2	**Alimony Paid Third Year**	**10,000**
3	Floor	15,000
4	Add Lines 2 & 3	25,000
5	Subtract Line 4 from Line 1	25,000
6	**Alimony Paid First Year**	**75,000**
7	Adjusted Alimony Paid Second Year	25,000
	Subtract Line 5 from Line 1	
8	Alimony Paid in Third Year	10,000
9	Add Lines 7 & 8	35,000
10	Divide Line 9 by 2	17,500
11	Floor	15,000
12	Add Lines 10 & 11	32,500
13	Subtract Line 12 from Line 6	42,500
14	**Recaptured Alimony:**	**67,500**
	Add Lines 5 & 13	

In summary, *H* will deduct $75,000 in year one, $50,000 in year two, and $10,000 in each of years three through ten. In addition, *H* will also have recapture income of $67,500 in year three, which *H* will include in gross income. *W* will have income of $75,000 in year one, $50,000 in year two, and $10,000 in each of years three through ten. In addition, *W* will deduct $67,500 in year three.

3. Arrearages

a. Deductibility of Lump Sum Payment

If the payor spouse is in arrears in the payment of alimony and makes a lump sum payment in discharge of the arrearage, the character of the underlying obligation which the arrearage payment discharges, and not the lump sum payment, determines whether the lump sum payment is deductible.[203]

For example, if a lump sum payment discharges past due alimony, it should be deemed current alimony.[204] Thus, if a payor spouse and payee spouse are cash basis taxpayers, as is the usual case, a lump sum payment of alimony arrearage should be taxable to the payee spouse in the year of receipt and deductible by the payor spouse in the year of payment.

b. Planning

This tax treatment regarding the payment of arrearage of alimony may cause a bunching of the payee spouse's income which, because of the graduated income tax rate structure, may leave the payee spouse with less after-tax dollars than anticipated. Therefore, if you represent the payee spouse, it would appear to be advisable to insert a clause in the decree or agreement providing for the payment of damages to the payee spouse in an amount at least equal to the amount of after-tax dollars lost as a result of the arrearage payments. This clause should not, however, provide for the payment of the payee spouse's taxes by the payor spouse, since payment of the payee spouse's taxes by the payor spouse may be deemed income to the payee spouse, thus pyramiding taxes on taxes.[205] Moreover, as noted earlier, this may invoke the frontend loading rules. Thus, the payor spouse should avoid bunching income because of the recapture rule, but if the payments are made under a decree for support, the recapture rules do not apply and bunching may be warranted for tax planning.

---

203. *E.g.*, Davis v. Comm'r, 41 T.C. 815 (1964); Stroud v. Comm'r, T.C. Memo. 1993-317 (arrearage payments made in subsequent years retain the same character as payments due under the original support agreement).

204. Dalton v. Comm'r, 34 T.C. 879 (1960); Capodanno v. Comm'r, 69 T.C. 638 (1978), *aff'd*, 602 F.2d 64 (3d Cir. 1979).

205. *See* Rev. Rul. 58100, 1958-1 C.B. 3.

c. Effect of Amendment Nunc Pro Tunc

Payments made under a decree that is amended nunc pro tunc by a Court of competent jurisdiction to reflect correctly the Court's intention at the time of its entry are also deductible retroactively.[206] But see *Graham v. Commissioner*,[207] where the Court denied retroactive effect to a nunc pro tunc amendment of a divorce court altering the character of the payments from alimony to child support on the grounds that state law (Kentucky) permitted nunc pro tunc amendments only to correct clerical errors and not judicial errors.[208]

d. Amount Allocable to Arrearage

If a lump sum payment represents arrearage that the payor spouse desires to deduct, the agreement should specify the amount of the payment allocable to the arrearage.

e. Failure to Make Timely Payments

The failure of the payor spouse to make timely payments may cause excess front-end loading problems because of the application of the minimum term and recapture rules just discussed.

f. Priority in Application of Payments

When any payment is for both alimony and child support and the payment is less than the amount specified in the divorce or separation instrument, the payment is applied first to the child support and then to alimony.[209]

4. Year of Inclusion and Deduction

Payments are includable in the payee spouse's income only for the taxable year in which the payments are received (assuming, of course, that the payee spouse is a cash-basis taxpayer, which is the norm). Thus, the payee spouse is treated as a cash basis taxpayer even if he or she files returns on the accrual basis.[210] If, however, the alimony payments are to be made by an estate or trust, such alimony payments are to be included in the gross income of the payee spouse for the taxable year in which they are includible according to the rules pertaining to income of estates and trust as provided in Sections 652, 662, and

---

206. Newman v. Comm'r, 68 T.C. 494 (1977).
207. 79 T.C. 415 (1982).
208. *See also* Hayes v. Comm'r, 101 T.C. 593 (1993) (discussed at Chapter V.C.4.e.(2)(b)(iii)). *See* Temp. Prop. Treas. Reg. § 1.711T(A22).
209. I.R.C. § 71(c)(3).
210. Prop. Treas. Reg. § 1.71-1(b)(5).

682, whether or not such payments are made out of the income of such estates or trusts.[211]

Payments are deductible by the payor spouse in the year paid, again assuming the taxpayer is a cash basis taxpayer.[212]

If the recapture rule applies:

(a) the payor spouse must include the excess amount in gross income for his or her third taxable year,[213] and

(b) the payee spouse may deduct the excess amount in computing adjusted gross income for his or her third taxable year. The payee spouse must compute the excess amount by reference to the date when payments were made and not when payments were received.[214]

Generally, alimony is includable in income by the payee spouse and deductible by the payor spouse in the same year. *Burkes v. Commissioner*,[215] however, illustrates where such consistent timing may not apply. Under a divorce judgment, *H* was to pay *W* $60,000 as "additional alimony" toward attorney's fees. Late in the year, *W* filed a garnishment against *H*, and *H*'s wages were garnished. The Court issued payment to *W*'s counsel in two parts, one in late December 1990 and one in early January 1991. *W*'s attorney deposited the two checks into a trust account and disbursed the proceeds to *W* in 1991. *H* paid *W* the balance of the attorney's fees in 1991.

The issue before the Court was the year in which the funds were includable in the gross income of *W*. Applying the doctrine of constructive receipt, the Court held that the payment to *W*'s counsel in late December 1990 was income to *W* in 1990, even though she did not receive the funds until 1991, because the attorney was *W*'s agent and received the amounts from the Court on *W*'s behalf. The balance was includable in *W*'s 1991 income. *H*, on the other hand, was allowed to deduct in 1990 the amount garnished from his wages in 1990, and to deduct in 1991 the amount he paid *W* in 1991.

Thus, due to the time between the garnishment and payment to *W*'s attorney in 1990, and her receipt of those amounts in 1991, *H* could deduct the

211. *Id.*

212. I.R.C. § 215; The payor spouse has the burden of proving the payments were made. Cancelled checks are acceptable evidence; uncorroborated self-serving testimony is not. *See* Croteau v. Comm'r, T.C. Memo. 1998-9. *See* Melvin v. Comm'r, T.C. Memo. 2008-115 ("Advance" payments made in 1985 were not deductible in 2003. Payments are deductible in year of payment. Thus, since the taxpayer made no payments of alimony in 2003, the taxpayer was not entitled to a deduction in 2003); Jonas III v. Comm'r, T.C. Memo. 2009-49 (payor spouse not entitled to deduction for year in issue because payor spouse did not make any payments to payee spouse for year in issue).

213. Temp. Prop. Treas. Reg. § 1.71-1T(A-24).

214. *Id.*

215. T.C. Memo. 1998-61.

garnished amount in 1990, whereas *W* had to include most of the garnished amount in income in 1990, and the rest in 1991.

The payor spouse is not required to withhold income taxes on alimony payments made to the payee spouse. Thus, if you are counsel to the payee spouse, you should advise the payee spouse that he or she is responsible for the payment of Federal income taxes on the payments received, and that the payee spouse should make quarterly estimated payments of tax to cover any tax on the alimony payments.[216] Failure to do so will cause the payee spouse to incur substantial penalty and interest on the missed quarterly payment. Thus, the payee spouse should be advised that each alimony payment is not his or hers to spend in full, but a portion of the payment should be set aside to make estimated tax payments.

An exception to the non-withholding rule is where the payee spouse is a nonresident alien. In such instance, the tax should be withheld equal to 30 percent of the alimony payment.[217]

5. Resolving Disputes Concerning Payments to Former Spouse

In *Barrett v. United States*,[218] the district Court held that two payments made to resolve a past alimony arrearage and a future alimony obligation were not deductible under I.R.C. § 71(b) because the payments were lump sum alimony, which did not satisfy the requirement of I.R.C. § 71(b)(1)(D).

In *Kitch v. Commissioner*,[219] the Tax Court held that payments made by the estate of the payor spouse to the estate of the payee spouse to resolve an alimony delinquency were fully includable in the income of the payee spouse's estate as income in respect of a decedent under I.R.C. § 691. The amount of income recognized was not limited by I.R.C. § 682(b) to the distributable net income of the payor spouse's estate.

6. The Rules of I.R.C. § 215

a. Law Prior to the Tax Cuts and Jobs Act of 2017

For pre-2019 divorce or separation instruments, I.R.C. § 215(a) allows the payor spouse to deduct the amount of alimony or separate maintenance meeting the requirements of I.R.C. § 71 in computing the amount of the payor spouse's adjusted gross income.

However, I.R.C. § 215(c), as amended, adds a provision permitting the Secretary of the Treasury to prescribe regulations under which (i) any individual receiving alimony or separate maintenance payments is required to furnish his

216. I.R.C. § 6654.
217. Section 1441(a).
218. 878 F. Supp. 892 (S. D. Miss. 1995).
219. 104 T.C. 1 (1995).

or her taxpayer identification number to the person making the payments;[220] and (ii) the individual making the payments is required to include the payee's taxpayer identification number on his or her return for the taxable year in which the payments are made,[221] except where the payee spouse is a foreign person who does not have a U.S. tax identification number.

Temp. Treas. Reg. § 1.2151T (August 31, 1984) has been promulgated under the authority of I.R.C. § 215(c). It requires the payor spouse to include on his or her first filed return of tax (Form 1040) for the taxable year in which the payment is made the payee's Social Security number. The payee is required to furnish the number to the payor.

In PLR 200251004, however, the IRS held that the payor spouse may deduct alimony payments even when the payor spouse does not include the recipient's tax identification number on the payor spouse's tax return. Pursuant to I.R.C. § 215(c), the IRS propounded regulations that require the payor spouse to include on his or her return the payee spouse's Social Security number. In the PLR, however, the IRS acknowledged that foreign alimony recipients usually do not have taxpayer identification numbers. Procedurally, such persons may obtain a taxpayer identification number. However, in many cases there may be no effective way to force the foreign recipients of alimony to obtain a tax identification number for their respective payors. Thus, the IRS concluded that it would not deny the deduction for noncompliance of the tax identification provision under either the statute or the implementing regulations.

I.R.C. § 215 also provides that no deduction is allowed with respect to any payment if, by reason of I.R.C. § 682 (relating to income from trusts), the amount thereof is not includable in the individual's gross income.[222]

In a case involving pure chutzpah, the taxpayers were denied an alimony deduction for payments made as guarantors of their daughter's divorce agreement. The taxpayers were not the divorcing parties, their daughter was and therefore they did not meet any of the tests of Section 71 to characterize the payments as alimony.[223]

In an interesting case, the IRS determined that the taxpayer received a "double deduction" by excluding from gross income health insurance premiums pursuant to an employer's cafeteria plan, and then deducting those payments as alimony, which his spouse included in gross income. The Tax Court disagreed. The Court looked to the parity created between Sections 71 and 215, that if the one spouse included the payments in income, the other spouse would be entitled to an alimony deduction, and concluded that an alimony

220. I.R.C. § 215(c)(1).
221. I.R.C. § 215(c)(2).
222. I.R.C. § 215(d).
223. Berger v. Comm'r T.C. Memo 2021.89.

deduction was appropriate for premiums paid for his ex-wife's insurance, even if the wife excluded the premiums from gross income.[224]

Caution is advised in claiming an alimony deduction to which the taxpayer is not entitled because penalties may be added to the deficiency. In *Shelton v. Commissioner*,[225] the decree of divorce provided that each party waived alimony from the other. The husband nevertheless claimed an alimony deduction for military separation payments he made to his spouse. In addition to denying the alimony deduction, the Court held that the taxpayer was subject to the accuracy-related penalty because he did not act with reasonable cause and in good faith since the divorce decree specifically stated that neither party was entitled to alimony.

To be entitled to an alimony deduction, the taxpayer must be able to substantiate the deduction. Entitlement to claim a deduction in prior years does not entitle the taxpayer to the deduction in a subsequent year without adequate substantiation in the subsequent year.[226]

b. Law As a Result of the Tax Cuts and Jobs Act of 2017

As noted earlier in Chapter 1.A. under the Tax Cuts and Jobs Act of 2017 (PL 115-97, 12.22.2017), the deduction by the payor spouse for the payment of alimony and the inclusion of alimony payments in the gross income of the payee spouse will not apply for divorce or separation instruments executed after December 31, 2018.

224. Leyh v. Comm'r 157 T.C. No.7 (2021).
225. T.C. Memo. 2011-266
226. Polz v. Comm'r, T.C. Memo. 2011-117.

2 Child Support

A. Law as a Result of Tax Cuts and Jobs Act of 2017

The Tax Cuts and Jobs Act of 2017 (TCJA 2017) repealed Section 71 for divorce or separation instruments entered into after December 31, 2018, or for instruments executed before January 1, 2019, if the divorce or separation instrument is modified after December 31, 2018, and the modification expressly provides that Section 71 applies as in effect before its repeal by the TCJA 2017. Thus, under post-2018 divorce or separation instruments, there is no need to distinguish between payments of child support and payments of alimony, for tax purposes, because both types of payments are not deductible by the payor spouse, nor are such payments includible in the gross income of the payee spouse. As a result of TCJA 2017, there is no longer a necessity to distinguish payments between alimony and child support for purposes of Federal income taxation. The following discussion applies to divorce or separation instruments entered into before January 1, 2019.

B. Law Prior to Tax Cuts and Jobs Act of 2017

Divorce or separation instruments executed before January 1, 2019, follow the rules in effect prior to TCJA of 2017. If a divorce or separation instrument is modified after December 31, 2018, the instrument still follows the law in effect prior to TCJA 2017 so long as the modifications do not change the terms of the payments. As a result, the law in effect prior to TCJA 2017 is discussed here because of pre-2019 divorce or separation instruments, which are not modified after 2018 to make the provisions of TCJA 2017 applicable.

I.R.C. § 71(c)(1) provides that the payee spouse's gross income does not include any payment that the divorce or separation instrument fixes, in terms of an amount of money or a part of the payment, as a sum that is payable for the support of all children of the payor spouse.[1] Thus, child support can be for a minor child or an adult child.

Concomitantly, the payor spouse cannot deduct child support payments, since child support payments are not includible in the payee spouse's gross income.[2]

In *Bogard v. Commissioner*,[3] Federal law and not State law controlled to determine whether payments were alimony or child support. Moreover, the choice of law rules are not applicable to determine the character of the payments. Thus, where the State in which the divorce occurs treats the payment as alimony, and the payee spouse moves to another State that treats the payments as child support, the payments are treated as alimony for purposes of Federal income taxation, because the payments are characterized as alimony under I.R.C. § 71.[4]

1. Specific Designation

a. General Rule

For payments to qualify as child support rather than as alimony, the amount attributable to child support must be fixed (or treated as fixed) in the decree or agreement.[5] If the amount is not designated specifically, all payments are deemed alimony, even if the parties intend part of the payment to be child support.[6]

b. Fixed or Treated as Fixed

A payment that, under the terms of the divorce or separation instrument, is fixed (or treated as fixed) as payable for the support of a child of the payor spouse does not qualify as an alimony or separate maintenance payment. Thus, such a payment is not deductible by the payor spouse nor includible in the gross income of the payee spouse.[7]

(1) Fixed

A payment is "fixed" as payable for the support of a child of the payor spouse if the divorce or separation instrument specifically designates some sum or

1. *See also* Temp. Prop. Treas. Reg. § 1.711T(A15).
2. *Id.*
3. 59 T.C. 97 (1972). See text at Chapter 1, B.3(c)(2)(a).
4. Cain v. Comm'r, T.C. Memo. 1976-175.
5. I.R.C. § 71(c)(l); Comm'r v. Lester, 366 U.S. 299 (1961).
6. Zinsmeister v. Comm'r, T.C. Memo. 2000-364 (2000) (Amounts specified for payment of the child's trombone, graduation expense and dental work were treated as child support and not alimony because they were fixed for the support of the child.).
7. Temp. Prop. Treas. Reg. § 1.711T(A15).

portion (which sum or portion may fluctuate) as payable for the support of a child of the payor spouse.[8]

The key word is "fixed," which means that of the total amount paid to the payee spouse for alimony and/or child support, the amount allocated between alimony and child support can be determined with absolute mathematical certainty. Absent such certainty, the payments will be treated as alimony. Thus, as the following examples indicate, child support need not be fixed numerically; all that is required is that it be mathematically determinable.

If the divorce or separation instrument states that ten (10) percent of each payment to the payee spouse is for child support, ten (10) percent of each payment is "fixed" as child support and will be characterized as child support for purposes of Federal income taxation. Moreover, if the payor spouse agrees to pay the payee spouse an amount necessary to pay for their child's college education, those payments will be treated as child support because they "fix" the payments to be made as child support.

In *Freyre v. United States*,[9] the order of the Court required the taxpayer to pay his spouse $1,460.50 per month "as and for support." The taxpayer deducted this amount on his return as alimony. The IRS disallowed this deduction and claimed that the payment was nondeductible child support. The lower court agreed with the IRS. The Sixth Circuit reversed and agreed with the taxpayer, holding that the court order did not "specifically designate" or "fix" the monthly payment as child support. The Court concluded that the monthly payment is considered alimony and thus is deductible by the taxpayer.[10]

Freyre presents an excellent example of the care counsel must take in reviewing court orders. In *Freyre*, the divorce decree noted that the parties agreed that the husband would pay the wife $1,460.50 per month for child support. The wife's counsel prepared a consent order, signed by the attorneys for the husband and wife, which required the husband to pay the wife $1,460.50 per month "as and for support." The word "child" appears to have been accidently omitted before the word "support." The Court, although sympathetic to the government's position that the monthly payment of $1,460.50 should be treated as alimony ("it is unlikely, that, in drafting the consent order, the parties intentionally omitted the word 'child' to substantially alter their agreement"), the statute and the regulations provide that for a payment to constitute child support the divorce instrument must specifically designate a payment as child support. Therefore, regardless of any previous agreement or mistake in drafting, the Court reluctantly held that the $1,460.50 monthly payment constituted

8. I.R.C. § 71(c)(1); Temp. Prop. Treas. Reg. § 1.711T(A16).

9. 135 Fed. Appx. 863 (6th Cir. 2005).

10. *See also* Raymond v. Comm'r, T.C. Memo. 1997-219 (Payments of $X to W which she used solely for support of children were child support and not alimony because the support order did not fix in terms of money that any of the payments were for the support of the children.).

alimony and not child support, deductible by the husband and taxable to the wife. Query whether the result could have been avoided by having the decree amended nunc pro tunc.[11]

In *Delong v. Commissioner*,[12] the Court ordered the husband to pay the wife family support payments of $3,000 per month. The Court indicated that the family support payments were for both spousal support and child support. It did not allocate any specific portion of the family support payments as spousal support or child support. The Service argued that because the family support payments were partly for child support, some of the family support payments constituted child support and hence were not deductible by the payor spouse. The Court, relying upon *Lester v. Commissioner*, held that an unallocated award of spousal and child support does not "fix" any portion of the payment as a sum that is payable for the support of the payor spouse's children. State law may also be considered by the courts to determine if unallocated support payments constitute alimony or child support. In *Hawley v. Commissioner*,[13] the Court looked to Pennsylvania law to determine that the unallocated payments would not have terminated on the death of the payee spouse and therefore the payments were held to be child support and not alimony for purposes of Federal income taxation.

Examples. The following four examples give some guidance on whether a payment is considered to be "fixed" and hence constitutes child support.

(i) If the decree or agreement provides "$100 to my child," "$100 to my wife for use of my child," "10% of each payment for the use of my child," "payment of our child's educational expenses" should all result in the payments being characterized as child support because they are mathematically determinable. On the other hand, "$100 for family support" is treated as alimony, since the amount allocable to child support is not mathematically determinable; although the parties can treat this $100 as child support by making the nonalimony election provided by I.R.C. § 71(b)(1)(B).

(ii) If the decree or agreement provides for the payment of "$200 per month to my spouse Penelope (until her death or remarriage) and our child Ralph," each monthly payment of $200 will be characterized as alimony, notwithstanding that a portion of the payment may have been intended as child support and may be mathematically determinable as such, because no amount was fixed for the support of the child.

11. See discussion in Chapter 1, B.3.c(1)(c).
12. T.C. Memo. 2013-70.
13. Gilbert v. Comm'r, T.C. Memo. 2003-92, *aff'd* subnon, Hawley v. Comm'r, 94 Fed. Appx. 126 (C.A. 3, 2004). *See also* Wignall v. Comm'r, Spring v. Comm'r, discussed at Chapter 1, B.1.f(2).

(iii) On the other hand, if the preceding provision were altered to read "$100 per month to my spouse Penelope (until her death or remarriage) and $100 per month to my child Ralph," for purposes of Federal income taxation $100 would be characterized as alimony and $100 as child support, because a specific amount was fixed for the support of the child.

(iv) If, however, the decree or instrument provides that each monthly payment of $200 is "for Ralph" or "the support of Ralph" or other language that clearly indicates the full $200 per month is for the child, the entire payment will be treated as child support because, again, a specific, mathematically determinable amount was fixed for child support.[14]

(2) Treated as Fixed

A payment is "treated as fixed" as payable for the support of a child of the payor spouse if the payment specified in the instrument is reduced:

(i) On the happening of a contingency specified in the instrument relating to a child of the payor,[15] or

(ii) At a time that can clearly be associated with such a contingency related to the child.[16] A payment may be treated as fixed as payable for the support of a child of the payor spouse even if other separate payments specifically are designated as payable for the support of a child of the payor spouse.[17] Section 71(c)(2) overrules *Commissioner v. Lester*, though its reasoning is still applicable, since it is still cited for its proposition.[18]

---

14. Zinsmeister v. Comm'r, T.C. Memo. 2000-364 (2000). Amounts specified for the payment of the child's broken trombone, graduation expenses, and dental work are treated as child support and not alimony, because they were fixed for the support of the child.

15. I.R.C. § 71(c)(2)(A).

16. I.R.C. § 71(c)(2)(B); Temp. Prop. Treas. Reg. § 1.711T(A16).

17. Temp. Prop. Treas. Reg. § 1.711T(A16).

18. 366 U.S. 299 (1961). Lester involved a written agreement in which the payor-taxpayer was to make payments for spousal support and child support. The agreement did not allocate the amount payable for spousal support or the amount payable for child support. The U.S. Supreme Court held that an agreement which required the payments to be reduced by one-sixth (1/6) of the payments payable for the support of the taxpayer's children upon a child's marriage, emancipation, or death did not adequately "fix" the payments as child support. The Court interpreted the word "fix" to mean that the amount allocable to child support must be "specifically designated" in the agreement and not left to "determinations by inference or conjecture." Note that this analysis has been revised by I.R.C. § 71(c)(2)(B).

(3) Contingency Relating to a Child of the Payor—I.R.C. § 71(c)(2)(A)

A contingency relates to a child of the payor if it depends on any event relating to that child, regardless of whether such an event is certain or likely to occur.[19] Events that relate to a child of the payor include the following: the child's attaining a specified age or income level, dying, marrying, leaving school, leaving the spouse's household, or gaining employment.[20] Payments pursuant to a divorce judgment that would cease when the taxpayer's youngest child reaches the age of 18 years are treated as child support.[21]

Example. Assume *H* agrees to pay *W* $4,000 per month for life. The agreement further provides that when any of the contingencies in I.R.C. § 71(c)(2)(B) occur, the payments will be reduced by $1,000 per month. Thus, $3,000 of each $4,000 monthly payment is alimony, and $1,000 of each $4,000 monthly payment is child support. Then, when the payments are reduced to $3,000 per month, the full amount of each payment is treated as alimony. See *Hammond v. Commissioner*,[22] where the payor spouse was ordered to pay the payee spouse $2,000 per month as alimony ending on their son's 18th birthday, or the remarriage of the payee spouse. The Court held that the payments fit squarely under I.R.C. § 71(c) and thus constituted child support and not alimony.

If a divorce instrument contains both a child-related contingency and a spouse-related contingency, the child-related contingency is triggered by a contingency relating to a child without regard to the existence of other contingencies. In such a situation, the provisions of Section 71(c)(2)(A) are met and the payment is deemed child support and not alimony.[23]

If, on the other hand, the payments are to increase by $1,000 per month on the happening of any of the contingencies, the full amount will be alimony and none of the payments will be deemed child support because the statute speaks

19. Temp. Prop. Treas. Reg. § 1.71-1T(A-17).

20. I.R.C. § 71(c)(2)(A); Temp. Prop. Treas. Reg. § 1.71-1T(A-17).

21. Hammond v. Comm'r, T.C. Memo. 1998-53; Israel v. Comm'r, T.C. Memo. 1995-500; Fosberg v. Comm'r, T.C. Memo. 1992-713 (Payments which are deemed alimony but which are reduced by one-third if the child resides with the payor for more than one year. Held: two-thirds of payments constitute child support because of the contingency of the child residing with the payor for at least one half the year.); Rojas v. Comm'r. T.C. Memo. 2022-77 (A provision in a divorce instrument requiring the payor spouse to make support payments "until both minor children emancipate" is a child related contingency that encompasses the types of contingencies expressly specified in Section 71(c)(2)(A). Such a provision characterizes the payments as child support which are not included in the gross income of the payee spouse and which are not deductible as alimony by the payor spouse under Section 215.)

22. T.C. Memo. 1998-53.

23. Rojas v. Comm'r. T.C. Memo. 2022.77 (Payments continue "until both minor children emancipate or the Petitioner remarries" triggers the application of the child contingency provision of Section 71(c)(2)(A). Thus, payments under such a mixed provision are deemed child support and not alimony.).

of a reduction, not an increase. By utilizing an increase, the payor can transmute what otherwise appears to be nondeductible child support to deductible alimony.

If the contingency does not relate to the child, the amount to be reduced as a result of the contingency will not be deemed to be child support. For example, if the $1,000 reduction in payments is to occur when the mother of the payee dies, the $1,000 will not be deemed child support since the contingency does not relate to the child. A provision in a divorce instrument that allows for a modification of child support is not a contingency related to the child.[24] If a divorce or separation instrument contains both a child-related contingency and a spouse-related contingency, the child-related contingency is triggered by a contingency related to a child without regard to the existence of other contingencies. In such a situation, the provisions of Section 71(c)(2)(A) are met and the payment is deemed child support and not alimony.[25]

(4) Time Associated with a Contingency—I.R.C. § 71(c)(2)(B)

There are two situations (described next) in which payments that would otherwise qualify as alimony or separate maintenance payments are *presumed* to be reduced at a time clearly associated with the happening of a contingency relating to a child of the payor. In all other situations, reductions in payments are not treated as clearly associated with the happening of a contingency relating to a child of the payor.[26]

The first situation is where the payments are to be reduced not more than six months before or after the date the child is to attain the age of 18, 21, or the local age of majority.[27] The contingency must relate to an event related to the child and not to an event related to the payee spouse.[28] This situation applies only where alimony is reduced on a future date. Also, this situation applies on

---

24. Heller v. Comm'r, T.C. Memo. 1994-463 (Payment of $1,700 per month as child support and $1,700 per month as spousal support, provided that if payee spouse seeks a modification of child support and an increase in child support is ordered by the Court, the Court is to reduce the payee's spousal support by $1 for every $1 of increased child support. Held: the $1,700 per month is alimony and not child support.). In reaching this conclusion, the Court first held that the ability to modify child support rises to the level of a contingency related to a child. The Court then held that a modification which increases the amount of child support with a corresponding decrease in spousal support does not qualify as a contingency relating to a child attaining a specified income level.

25. Rojas v. Comm'r., T.C. Memo. 2022-77 (Payments continue "until both minor children emancipate or the Petitioner remarries" triggers the application of the child contingency provision of Section 71(c)(2)(A). Thus, payments under such a mixed provision are deemed child support and not alimony).

26. Temp. Prop. Treas. Reg. § 1.711T(A18).

27. *Id.*

28. *Id.*

a reduction-by-reduction basis, so that it may apply to some reductions but not to others.[29]

To illustrate, in *Schilling v. Commissioner*,[30] the separation agreement provided that the payor spouse would pay the payee spouse spousal support of $2,450 per month for six years. The agreement further provided that the amount would decrease by $125 per month when child *A* turned age 18 or left for college, by $200 per month when child *B* turned age 18 or left for college, and $200 per month when child C turned age 18 or left for college. The amount equal to each reduction was held to be child support because each of the first three reductions was made because a child either reached age 18 or left for college. The amount equal to the fourth reduction, when all spousal support payments ceased, was held not to be a reduction clearly associated with a contingency relating to a child of the payee and no presumption applied.

Further, in *Maes v. United States*,[31] alimony payments were scheduled to decrease when the parties two children reached age 20. This was not referenced in their agreement. The wife argued that because the payments decreased in years that their children reached age 20, the payments should be characterized as nondeductible child support. The Court held that the payments constituted alimony and not child support because the decree lacked any reference to the reductions relating to the children turning age 20. A letter from their accountant corroborated this and stated that the parties intended the payments to constitute alimony and the reductions were not clearly associated with a contingency related to an event in the life of a child and therefore were not child support.

If a divorce or separation instrument contains a separately allocated child support provision, other payment provisions contained in the decree may still be deemed child support if the provision contains an explicit contingency related to a child of the payor spouse. In *Hammond v. Commissioner, supra*, the divorce decree awarded the payee spouse child support payments of $1,150 per month until the child attained age 18, died, married, or joined the military. The decree also awarded the payee spouse alimony of $2,000 per month ending on the child's 18th birthday or the remarriage of the payee spouse, whichever came first. The Court held that the payments of $2,000 were nondeductible child support, and not alimony, even though characterized as such in the decree because the termination of the $2,000 monthly payments to the payee spouse coincided with the child's 18th birthday. The payor spouse agreed that the payments of $2,000 per month were alimony and not child support because

29. *See* Schilling v. Comm'r, T.C. Memo. 2012-256 where the Court applied four reductions separately and found that the situation applied to the first three reductions, but not the fourth.
30. T.C. Memo. 2012-256.
31. (D. Mont., October 13, 2010) (CV 09-42-H-DWM).

the payor spouse was required to pay $1,150 per month as separately allocated, fixed payments for child support. Thus, the payor spouse argued that Section 71(c)(2) should not operate to convert alimony payments to child support when child support payments are already fixed. The Court summarily dismissed this argument finding no authority to support it.

In *Johnson v. Commissioner*,[32] the payor spouse was required to pay the payee spouse monthly spousal support plus 40 percent of his gross bonus. Both payments were to terminate on the earliest to occur of (i) the graduation from high school of the youngest son, (ii) the remarriage of the payee spouse, or (iii) the death of either spouse. The decree further provided that the spousal support payments were to be deductible by the payor spouse and includible in the gross income of the payee spouse. The decree also required the payor spouse to pay $500 per month for the support of his minor children until one of a series of events occurred, including graduation from high school. The payor spouse claimed an alimony deduction for the monthly spousal support and for the bonus payment. The payee spouse included these amounts in income. The IRS disallowed the alimony deductions to the payor spouse. The Court agreed with the IRS because it was clear that the support payments would terminate upon the graduation of the youngest child from high school. The fact that the decree specified that the payments were deductible by the payor spouse was not controlling. And the Court gave no value to the argument of the payor spouse that the graduation of the youngest child from high school was intended as a mere reference point for termination of spousal support.

The second situation is where the payments are to be reduced on two or more occasions that occur not more than one year before or after a different child of the payor spouse attains a certain age between the ages of 18 and 24, inclusive. The certain age referred to in the preceding sentence must be the same for each such child, but need not be a whole number of years.[33] This situation applies only where there is more than one child.

(a) Rebuttable Presumption

The presumption in the two situations just described that payments are to be reduced at a time clearly associated with the happening of a contingency relating to a child of the payor may be rebutted (either by the IRS or by taxpayers) by showing that the time at which the payments are to be reduced was determined independently of any contingencies relating to the children of the payor.[34]

32. T.C. Memo. 2014-67.
33. Temp. Prop. Treas. Reg. § 1.71-1T(A-18).
34. *Id.*

The presumption in the first situation will be rebutted conclusively if the reduction is a complete cessation of alimony or separate maintenance payments during the third postseparation year or upon the expiration of a 36-month period. The presumption may also be rebutted in other circumstances, for example, by showing that alimony payments are to be made for a period customarily provided in the local jurisdiction, such as a period equal to one-half the duration of the marriage.[35]

Note: The regulation refers to the "sixth" postseparation year and a "72"-month period. However, these time frames were changed by the 1986 Tax Reform Act (TRA) to three postseparation years.

The leading case regarding rebutting the presumption of a time associated with the happening of a contingency in the life of a child under I.R.C. § 71(c)(2)(B) is *Hill v. Commissioner.*[36] This case and *Shephard v. Commissioner,*[37] provide guidance for rebutting the presumption created by I.R.C. § 71(c)(2)(B).

The issue before the Court in *Hill* was whether monthly payments from August 1, 1990, to January 31, 1992, constituted alimony, as the Service contended, or child support, as the taxpayer contended. The dates are important because the youngest daughter of the parties was born on December 21, 1973. The parties agreed that the case should be decided under I.R.C. § 71(c)(2)(B) and Prop. Temp. Treas. Reg. § 1.71-1T(A-18). The Service conceded that the payments were "presumed" to be child support under the temporary regulations because the decree eliminated alimony on January 31, 1992, which was within six months of the youngest daughter's 18th birthday.

The evidence indicated that the decree did not refer to the daughter's 18th birthday, nor did the parties discuss the daughter's 18th birthday when they negotiated their agreement. Based on the evidence, the Court concluded that the date for termination of payments, January 31, 1992, which was within six months of the youngest daughter's 18th birthday, was a "coincidence" and not a contingency related to the daughter. Thus, the Court concluded the payments were not presumed to be child support.

In so holding, the Court rejected the taxpayer's contention that the Service must show that the parties chose the termination date based on a specific event in the daughter's or husband's life other than the daughter's 18th birthday. According to the Court, the regulation does not require that payments

35. *Id.*

36. T.C. Memo. 1996-179.

37. T.C. Memo. 2000-174.

terminate based on a specific event to overcome the presumption that payments that terminate within six months of a child's 18th birthday are child support. According to the Court, the regulation provides that a party may overcome the presumption by showing that the dates the payments are to be reduced was chosen independently of any contingencies relating to the children. This the Service has done, said the Court, by showing that it was a mere "coincidence" that January 31, 1992, the date chosen, was within six months of the daughter's 18th birthday. Consequently, the payments were deemed to constitute alimony and not child support, because not only had the presumption been rebutted, but all the other tests of alimony had been met.

In *Shepard*, the settlement agreement, which was executed on April 17, 1989, required the husband to make monthly payments characterized as "alimony for the support and maintenance of wife" for ten years beginning May 1, 1989, and ending April 30, 1999. The end of the ten-year period was within six months (September 5, 1999) of the 18th birthday of the parties' daughter. The taxpayer argued that the payments were child support under the "time associated with a contingency" provision of I.R.C. § 71(c)(2)(B). The Service conceded that the payments were presumed to be child support because they terminated within six months of the daughter's 18th birthday. The Service maintained, however, that the presumption is overcome by the facts surrounding the settlement negotiations. The Court agreed with the Service that the presumption that the payments were child support was overcome by evidence that the termination of the payments was determined independently of any contingency relating to the children. According to the Court, the alimony provision made no reference to the daughter's 18th birthday, nor did proposed offers from the taxpayer's attorney. The settlement offers suggested that the only dispute was the amount of alimony and not the length of time over which the payments would be made, nor was there any evidence of discussions between the parties regarding their daughter's 18th birthday. Relying upon *Hill v. Commissioner*, supra, the Court found that it was a mere coincidence that the ten-year term ended within six months of the daughter's 18th birthday.

(b) Avoiding the Problem, Example 1

A decree of divorce or written separation agreement provides that *H* is to pay *W* $1,000 per month until May 19, 1996 (the date of their only child's 18th birthday), at which time the payments will decrease to $600 per month. As a result of the first situation, $600 per month is treated as alimony and $400 per month is treated as child support. If the reduction occurred before December 19, 1995, or after November 19, 1996, this situation could be avoided. Thus, where a reduction in alimony is contemplated by the agreement, it is important to know the birthdate of the child.

(c) Avoiding the Problem, Example 2

A and *B* are divorced on July 1, 1985, when their children, *C* (born July 15, 1970) and *D* (born September 23, 1972), are 14 and 12, respectively. Under the divorce decree, *A* is to make alimony payments to *B* of $2,000 per month. Such payments are to be reduced to $1,500 per month on January 1, 1991, and to $1,000 per month on January 1, 1995. On January 1, 1991, the date of the first reduction in payments, *C* will be 20 years, five months, and 17 days old. On January 1, 1995, the date of the second reduction in payments, *D* will be 22 years, three months, and nine days old. Each of the reductions in payments is to occur not more than one year before or after a different child of *A* attains the age of 21 years and four months. (Actually, the reductions are to occur not more than one year before or after *C* and *D* attain any of the ages 21 years, three months, and nine days through 21 years, five months, and 17 days.)[38]

Accordingly, the reductions are presumed clearly to be associated with the happening of a contingency relating to *C* and *D*. Unless this presumption is rebutted, payments under the divorce decree equal to the sum of the reductions ($1,000 per month) will be treated as fixed for the support of the children of *A* and therefore will not qualify as alimony or separate maintenance payments.

To avoid this result, either the first reduction should be made earlier, or the second reduction later, so that the ages of *C* and *D* at the time of the reductions are more than two years apart. Thus, if the first reduction were made on or before September 1, 1990, the two-year range would be exceeded. The same avoidance could result if the second reduction were made on or after April 1, 1995.

An easier way to avoid the second situation is to not have the reductions occur between ages 18 and 24. Thus, by having one reduction occur before a child is age 18 or after the child is age 24, the second situation can be avoided. But the first situation may apply.

(5) Planning Specific Designation

The two methods offered in the regulations are preferable to the solutions offered in *Hill*, and *Shepherd*, discussed in (4)(a) above because those cases rely upon the "coincidence test," which can only be established after lengthy discovery and perhaps judicial intervention, at great cost to the taxpayer. Thus, where there is to be a decrease in payments, the practitioner must be aware of the ages of the children of the payor spouse and avoid reducing the payments within the proscribed time periods. The drawing of a family timeline, including the dates of the ages of the children and the dates of the reduction in payments can be helpful in avoiding this trap for the unwary.

38. Prop. Temp. Treas. Reg. 1.71-1T(c)(A-18).

Where the decree or agreement provides for the payment of both alimony and child support, the draftsman should specifically designate the amount attributable to each to ensure the desired tax result for the client. Language in an instrument that states that the parties intend for the payments to be treated as alimony does not make the payments alimony if they are in fact child support. Thus, if the tests for child support are met, the payments will be treated as child support even if the language labels the payments as taxable alimony.[39]

On the other hand, the parties may intend to make the payments unallocated between the payee spouse and the children or to specifically allocate the payments to alimony. By so doing, the payments will constitute alimony, taxable to the payee spouse and deductible to the payor spouse. Such unallocated payments may be beneficial to the parties by allowing the shifting of taxes to the lower bracket spouse, while allowing a deduction to the higher bracket spouse, resulting in a tax savings in which all the parties can share. The practitioner should be careful in intending this result, because it may conflict with State law that may require the payment of some child support. Then, the payor may be called on to pay additional support in a subsequent support modification suit. This technique was recognized by Judge Marvel in *Miller v. Commissioner*,[40] where the Court stated:

> Unallocated family support is a technique sometimes used in domestic relations cases to encourage sensible cash-flow planning between separated spouses. If used correctly, the technique enables the parties to achieve a higher net transfer of funds to the payee spouse because the payor spouse, who is generally in a higher tax bracket, reaps an economic benefit from the larger tax deduction obtained when unallocated family support payments are structured to be deductible as alimony. See generally H. Rept. 98-432 (Part 2), at 1495 (1984). These unallocated payments, while typically temporary, can facilitate the economic transition that must occur as a result of a divorce or separation, provided the parties understand and agree to the tax consequences.

(6) Amendments

If the amount of child support is not specifically designated, but a court of competent jurisdiction permits the decree or agreement to be amended so that the intent of the parties can be specifically designated, thus redesignating alimony payments as child support or child support payments as alimony, the amendment applies prospectively and not retroactively,[41] unless due to any

39. Priv. Ltr. Rul. 9251033.

40. T.C. Memo. 1999-273.

41. Wilson v. Comm'r, 49 T.C. 1 (1967); Martin v. Comm'r, T.C. Memo. 1973-228. *See* Gordon v. Comm'r, 70 T.C. 525 (1978) and cases cited therein.

error in the divorce decree that is corrected nunc pro tunc.[42] This could cause application of the recapture rule.

(7) Child Defined

Payments can be made to a child of the payor who has reached the age of majority and still qualify as child support if all the other tests are met. The "child" must be a child of the payor spouse.

(8) Property Transfers

A transfer of property for support of a child qualifies as child support. Moreover, the transfer will not be subject to gift tax if it falls within I.R.C. § 2516.[43]

(9) Kiddie Tax

The "kiddie tax" was enacted by the 1986 TRA. It was recently amended by the Tax Acts and Jobs Act of 2017 for tax years 2018 through 2025.[44] The purpose for the kiddie tax is to stop parents from transferring income-producing assets to their children that would be taxed to the children at a lower tax rate than their parents. It accomplishes this by providing that children with investment income may be subject to tax on that income at their parent's top marginal tax rate if it results in a higher tax than would apply at the child's rate.[45] These special tax rules do not apply to the earned income of the child. As a result of the Tax Cuts and Jobs Act of 2017, for tax years beginning after December 31, 2017, and before January 1, 2026, the net unearned income of the child is taxed as ordinary income and capital gains rates applicable to estates and no longer will the parents rate be used. Thus, assuming the child has no earned income, the first $1,250 of earned income is not taxed in 2021 (increased from $1,150 in 2022), the next $1,250 (increased from $1,150 in 2022) is taxed at the child's tax rate, and the excess above $2,500 (increased from $2,300 in 2022) is taxed at the parent's tax rate.[46] Alternatively, the kiddie tax applies if the child has earned income in excess of $13,850 in 2023 (the standard deduction for a taxpayer filing single in 2023), up from $11,500 in 2022. Thus, the kiddie tax generally applies in 2023 if the child has more than $2,500 of unearned income. As under pre-2017 Act law, the child's taxable income is taxed based upon the taxpayer's bracket.

---

42. Johnson v. Comm'r, 45 T.C. 530 (1966); Rev. Rul. 71416, 19712 C.B. 83. *See also* Newman v. Comm'r, 68 T.C. 494 (1977). See text at Chapter 1, B.3.c(1)(b).

43. See discussion at Chapter 11, B.2.

44. Pub.1., 115.97, Title I, §§ 11001(a), 11002(a)–(c), 14223(a), 31 Stat. 2054 (12.22.17).

45. I.R.C. § 1(g)(1).

46. Rev. Proc. 2022-38, 2022-45 I.R.B. 445.

For tax years 2018 through 2025, the kiddie tax applies if the following five tests are met. First, the child must meet one of three age tests. The child must be (i) under the age of 18 before the close of the tax year; or (ii) age 18 before the close of the tax year and the child's earned income is less than one-half of his or her own support for the year; or (iii) the child is age 19 through 23 at the end of the tax year, is a full-time student, and the child's earned income for the taxable year is less than one-half of his or her own support.[47] Second, either parent of the child must be alive at the close of the taxable year.[48] Third, the child must not file a joint return for the taxable year.[49] Fourth, the child's unearned income for the tax year must be more than $2,500 for tax year 2023.[50] Fifth, the child is required to file an individual income tax return.[51] In the case of parents who are not married, the additional tax is based on the taxable income of the custodial parent (including that of the spouse of the parent if the custodial parent remarries and files a joint return with his or her new spouse).[52] In the case of parents who are married filing separately, the additional tax is based on the taxable income of the parent with the greater taxable income.[53] Form 8615 is used by the child to calculate the kiddie tax and is attached to the child's, not the parent's, Form 1040. The instructions to Form 8615 provide useful examples and worksheets to compute the kiddie tax. Generally, the child's tax is the greater of (a) the sum of (i) the share of the tentative tax based on the parent's tax plus (ii) the child's taxable income in excess of earned income if figured at the child's tax rate, or (b) the tax on the child's taxable income figured at the child's tax rate. In addition, if the child is required to file Form 8615, the child may also be required to file Form 8960 if the child is subject to the net investment income tax. The NIIT, which is imposed by Section 1441, is a tax of 3.8 percent on the lesser of (i) investment income or (ii) the excess of modified adjusted gross income over the threshold amount (which is $250,000 for married filing jointly, or a qualifying widow or widower with a dependent child, $200,000 for single or head of household, and $125,000 for married filing separately).

The parents of a child may elect to include on their return the unearned income of a child to avoid the kiddie tax.[54] The purpose for this election is so that the parents do not have to disclose their tax bracket to the child. To make

47. I.R.C. § 1(g)(2)(A)
48. I.R.C. § 1(g)(2)(B)
49. I.R.C. § 1(g)(2)(C)
50. I.R.C. § 1(g)(2)(A); Rev. Proc. 2022-38, 2022-45, I.R.C. 445.
51. I.R.C. § 1(g)(1). This is determined by excluding the child's standard deduction of $13,850 and taxing the next $13,850 at the child's marginal tax rate for tax year 2023.
52. I.R.C. § 1(g)(5)(A); Temp. Prop. Treas. Reg. § 1.1(i)1T(A12 and A-13).
53. I.R.C. § 1(g)(5)(B).
54. I.R.C. § 1(g)(7).

the election, the following four tests must be met in addition to meeting the aforesaid five tests. First, the child must have gross income for the taxable year only from interest and dividends.[55] Second, the child's gross income must be less than $11,500 in 2022 or less than $12,500 in 2023.[56] Third, no estimated tax payment for such year is made in the name and TIN of the child, no back-up withholding has taken place, or no overpayment from the previous tax year was applied to the current tax year under the child's name and Social Security number.[57] Fourth, the parents of such child makes the election using Form 8814, and attaches such form to their tax return.[58] When these tests have been met, the parents may elect to report the child's unearned income on their return, rather than the child's return, thus avoiding disclosure of their tax bracket, which may, perhaps, be lower than the child's, resulting in a tax savings to the family unit. In the case of parents who filed married filing separate, the individual with the greater taxable income is the parent whose income is taken into account.[59] If the election is made, the child will not have to report such income on the child's tax returns, if the child is otherwise required to file a tax return.

There are at least two ways the child or the parents may avoid or reduce the kiddie tax. First, if the child has earned income, the child can avoid or reduce the child's tax by establishing a traditional or ROTH IRA and contributing the maximum allowable amount to the IRA. Second, instead of gifting income producing assets to the child, the parents can gift the funds to a Section 529 Plan for the child's education.

2. Arrearages

a. Application of Payment

I.R.C. § 71(c)(3) provides that if both alimony and child support are required by the decree or the agreement, and if any payment is less than the amount specified in the decree or agreement, the payment is applied first to child support and the balance to alimony.

---

55. I.R.C. § 1(g)(7)(A)(i)

56. I.R.C. § 1(g)(7)(A)(ii), Rev. Proc. 2022-38, *supra.* The same $1,250 amount is used for purpose of I.R.C. § 1(g)(7) to determine whether a parent may elect to include a child's gross income in the parent's gross income and to calculate the kiddie tax. For example, one of the requirements of the parental election is that a child's gross income is more than the amount referenced in I.R.C. § 1(g)(4)(A)(ii)(I) but less than ten times the amount. Thus, a child's gross income for 2023 must be more than $1,250 but less than $12,500.

57. I.R.C. § 1(g)(7)(A)(iii). If the child is newly born and has not received a Social Security number, it is recommended that the child's birth certificate be attached to the return with a statement that the Social Security application is pending.

58. I.R.C. § 1(g)(7)(A)(iv). Parent means the custodial parent in the case of parents who are not married, and in the case of married individuals filing separately, the individual with the greater taxable income. I.R.C. § 1(g)(5).

59. I.R.C. § 1(g)(5)(B).

b. Example

For payments made pursuant to a pre-2019 divorce or separation instrument, if the decree requires "the payment of $100 per month to my spouse Penelope (until her death or remarriage) and $100 per month to my child Ralph," and the payor spouse pays only $2,000 during the year, $1,200 will be characterized as child support and $800 as alimony. The unpaid balance of $400 becomes an alimony arrearage, the tax consequences of which are discussed at Chapter 1, B.4.

In *Haubrich v. Commissioner*,[60] the Court held that alimony payments were not deductible because the payor owed child support for the same period for which the deduction was claimed. Thus, the payments had to be allocated first to child support before any amount could be allocated to alimony. And since the total payments for the tax year were less than the amount owed for child support and child support arrears, none of the payments could be allocated to alimony.

c. Consequences

This may invoke the alimony recapture rule and the alimony arrearage rule.

3. Making Child Support Deductible under Pre-2019 Divorce or Separation Instruments

Although child support is not deductible, it may be made indirectly deductible. For example, where the agreement provides for monthly payments to the payee spouse of $500 for the support of the payee spouse and the children and is increased by $100 per month (at approximately the time the child is expected to attend college), all payments may be alimony, even though the intent of the parties is that some portion of each payment constitutes child support.[61]

Even though the amount intended as child support can be determined with mathematical specificity, an increase rather than a reduction is occurring, and I.R.C. § 71(c)(2) refers only to a "reduction," thus inferentially permitting an increase. The key is that the payments are made to the payee spouse who has unfettered discretion over their control and disposition. Under this reasoning, a payor spouse can deduct the educational expenses of his or her children.[62]

Notwithstanding any potential tax savings that may be obtained by failing to fix specifically the amount allocable to child support, the nontax aspects of the transaction must not be overlooked. For "child support" to be deductible, the payee spouse must have unrestricted use of the money. If the payee spouse

---

60. T.C. Memo. 2008-299. *See also* Hazam v. Comm'r, T.C. Memo. 2000-71 and Thornton v. Comm'r, T.C. Memo. 1992-286.

61. *E.g.*, Kauffman v. Comm'r, T.C. Memo. 1979-376 (1979). *See also* Priv. Ltr. Rul. 8142212.

62. *See* West v. United States, 413 F.2d 294 (4th Cir. Va. 1969); Gotthelf v. Comm'r, 48 T.C. 690 (1967); Talberth v. Comm'r, 47 T.C. 326 (1966).

fails adequately to support the child, the payor spouse may then be responsible to provide for the child. Or, the payor spouse may want to feel as if he or she is actually supporting the child or may want to claim a dependency exemption for the child. These nontax considerations should not be overlooked in determining whether the payments should be characterized as alimony or child support.

3 Dependency Exemption for Child

A. Tax Cuts and Jobs Act of 2017

Interestingly, the Tax Cuts and Jobs Act of 2017 (TCJA 2017) did not repeal the dependency exemption as many at first believed happened, but it merely provided that the exempt amount is zero.[1] The purpose for this retention, rendered meaningless for purposes of claiming the dependency exemption, is because many of the provisions found in the dependency exemption provision of the Code are used in other sections of the Internal Revenue Code of 1986, as amended, such as the child tax credit, the household and dependent care credit, and the head of household provisions. Thus, it is important to discuss the provisions of the dependency exemption because of the impact its provisions still have on other provisions of the Code.

B. General Rule

1. In General

I.R.C. § 152(a) allows a personal exemption for each dependent of the taxpayer. That Section defines a dependent to mean a "qualifying child"[2] or a "qualifying relative."[3] Thus, to claim an individual as a dependent, the individual must be a qualifying child or qualifying relative. The tests for each are different. The following first discusses who is a "qualifying child," and then discusses who is a "qualifying relative."[4]

1. I.R.C. § 151(d)(5)(A).

2. *See* Chapter 3, A.1.b(1).

3. *See* Chapter 3, A.1.b(3). Prop. Treas. Reg. § 1.152-1(a) (1.18.17). On February 13, 2017, the IRS issued proposed regulations under § 2, 32, 63, and 152, effective as of January 18, 2017, Reg. 137604-07, IRS Bulletin 2017-7.

4. For an overview of the rules for claiming a dependent, *see* IRS Publication 504, Divorced or Separated Individuals, Table 3, p. 8 (2021). *See also* I.R.S. Publication 501, Dependents, Standard

The exemption may only be claimed by the custodial parent,[5] except in the limited circumstances involving divorced or separated parents, or parents who live apart at all times during the last six months of the taxable year.[6] The custodial parent is the parent with whom the child resides for the longest period of time during the taxable year.[7]

In addition to being characterized as a qualifying child or a qualifying relative, the dependent must satisfy the joint return, citizenship, and ineligible dependency tests.

I.R.C. § 152(b) sets forth three types of individuals who do not qualify as a dependent, and hence do not qualify as a qualifying child or a qualifying relative: First, if an individual is a dependent of a taxpayer for any taxable year of the taxpayer beginning in a calendar year, the individual is treated as having no dependents for any taxable year of the individual beginning in such taxable year.[8] An individual is not a dependent of a person if that person is not required to file an income tax return under Section 6012 and either does not file an income tax return or files an income tax return solely to claim a refund of estimated or withheld taxes.[9]

Second, an individual is not treated as a dependent of a taxpayer if such individual files a joint return with the individual's spouse under Section 6013 for the taxable year beginning in the calendar year in which the taxable year of the taxpayer begins,[10] other than solely to claim a refund of estimated or withheld taxes, with the individual's spouse under Section 6013 for the taxable year beginning in the calendar year in which that taxable year of the taxpayer begins.[11]

Finally, the term "dependent" does not include an individual who is not a citizen or national of the United States unless such individual is a resident of the United States or is a resident of a country contiguous to the United States (i.e., a child of a non-U.S. citizen who resides in Canada or Mexico).[12] However, a dependent does include a child if the child is legally adopted by the taxpayer or is lawfully placed with the taxpayer for legal adoption by the taxpayer if (i) for the taxable year of the taxpayer the child has the same principal place

---

Deduction and Filing Information, for a chart on the Rules For Claiming A Dependent, Table 5, page 10 (2021).

5. I.R.C. § 152(c)(4).
6. I.R.C. § 152(e)(1).
7. I.R.C. § 152(c)(4)(B)(i).
8. I.R.C. § 152(b)(1); Prop. Treas. Reg. § 1.152-1(a)(2)(i)(1.18.17).
9. *Id.*
10. I.R.C. § 152(b)(2). This restriction does not apply if a joint return was filed solely to obtain a refund and no tax liability would exist for either spouse if they filed separate returns. H. Rep. No. 108-696 at p. 55 n. 38 (2004) (Conf. Rept.).
11. Prop. Treas. Reg. § 1.152-2(a)(2)(ii) (1.18.17).
12. I.R.C. § 152(b)(3)(A); Prop. Treas. Reg. § 1.152-1(a)(2)(iii)(1.18.17).

of abode as the taxpayer; (ii) is a member of the taxpayer's household; and (iii) the taxpayer is a citizen or national of the United States.[13] A taxpayer and the child have the same principal place of abode for the taxpayer's taxable year if the taxpayer and child have the same principal place of abode for the entire portion of the taxable year following the placement of the child with the taxpayer.[14]

For taxable years beginning after October 13, 2020, a payment of alimony or separate maintenance to a payee spouse is not treated as a payment by the payor spouse for the support of any dependent. Similarly, the distribution of income of an estate or trust to a divorced or legally separated payee spouse is not treated as a payment by the payor spouse for the support of any dependent, except to the extent that such a distribution is in satisfaction of the amount or portion of income that, by the terms of a divorce decree, written separation agreement, or the trust instrument is fixed as payable for the support of the minor child of the payor spouse.[15]

a. Definition of "Qualifying Child"

I.R.C. § 152(c)(1) defines a "qualifying child" as an individual who meets the following five tests: (i) the relationship test, (ii) the place of abode test, (iii) the age test, (iv) the support test, and (v) the joint return test.[16] Each of these tests is discussed in the following paragraphs. This universal definition of a qualifying child applies to the filing status of head of household under Section 2(b); the child and dependent care credit under Section 21, the child tax credit under Section 24, the earned income credit under Section 32, and the dependency exemption under Section 151. Thus, it is important to determine of whom a child is a qualifying child so that person can receive a variety of tax benefits.

(1) Relationship Test

A qualifying child is an individual who is a child of the taxpayer or a descendant of such a child, or is a brother, sister, stepbrother, or stepsister of the taxpayer or a descendant of the taxpayer, or a descendant of any such relative.[17] A child includes a son, daughter, stepson, or stepdaughter of the taxpayer.[18] A child also includes an eligible foster child; i.e., an individual who is placed with the taxpayer by an authorized placement agency or by judgment decree, or

13. I.R.C. § 152(b)(3)(B), I.R.C. § 152(f)(1)(B); Prop. Treas. Reg. § 1.152-1(a)(2)(iii)(1.18.17).
14. Prop. Treas. Reg. § 1.152-1(a)(2)(iii)(1.18.17).
15. Treas. Reg. § 1.152-2(b)(1) and (2).
16. Prop. Treas. Reg. § 1.152-2(a) (1.18.17).
17. I.R.C. §§ 152(c)(1)(A), 152(c)(2). A child born out of wedlock who is acknowledged as a child of the parties is deemed a child for the relationship test. Rev. Rul. 54-498, 1934-2 C.B. 107. Prop. Treas. Reg. § 1.152-2(b)(1) and (2)(1.18.17).
18. I.R.C. § 152(f)(1)(A)(i); Prop. Treas. Reg. § 1.152-1(b)(1)(i)(1.18.17).

other order of any court of competent jurisdiction.[19] A son, daughter, stepson, or stepdaughter includes an individual who is a legally adopted individual of the taxpayer, or an individual who is lawfully placed with the taxpayer for legal adoption by the taxpayer.[20]

(2) Place of Abode Test

A qualifying child is an individual who has the same principal place of abode as the taxpayer for more than half the taxable year.[21] Generally, an individual has the same principal place of abode as the taxpayer for more than one-half of the taxable year if the individual resides with the taxpayer for more than one-half of the taxable year.[22] For purposes of the place of abode test, temporary absences[23] due to special circumstances, including absences due to illness, education, business, vacation, or military service, are not treated as absences.[24]

(3) Age Test

A qualifying child is an individual who (i) has not attained the age of 19 as of the close of the calendar year in which the taxable year of the taxpayer begins, or (ii) is a student[25] who has not attained the age of 24 as of the close of such taxable year, or (iii) is any age if permanently and totally disabled[26] at any time

---

19. I.R.C. §§ 152(f)(1)(A)(ii), 152(f)(1)(C); Prop. Treas. Reg. § 1.152-1(b)(1)(iii)(1.18.17).

20. I.R.C. § 152(f)(1)(B); Prop. Treas. Reg. § 1.152-1(b)(2) (1.18.17).

21. I.R.C. § 152(c)(1)(B). The husband could not claim the dependency exemption for his two minor children. They were not "qualifying children" because they did not share the same principal place of abode with the taxpayer for more than one-half of the taxable year. Alarcon v. Commissioner, T.C. Memo. 2011-245.

22. Prop. Treas. Reg. § 1.152-2(c)(1.18.17).

23. Prop. Treas. Reg. § 1.152-2(c)(1.18.17).

24. *See* Conference Report (H.R. Rept. No. 108-696 for H.R. 1308, 108th Cong, 2nd Sess., Pub. L. No. 108-311, I.R.C. § 201). Look to the number of nights a child spends with a parent to determine whether the child has the same principal place of abode as the parent for more than one-half the taxable year for purposes of § 152(c)(1)(B). Where the child resides with the non-custodial parent six out of every 14 nights during the school year, and alternating weeks during school break in the summer, the child is deemed to have spent more than half the nights with the custodial parent. Consequently, the child did not have the same principal place of abode as the noncustodial parent for more than half the tax year and therefore was not the qualifying child of the noncustodial parent for that year. Skitzki v Comm'r, T.C. Memo. 2019-106; *see also* Stapleton v Comm'r. T.C. Memo. 2015-171 (count the number of nights a child spends with a parent to determine whether the child had the same principal place of abode as the parent for more than half of the taxable year); and Phillips v. Comm'r. T. C. Memo 2011-199 (the children did not satisfy the principal place of abode test because they did not reside with the taxpayer for more than half the year).

25. *See* Chapter 3, B.1.b(5) for discussion of a student.

26. *See* Chapter 3, B.1.b(2) for discussion of a disabled person. Prop. Treas. Reg. § 1.152-2(d) (1.18.17).

during the calendar year.[27] No age limit applies to a permanently and totally disabled child.[28] To be a qualifying child, the individual must be younger than the taxpayer claiming the individual as a qualifying child.[29]

(4) Support Test

A qualifying child is an individual who has not provided more than one-half of his or her own support for the calendar year in which the taxable year of the taxpayer begins.[30] If the individual is a child of the taxpayer and a student, amounts received as a scholarship at an educational institution described in I.R.C. § 170(b)(1)(A)(ii) are not taken into account.[31]

(5) Joint Return Test

Finally, a qualifying child is an individual who has not filed a joint return (other than only to file a claim for refund of withheld tax or estimated tax paid) with his or her spouse under Section 6013 for the taxable year beginning in the calendar year in which the taxable year of the taxpayer begins.[32] For example, if the taxpayer's married child files a joint return with his or her spouse, the married child is not a qualifying child of the taxpayer unless the child filed a joint return solely to claim a refund of withheld tax or estimated tax paid.

b. Discussion of "Qualifying Child"

(1) Other Covered Provisions

This definition of a qualifying child applies for purposes of the dependency exemption, the child care credit, the dependent care credit, and head of household filing status. If the child is a qualifying relative (discussed in Chapter 3, B.1.c), the taxpayer may be able to claim the dependency exemption, but not the child tax credit, dependent care credit, earned income credit, or head of household status.

(2) Disabled

An individual is permanently and totally disabled if the individual is unable to engage in any substantial gainful activity by reason of any medically determinable physical or mental impairment which can be expected to result in death or

---

27. I.R.C. §§ 152(c)(1)(C), 152(c)(3)(A), and 152(c)(3)(B). Prop. Treas. Reg. § 1.152-2(d)(1)(1.18.17). See text at Chapter 3, B.1.b(5), for discussion of a student.

28. I.R.C. § 152(c)(3)(B). Prop. Treas. Reg. § 1.152-2(d)(2)(1.18.17)

29. I.R.C. § 152(e)(1)(C) and I.R.C. § 152(c)(3). Prop. Treas. Reg. § 1.152-2(d)(1.18.17)

30. I.R.C. § 152(c)(1)(D). Prop. Treas. Reg. § 1.152-2(e)(1.18.17)

31. I.R.C. § 152(f)(5). *See* IRS Publication 501, Dependents, Standard Deduction and Filing Instruction (2021) Worksheet 2, page 16, for a worksheet for determining support.

32. I.R.C. § 152(c)(1)(E). Prop. Treas. Reg. § 1.152-2(f)(1.18.17).

which has lasted or can be expected to last for a continuous period of not less than 12 months. An individual is not considered to be permanently and totally disabled unless he furnishes proof of the existence thereof. No age limit applies with respect to individuals who are totally and permanently disabled.[33]

(3) Multiple Claimants

I.R.C. § 152(c)(4) provides a Solomon-like rule for determining which taxpayer may claim a child as a qualifying child where two or more taxpayers claim the same individual as a qualifying child.[34] If an individual may be and is claimed as a qualifying child by two or more taxpayers for a taxable year beginning in the same calendar year, such individual is treated as the qualifying child of the taxpayer who is (i) the parent of the individual, or (ii) if the taxpayer is not the parent of the individual, the taxpayer with the highest adjusted gross income for the taxable year.[35] Adjusted gross income of each person who files a joint return is the total adjusted gross income shown on the return.[36]

If more than one eligible taxpayer is a parent of the individual (an "eligible parent"), any one of the eligible parents may claim the individual as a qualifying child. However, if more than one eligible parent claims the individual as a qualifying child, and those eligible parents do not file a joint return with each other, the individual is treated as the qualifying child of the eligible parent claiming the individual with whom the individual resides for the longest period of time during the taxable year. If the individual resides for the same amount of time during the taxable year with each eligible parent claiming the child, the individual is treated as the qualifying child of the eligible parent with the highest adjusted gross income who claims the individual.[37]

If at least one eligible taxpayer is a parent of the individual, but no eligible parent claims the individual as a qualifying child, the individual may be treated as the qualifying child of another eligible taxpayer only if that taxpayer's adjusted gross income exceeds both the adjusted gross income of each

33. *See* I.R.C. § 152(c)(3)(B) which refers to I.R.C. § 22(e)(3) for a definition of disability.

34. Prop. Treas. Reg. § 1.152-2(g)(1)(i)(1.18.17). *See* Hicks v. Commissioner, T.C. Memo 2022-10 for a discussion of the tie-breaker rule.

35. I.R.C. § 152(c)(4)(A); Prop. Treas. Reg. § 1.152-2(g)(1)(i)(1.18.17).

36. Prop. Treas. Reg. § 1.152-2(g)(2)(1.18.17). This provision allows a grandparent to claim a child as a qualifying child. For example, if a teenage child resides with her parent and grandmother for the entire year, but the grandparent's adjusted gross income is greater than the parent's adjusted gross income, if the mother agrees to allow the grandparent to claim the child as a qualifying child, then the grandparent can claim the teenager as a qualifying child. This will then enable the grandparent to claim the child tax credit, head of household filing status, child and dependent care credit, dependent care benefits, and the earned income credit if the grandparent qualifies for each of those benefits and the parent does not claim the child as a qualifying child for any of those tax benefits.

37. Prop. Treas. Reg. § 1.152-2(g)(1)(i)(1.18.17).

eligible parent of the individual and the adjusted gross income of each other eligible taxpayer, if any.[38]

Except as provided in the preceding two paragraphs, if there are two or more eligible taxpayers, only one of whom is the parent of the individual, the individual is treated as the qualifying child of the eligible parent.[39]

If no eligible taxpayer is a parent of the individual, the individual is treated as the qualifying child of the eligible taxpayer with the highest adjusted gross income for the taxable year. [40]

Notwithstanding the preceding, if the parents claiming any qualifying child do not file a joint return together, such child is treated as the qualifying child of (i) the parent with whom the child resided for the longest period of time during the taxable year; or (ii) if the child resides with both parents for the same amount of time during such taxable year, the child is treated as the qualifying child of the parent with the highest adjusted gross income for that taxable year.[41] According to the Conference Committee Report,[42] if the child's parents do not claim the child as a qualifying child, then the child is deemed a qualifying child with respect to the claimant, but only if the adjusted gross income of such claimant is higher than the highest adjusted gross income of any parent of any individual.[43]

Notwithstanding the rule of I.R.C. § 152(c)(4)(B), a child may be treated as the qualifying child of the noncustodial parent for certain purposes under the special rule of I.R.C. § 152(e), which is discussed at Chapter 3, C.3.

Except to the extent that Section 152(e) and Prop. Treas. Reg. § 1.152-5 (discussed later) apply, if more than one taxpayer may claim a child as a qualifying child, the child is treated as the qualifying child of only one taxpayer for purposes of head of household filing status under Section 2(b), the child and dependent care credit under Section 21, the child tax credit under Section 24, the earned income credit under Section 32, the exclusion from income for dependent care assistance under Section 129, and the dependency exemption under Section 151. Thus, the taxpayer claiming the individual as a qualifying child under any one of these sections is the only taxpayer who may claim any credit or exemption under these other sections for that same individual for a taxable year beginning in the same calendar year as the taxpayer's taxable year. If Section 152(e) applies, however, the noncustodial parent may claim the child as a qualifying child for purposes of the dependency exemption and the child

38. Prop. Treas. Reg. § 1.152-2(g)(1)(ii)(1.18.17).

39. Prop. Treas. Reg. § 1.152-2(g)(1)(iii)(1.18.17).

40. Prop. Treas. Reg. § 1.152-2(g)(1)(iv)(1.18.17).

41. I.R.C. § 152(c)(4)(A) and (B).

42. I.R.C. § 152(c)(4)(C); H. Rep. No. 108-696 for H.R. 1308, 108th Cong., 2d Sess., Pub. L. No. 108-311, I.R.C. § 201.

43. I.R.C. § 152(c)(4)(C).

tax credit, and another person may claim the child for purposes of one or more of these other provisions.[44]

The following six examples from the proposed regulations illustrate the rules in which a child who is eligible to be claimed as a qualifying child by more than one taxpayer. In the examples, each taxpayer uses the calendar year as the taxpayer's taxable year, the child is a qualifying child of each taxpayer, and except to the extent indicated, each taxpayer meets the requirements to claim the benefit(s) described in the example.[45]

Example 1. A and B, parents of Child C, are married to each other. A, B, and Child C share the same principal place of abode for the first eight months of the year. Thus, both parents satisfy the qualifying child residency test. For the last four months of the year, the parents live apart from each other, and B and Child C share the same principal place of abode. Section 152(e), relating to divorced or separated parents, does not apply. The parents file as married filing separately for the taxable year, and both parents claim their child as a qualifying child. Child C is treated as a qualifying child of B for all purposes, because the child resided with B for the longer period of time during the taxable year. Because Section 152(e) does not apply, Child C may not be treated as a qualifying child of A for any purpose.

Example 2. The facts are the same as in Example 1, except that B does not claim Child C as a qualifying child. Because A and B are not both claiming the same child as a qualifying child, Child C is treated as a qualifying child of A.

Example 3. Child C, Child C's parent (D), and Grandparent share the same principal place of abode. D is not married and is not a qualifying child or dependent of Grandparent, and Grandparent is not D's dependent. Section 152(e), relating to divorced or separated parents, does not apply. Child C meets the definition of a qualifying child of both D and Grandparent. D claims Child C as a qualifying child for purposes of the child and dependent care credit under Section 21, the earned income credit under Section 32, and the dependency exemption under Section 151. Grandparent claims Child C as a qualifying child for purposes of head of household filing status under Section 2(b).

Child C is treated as the qualifying child of D for all purposes, because D is eligible to claim and claims Child C as D's qualifying child. Because D is eligible to claim and claims Child C as D's qualifying child, Child C may not be treated as a qualifying child of Grandparent for any purpose. Grandparent erroneously claimed Child C as Grandparent's qualifying child for purposes of head of household filing status under Section 2(b). If D had not claimed Child as D's qualifying child for any purpose, Grandparent could have claimed Child C as Grandparent's qualifying child if Grandparent's adjusted gross income

44. Prop. Treas. Reg. § 1.152-2(g)(3)(1.18.17).
45. Prop. Treas. Reg. § 1.152-2(g)(4)(1.18.17).

(AGI) exceeded D's AGI. In that situation, Grandparent could have claimed Child C as Grandparent's qualifying child for purposes of any of the child-related tax benefits, provided that Grandparent had met the requirements of those sections.

Example 4. The facts are the same as in Example 3, except that Child C's parents, D and E, are married to each other and share the same principal place of abode with Child C and Grandparent for the entire taxable year. Child C meets the definition of a qualifying child of both parents and Grandparent. D and E file a joint return for the taxable year and do not claim Child C as a qualifying child for any purpose. Because D or E may claim Child C as a qualifying child but neither claims Child C as a qualifying child for any purpose, Grandparent may claim Child C as a qualifying child if Grandparent's AGI exceeds the total AGI reported on the joint return of D and E.

Example 5. The facts are the same as in Example 4, except that D and E are divorced from each other, E moved into a separate residence during that year and is the noncustodial parent, and Section 152(e), relating to divorced or separated parents, applies. E attaches to E's return a Form 8332 on which D agrees to release D's claim to a dependency exemption for Child C and E claims Child C as a qualifying child for purposes of the dependency exemption and the child tax credit. Child C is treated as a qualifying child of E for purposes of the dependency exemption and the child tax credit. Child C may be treated as a qualifying child of D for purposes of the earned income credit. If D claims Child C as a qualifying child for purposes of the earned income credit, Child C may not be treated as a qualifying child of Grandparent for any purpose.

Example 6. F and G, parents of two children, are married to each other. F, G, and both children share the same principal place of abode for the entire taxable year. F and G file as married filing separately for the taxable year. F claims the older child as a qualifying child for purposes of the child tax credit, dependency exemption, and the child and dependent care credit. G claims the younger child as a qualifying child for purposes of the same three tax benefits. The older child is treated as qualifying child of F and the younger child is treated as a qualifying child of G. The tiebreaker rule does not apply because F and G are not claiming the same child as a qualifying child.

Notice 2006-86[46] provides interim guidance under I.R.C. § 152(c)(4) for determining which taxpayer may claim a qualifying child when two or more taxpayers claim the same child under any of the following provisions:

(i) head of household filing status under I.R.C. § 2(b),
(ii) the child and dependent care credit under I.R.C. § 21,

46. 2006-2 C.B. 680. According to the Supplementary Information of Prop. Treas. Reg. § 1.152(1.18.17), the rule described in Notice 2006-86 that an individual is treated as the qualifying child of only one taxpayer for the listed child related benefits is still good law.

(iii) the child tax credit under I.R.C. § 24,
(iv) the earned income credit under I.R.C. § 32,
(v) the exclusion for dependent care assistance under I.R.C. § 129 (which incorporates by reference the definition of qualifying child or other qualifying individual under I.R.C. § 21), and
(vi) the dependency deduction under I.R.C. § 151.

The notice clarifies that if the special rule in I.R.C. § 152(e) applies, the tie-breaking rule in I.R.C. § 152(c)(4) applies to these provisions as a group, rather than on a section-by-section basis. The IRS and Treasury Department intend to issue regulations consistent with the guidance contained in the notice. The guidance in this notice applies until those regulations are effective.[47]

If I.R.C. § 152(e) applies, a child may be treated as the qualifying child of two taxpayers. A noncustodial parent may claim the child as a qualifying child under I.R.C. § 152(e) only for purposes of the child tax credit under I.R.C. § 24 and the dependency deduction under I.R.C. § 151. However, the noncustodial parent may not claim the child as a qualifying child under I.R.C. § 152(e) in determining head of household filing status under I.R.C. § 2(b), the earned income credit under I.R.C. § 32, the child and dependent care credit under I.R.C. § 21, or the exclusion from income for dependent care assistance under I.R.C. § 129. Only the custodial parent (or other eligible taxpayer) may claim the child as a qualifying child for those purposes.

Notice 2006-86 provides five examples that illustrate its applications. In the following examples, each individual is a citizen of the United States and uses a calendar taxable year, and the child is a qualifying child (as defined in I.R.C. § 152(c)) of each taxpayer. Unless otherwise indicated, these examples assume that each individual meets the other requirements for claiming a benefit described in the example.

Example 1. A child, mother, and grandmother share the same principal place of abode. The mother is not married and is not the qualifying child of the grandmother, and the grandmother is not the mother's dependent. The mother claims the child as a qualifying child for purposes of the earned income credit under I.R.C. § 32.

The child is treated as the qualifying child of the mother for purposes of the earned income credit. Because the mother claims the child as a qualifying child for purposes of the earned income credit, under I.R.C. § 152(c)(4)(A), the child may not be treated as the qualifying child of the grandmother for any purpose.

If, however, the mother does not claim the child as a qualifying child for any purpose, the child may be treated as the qualifying child of the grandmother for purposes of the earned income credit under I.R.C. § 32, as well as

47. The regulations became effective January 18, 2017. *See* 82 FR 6370.

head of household filing status under I.R.C. § 2(b), the dependency deduction under I.R.C. § 151, the child tax credit under I.R.C. § 24, the child and dependent care credit under I.R.C. § 21, and the exclusion from income for dependent care assistance under I.R.C. § 129, if applicable, assuming that no other taxpayer claims the child as a qualifying child.

Example 2. The facts are the same as in Example 1, except that the mother and father of the child are divorced, the father is the noncustodial parent, the mother has released the claim to the exemption to the father in a written declaration under I.R.C. § 152(e), and the father attaches the written declaration to his return and claims the child as a qualifying child for purposes of the dependency deduction and the child tax credit.

Under I.R.C. § 152(e), the child is treated as the qualifying child of the father for purposes of the dependency deduction and the child tax credit. The child is treated as the qualifying child of the mother for purposes of the earned income credit and, if applicable, head of household filing status, the child and dependent care credit, and the exclusion from income for dependent care assistance. The child may not be treated as the qualifying child of the grandmother for any purpose.

Example 3. The father and mother of a child are married to each other. The father, mother, and child share the same principal place of abode for the first eight months of the year. For the last four months of the year, the parents live apart from each other, and the mother and child share the same principal place of abode. The parents file separate tax returns for the taxable year. Consequently, neither parent may claim head of household filing status, an earned income credit, or a child and dependent care credit, because in general I.R.C. § 2(b) applies only to unmarried individuals, whereas I.R.C. §§ 32(d) and 21(e)(2) require married individuals to file a joint return. The father claims the child as a qualifying child for purposes of the dependency deduction under I.R.C. § 151 and the exclusion for dependent care assistance under I.R.C. § 129. The mother claims the child as a qualifying child for purposes of the dependency deduction under I.R.C. § 151, the child tax credit under I.R.C. § 24, and the exclusion for dependent care assistance under I.R.C. § 129.

Under the tie-breaking rule of I.R.C. § 152(c)(4)(B), the child is treated as the qualifying child of the mother because the child resided with the mother for the longer period of time during the taxable year. Therefore, the child is the qualifying child of the mother for purposes of the dependency deduction, the child tax credit, and the exclusion for dependent care assistance. I.R.C. § 152(e) does not apply because the mother and father are not divorced or separated under a decree of separate maintenance or written separation agreement at the end of the taxable year and did not live apart for the last six months of the calendar year. Therefore, the child may not be treated as the qualifying child of the father for any purpose.

If, however, the mother does not claim the child as a qualifying child for any purpose, the child is treated as the qualifying child of the father for purposes of the dependency deduction under I.R.C. § 151 and the exclusion for dependent care assistance under I.R.C. § 129.

Example 4. The facts are the same as in Example 3, except that the mother and father are separated under a written separation agreement at the end of the taxable year, the mother is the custodial parent and has released the claim to the exemption to the father in a written declaration under I.R.C. § 152(e), and the father attaches the Form 8332 to his return and claims the child as a qualifying child for purposes of the dependency deduction, the child tax credit, and the exclusion for dependent care assistance under I.R.C. § 129.

Because I.R.C. § 152(e) applies, the child is treated as the qualifying child of the father for purposes of the dependency deduction and the child tax credit. The child is not treated as the qualifying child of the father for purposes of the exclusion for dependent care assistance because the father is the noncustodial parent and, under I.R.C. § 21(e)(5), only the custodial parent may claim the child as a qualifying child for purposes of the exclusion for dependent care assistance. Therefore, the tie-breaking rule of I.R.C. § 152(c)(4)(B) applies, and the child is treated as the qualifying child of the mother for purposes of the exclusion for dependent care assistance.

Example 5. The father and mother of two children are married to each other. The father, mother, and both children share the same principal place of abode for the entire year. The father and mother file separate tax returns for the taxable year. Consequently, neither parent may claim head of household filing status, an earned income credit, or a child and dependent care credit, because in general I.R.C. § 2(b) applies only to unmarried individuals, whereas I.R.C. §§ 32(d) and 21(e)(2) require married individuals to file a joint return.

The father claims the older child as a qualifying child for purposes of the child tax credit, dependency deduction, and exclusion for dependent care assistance. The mother claims the younger child as a qualifying child for purposes of the child tax credit, dependency deduction, and exclusion for dependent care assistance.

The older child is treated as the qualifying child of the father and the younger child is treated as the qualifying child of the mother. The tie-breaking rule of I.R.C. § 152(c)(4)(B) does not apply because no two taxpayers are claiming the same child as a qualifying child for any of the benefits.

(4) Planning

Although at first blush it may seem to be a bonanza to allocate the dependency exemption to the parent with the highest adjusted gross income, this may turn into a trap, because that parent's adjusted gross income may involve the phase-out rule and some or all of the exemption may be lost to both parents. In that instance, it would appear advisable for the parents to attempt to allocate the dependency exemption to the parent with the lowest adjusted gross income.[48]

(5) Student

I.R.C. § 152(f)(2) defines a "student" to mean an individual who during five calendar months during the calendar year in which the taxable year of the taxpayer begins: (i) is a full time student at an educational organization described in I.R.C. § 170(b)(1)(A)(ii) (i.e., an educational organization that normally maintains a regular faculty and curriculum and normally has a regularly enrolled body of pupils or students in attendance at the place where its educational activities are regularly carried on), or (ii) is pursuing a full-time course of institutional on-farm training under the supervision of an accredited agent of such educational institution or of a State or political subdivision of a State. A full-time student is one who is enrolled for the number of hours or courses that the educational organization considers full-time attendance.[49] A school includes an elementary school, junior or senior high school, college, university, technical, trade or mechanical school. An educational organization does not include on-the-job-training schools, a correspondence school, or a night school.[50] The five months do not have to be consecutive.[51] Night school attendance alone without full-time studies does not qualify.[52] For purposes of the support test to determine if an individual who is a qualifying child or qualifying relative under I.R.C. §§ 152(c)(1)(D) and 152(c)(1)(C) in the case of an individual is a child of the taxpayer and a student, amounts received as a scholarship for study at a previously described educational institution is not taken into account as an item of support.[53]

(6) Household Status

An individual is not treated as a member of the taxpayer's household if at any time during the taxable year of the taxpayer the relationship between the individual and the taxpayer is in violation of local law.[54]

---

48. *See* Chapter 3, B.2.a.
49. Prop. Treas. Reg. § 1.152-1(b)(2). Thus, the definition of full-time student depends upon the educational institution the child attends, since each educational institution defines "full-time" differently.
50. I.R.C. § 152(f)(2), I.R.C. § 170(b)(1).
51. Prop. Treas. Reg. § 1.152-1(b)(2).
52. Prop. Treas. Reg. § 1.151-3(b).
53. I.R.C. § 152(f)(5).
54. I.R.C. § 152(f)(3).

c. Definition of "Qualifying Relative"

An individual who does not meet the definition of a "qualifying child" may still qualify as a dependent if the individual is a "qualifying relative." I.R.C. § 152(d) sets forth four tests (relationship test, gross income test, support test, and nonqualifying child test) for an individual to qualify as a "qualifying relative."[55] There is no age test for a qualifying relative as there is for a qualifying child. Each of those tests is discussed following.

(1) Relationship Test

The relationship test is met if any of the following individuals bears any of the following relationships with respect to the taxpayer:

(i) a child or a descendant of a child;
(ii) a brother, sister, stepbrother, or stepsister;[56]
(iii) the father or mother or an ancestor of either;
(iv) a stepfather or stepmother;
(v) a son or daughter of a brother or sister of the taxpayer (i.e., a nephew or niece of the taxpayer);
(vi) a brother or sister of the father or mother of the taxpayer (i.e., an uncle or aunt of the taxpayer);
(vii) a son-in-law, daughter-in-law, father-in-law, mother-in-law, brother-in-law, or sister-in-law; or
(viii) an individual (other than an individual who at any time during the taxable year was the spouse, determined without regard to I.R.C. § 7703, of the taxpayer) who, for the taxable year of the taxpayer, has the same principal place of abode as the taxpayer and is a member of the taxpayer's household.[57]

Thus, an individual does not have to live with you for the entire year as a member of your household if the person is related to the taxpayer in some of the above listed ways to be deemed a "qualifying relative." The relationship test for a qualifying relative is broader than the relationship test for a qualifying child.[58]

---

55. I.R.C. § 152(d)(1)(A)–(D); Prop. Treas. Reg. § 1.152-3(a)(1.18.17). *See* Table 3 of IRS Publication 504, Divorced or Separated Individuals (2021).

56. "Brother" and "sister" include a brother or sister by the half-blood. I.R.C. § 152(f)(4).

57. I.R.C. §§ 152(d)(1)(A)–(D); I.R.C. § 152(d)(2).

58. *Compare,* I.R.C. § 152(c)(1) and (2) *with* I.R.C. § 152(d)(1) and (2). Prop. Treas. Reg. § 1.152-2(b)(1.18.17). Notwithstanding the foregoing, the key to the relationship test to be a qualifying relative is that the person whom the taxpayer is seeking to treat as his/her qualifying relative cannot be the taxpayer's qualifying child or the qualifying child of any other taxpayer.

(2) Gross Income Test

Section 152(d)(1)(B) provides that the gross income test requires the gross income for the calendar year in which such taxable year begins to be less than the exempt amount. (As noted earlier, and as provided in Notice 2018-70, Section 151(d)(5)(A) provides that for taxable years beginning after December 31, 2017, and before January 1, 2026, the term "exemption amount" is zero, thereby suspending the deduction for personal exemptions. Section 151(d)(B), however, provides that for any other provision of the Code, the reduction of the exemption amount to zero will not be taken into account in determining whether a deduction is allowed or allowable, or whether a taxpayer is entitled to a deduction under Section 151. The Conference Report[59] states that the reduction of the personal exemption to zero shall not alter the operation of other provisions of the Code which refer to a taxpayer allowed a deduction under Section 151. For example, Section 24(a) allows credit against tax with respect to each qualifying child of the taxpayer of which the taxpayer is allowed a deduction under Section 151. A qualifying child, as defined under Section 152(c), remains eligible for the child tax credit under Section 24, notwithstanding that the deduction under Section 151 has been reduced to zero.) For example, Section 24(a) allows a credit against tax with respect to each qualifying child of the taxpayer for which the taxpayer is allowed a deduction under Section 152(a). A qualifying child, as defined under Section 152(c), remains eligible for the child tax credit under Section 24, notwithstanding that the deduction under Section 151 has been reduced to zero. Notice 2018-70, was issued as a result of the Tax Cuts and Job Act of 2017 to provide that the gross income test for a qualifying relative is $4,150 as adjusted for inflation in future years in which the dependency exemption is zero. The gross income for 2018 was $4,150, for 2019 was $4,200, for 2020 and 2021 was $4,300, and for 2022 is $4,400. See Treas. Reg. § 1.152-3(c)(1) amended October 13, 2020, 85 FR64383 (10.13.20). Treas. Reg. § 1.152-2(1) approved September 8, 2020, adopts Notice 2018-70 for purposes of establishing the exempt amount in defining a qualifying relative.[60] Gross income is income from money, property, or nonexempt services. Thus, the exempt amount referenced in Section 152 is $4,150 (adjusted for inflation), rather than zero for purposes of the gross income test in determining who is a qualifying relative. Gross income includes a partner's share of the gross income of a partnership, taxable unemployment compensation and Social Security benefits, and amounts received in scholarships.

59. Conference Report to Accompany HR 1, Report 115-416, 115th Cong., 1st Sess. (12.15.14), at 202, n.16.

60. I.R.C. § 152(d)(1)(B), Prop. Treas. Reg. § 1.152-3(c)(1)(1.18.17). "Gross income" means gross income under § 61. It does not include exempt income such as income from municipal bonds. There is a special rule, discussed above, defining gross income of a person who is permanently and totally disabled. Prop. Treas. Reg. § 1.152-3(c)(2)(1.18.17); I.R.C. § 151 (d)(5).

There is a special rule relating to handicapped dependents for purposes of the gross income test for determination of a qualifying relative. It provides that the gross income of an individual who is permanently and totally disabled[61] at any time during the taxable year does not include income attributable to services performed by the individual at a sheltered workshop if (i) the availability of medical care at the workshop is the principal reason for the individual's presence there, and (ii) the income arises only from activities at the workshop that are incident to such medical care.[62] A "sheltered workshop" is a school that (i) provides special instructions or training designed to alleviate the disability of the individual, and (ii) is operated by an organization described in Section 501(1)(3).[63]

(3) Support Test

The support test requires the taxpayer to provide more than one-half the individual's support for the calendar year in which such taxable year begins.[64] For purposes of the support test if more than half of an individual's support is provided by two or more persons together, a taxpayer is treated as having contributed over half of the support for that calendar year if:

(i) No one person contributed over half such support,

(ii) Over one-half of such support is received from two or more persons each of whom, but for the fact that any such person alone did not contribute over one-half of such support, would have been entitled to claim such individual as a dependent for a taxable year beginning in such calendar year,

(iii) The taxpayer claiming the individual as a qualifying relative contributes more than ten (10) percent of individual's support, and

(iv) Each person described in (ii) (other than the taxpayer) who contributed more than ten (10) percent of support for the individual furnishes

61. I.R.C. § 22(e)(3) defines an individual as being permanently and totally disabled if the individual is unable to engage in any substantial gainful activity by reason of any medically determinable physical or mental impairment which can be expected to result in death or which has lasted or can be expected to last for a continuous period of not less than 12 months. An individual is not considered to be permanently and totally disabled unless the individual furnishes proof of the existence of such disability in such form and manner, and at such times, as the IRS may require.

62. I.R.C. § 152(d)(4)(A); Prop. Treas. Reg. § 1.152-3(c)(2)(1.18.17). *See* IRS Publication 501, Dependents, Standard Deduction and Filing Instruction (2021) Worksheet 2, page 16, for a worksheet for determining support.

63. I.R.C. § 151(d)(4)(B); Prop. Treas. Reg. § 1.152-3(d)(2)(1.18.17).

64. I.R.C. § 152(d)(1)(C), Prop. Treas. Reg. § 1.152-3(d)(1)(1.18.17). *See* Worksheet 2 in Publication 501, Dependents, Standard Deduction and Filing Information, p. 16 (2021) for help in determining whether the taxpayer provided more than half of a person's support.

> to the taxpayer claiming the individual as a dependent a written declaration that such person will not claim such individual as a dependent for any taxable year beginning in such taxable year.[65]

The impact of this provision is that where more than half the support of the individual is provided by two or more persons, each of whom would be entitled to claim the dependency exemption for the individual, those persons may agree among themselves that one of those persons who contributed more than ten (10) percent of the individual's support will be deemed to have met the support test and may claim the individual as his or her dependent for purposes of the dependency exemption. The persons who contributed more than ten (10) percent of the individual's support but who do not intend to claim the individual as a dependent must sign a waiver, in the form prescribed by the regulations, granting the exemption to one of the ten percenters. Form 2210 may be used for this purpose.

For purposes of the qualifying relative rule: (i) payments to a spouse that are includible in the gross income of the payee spouse under I.R.C. §§ 71 or 682 (pertaining to alimony trusts) as alimony or separate maintenance payments[66] are not treated as a payment by the payor spouse for the support of any dependent, and (ii) in the case of remarriage of a parent, support of a child received from the parent's spouse is treated as received from the parent.[67] Any support provided to or for the benefit of an individual by a stepparent of the individual is treated as support provided by the individual's parent who is married to the stepparent.[68]

The funds of a qualifying relative are not deemed provided by the qualifying relative unless the funds are actually spent for support. If any of the funds are withheld for investment they are not deemed spent for support by the qualifying relative. Tax exempt income, however, is included in determining the providing of support. This includes not only interest from municipal bonds under Section 103, but also nontaxable life insurance proceeds, Social

---

65. I.R.C. § 152(d)(3), Prop. Treas. Reg. § 1.152-3(d)(4)(1.18.17).

66. "Alimony or separate maintenance payments" mean: (1) payments of cash, (2) received by (or on behalf of) a spouse under a divorce or separation instrument defined in Section 121(d)(3)(C) (instead of Section 71 which was repealed by TCJA 2017), (3) in the case of an individual legally separated from his or her spouse under a decree of divorce or of separate maintenance, (4) the payee and the payor spouses are not members of the same household at the time the payment is made, and (5) there is no liability to make such payments for any period after the death of the payee spouse and there is no liability to make any payment in cash or property as a substitute for such payments after the death of the payee spouse. Those requirements are the same as alimony tests 1, 2, 3, 5, and 6 under Section 71 in effect prior to TCJA 2017 (see Chapter 1, B.3.a,b,c,e,f).

67. I.R.C. § 152(d)(5)(A)(ii). The rule in (i) applies to the law in effect prior to TCJA 2017.

68. Prop. Treas. Reg. § 1.152-3(d)(3)(1.18.17).

Security proceeds, and government benefits such as food stamps and housing are treated as provided by a third party.[69]

If the taxpayer provides a person with lodging, the taxpayer is deemed to have provided support equal to the fair rental value of the place provided to that person. Fair rental value is deemed the amount the taxpayer could reasonably expect to receive from a third party for the use of the same space. Actual expenses incurred are disregarded in determining fair rental value. Equivalent rent to a third party is the controlling test.

On the other hand, if the taxpayer provides property or support, one looks to the fair market value of the property to determine the value of the property provided in determining support. Fair market value of the property is the price between a willing buyer and a willing seller when both act without compulsion and both have reasonable knowledge of all the relevant facts.[70]

Child care expenses paid to provide child care are deemed an item of support. On the other hand, Federal, State, and Local income taxes and Social Security and Medicare taxes paid by the person from his/her funds are not included in support, nor are payments of life insurance premiums or funeral arrangements or scholarships received by a child included as items of support.

(4) Not a Qualifying Child of Another

The last test to qualify as a qualifying relative requires the individual to not be a qualifying child of the taxpayer or of any other taxpayer for any taxable year beginning in the calendar year in which such taxable year begins.[71] An individual is not a qualifying child of that person if that person is not required to file an income tax return and does not file an income tax return or files an income tax return solely to claim a refund of estimated or withheld taxes.[72] The qualifying relative test does not have an age test like the qualifying child test. Thus, a qualifying relative can be any age.

The following six examples from the proposed regulations[73] illustrate the fourth test—"not a qualifying child test." In each example, each taxpayer uses the calendar year as the taxpayer's taxable year and each taxpayer meets the requirements to claim the benefits described in the example.

Example 1. For the taxable year, B provides more than one-half of the support of an unrelated friend, C, and C's three-year-old child, D, who are members of B's household. No taxpayer other than C is eligible to claim D as a qualifying child. C has no gross income, is not required by Section 6012 to file a

69. *See* Lutter v. Commissioner, 61 T.C. 685 (1974) *aff'd. per curiam* 514 F.2d 1095 (C.A.7 1975).

70. Rev. Rul. 59-60, 1959-1 C.B. 237.

71. I.R.C. § 152(d)(1)(D), Prop. Treas. Reg. § 1.152-3(e)(1.18.17). *See* Notice 2008-5, at Chapter 3, C(4)d.

72. Prop. Treas. Reg. § 1.152-3(e)(1)(1.18.17).

73. Prop. Treas. Reg. § 1.152-3(e)(2)(1.18.17).

Federal income tax return, and does not file a Federal income tax return for the taxable year. Because C does not have a filing requirement and does not file an income tax return, D is not treated as a qualifying child of C, and B may claim both C and D as B's qualifying relatives.

Example 2. The facts are the same as in Example 1, except that C has earned income of $1,500 during the taxable year, had income tax withheld from wages, and is not required by Section 6012 to file an income tax return. C files an income tax return solely to obtain a refund of withheld taxes and does not claim the earned income credit under Section 32. Because C does not have a filing requirement and files only to obtain a refund of withheld taxes, D is not treated as a qualifying child of C, and B may claim both C and D as B's qualifying relatives.[74]

Example 3. The facts are the same as in Example 2, except that C's earned income is more than the amount of the dependency exemption for that year. C files an income tax return for the taxable year to obtain a refund of withheld taxes and claims the earned income credit. Because C filed an income tax return to obtain the earned income credit and not solely to obtain a refund of withheld taxes, D is a qualifying child of a taxpayer C, and B may not claim D as a qualifying relative. B also may not claim C as a qualifying relative because C fails the gross income test.

The IRS issued Notice 2008-5[75] to provide guidance under I.R.C. § 152(d) for determining whether an individual is a qualifying relative for whom the taxpayer may claim a dependency exemption deduction under I.R.C. § 151(c). I.R.C. § 152(d)(1)(D) provides that an individual is not a qualifying relative of the taxpayer if the individual is a qualifying child of any other taxpayer. The notice clarifies that an individual is not a qualifying child of "any other taxpayer" if the individual's parent (or other person with respect to whom the individual is defined as a qualifying child) is not required by I.R.C. § 6012 to file an income tax return and (i) does not file an income tax return, or (ii) files an income tax return solely to obtain a refund of withheld income taxes.

I.R.C. § 152(d)(1) provides, in part, that to be a "qualifying relative" of a taxpayer, an individual must: (i) bear a certain relationship to the taxpayer, (ii) have gross income for the calendar year that is less than the exemption amount (as defined in I.R.C. § 151(d)), and (iii) derive over one-half of his or her support for the calendar year from the taxpayer. In addition, I.R.C. § 152(d)(1)(D) requires that the individual not be a qualifying child of the taxpayer or of "any other taxpayer" for the taxable year. I.R.C. § 152(d)(2)(H) provides that a qualifying relative may include an individual who has the same principal place of abode as the taxpayer and who is a member of the taxpayer's

74. Prop. Treas. Reg. § 1.152-3(e)(2)(1.18.17).
75. 2008-21 I.R.B. 256.

household. The IRS, therefore, concludes that a taxpayer otherwise eligible to claim a dependency exemption deduction for an unrelated child is not prohibited by I.R.C. § 152(d)(1)(D) from claiming the deduction if the child's parent (or other person with respect to whom the child is defined is a qualifying child) is not required by I.R.C. § 6012 to file an income tax return and (i) does not file an income tax return, or (ii) files an income tax return solely to obtain a refund of withheld income taxes.[76]

For purposes of I.R.C. § 152(d)(1)(D), an individual is not a qualifying child of "any other taxpayer" if the individual's parent (or other person with respect to whom the individual is defined as a qualifying child) is not required by I.R.C. § 6012 to file an income tax return and (i) does not file an income tax return, or (ii) files an income tax return solely to obtain a refund of withheld income taxes.

Notice 2008-5 provides three examples that illustrate its application. In each example the taxpayer is not related or married to his friend and is not the biological or adopted father of the friend's child.

Example 1. Alex supports as members of his household for the taxable year an unrelated friend, Bev, and her three-year-old child, Chris. Bev has no gross income, is not required by I.R.C. § 6012 to file an income tax return, and does not file an income tax return for the taxable year. Accordingly, because Bev does not have a filing requirement and did not file an income tax return, Chris is not treated as a qualifying child of Bev or any other taxpayer, and Alex may claim both Bev and Chris as his qualifying relatives, provided all other requirements of I.R.C. §§ 151 and 152 to qualify for the deduction are met.

Example 2. Same facts as Example 1, except that Bev has earned income of $1,500 during the taxable year 2006, had income tax withheld from her wages, and is not required by I.R.C. § 6012 to file an income tax return. With one qualifying child, Bev may claim the earned income credit (EIC) in the amount of $519 for the taxable year. Bev files an income tax return solely to obtain a refund of withheld income taxes and does not claim the EIC. Accordingly, because Bev does not have a filing requirement and filed only to obtain a refund of withheld income taxes, Chris is not a qualifying child of Bev or any other taxpayer, and Alex may claim both Bev and Chris as his qualifying relatives, provided all other requirements of I.R.C. §§ 151 and 152 to qualify for the deduction are met.

Example 3. Same facts as Example 1, except that Bev has earned income of $8,000 during the taxable year 2006, had income tax withheld from her wages, and is not required by I.R.C. § 6012 to file an income tax return for the taxable year. With one qualifying child, Bev may claim the EIC in the amount of

76. *See* Rev. Rul. 54-567, 1954-2 C.B. 108, *aff'd*, Rev. Rul. 65-34, 1965-1 C.B. 86.

$2,729 for the taxable year. Bev files an income tax return for the taxable year to obtain a refund of withheld income taxes, and Bev claims the EIC on the return. Accordingly, because Bev filed an income tax return to obtain the EIC, and not solely to obtain a refund of withheld income taxes, Chris is a qualifying child of another taxpayer, Bev, and Alex may not claim Chris as a qualifying relative.

(5) Miscellaneous

In addition to the specific tests that must be met to be deemed a qualifying relative, the general tests applicable to all dependents must be met, such as the non-joint return test and the citizenship test, which are discussed under the preceding "qualifying child" rules.

d. Special Rules for a Qualifying Child and a Qualifying Relative

There are special rules that apply both to a qualifying child and a qualifying relative. These special rules include a support test, relationship test, and place of abode test, which are discussed next.

(1) Support Test

(a) In General

The term "support" includes food, shelter, clothing, medical and dental care, education, and similar items. Support does not include an individual's Federal, State, and Local income taxes paid from the individual's own income or assets, Social Security and Medicare taxes under Section 3101 paid from the individual's own income, life insurance premiums, or funeral expenses. In determining whether an individual provided more than one-half of the individual's own support for purposes of Treasury Regulations § 1.152-2(e), or whether a taxpayer provided more than one-half of an individual's support for purposes of Treasury Regulations § 1.152-3(d), the amount of support provided by the individual, or the taxpayer, is compared to the total amount of the individual's support from all sources. For these purposes, except as otherwise provided in this paragraph, the amount of an individual's total support is the amount of support from all sources and includes support the individual provides and amounts that are excludable from gross income. Generally, the amount of an item of support is the amount of expense paid or incurred to furnish the item of support. If the item of support furnished is property or a benefit, such as lodging, however, the amount of the item of support is the fair market value of the item.[77]

77. Prop. Treas. Reg. § 1.152-4(a)(1)(1.18.17).

(b) Payments Made during the Year for Unpaid or Future Support

For purposes of determining the amount of support provided in a calendar year, an amount paid in a calendar year after the calendar year in which the liability is incurred is treated as paid in the year of payment. An amount paid in a calendar year before due, whether made in the form of a lump sum payment in settlement of a person's liability for support, is treated as support paid during the calendar year of payment rather than the calendar year when payment is due. A payment of a liability from amounts set aside in trust in a prior year is treated as made in the year in which the liability is paid.[78]

(c) Governmental Payments

(i) Governmental Payments as Support. Except as provided as follows, governmental payments and subsidies for an item of support are support provided by a third party, the government.[79] For example, payments of Temporary Assistance for Needy Families (42 U.S.C. 601-619), low-income housing assistance (42 U.S.C. 1437f), Supplemental Nutrition Assistance Program benefits (7 U.S.C. Chapter 51), Supplemental Security Income payments (42 U.S.C. 1381-1383f), foster care maintenance payments, and adoption assistance payments are governmental payments and subsidies for an item of support.

(ii) Governmental Payments Based on a Taxpayer's Contributions. Except as provided as follows, governmental payments based on a taxpayer's earnings and contributions into the Social Security system are support provided by the individual for whose benefit the payments are made to the extent those payments are used for that individual's support.[80] For example, Social Security old age benefits under Section 202(b) of Title II of the Social Security Act (SSA) (42 J.S.C. 402) are governmental payments based on a taxpayer's earnings and contributions into the Social Security system. Similarly, Social Security survivor and disability insurance benefits paid under Section 202(d) of the SSA to, or for the benefit of, the child of a deceased or disabled parent are treated as support provided by the child to the extent those payments are used for the child's support.[81]

(iii) Payments Used for Support of Another Individual. Governmental payments and subsidies just described in (i) immediately preceding and governmental payments just described in (ii), immediately pre-

78. Prop. Treas. Reg. § 1.152-4(a)(2)(1.18.17).
79. Prop. Treas. Reg. § 1.152-4(a)(3)(i)(A)(1.18.17).
80. Prop. Treas. Reg. § 1.152-4(a)(3)(ii)(A)(1.18.17).
81. Prop. Treas. Reg. § 1.152-4(a)(3)(iii)(B)(1.18.17).

ceding that are used by the recipient or other intended beneficiary to support another person are support of that person provided by the recipient or other intended beneficiary, rather than support provided by a third party, the government.[82]

(d) Medical Insurance

Medical insurance premiums, including Part A Basic Medicare premiums, if any, under Title XVIII of the Social Security Act (42 U.S.C. 1395c to 1395i-5), Part B supplemental Medicare premiums under Title XVIII of the Social Security Act (42 U.S.C. 395w-6), Part C Medicare = Choice Program premiums under Title XVIII of the Social Security Act (42 U.S.C. 1395w-21 to 1395w-29), and Part D Voluntary Prescription Drug Benefit Medicare premiums under Title XVIII of the Social Security Act (42 U.S.C. 1395w-101 to 1395w-154), are treated as support. Medical insurance proceeds, including benefits received under Medicare Part A, Part B, Part C, and Part D, are not treated as items of support and are disregarded in determining the amount of the individual's support. Services provided to an individual under the medical and dental care provisions of the Armed Forces Act (U.S.C. Chapter 55) are not treated as support and are disregarded in determining the amount of the individual's support.[83]

(e) Medical Care Payments from Personal Injury

Payments for the medical care of an injured individual from a third party, including a third party's insurance company, in satisfaction of a legal claim for the personal injury of the individual are not treated as items of support and are disregarded in determining the amount of the individual's support.[84]

(f) Scholarships

Amounts a student who is the child of the taxpayer receives as a scholarship for study at an educational organization described in Section 170(b)(1)(A)(ii) are not treated as an item of support and are disregarded in determining the amount of the student's support.[85]

(2) Relationship Test

(a) Joint Return

A taxpayer may satisfy the relationship test relating to a qualifying child or qualifying relative if a described relationship exists between an individual and the taxpayer claiming that individual as a qualifying child or qualifying

---

82. Prop. Treas. Reg. § 1.152-4(a)(3)(ii)(B)(1.18.17).
83. Prop. Treas. Reg. § 1.152-4(a)(4)(1.18.17).
84. Prop. Treas. Reg. § 1.152-4(a)(5)(1.18.17).
85. Prop. Treas. Reg. § 1.152-4(a)(6)(1.18.17).

relative, even though the taxpayer files a joint return with his or her spouse who does not have a described relationship with the individual.[86]

(b) Divorce or Death of Spouse

If the relationship between the taxpayer and an individual claimed by that taxpayer as a dependent results from a marriage, the taxpayer's qualifying relationship with the individual continues after the termination of the marriage by divorce or death.[87]

(3) Principal Place of Abode Test

(a) In General

The term "principal place of abode" of a person means the primary or main home or dwelling where the person resides. A person's principal place of abode need not be the same physical location throughout the taxable year and may be temporary lodging such as a homeless shelter or relief housing resulting from displacement caused by a natural disaster.[88]

(b) Temporary Absence

The taxpayer and an individual have the same principal place of abode despite a temporary absence by either person because of special circumstances. An absence is temporary if the person would have resided at the place of abode. An individual who does not reside with the taxpayer because of a temporary absence is treated as residing with the taxpayer. For example, a nonpermanent failure to occupy the abode by reason of illness, education, business, vacation, military service, institutionalized care for a child who is totally and permanently disabled (as defined in Section 22(e)(3)), or incarceration may be treated as a temporary absence because of special circumstances. If an infant must remain in a hospital for a period of time after birth and would have resided with the taxpayer during that period but for the hospitalization, the infant is treated as having the same principal place of abode as the taxpayer during the period of hospitalization.[89]

(c) Residing with Taxpayer for More than One-Half of the Taxable Year

(i) In General. An individual has the same principal place of abode as the taxpayer for more than one-half of the taxable year if the individual

86. Prop. Treas. Reg. § 1.152-4(b)(1)(1.18.17).
87. Prop. Treas. Reg. § 1.152-4(b)(2)(1.18.17).
88. Prop. Treas. Reg. § 1.152-4(c)(1)(1.18.17).
89. Prop. Treas. Reg. § 1.152-4(c)(2)(1.18.17).

resides with the taxpayer for at least 183 nights during the taxpayer's taxable year, or 184 nights if the taxable year includes a leap day.[90]

(ii) Nights of Residence. For purposes of determining whether an individual resides with the taxpayer for more than one-half of the taxable year, an individual resides with a taxpayer for a night if the individual sleeps (i) at the taxpayer's principal place of abode, whether or not the taxpayer is present; or (ii) in the company of the taxpayer when the individual does not sleep at the taxpayer's principal place of abode (for example, when the taxpayer and the individual are on vacation).[91]

(iii) Night Straddling Two Taxable Years. If an individual resides with a taxpayer for a night that extends over two taxable years, that night is allocated to the taxable year in which the night begins.[92]

(iv) Exception for a Parent Who Works at Night. If, in a calendar year, because of a taxpayer's nighttime work schedule, an individual resides for at least 183 days, or 184 days if the taxable year includes a leap day, but not nights with the taxpayer, the individual is treated as residing with the taxpayer for more than one-half of the taxable year.[93]

(v) Absences. An individual who does not reside with a taxpayer for a night because of a temporary absence is treated as residing with the taxpayer for that night if the individual would have resided with the taxpayer for that night but for the absence.[94]

(d) Examples

The following six examples from the regulations illustrate the principal place of abode rules. In each example, each taxpayer uses the calendar year as the taxable year, and Section 152(e), which contains the special rule for divorced or legally separated parents, does not apply.[95]

---

90. Prop. Treas. Reg. § 1.152-4(c)(2)(1.18.17).

91. Prop. Treas. Reg. § 1.152-4(c)(ii)(A)(1.18.17). Look to nights a child spends with a parent to determine whether the child has the same principal place of abode as the parent for more than one-half the taxable year for purposes of § 152(c)(1)(B). Where child resides with noncustodial parent six out of every 14 nights during the school year, and alternating weeks during school break in the summer, child is deemed to have spent more than half the nights with the custodial parent. Consequently, the child did not have the same principal place of abode as the noncustodial parent for more than half the tax year and therefore was not the qualifying child of the noncustodial parent for that year.

92. Prop. Treas. Reg. § 1.152-4(c)(ii)(B)(1.18.17).

93. Prop. Treas. Reg. § 1.152-4(c)(ii)(C)(1.18.17).

94. Prop. Treas. Reg. § 1.152-4(c)(3)(ii)(D)(1.18.17).

95. Prop. Treas. Reg. § 1.152-4(c)(4)(1.18.17).

Example 1. B and C are the divorced parents of Child. In 2015, Child sleeps at B's principal place of abode for 210 nights and at C's principal place of abode for 155 nights. Child resides with B for at least 183 nights during 2015 and has the same principal place of abode as B for more than one-half of 2015.

Example 2. D and E are the divorced parents of Child, and Grandparent is E's parent. In 2015, Child resides with D for 140 nights, with E for 135 nights, and with Grandparent for the last 90 nights of the year. None of these periods is a temporary absence. Child does not have the same principal place of abode as D, E, or Grandparent for more than one-half of 2015.

Example 3. The facts are the same as in Example 2, except that for the 90-day period that Child lives with Grandparent, E is temporarily absent on military service. Child would have lived with E if E had not been absent during that period. Child is treated as residing with E for 225 nights in 2015 and, therefore, Child has the same principal place of abode as E for more than one-half of 2015.

Example 4. The facts are the same as in Example 2, except that, for the last 90 days of the year Child, who is 18 years of age, moves into Child's own apartment and begins full-time employment. Because Child's absence is not temporary, Child is not treated as residing with D or E for the 90 nights. Therefore, child does not have the same principal place of abode as D or E for more than one-half of 2015.

Example 5. F and G are the divorced parents of Child. In 2015, Child sleeps at F's principal place of abode for 170 nights and at G's principal place of abode for 170 nights. Child spends 25 nights of the year away from F and G at a summer camp. Child would have spent those nights with F if Child had not gone to summer camp. Child is treated as residing with F for 195 nights and, therefore, Child has the same principal place of abode as F for more than one-half of 2015.

Example 6. H and J are the divorced parents of Child. In 2015, Child sleeps at H's principal place of abode for 180 nights and at J's principal place of abode for 180 nights. For five nights during that year, Child sleeps at Grandparent's abode or at the house of a friend. Child would have spent all five nights at H's house if Child had not slept at Grandparent's or a friend's house. Child is treated as residing with H for 185 nights and, therefore, Child has the same principal place of abode as H for more than one-half of 2015.

(e) Residence for a Portion of a Taxable Year because of Special Circumstances

If an individual is born or dies during a taxpayer's taxable year, the residency test for a qualifying child is treated as met if the taxpayer and the individual have the same principal place of abode for more than one-half of the portion of the taxable year during which the individual is alive. If an individual is born or dies during a taxpayer's taxable year, the relationship test for a qualifying relative who is a member of the taxpayer's household is treated as met if the taxpayer and the individual have the same principal place of abode for the entire portion of the taxable year during which the individual is alive.[96]

If, during a taxpayer's taxable year, the taxpayer adopts a child, a child is lawfully placed with a taxpayer for legal adoption by that taxpayer, or an eligible foster child is placed with a taxpayer, the residency test for a qualifying child and the residency requirement under Treas. Reg. § 1.152-1(a)(2)(iii) for a child who is not a citizen or national of the United States are treated as met if the taxpayer and the child have the same principal place of abode for more than one-half of the portion of the taxable year as required for a qualifying child, or for the entire taxable year as required for a noncitizen, following the placement of the child with the taxpayer.[97]

(f) Missing Child

(i) Qualifying Child. A child of the taxpayer who is presumed by law enforcement authorities to have been kidnapped by someone who is not a member of the family of either the child or the taxpayer, and who had for the taxable year in which the kidnapping occurred the same principal place of abode as the taxpayer for more than one-half of the portion of the taxable year before the date of the kidnapping, is treated as meeting the residency test for a qualifying child of the taxpayer for all taxable years ending during the period that the child is missing. Also, the child is treated as meeting the residency test in the year of the child's return if the child has the same principal place of abode as the taxpayer for more than one-half of the portion of the taxable year following the date of the child's return.[98]

(ii) Qualifying Relative. A child of the taxpayer who is presumed by law enforcement authorities to have been kidnapped by someone who is not a member of the family of either the child or the taxpayer, and who was a qualifying relative of the taxpayer for the portion of the taxable year before the date of the kidnapping, is treated as a qualifying relative of the taxpayer for all taxable years ending during the period that the child is missing. Also, the child is treated as a qualifying relative of the taxpayer in the year of the child's return if the child is a qualifying relative of the taxpayer for the portion of the taxable year following the date of the child's return.[99]

96. Prop. Treas. Reg. § 1.152-4(d)(1)(1.18.17).
97. Prop. Treas. Reg. § 1.152-4(d)(2)(1.18.17).
98. Prop. Treas. Reg. § 1.152-4(e)(1)(1.18.17).
99. Prop. Treas. Reg. § 1.152-4(e)(2)(1.18.17).

(iii) Age Limitation. The special rules for a missing qualifying child or qualifying relative cease to apply as of the first taxable year of the taxpayer beginning after the calendar year in which there is a determination that the child is dead or, if earlier, in which the child would have attained age 18.[100]

(iv) Application. Prop. Treas. Reg. § 1.152-4(e) pertaining to a missing child applies solely for purposes of determining surviving spouse or head of household filing status under Section 2, the child tax credit under Section 24, the earned income credit under Section 32, and the dependency exemption under Section 151.[101]

2. Exemption Amount

The personal exemption for an individual, spouse, and each dependent is indexed for inflation beginning in 1990.[102] The exemption amount for 2016 and 2017 was $4,150.[103] The exemption amount for 2018 before enactment of TCJA 2017 was also $4,150. As a result of TCJA 2017, however, for tax years beginning after December 31, 2017, and before January 1, 2026, the exemption amount for claiming the dependency exemption is *zero*. The dependency exemption was not repealed; only the exempt amount was set at zero.[104] Even though the exempt amount is zero, the dependency exemption rules are still important because they determine whether the taxpayer can claim the child tax credit, the dependent care credit, or head of household status. In effect, for taxable years 2018 through 2025, Congress united two exemption amounts. The first exemption amount is zero for the dependency exemption, but for other provisions of the Code that reference the personal exemption, the exemption amount is not zero, but is $4,150 in 2018 indexed for inflation.[105] Thus, in determining who is a dependent for the child tax credit, dependent care credit

100. Prop. Treas. Reg. § 1.152-4(e)(3)(1.18.17).

101. Prop. Treas. Reg. § 1.152-4(e)(4)(1.18.17).

102. I.R.C. § 151(d).

103. Rev. Proc. 2017-58(§ 3.24), IRB 2017-45, modified and superseded by Rev. Proc. 2018-18, 2018-10 IRB 392; Rev. Proc. 2016-55 (§ 3.24(1)), IRB 2016-45 and Rev. Proc. 2015-53, (§ 3.24(1)), 2015-44, IRB 615. The exemption amount for 2008 was $3,500 (Rev. Proc. 2008-69, 2008-45 I.R.B. § 1107); for 2009 the exemption amount was $3,650 (Rev. Proc. 2012-15 and Rev. Proc. 2013-35). The exemption amount for 2010 was also $3,650.00. For 2011 the exemption amount was increased to $3,700.00 (*see* Rev. Proc. 2011-12, IRB 2011-2 297), and for 2012 the exemption amount was $3,800.00 (*see* Rev. Proc. 2011-52, IRB 2011-45). For 2013 the exemption amount was $3,900, for 2014 the exemption amount was $3,950, for 2015 the exemption amount was $4,050, and for 2016 the exemption amount was $4,000.

104. Tax Cuts and Jobs Act of 2017, PL 115-97, 12/22/2017, Section 11041(a)(2).

105. I.R.C. § 151(d)(5)(B) (The reduction of the exemption amount to zero will not be taken into account in determining whether a deduction is allowed or allowable. According to H.R. Rep. No. 115-466 at 203 (2017), the reduction of the exemption amount to zero does not affect those Code provisions which refer to a taxpayer allowed deduction under Section 151, including

and head of household the amount is $4,200 for 2019, $4,300 for 2020, $4,300 for 2021, $4,400 for 2022, and $4,700 for 2023.

a. Phaseout

For tax years prior to 2018, the personal exemption is phased out for high income taxpayers for tax years after 2017 and before 2026. For tax years between 2018 and 2025 there is no need for the phaseout of the personal exemption because the personal exemption for those years is zero. The phaseout resumes in tax year 2026. The phaseout affects all exemptions that may be claimed on a return, including those for a spouse and dependent. The purpose of the phaseout is to limit any benefit that high-income taxpayers may obtain as a result of the lowering of the tax brackets. The personal exemption of a taxpayer whose adjusted gross income (AGI) exceeds the threshold amounts set forth in Table 3.1 is reduced by 2 percent for each $2,500 (or fraction thereof) by which the adjusted gross income of a taxpayer exceeds the threshold amount.[106] For married filing separate taxpayers, the $2,500 is reduced to $1,250.[107] The exemption is eliminated completely when the taxpayer's AGI exceeds the threshold amount by more than $150,000 ($75,000 for married couple filing separately). The phaseout of the personal exemption, via the surtax, for tax years beginning after 2017 and before 2026, begins at the levels of taxable income shown in Table 3.1.

Table 3.1 Phaseout Table

	For 2016[108]		For 2017[109]	
Filing Status	**Phaseout Begins After AGI of**	**Phaseout Ends After AGI of**	**Phaseout Begins After AGI of**	**Phaseout Ends After AGI of**
Married filing jointly or surviving spouse	$311,300	$433,800	$313,800	$436,300
Heads of household	$285,350	$407,850	$287,650	$410,150
Single taxpayer	$259,400	$381,900	$261,500	$384,000
Married filing separately	$155,650	$216,900	$156,900	$218,150

the child tax credit under Section 24.). *See also* Notice 2018-70 discussed at Chapter 3, B.C(2), *supra*.

106. I.R.C. § 151(d)(3)(A) and (B)
107. I.R.C. § 151(d)(3)(B).
108. Rev. Proc. 2013-15, § 2.11, 2013-5, I.R.B. 444
109. Rev. Proc. 2013-35, § 3.23(2), I.R.B. 2013-47.

The ending phaseout amounts, which are the same as the phaseout amounts for itemized deductions, are $122,500 above the beginning phaseout amounts, except for married filing separate, which is $61,250 above the beginning phaseout amounts.

For 2018 through 2025, there is no limitation on the dependency exemption, as that limitation was eliminated by TCJA 2017 setting the dependency amount at zero. Thus, since the personal exemption is zero between 2018 and 2025, the phaseout amount is also zero (exemption amount of zero reduced by the applicable percentage equals zero).[110]

b. Example

Mr. and Mrs. Married file a joint Federal income tax return for 2017. They have adjusted gross income of $401,000. They have two children. They are entitled to claim four exemptions for a total of $16,200 (4 × $4,050). As a result of the phaseout, however, their exemptions are reduced to $15,860, determined as follows:

Adjusted gross income	$ 401,000
Threshold amount	313,800
Difference	87,200
Divided by	2,500
Quotient	35
Multiplied	× 2%
Product	7
Pre-phaseout exemption	16,200
Exemption reduction (100%)	1,620
Phaseout of exemption reduction (two thirds)	1,080
Exemption reduction	340
Exemption allowed	$ 15,860

C. Exemption for Divorced or Separated Parents

1. Legislative History

The general rule of I.R.C. § 151 was the cause of a substantial amount of litigation between divorced or separated parents in which the IRS was a wonted but unwanted party. To alleviate the onerous burden placed on the IRS, Congress, in 1966, added I.R.C. § 152(e) to the Code, which establishes the support test for

110. I.R.C. § 151(d)(3)(A) and (B).

a child of separated or divorced parents.[111] In 1984, Congress again amended the dependency exemption provision for a child of divorced or separated parents in order to provide a clear standard for determining entitlement to the dependency exemption where the parents are separated or divorced. The standard was further amended by the 2004 Working Families Tax Relief Act and the 2005 Gulf Zone Opportunity Act. The following discusses the provisions to the dependency exemption for divorced or separated parents as a result of those legislations.

2. General Rule—Custodial Parent

I.R.C. § 152(e)(1) sets forth the general rule for divorced or separated parents, or never married parents not living together,[112] and provides that where the parents of a qualifying child do not file a joint return, the custodial parent is entitled to the dependency exemption for a qualifying child or qualifying relative.[113] Thus, the custodial parent is entitled to the dependency exemption as between divorced or separated parents, or parents who are never married. On the other hand, the child is treated as the qualifying child or qualifying relative of the noncustodial parent if:

a. The child receives over one-half of the child's support during the calendar year from the child's parents.
b. The child's parents are:
    (i) Divorced or legally separated under a decree of divorce or separate maintenance, or
    (ii) Separated under a written separation agreement or,
    (iii) Live apart at all times during the last six months of the taxable year.[114]

---

111. H. Rep. No. 102, 90th Cong., 1st Sess., 19672 C.B. 590.

112. King v. Comm'r, 121 T.C. 245 (2003), *see also* Hughes v. Comm'r, T.C. Memo. 2000-143, and Brignal v. Comm'r, T.C. Memo. 1999-387 where I.R.C. § 152(e) was applied to parents who were never married, though it does not appear that the IRS argued in these cases that I.R.C. § 152(e) did not apply.

113. Prop. Treas. Reg. § 1.152-5(a)(1.18.17).

114. Prop. Treas. Reg. § 1.152-4(b)(2)(i)(A)–(C)(1.18.17). Living apart means living in separate residences, not just separate bedrooms. Chiosie v. Comm'r, T.C. Memo. 2000-117. Also, this provision allows the special rule of I.R.C. §152(e) to apply to parents who have never been married. King v. Comm'r, 121 T.C. 245 (2003). In *King v. Comm'r*, a pre-2004 Act provision case, the court held that I.R.C. § 152(e)(1) applies to parents who have never been married. In *King*, the Court found that I.R.C. § 152(e)(1)(A)(iii) applied because the parents lived apart at all times during the last six months of the calendar year. Based on this finding, the Court concluded that the child was treated as receiving over half her support during the calendar from the parent having custody for the greater portion of the calendar year. The Court held that since the child is treated as receiving over half her support from the custodial parent, the non-custodial parent could claim the dependency deduction if the custodial parent executed a valid written declaration under I.R.C. § 152(e)(2) releasing the claim to the deduction to the noncustodial parent. Thus, the Court

(iv) The child is in the custody of one or both of the child's parents for more than one-half of the calendar year.[115]

(v) The custodial parent releases the dependency exemption to the noncustodial parent,[116] or a "qualified pre-1985 instrument"[117] is entered into between the parents which provide that the noncustodial parent shall be entitled to the dependency exemption.[118]

As discussed a little later in the chapter, if all four tests are met, then the noncustodial parent can claim the child as a dependent and claim the child as a qualifying child for the child tax credit, refundable child tax credit, or the additional child tax credit. But meeting the four tests does not qualify the noncustodial parent to claim head of household status, the child and dependent care credit, the earned income credit, or health coverage tax credit.

a. Definition of "Custodial Parent"

A child is considered to be in the custody of one or both parents for more than one-half the calendar year if one or both parents have the right, under state law, to physical custody of the child for more than one-half of the calendar year.[119] The custodial parent is the parent having custody of the child for the greater portion of the calendar year.[120] The regulations further define who is the custodial parent by providing that the custodial parent is the parent with whom the child resides for the greater number of nights during the calendar year.[121] The noncustodial parent is then defined as the parent who is not the custodial parent.[122]

Where time spent between the parents is substantially evenly split and may be the deciding factor as to which parent is deemed the custodial parent, it is recommended that the parties keep a log of the time each parent spends with the child.

---

held that the custodial parent could release the dependency exemption to the noncustodial parent, even though the parties had never been married. The case involved tax years 1998 and 1999. It should be noted that the Form 8332 for the years in issue provided that it should not be used by taxpayers who were never married to each other. This form was revised by the IRS in December 2000. Thus, the Court's holding would appear to negate the forms requirement that the parties be married in order to release the dependency exemption. The most recent revision to the form was October 2018 which reflected the suspension of the exemption amount. Prior revisions took place in 2010, 2009, 2007, 2006, and 2003. The general instructions to each form describes the revisions in that revised form.

115. I.R.C. § 152(e)(1)(A) and (B); Prop. Treas. Reg. § 1.152-4(b)(2)(i)(1.18.17).
116. I.R.C. § 152(e)(2); Prop. Treas. Reg. § 1.152-5(b)(3)(i)(1.18.17).
117. I.R.C. § 152(e)(3); Prop. Treas. Reg. § 1.152-5(b)(3)(ii)(1.18.17).
118. I.R.C. § 152(e)(1)(B).
119. Prop. Treas. Reg. § 1.152-5(c)(1.18.17).
120. I.R.C. § 152(e)(4)(A).
121. Prop. Treas. Reg. § 1.152-5(d)(1)(1.18.17).
122. *Id.*

A child is treated as residing with neither parent if the child is emancipated under local law.[123] On the other hand, a child is treated as residing with a parent for the night if the child sleeps (i) at the residence of that parent, whether or not the parent is present, or (ii) in the company of the parent when the child does not sleep at a parent's residence (for example, when the parent and child are on vacation together).[124] A night that extends over two taxable years is allocated to the taxable year in which the night begins.[125] In *Harris v. Commissioner*,[126] the Court had to determine with whom the child resided for the longer period of time during the taxable year in issue in order to determine which parent was the custodial parent. Although there was no log to determine how many nights the child resided with his father or mother, based upon the testimony of the parties, the Court determined that the child resided at the father's residence or in the company of the father at the father's great aunt's house a greater number of nights during the years in issue than the child slept at his mother's residence or in her company. Consequently, the Court concluded that the father was the custodial parent, that the child was the qualifying child of the father, and that the father was entitled to the dependency exception for the years in issue.

A child who does not reside with a parent for a night is treated as residing with the parent with whom the child would have resided for the night but for the absence.[127] A child who does not reside with a parent for a night is treated as not residing with either parent for that night if it cannot be determined with which parent the child would have resided or if the child would not have resided, with either parent for the night.[128]

If a child is in the custody of one or both parents for more than one-half the calendar year and the child resides with each parent for an equal number of nights during the calendar year, the parent with the higher adjusted gross income for the calendar year is treated as the custodial parent.[129]

If, in a calendar year, due to a parent's nighttime work schedule, a child resides for a greater number of days, but not nights, with the parent who works at night, that parent is treated as the custodial parent.[130] On a school day, the child is treated as residing at the primary residence registered with the school.[131]

---

123. Prop. Treas. Reg. § 1.152-5(d)(1)(1.18.17).
124. Prop. Treas. Reg. § 1.152-5(d)(1)(i) and (ii)(1.18.17).
125. Prop. Treas. Reg. § 1.152-5(d)(2)(1.18.17). Thus, a child who resides with a parent for New Year's Eve 2014 is considered to have spent the night with the parent in 2014, notwithstanding that the night carries over to 2015.
126. T.C. Memo. 2014-69.
127. Prop. Treas. Reg. § 1.152-5(d)(3)(i)(1.18.17).
128. Prop. Treas. Reg. § 1.152-5(d)(3)(ii)(1.18.17).
129. Prop. Treas. Reg. § 1.152-5(d)(4)(1.18.17).
130. Prop. Treas. Reg. § 1.152-5(d)(5)(1.18.17).
131. *Id.*

In *Nieto v. Commissioner,*[132] the mother was deemed the custodial parent since she had physical custody for the entire year, even though the decree awarded custody to the father. In *Maher v. Commissioner,*[133] the Court awarded the dependency exemption to the husband, even though a court order gave the parties "joint legal custody" but gave the wife "primary physical custody" of both children, because the children resided with the husband for most of the year and, therefore, he was deemed the custodial parent for purpose of Federal income taxation.

In *McCullar v. Commissioner,*[134] the decree named the husband and wife as joint managing conservators of their daughter and gave the wife primary control and custody of the child. Both the husband and wife claimed a dependency exemption deduction for the child. Based on a log the husband kept of time he spent with his daughter, the Court found that he spent more than fifty (50) percent of the time with his daughter. This qualified him to be deemed the custodial parent and therefore entitled him to the dependency exemption. As a result, he was also entitled to claim the child tax credit and head of household status.

b. Support

The general rule granting the dependency exemption to the custodial parent applies without regard to whether the custodial parent actually furnishes over half the support for the child during the year in issue. Thus, even if the noncustodial parent furnishes over half the child's support, the custodial parent is still entitled to the dependency deduction. The key to the custodial parent receiving the dependency exemption is not the amount of support such parent expends on the child, but rather who has custody of the child for the greater number of nights during the calendar year.[135]

3. Exceptions—Noncustodial Parent

a. General Rule

The noncustodial parent (cleverly defined as "the parent who is not the custodial parent")[136] may claim the dependency exemption for a child as a qualifying relative pursuant to I.R.C. § 152(e)(1) if the following four tests are met:

132. T.C. Memo. 1992-296 (1992).
133. T.C. Memo. 2003-85 (2003).
134. T.C. Memo. 2003-272 (2003).
135. I.R.C. § 152(c)(B)(4)(i); I.R.C. 152(e)(1)
136. I.R.C. § 152(e)(4)(B); Prop. Treas. Reg. § 1.152-4(d)(1)(1.18.17).

(i) the child receives over one-half of the child's support for the calendar year from the child's parents,[137] and

(ii) the child is in the custody of one or both parents for more than one-half of the calendar year,[138] and

(iii) the parents:

(a) are divorced or legally separated under a decree of divorce or separate maintenance,

(b) are separated under a written separation agreement, or

(c) live apart at all times during the last six months of the calendar year whether or not they are or were ever married;[139] and

(iv) (a) the custodial parent signs a written declaration that the custodial parent will not claim the child as a dependent for any taxable year beginning in the calendar year and the noncustodial parent attaches the declaration to the noncustodial parent's tax return for the taxable year beginning during such calendar year,[140] (the "release test") or

(b) a qualified pre-1985 instrument between the parents, effective for the taxable beginning in that calendar year provides that the noncustodial parent is entitled to the dependency exemption for the child and the noncustodial parent provides at least $600 for the support of the child during the calendar year.[141] Amounts expended for the support of a child or children are treated as received from the noncustodial parent to the extent that the noncustodial parent provided amounts for such support[142] (the "qualified pre-1985 instrument test").

Thus, if only the first three tests are met, the custodial parent is entitled to the dependency exemption. But if the first three tests and either of the fourth tests (the release test of I.R.C. § 152(e)(2) or the qualified pre-1985 instrument test of I.R.C. § 152(e)(3)) are met, the dependency exemption may be claimed by the noncustodial parent.

Thus, a child who does not meet the tests to be a qualifying child of either parent will be deemed to be the qualifying relative of his or her noncustodial parent if the preceding four tests are met.

---

137. I.R.C. § 152(e)(1)(A); Prop. Treas. Reg. § 1.152-5(b)(2)(i)(1.18.17).

138. I.R.C. § 152(e)(1)(B); Prop. Treas. Reg. § 1.152-5(b)(2)(i)(1.18.17).

139. I.R.C. § 152(e)(1)(A)(i)–(iii); Prop. Treas. Reg. § 1.152-4 (b)(2)(i)(A)–(C)(1.18.17); King v. Comm'r, 121 T.C. 245 (2003) (I.R.C. § 152(e) applied to parents who were never married). See text at Chapter 3, C.2, *supra*.

140. I.R.C. § 152(e)(4)(B); Prop. Treas. Reg. § 1.152-5(d)(1)(1.18.17).

141. I.R.C. § 152(e)(3)(A); Prop. Treas. Reg. § 1.152-5(b)(3)(i)(1.18.17).

142. I.R.C. § 152(e)(3) flush language; Prop. Treas. Reg. § 1.152-5(b)(3)(i)(1.18.17).

b. Qualified Pre-1985 Instruments

(1) Tests

The qualified pre-1985 instrument test provides that the noncustodial parent is entitled to the dependency exemption for a qualifying child or qualifying relative if:

(i) A qualified pre-1985 instrument between the parents applicable to the taxable year beginning in such calendar year provides that the non-custodial parent is entitled to the dependency exemption, and

(ii) The noncustodial parent provides at least $600 for the support of the child during the calendar year.[143] For this purpose, amounts expended for the support of a child or children are treated as received from the noncustodial parent to the extent that such parent provided amounts for such support.[144]

In *Zion v. Commissioner*,[145] the custodial parent signed a settlement agreement in 1978 stating she would not claim the children as dependents, and the noncustodial parent paid in excess of $600 for child support for each of the three children. The Court held that the noncustodial parent was entitled to the dependency exemption under the qualified pre-1985 instrument exception because the instrument provided that the noncustodial parent was entitled to claim the dependency exemption and the noncustodial parent paid more than $600 for the support of the child during the calendar year. On the other hand, where the noncustodial parent could not establish that he paid in excess of $600 for support of the child, the Court held that he failed to meet the tests of I.R.C. § 152(e)(3) and therefore was not entitled to the dependency exemption.[146]

(2) Definition

A qualified pre-1985 instrument is:

(i) a decree of divorce or separate maintenance, or a written separation agreement;

(ii) which is executed before Jan. 1, 1985;

(iii) which on Jan. 1, 1985 provides that the noncustodial parent is entitled to the dependency exemption; and

(iv) which is not modified on or after Jan. 1, 1985 to expressly provide that I.R.C. § 152(e)(3) does not apply to such decree or agreement.[147]

143. I.R.C. § 152(e)(3).
144. I.R.C. § 152(e)(3)(A)(ii) flush language.
145. T.C. Memo. 1991-119.
146. Swonder v. Comm'r, T.C. Memo. 1994-430.
147. I.R.C. § 152(e)(3)(B).

(3) Planning—Modification of Instrument

The parties can elect whether the custodial or noncustodial parent should receive the dependency exemption where a qualified pre-1985 instrument is involved. To elect to give the dependency exemption to the custodial parent, the parties should modify the instrument to provide expressly that the custodial parent is entitled to the dependency exemption.

To elect to give the dependency exemption to the noncustodial parent, the parties should make sure that the agreement grants the dependency exemption to the noncustodial parent, the noncustodial parent should pay at least $600 for the support of the child, and the portion of the agreement granting the noncustodial parent the dependency exemption should provide that it may not be modified.

(4) Application

This exception applies only to:

(i) a qualifying child or qualifying relative as defined under the general rule above;[148]

(ii) whose parents meet the marital division test set forth in the general rule above (i.e., divorced or legally separated under a decree of divorce or separate maintenance or separated under a written separation agreement);[149]

(iii) who receives over half of his or her support from either or both parents;[150] and

(iv) who is in the custody of either or both parents for more than half the calendar year.[151]

c. Release of Exemption by Custodial Parent

(1) Tests

The second exception provides that the noncustodial parent is entitled to the dependency exemption if the custodial parent signs a written declaration (in such manner and form as the IRS prescribes by regulation[152]) that the custodial parent will not claim the child as a dependent for any taxable year beginning in such calendar year, and the noncustodial parent attaches such written declaration to the income tax return of the noncustodial parent for the taxable year

---

148. I.R.C. § 152(e); I.R.C. § 152(c)(1); I.R.C. § 152(d).

149. I.R.C. § 152(e)(1)(A)(i) and (ii).

150. I.R.C. § 152(e)(1)(A).

151. I.R.C. § 152(e)(1)(B).

152. I.R.C. § 152(e)(2). Such language makes the regulation promulgated as a result thereof more akin to legal legislation than regulation and the Courts are more likely to give such regulation effect than one that is not promulgated pursuant to such legislation.

beginning during such calendar year.[153] This exception applies only to: a qualifying child or qualifying relative as defined under the aforementioned general rule; whose parents meet the marital division test set forth in the general rule; who receives over half his or her support from either or both parents; and who was in the custody of either or both parents for more than half the calendar year.[154]

The effect of meeting these tests is that the child is treated as being the "qualifying child" or "qualifying relative" of the noncustodial parent for the calendar year.[155] The preceding rules supersede the rule that a qualifying child have the same principal place of abode as the taxpayer,[156] the multiple claimant rule of I.R.C. § 152(c)(4), and the support rule for qualifying relatives found in I.R.C. § 152(d)(1)(C).

(2) Compliance

The release is not required to be included in the decree of divorce or separate maintenance or written separation agreement. All that is required is for the custodial parent to sign a written declaration that the custodial parent will not claim the child as a dependent for the taxable year and, as noted below, for the noncustodial parent to attach the written declaration to his or her return for the taxable year.[157] The written declaration must be an unconditional release of the custodial parent's claim to the child as a dependent for the year or years for which the declaration is effective.[158] A declaration is not unconditional if the custodial parent's release of the right to claim the child as a dependent requires the satisfaction of any condition, including the noncustodial parent's meeting of an obligation such as the payment of support.[159] A written declaration must

153. I.R.C. § 152(e)(2)(A) and (B); Prop. Treas. Reg. § 1.152-4(e). *See* Brown v. Comm'r, T.C. Memo. 1992-548 (1992) and Rownd v. Comm'r, T.C. Memo. 1994-465 (1994), where the Court denied the exemption to the noncustodial parent where the release was oral and no attachment was made to the noncustodial parent's tax return. *See* Barrett v. Comm'r, T.C. Memo. 2008-784 where the Court held that because the custodial parent never executed a written declaration releasing her right to claim the children as dependents, the noncustodial parent was not entitled to the dependency exemption.

154. Thus, as discussed in the text, the release exception does not apply if more than half the child's support is treated as received under a multiple support agreement pursuant to I.R.C. § 152(e)(5).

155. I.R.C. § 152(e)(1).

156. I.R.C. § 152(c)(1)(B).

157. I.R.C. § 152(e)(2)(A).

158. Prop. Treas. Reg. § 1.152-5(e)(2)(i)(1.18.17). Boltinghouse v. Comm'r, T.C. Memo. 2003-134 (separation agreement signed by both parents which unconditionally grants the dependency exemption to the noncustodial parent met the requirements of a written declaration under I.R.C. § 152(e)(2)(A) because it conformed in substance to Form 8332).

159. *Id.* Thomas v. Comm'r, T.C. Memo. 2010-11 (release of exemption conditioned on payment of child support does not conform to Form 8332 or I.R.C. § 152(e)(2)); Hanson v. Comm'r, T.C. Memo. 2012-352 (Divorce settlement provides that "so long as [noncustodial parent] is

name the noncustodial parent to whom the exemption is released,[160] and must specify the year or years for which it is effective.[161] A written declaration that specifies all future years is treated as specifying the first taxable year after the taxable year of execution and all subsequent taxable years.[162]

The regulations require that the written declaration be made on a form designated by the IRS.[163] The written declaration should be made on IRS Form 8332,[164] which is the form designated by the IRS.[165] Thus, it is recommended that only this form be used. Form 8332 may be used by parents who are divorced or separated, or by parents who were never married, provided they live apart at all times during the last six months of the calendar years.[166]

Any declaration made other than on Form 8332 must conform to the substance of such form and must be a document executed for the sole purpose of serving as a written declaration to release the dependency exemption.[167] However, there is no reason not to use Form 8332. The failure to use Form 8332, and to complete it and attach it in accordance with the regulations has generated a substantial number of cases, most of which have been lost by the noncustodial parent. Many of these cases are cited in the following materials and footnotes.

Generally, Form 8332 requires (i) the name of the child for whom the release is to apply; (ii) the year or years released; (iii) an unconditional statement by the custodial parent that he/she will not claim the dependency exemption;

---

current on child support payments, the noncustodial parent shall be entitled to claim the child as a dependent." Because that sentence did not contain an unconditional release, the noncustodial parent was not entitled to claim the dependency exemption); Gessic v. Comm'r, T.C. Memo. 2010-88 (Release of dependency exemption was conditional. Separation agreement provided that as long as noncustodial parent's child support payments were current he could receive the dependency exemption); Horn v. Comm'r, T.C. Memo. 2001-290 (Handwritten note indicating custodial gave exemption to noncustodial parent "only if it does not interfere with my ability to receive Federal Student Aid" was not unconditional and therefore did not meet the tests of Section 152(e)(2)).

160. Prop. Treas. Reg. § 1.152-5(e(2))(i)(1.18.17).

161. White v. Comm'r, T.C. Memo. 1996-438 (letter which failed to state the years for which the claim to the exemption was released did not substantially conform to Form 8832). Briscoe v. Comm's, T.C. Memo. 2011-165 (Court order of support did not contain the years to which the exemption applied).

162. *Id.*

163. Prop. Treas. Reg. § 1.152-5(d)(1)(ii)(1.18.17).

164. Prop. Treas. Reg. § 1.152-5(e)(1)(ii)(1.18.17). *See* Miller v. Comm'r, 114 T.C. 184 (2000) which approves the regulation and the Form 8332. I.R.C. § 152(e)(2)(A) requires the use of a form "in such manner and form as the Secretary may by regulation prescribe." This provision elevates the regulation to the status of quasi-legislation. Thus, it will be strictly construed and enforced by the Courts.

165. See www.irs.gov. search form 8332 to obtain a copy of this form.

166. I.R.C. § 1.152(e)(1)(A)(iii); King v. Comm'r, T.C. Memo 2003-12. For a discussion of *King v. Comm'r,* see note in Chapter 3, C.3.a.

167. Hanson v. Comm'r, T.C. Memo. 2012-352 (divorce settlement did not conform to the substance of Form 8332); Walters v. Comm'r, T.C. Memo. 2012-268.

(iv) the form must be signed and dated by the custodial parent along with his/her Social Security number; and (v) the name and Social Security number of the noncustodial parent to whom the exemption is released. If the child is newly born and does not have a Social Security number, the child's birth certificate should be attached to the form, with notice that the application for a Social Security number is pending. Rather than completing all this information on a conforming form, it is easier and more accurate to just use Form 8332. Thus, it is recommended that Form 8332 be used since all the required information is listed on the Form and the IRS has approved the use of the Form.[168] A court order or decree of divorce or a written separation agreement may not serve as a written declaration[169] under I.R.C. § 152(e)(2)(A) because it is signed by a judge and not by the custodial parent.[170]

The noncustodial parent must attach the written declaration (Form 8332 or similar written statement) to the noncustodial parent's tax return for each taxable year for which the child is claimed as a dependent.[171] If the noncustodial parent fails to attach Form 8332, or a similar written declaration to his original tax return, the taxpayer may not claim his child as a dependent.[172] According to the regulations,[173] noncustodial parent must attach a copy of the written declaration to the parent's original or amended return for each taxable year for which the noncustodial parent claims an exemption for the child. A noncustodial parent may submit a copy of the Form 8332 or written declaration to the IRS during an examination or with an amended return to substantiate a claim

168. *Cf.*, Armstrong v. Comm'r, 139 T.C. 468 2012)(n.5); Gessic v. Comm'r, T.C. Memo. 2010-88; Hanson v. Comm'r, T.C. Memo. 2012-252.

169. Prop. Treas. Reg. § 1.152-5(e)(1)(ii)(1.18.17). *See* Appendix C. *When More Than One Person Files a Return Claiming the Same Qualifying Child (Tie-Breaker Rule).*

170. Hanson v. Comm'r, T.C. Memo. 2012-352; Gessic v. Comm'r, T.C. Memo. 2010-88; Thomas v. Comm'r, T.C. Memo. 2010-11; Moody v. Comm'r, T.C. Memo. 2012-268.

171. I.R.C. § 152(e)(2)(B). Noncustodial parent not entitled to dependency exemption because custodial parent never executed Form 8332 even though the divorce decree granted the dependency exemption to the noncustodial parent if he were current on his child support payments (which he was). Espinoza v. Comm'r, T.C. Memo. 2011-108; CCA200925041. *See* Nixon v. Comm'r, T.C. Memo. 2011-249 (Noncustodial parent not entitled to dependency exemption because he failed to attach a properly executed Form 8332 to his return. He attached an unsigned Form 8332 to his return which his former spouse refused to sign even though a court order allowed him the dependency exemption for one of his children every year and for the other child every other year.) *Planning*: Have the custodial parent pre-sign Form 8332 for years the dependency exemption is to be released to the noncustodial parent. In Brissett v. Comm'r, T.C. Memo. 2003-310 (noncustodial parent denied dependency exemption because he failed to attach to his tax return Form 8332 which had been signed by the custodial parent); Hanson v. Comm'r, T.C. Memo. 2012-352; Doby v. Comm'r, T.C. Memo. 2003-33; Norwood v. Comm'r, T.C. Memo. 2003-63; Walters v. Comm'r, T.C. Memo. 2012-230; Israel v. Comm'r, T.C. Memo. 2012-185.

172. Demar v. Comm'r, T.C. Memo. 2019-91. Noncustodial parent cannot claim depending exemption where he failed to attach Form 8332 to his return. Skitzki v. Comm'r, T.C. Memo. 2019-106.

173. Prop. Treas. Reg. § 1.152-5(e)(2)(i)(1.18.17).

to a dependency exemption for a child, provided the custodial parent either did not claim the dependency exemption or filed an amended return removing the claim to the dependency exemption.[174] A copy of a written declaration attached to an amended return, or provided during an examination, will not meet the requirement of Prop. Treas. Reg. § 1.152-5(e)(1) if the custodial parent signed the written declaration after the custodial parent filed a return claiming a dependency exemption for the child for the year at issue, and the custodial parent has not filed an amended return to remove that claim to a dependency exemption for the child.[175]

The following three examples illustrate the rules for the child of divorced or separated parents, or parents who live apart.[176]

Example 1. Custodial parent (CP) files her 2015 return on March 1, 2016, and claims a dependency exemption for Child. At noncustodial parent's (NCP) request, CP signs a Form 8332 for the 2015 tax year on April 15, 2016. On April 15, NCP files his return claiming a dependency exemption for Child and attaches the signed Form 8332 to his return. NCP is allowed a dependency exemption for Child for 2015, and CP is not allowed a dependency exemption for Child for that year.

Example 2. The facts are the same as in Example 1, except NCP files on April 15, 2016, a request for an extension to file his tax return because he does not have a signed Form 8332. CP signs the Form 8332 for the 2015 tax year in August of 2016, and NCP files his return a week later. NCP claims a dependency exemption for Child and attaches the signed Form 8332 to his return. NCP is allowed a dependency exemption for Child for 2015, and CP is not allowed a dependency exemption for Child for that year.

Example 3. CP files his 2015 return on March 1, 2016, and claims a dependency exemption for Child. NCP files her return on April 15, 2016, and does not claim a dependency exemption for Child, even though her divorce decree allocates the dependency exemption for Child to her. CP signs a Form 8332 for the 2015 tax year in August of 2016, and NCP files an amended return a week later and attaches the signed Form 8332 to her amended return claiming a dependency exemption for Child. NCP is not allowed a dependency exemption for Child for 2015 if CP has not amended his return to remove a claim to the dependency exemption for Child for that year.

---

174. Prop. Treas. Reg. § 1.152-5(e)(2)(i) (1.19.2017).

175. *See* Paulson v. Comm'r, T.C. Memo. 1996-560 where the noncustodial parent was denied the dependency exemption because he failed to attach Form 8332 to his return for the years he claimed the dependency exemption. Brissett v. Comm'r, T.C. Memo. 2003-310 (noncustodial parent denied dependency exemption because he failed to attach to his tax return the Form 8332 that had been signed by the custodial parent); Hanson v. Comm'r, T.C. Memo. 2012-352 (divorce settlement did not conform to the substance of Form 8332); Walters v. Comm'r, T.C. Memo. 2012-268.

176. Treas. Reg. § 1.152-5(e)(2)(ii).

In *Shenk v. Commissioner*,[177] the Court held that since the custodial parent did not execute, and the noncustodial parent did not attach to his return, Form 8332 or equivalent release, the noncustodial parent was not entitled to the dependency exemption or child tax credit.

Care should be taken in completing Form 8332 to ensure that the declaration is clear and unambiguous and follows explicitly the dictates of the regulations.[178] A court order awarding the dependency exemption to the noncustodial parent does not satisfy the requirements of I.R.C. § 152(e) or the regulations. In *Miller v. Commissioner*,[179] the State Court issued permanent orders providing that the husband "shall claim both of [the] children on his tax returns as exemptions." In accordance with the permanent orders, the husband claimed the dependency exemptions for the children. He did not, however, attach a completed Form 8332 signed by the wife. Rather, he attached the permanent orders to his returns as support for the claimed dependency exemptions. The wife did not sign the permanent orders consenting to the release of the dependency exemptions. The permanent orders were signed by her attorney as to form only. The Tax Court held that the permanent orders do not qualify as a written declaration signed by the custodial parent consenting to the release of the dependency exemptions to the noncustodial spouse and confirming that the custodial parent will not claim the children as dependents. Thus, attaching the permanent orders to the husband's tax returns did not satisfy the requirements of I.R.C. § 152(e)(2). Consequently, the husband was not entitled to claim the dependency exemption for his minor children. For another decision adverse to the husband disallowing the deduction of alimony, see *Prater v. Commissioner*.[180] In *Paulson v. Commissioner*,[181] the Court held that a State Court judgment allowing the dependency exemption to the

177. 140 T.C. No. 10 (2013).

178. In Briscoe v. Comm'r, T.C. Memo. 2011-9 the Court held that the noncustodial parent was not entitled to the dependency exemption. The noncustodial parent did not attach Form 8332, but rather attached a support order which the Court held did not contain the elements contained in Form 8332 because it did not specify the years to which it applied and did not contain the former wife's Social Security number or signature, nor any other document stating she would not claim the child as her dependent. In fact, she did claim the child as her dependent for the year in issue. *See* Cafarelli v. Comm'r, T.C. Memo. 1994-265 (1994), in which the Tax Court determined that a reference in Form 8332 to "All Future Years" did not include the 1989 year even though the custodial parent was under a legal obligation imposed by the divorce decree and related marital settlement agreement to release the exemption. *See also* White v. Comm'r, T.C. Memo. 1996-438 (1996), where a letter signed by the wife transferring the dependency exemption to the noncustodial parent did not contain the specific items of information required by former Temp. Prop. Treas. Reg. § 1.152-4T(a)(A-3) now (Prop. Treas. Reg. § 1.152-4(e)(1)) and failed to conform to the substance of Form 8332.

179. 114 T.C. 184 (2000).

180. T.C. Memo. 1993-273 (1993).

181. T.C. Memo. 1996-560.

noncustodial parent was not sufficient, especially where it provided that the custodial parent was required to execute Form 8332.

In *Loffer v. Commissioner*,[182] the decree of divorce provided that the husband (the noncustodial parent) and the wife (the custodial parent) were each entitled to claim one of the two children as a dependent for Federal income tax purposes. The husband claimed his daughter as a dependent on his Federal income tax return. The IRS denied the claim because the husband did not attach Form 8332 to his Federal income tax return. The taxpayer argued that the copy of the divorce decree that he attached to his Federal income tax return substantially conformed to the substance of Form 8332 and should satisfy the written declaration requirement of I.R.C. § 152(e)(2) and Treas. Reg. § 1.152-4T(a). The Court agreed with the IRS and held that the divorce decree in issue did not substantially conform to Form 8332 since it did not contain all the information required by the Form and the Regulations and did not specify which child the husband was to claim as a dependent and no year was specified.

A handwritten note from the custodial parent to the noncustodial parent giving the noncustodial parent the exemption "only if it does not interfere with my ability to receive Federal student aid" is not a valid release pursuant to I.R.C. § 152(e)(2) because it does not meet the substance of Form 8332, nor does it identify the years to which it was meant to apply, and is not unconditional.[183] An oral agreement between the parents entitling the noncustodial parent to claim the dependency exemption for the children does not meet the tests I.R.C. § 152(e)(2)(A).[184] Use Form 8332 to have the custodial parent release the dependency exemption to the noncustodial parent. If Form 8332 is not used, the document used must contain substantially the same information required by Form 8332, particularly the signature of the custodial parent. Thus, such a document should include the names of the children for which the exemption claims are released, the years for which the claims are released, the signature of the custodial parent confirming his or her consent, the Social Security number of the custodial parent, the date of the custodial parent's signature, and the name and the Social Security number of the parent claiming the exemption. Rather than prepare such a document, it is recommended that Form 8332 be used.

Although Form 8332 requires the custodial parent's Social Security number, neither the Code nor the Regulations require this. Thus, where the custodial

182. T.C. Memo. 2002-298 (2002). *See also* Thomas v. Comm'r, T.C. Memo. 2010-11 (Copy of decree attached to return, which was conditional on payment of child support, did not conform to substance of Form 8332 or satisfy the requirements of I.R.C. § 152(e)(2).).

183. Horn v. Comm'r, T.C. Memo. 2002-290 (2002).

184. Brown v. Comm'r, T.C. Memo. 1992-548; Noah v. Comm'r, T.C. Memo. 1998-384 (Oral agreement to release dependency exemption to noncustodial parent does not satisfy requirements of I.R.C. § 152(e)(2)(A).).

parent signed Form 8332 but her Social Security number was not completed on the Form, nor was the Form dated, the Court held this was not defective and that the custodial parent had released the dependency exemption to the noncustodial parent.[185] It should be noted that in *Miller v. Commissioner*,[186] the Court held that requiring the taxpayer to provide the Social Security number of dependent children as a condition to allowing the dependency exemption does not violate the taxpayer's right to free exercise of religion. Nonetheless, it is recommended that the custodial parent's Social Security number be inserted on the Form 8332 to avoid the risk of audit or a wayward judicial decision.

The Tax Court has repeatedly emphasized the importance of the custodial parent's signature on the declaration.[187] The failure of the custodial parent to sign the Form 8332 renders the release invalid. If the custodial parent does not execute such a declaration, the custodial parent, and not the noncustodial parent, is entitled to claim the dependency exemption.[188]

An unsigned and undated Form 8332 attached to a filed Federal income tax return is invalid as a release of the custodial parent's claim to the exemption.[189] Thus, be sure to have the custodial parent sign Form 8332.

Where both the custodial and noncustodial parents have claimed a dependency exemption for the same child for the same year, a declaration signed by the custodial parent after the period of limitations for assessments has expired that the custodial parent will not claim the child as a dependent does not qualify as a declaration under I.R.C. § 152(e)(2)(A).[190] In such a situation, where the custodial parent claimed the child as a dependent, the three-year period of limitations has expired, the custodial parent could not issue a declaration that she would not claim the child as a dependent. To allow the custodial parent to

---

185. *See* Boltinghouse v. Comm'r, T.C. Memo. 2003-14 (2003), where the failure to attach the custodial parent's Social Security number to the return of the noncustodial parent, as required on Form 8332, did not invalidate the release of the exemption. *See* Bramante v. Comm'r, T.C. Memo. 2002-228 (2002) (failure to list the custodial parent's Social Security number on the Form 8832 or the returns of them or custodial parent did not invalidate the release of the exemption, even though the Form requires it.). *But see* Thomas v. Comm'r, T.C. Memo 2010-11 (Decree did not contain either parents' Social Security number or date of signature of custodial parent releasing the exemption); White v. Comm'r, T.C. Memo 1996-438 (Letter did not contain parents' Social Security numbers or years released). It may be gleaned from the foregoing that the failure to include the parents' Social Security number on Form 8332 is not fatal, whereas failure to do so on a document other than Form 8332, such as an order, decree or later may be fatal.

186. 114 T.C. 184 (2000).

187. Miller v. Comm'r, 114 T.C. Memo. 184, 191-194 (2000); Himes v. Comm'r, T.C. Memo. 2010-97; Neal v. Comm'r, T.C. Memo. 1999-97; Moody v. Comm'r, T.C. Memo. 2012-268. Allred v. Comm'r, T.C. Memo. 2014-54.

188. Barrett v. Comm'r, T.C. Memo. 2008-284.

189. Horn v. Comm'r, T.C. Memo. 2002-290 (2002); Neal v. Comm'r, T.C. Memo. 1999-97; Nixon v. Comm'r, T.C. Memo. 2011-249; Philemond v. Comm'r, T.C. Memo. 2012-29; Santana v. Comm'r, T.C. Memo. 2012-49; Moody v. Comm'r, T.C. Memo. 2012-268.

190. Shenk v. Comm'r, 140 T.C. No. 10 (2013).

issue a declaration after the expiration of the period of limitations would allow both parents to claim the declaration, which the statute does not permit. Such a latent declaration would be contrary to fact since the custodial parent had already claimed the deduction. To comply with the statute, the custodial parent must agree not to claim the child as a dependent in the future, not in the past, as required by the statute.

In *Shenk*, the Court speculated that if before the expiration of limitations, the custodial parent filed an amended return on which she disclaimed the deduction and agreed not to claim the exemption, this may comply with law. This same result may occur even if no amended return were filed, since the custodial parent would still be susceptible to IRS assessment. But once the period of limitations for assessment has expired and the custodial parent's claim of the child as a dependent cannot be disturbed, any statement by her that she will not claim the child as a dependent "would be absurd." Thus, the outside limit for the custodial parent to issue a declaration that she will not claim the child as a dependent is the custodial parent's period of limitations.[191]

(3) Length of Release

The exemption may be released for a single year, for a number of specified years (for example, alternate years), or for all future years, as specified in the declaration.[192] If the exemption is released for more than one year, the original written release must be attached to the return of the noncustodial spouse for the first taxable year in which the release is effective and a copy of such release must be attached to his or her return for each succeeding taxable year for which he or she claims the dependency exemption.[193] The release must be completely and accurately filled in. Where Form 8332 was signed on January 5, 1990, but Part I on the form pertaining to the current year was left blank, and in Part II on the form the words "all future years" were inserted, the Tax Court, in *Cafarelli v. Commissioner*,[194] held that the release was not effective for 1989 even though it was signed before the parties' 1989 Federal income tax returns were filed.

In *Boltinghouse v. Commissioner*,[195] the separation agreement gave custody of both children to the wife and provided that the husband could claim one of the children as a dependent on his return. The husband claimed the child as dependent on his return and the child tax care credit for the child. A copy of the separation agreement was attached to the return. The IRS disallowed the dependency exemption and child tax credit arguing that the agreement did not entitle the husband to claim the child, unconditionally, as a dependent,

191. *Id.* at 13–15.
192. Treas. Reg. § 1.152-5(e)(1)(i).
193. Treas. Reg. § 1.1525(e)(2).
194. T.C. Memo. 1994-265.
195. T.C. Memo. 2003-14.

and the agreement was not incorporated into the decree. The taxpayer argued that attaching a copy of the separation agreement to their return satisfied the requirements of I.R.C. § 152(e)(2). The Court agreed with the taxpayer. The Court first held that I.R.C. § 152(e)(2) does not require a spouse's waiver of her claim to a dependency exemption to be incorporated into a divorce decree. The Court then held that the separation agreement conformed to the substance of Form 8332. The Court found the agreement unconditionally entitled the husband to the exemption and that it was to apply to all returns filed after the divorce has been finalized. The Court then distinguished the case from *Cafarelli v. Commissioner*[196] and *Loffer v. Commissioner*,[197] because in those cases the Court could not determine the years to which the waiver of the exemption applied, whereas in the instant case it was clear it applied to the current year and all future years.

(4) Revocation of Written Declaration

A parent may revoke a written declaration by providing written notice of the revocation to the other parent. The parent revoking the written declaration must make reasonable efforts to provide actual notice to the other parent. Mailing the revocation to the last known address of the other parent should satisfy this requirement. The revocation may be effective no earlier than the table year that begins in the first calendar year after the calendar year in which the parent revoking the written declaration provides, or makes reasonable efforts to provide, the written notice.[198]

The revocation may be made on Form 8332 or successor form designated by the IRS whether or not the written declaration was made on a form designated by the IRS. A revocation not on that form must conform to the substance of the form and must be a document executed for the sole purpose of serving as a revocation under this section. The revocation must specify the year or years for which the revocation is effective. A revocation that specifies all future years is treated as specifying the first taxable year after the taxable year the revocation is executed and all subsequent taxable years.

The parent revoking the written declaration must attach a copy of the revocation to his/her original or amended return for each taxable year for which the parent claims a child as a dependent as a result of the revocation. The parent revoking the written declaration must keep a copy of the revocation and evidence of delivery of the notice to the other parent, or of the reasonable

---

196. T.C. Memo. 1994-265.

197. T.C. Memo. 2002-298.

198. Treas. Reg. § 1.152-5(e)(3)(i). It is recommended that not only should the notice of revocation be sent to the last known address of the other parent by first class mail, postage prepaid, but also notice should be sent by certified mail, return receipt requested or by recognized overnight national carrier such as Federal Express or UPS.

efforts to provide actual notice. A parent may submit a copy of a revocation to the IRS during an examination to substantiate a claim to a dependency exemption for the child.[199]

A written declaration or revocation that fails to satisfy the requirements of Treas. Reg. § 1.152-5(e) has no effect.[200]

A written declaration executed in a taxable year beginning on or before July 2, 2008, that satisfies the requirements for the form of a written declaration in effect at the time the written declaration is executed will be treated as meeting the requirements of Treas. Reg. § 1.152-5(e)(1) and (3). The revocation applies without regard to whether a custodial parent executed the written declaration in a taxable year beginning on or before July 2, 2008.[201] In *Swint v. Commissioner*,[202] the Court, relying upon Treas. Reg. § 1.152-4(e)(5) held that since the State Court filed an entry in 1988, it had to look at the requirements for a form of a written declaration that was in effect at the time the written declaration was filed. At the time the Court entry was filed in 1998 there was no prohibition on using a court order or decree or separation agreement as a written declaration releasing the dependency exemption to the noncustodial parent, provided the other requirements for a written declaration were met. The Court held that although the Court entry qualified as a written declaration, it did not satisfy the requirements for the form of a written declaration in effect at the time the agreed entry was executed because it was not signed by the custodial parent and was not unconditional. Thus, the noncustodial parent was not entitled to the dependency exemption.

If I.R.C. § 152(e) and Treas. Reg. § 1.152-(4)(e)(3) apply, a child is treated as the dependent of both parents for purposes of I.R.C. §§ 105(b), 132(h)(2)(B), and 213(d)(5).[203]

(5) Planning

Where the custodial parent is uncertain that the noncustodial parent will actually make the support payments, it would appear to be advisable for the custodial parent to make an annual rather than permanent declaration to give up the dependency exemption. Recall that the release must be unconditional; conditioning it to the payment of support will nullify the release.[204]

Where the custodial parent is in a lower income tax bracket than the noncustodial parent, the custodial parent should consider transferring the exemption to the noncustodial parent in exchange for additional dollars. For example,

199. Treas. Reg. § 1.152-5(e)(3)(ii).
200. Treas. Reg. § 1.152-5(e)(4).
201. Treas. Reg. § 1.152-5(e)(5).
202. 142 T.C. No. 6 (2.24.14).
203. Treas. Reg. § 1.152-5(f).
204. *See* Prop. Treas. Reg. § 1.152-5(e)(1) discussed *supra*, at Chapter 3, C.3.c(2).

if the noncustodial parent is in the thirty-six (36) percent bracket and the custodial parent is in the fifteen (15) percent bracket, the exemption is worth $882 to the noncustodial parent, but only $367.50 (15 percent of $2,450) to the custodial parent. By shifting the exemption to the noncustodial parent, the parties can save $514.50, in which they can both share by having the noncustodial pay the custodial parent all or some of the tax savings. The noncustodial parent should take care to be aware that all or some of the personal exemption allocated to it will be subject to the phaseout rules of Section 151(d)(3) and thus the noncustodial parent could lose some of the dependency exemption.[205]

(6) Multiple Support Agreements

I.R.C. § 152(e)(5) provides that the special rule of I.R.C. § 152(e) for divorced, separated, or never married parents does not apply where more than one-half the support of the child is treated as having been received from a taxpayer under the multiple support agreement provisions of I.R.C. § 152(d)(3). Thus, a noncustodial parent who cannot claim a child as a dependent under the release rule or the qualified pre-1985 instrument rule of I.R.C. § 152(e)(2) or (3) may nonetheless be able to claim the child if the multiple support rule of I.R.C. § 152(d)(3) applies. The multiple support provision of I.R.C. § 152(d)(3) provides that more than half of the support of an individual for the calendar year is treated as received from the taxpayer if:

(i) No one person contributed more than one-half of such support,
(ii) More than one-half of such support was received by two or more persons, each of whom would have been entitled to claim such individual as a dependent for a taxable year beginning in such calendar year even though such person alone did not contribute more than one-half of such support,
(iii) The taxpayer contributed more than 10 percent of such support, and
(iv) Each person described in (ii), other than the taxpayer, who contributed more than 10 percent of such support files a written declaration with the IRS, in the manner prescribed by the IRS by regulation, that such person will not claim such individual as a dependent for any taxable year beginning in such calendar year.

(7) Medical Expenses

The exemption may be transferred to the noncustodial parent, but the custodial parent may still claim a medical expense deduction for medical expenses paid for the child.[206]

205. See Chapter 3, B.2.a.
206. Rev. Proc. 2008-48, 2008-36 I.R.B. 586. *See also* B. Medical Expenses at Chapter 9, B.

4. Custody

The custodial parent is defined as the parent having custody for a greater portion of the calendar year.[207]

The noncustodial parent is defined as the parent who is not the custodial parent (i.e., the one who has custody for the lesser portion of the calendar year).[208]

5. Child Deemed Dependent of Both Parents

Rev. Proc. 2008-48[209] provides that if certain tests are met, a child will be deemed the dependent of both parents who are divorced, separated, or living apart for purposes of I.R.C. §§ 105(b), 106(a), 132(h)(2)(B), 213(d)(5), 220(d), and 223(d)(2), where the custodial parent has not released the claim to the dependency exemption pursuant to I.R.C. § 152(e)(2).

I.R.C. § 105(b) provides an exclusion from gross income to employees for certain employer-provided medical expense reimbursements, including expenses incurred by the employee for the medical care (as defined in I.R.C. § 213(d)) of the employee, the employee's spouse, or the employee's dependent (as defined under I.R.C. § 152 determined without regard to subsections 152(b)(1), (b)(2), and (d)(1)(B)).

I.R.C. § 106(a) provides that the gross income of an employee does not include employer-provided coverage under an accident or health plan.

I.R.C. § 132(a)(1) and (2) provides an exclusion from gross income for certain fringe benefits that qualify as no-additional-cost services or qualified employee discounts. I.R.C. § 132(h)(2)(A) provides that use of the fringe benefit by the employee's spouse or dependent is treated as use by the employee. For this purpose, dependent child means any child (as defined in I.R.C. § 152(f)(1)) of the employee (i) who is a dependent of the employee, or (ii) both of whose parents are deceased and who has not attained age 25.

I.R.C. § 213(a) allows a deduction for medical expenses of the taxpayer, the taxpayer's spouse, or the taxpayer's dependent (as defined under I.R.C. § 152 determined without regard to subsections (b)(1), (b)(2), and (d)(1)(B)).

I.R.C. §§ 220(f)(1) and 223(f)(1) allow an exclusion from gross income for distributions from Archer Medical Savings Accounts (MSAs) and Health Savings Accounts (HSAs), respectively, if the distributions are used to pay qualified medical expenses.

For purposes of I.R.C. §§ 105(b), 132(a)(1) and (2), and 213(a), any child to whom I.R.C. § 152(e) applies is treated as a dependent of both parents. I.R.C. §§ 220(d)(2) and 223(d)(2) do not include a similar rule. However, I.R.C.

207. I.R.C. § 152(e)(4)(A); Prop. Treas. Reg. § 1.152-5(d)(1).
208. I.R.C. § 152(e)(4)(B); Prop. Treas. Reg. § 1.152-5(d)(1).
209. 2008-36 I.R.B. 586.

§§ 220(d)(2)(A) and 223(d)(2)(A) define medical care by reference to I.R.C. § 213(d), and under I.R.C. § 213(d)(5), a child to whom I.R.C. § 152(e) applies is treated as the dependent of both parents.

I.R.C. § 152(e) provides that, in the absence of a qualified pre-1985 instrument,[210] a child may be treated as the dependent of the noncustodial parent only if the custodial parent releases the claim to the exemption.[211] If the custodial parent does not release the claim, the right to the exemption is determined under the general rules of I.R.C. § 152(c) or (d).

Consequently, if a custodial parent does not release the claim to the exemption, only the taxpayer who is entitled to claim the child as a dependent under I.R.C. § 152(c) or (d) may treat the child as a dependent for purposes of I.R.C. §§ 105(b), 132(h)(2)(B), and 213(d)(5). This guidance provides a limited exception to that conclusion.

If taxpayers who: (i) are divorced, legally separated under a decree of divorce or separate maintenance, legally separated under a written separation agreement, or live apart at all times for the last six months of the calendar year; and (ii) are the parents of a child who (a) receives more than one-half of the child's support during the calendar year from the child's parents; (b) is in the custody of one or both parents for more than one-half of the calendar year; and (c) qualifies under I.R.C. § 152(c) or 152(d) as a qualifying child or qualifying relative of one of the child's parents, (iii) then the IRS will treat a child of such taxpayers as the dependent of both parents under I.R.C. §§ 105(b), 106(a), 132(h)(2)(B), 213(d)(5), 220(d)(2), and 223(d)(2), whether or not the custodial parent releases the claim to the exemption under I.R.C. § 152(e)(2).[212] Rev. Proc. 2008-48 is effective Aug. 18, 2008. However, taxpayers may apply Rev. Proc. 2008-48 in any taxable year beginning after December 31, 2004, for which the period of limitation on credit or refund under I.R.C. § 6511 has not expired as of August 18, 2008.

6. Examples

Treas. Reg. § 1.152-5(g) provides 20 examples that illustrate which parent is entitled to the dependency exemption. The examples assume that each taxpayer's taxable year is the calendar year, one or both of the child's parents provide more than one-half of the child's support for the calendar year, one or both parents have the right under state law to physical custody of the child for more than one-half of the calendar year, and the child otherwise meets the requirements of a qualifying child under I.R.C. § 152(c) or a qualifying relative

210. *See* I.R.C. § 152(e)(3).
211. I.R.C. § 152(e)(2).
212. Rev. Proc. 2008-48, 1008-36 I.R.B. 586.

under I.R.C. § 152(d). In addition, in each of the examples, no qualified pre-1985 instrument or multiple support agreement is in effect.

The 20 examples are reproduced here.

Example 1: Custodial Parent Effectively Releases Exemption to Noncustodial Parent. Bob and Carol are the divorced parents of Chris. In 2009, Chris resides with Bob for 210 nights and with Carol for 155 nights. Bob executes a Form 8332 for 2009 releasing Bob's right to claim Chris as a dependent for that year, which Carol attaches to Carol's 2009 return. Bob is considered the custodial parent of Chris in 2009 because Bob is the parent with whom Chris resides for the greater number of nights in 2009. Since Bob meets the tests for releasing the claim by the custodial parent, Carol may claim Chris as a dependent.

Example 2: Failure to Properly Execute Form 8332. The facts are the same as in Example 1 except that Bob does not execute an IRS Form 8332 or similar declaration for 2009. Therefore, I.R.C. § 152(e) and this regulation do not apply. Whether Chris is the qualifying child or qualifying relative of Bob or Carol is determined under I.R.C. § 152(c) or (d) (which define who is a qualifying child or qualifying relative).

Example 3: Third-Party Custody. Dave and Ellen are the divorced parents of Adam under a custody decree. Grandmother has the right under state law to physical custody of Adam from January 1 to July 31, 2009. Because Dave and Ellen do not have the right under state law to physical custody of Adam for more than one-half of the 2009 calendar year, Adam is not in the custody of one or both parents for more than one-half of the calendar year. Therefore, I.R.C. § 152(e) and the regulations do not apply, and whether Adam is the qualifying child or qualifying relative of Dave, Ellen, or Grandmother is determined under I.R.C. § 152(c) or (d) (which define who is a qualifying child or qualifying relative).

Example 4: Multiple Claimants; Effective Release. The facts are the same as in Example 3, except that Grandmother has the right to physical custody of Adam from January 1 to March 31, 2009, and, as a result, Adam resides with Grandmother during this period. Dave and Ellen jointly have the right to physical custody of Adam from April 1 to December 31, 2009. During this period, Adam resides with Dave for 180 nights and with Ellen for 95 nights. Dave executes an IRS Form 8332 for 2009 releasing Dave's right to claim Adam as a dependent for that year, which Ellen attaches to Ellen's 2009 return. Adam is deemed to be in the custody of Dave and Ellen for more than one-half of the calendar year, because Dave and Ellen have the right under state law to physical custody of Adam for more than one-half of the calendar year. The nights that Adam resides with Grandmother are not allocated to either parent. Adam resides with Dave for a greater number of nights than with Ellen during the calendar year and, therefore, Dave is the custodial parent. Because the release of the claim by the custodial parent has been met, Ellen may claim Adam as a dependent.

Example 5: Qualified Absence; Effective Release. The facts are the same as in Example 4, except that Dave is away on military service from April 10 to June 15, 2009, and September 6 to October 20, 2009. During these periods Adam resides with Grandmother in Grandmother's residence. Adam would have resided with Dave if Dave had not been away on military service. Grandmother claims Adam as a dependent on Grandmother's 2009 return. Under the regulations, Adam is treated as residing with Dave for the nights that Dave is away on military service. Because the release of the claim by the custodial parent has been met, Ellen, not Grandmother, may claim Adam as a dependent.

Example 6: Emancipated Child. Fred and Gail are the divorced parents of Jane. In May of 2009, Jane turns age 18 and is emancipated under the law of the state where Jane resides. Therefore, in 2009 and later years, Fred and Gail do not have the right under state law to physical custody of Jane for more than one-half of the calendar year, and Jane is not in the custody of Fred and Gail for more than one-half of the calendar year. I.R.C. § 152(e) and the regulations do not apply, and whether Jane is the qualifying child or qualifying relative of Fred or Gail is determined under I.R.C. § 152(c) or (d).

Example 7: Emancipated Child; Effective Release. The facts are the same as in Example 6, except that Jane turns age 18 and is emancipated under state law on August 1, 2009, resides with Fred from January 1, 2009, through May 31, 2009, and resides with Gail from June 1, 2009, through December 31, 2009. Fred executes an IRS Form 8332 releasing Fred's right to claim Jane as a dependent for 2009, which Gail attaches to Gail's 2009 return. Jane is deemed to be in the custody of Fred and Gail for more than one-half of the calendar year. Jane is treated as not residing with either parent after Jane's emancipation. Therefore, Jane resides with Fred for 151 nights and with Gail for 61 nights. Thus, Gail may claim Jane as a dependent.

Example 8: Deemed Residence. Hilary and John are the divorced parents of Ken. Ken generally resides with Hilary during the week and with John every other weekend. Ken resides with John in Hilary's residence for ten consecutive nights while Hilary is hospitalized. Ken is deemed to reside with Hilary for those ten nights.

Example 9: Deemed Residence. Kathy and Lou, who are separated under a written separation agreement, are the parents of Nancy. In August 2009, Kathy and Nancy spend ten nights together in a hotel while on vacation. Nancy is deemed to reside with Kathy for the ten nights that Kathy and Nancy are on vacation.

Example 10: Allocation between Taxable Years. Mark and Nora are the divorced parents of Nick. On December 31, 2009, Nick attends a party at Mark's residence. After midnight on January 1, 2010, Nick travels to Nora's residence, where Nick sleeps. Nick is deemed to reside with Nora for the night of December 31, 2009, to January 1, 2010, because Nick sleeps at Nora's residence that night. However, the night of December 31, 2009, to January 1, 2010, is allocated to taxable year 2009 for purposes of determining whether Nick resides with Mark or Nora for a greater number of nights in 2009.

Example 11: Non-married Parents; Qualified Absence. Ollie and Pat, who never married, are the parents of Ronnie. In 2009, Ronnie spends alternate weeks residing with Ollie and Pat. During a week that Ronnie is residing with Ollie, Ollie gives Ronnie permission to spend a night at the home of a friend. The night Ronnie spends at the friend's home is treated as a night that Ronnie resides with Ollie.

Example 12: Non-married Parents; Qualified Absence; Undeterminable Residence. The facts are the same as in Example 11, except that Ronnie also resides at summer camp for six weeks. Because Ronnie resides with each parent for alternate weeks, Ronnie would have resided with Ollie for three weeks and with Pat for three weeks of the period that Ronnie is at camp. Ronnie is treated as residing with Ollie for three weeks and with Pat for three weeks for the six weeks Ronnie resides at summer camp.

Example 13: Undeterminable Residence. The facts are the same as in Example 12, except that Ronnie does not spend alternate weeks residing with Ollie and Pat, and it cannot be determined whether Ronnie would have resided with Ollie or Pat for the period that Ronnie is at camp. Ronnie is treated as residing with neither parent for the six weeks Ronnie resides at summer camp.

Example 14: Nighttime Residence; Effective Release. Quentin and Rita are the divorced parents of Sam. Quentin works from 11:00 p.m. to 7:00 a.m. Sunday through Thursday nights. Because of Quentin's nighttime work schedule, Sam resides with Rita Sunday through Thursday nights and with Quentin Friday and Saturday nights. Therefore, in 2009, Sam resides with Rita for 261 nights and with Quentin for 104 nights. Sam spends all daytime hours when Sam is not in school with Quentin and Quentin's address is registered with Sam's school as Sam's primary residence. Quentin executes an IRS Form 8332 for 2009 releasing Quentin's right to claim Sam as a dependent for that year, which Rita attaches to Rita's 2009 return. Quentin is deemed the custodial parent of Sam in 2009. Sam resides with Rita for a greater number of nights than with Quentin due to Quentin's nighttime work schedule, and Sam spends a greater number of days with Quentin. Therefore, since the nighttime rule applies and not the general rule, and the release rule also applies, Rita may claim Sam as a dependent.

Example 15: Effective Release; Revocation of Release. In 2009, Sarah and Tom, the parents of Jacob, execute a written separation agreement. The agreement provides that Jacob will live with Sarah and that Tom will make monthly child support payments to Sarah. In 2009, Jacob resides with Sarah for 335 nights and with Tom for 30 nights. Sarah executes a letter declaring that Sarah will not claim Jacob as a dependent in 2009 and in subsequent alternate years. The letter contains all the information requested on IRS Form 8332, does not require the satisfaction of any condition such as Tom's payment of support, and has no purpose other than to serve as a written declaration under I.R.C. § 152(e) and the Regulations. Tom attaches the letter to Tom's return for 2009 and 2011.

In 2010, Tom fails to provide support for Jacob, and Sarah executes a Form 8332 revoking the release of Sarah's right to claim Jacob as a dependent for 2011. Sarah delivers a copy of the IRS Form 8332 to Tom, attaches a copy of the IRS Form 8332 to Sarah's tax return for 2011, and keeps a copy of the IRS Form 8332 and evidence of delivery of the written notice to Tom.

Tom may claim Jacob as a dependent for 2009 because Sarah releases the right to claim Jacob as a dependent by executing the letter, which conforms to form of the written declaration, and Tom attaches the letter to Tom's return. In 2010, Sarah revokes the release of the claim in accordance with the Regulations, and the revocation takes effect in 2011, the taxable year that begins in the first calendar year after Sarah provides written notice of the revocation to Tom. Therefore, in 2011, I.R.C. § 152(e) and the Regulations do not apply, and whether Jacob is the qualifying child or qualifying relative of Sarah or Tom is determined under I.R.C. § 152(c) or (d).

Example 16: Conditional Release. The facts are the same as Example 15, except that the letter expressly states that Sarah releases the right to claim Jacob as a dependent only if Tom is current in the payment of support for Jacob at the end of the calendar year. The letter does not qualify as a written declaration because Sarah's agreement not to claim Jacob as a dependent is conditioned on Tom's payment of support, and a written declaration must be unconditional. Therefore, the Regulations do not apply, and whether Jacob is the qualifying child or qualifying relative of Sarah or Tom for 2009 as well as 2011 is determined under I.R.C. § 152(c) or (d).

Example 17: Failure to Specify Year of Releas. Ursula and Vince are the divorced parents of Lisa. Lisa resides with Ursula for more nights than with Vince in 2009 through 2011. In 2009, Ursula provides a written statement to Vince declaring that Ursula will not claim Lisa as a dependent, but the statement does not specify the year or years it is effective. Vince attaches the statement to Vince's returns for 2009 through 2011.

Because the written statement does not specify a year or years, it is not a written declaration that conforms to the substance of IRS Form 8332. Thus, the statement has no effect. I.R.C. § 152(e) and the regulations do not apply, and whether Lisa is the qualifying child or qualifying relative of Ursula or Vince is determined under I.R.C. § 152(c) or (d).

Example 18: Unsigned Form 8332. Wanda and Xavier are the divorced parents of Paul. In 2009, Paul resides solely with Wanda. The divorce decree requires Xavier to pay child support to Wanda and requires Wanda to execute an IRS Form 8332 releasing Wanda's right to claim Paul as a dependent. Wanda fails to sign an IRS Form 8332 for 2009, and Xavier attaches an unsigned Form 8332 to Xavier's return for 2009.

The order in the divorce decree requiring Wanda to execute an IRS Form 8332 is ineffective to allocate the right to claim Paul as a dependent to Xavier. Furthermore, the unsigned Form 8332 does not conform to the substance of IRS Form 8332, and the Form 8332 has no effect. Therefore, I.R.C. § 152(e) and the Regulations do not apply, and whether Paul is the qualifying child or qualifying relative of Wanda or Xavier is determined under I.R.C. § 152(c) or (d).

If, however, Wanda executes an IRS Form 8332 for 2009, and Xavier attaches the Form 8332 to Xavier's 2009 return, then Xavier may claim Paul as a dependent in 2009.

Example 19: Separation Agreement; Written Declaration. Yale and Zoe are the divorced parents of Max. In 2003, Yale and Zoe enter into a separation agreement, which is incorporated into a divorce decree, under which Yale, the custodial parent, releases Yale's right to claim Max as a dependent for all future years. The separation agreement satisfies the requirements for the form of a written declaration in effect at the time it is executed. Zoe attaches a copy of the separation agreement to Zoe's returns for 2003 through 2009.

A separation agreement may not serve as a written declaration. However, a written declaration executed in a taxable year beginning on or before July 2, 2008, that satisfies the requirements for the form of a written declaration in effect at the time the written declaration is executed will be treated as meeting the requirements of the regulation. Therefore, the separation agreement may serve as the written declaration for 2009, and Zoe may claim Max as a dependent in 2009 and later years.

Example 20: Revocation of Release. The facts are the same as in Example 19, except that in 2009 Yale executes an IRS Form 8332 revoking the release of Yale's right to claim Max as a dependent for 2010. Yale complies with all the requirements of the Regulations.

Although Yale executes the separation agreement releasing Yale's right to claim Max as a dependent in a taxable year beginning on or before July 2, 2008, Yale's execution of the IRS Form 8332 in 2009 is effective to revoke the release. Therefore, I.R.C. § 152(e) and the regulations do not apply in 2010, and whether Max is the qualifying child or qualifying relative of Yale or Zoe is determined under I.R.C. § 152(c) or (d).

7. Items of Support

Determining whether an item constitutes support is important to determine whether an individual is a qualifying child or a qualifying relative. For purposes of the qualifying child requirement, the support test provides that the dependent cannot provide more than half of his or her support for the calendar year in which the taxable year of the taxpayer begins,[213] whereas for purposes of the qualifying relative requirement the support test provides that the taxpayer must provide more than half the dependent's total support for the calendar year in which the taxable year of the taxpayer begins.[214] Notwithstanding the foregoing rules, a taxpayer may claim an individual as a dependent even if the taxpayer does not provide more than half of the dependent's support if the individual is covered by a multiple support agreement.[215]

In determining support, one looks to all sources of support, including those the dependent provides, and whether the source is taxable or exempt sources. Support includes food, shelter, clothing, medical and dental care, and education.[216] In addition, the Courts have held that support includes, inter alia, entertainment, transportation, child care expenses, toys, laundry, summer camp, vacations, and music lessons. The IRS has held that support includes payment for a child's wedding.[217] Expenses incurred for singing, dancing, and dramatic lessons also constitute items of support.[218]

On the other hand, luxury items probably do not qualify. Airplane fares paid by the taxpayer to fly his children to Florida to visit him and a pro rata portion of the rental value of his Florida home and utility expenses for the period during which his children visit him are not items of support.[219]

Amounts expended by the noncustodial parent during periods of visitation for food, clothing, spending allowances, and recreation may be deemed part of the child's support.[220]

Generally, amounts expended for support are valued at cost.[221] Items of support furnished in the form of property or lodging are valued at fair market value, which includes the fair rental value of the accommodations, with or

---

213. I.R.C. § 152(c)(1)(D).
214. I.R.C. § 152(d)(1)(C).
215. I.R.C. § 152 (d)(3).
216. Prop. Treas. Reg. § 1.1521(a)(2)(i).
217. Rev. Rul. 76184, 19761 C.B. 44.
218. McKay v. Comm'r, 34 T.C. 1080 (1960).
219. Hopkins v. Comm'r, T.C. Memo. 1999-54 (1999). *See also* McKay v. Comm'r, 34 T.C. 1080 (1960) (traveling expenses incurred on weekend visits with child are expenditures for the taxpayer's personal benefit and not for the child's support).
220. Gillespie v. Comm'r, T.C. Memo. 1966-181 (1966). *See also* Vance v. Comm'r, 36 T.C. 547 (1961).
221. Prop. Treas. Reg. § 1.1521(a)(2)(i).

without the cost of utilities allocable to the dependent.[222] Compare *Hopkins v. Commissioner*[223] (pro rata portion of the rental value of the taxpayer's home for the period during which his children visited him are not items of support) with *Blarek v. Commissioner*[224] (fair rental value of room furnished one of the parents' of the taxpayers who lived with the taxpayers constitutes an item of support) and *McKay v. Commissioner*[225] (fair rental value of child's room in house that child resides in with mother constitutes an item of support). The distinguishing feature between these cases is that the fair rental value of a portion of the custodial parent's home where the child resides is deemed an item of support, but not the home where the child visits the noncustodial parent.

The cost of purchasing a car for a child is considered an item of support if the title to the car is registered in the child's name. If the car is registered in the parent's name but the parent pays the cost of operating and maintaining the car, the cost of the car is not deemed an item of support, but the costs of operation and maintenance are deemed items of support.[226]

A similar situation exists with student loans. If the student takes out the loan the loan is not deemed an item of support, but if the taxpayer takes out the loan, it will count as an item of support.[227]

In the case of the remarriage of a parent, support of a child received from the parent's spouse is treated as received from the parent.[228]

Third-party medical payments made pursuant to private health insurance or Part A Medicare benefits received by a beneficiary are excluded from the computation of whether a third party provided more than one-half of the support of the beneficiary,[229] as are payments received pursuant to Medicaid for extraordinary medical expenses such as nursing care.[230] Moreover, the proceeds of health insurance coverage purchased by the noncustodial parent cannot be included by the noncustodial parent in computing the amount of support provided by such parent, but the cost of the premiums for health insurance coverage can be included as an item of support.[231]

---

222. Prop. Treas. Reg. § 1.1521(a)(2)(i).
223. 55 T.C. 538 (1970).
224. 23 T.C. 1037 (1955).
225. 34 T.C. 1080 (1960).
226. Rev. Rul. 77-282,1977-2 C.B. 52.
227. McCauley v. Comm'r, 56 T.C. Memo. 48 (1971).
228. I.R.C. § 152(e)(6).
229. Turecamo v. Comm'r, 64 T.C. 720 (1975), *aff'd*, 554 F.2d 564 (2d Cir. 1977), *acq.*, Rev. Rul. 79173, 19791 C.B. 861.
230. Archer v. Comm'r, 73 T.C. 963 (1980).
231. McGuire v. Comm'r, 77 T.C. 765 (1981). *Cf.* Samples v. United States, 226 F. Supp. 115 (N.D. Ga. 1963) where medical payments received under a health insurance policy maintained by the employer of the noncustodial parent were deemed an item of support from the noncustodial parent.

Payments provided by Federal and State agencies in the form of AFDC payments, Medicaid, food stamps, and subsidized housing are included in the computation of support. When these sources of funds are more than those provided by the taxpayer, the taxpayer will not be considered to have provided more than one-half the support of the taxpayer's dependents. Therefore, the taxpayer is not entitled to the dependency exemption.[232]

8. Proof of Support

Payments made by the noncustodial parent to the custodial parent for child support are treated as having been used for support of the child even if not actually expended on the child.[233] For example, if the decree provides that the payor spouse is to pay $200 per month for child support, and the payor pays this sum to the payee spouse, but the payee spouse places the proceeds in a special education fund for the child, the payor spouse is deemed to have provided child support of $200.[234]

Thus, it is whether the payment is made by the noncustodial parent, and not how the proceeds are applied by the custodial parent, that controls. This would appear to be important if the first exception to the general rule applies. In addition, I.R.C. § 152(d)(5)(A) provides that any payment to the payee that is includible in payee's gross income as alimony cannot be treated as a payment for child support by the payor spouse. Thus, as noted earlier in Chapter 2, Child Support, where the child support payments are not specifically designated, the lump sum payment is deductible by the payor spouse as alimony but is not considered payment of child support for purposes of the dependency exemption.

Support provided by a parent and his or her new spouse may be combined in computing the total support provided by that parent. Thus, if a parent remarries, support that a child receives from the parent's spouse is treated as received from the parent.[235]

9. Arrearages

a. General Rule

The general rule regarding arrearage payments of child support is that payments for child support are deemed support in the year paid.

232. Williams v. Comm'r, T.C. Memo. 1996-126 (1996).
233. *See* Prop. Treas. Reg. § 1.1525. *See also* Coltman v. Comm'r, T.C. Memo. 1978-181 (1978).
234. Rev. Rul. 7143, 19711 CB. 44.
235. I.R.C. § 152(d)(5)(B).

b. Two Exceptions to General Rule

There are two exceptions to this general rule. First, if the payor spouse is in arrears in his or her child support payments and, in a subsequent year, he or she makes a lump sum child support payment that exceeds his or her support obligation in such subsequent year, the lump sum payment does not constitute child support for either the year paid or the year due for purposes of the dependency exemption.[236] Rather, the excess is considered a reimbursement to the payee spouse for amounts payee expended for the prior year's child support. No amount is treated as an arrearage payment to the extent there is an unpaid liability (determined without regard to such payment) with respect to the support of a child for the taxable year of payment.[237]

Second, if the lump sum payment made in the current year does not exceed the payor spouse's support obligation for the current year, the amount of his or her contribution for child support is presumed to be support in the year of payment, unreduced by arrearage included in the payment if the money is actually spent for child support.[238]

The first exception precludes the payor spouse from claiming a dependency exemption to which he or she might not ordinarily be entitled, by shifting child support from one year to another.

The second exception does not preclude the payor spouse from claiming a dependency exemption in the current year merely because he or she is in arrears.[239]

Payments made prior to any calendar year (whether or not made in the form of a lump sum payment in settlement of the parent's liability for support) are not treated as made during such calendar year, but payments made during any calendar year from amounts set aside in trust by a parent in a prior year are treated as made during the calendar year in which paid.[240]

---

236. Prop. Treas. Reg. § 1.1521(a)(2)(iii)(a); Lovett v. Comm'r, 18 T.C. 477 (1952). *See also* Casey v. Comm'r, 60 T.C. 68 (1973).

237. Prop. Treas. Reg. § 1.1521(a)(2)(iii)(a).

238. Gajda v. Comm'r, 44 T.C. 783 (1965); Meshulam v. Comm'r, T.C. Memo. 1976-111 (1976) (payment of more than $600 per child per year but less than amount provided in agreement). *See also* Prop. Treas. Reg. § 1.1521(a)(2).

239. Labay v. Comm'r, 55 T.C. 6, 9 (1970), *aff'd*, 450 F.2d 280 (5th Cir. 1971).

240. Prop. Treas. Reg. § 1.1521(a)(2)(iii)(b).

4 Tax Credits

There are two credits that may be helpful to taxpayers with dependents. The first is the child tax credit provided for under Section 24, and the second is the child and dependent care credit provided for under Section 21. A tax credit, unlike a deduction, is a dollar for dollar offset against a tax liability, whereas a deduction is a percentage offset against tax depending upon the taxpayer's tax rate. Each of these two credits is discussed here.

A. Child Tax Credit

An additional element of tax planning in divorce and separation cases is created by the child tax credit. The child tax credit was enacted as part of the Taxpayer Relief Act of 1997 (1997 Act) and is codified as I.R.C. § 24.[1] It is available in addition to the child and dependent care credit discussed in Part B of this chapter. The child tax credit has become the new political football of tax legislation. It seems that every time Congress meets it introduces legislation to revise or expand the credit, and sometimes the proposed legislation has passed successfully, such as in 2017 and 2021.[2] As a result the reader should research this section because Congress is likely to amend it in the future.

1. Taxpayer Relief Act of 1997, P.L. 105-34, 8/5/97 ("1997 Act") § 101(b). The tax credit has been amended a number of times. See, Tax Relief, Unemployment Insurance Reauthorization and Job Creation Act of 2010, P.L. 111-312, 12/17/2010; American Recovery and Reinvestment Act of 2009, P.L. 111-5, 2/17/2009; Emergency Economic Stabilization Act of 2008, P.L. 110-343, 10/3/2008; Working Families Tax Relief Act of 2004, P.L. 108-311, 10/4/2004; Job and Growth Tax Relief Reconciliation Act of 2003, P.L. 108-27, 5/28/2003; Job Creation and Worker Assistance Act of 2002, P.L. 107-147, 3/9/2002; Economic Growth and Tax Relief Reconciliation Act of 2001, P.L. 107-16, 6/7/2001; Tax and Trade Relief Extension Act of 1998, P.L. 105-277, 10/21/98; IRS Restructuring and Reform Act of 1998, P.L. 105-206, 7/22/98.

2. See Congressional Research Service, CRS Reports.Congress.gov for the legislative history of the child tax credit.

1. General Rule

I.R.C. § 24(a) permits a taxpayer to claim a credit equal to $2,000 against income tax for each "qualifying child" of the taxpayer[3] who is under the age of 17 for which the taxpayer is allowed a dependency exemption under Section 151 for tax years 2018 to 2025 (except tax year 2021).[4] For tax year 2021 only, the American Rescue Plan Act of 2021 increased the amount of the credit to $3,600 for each qualifying child under the age of six, and to $3,000 per child for each qualifying child six years of age or over and under 18 years of age. (Note that after tax year 2025, the maximum amount of the credit reverts to $1,100.)[5] The maximum amount of the credit for any tax year is not adjusted for inflation.

---

3. I.R.C. § 152(c)(i). See text at Chapter 3, B.1, and at Chapter 4, A.2.

4. The amount of the credit was increased from $1,000 to $2,000 by the Tax Cuts and Jobs Act of 2017 for tax years beginning in 2018. This change and others made by the 2017 Act expires after December 31, 2025. The amount of the credit was $500 per qualifying child ($400 in the case of the taxable year beginning in 1998). The Tax Act of 2001 increased the minimum credit to $600 in years 2001–2004, $700 in years 2005–2008, $800 in 2009, and $1,000 in 2010 and thereafter. The 2003 and 2004 Acts increased the child tax credit allowable per child as follows:

2001 Act Taxable Year Beginning In	2003 Act Per Child Credit Amount Is	2004 Act Per Child Credit Amount Is
2003–2004	$1,000	
2005–2008	$700	$1,000
2009	$800	$1,000
2010	$1,000	$1,000

Thus, The Working Families Tax Relief Act of 2004 increased the child tax credit to $1,000 for each qualifying child for tax years beginning in 2005 and thereafter.

5. The American Rescue Plan Act of 2021 (ARPA) PL 117-2, Title IX, §§ 9611(a), (b)(2),9612, 135 Stat.144,148,150 (3.11.21). Summarily, ARPA increased the credit from $2,000 to $3,600 for a qualifying child under the age of six, and to $3,000 for qualifying children six years or older but under 18 for tax year 2021. It also provides the $3,000 credit for 17-year-olds. See FAQs IRS Fact Sheet 2022-6 (Jan. 2022), updated March 18, 2022, and further updated July 14, 2022 at Fact Sheet 2022-32. The FAQs were issued to assist taxpayers who received the Advance Child Tax Credit or who were eligible to receive the child tax credit in preparing their 2021 Federal income tax returns. The FAQ was modified by FS 2022-17 (March 18, 2022) to reflect that IRS Publication 972, Child Tax Credit, had become obsolete. The modified FAQ provided that Schedule 8812 would be used to calculate the Child Tax Credit and the adjustments to the credit for 2021 only. See the Final Audit Report of the Treasury Inspector General for Tax Administrators of the Department of the Treasury for results of its review of the implementation of the expanded Child and Dependent Care Credit Eligibility requirements. The audit was undertaken because of the size of the refundable credits for 2021. It should be noted that FAQs will not be relied on or used by the IRS to resolve a case, because the FAQs are not published in the Internal Revenue Bulletin, but a taxpayer who reasonably in good faith relies on the FAQ will not be subject to a penalty that provides a reasonable cause standard for relief, including the negligence penalty or other accuracy related penalty to the extent that reliance results in an underpayment of tax. See FS 2021-13, November 2021.

For tax years 2018 through 2025, the amount of the credit is increased by $500 for each dependent of the taxpayer other than a qualifying child (i.e., as qualifying relative not adjusted for inflation).[6] But this adjustment does not apply if the individual is not a citizen or national of the United States, unless the individual is a resident of the United States.[7] These dependents include dependent children who are age 16 or older at the end of the tax year and dependents who do not have the required SSN, or parents or other qualifying relatives supported by the taxpayer.[8] The child care credit is claimed using Schedule 8812.[9]

Example. Assume for a year other than 2021, the parents have a ten-year-old son, 14-year-old daughter, and 18-year-old daughter who all live home with them. Assume they also have a 20-year-old full-time college student. The amount of their credit would be $4,000 for the two children under age 17, and $1,000 for the two children over age 16, for a total credit of $5,000.

However, the amount of the credit allowable is reduced for each qualifying child (but not below zero) by $50 for each $1,000 (or fraction thereof) by which the taxpayer's "modified adjusted gross income" exceeds the "threshold amount."[10] "Threshold amount" means (i) $110,000 in the case of a joint return; (ii) $75,000 in the case of an unmarried taxpayer; and (iii) $55,000 in the case of a married taxpayer filing separate returns.[11] For tax years beginning after December 31, 2017, and before January 1, 2026, the threshold amount is $400,000 in the case of a joint return and $200,000 in the case of any other return,[12] except that for tax year 2021, the threshold amount is $150,000 for a joint return, $112,500 for head of household return, and $75,000 for a single return.[13] The value of the credit is further reduced by 5 percent of the adjusted gross income in excess of $200,000 for a single taxpayer or $400,000 for taxpayers filing a joint return. The threshold amount is not indexed for inflation. "Modified adjusted gross income" means adjusted gross income increased by any amount excluded from gross income under Section 911, 931, or 933.[14] Section 911 excludes from gross income (i) amounts received by an individual from sources within a foreign country that constitutes earned income attributable to services performed by the individual during the periods the taxpayer

---

6. I.R.C. § 24(h)(1) and (h)(4)(A). Tax Cuts and Jobs Act of 2017, § 11022(a).
7. I.R.C. § 24(h)(4)(B).
8. See Chapter 3, B.1.a–c for a full discussion of a qualifying child and a qualifying relative.
9. See FAQ issued by the Internal Revenue Service in Fact Sheet 2022-17 (Mar. 8, 2022) for how to complete Schedule 8812 in order to claim the nonrefundable portion of the child tax credit calculation when the taxpayer is exempt from Social Security and Medicare tax.
10. I.R.C. § 24(b)(1).
11. I.R.C. § 24(b)(2).
12. Section 24(h)(3). Tax Cuts and Jobs Act of 2017, Section 11022(a).
13. I.R.C. § 24(i)(4)(B).
14. *Id.*

was a U.S. citizen who is a bona fide resident of a foreign country or countries for an uninterrupted period that includes an entire year, or who is a U.S. citizen or resident who is present in a foreign country or countries for at least 330 days during any 12-month consecutive period; and (ii) the housing cost of such individual. Section 931 excludes from gross income the income of a person who is a bona fide resident of Guam, American Samoa, and the Northern Mariana Islands during the entire taxable year; income derived from sources within any such possession; and income effectively connected with a trade or business by such individual within any such possession. Section 933 exempts from gross income, in the case of an individual who is a bona fide resident of Puerto Rico during the entire taxable year, income derived from sources within Puerto Rico (except accounts received for services performed as an employee of the United States or any agency thereof). Such individual is not allowed as a deduction (except the dependency exemption) or any credit properly allowable to or chargeable against amounts excluded from gross income under Section 933.

As between divorced and separated spouses, the custodial parent is entitled to claim the child tax credit, unless the custodial parent releases the exemption to the noncustodial parent (as discussed in Chapter 3, C.3.c.), in which case the noncustodial parent may claim this credit.[15] Generally, the dependency exemption and the child care credit run together. The determination of marital status is made as of the close of the taxable year, provided that if a spouse deceases during the taxable year, marital status is determined as of the date of death.[16] An individual legally separated from his or her spouse under a decree of divorce or separate maintenance is not considered married.[17]

A special rule exists for certain married individuals who live apart.[18] Although married, such individuals are treated as not married if the following five tests are met. First, the individual is married as just described.[19] Second, the individual files a separate return.[20] Third, the individual maintains as his or her home a household that constitutes for more than one-half the taxable year the principal place of abode of a child with respect to whom such individual is entitled to a dependency deduction for the taxable year (or would be so entitled except for the release rule and the pre-1985 qualified retirement rule

15. Allred v. Comm'r, T.C. Memo. 2014-54; George v. Comm'r, 139 T.C. 508 (2012) (custodial parent not entitled to child tax credit because she released the dependency exemption to the noncustodial parent).

16. I.R.C. § 24(b)(2) Flush language; I.R.C. § 7703(a)(1).

17. I.R.C. § 7703(a)(2).

18. I.R.C. § 7703(b)(1).

19. *Id.*

20. *Id.*

of I.R.C. § 152 (e)).[21] Fourth, the individual furnishes more than one-half of the cost of maintaining such household during the taxable year.[22] Fifth, during the last six months of the taxable year, the individual's spouse is not a member of the taxpayer's household.[23]

Notwithstanding any of the foregoing, the child tax credit may not exceed the sum of the taxpayer's regular tax liability for the taxable year reduced by the foreign tax credit (allowable under Section 27), and the alternative minimum tax (imposed under Section 55).[24]

2. Definition of Qualifying Child

The key provision of I.R.C. § 24 is found in subsection (a), which requires the child to be the "qualifying child" of the taxpayer (as defined in I.R.C. § 152(c)) who is under the age of 17 years in order for the taxpayer to be entitled to claim the child tax credit. This requirement has garnered the most litigation among taxpayers claiming entitlement to the child tax credit.[25]

A "qualifying child" means any individual if the child is a qualifying child of the taxpayer as defined in I.R.C. § 152(c), and the child has not attained the age 19 (age 17 for the child tax credit).[26] I.R.C. § 152(c) defines a qualifying child as an individual who meets the following seven tests:

(i) Is a child of the taxpayer (including a son, daughter, stepchild, foster child, adopted child, or stepchild) or a descendant of such a child (including a grandchild, niece, or nephew), or is a brother, sister, stepbrother, or stepsister of the taxpayer, or a descendant of any such relative;[27]

(ii) Has the same principal place of abode as the taxpayer for more than half the taxable year;[28]

21. *Id.*

22. I.R.C. § 7703(b)(2).

23. I.R.C. § 7703(b)(3).

24. Section 26(a). Note that the regular tax is computed under Section 1, but excludes 25 taxes imposed under the income tax, such as the accumulated earnings tax under Section 531 and the personal holding company tax under Section 541.

25. *E.g.*, Swint v. Comm'r, 142 T.C. 131 (2014); Shenk v. Comm'r, 140 T.C. 200 (2013); Longino v. Comm'r, T.C. Memo. 2013-80; Volkovan v. Comm'r, T.C. Memo. 2013-37; Powers v. Comm'r, T.C. Memo. 2005-152; Luckens v. Comm'r, T.C. Memo. 2008-159. Note that if the minor children are a "qualifying relative" of the taxpayer instead of being a "qualifying child," the taxpayer is not eligible to claim the child tax credit. LaTisha v. Comm'r, T.C. Memo. 2013-16.

26. I.R.C. § 24I(1).

27. I.R.C. §§ 152(c)(1)(A), 152(c)(1)(A).

28. I.R.C. § 152(c)(1)(B). Temporary absences by the taxpayer or the child, such as school, vacation, business, medical care, or military service count as time the child lived with the taxpayer.

(iii) Has not attained the age of 17 as of the close of the calendar year in which the taxable year of the taxpayer begins, or is a student who has not attained the age of 24 as of the close of such taxable year;[29]

(iv) Has not provided more than one-half of such individual's own support for the calendar year in which the taxable year of the taxpayer begins;[30]

(v) Has not filed a joint return with the individual's spouse for the taxable year unless the return is made solely to claim a refund;

(vi) Is claimed as a dependent on the taxpayer's return;[31] and

(vii) Is a U.S. citizen, national, or resident.[32]

As noted earlier, for the child care credit, age 17 and not age 19 controls.[33] According to Rev. Proc. 2003-72,[34] a child attains an age on the anniversary of the date that the child was born. In addition, the qualifying child must be a U.S. citizen, national, or resident.[35]

The effect of the foregoing is that in the case of divorced or separated parents, the parent who claims the dependency exemption (the custodial parent, or the noncustodial parent if the dependency exemption is released by the custodial parent) is entitled to claim the credit. For non-divorced or separated parents, the parent who is the parent of a qualifying child is entitled to claim the credit because this parent can claim the dependency exemption for the child. Thus, in both situations the parent who claims the dependency exemption may claim the child tax credit.[36] The phaseout amount for the dependency exemption and the child tax credit are different. As a result of this difference, releasing or not releasing the dependency exemption to the noncustodial parent may result in the loss of the credit. If a child is not a qualifying child as defined in Section 24 for purposes of the dependency exemption, then the noncustodial parent is not entitled to the child tax credit.[37]

---

29. I.R.C. §§ 152(c)(1)(C), 152(c)(3)(A), I.R.C.§ 24(c)(i). Shinault v. Comm'r, T.C. Memo. 2006-136. *But see* Rodriquez v. U.S., [III AFTR 2d 2013-2222] (D. TX 2013) where the taxpayer was denied the credit for his daughter who was over age 17.

30. I.R.C. § 152(c)(1)(D). *See also* Chapter 3, B.1.a. and c. for a discussion of a "qualifying child."

31. Denial of dependency deduction precludes claiming the child tax credit. Note v. Comm'r, T.C. Memo. 2014-54.

32. I.R.C. § 24(c)(2). *See* Carlebach v. Comm'r, 139 T.C. 1 (2003) and Stern v. Comm'r, T.C. Memo. 2012-204 where the child tax credit was denied because children resided in Israel and were not U.S. citizens. For a more detailed discussion of a "qualifying child" see text at Chapter 3, B.1.a. and c et. seq. *See also* IRS Tax Tip 2014-18(2/21/14).

33. I.R.C. § 24(c)(1).

34. 2003-2 C.B.346.

35. I.R.C. § 24(c)(2).

36. I.R.C. § 24(a); Notice 2006-86, 2006-2 C.B. 680; George v. Comm'r, 139 T.C. 508 (2012).

37. Nixon v. Comm'r, T.C. Memo 2011-249.

A taxpayer who may claim an individual as a qualifying relative, as opposed to a qualifying individual, may not claim the individual for purposes of the child tax credit, because the dependent must be a qualifying individual.[38]

3. Refundable Credit

Although the child tax credit was first enacted in 1997, it was first made refundable in 2001. It was designed to work in conjunction with the earned income credit. Although generally the child tax credit is nonrefundable, in certain cases involving low-income taxpayers any unused child tax credit is refundable.[39] The child tax credit is refundable to the extent of the greater of the following.

The aggregate credits allowed to a taxpayer under Sections 31 through 36B are increased by the lesser of:[40]

(i) the child tax credit that would be allowed under the child tax credit provisions of Section 24 determined without regard to the refundable provision of Section 24(d) and the limitations under Section 26(a) ($1,000),[41] or

(ii) the amount by which the aggregate amount of nonrefundable personal credits would increase if the limitation imposed by Section 26(a) were increased by the greater of:[42]

    (a) 15 percent (increased from 10 percent as described below) of the taxpayer's earned income (as defined in Section 32 pertaining to the earned income credit), which is taken into account in computing taxable income for the taxable year that exceeds $2,500,[43] or

    (b) for a taxpayer with three or more qualifying children, the excess, if any, of the taxpayer's Social Security taxes[44] for the tax year

38. LaTisha v. Comm'r, T.C. Memo. 2013-16; Notice 2008-5, 2008-2; I.R.B. 256 and CCA 200812024.

39. I.R.C. § 24(d). Due diligence can be established by getting and keeping the providers Form W-10 or one of the other sources of information listed in the text. See IRS Publication 503, Child and Dependent Care Expenses.

40. I.R.C. § 24(d)(1).

41. I.R.C. § 24(d)(1)(A).

42. I.R.C. § 24(d)(1)(B).

43. I.R.C. § 24(d)(1)(B)(i); I.R.C. § 24(h)(6). The $2,500 floor applies for taxable years 2018 through 2025. Thereafter, it reverts to $3,000. This means a family must earn at least $2,500 to claim the credit. For any taxable year beginning in a calendar year after 2001, the amount set forth in I.R.C. § 24(d)(1)(B)(i) is increased by an amount equal to the amount stated in I.R.C. § 24(d)(1)(B)(i), multiplied by the cost-of-living adjustment determined under I.R.C. § 1(f)(3) for the calendar year in which the taxable year begins in I.R.C. § 1(f)(3)(B). Any increases so determined are rounded to the nearest multiple of $50.

44. *See* I.R.C. § 24(d)(2) defines Social Security taxes to mean, with respect to any taxpayer for any taxable year: (i) the amount of taxes imposed by Sections 3101 and 3201(a) on amounts received by the taxpayer during the calendar year in which the taxable year begins; (ii) 50 percent of the taxes imposed by § 1401 (pertaining to tax on self-employment income) on the

over the taxpayer's earned income credit under Section 32 for the tax year.[45]

Thus, for tax years prior to 2018 the child tax credit is refundable to the extent of the lesser of the $1,000 credit per child under the age of 17 or 15 percent of the taxpayer's earned income in excess of $2,500[46] for tax years between 2018 through 2025 per the Tax Cut and Jobs Act of 2017. For example, if a husband and wife have earned income of $16,000, the $1,000 credit is fully refundable because 15 percent of the excess of their earned income over $3,000 is greater than the $1,000 credit to which they would otherwise be entitled. As noted later, the refund may not exceed $1,400 per qualifying child.

The amount of the portion of the refundable credit allowed under Section 24(d) is not treated as a credit allowed under Sections 31 through 36B, and reduces the amount of the credit otherwise allowable under Section 24(a) without regard to Section 26(a) (pertaining to limitations on allowable credits). For purposes of Section 24(d)(1)(B) immediately preceding any amount excluded from gross income by reason of Section 112 (pertaining to combat zone compensation) is treated as earned income, which is taken into account in computing taxable income for the taxable year.[47]

According to the Committee Reports, the refundable credit does not constitute income.[48]

Notwithstanding the foregoing, for tax years 2018 through 2020, the maximum amount of the refundable portion of the credit for low-income taxpayers was $1,400 per qualifying child under the age of 17, adjusted for inflation (determined under Section 1(f)(3), thus increasing the amount to $1,500 per qualifying child for tax year 2022).[49] The child tax credit is phased-in based on 15 percent of earned income in excess of $2,500 of earned income (lowered from $3,000 of earned income) not to exceed the maximum child tax credit.

The American Rescue Plan Act of 2021 expanded the child tax credit for tax year 2021. It did this by enacting I.R.C. § 7527 A, which provided for an advance child tax credit payment. These payments are early payments from the IRS of 50 percent of the estimated amount of the child tax credit that the taxpayer could have properly claimed on the taxpayer's 2021 Federal income

---

self-employment income of the taxpayer of the taxable year; and (iii) 50 percent of the taxes imposed by § 3211(a) (pertaining to the tax on employee representatives under the Railroad Retirement Tax Act) on amounts received by the taxpayer during the calendar year in which the taxable year begins. Social Security taxes do not include any taxes to the extent the taxpayer is entitled to a special refund of such taxes under § 6413(c) (pertaining to the refund of the multi-employer tax).

45. I.R.C. § 24(d)(1)(B)(ii).
46. For tax years before 2018 and after 2025, the earned income amount will revert to $3,000.
47. I.R.C. § 24(d) flush language.
48. Conference Report 108-696, Pub. L. No. 108-311 (Oct. 4, 2004).
49. I.R.C. § 24(h)(5)(A) and (B).

tax return.[50] The advance payments were based on information contained on the taxpayer's 2019 or 2020 Federal income tax return. The balance of the payments will have been made when the taxpayers filed their 2021 Federal income tax return. Rev. Proc. 2022-12[51] provides procedures for individuals who were not required to file a Federal income tax return for tax year 2021 to claim the child tax credit. The payments could only be made between July and December 2021.

For tax year 2021 only, the child tax credit is fully refundable. The phase-in for low income taxpayers was eliminated so that low income taxpayers could receive the maximum credit as a refund.

Because the advance child tax credit can only be claimed on a taxpayer's 2021 Federal income tax return, and the payments could only be received between July 2021 and December 2021, the advance child tax credit will not be discussed further. If the reader desires more information about this credit, the reader is directed to Fact Sheet 2022-32 (July 14, 2022), which was issued to provide general information to taxpayers and tax professionals in claiming the credit in the preparation and filing of the taxpayer's 2021 Federal income tax return.

4. Identification Requirement

No child tax credit is allowable on an original or amended return for any qualifying child unless the taxpayer includes the name and taxpayer identification number for the qualifying child on the taxpayer's return for the taxable year the child tax credit is claimed.[52] Thus, the child must have a Social Security number to qualify for the credit. In addition, the taxpayer identification number must have been issued by the Social Security Administration to a citizen of the United States on or before the due date for filing such return (including extensions).[53] The child tax credit is not allowed if the identifying number of the taxpayer claiming the credit was issued after the due date for filing the return for the taxable year.[54] If the identification requirement is not met, the IRS may use its summary assessment procedure applicable to returns containing mathematical or clerical errors to recalculate the taxpayer's tax liability.[55]

If a qualifying child is not allowed the child tax credit because the child does not have a Social Security number, the child is treated as a dependent to whom the partial tax credit under Section 24(h)(4)(A) (described earlier)

---

50. See IRS Fact Sheet 2022-32 (July 14, 2022), superseding FS 2022-29 (May 2022) for FAQs for the 2021 child tax credit and advance child tax credit payments.
51. 2022-7 I.R.B. 494.
52. I.R.C. § 24(e)(1), § 24(h)(7).
53. *Id.*
54. I.R.C. § 24(e)(2).
55. I.R.C. § 6213(g)(2)(L),

applies.[56] In other words, it would appear that if the qualifying child does not have a Social Security number, the qualifying child is characterized as a non-qualifying child dependent and the taxpayer can claim the partial $500 credit allowed by Section 24(h)(4)(A).

5. Full Taxable Year

A full tax year is required to claim the credit. Except for a short tax year caused by the death of the taxpayer, no child tax credit is allowed for a taxable year covering a period of less than 12 months.[57] In addition, no tax credit is allowed for ten taxable years after the taxable year in which the IRS determines that the taxpayer's claim of credit was due to fraud[58] or for two taxable years after the taxable year in which the IRS determines that the taxpayer's claim of credit was due to reckless or intentional disregard of the rules and regulations.[59] Finally, in the case of a taxpayer who is denied the child care credit for any taxable year because of a deficiency determination, no credit is allowed for any subsequent taxable year unless the taxpayer provides such information as the IRS may require to demonstrate eligibility for the credit.[60]

6. Summary

In IRS Tax Tip 2015-26 (February 25, 2015), the IRS issued the top six things to know about the child tax credit. These tips are still applicable, except as amended by the Tax Cuts and Jobs Act of 2017.

a. Amount

The child tax credit may help reduce the taxpayer's Federal income tax by up to $2,000 for each qualifying child that the taxpayer is eligible to claim on his or her tax return. The Tax Cuts and Jobs Act of 2017 increased the tax credit to $2,000 for each qualifying child for tax years 2018 through 2025.[61]

b. Additional Child Tax Credit

If the taxpayer qualifies and gets less than the full child tax credit, the taxpayer could receive a refund even if the taxpayer owes no tax with the additional child tax credit. Under the Tax Cuts and Jobs Act of 2017, the refundable portion of the credit is limited to $1,400 per qualifying child for tax years 2018

56. Section 24(h)(4)(C). Tax Cuts and Jobs Act of 2017, Section 11022(a).
57. I.R.C. § 24(f).
58. I.R.C. § 24(f)(1)(B)(i).
59. I.R.C. § 24(g)(1).
60. I.R.C. § 24(g)(2).
61. I.R.C. § 24(h)(2). Tax Cuts and Jobs Act of 2017, Section 11022(a).

through 2025.[62] For tax year 2021, the credit was increased to $3,000 for a qualifying child between the ages of 6 and 17.

c. Qualifications

For this credit to be available, a qualifying child must pass seven tests:

(i) Age test. The child must have been under age 17 at the end of the calendar year in which the credit is claimed, except see preceding for tax year 2021.

(ii) Relationship test. The child must be the taxpayer's son, daughter, stepchild, foster child, adopted child, brother, sister, stepbrother, or stepsister. The child may be a descendant of any of these individuals. A qualifying child may also include the taxpayer's grandchild, niece, or nephew.

(iii) Support test. The child must not have provided more than half of his or her own support for the year.

(iv) Dependent test. The child must be a dependent that the taxpayer claims on his or her Federal tax return.

(v) Joint return test. The child cannot file a joint Federal income tax return for the year, unless the only reason the child is filing a joint Federal income tax return is to claim a refund.

(vi) Citizenship test. The child must be a U.S. citizen, a U.S. national, or a U.S. resident alien.

(vii) Residence test. In most cases, the child must have lived with the taxpayer for more than half of the tax year.

d. Limitations

The child tax credit is subject to income limitations. The limits may reduce or eliminate the credit depending on the taxpayer's filing status and income.

e. Schedule 8812

If the taxpayer qualifies to claim the child tax credit, the taxpayer must complete and attach Schedule 8812 with his or her tax return. For example, if the taxpayer claims a credit for a child with an individual taxpayer identification number, the taxpayer must complete Part I of Schedule 8812. If the taxpayer qualifies to claim the additional child tax credit, the taxpayer must complete and attach Schedule 8812.[63]

---

62. I.R.C. § 24(h)(5)(A) and (B). Tax Cuts and Jobs Act of 2017, Section 11022(a).

63. See FAQ issued by the Internal Revenue Service in Fact Sheet 2022-17 (March 8, 2022) for how to complete Schedule 8812 in order to claim the nonrefundable portion of the child tax

f. Due Diligence

Tax return preparers should be aware of Form 8867, which contains a due diligence checklist for the child tax credit (among others) that must be attached to the taxpayers tax return.

B. Child and Dependent Care Credit

1. Introduction

A second credit relating to dependents is the dependent care credit. The purpose for this credit is to assist the taxpayer and his or her spouse to be gainfully employed by helping the parents pay for the care of eligible children and other dependents while the parents are at work. This credit is available for expenses relating to "qualifying individuals" as hereinafter defined. The credit is claimed on IRS Form 2441. The credit is in addition to the child tax credit discussed in Part A of this chapter. Based on the following requirements, the maximum credit for tax year beginning after 2021 is $1,050 if there is one qualifying individual and $2,100 if there are two or more qualifying individuals. This is a decrease from tax year 2021 when the maximum credit was $4,000 for one qualifying individual and $8,000 for two or more qualifying individuals.

I.R.C. § 21(a)(1) provides that an individual taxpayer who has one or more qualifying individuals (as defined later) is entitled to a credit equal to the "applicable percentage" of the "employment related expenses" paid by the individual during the taxable year.[64]

The amount of the credit is equal to the applicable percentage of the employment-related expenses that may be taken into account by the taxpayer during the taxable year (but subject to the limits prescribed in Treas. Reg. § 1.21-2). Applicable percentage means 35 percent reduced (but not below 20 percent) by 1 percentage point for each $2,000 (or fraction thereof) by which the taxpayer's adjusted gross income for the taxable year exceeds $15,000.[65] For example, if a taxpayer's adjusted gross income is $31,850, the applicable percentage is 26 percent.[66] As a result of the preceding, the 35 percent credit is available to taxpayers who have adjusted gross income of $15,000 or less, and the 20 percent credit is reached when a taxpayer has adjusted gross income of $43,000, after which the credit is no longer available.

Expenses may be taken into account, regardless of the taxpayer's method of accounting in the taxable year the services are provided or the taxable year

---

credit calculation when the taxpayer is exempt from Social Security and Medicare tax. FS 2022-17 was superseded by FAQs that were posted in FS 2022-29 (Mar. 20, 2022).

64. I.R.C. § 21(b)(1).
65. I.R.C. § 21.
66. Prop. Treas. Reg. § 1.21-1(a)(2).

the expenses are paid, whichever is later.[67] The requirements of I.R.C. § 21 and Treas. Reg. §§ 1.21-1 through 1.21-4 are applied at the time the services are provided, regardless of when the expenses are paid.[68]

Example 1. In December 2007, *B* pays for the care of her child for January 2008. *B* may claim the credit in 2008, the later of the years in which the expenses are paid and the services performed.

Example 2. The facts are the same as in Example 1, except that *B*'s child turns 13 on February 1, 2008, and *B* pays for the care provided in January 2008 on February 3, 2008. The determination of whether the expenses are employment-related expenses is made when the services are performed. Assuming other requirements are met, the amount *B* pays will be an employment-related expense under I.R.C. § 21, because *B*'s child is a qualifying individual when the services are performed, even though the child is not a qualifying individual when *B* pays the expenses.

Eight tests must be met to qualify for the child and dependent care credit.

(i) The care must be for one or more qualifying individuals. These persons are to be identified on Form 2441.

(ii) The taxpayer must have earned income during the taxable year. If the taxpayer is married, the spouses must file a joint Federal income tax return and both the taxpayer and the taxpayer's spouse must have earned income (except for a spouse who is a student or who is unable to care for himself or herself).

(iii) The taxpayer must pay employment-related expenses to enable the taxpayer (and the taxpayer's spouse if filing jointly) to work or search for work.

(iv) The taxpayer must make payments to someone the taxpayer and the taxpayer's spouse cannot claim as a dependent. Some persons to whom payments cannot be made are to a spouse, the parent of a qualifying child under the age of 13, or to the taxpayer's child unless the child is not the taxpayer's dependent is 19 years of age or older by the end of taxable year.

(v) The identity of the care provider must be reported on the taxpayer's return.[69]

(vi) There are limits on the amount the taxpayer can exclude or deduct. These tests are discussed later in the chapter.

---

67. Prop. Treas. Reg. § 1.21-1(a)(3).

68. Prop. Treas. Reg. § 1.21-1(a)(4).

69. See IRS Publication 503, Child and Dependent Care Expenses (2021). The Publication has an excellent chart to help determine if you can claim the credit (Figure A). It also has an excellent worksheet to figure the credit you may claim for earlier year expenses paid in a later year (Worksheet A).

(vii) The taxpayer's filing status may be single, head of household, or qualifying widow or widower with a dependent child, or joint return if married (subject to certain exceptions).

(viii) The total amount excludable must be less than $3,000 for the care of one qualifying person, or $6,000 for the care of two or more qualifying persons.[70]

2. Qualifying Individual

Three types of persons may constitute a qualifying individual.

First, a dependent of the taxpayer who is under the age of 13 when the care is provided, and with respect to whom the taxpayer is entitled to a dependency exemption under I.R.C. § 152(a)(1) (i.e., a qualifying child).[71] For purposes of the credit, a child attains a given age on the anniversary date of the child's birth.[72] To qualify as a dependent for a parent's taxable year, a child must be a U.S. citizen or a resident at some time during the year.[73]

Second, the dependent of the taxpayer who is physically or mentally incapable of caring for himself or herself, and who has the same principal place of abode as the taxpayer for more than one-half the taxable year.[74] An individual is physically or mentally incapable of self-care if, as a result of a physical or mental defect, the individual is incapable of caring for the individual's hygiene or nutritional needs, or requires full-time attention of another person for the individual's own safety or the safety of others. The inability of an individual to engage in any substantial gainful activity or to perform the normal household functions of a homemaker or care for minor children by reason of a physical or mental condition does not of itself establish that the individual is physically or mentally incapable of self-care.[75]

Third, the spouse of the taxpayer, if the spouse is physically or mentally incapable of caring for himself or herself and the spouse has the same principal

70. See IRS Publication 503, Child and Dependent Care Credit (2021), Figure A, for an excellent chart to help you determine whether you can claim the child and dependent care credit.

71. I.R.C. § 21(b)(1)(A); Prop. Treas. Reg. § 1.21-1(b)(1)(i). There is no age limit if the child is incapacitated.

72. Rev. Rul. 2003-72, 2003-2 C.B. 346.

73. Carlebach v. Comm'r, 139 T.C. 1 (2002).

74. I.R.C. § 21(b)(1)(B); Prop. Treas. Reg. § 1.21-1(b)(1)(ii) The Working Families Tax Relief Act of 2004 eliminated the requirement that the taxpayer maintain a household in order to claim the dependent care credit, and instead inserted a principal place of abode test. Thus, a taxpayer may claim the dependent care credit with respect to a child who lives with the taxpayer for more than half the year, even if the taxpayer does not provide more than one-half of the cost of maintaining the household. For taxable years beginning after Dec. 31, 2004, a qualifying individual must have the same principal place of abode as the taxpayer for more than one-half of the taxable year. For taxable years beginning before Jan. 1, 2005, the taxpayer must maintain a household that includes one or more qualifying individuals.

75. Prop. Treas. Reg. § 1.21-1(b)(4).

place of abode as the taxpayer for more than one-half the taxable year.[76] The principal place of abode requirement was added by the Working Families Tax Relief Act of 2004. Treas. Reg. § 1.21-1(b)(1) defines a qualifying individual for taxable years beginning after December 31, 2004, whereas Treas. Reg. § 1.21-1(b)(2) defines a qualifying individual for taxable years beginning before January 1, 2005.[77] An individual is not treated as having the same principal place of abode as the taxpayer if, at any time during the taxable year of the taxpayer, the relationship between the individual and the taxpayer violates local law.[78]

The status of an individual as a qualifying individual is determined on a daily basis. An individual is not a qualifying individual on the day the status terminates.[79] The individual who is claimed as a dependent for purposes of the credit must be a qualifying individual and not a qualifying relative of the taxpayer.[80] Example: C pays $420 for the care of her child, a qualifying individual, to be provided from January 2 through January 31, 2018 (21 days of care). On January 20, 2018, C's child turns 13 years old. C's child is a qualifying individual from January 2 through January 19, 2018 (13 days of care). C may take into account $260, the pro rata amount C pays for the care of her child for 13 days, under Section 21.[81]

3. Applicable Percentage

The child and dependent care credit is equal to the "applicable percentage" of "employment related expenses." The *applicable percentage* is 35 percent. The 35 percent rate is reduced (but not below 20 percent) by 1 percentage point for each $2,000 (or fraction thereof) by which the taxpayer's adjusted gross income for the taxable year exceeds $15,000.[82] The American Rescue Plan Act of 2021 increased the applicable percentage from 35 percent to 50 percent and increased the taxpayer's adjusted gross income from $15,000 to $125,000 for 2021.[83] See Child and Dependent Care FAQs issued August 29, 2011, for information about eligibility for and claiming the credit. These FAQs were updated on January 11, 2022, and can be found at IR 2022-10. For tax year 2021 only, the phaseout percentage means 20 percent reduced (but not below zero) by 1 percentage point for each $2,000 or fraction thereof by which the taxpayer's

76. I.R.C. § 21(b)(1)(C); Prop. Treas. Reg. § 1.21-1(b)(1)(iii).
77. Prop. Treas. Reg. § 1.21-1(a)(1);
78. I.R.C. § 21(e)(1); Prop. Treas. Reg. § 1.21-1(g).
79. Prop. Treas. Reg. § 1.21-1(b)(3).
80. Notice 2008-5, 2008-2, I.R.B. 256, CCCA 200812024.
81. Prop. Treas. Reg. § 1.21-1(b)(6).
82. I.R.C. § 21(a)(2). For tax year beginning after Dec. 31, 2002, the Tax Act of 2001 increased the applicable percentage from 30% to 35% and the phaseout threshold increased from $10,000 to $15,000. Section 204 of the Economic Growth and Tax Relief Reconciliation Act of 2001, P.L. 107-16 (6/07/2001).
83. I.R.C. §21(g)(3). Pub. L. 117-2, Title IX, § 9631(a) (Mar. 11, 2021).

adjusted gross income for the taxable year exceeds $400,000.[84] For tax year 2022, the income phaseout amounts revert to the pre-2021 levels just described.

4. Employment-Related Expenses

a. General Rule

Employment-related expenses include amounts paid for household services, and for the care of a qualifying individual, but only if such expenses are incurred to enable the taxpayer to be gainfully employed for any period for which there are one or more qualifying individuals with respect to the taxpayer.[85] The expenses must be for the care of a qualifying individual or household services provided during periods in which the taxpayer is gainfully employed or is in active search of gainful employment. Employment may consist of services within or outside the taxpayer's home and includes self-employment. An expense is not employment related merely because it is paid or incurred while the taxpayer is gainfully employed. The purpose of the expense must be to enable the taxpayer to be gainfully employed. Whether the purpose of an expense is to enable the taxpayer to be gainfully employed depends on the facts and circumstances of the particular case. Work as a volunteer or for a nominal consideration is not gainful employment.[86]

Expenses paid for a period during only part of the year in which the taxpayer is gainfully employed or in active search of gainful employment must be allocated on a daily basis.[87] For example, if you work or look for work only two months and 15 days during the year and pay expenses of $250 per month, work related expenses are limited to $625 (two and a half months × $250).

There are special rules for short temporary absences and for a taxpayer who is employed part time.[88] A taxpayer who is gainfully employed is not required to allocate expenses during a short, temporary absence from work, such as for vacation or minor illness, provided that the caregiving arrangement requires the taxpayer to pay for care during the absence. An absence of two consecutive calendar weeks is a short, temporary absence. Whether an absence longer than two consecutive calendar weeks is a short, temporary absence is determined based on all the facts and circumstances.[89] For example, if the taxpayer is ill and misses four months of work but receives sick pay during the period of absence, and the taxpayer continues to pay the service provider for care of the taxpayer's children, the absence is not considered a temporary absence, and

84. I.R.C. § 21(g)(4)(B). In I.R.C. 2021-106 (May 11, 2021) the Service issued an overview of the tax provisions in the American Rescue Plan Act of 2021.

85. I.R.C. § 21(b)(2)(A); Prop. Treas. Reg. § 1.21-1(c)(1).

86. Prop. Treas. Reg. § 1.21-1(c)(1).

87. Prop. Treas. Reg. § 1.21-1(c)(2)(i).

88. Prop. Treas. Reg. § 1.21-1(c)(2).

89. Prop. Treas. Reg. § 1.21-1(c)(2)(ii).

the expenses paid to the service provider are not considered work related and hence are not available for the credit.

A taxpayer who is employed part-time generally must allocate expenses for dependent care between days worked and days not worked. Thus, this is done on a daily basis.[90] However, if a taxpayer employed part-time is required to pay for dependent care on a periodic basis (such as weekly or monthly that includes both days worked and days not worked), the taxpayer is not required to allocate the expenses. A day on which the taxpayer works at least one hour is a day of work.[91] It does not matter whether the taxpayer works day or night, so long as the expenses are incurred to allow the taxpayer to be gainfully employed.

The regulations provide six examples to illustrate these provisions.[92]

Example 1. D works during the day and her husband, E, works at night and sleeps during the day. D and E pay for care for a qualifying individual during the hours when D is working and E is sleeping. The amount paid by D and E for care may be for the purpose of allowing D and E to be gainfully employed and may be an employment-related expense under Section 21.

Example 2. F works at night and pays for care for a qualifying individual during the hours when F is working. The amount paid by F for care may be for the purpose of allowing F to be gainfully employed and may be an employment-related expense under Section 21.

Example 3. G, the custodial parent of two children who are qualifying individuals, hires a housekeeper for a monthly salary to care for the children while G is gainfully employed. G becomes ill and as a result is absent from work for four months. G continues to pay the housekeeper to care for the children while G is absent from work. During this four-month period, G performs no employment services, but receives payments under her employer's wage continuation plan. Although G may be considered to be gainfully employed during her absence from work, the absence is not a short, temporary absence, and her payments for household and dependent care services during the period of illness are not for the purpose of enabling her to be gainfully employed. G's expenses are not employment-related expenses, and she may not take the expenses into account under Section 21.

Example 4. To be gainfully employed, H sends his child to a dependent care center that complies with all state and local requirements. The dependent care center requires payment for days when a child is absent from the center. H takes eight days off from work as vacation days. Because the absence is less than two consecutive calendar weeks, H's absence is a short, temporary

90. Prop. Treas. Reg. § 1.21-1(c)(2)(iii).
91. Prop. Treas. Reg. § 1.21-1(c)(2)(iii).
92. Prop. Treas. Reg. § 1.21-4(c)(3).

absence. H is not required to allocate expenses between days worked and days not worked. The entire fee for the period that includes the eight vacation days may be an employment-related expense under Section 21.

Example 5. J works three days per week and her child attends a dependent care center (that complies with all state and local requirements) to enable her to be gainfully employed. The dependent care center allows payment for any three days per week for $150 or five days per week for $250. J enrolls her child for five days per week, and her child attends the care center for five days per week. J must allocate her expenses for dependent care between days worked and days not worked. Three-fifths of the $250, or $150 per week, may be an employment-related expense under Section 21.

Example 6. The facts are the same as in Example 5, except that the dependent care center does not offer a three-day option. The entire $250 weekly fee may be an employment-related expense under Section 21.

To qualify for the child and dependent care credit, the expenses must be for the care of a qualifying individual. Expenses are for the care of a qualifying individual if the primary function is to ensure the individual's well-being and protection. Not all expenses relating to a qualifying individual are provided for the individual's care. Amounts paid for food,[93] lodging, clothing, or education are not for the care of a qualifying individual. If, however, the care is provided in such a manner that the expenses cover other goods or services that are incidental to and inseparably a part of the care, the full amount is for care.[94] On the other hand, if the taxpayer incurs expenses for meals for a housekeeper who eats in the home because of employment, the cost of the meals for the housekeeper is deemed a work-related expense.

If an expense is partly for household services or for the care of a qualifying individual and partly for other goods or services, a reasonable allocation must be made. Only so much of the expense that is allocable to the household services or care of a qualifying individual is an employment-related expense. An allocation must be made if a housekeeper or other domestic employee performs household duties and cares for the qualifying children of the taxpayer and also performs other services for the taxpayer. No allocation is required, however, if the expense for the other purpose is minimal or insignificant or if an expense is partly attributable to the care of a qualifying individual and partly to household services.[95]

Expenses for household services may be employment-related expenses if the services are provided in connection with the care of a qualifying individual.

---

93. Amounts paid for food are not employment related expenses for child care. Houston v. Comm'r, T.C. Memo. 1983-635 (Payment for school lunches are not payments that can be claimed for the credit.).

94. Prop. Treas. Reg. § 1.21-1(d)(1); I.R.C. § 21(b)(2)(A).

95. Prop. Treas. Reg. § 1.21-1(d)(2).

The household services must be the performance in and about the taxpayer's home of ordinary and usual services necessary to the maintenance of the household and attributable to the care of the qualifying individual. Services of a housekeeper are household services if part of those services is provided to the qualifying individual. Services provided by chauffeurs, bartenders, or gardeners are not household services.[96]

The manner of providing care need not be the least expensive alternative available to the taxpayer. The cost of a paid caregiver may be an expense for the care of a qualifying individual even if another caregiver is available at no cost.[97]

Employment-related expenses do not include any amount paid for services outside the taxpayer's household at a camp where the qualifying individual stays overnight.[98] The cost of a day camp or similar program may be for the care of a qualifying individual and an employment related expense even if the day camp specializes in a particular activity. Summer school and tutoring programs are not for the care of a qualifying individual and the costs are not employment-related expenses.[99]

The cost of transportation incurred by a dependent care provider of a qualifying individual to or from a place where care of that qualifying individual is provided may be for the care of the qualifying individual. The cost of transportation not provided by a dependent care provider is not for the care of the qualifying individual.[100]

Expenses for a child in nursery school, preschool, or similar programs for children below the level of kindergarten are for the care of a qualifying individual and may be employment-related expenses. Expenses for a child in kindergarten or a higher grade are not for the care of a qualifying individual. However, expenses for before- or after-school care of a child in kindergarten or a higher grade may be for the care of a qualifying individual.[101]

Expenses for overnight camp are not employment related expenses.[102] On the other hand, the cost of a day camp or similar program may be an employment-related expense if it cares for a qualifying individual.[103]

---

96. Prop. Treas. Reg. § 1.21-1(d)(3).
97. Prop. Treas. Reg. § 1.21-1(d)(3).
98. I.R.C. § 21(b)(2)(A) flush language. *See also* Prop. Treas. Reg. § 1.21-1(d)(6).
99. Prop. Treas. Reg. § 1.21-1(d)(7).
100. Prop. Treas. Reg. § 1.21-1(d)(8); I.R.C. § 21(b)(2)(A). Commuting expenses (Kourovklis v. Comm'r, T.C. Memo 1986-68), expenses for airfare to spend vacation with grandparents (Perry v. Comm'r, 92 T.C. 470 (1989)), and cleaning expenses (Knuston v. Comm'r, T.C. Memo. 1990-440) are not eligible for the credit.
101. Prop. Treas. Reg. § 1.21-1(d)(5).
102. Prop. Treas. Reg. § 1.21-1(d)(6).
103. Prop. Treas. Reg. § 1.21-1(d)(7)(i).

Summer school and tutoring programs are not for the care of a qualifying individual and therefore the costs are not employment-related expenses.[104]

The cost of transportation by a dependent care provider of a qualifying individual to or from a place of care for the qualifying individual is an employment-related expense if it is for the care of the qualifying individual. But the cost of the transportation must be provided by the dependent care provider to be deemed care for a qualifying individual.[105]

Taxes under I.R.C. § 3111 (relating to the Federal Insurance Contributions Act [FICA]) and I.R.C. § 3301 (relating to the Federal Unemployment Tax Act [FUTA]) and similar state payroll taxes are employment-related expenses if paid for wages that are employment-related expenses.[106]

The additional cost of providing room and board for a caregiver over usual household expenditures may be an employment-related expense.[107]

Expenses that relate to but are not directly for the care of a qualifying individual, such as application fees, agency fees, and deposits, may be for the care of a qualifying individual and may be employment-related expenses if the taxpayer is required to pay the expenses to obtain the related care. However, forfeited deposits and other payments are not for the care of a qualifying individual if care is not provided.[108]

The following six examples from the Regulations illustrate the preceding rules.[109]

Example 1. To be gainfully employed, *E* sends his three-year-old child to a preschool. The preschool provides lunch and snacks. *E* is not required to allocate expenses between care and the lunch and snacks because the lunch and snacks are incidental to and inseparably a part of the care. Therefore, *E* may treat the full amount paid to the preschool as payment for the care of his child.

Example 2. *F*, a member of the armed forces, is ordered to a combat zone. To be able to comply with the orders, *F* places her ten-year-old child in boarding school. The school provides education, meals, and housing to *F*'s child in addition to care. *F* must allocate the cost of the boarding school between expenses for care and expenses for education and other services not constituting care. Only the part of the cost of the boarding school that is for the care of *F*'s child is an employment-related expense under I.R.C. § 21.

Example 3. To be gainfully employed, *G* employs a full-time housekeeper to care for *G*'s two children, ages 9 and 13 years. The housekeeper regularly

104. Prop. Treas. Reg. § 1.21-1(d)(7)(ii).
105. Prop. Treas. Reg. § 1.21-1(d)(8)).
106. Prop. Treas. Reg. § 1.21-1(d)(9).
107. Prop. Treas. Reg. § 1.21-1(d)(10).
108. Prop. Treas. Reg. § 1.21-1(d)(8)–(11).
109. Prop. Treas. Reg. § 1.21-1(b)(12).

performs household services of cleaning and cooking and drives G to and from G's place of employment, a trip of 15 minutes each way. The chauffeur services are not a household service. G is not required to allocate a portion of the expenses of the housekeeper to the chauffeur services, however, because the chauffeur services are minimal and insignificant. Further, no allocation is required to determine the portion of the expenses attributable to the care of the 13-year-old child (not a qualifying individual) because the household expenses are in part attributable to the care of the nine-year-old child. Accordingly, the entire expense of employing the housekeeper is an employment-related expense. The amount that G may take into account as an employment-related expense under I.R.C. § 21, however, is limited to the amount allowable for one qualifying individual.

Example 4. To be gainfully employed, *H* sends her nine-year-old child to a summer day camp that specializes in computer instruction and activities. The full cost of the summer day camp may be for care although it specializes in a particular activity, computers.

Example 5. *J* pays a fee to an agency to obtain the services of an au pair to care for *J*'s qualifying children to enable *J* to be gainfully employed. The au pair begins caring for *J*'s children. The fee paid may be an employment-related expense.

Example 6. *K* places a deposit with a preschool to reserve a place for her child. *K* sends the child to another preschool and forfeits the deposit. The forfeited deposit is not an employment-related expense.

b. Exceptions

Employment-related expenses that are incurred for services outside the taxpayer's household are taken into account only if incurred for the care of:

(i) A qualifying individual as just described, or
(ii) A qualifying individual, other than a dependent of the taxpayer who has not attained the age of 13 years who regularly spends at least eight hours each day in the taxpayer's household.[110]

c. Dependent Care Centers

Employment-related expenses that are incurred for services provided outside the taxpayer's household by a dependent care center are taken into account only if (i) such center complies with all applicable laws and regulations of the state or unit of local government, such as licensing units and building and fire code regulations, and (ii) a qualifying individual (other than a dependent of

110. I.R.C. § 21(b)(2)(B); Prop. Treas. Reg. § 1.21-1(e)(1).

the taxpayer who has not attained the age of 13 years) who regularly spends at least eight hours each day in the taxpayer's household.[111]

A dependent care center means any facility that (i) provides care for more than six individuals (other than individuals who reside at the facility) on a regular basis during the taxable year of the taxpayer, and (ii) receives a fee, payment, or grant for providing services for any of the individuals (regardless of whether the facility is operated for profit).[112] For those purposes, a facility is presumed to provide full-time or part-time care for six or fewer individuals on a regular basis during the taxpayer's taxable year if the facility has six or fewer individuals (including the taxpayer's qualifying individual) enrolled for full-time or part-time care on the day the qualifying individual is enrolled in the facility (or on the first day of the taxable year the qualifying individual attends the facility if the qualifying individual was enrolled in the facility in the preceding taxable year) unless the IRS demonstrates that the facility provides full-time or part-time care for more than six individuals on a regular basis during the taxpayer's taxable year.[113]

d. Reimbursable Expenses

Reimbursed employment-related expenses, for example, under a dependent care assistance program, may not be taken into account for purposes of the credit.[114] For example, if the taxpayer incurs work-related expenses of $4,000 and is reimbursed $3,000, only $1,000 is available to determine the credit allowable.

5. Expenses Qualifying as Medical Expenses

A taxpayer may not take an amount into account as both an employment-related expense under I.R.C. § 21 and an expense for medical care under I.R.C. § 213.[115] In other words, the taxpayer can use the expense as a medical deduction or a child and dependent care credit, but not as both. If the taxpayer uses these expenses to determine the credit and the expenses exceed the earned income limit and dollar limit discussed later, the excess can be added to the taxpayer's medical expenses. On the other hand, if the total expenses are applied to the medical expense deduction, they cannot be used to determine the credit allowable.

Example. *S* has $6,500 of employment-related expenses for the care of his child who is physically incapable of self-care. The expenses are for services

111. I.R.C. § 21(b)(2)(C); Prop. Treas. Reg. § 1.21-1(e)(2).
112. I.R.C. § 21(b)(2)(D); Prop. Treas. Reg. § 1.21-1(e)(2)(i)(B)(ii).
113. Prop. Treas. Reg. § 1.21-1(e)(2)(ii).
114. Prop. Treas. Reg. § 1.21-1(f).
115. Prop. Treas. Reg. § 1.21-1(j)(1).

performed in *S*'s household that also qualify as expenses for medical care, under I.R.C. § 213. Of the total expenses, *S* may take into account $3,000 under I.R.C. § 21. *S* may deduct the balance of the expenses for medical care, or $3,500, under I.R.C. § 213 to the extent the expenses exceed 10 percent of *S*'s adjusted gross income.[116]

If, however, *S* first takes into account the $6,500 of expenses under Section 213, *S* deducts $500 as an expense for medical care, which is the amount by which the expenses exceed 10 percent of *S*'s adjusted gross income. *S* may not take into account the $6,000 balance as employment-related expenses under Section 21 because *S* has taken the full amount of the expenses into account in computing the amount deductible under Section 213.[117]

6. Dollar Limit

The amount of employment-related expenses incurred in any taxable year that may be taken into account may not exceed (i) $3,000 if there is one qualifying individual with respect to the taxpayer for the taxable year, or (ii) $6,000 if there are two or more qualifying individuals with respect to the taxpayer for such taxable year.[118] The American Rescue Plan Act of 2021 increased the credit up to $8,000 for one qualifying person and $16,000 for two or more qualifying persons for tax year 2021.[119] See Child and Dependent Care FAQs issued August 29, 2021, for information about eligibility for and claiming the credit. The dollar limit is a yearly limit. Those dollar limits are reduced by the aggregate amount excludable from gross income under I.R.C. § 129 (pertaining to the dependent care assistance program) for the taxable year.[120] A taxpayer may take into account the total amount of employment-related expenses that do not exceed the annual dollar limitation even though the amount of employment-related expenses attributable to one qualifying individual is disproportionate to the total employment-related expenses. For example, a taxpayer with expenses of $4,000 for one qualifying individual and $1,500 for a second qualifying individual may take into account the full $5,500.[121] A taxpayer is not required to prorate the annual dollar limitations if a qualifying individual ceases to qualify (for example by turning age 13) during the taxable year. However, the taxpayer may take into account only amounts that qualify as employment-related expenses before the disqualifying event.[122]

---

116. Prop. Treas. Reg. § 1.21-1(j)(2); Example 1.
117. *Id.* at Example 2.
118. I.R.C. § 21(c); Prop. Treas. Reg. § 1.21-2(a)(1).
119. I.R.C. § 21(g)(2). Pub. L. 117-2; Title IX, § 9631(a) (Mar. 11, 2021).
120. I.R.C. § 21(c); Prop. Treas. Reg. § 1.21-2(a)(2).
121. Prop. Treas. Reg. § 1.21-2(a)(3).
122. Prop. Treas. Reg. § 1.21-2(a)(4).

7. Earned Income Limitation

a. General

Except as otherwise provided in I.R.C. § 21(d)(1), the amount of the employment-related expenses incurred during any taxable year that may be taken into account may not exceed (i) in the case of an individual who is not married at the close of such year, such individual's earned income for such year, or (ii) in the case of an individual who is married at the close of such year, the lesser of such individual's earned income or the earned income of his or her spouse for such year.[123] A taxpayer must take into account only the earned income of a spouse to whom the taxpayer is married at the close of the taxable year. The spouse's earned income for the entire taxable year is taken into account, however, even though the taxpayer and the spouse were married for only part of the taxable year. The taxpayer is not required to take into account the earned income of a spouse who died or was divorced or separated from the taxpayer during the taxable year.[124] For example, if the taxpayer has earned income of $18,000 for the year and his/her spouse has income of $2,000 for the year, and the taxpayer pays $3,000 for the care of his/her six-year-old child, the amount of expenses that can be used to determine the taxpayer's credit is $2,000 (the lesser of the taxpayer's earned income or the spouse's earned income).

Earned income is defined in I.R.C. § 32 pertaining to the earned income credit.[125] Thus, to claim the credit, the taxpayer (and the taxpayer's spouse if they file jointly) must have earned income from wages, salaries, or other taxable employee compensation, or net earnings from self-employment. Earned income does not include pensions and annuities, Social Security benefits, worker's compensation, interest and dividends, unemployment compensation, scholarships, or child support payments among others.

b. Special Rule for Spouse Who Is Full-time Student or Incapable of Self-care

In the case of a spouse who is a full-time student or is a qualifying individual who is physically or mentally incapable of caring for himself or herself and who has the same principal place of abode as the taxpayer for more than one-half of the taxable year,[126] such spouse is deemed for each month during which such spouse is a full-time student at an educational institution, or is such a qualifying individual to be gainfully employed and to have earned income of not less than (i) $250 if the $3,000 limit applies for the taxable year, or (ii) $500

123. I.R.C. § 21(d)(1); Prop. Treas. Reg. § 1.21-2(b)(1).
124. Prop. Treas. Reg. § 1.21-2(b)(2).
125. Prop. Treas. Reg. § 1.21-2(b)(3).
126. I.R.C. § 21(b)(1)(C).

if the $6,000 limit applies for the taxable year.[127] In the case of any husband and wife, this special rule applies with respect to only one spouse for any one month.[128]

A full-time student is an individual who is enrolled at and attends an educational institution during each of five calendar months of the taxpayer's taxable year for the number of course hours considered by the school to be a full-time course of study. The enrollment for five calendar months does not have to be consecutive.[129] A school includes a high school, college, university, or technical school, but not a correspondence school or on-the-job training school.

c. Examples

The Regulations provide the following three examples to illustrate the preceding rules.

Example 1. T, who is married to U, pays employment-related expenses of $5,000 for the care of one qualifying individual. T's earned income for the taxable year is $40,000 and her husband's earned income is $2,000. T did not exclude any dependent care assistance under Section 129. T may take into account under Section 21 only the amount of employment-related expenses that does not exceed the lesser of her earned income or the earned income of U, or $2,000.

Example 2. The facts are the same as in Example 1 except that U is a full-time student at an educational organization within the meaning of Section 170(b)(1)(A)(ii) for nine months of the taxable year and has no earned income. U is deemed to have earned income of $2,250. T may take into account $2,250 of employment-related expenses under Section 21.

Example 3. For all of 2007, V is a full-time student and W, V's husband, is an individual who is incapable of self-care. V and W have no earned income and pay expenses of $5,000 for W's care. V or W may be deemed to have $3,000 of earned income. However, earned income may be attributed to only one spouse. Under the limitation in Treas. Reg. § 1.21-2(b)(1)(iii), the lesser of V's and W's earned income is zero. V and W may not take the expenses into account under Section 21.[130]

8. Community Property Laws

Community property laws are disregarded in determining earned income for the child and dependent care credit.

---

127. I.R.C. § 21(d)(2); Prop. Treas. Reg. § 1.21-2(b)(4)(i)–(iii).
128. I.R.C. § 21(d)(2) Flush language; Prop. Treas. Reg. § 1.21-2(b)(4)(iii).
129. *See* I.R.C. § 152(f)(2), and the regulations thereunder. Prop. Treas. Reg. § 1.21-2(b)(4)(ii).
130. Prop. Treas. Reg. § 1.21-2(c), Examples 1–3.

9. Principal Place of Abode

For purposes of this credit, an individual is not deemed to have the same principal place of abode of the taxpayer if at any time during the taxable year of the taxpayer the relationship between the individual and the taxpayer is in violation of local law.[131]

10. Married Couples Must File Joint Return

If the taxpayer is married at the close of the taxable year, the credit is allowed only if the taxpayer and his or her spouse file a joint return for the taxable year.[132] If the taxpayer is legally separated under a decree of divorce or separate maintenance or certain married taxpayers living apart,[133] the joint return requirement does not apply.[134] Thus, such taxpayer, even though married, is not required to file a joint return with his or her spouse in order to claim the credit.

11. Marital Status

Generally, married couples must file a joint return to claim the credit. An individual legally separated from his or her spouse under a decree of divorce or of separate maintenance is not considered as married for purposes of the credit.[135] A taxpayer who is treated as not married is not required to take into account the earned income of the taxpayer's spouse for purposes of applying the earned income limitation on the amount of employment-related expenses.[136] Thus, such taxpayer need only use his/her income in figuring the earned income limit. If a married taxpayer dies during the taxable year and the survivor is eligible to file a joint return with respect to the deceased spouse under I.R.C. § 6013(a)(3), the credit is allowed for the year only if a joint return is made. If a joint return is filed as a surviving spouse, the taxpayer may take into account the earned income of the deceased spouse. If, however, the surviving spouse

131. I.R.C. § 21(e)(1).

132. I.R.C. § 21(e)(2); Prop. Treas. Reg. § 1.21-3(a). Credit denied where married spouses filed separate return *Rodriguez v. U.S.*, 111 AFTR2d 2013-2222 (DC TX, 2013); Carlebach v. Comm'r, 139 T.C. 1 (2012).

133. I.R.C. § 21(e)(3).

134. Prop. Treas. Reg. § 1.21-3(b).

135. I.R.C. § 21(e)(3); Prop. Treas. Reg. § 1.21-3(b). See Chapter 1, B.3.c. for the definition of a "decree of divorce or separate maintenance."

136. Prop. Treas. Reg. § 1.21-3(b). *See* Hopkins v. Comm'r, T.C. Memo. 1992-326 (Wife not entitled to the credit because she was married at the end of the year, did not file a joint return with her husband, and they were not living apart since they were living in the same household during the last six months of the taxable year). This provision does not apply if the parties are not married. Sharer v. Comm'r, T.C. Memo. 1994-453.

remarries before the end of the taxable year in which the deceased spouse dies, a credit may be allowed on the decedent spouse's separate return.[137]

12. Certain Married Individuals Living Apart

An individual who is married but who lives apart from his or her spouse is not considered as married if:

(i) The individual is married and files a separate return:
(ii) Maintains as his or her home a household that constitutes for more than one-half of the taxable year the principal place of abode of a qualifying individual with respect to whom the individual is entitled to claim a dependency exemption, and
(iii) Furnishes over half of the cost of maintaining such household during the taxable year, and
(iv) During the last six months of such taxable year such individual's spouse is not a member of such household.[138] So, too, is a taxpayer who is separated from his/her spouse, even if not under a written separation agreement or decree of divorce or separate maintenance, and who files a separate return considered eligible to claim the credit.

For example, wife is separated but not under a decree of divorce or separate maintenance agreement. Wife files as married filing separate. She maintains a home for herself and her disabled brother who is permanently and totally disabled and unable to care for himself. The brother earns $5,600 in interest income. Therefore, wife can't claim him as a dependent (his gross income is greater than the exemption amount, $4,050). And, because she isn't able to claim him as a dependent and she is still married as of the end of the year, she can't use the head of household filing status. Thus, her filing status is married filing separately and her brother qualifies as a qualifying person for the child and dependent care credit. Wife is able to claim the credit for child and dependent care expenses even though she uses the married filing separate filing status because she did not live with her spouse for the last six months of the year; maintained a home for herself and her brother (a qualifying individual) since she separated from her spouse; maintained her own household and provided more than half of the cost of maintaining that home for her and her brother; and paid an adult daycare center to care for her brother to allow her to work.

137. Prop. Treas. Reg. § 1.21-3(c).
138. I.R.C. § 21(e)(4).

13. Special Dependency Test in Case of Divorced or Separated Parents or Parents Living Apart, and So On

There is a special dependency test for divorced or separated parents or parents living apart that allocates the credit to the custodial parent if (i) the child is under the age of 13 years or is physically or mentally incapable of caring for himself or herself; and (ii) the child receives more than one-half of his or her support during the calendar year from one or both parents who are divorced or legally separated under a decree of divorce or separate maintenance, are separated under a written separation agreement, or live apart at all times during the last six months of the calendar year; and (iii) the child is in the custody of one or both parents for more than one-half of the calendar year.[139]

A child who meets these tests is the qualifying individual of only one parent in any taxable year and is the qualifying child of the custodial parent even if the noncustodial parent may claim the dependency exemption for that child for that taxable year.[140] The custodial is the parent having custody for the greater portion of the calendar year.[141] Thus, the noncustodial parent under I.R.C. § 152(e) cannot claim the child and dependent care credit, even if the noncustodial parent incurs employment-related expenses. Only the custodial parent under I.R.C. § 152(e) (relating to divorced or separated spouses) may claim this credit, even if the custodial parent releases the dependency exemption to the noncustodial parent or there is a pre-1985 instrument in effect.[142]

14. Payments to Related Individuals

No credit is allowed for any amount paid by the taxpayer to certain related individuals. A related individual is one:

(i) with respect to whom, for the taxable year, a dependency deduction under I.R.C. § 151(c) (relating to deduction for personal exemptions for dependents) is allowable either to the taxpayer or the taxpayer's spouse,

(ii) who is a child of the taxpayer[143] who has not attained the age of 19 at the close of the taxable year,

---

139. I.R.C. § 21(e)(5); Prop. Treas. Reg. § 1.21-1(b)(5).

140. *See* I.R.C. § 21(e)(5); Prop. Treas. Reg. § 1.21-1(b)(5)(ii).

141. *See* I.R.C. § 152(e)(4)(A), Prop. Treas. Reg. § 1.21-1(b)(5)(ii) .

142. I.R.C. § 21(e)(5). *See also* Prop. Treas. Reg. § 1.21-1(b)(5)(ii). See Chapter 3, B.3.c. for a discussion of the release rule and Chapter 3, B.3.b., for a discussion of the pre-1985 qualified instrument rule.

143. "Child" is defined in I.R.C. § 151(f) as the son, daughter, stepson, stepdaughter, eligible foster child, or adopted child of the taxpayer.

(iii) who is the spouse of the taxpayer at any time during the taxable year, or

(iv) who is the parent of the taxpayer's child who is a qualifying individual.[144] For purposes of disallowing the credit for amounts paid to a related individual, the term "taxable year" means the taxable year of the taxpayer in which the service is performed.[145]

The foregoing does not apply to services performed by partnerships or other entities. If, however, the partnership or other entity is established or maintained primarily as a mechanism to permit the taxpayer to claim the credit by avoiding payments to related individuals, the payments of employment-related expenses are treated as made directly to each partner or owner in proportion to that partner's or owner's ownership interest. Whether a partnership or other entity is established or maintained to avoid losing the credit by making payments to related individuals is determined based on the facts and circumstances, including whether the partnership or other entity is established for the primary purpose of caring for the taxpayer's qualifying individual or providing household services to the taxpayer.[146]

The regulations provide the following three examples to illustrate the foregoing rules:

Example 1. During 2007 X pays $5,000 to her mother for the care of X's five-year-old child who is a qualifying individual. The expenses otherwise qualify as employment-related expenses. X's mother is not her dependent. X may take into account under Section 21 the amounts paid to her mother for the care of X's child.

Example 2. Y is divorced and has custody of his five-year-old child, who is a qualifying individual. Y pays $6,000 during 2007 to Z, who is his ex-wife and the child's mother, for the care of the child. The expenses otherwise qualify as employment-related expenses. Y, however, may not take into account under Section 21 the amounts paid to Z because Z is the child's mother.

Example 3. The facts are the same as in Example 2, except that Z is not the mother of Y's child. Y may take into account under Section 21 the amounts paid to Z.[147]

---

144. I.R.C. § 21(e)(6); Prop. Treas. Reg. § 1.21-4(a)(1)–(4). *See* Langlois v. Comm'r, T.C. Memo. 1988-415 (Credit allowed for payment to daughter, age 20, who was not claimed as a dependent by the taxpayer, for babysitting services.).

145. I.R.C. § 21(e)(6).

146. Prop. Treas. Reg. § 1.21-4(b).

147. Prop. Treas. Reg. § 1.21-4(c).

15. Student

The term "student" means an individual who during each of five calendar months during the taxable year is a full-time student at an educational organization.[148]

16. Educational Organization

The term "educational organization" means an educational organization that normally maintains a regular faculty and curriculum and normally has a regularly enrolled body of pupils or students in attendance at the place where its educational activities are regularly carried on.[149]

17. Identifying Information Required with Respect to Service Provider

No credit is allowed for any amount paid to any person unless (i) the name, address, and taxpayer identification number of such person are included on the return claiming the credit;[150] or (ii) if such person is an exempt organization described in I.R.C. § 501(c)(3) and is exempt from tax under I.R.C. § 501(a), the name and address of such person are included on the return claiming the credit.[151] In the case of a failure to provide the information required under the preceding sentence, the preceding sentence does not apply if it is shown that the taxpayer exercised due diligence in attempting to provide the information so required.[152] If the qualifying person is a nonresident or resident alien who does not have, or cannot obtain, a Social Security number, then that person's ITIN should be used.[153]

The taxpayer may use Form W-10, Dependent Care Provider's Identification and Certification, to request the required information from the care provider. If Form W-10 is not used, the taxpayer may obtain the information from one of the sources listed in the instructions to Form W-10, including (i) a copy of the provider's Social Security number; (ii) a copy of the provider's

148. I.R.C. § 21(e)(7).

149. I.R.C. § 21(e)(8).

150. I.R.C. § 21(e)(9)(A). The requested information is required to be reported on IRS Form 2441. See Part I of the Form.

151. I.R.C. § 21(e)(9)(B).

152. I.R.C. § 21(e)(9). According to the Conference Committee Report to H.R.1, Rep. 115-466, 115th Cong., 1st Session, p. 232 (2017), the taxpayer could show that he or she exercised due diligence by, for example, obtaining and retaining a copy of the Social Security card or driver's license (in a state where the driver's license includes the Social Security number) of the dependent care provider. Alternatively, the taxpayer could show that he or she exercised due diligence by obtaining and retaining the required information from recently printed letterhead or printed invoice from the dependent care provider.

153. An ITIN (Individual Taxpayer Identification Number) is issued by the IRS to individuals who do not have, and are not eligible to obtain, a Social Security number. It is obtained by filing Form W-7.

completed Form W-4 if the care provider is a household employee, (iii) a copy of the statement furnished by the taxpayer's employer if the provider is on the employer's dependent care plan, or a letter or invoice from the provider if it contains the necessary information.[154]

If the provider refuses to provide the identifying information, the taxpayer should report on Form 2441 whatever information the taxpayer has, and then attach a statement to the form explaining that the information was requested from the care provider, but the care provider did not provide the information.[155]

18. Identifying Information Required with Respect to Qualifying Individual

No credit is allowed with respect to any qualifying individual, unless the taxpayer identification number of such individual is included on the tax returns of the taxpayer claiming the credit.[156] This is not a procedural requirement, but a substantive requirement. Thus, there is no "waffle room" for failure to include the TIN, which will be very costly to the taxpayer.

19. Employment Taxes

If the taxpayer pays someone to come to the taxpayer's home to care for the taxpayer's dependent or spouse, the taxpayer may be considered a household employer who has to withhold and pay employment taxes. The taxpayer may not be considered a household employer, however, if the services are provided at the home or place of business of the care provider.

20. Substantiation

A taxpayer claiming a credit for employment-related expenses must maintain adequate records or other sufficient evidence to substantiate the expenses in accordance with I.R.C. § 6001 and the regulations thereunder.[157]

21. Refundable Credit

The American Rescue Plan Act of 2021 added Section 21(g) for tax year 2021.[158] Section 21(g) provides that the credit is refundable in certain if the taxpayer, or either spouse in the case of a joint return, has a principal place of abode in

---

154. IRS Publication 503, Child and Dependent Care Expenses (2021).

155. *Id.*

156. I.R.C. § 21(e)(10).

157. Prop. Treas. Reg. § 1.21-1(k). Turay v. Comm'r, T.C. Memo. 1999-315 (Child care credit disallowed because taxpayer failed to provide documentation to substantiate the amount of child care expenses paid or incurred, or that such expenses were incurred so the taxpayer could be gainfully employed.).

158. The American Rescue Plan Act of 2021, PL117.2, Title IX, Part 4, Section 9631.

the United States for more than half the tax year, the child and dependent care credit shall be treated as a refundable credit instead for credit against tax.[159] For purposes of Section 21(c) the amount of employment-related expenses in any taxable year may not exceed $8,000 if there is one qualifying individual, and $16,000 if there are two or more qualifying individuals with respect to the taxpayer for the taxable year.[160] Furthermore, the applicable percentage is increased from 35 percent to 50 percent and the adjusted gross income floor is increased from $15,000 to $125,000.[161] Finally, the phaseout of the applicable percentage was revised to provide that the applicable percentage is 35 percent reduced (but not below 20 percent) by 1 percentage point for each $2,000 (or fraction thereof) by which the taxpayer's adjusted gross income for the taxable year exceeds $400,000.[162] Thus, the maximum credit is $4,000 if there is one qualifying individual and $8,000 if there are two or more qualifying individuals. In addition, as noted earlier the credit is subject to a two-part phaseout at the 50 percent credit rate. Under the first phase-out, the 50 percent credit rate is reduced, but not below 20 percent, by 1 percentage point for each $2,000 (or fraction thereof) of adjusted gross income above $125,000. Under the second phaseout, the 20 percent rate is reduced, but not below zero, by 1 percentage point for each $2,000 (or fraction thereof) of adjusted gross income above $400,000. Thus, for taxpayers with adjusted gross income between $183,000 and $400,000, the credit is 20 percent, and for taxpayers with adjusted gross income above $483,000, the credit is fully phased out.

To note again, this credit was refundable only for tax year 2021.

22. Due Diligence Checklist

Tax return preparers should be aware of Form 8867, which contains a due diligence checklist for the additional child tax credit, credit for other dependents, and head of household filing status that the preparer must complete and attach to the taxpayer's tax return.

23. Summary

If the taxpayer paid someone to care for his or her child, spouse, or dependent last year, the taxpayer may be able to claim the child and dependent care credit on his or her Federal income tax return. Following are ten things (issued in IRS Tax Tip 2014-18 (2.21.13)) that the IRS wants taxpayers to know about claiming a credit for child and dependent care expenses.

159. I.R.C. § 21(g)(1).
160. I.R.C. § 21(g)(2)(A) and (B).
161. I.R.C. § 21(g)(3)(A) and (B).
162. I.R.C. § 21(g)(4).

(i) The care must have been provided for one or more qualifying persons. A qualifying person is the taxpayer's dependent child who is age 13 or younger when the care was provided. Additionally, the taxpayer's spouse and certain other individuals who are physically or mentally incapable of self-care may also be qualifying persons. The taxpayer must identify each qualifying person on the taxpayer's tax return.

(ii) The care must have been provided so the taxpayer and his/her spouse, if married, filing jointly, could work or look for work. This rule applies to the taxpayer's spouse if the parties file a joint return.

(iii) The taxpayer and his/her spouse, if they file jointly, must have earned income from wages, salaries, tips, other taxable employee compensation, or net earnings from self-employment. One spouse may be considered as having earned income if they were a full-time student or were physically or mentally unable to care for themselves.

(iv) The payments for care cannot be paid to the taxpayer's spouse, to the parent of the taxpayer's qualifying person, to someone the taxpayer can claim as a dependent on his/her return, or to his/her child who will not be age 19 or older by the end of the year even if he or she is not taxpayer's dependent. The taxpayer must identify the care provider(s) on the taxpayer's tax return.

(v) The taxpayer's filing status must be single, married filing jointly, head of household, or qualifying widow(er) with a dependent child.

(vi) The qualifying person must have lived with taxpayer for more than half of the year. There are exceptions for the birth or death of a qualifying person, or a child of divorced or separated parents.

(vii) The credit can be up to 35 percent of the taxpayer's qualifying expenses, depending on the taxpayer's adjusted gross income.

(viii) The taxpayer may use up to $3,000 of expenses paid in a year for one qualifying individual or $6,000 for two or more qualifying individuals to figure the credit.

(ix) The qualifying expenses must be reduced by the amount of any dependent care benefits provided by the taxpayer's employer that the taxpayer deducted or excluded from taxpayer's income.

(x) If the taxpayer pays someone to come to the taxpayer's home and care for the taxpayer's dependent or spouse, the taxpayer may be a household employer and may have to withhold and pay Social Security and Medicare tax and pay Federal unemployment tax.

5 Community Property

A. Treatment of Income

Special rules govern income and property rights for individuals who are domiciled in a community property state. Those states are Arizona, California, Idaho, Louisiana, Nevada, New Mexico, Texas, Washington, and Wisconsin. Generally, spouses who reside in a community property state are each responsible for tax on one-half of the community income.

Generally, married individuals domiciled in a community property state who do not file a joint Federal income tax return must report half the total community income earned by them during the taxable year, unless one of the following three exceptions applies.[1] First, the spouses live apart as provided in Section 66(a).[2] Second, the IRS denies a spouse the Federal income tax benefits resulting from the operation of community property law where spouses are not notified under Treas. Reg. § 1.66-3 because that spouse acted as if he/she were solely entitled to the income and failed to notify his or her spouse of the nature and amount of the income prior to the due date for the filing of his or her spouse's returns.[3] Finally, a requesting spouse seeking innocent spouse relief qualifies for traditional relief or equitable relief from Federal income tax liability resulting from the operation of the community property laws.[4] When a taxpayer reports income under the foregoing rules, all community income for the calendar year is treated in accordance with the rules under Section 879(a) (which provides for the allocation of earned income, trade or business income, and community income where one or both spouses of a married couple are nonresident aliens who have community income for the taxable year).[5]

1. Treas. Reg. § 1.66-1(a).
2. Treas. Reg. § 1.66-1(a)(1).
3. Treas. Reg. § 1.66-1(a)(2).
4. Treas. Reg. § 1.66-1(a)(3) and (4)
5. Treas. Reg. § 1.66-1(b)(2).

The foregoing rules apply only to community income as defined by state law. The foregoing rules do not apply to income that is not community income. For example, the foregoing rules do not apply to income from property that was formally community property but has ceased to be community property under state law, becoming, instead, separate property, tenancy in common property, or property held as joint tenants with rights of survivorship.[6] It should be noted that Section 66(a) does not permit inclusion on an item-by-item basis.[7]

Transferee liability rules do apply to community income. The provisions of Section 66 regarding the treatment of community income do not negate liability that arises under the operation of other laws. Accordingly, a spouse who is not subject to Federal income tax on community income may still remain liable for unpaid tax to the extent provided by Federal transferee liability or property laws under Section 6901 or State transferee or property laws other than community property laws.[8]

Section 66(a) provides a special rule for the treatment of community income where the spouses live apart if the following five tests area met. First, the spouses are married to each other at any time during a calendar year. Second, the individuals live apart at all times during the calendar. Third, the individuals do not file a joint return with each other for the taxable year. Fourth, one or both of the spouses have earned income for the calendar year that is community income. Fifth, no portion of such earned income is transferred, directly or indirectly, between the individuals before the close of the taxable year.[9] If the five tests are met, any community income of the individuals for the calendar year is treated in accordance with the rules of Section 879(a).[10] As noted earlier, Section 879(a) provides special rules for the allocation of earned income, trade or business income, and community income where one or both persons of a married couple are nonresident aliens who have community income for the taxable year.

Living apart requires that the spouses maintain separate residences at all times during the calendar year. Spouses who maintain separate residences due to temporary absences are not considered to be living apart. On the other hand, spouses who are not maintaining the same household under Treas. Reg.

6. Treas. Reg. § 1.66-1(b)(1).
7. Treas. Reg. § 1.66-1(b)(2).
8. Treas. Reg. § 1.66-1(c).
9. Treas. Reg. § 1.66-2(a). Transferred income does not include de minimis amounts of earned income that are transferred between spouses. In addition, any amount of earned income transferred for the benefit of the spouses' children is not treated as an indirect transfer to one spouse. Finally, income transferred between spouses is presumed to be a transfer of earned income, though this transfer may be rebutted. Treas. Reg. § 1.66-2(c). Treas. Reg. §1 .66-2(d) offers two examples to illustrate transfer of earned income.
10. *Id.*

§ 1.6015-3(b) are considered to be living apart.[11] That regulation provides that spouses are members of the same household during either spouses temporary absence from the household if it is reasonable to assume that the absent spouse will return to the household and the household is maintained in anticipation of such return. Examples of temporary absences include absence due to illness, incarceration, business, vacation, military service, or education.[12] A husband and wife who reside in the same dwelling are considered members of the same household. A husband and wife who reside in two separate dwellings are considered members of the same household if the spouses are not estranged or one spouse is temporarily absent from the household.[13] It would seem that for this rule to apply, the spouses should maintain a third common residence, to which they would return, but the regulations do not so require. Compare this rule for living separate and apart with the rule of Section 71(b)(1)(c), which requires, for alimony purposes, that the spouses not be members of the same household.[14]

The IRS may disallow any of the benefits of any community property law to any taxpayer with respect to any item of community income if that spouse acted as if he or she was solely entitled to the income and failed to notify his or her spouse before the due date, including extensions, for filing the return of his or her spouse for the taxable year in which the income was derived.[15] Whether a spouse has acted as if he or she were solely entitled to the item of income is based on all facts and circumstances, which focuses on whether the taxpayer used or made available the item of income for the benefit of the marital community.[16] The effect of the denial is the item of community income denied will be includible, in its entirety, in the gross income of the spouse to whom the IRS denied the Federal income tax benefits resulting from community property law. The tax liability arising from the inclusion of the item of community income is assessed pursuant to Section 6212 against this spouse.[17]

The provisions of Section 66(b) may be illustrated by the following three examples:

Example 1. H and W are married and are domiciled in State A, a community property state. W's Form W-2 for taxable year 2020 showed wage income of $35,000. W also received a Form 1099-INT, "Interest Income," showing W received $1,000 of interest income in taxable year 2020. W's wage income was directly deposited into H and W's joint account, from which H and W paid

11. Treas. Reg. § 1.66-2(b).
12. Treas. Reg. § 1.6015-3(b)(1).
13. Treas. Reg. § 1.6015-3(b)(2).
14. See text at Chapter 1, B.3.e.
15. I.R.C. §1.66(b); Treas. Reg. § 1.66-3(a).
16. Treas. Reg. § 1.66-3(a).
17. Treas. Reg. § 1.66-3(b).

bills and household expenses. W did not inform H of her interest income or that she received the Form 1099-INT, but W gave H a copy of the W-2 when she received it in January 2021. W did not use her interest income for bills or household expenses. Instead, W gave her interest income to her brother, who was unemployed. Neither the separate return filed by H nor the separate return filed by W included the interest income. In 2022, the IRS audits both H and W. The IRS may raise Section 66(b) as to W's interest income, denying W the Federal income tax benefit resulting from community property law as to this item of income.

Example 2. H and W are married and are domiciled in State B, a community property state. For taxable year 2022, H receives $45,000 in wage income that H places in a separate account. H and W maintain separate residences. H's wage income is community income under the laws of State B. That same year, W loses her job, and H pays W's mortgage and household expenses for several months while W seeks employment. Neither H nor W files a return for 2020, the taxable year for which the IRS subsequently audits them. The IRS may not raise Section 66(b) and deny H the Federal income tax benefits resulting from the operation of community property law as to H's wage income of $45,000, as H has not treated this income as if H were solely entitled to it.

Example 3. H and W are married and domiciled in State C, a community property state. H and W do not file a joint return for taxable year 2020. H's and W's earned income for 2020 is community income under the laws of State C. H receives $50,000 in wage income in 2020. In January 2021, H receives a Form W-2 that erroneously states that H earned $45,000 in 2020. H provides W with a copy of his Form W-2 in February 2021. W files for an extension prior to April 15, 2021. H receives a corrected Form W-2 reflecting wages of $50,000 in May 2021. H provides a copy of the corrected Form W-2 to W in May 2021. W files a separate return in June 2021 but reports one-half of $45,000 ($22,500) of wage income that H earned. H files a separate return reporting half of $50,000 ($25,000) in wage income. The IRS audits both H and W. Even if H had acted as if he were solely entitled to the wage income, the IRS may not raise Section 66(b) as to this income because H notified W of the nature and amount of the income prior to the due date of W's return (including extensions).[18]

B. Alimony

Payments that may otherwise qualify as alimony are not deductible by the payor spouse under the rules in effect for taxable years ending before 2019 if they are the payee spouse's part of community income. On the other hand,

18. Treas. Reg. § 1.66-3(c).

the payments are deductible by the payor spouse and includible in the gross income of the payee spouse only to the extent they are more than the payee spouse's part of community income. For example, assume H and W are domiciled in community property State A. They are separated, but for less than the entire year. They enter into a written separation agreement in which H agrees to pay W $48,000 of H's $80,000 community income. W has no community income. Under State law, the earnings of a spouse living separate and apart from the other spouse constitutes community property. H and W file separate returns. On their separate returns, each must report $40,000 of the community income. In addition, W must report $8,000 in gross income as alimony, and H can deduct $8,000 as alimony paid for taxable years ending before 2019.

6 Property Settlements

A. Introduction

In lieu of, or in addition to, alimony payments made by the payor spouse to the payee spouse, the parties may agree to transfer property from one spouse to the other in exchange for the transferee spouse's marital rights.

The tax consequences of a property settlement payment differ from those of alimony payments because the property settlement is not made as a result of the marital or family obligation of support imposed on the payor spouse, but is treated as made to the payee spouse due to his or her interest in family property. Thus, the transfer payment is neither taxable to the payee spouse nor deductible by the payor spouse as alimony.[1]

Oftentimes, a study of the history of the law aids in understanding the current law. Such is the case with the tax aspects of the transfer of property as part of a separation or divorce. The following first discusses the prior law, and then the current law, which was enacted by the Tax Reform Act of 1984. The current law was not changed by the Tax Cuts and Jobs Act of 2017.

B. Prior Law (before 1984 TRA)

1. Transferor

a. Appreciated Property

The law regarding transfers of appreciated property in a separation or divorce proceeding prior to the Tax Reform Act of 1984, for taxable years ending before

1. Yoakum v. Comm'r, 82 T.C. 128 (1984). *See* Riley v. Commissioner, T.C. Memo. 1979-237, *aff'd*, 649 F.2d 768 (C.A. 10, 1981), where the Court listed five factors as being indicative of property settlement payments: (i) the presence of a fixed sum, (ii) the payments are not related to the income of the payor spouse, (iii) the payments are made without regard to the death or remarriage of the payee spouse, (iv) the payee spouse relinquished property interests in return for the property payments, and (v) the payor spouse's obligation to make the payments is secured.

January 1, 1985, was governed by *United States v. Davis*.[2] In *Davis* the husband agreed to transfer to his wife, inter alia, 1,000 shares of stock in E.I. du Pont De Nemours & Co (the "duPont stock"). The wife agreed to accept the duPont stock "in full settlement and satisfaction of any and all claims and rights against the husband whatsoever (including but not by way of limitation, dower and all rights under the laws of testacy and intestacy. . . ."[3] The shares of duPont stock had a fair market value in excess of basis. The threshold question before the Court was "whether the transfer in issue was an appropriate occasion for taxing the accretion [in value] to the stock. . . ."[4] "The problem confronting [the Court] is simply *when* is such accretion to be taxed. Should the economic gain be presently assessed against the taxpayer, or should this assessment await a subsequent transfer of the property by the wife?"[5]

The taxpayer asserted that the disposition was comparable to a nontaxable division of property between two co-owners. The Service contended that the disposition resembled a taxable transfer of property in exchange for the release of an independent legal obligation.

The Court first held that the transferor realized and recognized gain on the transfer of appreciated property to the transferee in exchange for the release of the transferee's marital rights pursuant to a property settlement agreement.

Gain realized is the excess of the "amount realized" from the transfer of the property over its adjusted basis.[6] The amount realized is the sum of money received plus the fair market value of property (other than money) received.[7]

The Court held that the "amount realized" by the transferor from the transfer of property was equal to the release of the wife's inchoate marital rights. The Court of Claims,[8] in the decision below, had held that these rights were not susceptible of valuation. In *Davis*, the Supreme Court held that the value of the marital rights released by the payee spouse was susceptible of valuation inasmuch as it was presumed to have been equal to the value of the appreciated property transferred. The Court reasoned that absent a readily ascertainable value, it is accepted practice to hold that the values of the two properties exchanged in an arm's length transaction are either equal in fact or presumed to be equal. According to the Court, "once it is recognized that the transfer was a taxable event, it is more consistent with the general purpose and scheme of

2. 370 U.S. 65 (1962).
3. *Id.* at 67.
4. *Id.* at 68.
5. *Id.* at 70. The question posed by the Court was prescient, since, as noted later, the Tax Reform Act of 1984 answered this question in Section 1041 by providing that the assessment should await a subsequent transfer of the property by the transferee spouse. But it would take the Congress 22 years to address this question.
6. I.R.C. § 1001(a).
7. I.R.C. § 1001(b).
8. 152 Cl. Ct. 805, 287 F.2d. 168 (1961).

the taxing statutes to make a rough approximation of the gain realized thereby than to ignore altogether its tax consequences.[9]

The Court then went on to determine the basis of the property to the transferee spouse.

> Our present holding that the value of these rights is ascertainable eliminates this problem [of determining the basis of the property in the hands of the transferee spouse]; for the same calculation that determines that the amount received by the husband fixes the amount given up by the wife and the figure, *i.e.*, the market value of the property transferred by the husband, will be taken by her as her tax basis for the property received.[10]

Thus, the value of the wife's marital rights received by the husband in exchange for the duPont stock, and the basis of the duPont stock in the hands of the wife are deemed to be identical and are deemed to be equal to the value of the duPont shares transferred.

For example, if the transferor owned vacant real estate with a fair market value of $200,000 and an adjusted basis of $50,000 and, pursuant to a property settlement, the transferor transferred the property to the transferee in exchange for the release of transferee's marital rights, the amount realized and recognized by the transferor (i.e., the fair market value of the release of the wife's marital rights) would be $200,000. The transferor would realize taxable gain of $150,000 and the basis of the property in the hands of the transferee would be $200,000 (its cost).

Although one could not state with certainty, it was possible for the transferor to have avoided these adverse tax consequences by having the transferee, in the written separation agreement, assign a value to the marital rights the transferee was releasing at least equal to the transferor's basis in the assets the transferor was transferring. Although the transferee would have then received a basis in the property less than its fair market value, thereby triggering a taxable event upon subsequent disposition of the property (as noted later), agreeing to assign a lower value to transferee's marital rights than was otherwise presumed may have given the transferee leverage for other matters in dispute.

In addition, the transferor may have avoided such adverse income tax consequences if the property transferred was deemed a nontaxable division of marital property between coowners such as usually occurs in community property jurisdictions. According to the IRS in Rev. Rul. 74-347,[11] property is deemed coowned if title is taken jointly under State property law, the State is a community property jurisdiction, or State property law is found to be similar to

9. 370 U.S. 65 at 72.
10. 370 U.S. 65 at 73.
11. 19742 C.B. 26.

community property law. The issue in Rev. Rul. 74-347 was whether under the divorce decree the unequal division of jointly owned property which awarded the wife an excess of jointly owned property constituted a taxable transfer by the husband in satisfaction of the wife's marital rights and, if so, the amount of gain realized by the husband on the transfer. According to the Service, only jointly owned property of the husband and wife was within the scope of the term "co-ownership." As a result of this analysis, the Service held that since the wife's interest in the husband's separately owned property was not the equivalent of co-ownership, the division of jointly owned property awarded to the wife constituted a taxable exchange of a portion of the husband's jointly owned property in exchange for the wife's marital rights in the husband's jointly owned property. Prior to the enactment of Section 1041, Rev. Rul. 74-374 was the primary way to transfer appreciated property from one spouse to the other without the transferor spouse recognizing income as a result of the transfer.

It would appear that the parties could select the jointly owned assets that caused the excess. For example, in *Carrieres v. Commissioner*,[12] the U.S. Tax Court stated that the payor spouse and the payee spouse could, by agreement between them, select the jointly owned assets that caused the excess. The result would be that the payor spouse and the payee spouse could select for the excess jointly owned property which had an adjusted basis and fair market value which were relatively equal, with the result that little if any gain would be realized.

The assets transferred by the payor spouse were valued at the date of the transfer unless substantial burdens and benefits of ownership were previously transferred.[13]

The character of the gain depended on the character of the asset transferred.

- If the property transferred was a capital asset or I.R.C. § 1231 property, the gain was capital.
- If, however, the property transferred was subject to recapture of depreciation or investment tax credit, all or part of the gain may have been ordinary.[14]
- Moreover, if the property transferred was subject to depreciation and the transfer was made while the parties were still married, I.R.C. § 1239 required that gain recognized from the transfer of such property be characterized as ordinary income.

12. 64 T.C. 959 (1975), *aff'd*, 552 F.2d 1350 (9th Cir. 1977).
13. *See* United States v. Davis, 370 U.S. 65 (1962).
14. *E.g.*, I.R.C. §§ 47, 1245, and 1250.

See also Rev. Rul. 81292,[15] where the IRS held that an approximately equal division of the total value of jointly owned property under a divorce property settlement agreement in a noncommunity property state was considered neither a sale nor exchange, but rather was considered a nontaxable division of jointly owned property where some assets were transferred in their entirety to one spouse or the other. The basis and holding period of each asset was the same as when the property was jointly owned. And see Rev. Rul. 7683,[16] which reached the same result with respect to community property in a community property state.

The difference between Rev. Rul. 81292 and Rev. Rul. 74347 is that under Rev. Rul. 81292 there was an approximately equal division of the jointly owned property, whereas under Rev. Rul. 74347 the transferee spouse received more jointly owned property than the transferor spouse, although they each received property of equal value because the transferor retained ownership of his separately owned property, which was approximately equal in value to the difference between the value of the jointly owned property that the transferee received and the value of the jointly owned property that the transferor received. Confusion abounded in this area, however, because Rev. Rul. 81292 spoke of "total value", whereas *Carrieres v. Commissioner*[17] and Rev. Rul. 7683,[18] to which Rev. Rul. 81292 refers, pertained to "total net fair market value" (i.e., fair market value less encumbrances) (though the terms "total value," "fair market value," and "total net fair market value" appeared to be used interchangeably). Note that *Carrieres* and Rev. Rul. 7683 involved community property in a community property state, though this would not seem to have made a difference.

Where a divorce Court ordered the transferor to transfer to the transferee assets the transferor acquired during the marriage by gift or purchase from the transferee and the transferee's parents, the transfer was in the nature of a division of property and not a taxable transaction.[19] The Court, in what appears to be a result-oriented decision, determined that although the "transfer enforced by the divorce Court [Connecticut] was not a 'division of property' in the ordinary meaning of those words, neither was the transfer ordered to discharge [the husband's] marital obligations to [the wife]."[20] Thus, the Court refused to

---

15. 1981-2 C.B. 158.
16. 1976-1 C.B. 213 (No gain or loss recognized from approximately equal division of fair market value of community property in a community property state under a divorce settlement agreement that provides for transfer of some assets in their entirety to one spouse or the other.).
17. 64 T.C. 959 (1975), *aff'd*, 552 F.2d 1350 (9th Cir. 1977).
18. 1976 C.B. 213.
19. Cook v. Comm'r, 80 T.C. 512 (1983), *aff'd without op.*, 742 F.2d 1431 (2d Cir. 1984).
20. 80 T.C. 512 at 527.

impose a tax where the divorce judge intended to return to the payee spouse property he thought belonged to her regardless of legal title.

As discussed later in the chapter, the 1984 TRA substantially revised the preceding rules and rendered unnecessary the application of the foregoing cases and rulings.

b. Depreciated Property

If the property had depreciated in value so that its basis exceeded its fair market value, I.R.C. § 267 precluded the transferor from recognizing a loss if the transfer was made to the transferee while the parties were still married. Thus, it was advisable not to transfer depreciated property between the spouses until the marriage was fully dissolved.

Even if the transfer was made after the divorce, the loss deduction may have been barred by I.R.C. § 165(c) as a transaction not entered into for profit if the transfer is deemed to be a part of the divorce.[21]

Accordingly, to ensure loss treatment, it was advisable for the transferor to sell the depreciated property to a third party and to give the cash proceeds to the transferee.

Even though I.R.C. § 267 was applicable to loss property transferred between spouses prior to a divorce, I.R.C. § 267(d) could be used by the transferee spouse to reduce the transferee's gain when the transferee ultimately disposed of such property.[22]

2. Transferee

Generally, the transferee neither realized nor recognized gain on the receipt of appreciated property from the transferor in exchange for the release of his or her marital rights, inasmuch as the value of the property received was presumed to be equal in value to the marital rights relinquished and the basis of the marital rights released was presumed to be equal to the fair market value of the marital rights released.[23]

Where the transferor recognized gain on the transfer of appreciated property, the transferee received a stepped-up basis equal to the fair market value of the property transferred.[24] Where, however, the transferor did not recognize gain, carryover basis applied with respect to the property received by

21. Compare Pulliam v. Comm'r, 39 T.C. 883 (1963), *aff'd*, 329 F.2d 97 (10th Cir. 1964) (loss on transfer of family residence incident to divorce is nondeductible) with Robertson v. Comm'r, 55 T.C. 862 (1971) (loss on transfer of interest in motel to transferee incident to a divorce is deductible).

22. Siewert v. Comm'r, 72 T.C. 326 (1979).

23. United States v. Davis, 370 U.S. 65 (1962); Rev. Rul. 67-221, 1967-2 C.B. 63.

24. Rev. Rul. 67-221, 1967-2 C.B. 63.

the transferee.[25] For example, in the hypothetical just described the transferee would not have realized or recognized gain on receipt of the vacant land. Moreover, the transferee's basis in the vacant real estate received from the transferor pursuant to a property settlement would have been its cost, that is, $200,000. Thus, if the transferee immediately resold the property for $200,000, the transferee would incur no Federal income tax liability. If, however, the transaction had been tax free to the transferor, the basis of the land in the hands of the transferee would have been $50,000, so that the transferee would have recognized the gain on the immediate resale.

As discussed later in the chapter, the 1984 TRA substantially revised the preceding rules and rendered them inapplicable.

C. Current Law

1. Introduction

a. Summary of Changes

The 1984 TRA completely revised the Federal income tax consequences respecting the transfer of property between separated or divorced spouses by adding I.R.C. § 1041 to the Code, which provides that no gain or loss is recognized on a transfer of property from an individual to (or in trust for the benefit of) a spouse, or a former spouse if that transfer is incident to a divorce. The 1984 TRA accomplished these revisions by:

- shifting the tax burden on the transfer of appreciated property from the transferor to the transferee;
- providing that property transfers cannot qualify as alimony;
- eliminating the requirement under prior law that alimony payments had to be made in discharge of the transferor's legal obligation of support imposed on him or her because of the marital or family relationship; and
- treating the transfers of property acquired by the transferee as a gift and employing a carryover basis concept as gifts.

Thus, no gain or loss is recognized to the transferor spouse on the transfer of property to a spouse, or former spouse incident to a divorce,[26] and the basis of the property in the hands of the transferee spouse is the same as the basis of the property in the hands of the transferor spouse (i.e., carryover basis).[27]

This rule applies to the transfer of "property," which includes both real and personal property, and tangible and intangible property. It does not apply to

25. *See also* Rev. Rul. 67221, 19672 C.B. 63.
26. I.R.C. § 1041(a).
27. I.R.C. § 1041(b)(2); I.R.C. § 1015(e).

the transfer of property in exchange for services, but only to property transferred for cash or other property.

b. Cash or Property Transfers

For payments made pursuant to the Tax Cuts and Jobs Act of 2017, which denies an alimony deduction to the payor spouse and excludes an alimony payment from the gross income of the payee spouse for years 2018 through 2025 for divorce or separation instruments executed after 2018, it no longer matters whether a payment of cash or property is characterized as an alimony payment or a property settlement (except for basis issues as discussed in Chapter 6, C.6.c.,[28] *transfers of property* can qualify only as a property settlement, whereas *transfers of cash* can qualify as either alimony or a property settlement, depending upon the intent of the parties.[29] Note, however, that where large amounts of cash are involved, the statute presumes that all or a part of such payments of cash are in the nature of a property settlement rather than in the nature of an alimony payment by application of the excess front-end loading rules discussed in Chapter 1, B.2.i. Moreover, cash payments are presumed to be alimony payments unless the decree or agreement provides otherwise.[30] This, of course, assumes that all other tests necessary for the payments to constitute alimony are met. Thus, it is important to specify whether a cash payment constitutes a property settlement or an alimony payment. It would also appear advisable to place the property settlement provisions and alimony provisions in separate parts of the agreement or decree to avoid confusion.

c. Nonresident Alien

I.R.C. § 1041 is not available if the transferee spouse is a nonresident alien.[31] Thus, if property is transferred to a spouse who is a nonresident alien, gain or

---

28. For payments under the law prior to the Tax Cuts and Jobs Act of 2017, for tax years before 2018 and after 2025, transfers of property could (and presumably will) qualify only as a property settlement, whereas transfers of cash could qualify as either alimony or a property settlement, depending upon the intent of the parties, Temp. Prop. Treas. Reg. § 1.1041-1T(a)(A-4); I.R.C. § 71(b)(1). See Chapter 1, B.2.a. Note, however, that where large amounts of cash were involved, the statute presumed that all or a part of such payments of cash were in the nature of a property settlement rather than in the nature of an alimony payment by application of the excess frontend loading rules discussed at excess front-end loading rules, Chapter 1, B.2.i. Moreover, cash payments were presumed to be alimony payments unless the decree or agreement provided otherwise. This, of course, assumed that all other tests necessary for the payments to constitute alimony were met. Thus, under prior law it was important to specify whether a cash payment constituted a property settlement or an alimony payment. It would still appear to be advisable to place the property settlement provisions and alimony provisions in separate parts of the agreement or decree to avoid confusion.

29. Temp. Prop. Treas. Reg. § 1.10411T(a)(A4); I.R.C. § 71(b)(1). *See* Chapter 1, B.2.a.

30. *See* Placement in the Agreement at Chapter 1, B.3.c.(2)(e).

31. I.R.C. § 1041(d); Temp. Prop. Treas. Reg. § 1.10411T(a)(A3).

loss is recognized by the transferor spouse. The transferor must withhold 30 percent of the tax.[32] On the other hand, Section 1041 would appear to apply to transfers from a nonresident alien to a U.S. resident or citizen.

d. Spouse and Former Spouses

I.R.C. § 1041 applies to transfers between spouses, and to transfers between former spouses but only if the transfer is "incident to the divorce." Annulments and cessations of marriages that are void ab initio due to violations of state law are divorces for purposes of I.R.C. § 1041.[33]

e. Transfer between Spouses during Marriage

I.R.C. § 1041 is not limited to transfers of property incident to divorce. I.R.C. § 1041 applies to any transfer of property between spouses regardless of whether the transfer is a gift or is a sale or exchange between spouses acting at arm's length (including a transfer in exchange for the relinquishment of property or marital rights or an exchange otherwise governed by another nonrecognition provision of the Code). A divorce or legal separation need not be contemplated between the spouses at the time of the transfer, nor must a divorce or legal separation ever occur.[34] The regulations provide three examples to illustrate the foregoing rules.[35]

Example 1. *A* and *B* are married and file a joint return. *A* is the sole owner of a condominium unit. A sale or gift of the condominium from *A* to *B* is a transfer which is subject to the rules of I.R.C. § 1041. No gain or loss is recognized on the transfer of the property from *A* to *B*.

Example 2. *A* and *B* are married and file separate returns. *A* is the owner of an independent sole proprietorship, X Company. In the ordinary course of business, *X* Company makes a sale of property to *B*. This sale is a transfer of property between spouses and is subject to the rules of I.R.C. § 1041. Thus, no gain is recognized by *A* on the sale of property to *B*. The same result would apply if *X* were a limited liability company which is wholly owned by *A*.

Example 3. Assume the same facts as in example 2, except that *X* Company is a corporation wholly owned by *A*. This sale is not a sale between spouses subject to the rules of I.R.C. § 1041. However, in appropriate circumstances, general tax principles, including the step-transaction doctrine, may be applicable in recharacterizing the transaction.[36]

---

32. I.R.C. § 1441. *See* Chapter 6, C.6.c. and f. Transferee.
33. Temp. Prop. Treas. Reg. § 1.10411T(b)(A8).
34. Temp. Prop. Treas. Reg. § 1.10411T(a)(A2).
35. *Id.*
36. *Id.*

f. Transfer after Marriage Ceases

A transfer of property acquired after the marriage ceases may be governed by I.R.C. § 1041.[37] Thus, property transferred to a former spouse incident to a divorce does not have to have been owned by the transferor spouse during the marriage for the transfer to qualify under Section 1041.

g. Prenuptial Agreements

I.R.C. § 1041 should not apply to prenuptial agreements. Thus, a transfer by *A* of property with a fair market value of $100 and a basis of $20 in exchange for *B*'s release of any rights *B* may have upon marriage pursuant to a prenuptial agreement will result in gain realized and recognized to *A* of $80. *B* will receive a stepup in basis of the property equal to its fair market value of $100.[38]

h. Time of Transfer

The date of transfer of property is the date of physical delivery or divestment of legal title.[39]

2. Income from Property

Income payments received by the payee spouse, whether from the payor spouse directly or from property transferred to the payee spouse from the payor spouse, are includible in the payee spouse's gross income.[40] Section 1041 does not provide for the exclusion of income, only for the exclusion of gain realized in certain circumstances.[41] Thus, interest on an installment sale from the husband to the wife is taxable to wife.[42] Generally, such payments will be taxable to the payee spouse as interest income under Section 61 and not as alimony under I.R.C. § 71.[43]

The payor spouse may deduct those payments that are made directly or indirectly. The payor spouse receives a deduction for payments from the income from transferred property and is not taxable on the income from such transferred property.

---

37. Temp. Prop. Treas. Reg. § 1.10411T(a)(A5).
38. *See, e.g.*, Rev. Rul. 67221, 19672 C.B. 63.
39. Godlewski v. Comm'r, 90 T.C. 200 (1988) (Look to the date the deed was executed to determine the date of transfer); Harrington v. Comm'r, T.C. Memo. 1994-258 (1994) (Look to the date property is transferred, not the date of the decree or separation agreement.).
40. I.R.C. §§ 71(b)(2)(A), 215.
41. Gibbs v. Comm'r, T.C. Memo. 1997-196.
42. *Id.*
43. *Id.*

3. General Rule

I.R.C. § 1001(a) provides that gain from the sale or exchange of property is the excess of the amount realized therefrom over the adjusted basis of the property, and loss from the sale or exchange of property is the excess of the adjusted basis of the property over the amount realized.

I.R.C. § 1001(b) provides that the amount realized from the sale or other disposition of property is the sum of money received plus the fair market value of the property (other than money) received.

I.R.C. § 1001(c) provides that: "[E]xcept as otherwise provided in [the income tax laws], the entire amount of gain or loss realized . . . on the sale or exchange of property is recognized [i.e., taxed]." I.R.C. § 1041, discussed in this Part, is an exception to I.R.C. § 1001(c).

4. Transferor

a. Property

Only transfers of property fall within I.R.C. § 1041. The property can be real or personal, tangible or intangible.[44] Transfers of services are not governed by I.R.C. § 1041.[45] The property transferred to a former spouse does not have to have been owned by the transferor spouse during the marriage.[46] Thus, a transfer of property acquired after the marriage ceases may also fall within the ambit of I.R.C. § 1041.[47]

b. Appreciated Property

(1) General Rule

I.R.C. § 1041(a) provides that the transferor realizes, but does not recognize, gain or loss on a transfer of property from an individual to (or in trust for the benefit of) (i) a spouse, or (ii) a former spouse, but only if the transfer to the former spouse is incident to the divorce.[48] Thus, transfers between spouses during the marriage, and to former spouses incident to a divorce, are nontaxable.

I.R.C. § 1041 applies to any transfer of property between spouses regardless of whether the transfer is a gift, or is a sale or exchange between spouses acting at arm's length (including a transfer in exchange for the relinquishment of

---

44. Temp. Prop. Treas. Reg. § 1.1041-1T(a)(A-4) (Transfer of one-half interest in proprietorship and one-half interest in partnership is property under I.R.C. § 1041 and the transferor does not recognize gain on the transfer of such property to the transferee.).

45. Temp. Prop. Treas. Reg. § 1.10411T(a)(A4).

46. See text at Chapter 6, C.1.f.

47. Temp. Prop. Treas. Reg. § 1.10411T(a)(A5).

48. I.R.C. § 1041(a)(l); Balding v. Comm'r, 98 T.C. 368 (1992). The *Balding* case gives an excellent discussion of the purpose, scope, and background of I.R.C. § 1041.

property or marital rights or an exchange otherwise governed by another non-recognition provision of the Code). This specifically applies to, and overrules, *Davis* and *Davis*-type transactions.[49] Thus, Section 1041 applies to transfers for the release of marital rights, as well as to the transfer of items of property that are not for the release of marital rights.

A divorce or legal separation need not be contemplated between the spouses at the time of the transfer, nor must a divorce or legal separation ever occur.[50] Thus, as noted earlier, Section 1041 applies to transfers between spouses while married whether or not incident to a divorce.

(2) Incident to a Divorce

A transfer of property is *incident to a divorce* if such transfer meets either of the following two tests:

First, the transfer occurs within one year after the date on which the marriage ceases.[51] This applies to property acquired within one year after the marriage ceases, and even if the transfer is not related to the cessation of the marriage.[52]

Thus, a transfer of property occurring not more than one year after the date on which the marriage ceases need not be related to the cessation of the marriage to qualify for I.R.C. § 1041 treatment.[53]

Second, the transfer is related to the cessation of the marriage.[54]

The first test, transfers within one year after the date on which the marriage ceases, establishes a conclusive presumption that the transfer is incident to a divorce, whereas the second test, transfers related to the cessation of the marriage, is based upon the facts and circumstances of each case. This second test is discussed in the following details.

(a) Transfers Related to Cessation of Marriage

Transfers related to the cessation of a marriage are divided into two time periods: (i) those transfers that take place within six years of the cessation of the marriage, and (ii) those transfers that take place more than six years after the cessation of the marriage.

---

49. Temp. Prop. Treas. Reg. § 1.10411T(a)(A2).
50. *Id.*
51. I.R.C. § 1041(c)(l). *See* Mehriary v. Comm'r, T.C. Memo. 2015-126 where the Court denied the taxpayer a loss on the transfer of real property to her husband because the property was transferred 362 days after the final judgment of divorce was entered. The Court found that the transfer was incident to a divorce because the transfer occurred within one year after the date on which the marriage ceased.
52. Temp. Prop. Treas. Reg. § 1.10411T(b)(A5&6).
53. Temp. Prop. Treas. Reg. § 1.10411T(b)(A6).
54. I.R.C. § 1041(c)(2). *See also* Temp. Prop. Treas. Reg. § 1.10411T(b)(A6).

(i) Transfers Not More than Six Years

A transfer of property is treated as related to the *cessation of the marriage* if the transfer is pursuant to a divorce or separation instrument, as defined in I.R.C. § 71(b)(2),[55] and the transfer occurs not more than six years after the date on which the marriage ceases. A divorce or separation instrument includes a modification or amendment to such decree or instrument.[56]

In PLR 9348020, the Service held that a sale of property from *W* to *H* pursuant to a right of first refusal was protected by Section 1041 where the sale took place within six years from the date the marriage ceased. The marital settlement agreement provided that certain real property would be sold to a third party, provided that *H* was given a right of first refusal to purchase *W*'s tenant in common interest in the property. *H* eventually purchased *W*'s interest in the property. The Service held that because the marital settlement agreement provided that *H* could purchase *W*'s interest in the property before it was sold to a third party, and because the sale would occur within six years after the cessation of the marriage, *W*'s sale of her interest in the property to *H* was treated as related to the cessation of the marriage under Section 1041.

The sale of the marital home by *W* to *H* pursuant to *H*'s right of first refusal contained in the divorce decree constitutes a transfer of property to a spouse incident to a divorce within the meaning of I.R.C. § 1041(a)(2).[57]

In *Young v. Commissioner*,[58] the Fourth Circuit Court of Appeals held that a transfer of land by a husband to his former wife four years after the divorce was a transfer "incident to a divorce." The parties were divorced in 1988. In 1989, they entered into an agreement to resolve their property claims. Under the agreement, the husband delivered a note to the wife for $1.5 million payable in five annual installments, secured by a deed of trust on 71 acres of land the husband received as part of the 1989 settlement agreement. In 1990, the husband defaulted under the 1989 agreement. The wife brought an action against the husband and the Court entered judgment for the wife. Before executing the judgment, the parties entered into a 1992 settlement agreement pursuant to which the husband agreed to transfer 59 acres of the 71 acres that

55. *See* Chapter 1, B.2.c.

56. Temp. Prop. Treas. Reg. § 1.10411T(b)(A7). *See* Priv. Ltr. Rul. 9348020.

57. Priv. Ltr. Rul. 8833018. In the PLR, H transferred the marital home to W with instructions to sell it. H was awarded the right of first refusal which he exercised. The Service held that the sale by W to H pursuant to the right of first refusal contained in the divorce decree constituted a transfer of property to a spouse "incident to a divorce." *See also* PLR 9348020 (Pursuant to a marital settlement agreement, H and W held properties as tenants in common. The MSA gave H the right of first refusal to purchase W's entire interest in any of the properties. H exercised the right of first refusal. The Court held the transfer qualifies under § 1041 since it was related to the cessation of the marriage. Thus, W recognizes no gain or loss on the transfer of the property to H, and H's basis in the property equals W's basis in the property immediately prior to the transfer.).

58. 240 F.3d 389 (4th Cir. 2001), *aff'g* 113 T.C. 152 (1999).

had collateralized his $1.5 million note and 16.7 adjoining acres. The husband retained an option to repurchase the land for $2.2 million. The husband assigned the option to a third party who exercised the option and bought the land from the wife for $2.2 million.

The wife reported no capital gain from the sale of the property, nor the $300,606 portion of the price that went directly to pay her legal fees. The husband also reported no gain from his transfer of property. The IRS asserted deficiencies against both the husband and the wife.

The Tax Court held that the 1992 property transfer was incident to the divorce and concluded that the husband realized no gain through the transfer of the property to his former wife. The Court held that the wife took the property with carryover basis and should have recognized gain on the subsequent sale of the property, including the portion of the proceeds which was paid directly to her attorney.

The wife had argued that the 1992 agreement did not affect the division of marital property because she was a judgment creditor. The Fourth Circuit held that the only status relevant for I.R.C. § 1041 purposes is "spouse" or "former spouse." I.R.C. § 1041 looks to the status of the parties, and the character of and reason for the transfer, and not the status of the transferee as a creditor, lienholder, devisee, trust beneficiary, or otherwise. Thus, an order from a divorce Court that specifically modifies an original divorce or separation agreement is considered related to the cessation of the marriage, even if the order of modification occurs years after the divorce.

In *Belot v. Commissioner*, the husband and wife owned three dance studios. In January 2007, the family Court entered a dual judgment of divorce. In April 2008, the parties entered into a settlement agreement pursuant to which the wife agreed to purchase all of the husband's interests in the three dance studios. The husband reported the sales under Section 1041. The Service, however, contended that the transfer was not protected by Section 1041 because the transfer did not relate to the divorce instrument as required by the first three sentences of Temp. Prop. Treas. Reg. § 1.1041-1T(b)(A-7). The Service's argument was that this was a separate transaction governed by the 2008 agreement and therefore was not part of any divorce or separation instrument.

The Court referred to the regulation that any transfer not pursuant to a divorce or separation is presumed not related to the cessation of the marriage, but that the presumption could be rebutted by showing that the transfer was made to affect the division of property owned by the former spouses at the time of cessation of the marriage. Relying on the regulation the Court disagreed with the Service and held that the taxpayer rebutted the presumption pursuant to the fourth sentence of the regulation that the "transfer" was made to affect the division of property owned by the former spouses at the time of the cessation of the marriage.

In *Belot*, as in *Young*, a second settlement agreement was negotiated by the parties, the terms of which were different from those contained in their first settlement agreement. The Court, in both cases, found that the transfers in both cases were made to "effect the division of property owned by the former spouses at the time of the cessation of the marriage" and were "related to the cessation of the marriage" as required by Section 1041.

In *Walker v. Commissioner*,[59] the issue before the Court was whether the wife was entitled to protection under I.R.C. § 1041 from the sale of property she received from her husband as part of a marital settlement agreement. The husband and wife jointly owned a 50 percent interest in real property. The other 50 percent interest had been conveyed by them to a trust for the benefit of their children and grandchildren. Pursuant to the marital settlement agreement, they severed their joint ownership interest in the property and conveyed a separate 25 percent to each of them. Thereafter, the husband and wife conveyed to the wife one half of their previously jointly owned 50 percent interest in the property, so that the wife owned an undivided 50 percent interest in the property and the trust owned the other 50 percent undivided interest in the property. Shortly after the deed that conveyed the husband's interest in the property to the wife was recorded, the wife and the trust conveyed the property to a thirdparty purchaser. The closing statement was signed by the wife and the trust as sellers of 50 percent interests in the property.

The wife did not report the gain on the sale to the third-party purchaser of the 25 percent interest in the property that had been transferred to her from her husband. She contended that under I.R.C. § 1041, she was liable for tax on only the 25 percent of the gain that resulted from the sale of the property that she had previously owned and not the property that she had acquired from her husband. The wife argued that the quit claim deed that she received from her husband constituted a written request from him that she sell his 25 percent interest in the property to a disinterested third party; therefore, she contended that the sale of the property to a third-party purchaser took place "on behalf of" her husband pursuant to Temp. Prop. Treas. Reg. § 1.10411T(c)(A9). Accordingly, she concluded that she should receive nonrecognition treatment as to the 25 percent interest in the property that she sold on behalf of her husband.

The Court divided the transaction into two parts. The first transaction involved the husband's transfer of his 25 percent interest in the property to the wife in consideration for a settlement agreement. The second transaction involved the wife's sale of her undivided 50 percent interest in the property to an unrelated third party. The Court held that the husband's transfer of his 25 percent interest in the property to his wife took place "incident to their

59. T.C. Memo. 2003-335.

divorce" because it occurred within one year after the date on which the marriage ceased. The Court then held that the wife's sale of her undivided 50 percent interest in the property was not a transaction that fell within the meaning of I.R.C. § 1041(a) because it was not a transfer "to or on behalf of" her spouse or former spouse incident to a divorce. The Court reasoned that the husband's transfer of his 25 percent interest in the property to the wife satisfied his specific legal obligation that he owed to the wife. The wife's subsequent sale of her interest in the property, however, did not satisfy any other legal obligation or liability that the husband owed to her or anyone else. Thus, the wife did not make the sale "in the interest of" or "as a representative of" the husband. Therefore, the wife's sale of her interest in the property was not made "on behalf" the husband. Accordingly, the Court held that Temp. Prop. Treas. Reg. § 1.10411T(c)(A9) did not apply to this case.

(ii) Transfers More than Six Years

Any transfer not pursuant to a divorce or separation instrument and any transfer occurring more than six years after the cessation of the marriage is presumed to be not related to cessation of the marriage. This presumption may be rebutted only by showing that the transfer was made to effect the division of property owned by the former spouses at the time of the cessation of the marriage. For example, the presumption may be rebutted by showing that (i) the transfer was not made within the one-year and six-year periods described earlier because of factors that hampered an earlier transfer of property, such as legal or business impediments to transfer or disputes concerning the value of the property owned at the time of the cessation of the marriage, and (ii) the transfer is effected promptly after the impediment to transfer is removed.[60]

A series of private letter rulings by the IRS offers guidance on whether transfers made more than six years after cessation of the marriage is deemed related to the cessation of the marriage and hence falls within the ambit of Section 1041. In PLR 200233022, the parties executed a marital settlement prior to 1984 that was incorporated into their decree of divorce, which was also before 1984. After 1984 the parties entered into a second agreement that was executed after 1984. Because the second agreement was entered into after 1984, the Service held that Section 1041 would apply to the transfer of property. Under the second agreement, any transfers of property between the spouses would occur more than six years from the date of cessation of the marriage. The reason for the second agreement was to prevent or resolve differences that may arise between one spouse and the heirs or representatives of the other spouse's estate. According to the Service, the differences were not the product of disputes between the former spouses concerning the division of marital property

60. Temp. Prop. Treas. Reg. 1.1041-1T(b) (A-7).

owned by them at the time of the divorce. Nor was there any indication of any legal or business implements to an earlier transfer of property or to the earlier resolution of the areas of concern. The Service looked to Temp. Prop. Treas. Reg. § 1.1041-1T(A-7), which recognizes that a divorce or separation instrument includes a modification or amendment to the decree. Consequently, any order from the divorce Court that specifically modifies an original divorce or separation instrument must be considered related to the cessation of the marriage, even if such order occurs many years after the divorce. Accordingly, the Service concluded that transfers that occurred more than six years after the cessation of the marriage were related to the cessation of the marriage within the meaning of Section 10471(c)(2) and Temp. Prop. Treas. Reg. § 1.1041-1T(A-7).

In Priv. Ltr. Rul. 20022102, the IRS ruled that a transfer of stock in a closely held company was related to the cessation of the marriage even though it occurred more than six years after the cessation of the marriage. The IRS's reasoning was twofold. First, the stock transfer from the husband to the wife was being made to effect the division of marital property owned by them at the time of the divorce, and a court order at the time of the divorce allocated a percentage of the shares to the wife. Second, the parties had compelling business reasons to delay the transfer for more than six years from the cessation of the marriage, such as maintaining investor confidence in the company, enhancing the marketability of the stock, and facilitating future growth.[61]

In PLR 9235026, the Service held that a delay in transfer of property caused by a dispute between the parties concerning the purchase price and payment terms constituted a rebuttable presumption that the transfer occurring more than six years after the cessation of the marriage was related to the cessation of the marriage. In the ruling the wife transferred her interest in a business and in real property held by the business pursuant to a marital settlement agreement, which was ultimately approved by the Court granting the divorce. The purchase price for the business interest and the real property was payable in 120 equal consecutive monthly installments of principal and interest. The Service ruled that the transfer was related to the cessation of the marriage even though the transfer occurred more than six years after the date on which the marriage

61. *See also* Priv. Ltr. Rul. 9644053 (To equalize the distribution of assets without selling stock in their closely held corporation, the property settlement agreement between the husband and the wife contained an annuity agreement pursuant to which annuity payments were to be paid to one spouse during that spouse's lifetime. Since the annual payments could be made for the remainder of the payee spouse's life, the Service said it was possible that of the payments could be made more than six years after cessation of the marriage. The Service accepted the taxpayer's representation that there were "compelling business reasons" why the annuity would be paid over the lifetime of the payee spouse. Thus, because said business reasons existed to explain why the payments would be spread over the payee's lifetime, the payments were deemed related to the cessation of the marriage even though such payments would occur more than six years after the cessation of the marriage.).

ceased. The Service's reasoning was threefold. First, the transfer of the business and real property was made to effect the division of property owned at the time of the cessation of the marriage. Second, the reason the transfer was not effected within the six-year period was due to a dispute concerning the purchase price and payment terms that resulted in litigation that was not settled until more than six years after the date on which the marriage ceased. Finally, the transfer of the business and the real property from the wife to the husband was completed immediately after the dispute was resolved.

On the other hand, in PLR 9306015, the Service ruled that the transfer by a former spouse of his one-half interest in the marital home more than six years after the date on which the marriage ceased was not covered by Section 1041. In this PLR, the judgment of divorce permitted the taxpayer to remain in the marital home until the youngest child finished high school or reached the age of 18, or until the taxpayer remarried, cohabitated, or no longer maintained the home as her principal residence. The taxpayer could sell the house sooner if she chose. When the house was sold, the husband and wife were to split the net proceeds equally. The judgment of divorce did not require the taxpayer to transfer her interest in the house to her husband or preclude her from doing so. Pursuant to a consent order amending the original divorce instrument more than eight years after the divorce became final, the taxpayer transferred her interest in the house to her former spouse. The Service's reasoning for failing to hold that Section 1041 applies was twofold. First, the divorce instrument did not provide that the transfer of the taxpayer's interest in the house would be made to her former spouse. Rather, the Service determined that the original divorce instrument clearly contemplated that the house would be sold to a third party. It was not until the consent order amending the divorce decree more than eight years after the divorce that there was any contemplation of a sale between spouses. Second, there was no legal impediment to an earlier transfer of the taxpayer's interest in the house by the taxpayer to her former spouse. Thus, the Service concluded that the sale of the taxpayer's interest in the house to his former spouse was not a transfer made to effect a division of marital property, but an arm's length transaction between two parties who happen to be former spouses.

In Priv. Ltr. Rul. 200442003 the IRS held that the payment of a lump sum to the wife in exchange for her community interest in a nonqualified deferred compensation plan payable to the husband by his company constituted a nontaxable transfer between former spouses that was related to the cessation of their marriage under I.R.C. § 1041. During the marriage, the husband was a participant in a deferred compensation plan under the company's Supplemental Executive Retirement Plan (SERP), a nonqualified employee benefit plan. The wife had a community property interest in the SERP. Under the marital settlement agreement the husband was to transfer to the wife all of her right, title, and interest in items of community party, including her community property interest in the SERP. The Court awarded the wife one-half of her community property interest in the husband's SERP. The order provided that the wife was to receive a pro rata portion of each payment, if any, as each payment is received. Several years after the court order, the husband reached the age of eligibility for retirement, but had not yet retired from the company. Therefore, no amounts were yet payable under the SERP. The wife wanted to commence receiving her share of the benefits under the SERP, but because the husband had not yet retired, no amounts were yet payable under the SERP. After a lengthy period, the Court approved a stipulation that provided that the husband would pay the wife a lump sum in full satisfaction of her claims with respect to the SERP. The final order provided that the parties intended that neither would have any gift or income tax consequences from the lump sum payment. As a result of the amended decree, the husband paid a lump sum into a trust fund held by his attorney. Funds were invested in tax exempt investments as agreed upon by the parties. There was to be no distribution from the trust unless a private letter ruling was received from the IRS.

The IRS held that the transfer by the husband to the wife (through the trust account) of a lump sum (including earnings held in the trust) and the transfer to the husband by the wife of her interest in the SERP constituted transfers between former spouses that were "incident to a divorce" within the meaning of I.R.C. § 1041(a) because they related to the cessation of their marriage. According to the IRS, any transfer of property under the final order regarding the SERP clearly occurred outside the six-year rule set forth in Temp. Prop. Treas. Reg. § 1.1041-IT(b)(A-7). Consequently, any order from the divorce that specifically modified an original divorce or separation instrument must be considered related to the cessation of the marriage, even if the order occurs after the divorce. In this case, the parties received an order amending their original divorce instrument to incorporate the terms and provisions of a Court approved stipulation and order with respect to the division of the SERP. Pursuant to Temp. Prop. Treas. Reg. § 1.1041-1T(b)(A-7), the IRS concluded that the transfers were related to the "cessation of the marriage" within the meaning of I.R.C. § 1041(c)(2) and are therefore considered "incident to the divorce." Thus, the transfers by the husband to the wife (through the husband's attorney's trust account) of a lump sum (including the earnings held in trust by the husband's attorney) and the wife's transfer to the husband of her interest in the SERP were pursuant to I.R.C. § 1041 and no gain or loss would be recognized by the husband or the wife.

In PLR 202137005 and PLR 202137006, the spouses entered into an agreement to effect a complete and total division of their property in anticipation of divorce. Pursuant to the agreement, the taxpayer paid the spouse annually with some payments extending beyond the six-year presumptive period. The

Service found that the parties had structured their agreement to extend the transfer beyond the six-year period for reasons the Service found reasonable in light of all the circumstances. Unfortunately, the ruling gives little guidance for grounds to rebut the presumption because it does not state the reasons the payments extended beyond the six-year period, or why the payments were reasonable. The result would seem to be based upon the notion that the payments beyond the six-year period were intended to effect a complete and total division of property between the taxpayer and the spouse.

(3) ITC Recapture

Investment tax credits will not be recaptured by the transferor, because the transfer is treated as a gift for purposes of Section 1041.[62] Rather, recapture will result to the transferee upon a subsequent disposition of the property by the transferee.[63]

(4) Depreciation Recapture

The transfer of the property will not trigger depreciation recapture to the transferor because Section 1041 treats the transfer as a gift, the carryover basis rules apply, and the depreciation recapture rules do not apply to gifts.[64] However, depreciation recapture will result to the transferee upon a subsequent disposition of the property by the transferee or a change in the use of the property prior to the expiration of the recapture period.

(5) Life Insurance

In addition, the cash value of life insurance policies received in a property settlement are excludable from the gross income of the transferee spouse (whereas under prior law they were not so excluded) and the transfer of an installment obligation is not deemed a disposition of the obligation (whereas under prior law such a transfer was deemed a disposition), unless transferred to a trust.[65]

(6) Transfer of IRA

I.R.C. § 1041 does not, however, apply to a voluntary transfer of an IRA to a spouse. Thus, the transfer of an IRA from one spouse to another is treated as a taxable distribution to the transferor spouse and is included in the gross income of the transferor spouse.[66] On the other hand, the transfer of an interest in an IRA to a former spouse pursuant to a decree of divorce or written instrument

62. I.R.C. § 47(e)(1).
63. I.R.C. § 47(e)(2).
64. I.R.C. §§ 1245 and 1250.
65. I.R.C. § 453B(g).
66. Priv. Ltr. Rul. 8820086.

incident to a decree is not taxable.[67] Thus, the transfer of an IRA between married spouses results in a taxable distribution to the transferor spouse, whereas the transfer of an IRA to a former spouse incident to a divorce is a nontaxable distribution to the transferor spouse.

c. Depreciated Property

(1) General Rule

If the property has depreciated in value so that its basis exceeds its fair market value, I.R.C. § 1041 precludes the transferor from recognizing a loss if the transfer is made to (or in trust for the benefit of): (i) a spouse or (ii) a former spouse if the transfer to the former spouse is incident to the divorce.[68] As noted earlier, a transfer of property is incident to the divorce if the transfer occurs within one year after the date on which the marriage ceases,[69] or is related to the cessation of the marriage.[70]

A transfer of property occurring not more than one year after the date on which the marriage ceases need not be related to the cessation of the marriage to qualify for I.R.C. § 1041 treatment.[71]

A transfer of property is treated as related to the cessation of the marriage if the transfer is pursuant to a divorce or separation instrument as defined in I.R.C. § 71(b)(2), and the transfer occurs not more than six years after the date on which the marriage ceases.[72] A transfer more than six years after the cessation of the marriage may be related to the cessation of the marriage depending upon the facts and circumstances of the case.[73] A divorce or separation instrument includes a modification or amendment to such decree or instrument.[74]

Any transfer not pursuant to a divorce or separation instrument and any transfer occurring more than six years after the cessation of the marriage is presumed to be not related to cessation of the marriage. This presumption may be rebutted only by showing that the transfer was made to effect the division of property owned by the former spouses at the time of the cessation of the marriage. For example, the presumption may be rebutted by showing that (i) the transfer was not made within the one-year and six-year periods just described because of factors that hampered an earlier transfer of property, such as legal or business impediments to transfer or disputes concerning the value of the

---

67. I.R.C. § 408(d)(6).
68. I.R.C. § 1041(a).
69. I.R.C. § 1041(c)(1).
70. I.R.C. § 1041(c)(2); Temp. Prop. Treas. Reg. § 1.1041-1T(b)(A-6).
71. Temp. Prop. Treas. Reg. § 1.10411T(b)(A6). See discussion at Chapter 6, C.4.b.(2)(a).
72. Temp. Prop. Treas. Reg. § 1.1041-1T(b)(A-7).
73. *Id.*
74. Temp. Prop. Treas. Reg. § 1.10411T(b)(A7).

property owned at the time of the cessation of the marriage, and (ii) the transfer is effected promptly after the impediment to transfer is removed.[75]

Annulments and cessations of marriages that are void ab initio due to violations of state law are divorces for purposes of I.R.C. § 1041.[76]

The former test, transfers within one year, establishes a conclusive presumption, whereas the latter test, transfers in relation to cessation of the marriage, is based upon facts and circumstances.

(2) Planning

Not only must the practitioner be aware of and concerned with Section 1041(a), which disallows a loss recognized on the transfer of property to a spouse, or a former spouse incident to a divorce, but also the practitioner must be aware of I.R.C. § 165(c) and I.R.C. § 267. Section 165(c) limits as a deduction any loss sustained by an individual, unless (i) the loss was incurred in a trade or business; (ii) the loss was incurred in a transaction entered into for profit, even if not connected with a trade or business; or (iii) the loss arose from a fire, storm, shipwreck, or other casualty, or from a theft.

Since it is doubtful that any transfer between spouses occurs from one of those purposes, Section 165(c) is another statutory provision that would disallow losses on transfers between spouses. But even if it could be established that the transfer occurred as a result of one of the foregoing three types of transactions, Section 1041 would still block the loss.

Section 267 would also stand in the way of a taxpayer attempting to recognize a loss on the transfer of property to his or her spouse. I.R.C. § 267 precludes recognition of loss on the sale or exchange of property if the transfer is made to the transferee while the parties are still married. However, I.R.C. § 267 is no longer relevant, since I.R.C. § 1041 prevents the recognition of loss on the transfer.

Thus, it would appear to be advisable not to transfer depreciated property between the spouses until the marriage is fully dissolved. For the transferor to recognize a loss on the sale or exchange of depreciated property during the marriage, it would appear to be advisable for the transferor to sell the depreciated property to a third party and to give the cash proceeds to his or her spouse. However, it is possible that loss realized on the sale of depreciated property to a third party may not be recognized if it is deemed to be "incident to the divorce."

For example, if *H* sells property to *W* with a fair market value of $75,000 and a basis of $100,000, I.R.C. § 1041 prohibits *H* from recognizing the loss of

75. Temp. Prop. Treas. Reg. § 1.10411T(b)(A7).
76. Temp. Prop. Treas. Reg. § 1.10411T(b)(A8).

$25,000. *W*'s basis in the property will be $100,000.[77] When *W* later sells the property for $75,000, *W* will be able to claim the loss of $25,000. The same result follows if *H* makes a gift of the property to *W*. If, however, *H* sells the property to a third party, *H* may claim the $25,000 loss. But if the sale is to a third party is deemed to be incident to a divorce (e.g., through application of the step transaction doctrine), the sale may be disallowed under Section 1041.

A gift of depreciated property to a spouse may produce a better tax result than a gift to a nonspouse. As noted earlier, a gift of depreciated property by *H* to *W* results in no loss recognized by *H*, but a loss recognized by *W* of $25,000 on a subsequent sale of the property for $75,000. If, on the other hand, *H* had gifted the property to his child, who subsequently sold it for $75,000, the child could not claim the loss. This is because the basis of the gifted property in the hands of the child is the lesser of its basis or fair market value on the date of the gift.[78] Thus, the basis of the property in the hands of the child would be $75,000 and, when the property is sold by the child for its fair market value of $75,000, no tax gain or loss is recognized by the child.

(3) S Corporation Loss Pass Through

Before the American Jobs Creation Act of 2004, a stockholder in an S corporation could not deduct any losses passed through to the stockholder by the S corporation in excess of the stockholder's basis in his stock and debt of the corporation.[79] Any such loss remained in the corporation and was carried forward by the corporation for use by the stockholder in a subsequent year. The loss, however, was personal to the stockholder and could not be transferred to another stockholder.[80] Thus, if the stockholder transferred his stock, the suspended loss was lost. The American Jobs Creation Act of 2004 added I.R.C. § 1366(d)(2)(B), effective for tax years beginning after December 31, 2004, which provides a limited exception to the general rule. I.R.C. § 1366(d)(2)(B) provides that where there is a transfer of stock between spouses or for former spouses incident to a divorce, pursuant to I.R.C. § 1041(a), any suspended loss may be transferred to the transferee spouse or former spouse who may use it to the extent of the transferee's basis in the stock or debt in the corporation. As noted earlier, the basis of the transferee in the stock of the corporation will be

77. I.R.C. § 1041(b)(2); I.R.C. § 1015(e). *See* Ingham v. United States, 167 F.3d 1240 (9th Cir. 1999) discussed in Chapter 6, C.4.f.

78. I.R.C. § 1015(a).

79. Disallowed and suspended losses which inured to the transferor when that transferor owned stock in an S corporation cannot be carried over to and deducted by the transferee spouse if the transferee spouse receives the stock incident to a divorce. Priv. Ltr. Rul. 9552001.

80. I.R.C. § 1366(d)(2)(A).

the same as the basis of the stock in the hands of the transferor (i.e., carryover basis).[81]

d. Imputed Interest

The imputed interest rules of I.R.C. § 483 are not applicable to property settlements incident to a divorce.[82] Similarly, the imputed interest rules of I.R.C. § 7872 are not applicable.[83] Thus, unless interest on the unpaid balance of a property settlement is specifically stated, no deduction is allowed for that portion of each payment that represents imputed interest under I.R.C. § 483.

Interest payable on a property settlement payable on the installment method is includible in the gross income of the transferor and is not excludable under I.R.C. § 1041, because interest and tax-free gain on principal are "two distinct items that give rise to separate Federal income tax consequences."[84]

On the deductible side of the coin, I.R.C. § 1041 does not require the husband's indebtedness to his former wife to be characterized as personal interest under I.R.C. § 163(h)(1). Thus, such interest may be deductible if it qualifies as investment interest, passive activity interest, or qualified residence interest.[85]

---

81. I.R.C. § 1041(b)(2); I.R.C. § 1015. *See* Chapter 6, B.6.c.

82. McCormick v. Comm'r, T.C. Memo. 1987-418; Gammill v. Comm'r, 73 T.C. 921 (1980), *aff'd*, 710 F.2d 607 (10th Cir. 1982). *See also* Fox v. United States, 510 F.2d 1330 (3d Cir. Pa. 1975) and Rev. Rul. 76146, 1976-1 C.B. 144. In each of those cases the taxpayer attempted to deduct, as imputed interest under I.R.C. § 483, portions of installment payments to a former spouse that were made pursuant to a divorce settlement that did not provide for the payment of interest. In each of those cases it was held that § 483 did not apply to property settlements made incident to a divorce, and the taxpayers were not entitled to an interest deduction.

83. *But see* Craven v. United States, 70 F. Supp. 2d 1323 (D.C. Ga, 1999), *aff'd*, 215 F.3d 1201 (11th Cir. 2000), discussed at Chapter 6, C.4.e(2)(b)(v).

84. Gibbs v. Comm'r, T.C. Memo. 1997-196 (1997) (Transferee pays transferor $122,500 to equalize property division over 10 years with interest at 9 percent per annum. Held: interest is includible in income pursuant to I.R.C. § 61 and is not excludable under I.R.C. § 1041. In Gibbs, each payment received by the payee spouse under the divorce decree consisted partially of principal and partially of income. The Court held that the principal and interest portions of the installment payments received were "two distinct items that give rise to separate Federal income tax consequences." The Court held that the principal portion was subject to § 1041, but the interest portion was not.) *See also* Yankwich v. Comm'r, T.C. Memo. 2002-37 (The principal portion of the monthly payments allocated to principal was not taxable under § 1041; the portion of the monthly payments allocated to interest were taxable to taxpayer and were not protected by § 1041.).

85. Seymour v. Comm'r, 109 T.C. 279 (1997) (Husband agreed to pay $625,000 over ten years with interest at 10 percent per annum in exchange for her interest in home, stocks and miscellaneous property. Note was secured by the home. Held: Interest payments are not part of property settlement payment and therefore are not deductible under § 1041, but are deductible, if at all, under interest deduction rules of § 163(h)(2)(A)-(E). According to the Court, § 1041 does not require indebtedness to a former spouse to be characterized as personal interest for purposes of § 163(h)(1).) *See also* Armacost v. Comm'r, T.C. Memo. 1998-150 (1998) (interest on note from husband to ex-wife for her interest in property transferred to the husband under their separation agreement was deductible as investment interest to the extent the underlying indebtedness

e. Third-Party Transfers

(1) Tests

Transfers of property to third parties on behalf of a spouse or former spouse qualify as nontaxable transfers under I.R.C. § 1041 in the following three situations. The first situation is where the transfer to the third party is required by a divorce or separation instrument. The second situation is where the transfer to the third party is pursuant to the written request of the other spouse (or former spouse). The third situation is where the transferor receives from the other spouse (or former spouse) a written consent or ratification of the transfer to the third party. Such consent or ratification must state that the parties intend the transfer to the third party to be treated as a transfer to the nontransferring spouse (or former spouse) subject to the rules of I.R.C. § 1041 and must be received by the transferor prior to the date of filing of the transferor's first tax return for the taxable year in which the transfer was made.[86]

In the three situations just described, the transfer of property will be treated as made directly to the nontransferring spouse (or former spouse), and the nontransferring spouse will be treated as immediately transferring the property to the third party. The deemed transfer from the nontransferring spouse (or former spouse) to the third party is not a transaction that qualifies for nonrecognition of gain under I.R.C. § 1041.[87]

(2) Stock Redemptions

As discussed herein, stock redemptions in a divorce setting have been a constant thorn in the side of the IRS. This area first discusses the problem involved, then discusses the cases in the area and offers solutions, and finally concludes with a discussion of Temp. Prop. Treas. Reg. § 1.1041-2 issued January 10, 2003 (T.D. 9035), which is the IRS's attempt to resolve the problem from their viewpoint and to prevent the IRS from being whipsawed, as is evident in the discussion of the cases that follow.

(a) The Problem

Many domestic relations cases involve closely held businesses in which the husband and wife own the stock (or alternatively, one spouse owns all of the stock but the other spouse has an interest in the stock by reason of its characterization as marital property). Economic and business realities will often lead

---

was allocable to property that fits within I.R.C. § 163(h) such as interest allocable to investment property.).

86. Temp. Prop. Treas. Reg. § 1.10411T(c)(A9).

87. Temp. Prop. Treas. Reg. § 1.10411T(c)(A9); *see* Walker v. Comm'r, T.C. Memo. 2003-335 discussed at Chapter 6, C.4.b(2)(a)(i).

the spouses and their advisors to conclude that one spouse's interest in the business should be transferred to the other as part of the property settlement.

A problem that sometimes arises is that the remaining spouse may have insufficient other property to transfer to the departing spouse in exchange for the departing spouse's interest in the business. The only source of funds available to compensate the departing spouse for his or her interest in the business is the business itself. The issue for I.R.C. § 1041 purposes is whether a stock redemption in a divorce setting can be structured under I.R.C. § 1041 to be taxfree to both the remaining spouse and the departing spouse.

In the cases to be explored, the husband and wife owned stock in a closely held C corporation. Generally, the wife has her shares of stock in the corporation redeemed for cash and/or an installment payment note. The transaction is often viewed for Federal income tax purposes as occurring in one of two ways: in the first situation, the wife's stock is completely redeemed under I.R.C. § 302(b)(3) as a complete termination of a stockholder's interest in the corporation. The waiver of the stock attribution rules of I.R.C. § 318 pursuant to I.R.C. § 302(c) may still have to be applied, and the I.R.C. § 302(c)(iii) "triple iii agreement" may still have to be filed with the tax return. Under this transaction, the departing spouse receives long-term capital gain (assuming the appropriate holding period), and the remaining spouse has no Federal income tax consequences.

In the second situation, the departing spouse's stock is also completely redeemed under I.R.C. § 302(b)(3) as a complete termination of interest. And, the departing spouse receives payment from the corporation. Unlike the first situation, the wife argues that (i) she transferred her stock in the corporation to her husband, (ii) who then sold those shares to the corporation, and (iii) the husband paid the departing spouse for her shares of stock with funds he received from the corporation, (iv) so that the wife argues that the sale was to her husband and thus she recognizes no gain or loss pursuant to I.R.C. § 1041. As a result of the characterization, the IRS argues that the husband has dividend income under I.R.C. § 301 to the extent of the corporation's earnings and profits.

The following first discusses the cases in this area, then discusses private letter rulings issued in this area, and finally discusses Treas. Prop. Treas. Reg. § 1.1041-2, which applies specifically to redemption of stock in a divorce setting, notwithstanding Temp. Prop. Treas. Reg. § 1.104-1T(c) (Q&A-9). As discussed following, Treas. Reg. § 1.1041-2 supersedes Temp. Prop. Treas. Reg. § 1.104-1T(c) (Q&A-9) with respect to stock redemptions during a marriage or incident to a divorce. Temp. Prop. Treas. Reg. § 1.104-iT(c) (Q&A-9) remains applicable to transfers between spouses during a marriage or incident to a divorce except in stock redemption transactions where Treas. Reg. § 1.1041-2 controls.

(b) The Cases

Six cases have dealt with the issue of whether a redemption was a transfer on behalf of a spouse. In the first two cases, involving the Arnes family, the IRS was whipsawed, and collected from neither the husband nor the wife. The cases were decided under regulations in effect pre-Temp. Prop. Treas. Reg. § 1.1041-2. These cases are inserted for historical reference.

(i) *Arnes v. United States*

In *Arnes v. United States*,[88] the Ninth Circuit Court of Appeals had the opportunity to discuss the Federal income tax consequences to the wife of the following transaction: the husband and wife jointly owned stock in a corporation that operated a McDonald's franchise. The McDonald's franchise agreement required that the corporate stock be owned 100 percent by the owner-operator. The parties agreed that the wife's stock would be transferred to the husband. Because the corporation was the only source of cash to acquire the stock, a corporate redemption was structured and the wife's stock was redeemed as part of the property settlement. Pursuant to their divorce decree, the corporation redeemed all the wife's stock for $450,000. Mrs. Arnes reported the redemption of her stock as a taxable transaction to her and paid capital gains tax on the sale. However, she subsequently determined that the redemption was nontaxable under I.R.C. § 1041 and filed a refund claim.

Mrs. Arnes argued that the substance of the transaction was a direct transfer of her interest in the corporation to her husband. She cited Temp. Prop. Treas. Reg. § 1.10411T(c)(A9), contending that this was a transfer of property to a third person (i.e., the corporation) on behalf of her spouse or former spouse.

The IRS argued that I.R.C. § 1041 did not apply because it was not a transfer directly to one's spouse or a former spouse, nor was it a transfer made in trust for that person. Thus, the IRS claimed that the $450,000 was taxable to the wife.

The Ninth Circuit disagreed, reasoning that although the wife transferred her stock directly to the corporation, the transfer was on behalf of her husband pursuant to Temp. Prop. Treas. Reg. § 1.10411T(c)(A9). The Court found that the husband, not the corporation, was obligated to purchase the wife's stock. The Court also found that the redemption benefited the husband because he guaranteed the corporation's payments and the transfer limited her future community property claims against him. Thus, the Court concluded that the stock sale was on behalf of the husband and held in wife's favor. Thus, the IRS was ordered to issue a refund to the wife.

---

88. 981 F.2d 456 (9th Cir. 1992). *Compare*, Praegitzer v. Comm'r, T.C. Memo. 1997-79 (1997), where receipt of assets was not an integral or necessary step in the marital property settlement; therefore, distribution of cash and cancellation of indebtedness were not protected from taxation by I.R.C. § 1041.

(ii) *Arnes v. Commissioner*

In *Arnes v. Commissioner*,[89] the Tax Court had the opportunity to discuss the husband's tax consequences. The Court found that as a result of a separation agreement incorporated into the decree, the parties would cause the corporation to redeem the wife's stock and the corporation's obligation would be guaranteed by the husband.

The issue before the Court was whether the corporation's redemption of the wife's stock was a constructive dividend to the husband. This in turn depended upon whether, as the IRS argued, the corporation redeemed the wife's stock, which the husband was obligated to buy, in effect having the corporation satisfy the husband's obligation to purchase the wife's stock.

Since the Court found that the husband was a guarantor, not an obligor (although the Ninth Circuit found that the husband was obligated), it concluded that the corporation was not satisfying an obligation of the husband and, therefore, the corporation's payments to the wife were not constructive dividends. The Tax Court determined the primary-unconditional obligation test is the one to apply to determine whether, under Temp. Prop. Treas. Reg. § 1.1041-1T(c)(A-9), a transfer by a redeeming stockholder of her share of stock in a corporation was "on behalf of" the nontransferring stockholder spouse who remains as a stockholder in the corporation. Clearly, the Tax Court's findings, and not the Ninth Circuit's, are correct, for the separation agreement provides, in relevant part, that "the parties hereto shall cause the corporation owned by the parties . . . to redeem from wife 2,500 shares of stock . . . that she owns . . . that the obligations of the corporation . . . shall be . . . personally guaranteed by husband. . . ." In this case, the IRS could not collect the tax from the husband. Moreover, as a result of the inconsistent decisions in the two *Arnes* cases, the IRS did not collect tax from either the husband or the wife.

(iii) *Hayes v. Commissioner*

In *Hayes v. Commissioner*,[90] the husband and wife entered into a separation agreement that provided that the husband would purchase the wife's stock in a corporation that operated a McDonald's franchise in which they were the sole stockholders. The agreement was incorporated into the decree. After the agreement was executed, however, Mr. Hayes determined that he did not have the money to satisfy the payment obligation and that if he redeemed his stock to raise the cash, he would incur a substantial income tax liability. His attorney proposed that the corporation redeem the wife's stock instead, since the tax on her redemption would be less than the tax on his dividend distribution. On that same day, June 4, 1986, the corporation and the wife entered into an agreement pursuant to which the corporation agreed to redeem the wife's shares of

89. .102 T.C. 522 (1994).
90. .101 T.C. 593 (1993).

stock. The corporation made one payment on December 31, 1986, and a final payment on March 31, 1987. On March 3, 1987, the Court entered an order nunc pro tunc to correct the original decree by changing the terms requiring the husband to purchase the wife's stock to provide that the corporation agreed to purchase the wife's stock. Neither Mr. nor Mrs. Hayes reported any income from the redemption on their Federal income tax returns.

The Tax Court refused to give the nunc pro tunc order validity for tax purposes. The Court's reasoning was that the nunc pro tunc order was contrary to Ohio law because it changed retroactively the rights of the parties to the action, rather than simply correcting an error in the original judgment. The Tax Court went on to state that even if the nunc pro tunc order had been valid, Mr. Hayes would still have had a constructive dividend. The Tax Court further held that Mr. Hayes received a constructive dividend as a result of the redemption of Mrs. Hayes' stock because that redemption satisfied a primary and unconditional obligation to purchase that stock which was imposed on him by the original judgment.[91] Thus, the redemption of the wife's stock constituted a constructive dividend to the husband. As a result of its holding, the issue of whether the wife's redemption was shielded by I.R.C. § 1041 and Temp. Prop. Treas. Reg. § 1.10411T(c)(A9) was rendered moot.

(iv) *Blatt v. Commissioner*

In *Blatt v. Commissioner*,[92] stock in a corporation was owned equally by the husband and wife. The corporation redeemed all of the wife's stock pursuant to a decree of divorce that ordered the husband and wife to cause the corporation to redeem all of the wife's stock in the corporation for $45,384. The issue before the Court was whether the payment made by the corporation to the wife is taxable to her in the year of redemption, or whether it is not taxable to her under Section 1041.

The Court held that the redemption was not a transfer to a third party pursuant to Temp. Prop. Treas. Reg. § 1.10411T(c)(A9) and, therefore, the redemption proceeds were taxable to the wife in the year of the redemption. The Court reasoned that the redemption was a transaction between the wife and the corporation and was not "on behalf of" her husband, which the Court found to mean "in the interest of" or "as a representative of." The Court stated that a transfer that satisfies an obligation or liability of someone is a transfer "on behalf of" that person, which the Court found was not present in the instant case. The Court also refused to follow the Ninth Circuit's decision in *Arnes*, on the grounds that its facts were "easily distinguishable" from the instant case.

Judge Parr, in her dissent, reasoned that the redemption satisfied an obligation of the husband because he had an obligation to obey the Court order

91. *Id.*
92. 102 T.C. 77 (1994).

to cause the wife's stock to be redeemed. Thus, the dissent concludes that the transaction was part of a property settlement between spouses, which is entitled to nonrecognition treatment under I.R.C. § 1041.

Compare *Praegitzer v. Commissioner*,[93] where receipt of assets was not an integral or necessary step recorded in the marital property settlement; therefore, distribution of cash and cancellation of indebtedness were not protected from taxation by I.R.C. § 1041. In *Praegitzer*, husband and wife owned stock in Corporation *A*. Incident to their divorce, Corporation *A* spun off one of its businesses to the husband, which he then wholly owned. The spin-off corporation then paid distributed cash to the husband and forgave a debt owed to it by the husband. The IRS conceded that the reorganization was tax-free under I.R.C. §§ 355 and 368(a)(1)(D), but argued that the cash distribution and cancellation of indebtedness constituted taxable income to the husband. The taxpayer argued that the cash and cancelled debt owed to the corporation were incident to his divorce and thus tax free under I.R.C. § 1041. The taxpayer relied on *Arnes, supra*, but the Court held the facts were distinguishable from *Arnes*. The Court ruled that the cash distribution and forgiveness of indebtedness were not protected by I.R.C. § 1041, because they were done at his behest as the sole stockholder of the corporation. The marital agreement did not obligate him to do it. Rather, the cash distribution and cancellation of indebtedness were dividends to the husband taxpayer under I.R.C. §§ 301, 312, and 316.

(v) *Craven v. United States*

Craven v. United States[94] is another case involving the redemption of shares of stock in a corporation in connection with a divorce. The husband owned 51 percent and the wife owned 47 percent of the issued and outstanding shares of stock in a corporation. The parties separated and entered into a Settlement Agreement in which the wife agreed to transfer all of her shares of stock in the corporation to the corporation through redemption. The corporation agreed to pay the wife $4.8 million for her 47 percent stockhold interest in the corporation. The parties then entered into a Stock Redemption Agreement, which was incorporated into the Settlement Agreement, pursuant to which the corporation would issue a promissory note for $4.8 million evidencing that it was required to make monthly payments of $15,000 per month for ten years, a lump sum of $1 million in one year, a lump sum of $1 million in five years, and a final lump sum of $1 million in ten years. The payments were without stated interest, though the corporation was to prepare and deliver to the wife a Form 1099-INT to report to the wife the appropriate interest portion of the payments made under the promissory note. The husband personally guaranteed the promissory note by a Contract of Guaranty. In the Guaranty, the husband

93. T.C. Memo. 1997-79 (1997).

94. 70 F. Supp. 2d 1323, (N.D. Ga. 1999), *aff'd*, 215 F.3d 1201 (11th Cir. 2000).

acknowledged that the terms of the note were of "direct interest, benefit, and advantage" to him as the sole remaining stockholder of the corporation. The divorce record reflected that any payments not made by the corporation by the tenth of the month would be made by the husband, who guaranteed all payments. The corporation sent the wife Form 1099-INT reflecting imputed interest income on the note for the years in issue.

There were two issues before the Court. First, whether the stock redemption was exempt from Federal income taxation under I.R.C. § 1041 and, second, whether interest is imputed on the note issued to the wife by the corporation under I.R.C. § 1274. The wife, relying on *Arnes, supra,* contended that since the redemption was pursuant to her divorce, the transfer qualified for nonrecognition treatment. Her position was that she was required to redeem her stock because Georgia law obligates that the marital assets be equally divided between her husband and her, and that the redemption was "on behalf of her husband" since he was a guarantor of the corporation's note which, under Georgia law, made him a primary obligor of the note. The IRS, relying on *Blatt, supra,* argued that the wife's redemption was not "on behalf of" her former husband pursuant to Temp. Prop. Treas. Reg. § 1.1041-IT (A-9) and was outside the scope of I.R.C. § 1041.

The Court held that the wife was entitled to nonrecognition treatment under I.R.C. § 1041 for any proceeds she received as a result of the redemption of her stock in the corporation. The Court held that the instant case was more similar to *Arnes* than *Blatt* because the redemption of the wife's stock satisfied the husband's obligation under Georgia law to divide the marital property equitably. The Court noted that the husband personally guaranteed the note and that under Georgia law the husband was jointly and severally liable with the corporation for the payment of the promissory note. Thus, said the Court, like the settlement agreement in *Arnes*, the instant settlement agreement allowed for the redemption of the wife's stock to satisfy the husband's marital obligations.

The IRS then argued that, since under the Court's holding the husband cannot be considered to have received a constructive dividend, the stock redemption did not occur on his behalf. Under the argument, the IRS attempted to get the Court to hold that the husband received a constructive dividend as a result of the redemption. The Court refused to rule on this issue because the husband was not a party to the action. For whatever reason, the IRS had failed bring an action against the husband.

Finally, the Court held that the wife was taxable on the imputed interest.

On appeal, the Eleventh Circuit *affirmed* the district Court on the redemption issue (215 F.3d 1201, 2000), relying on *Read v. Commissioner*[95] (discussed in

95. 114 T.C. 14 (2000).

(vi) following), which was decided after the district Court's decision. It then reversed the district Court on the imputed interest issue. *Read* is discussed later. The Eleventh Circuit noted that a transfer of stock from the wife to the corporation is treated for purposes of Federal income taxation as a transfer from the wife to the husband to the corporation when the wife makes the transfer to the corporation "on behalf of" the husband. The Court said that three factors evidenced that the transfer was "on behalf of" the husband. First, the wife's stock was redeemed pursuant to the Marital Settlement Agreement. Second, the husband guaranteed the note. Third, in the guaranty the husband acknowledged that the terms of the promissory note were of "direct interest, benefit and advantage" to him. According to the Court, the first factor was conclusive of the matter, and the second and third factors were merely icing on the cake in order to qualify the transaction under I.R.C. § 1041. Finally, the Circuit Court reversed the District Court and held that I.R.C. § 1274 did not apply and that imputed interest is not taxed when the transferor receives nonrecognition treatment under I.R.C. § 1041.

(vi) *Read v. Commissioner*

Read v. Commissioner[96] is the most recent case in the area, and perhaps the most important. It contains a majority opinion, one concurring opinion, and four dissenting opinions. In *Read*, the Court, ruling in favor of the wife, rejected the primary unconditional obligation standard applied in redemption cases in a divorce setting, and applied the "on behalf of" standard set forth in Q&A-9 and as defined in *Blatt*.

According to the Court in its synopsis of the case, the Court held that the primary and unconditional obligation standard is not an appropriate standard to apply in order to determine whether *W*'s transfer of her X stock to X was transfer of property by *W* to a third party on behalf of *H* within the meaning of Q&A-9. The Court next held that the primary and unconditional obligation standard is not an appropriate standard to apply in any case involving a corporate redemption in a divorce setting in order to determine whether the transfer of property by the transferring spouse to a third party is on behalf of the nontransferring spouse within the meaning of Q&A-9. The Court further held that in applying the common, ordinary meaning of the phrase "on behalf of" in Q&A-9, *W*'s transfer of her X stock to X was a transfer of property by *W* to a third party on behalf of *H* within the meaning of that temporary proposed regulation. Finally, the Court held that pursuant to I.R.C. § 1041(a), no gain shall be recognized by *W* as a result of that transfer.

In *Read*, *H* and *W* were married. *H* owned 1,300 shares of voting stock and 13,000 shares of nonvoting stock of corporation MPP, and *W* owned 1,200

96. 114 T.C. 14 (2000).

shares of voting stock and 12,000 shares of nonvoting stock of MPP. Pursuant to a marital settlement agreement, *W* agreed to convey to *H* all her voting and nonvoting stock in MPP. *H*, or at his election, MPP or MPP's ESOP plan, agreed to purchase *W*'s shares at their appraised value of $838,724. The terms of payment were $200,000 in cash at closing and the balance of $638,724 to be evidenced by a promissory to be signed by the purchaser, but if the purchaser were MPP or its ESOP, *H* would guarantee the payment. Interest was fixed at 9 percent per annum. The balance was payable $50,000 at the end of 12 months, and $50,000 per year thereafter until the note was paid in full.

Pursuant to the decree of divorce, *H* elected to have the sale of *W*'s stock be redeemed by MPP instead of *H*, and that MPP make the down payment of $200,000 and issue the promissory note to *W* for the balance of $638,724 with interest at 9 percent per annum. As a result of the election, *W* sold all her shares of stock to MPP instead of to *H*. The board of directors of MPP then adopted a resolution approving the election by *H* in accordance with the terms just recited. Then, the corporation and *W* entered into a stock purchase agreement that the board of directors then adopted as a second resolution approving the redemption of *W*'s shares, the purchase price ($838,724), the payment terms, and the collateral security. Thereafter, pursuant to *H*'s election under the divorce decree, *W* transferred her voting and non-voting shares in MPP to MPP; MPP paid *W* $200,000; and MPP issued *W* a promissory note for the balance of $638,724. *H* then signed an individual guaranty in which he unconditionally guaranteed the payment of all sums under the promissory note, which, under Florida law, constituted an absolute guaranty. As a result, *H* was secondarily, but not primarily, liable on MPP's installment promissory note.

W did not report any income on the redemption of her stock by MPP, except for the interest payments under the promissory note. *H* did not report any income with respect to *W*'s transfer of MPP stock.

The IRS issued deficiencies against both the husband and the wife, thus making the IRS a stakeholder and letting *H* and *W* fight it out. The IRS determined that the principal payment under the promissory note made by MPP to *W* in the redemption of her MPP stock was reportable in income by *W* as long-term capital gain. The IRS also determined that the principal and interest payments made by MPP to *W* under the promissory note that MPP made to *W* were constrictive dividends to *H*.

W contended that her transfer of MPP stock to MPP was a transfer of property by her to a third party "on behalf of" *H* within the meaning of Temp. Prop. Treas. Reg. § 1.1041-IT(c) (Q&A-9). According to *W*, the transfer fits both the first and second situations of that regulation. Thus, according to her, she was entitled to nonrecognition treatment under I.R.C. § 1041.

H contended that the transfer of MPP stock was not a transfer of property to a third party "on behalf of" *H* within the meaning of the regulation just cited, and that the transfer did not fit within any of the three situations described in the regulation. Consequently, argued *H*, I.R.C. § 1041 does not provide protection to *W* and, therefore, the payments were not constructive dividends to *H*.

H, *W*, and MPP all relied on *Hayes, supra, Arnes, supra*, and *Blatt, supra*, as prescribing the tests to be met in order to determine whether *W*'s stock transfer constituted a transfer of property by *W* to MPP "on behalf of" *H*. According to them, those cases establish that the "on behalf of" test may be satisfied only if *H* has a primary and unconditional obligation to purchase *W*'s stock in MPP such that *H* received a constructive dividend (to the extent of MPP's earnings and profits) as a result of MPP's payment to *W*.

The Court rejected the taxpayers' argument that *Hayes*, *Arnes*, and *Blatt* require the application of the primary and unconditional obligation standard as to *H* in order to determine whether the "on behalf of" standard in Q&A-9 is met by *W*. The IRS pointed out, and the Court agreed, that the Court had not expressed an opinion on whether the "on behalf of" standard in Q&A-9 is the same as the primary and unconditional obligation standard in constructive dividend decisional law. The Court held that, under *Hayes* and *Arnes*, it only decided whether the redemption of *W*'s stock constituted a constructive dividend to *H* because *H* had a primary and unconditional obligation to buy *W*'s stock from her. In *Hayes*, the Court imposed the constructive dividend on *H* but did not impose a constructive dividend in *Arnes* because it held that Mr. Arnes did not have a primary and unconditional obligation to purchase Mrs. Arnes' stock on the ground that it had a primary and unconditional obligation to purchase *W*'s shares, which was satisfied by the corporation. It thus concluded that both cases were not decided under Q&A-9 and I.R.C. § 1041.

The Court then turned to the *Blatt* case, in which it determined whether a transfer of property by a transferring spouse to a third party was "on behalf of" the nontransferring spouse within the meaning of Q&A-9. The Court held that it "did not decide in *Blatt* that only if the primary and unconditional obligation standard is satisfied as to the nontransferring spouse (*H*) may transfer by a transferring spouse (*W*) to a corporation of the transferring spouse's stock in the corporation be considered to be a transfer of property by a spouse to a third party on behalf of the nontransferring spouse within the meaning of Q&A-9." The Court then referred to its illustration in *Blatt* of a transfer of property by a spouse to a third party that satisfies an obligation or a liability of the other spouse, which the Court indicated in *Blatt* was one type of transfer by a transferring spouse that constitutes a transfer of property to a third party "on behalf of" a nontransferring spouse within the meaning of Q&A-9 did not implicate the primary and unconditional objection standard. The Court stated that illustration was not intended to implicate the primary and unconditional obligation standard. The Court then noted that in *Blatt* it did not hold that satisfaction of the primary and unconditional obligation standard as to the nontransferring spouse was the only way in which the "on behalf of" standard in Q&A-9 could be met in the case involving a corporate redemption in a divorce setting. It is important to note that in *Read* the Court did not reverse its decision in *Blatt*. Thus, the Court rejected the taxpayer's reliance on *Hayes*, *Arnes*, and *Blatt* to support their view that, in the instant cases, the "on behalf of" standard in Q&A-9 is the same as the primary and unconditional obligation standard in constructive dividend decisional law.

The Court then held that the primary and unconditional obligation standard is not an appropriate standard to apply in order to determine whether the wife's transfer of her MPP stock to MPP was a transfer of property by the transferring spouse (*W*) to a third party (MPP) on behalf of the nontransferring spouse (*H*) within the meaning of Q&A-9. The Court further held that the "primary and unconditional obligation standard is not an appropriate standard to apply in any case involving a corporate redemption in a divorce setting in order to determine whether the transfer of property by the nontransferring spouse to a third party is 'on behalf of' the nontransferring spouse within the meaning of Q&A-9."

According to the Court, "the primary-and-unconditional-obligation standard does not require analysis of (or even address) the transfer that Q&A-9 requires be analyzed in order to determine whether that temporary regulation applies (provided that the other requirements of Q&A-9 and I.R.C. § 1041 are satisfied). The transfer that must be analyzed under constructive-dividend decisional law in order to determine whether the primary-and-unconditional-obligation standard is satisfied and whether a stockholder whose stock *is not being redeemed* received a constructive dividend is the transfer by the redeeming corporation of the redemption proceeds to the stockholder whose stock is being redeemed. In contrast, the transfer that must be analyzed under Q&A-9 in the present cases (and in any case involving a corporate redemption in a divorce setting) in order to determine whether the "on behalf of" standard in Q&A-9 is satisfied and whether the stockholder whose stock is being redeemed (here *W*, the transferring spouse) is not required to recognize gain or loss under I.R.C. § 1041 is the transfer by that transferring spouse of the stock being redeemed (property) to the redeeming corporation (here MPP, a third party). Only if that transfer is made on behalf of the spouse whose stock is now being redeemed (here *H*, the nontransferring spouse) does the transfer of property (here MPP stock) by the transferring spouse (here *W*) to a third party (here MPP) satisfy the "on behalf of" standard in Q&A-9." The Court then noted that "the judicially created primary and unconditional obligation standard is well established in the tax law. If, in issuing Q&A-9, the Treasury Department had intended that in the case of, and solely in the case of, a corporate redemption in a divorce setting the 'on behalf of' standard may be satisfied only by satisfaction of the primary and unconditional obligation standard, the Treasury Department would have expressly so indicated in Q&A-9. It did not."

Having rejected the taxpayers' argument that only if the primary and unconditional obligation standard is met as to *H* may the "on behalf of" standard in Q&A-9 be satisfied, the Court then raised the issue whether *W*'s transfer of her MPP stock to MPP was a transfer of property by the transferring spouse (*W*) to a third party (MPP) on behalf of the nontransferring spouse (*H*) within the meaning of Q&A-9. The Court decided that determination by applying the meaning of the phrase "on behalf of" in Q&A-9, which it cited with approval and on which it relied in *Blatt v. Commissioner*.[97]

The Court first turned to the issue of whether *W*'s transfer of her MPP stock to MPP satisfied a liability or an obligation of *H*, one of the ways in which it indicated in *Blatt* that a transfer of property would be considered a transfer of property by the transferring spouse to a third party on behalf of the nontransferring spouse within the meaning of Q&A-9. The Court found that it did not. Under the divorce judgment, *H*'s obligation to purchase *W*'s MPP stock for the consideration stated in that judgment was owed to *W*. *W*'s transfer of her MPP stock to MPP (i.e., the transferring spouse's transfer of property to a third party) did not satisfy that obligation of *H* to *W*.

The Court then determined whether under the common, ordinary meaning of the phrase "on behalf of," which it cited with approval and on which it relied in *Blatt*, *W*'s transfer of her MPP stock to MPP was a transfer of property by the transferring spouse to a third party on behalf of the nontransferring spouse within the meaning of Q&A-9. The Court had indicated in *Blatt* that the common, ordinary meaning of the phrase "on behalf of" in Q&A-9 is "in the interest of" or "as a representative of." Applying that meaning to the facts in the instant cases, the Court found that *W* was acting as *H*'s representative in transferring her MPP stock to MPP, and that *W* was acting in the interest of *H* in making that transfer to MPP in that she was following and implementing *H*'s direction as reflected in his election under the divorce judgment that she transfer her MPP stock to MPP. Absent *H*'s election, *W* was obligated under the divorce judgment to transfer that stock to *H*. The Court thus held that *W*'s transfer to MPP of her MPP stock was a transfer of property by *W* to a third party on behalf of *H* within the meaning of Q&A-9. The Court then considered "whether *W*'s February 5, 1986, transfer of MPP stock qualified as one of the three situations described in Q&A-9": The first situation in Q&A describes a transfer of property by the transferring spouse to a third party on behalf of the nontransferring spouse that is required by a divorce or separation instrument.

97. 102 T.C. at 82.

The court held that *W*'s transfer of her MPP stock to MPP was required by the divorce judgment and fit within the first situation described in Q&A-9. According to the Court, although that transfer was required by the divorce judgment only in the event that *H* elected that *W* transfer her MPP stock to MPP, instead of to *H*, once *H* made that election, which he did prior to *W*'s transfer of her MPP stock to MPP, that transfer was required by the divorce judgment. Thus, the Court held that Q&A-9 applies to *W*'s February 5, 1986, transfer of MPP stock and that, pursuant to I.R.C. § 1041(a), no gain was recognized by *W* as a result of that transfer "*H* and MPP indicated that if the Court were to find, as it just did, that I.R.C. § 1041 applied to *W*'s transfer of her MPP stock to MPP, the determinations in the respective notices of deficiency issued to *H* and to MPP relating to that transfer should be sustained. Consequently, those determinations have become moot, and the Court decided not to address them."

Judge Colvin, in a concurring opinion, concluded that *W* was deemed to have transferred her MPP stock to *H* who was deemed to have transferred it to MPP to be redeemed. Thus, it was assumed that MPP redeemed *H*'s stock and not *W*'s stock. Judge Colvin would, however, tax *H* as receiving a constructive dividend on the transfer of *W*'s stock to MPP under I.R.C. §§ 302(d), 301(a), and 316.

Judge Ruwe, in a dissenting opinion, concluded that the issue is whether MPP's redemption of "[*W*'s] stock satisfied a primary and unconditional obligation of *H*. If the answer is yes, Q&A-9 applies, [*W*] receives the benefit of I.R.C. § 1041, and *H* has a constructive dividend. If the answer is no, i.e., *H* had no primary and unconditional obligation to purchase *W*'s stock, then the Court should hold that Q&A-9 does not apply, the redemption of *W*'s stock did not result in a constructive dividend to *H*, and *W*'s transfer of stock to MPP should be treated as a redemption resulting in a taxable capital gain to *H*."

Judge Halpern in his dissent concludes that the issue is whether *H* had a primary and unconditional obligation to purchase *W*'s shares. Based on the facts, Judge Halpern concluded that since *H* had the right to assign his obligation to purchase *W*'s shares, *H*'s obligation to purchase *W*'s shares was not primary and unconditional. Since, according to Judge Halpern, *W* failed to prove that the transfer was to *H*, I.R.C. § 1041 was inapplicable, he would hold that *W* recognized gain on the transfer and that *H* had no item of gross income on account of the transfer.

Judge Beghe, in a dissenting opinion, took the position that the "on behalf of" standard of Q&A-9 should be equated with the primary and unconditional obligation standard of traditional redemption tax law. Judge Beghe then notes that "it has been difficult to reach consensus about how to write up this case, much less decide it, because one or another of four different approaches might be used to determine the relationship of the 'on behalf of' and 'primary and unconditional obligation' standards." He then summarized and commented on them as follows: His view was that the "primary and unconditional obligation standard of traditional redemption tax law and the "on behalf of" standard of Q&A-9 should govern the interpretation and application of the "on behalf of" standard. The correct application of this view in the case at hand would result in no taxable income to *H* because *H* never had the primary *and* unconditional obligation to purchase the stock; he was entitled under both the settlement agreement and the divorce decree to lay his purchase obligation off on MPP, which he did. . . . Furthermore, MPP became primarily and unconditionally obligated to purchase and pay for the stock, notwithstanding that *W* became entitled to *H*'s guaranty—his secondary obligation—and a pledge of the redeemed shares to secure the satisfaction of MPP's obligation."

Judges Laro and Marvel also dissented on the grounds that I.R.C. § 1041 does not apply to stock redemptions incident to a divorce. According to them, nowhere in Q&A-9, or in any of the other Q&A's, "do we read that a gain arising from a spouse's sale of assets to a third party qualifies for nonrecognition treatment under I.R.C. § 1041." Thus, they conclude that *W* should have recognized gain from the redemption of her stock. According to them, "Q&A-9 does not reach a transfer of property by a spouse to a third party where the transfer is, in substance and in form, a sale to the third party. Rather, Q&A-9 is limited to those situations in which a spouse transfers property to a third party in satisfaction of an obligation that is owed (or a gift that is made) by the nontransferring spouse to the third party. In the latter cases, Q&A-9 operates to tax the nontransferring spouse on the transfer to the third party, if and to the extent that the transfer is taxable, as if the nontransferring spouse had first received a gift of the property from the transferring spouse. Q&A-9 says nothing about affording similar treatment to any proceeds which are received by a transferring spouse from a third party pursuant to the property transfer. While it is true that Q&A-9 recognizes that some transfers of property by a spouse to a third party may qualify for nonrecognition treatment under I.R.C. § 1041, Q&A-9 requires that the transfers must be "on behalf of" the transferor spouse."

(c) Private Letter Rulings

Two private letter rulings have dealt with stock redemptions in connection with a divorce. In Priv. Ltr. Rul. 9427009, the husband owned 52 out of 105 shares of the common stock of the corporation. In a marital settlement agreement, *H* agreed to transfer 12 shares of common stock to *W*. The agreement provided that *W* could negotiate with the corporation to redeem her stock. *H* was not a party to the redemption agreement and had no obligation with respect to the redemption or to purchase *W*'s shares if the corporation failed to redeem her shares. *H*'s only obligation under the agreement was to transfer 12 shares to *W*. The next day, *W* and the corporation entered into a redemption agreement in which *W* transferred her 12 shares to the corporation in exchange for cash. *H* did not vote as a director to approve the redemption agreement.

The IRS determined that the form of the transaction was governed by *Blatt v. Commissioner*[98] rather than *Arnes v. Commissioner*,[99] and concluded that the redemption did not satisfy an obligation of *H*. As a result, *W*'s transfer of stock to the corporation was not "on behalf of" *H* within the meaning of Treas. Reg. § 1.10411T(c)(A9). Furthermore, the redemption of *W*'s stock did not result in a constructive dividend to *H*, because neither was *H* relieved of an obligation, nor did the redemption satisfy a primary, unconditional obligation on the part of *H* to buy *W*'s shares. As a result of the preceding, the transfer of the 12 shares by *H* to *W* incident to the divorce is a nonrecognition event under I.R.C. § 1041, with the consequence of carryover basis to *W*, resulting in a taxable redemption to *W* under I.R.C. § 302(b)(3).

A second private letter ruling is Priv. Ltr. Rul. 200222008. In that ruling, the husband owned 100 percent of the common stock in a C corporation. Pursuant to a marital settlement agreement between the husband and the wife, the husband was obligated to transfer 16 percent of the common stock in the corporation to the wife. The agreement then provided that the corporation and the wife would enter into a stock redemption agreement whereby the wife would transfer her stock in the corporation to the corporation in complete termination of her interest and the corporation would pay her for her stock. The husband personally guaranteed the obligation of the corporation. The wife agreed to be solely responsible for any capital gains tax arising from the redemption.

The issue before the Service was whether the husband's transfer of the stock to the wife, incident to their divorce, followed by the corporation's complete redemption of the wife's stock in the corporation is taxable to the wife under Section 302(b)(3) as a complete termination of interest and thus taxable to her as a capital gain, or is taxable to the husband under Section 301 as a constructive dividend with no taxable gain to the wife as a result of Section 1041.

The Service held that the husband's transfer of the stock to his wife was a nontaxable transaction governed by Section 1041, and the wife's receipt of cash in exchange for all her shares of stock in the corporation was a complete termination interest under Section 302(b)(3) taxable as capital gains to the wife. In arriving at this conclusion, the Service first determined that as a result of Section 1041, the form of the transaction should be respected in a divorce setting, whereas in a non-divorce setting the form of a transaction may not be respected. This meant that Section 1041 applied to the transfer of the shares of stock to the wife, and the redemption of her shares of stock, thus imposing

98. 102 T.C. 77 (1994).

99. 102 T.C. 522 (1994).

a capital gains tax on the wife and no tax on the husband. This ruling clearly reflects that the parties are free to negotiate between themselves which one will bear the tax burden—whether the husband sells some of his shares of stock in the corporation to the corporation causing him to recognize gain and then transfers the proceeds to the wife, or whether the husband transfers some of his shares to the wife in a tax-free transaction governed by Section 1041, followed by the sale of the shares of stock by the wife to the corporation in a transaction taxable to the wife under Section 302(b)(3). Thus, as a result of Treas. Reg. § 1.1041-1T (Q&A-9) the parties are able to shift the tax consequences between themselves.

In arriving at this conclusion, the Service spent substantial time analyzing the discussed tax cases and concluded that Section 1041 and the intent of the parties is best served by respecting the form of the redemption transaction, which is further supported by having the wife accept any tax burden associated with the redemption transaction.

(d) Treasury Regulation § 1.11041-2

On January 10, 2003, the IRS issued new regulations regarding transfers of stock on behalf of a spouse in a redemption setting. Because of its importance, the regulation is reproduced here. This regulation supersedes Temp. Prop. Treas. Reg. § 1041 (Q&A-9) with respect to stock redemptions during a marriage or incident to a divorce. For transactions other than stock redemptions, Temp. Prop. Treas. Reg. § 1041-1T (c)(Q&A-9) remains viable.

"*Introduction*—In response to the cases discussed above, and to prevent itself from being whipsawed, the IRS has finalized.[100]

Preamble to regulations—The preamble describes the background to the problem and the IRS's solution to the problem.

Background—As discussed earlier, under I.R.C. § 1.1041-IT(c), Q&A-9, of the Temporary Income Tax Regulations (Q&A-9), I.R.C. § 1041 applies to a transfer of property by the transferor spouse to a third party that is on behalf of the other spouse or former spouse (nontransferor spouse) if: (i) the transfer to the third party is required by the divorce or separation instrument; (ii) the transfer to the third party is pursuant to the written request of the nontransferor spouse; or (iii) the transferor spouse receives from the nontransferor spouse a written consent or ratification of the transfer to the third party. If Q&A-9 applies, a direct transfer of property to a third party is treated first as a transfer to the nontransferor spouse in a transaction governed by I.R.C. § 1041 and then as an immediate transfer by the nontransferor spouse to the third party in a transaction not governed by I.R.C. § 1041.

100. Prop. Treas. Reg. § 1.1041-2.

Q&A-9 has provided spouses and former spouses with the ability to shift between themselves the tax consequences of a sale of property outside the marital unit. However, the questions of what standard should be applied for purposes of determining whether a transfer of property is, or is not, 'on behalf of' the nontransferor spouse for purposes of I.R.C. § 1041, and whether the same standard should be applied for purposes of determining the tax treatment of the transferor spouse and the nontransferor spouse under provisions of the Internal Revenue Code other than I.R.C. § 1041, have become the source of much confusion and litigation in the context of certain stock redemptions. For instance, the U.S. Court of Appeals for the Ninth Circuit in *Arnes v. United States*[101] (regarding the tax treatment of the transferor spouse), and the Tax Court in *Arnes v. Commissioner*[102] (regarding the tax treatment of the nontransferor spouse), applied different standards to determine the tax treatment of the transferor spouse and the nontransferor spouse, respectively, in the context of a redemption of stock owned by the transferor spouse. Consequently, neither spouse was taxed on the redemption proceeds, a result that Congress clearly sought to avoid in enacting I.R.C. § 1041.

In the *Arnes* cases, a husband and wife owned all the stock of a corporation. The divorce instrument required the wife to tender her stock to the corporation for redemption. The Ninth Circuit held that the redemption was 'on behalf of' the husband and, therefore, was not taxable to the wife, because it found that the husband had an obligation under the property settlement to purchase the wife's stock and the husband was benefitted by the redemption. The Ninth Circuit did not address the tax treatment of the husband, although it implied that the husband might be taxable on the redemption.

The Tax Court in *Arnes* addressed whether the husband was taxable on the redemption. The Tax Court stated that the question was whether the husband had a constructive dividend; that is, whether he had a 'primary and unconditional obligation' to purchase the stock. The Court concluded that the husband did not have a primary and unconditional obligation to purchase the wife's stock and, therefore, the redemption of the wife's stock did not result in a constructive dividend to the husband. This conclusion, the Court stated, was supported by the IRS's position in Rev. Rul. 69-608, 1969-2 C.B. 42. Rev. Rul. 69-608 holds that a corporation's redemption of its stock from a shareholder (the first shareholder) results in a constructive distribution to another shareholder (the second shareholder) if the redemption is in satisfaction of the second shareholder's primary and unconditional obligation to purchase the first shareholder's stock. The majority opinion of the Tax Court in *Arnes* expressly declined to opine as to whether the 'on behalf of' standard of Q&A-9 is the

---

101. 981 F.2d 456 (9th Cir. 1992).
102. 102 T.C. 522 (1994).

same as the 'primary and unconditional obligation' standard applicable to constructive distributions.

The uncertainty has persisted in subsequent cases. In *Read v. Commissioner*,[103] the Tax Court rejected equating the 'primary and unconditional obligation' standard with the 'on behalf of' standard in Q&A-9 for purposes of determining the tax consequences of a stock redemption to the transferor spouse. The Tax Court concluded that the appropriate standard for determining whether a transfer of property to a third party by a transferor spouse was on behalf of the nontransferor spouse under Q&A-9 was whether the transferor spouse was acting, 'as the representative of' or 'in the interest of' the nontransferor spouse or whether the transfer satisfied a liability or an obligation of the nontransferor spouse.[104]

Because of these inconsistent standards, the IRS decided to amend the regulations to provide certainty in determining which spouse will be taxed on certain stock redemptions occurring during marriage or incident to divorce.

Explanation of provisions—The proposed regulations apply where, under current law, the 'primary and unconditional obligation' standard applicable to constructive distributions governs the tax consequences to one spouse or former spouse of a redemption of stock owned by the other spouse or former spouse. Accordingly, the proposed regulations provide that they apply only where the nontransferor spouse owns stock of the redeeming corporation either immediately before or immediately after the stock redemption.

The regulations provide that, if a corporation redeems stock owned by a transferor spouse, and the transferor spouse's receipt of property in respect of such stock is treated, under applicable tax law, as resulting in a constructive distribution to the nontransferor spouse, then the stock redeemed is deemed first to be transferred by the transferor spouse to the nontransferor spouse and then to be transferred by the nontransferor spouse to the redeeming corporation. I.R.C. § 1041 applies to the deemed transfer of the stock by the transferor spouse to the nontransferor spouse, provided the requirements of I.R.C. § 1041 are otherwise satisfied with respect to such deemed transfer. I.R.C. § 1041 does not apply to the deemed transfer of stock from the nontransferor spouse to the redeeming corporation. Any property actually received by the transferor spouse from the redeeming corporation in respect of the redeemed stock is deemed first to be transferred by the redeeming corporation to the nontransferor spouse in exchange for the stock in a transaction to which I.R.C. § 1041 does not apply, and then to be transferred by the nontransferor spouse to the transferor spouse in a transaction to which I.R.C. § 1041 applies, provided the requirements of I.R.C. § 1041 are otherwise satisfied with respect to such

103. 114 T.C. 14 (2000).
104. *See also* Blatt v. Comm'r, 102 T.C. 77 (1994).

deemed transfer. The tax consequences of the deemed transfer of stock from the nontransferor spouse to the redeeming corporation in exchange for the redemption proceeds from the redeeming corporation are determined under applicable provisions of the Internal Revenue Code (other than I.R.C. § 1041) as if such transfers had actually occurred.

Where applicable law does not treat a transferor spouse's receipt of property in respect of stock redeemed as resulting in a constructive distribution to the nontransferor spouse, the form of the stock redemption is respected. In other words, the transferor spouse and the redeeming corporation are respected as parties to the redemption transaction, and thus the transferor spouse, not the nontransferor spouse, is treated as a party to the redemption.

The approach of the regulations recognizes that applicable tax law currently imposes the primary and unconditional obligation standard, which has its origins in well-established case law including *Wall v. United States*,[105] and *Sullivan v. United States*,[106] for determining whether a shareholder has received a constructive distribution. The regulations are designed to remove inconsistencies caused by the simultaneous potential application of the 'on behalf of' standard of Q&A-9 for one spouse and the primary and unconditional obligation standard of the case law for the other spouse. Thus, for example, if the rules of the regulations had applied in the *Arnes* case, because the husband did not have a primary and unconditional obligation to purchase the wife's stock, the redemption would have been taxed in accordance with its form with the result that the wife would have incurred the tax consequences of the redemption.

The regulations provide a special rule that permits spouses and former spouses to treat a redemption of the transferor spouse's stock as a deemed transfer of the redeemed stock by the transferor spouse to the nontransferor spouse and then a deemed transfer of the redeemed stock by the nontransferor spouse to the redeeming corporation, and to treat any property actually received by the transferor spouse from the redeeming corporation in respect of the redeemed stock as first transferred by the redeeming corporation to the nontransferor spouse in exchange for the stock and then to be transferred by the nontransferor spouse to the transferor spouse. The special rule will apply if a divorce or separation instrument, or a written agreement between the transferor spouse and the nontransferor spouse, requires the transferor spouse and the nontransferor spouse to file their Federal income tax returns in a manner that reflects that the transferor spouse transferred the redeemed stock to the nontransferor spouse in exchange for the redemption proceeds and the corporation redeemed the stock from the nontransferor spouse in exchange for the redemption proceeds. Such divorce or separation instrument must be effective,

---

105. 164 F.2d 462 (4th Cir. 1947).
106. 363 F.2d 724 (8th Cir. 1966).

or the written agreement must be executed by both spouses or former spouses, prior to the date on which the nontransferor spouse files such spouse's first timely filed Federal income tax return for the year that includes the date of the redemption, but no later than the date such return is due (including extensions). The special rule is provided to give spouses and former spouses a means of ensuring the application of those Federal income tax consequences that would have resulted had applicable tax law treated the transferor spouse's stock redemption as resulting in a constructive distribution to the nontransferor spouse."

(e) The Regulations

On January 13, 2003, the Service issued Treas. Reg. § 1.1041-2 regarding redemptions of stock in a divorce setting. This regulation applies instead of Q&A-9, Treas. Reg. § 1.1041-1T(c). The regulations first discuss whether a redemption of stock results in a stock redemption or constructive dividend, the tax consequences of a redemption or a constructive dividend, the planning opportunities available to determine upon which spouse the tax burden falls, and finally discusses the effective date of the regulations. The regulations conclude with examples which illustrate their rules.

(i) *Redemptions of stock not resulting in constructive distributions.* Notwithstanding Q&A-9 of Treas. Reg. § 1.1041-IT(c), if a corporation redeems stock owned by the transferor spouse, and the transferor spouse's receipt of property in respect of such redeemed stock is not treated, under applicable tax law, as resulting in a constructive distribution to the nontransferor spouse, then the form of the stock redemption is respected for Federal income tax purposes. Therefore, the transferor spouse is treated as having received a distribution redemption transaction to which the nontransferor spouse is not a party.[107]

(ii) *Redemptions of stock resulting in constructive distributions.* Notwithstanding Q&A-9 of Treas. Reg. § 1.1041-IT(c), if a corporation redeems stock owned by a spouse or former spouse (transferor spouse), and the transferor spouse's receipt of property in respect of such redeemed stock is treated, under applicable tax law, as resulting in a constructive distribution to the other spouse or former spouse (nontransferor spouse), then the stock redeemed is deemed first to have been transferred by the transferor spouse to the nontransferor spouse and then to have been transferred by the nontransferor spouse to the redeeming corporation. Any property actually received by the transferor spouse from the redeeming corporation in respect of the redeemed stock is

107. Treas. Reg. § 1.1041-2(a)(1).

deemed first to have been transferred by the redeeming corporation to the nontransferor spouse in exchange for the redeemed stock and then to have been transferred by the nontransferor spouse to the transferor spouse.[108] Thus, the nontransferor spouse is treated as acquiring the shares from the transferor spouse in an exchange governed by Section 1041(a); the nontransferor spouse is then treated as transferring those shares to the corporation in exchange for a constructive distribution under Section 301 equal to the redemption proceeds received by the transferor spouse; and the nontransferor spouse is treated as transferring the constructive dividend tax free to the transferor spouse under Section 1041. The effect of all of this is that the nontransferor recognizes capital gain treatment if any of the tests of Section 302(b) apply, or as ordinary income if none of the tests of Section 302(b) apply. On the other hand, the transferor spouse has no tax consequence because of Section 1041.

(iii) *Tax consequences—Redemption of stock not resulting in constructive distribution.* I.R.C. § 1041 does not apply to any redemption of stock not resulting in a constructive distribution. See I.R.C. § 302 for rules relating to the tax consequences of certain stock redemptions.[109]

(iv) *Tax consequences—Redemption of stock resulting in constructive distribution.* The tax consequences of a stock redemption resulting in a constructive distribution are determined under applicable provisions of the Internal Revenue Code as if the parties had actually made such transfers. Accordingly, I.R.C. § 1041 applies to any deemed transfer of the stock and redemption proceeds between the transferor spouse and the nontransferor spouse, provided the requirements of I.R.C. § 1041 are otherwise satisfied with respect to such deemed transfer. I.R.C. § 1041, however, will not apply to any deemed transfer of stock by the nontransferor spouse to the redeeming corporation in exchange for the redemption proceeds. See I.R.C. § 302 for rules relating to the tax consequences of certain corporate redemptions.[110]

(v) *Special rule.* The regulations contain special rules that allow divorcing spouses to elect who between them should be responsible for the tax consequences in a redemption resulting from a divorce. In effect, they can shift the tax consequences from the nontransferror spouse to the transferor spouse. Notwithstanding applicable tax law, a transferor spouse's receipt of property in respect of the redeemed stock is treated as a distribution to the transferor spouse in redemption of

108. Prop. Treas. Reg. § 1.1041-2(a)(2).
109. Prop. Treas. Reg. § 1.1041-2(b)(2).
110. Prop. Treas. Reg. § 1.1041-2(b)(1).

such stock for purposes of redemption of stock not resulting in constructive distributions, and is not treated as resulting in a constructive distribution to the nontransferor spouse for purposes of redemption of stock resulting in constructive distributions if a divorce or separation instrument, or a valid written agreement between the transferor spouse and the nontransferor spouse, expressly provides that (i) both spouses or former spouses intend for the redemption to be treated, for Federal income tax purposes, as a redemption distribution to the transferor spouse; and (ii) such instrument or agreement supersedes any other instrument or agreement concerning the purchase, sale, redemption, or other disposition of the stock that is the subject of the redemption.[111]

Notwithstanding applicable tax law, a transferor spouse's receipt of property in respect of the redeemed stock is treated as resulting in a constructive distribution to the nontransferor spouse for purposes of redemptions of stock resulting in constructive distributions and is not treated as a distribution to the transferor spouse in redemption of such stock for purposes of redemption of stock not resulting in constructive distribution, if a divorce or separation instrument, or a valid written agreement between the transferor spouse and the nontransferor spouse, expressly provides that (i) both spouses or former spouses intend for the redemption to be treated, for Federal income tax purposes, as resulting in a constructive distribution to the nontransferor spouse; and (ii) such instrument or agreement supersedes any other instrument or agreement concerning the purchase, sale, redemption, or other disposition of the stock that is the subject of the redemption.[112]

For purposes of this special rule, a divorce or separation instrument must be effective, or a valid written agreement must be executed by both spouses or former spouses, prior to the date on which the transferor spouse or the nontransferor spouse files such spouse's first timely filed Federal income tax return for the year that includes the date of the stock redemption, but no later than the date such return is due (including extensions).[113]

(vi) *Effective date*. Except as otherwise provided in this paragraph, the regulations are applicable to redemptions of stock on or after January 13, 2003, except for redemptions of stock that are pursuant to instruments in effect before January 13, 2003. For redemptions of stock before Jan-

111. Treas. Reg. § 1.1041-2(c)(1).
112. Treas. Reg. § 1.1041-2(c)(2).
113. Treas. Reg. § 1.1041-2(c)(3).

uary 13, 2003 and redemptions of stock that are pursuant to instruments in effect before January 13, 2003, see Treas. Reg. § 1.1041-IT(c) (Q&A-9). However, these regulations are applicable to redemptions described in the preceding sentence of this paragraph if the spouses or former spouses execute a written agreement on or after August 3, 2001, that satisfies the requirements of one of the special rules with respect to such redemption. A divorce or separation instrument or valid written agreement executed on or after August 3, 2001, and before May 13, 2003, that meets the requirements of the special rule in Regulations project REG-107151-00 published in 2001-2 C.B.370 is treated as also meeting the requirements of the special rule in Treas. Reg. § 1.1041-2(c)(2).[114]

(f) Examples

Treas. Reg. § 1.1041-2(d) sets forth the following *four examples,* which illustrate the preceding rules:

Example 1. Corporation X has 100 shares outstanding. *A* and *B* each own 50 shares. *A* and *B* divorce. The divorce instrument requires *B* to purchase *A*'s shares, and *A* to sell *A*'s shares to *B* in exchange for $100. Corporation X redeems *A*'s shares for $100. Assume that, under applicable tax law, *B* has a primary and unconditional obligation to purchase *A*'s stock, and therefore the stock redemption results in a constructive distribution to *B*. Also assume that the special rule for the transferor spouse discussed above does not apply. Accordingly, *A* is treated as transferring *A*'s stock of Corporation X to *B* in a transfer to which I.R.C. § 1041 applies (assuming the requirements of I.R.C. § 1041 are otherwise satisfied). *B* is treated as transferring the Corporation X stock *B* is deemed to have received from *A* to Corporation X in exchange for $100 in an exchange to which I.R.C. § 1041 does not apply and I.R.C. §§ 302(d) and 301 apply, and *B* is treated as transferring the $100 to *A* in a transfer to which I.R.C. § 1041 applies.

Example 2. Assume the same facts as Example 1, except that the divorce instrument provides as follows: "*A* and *B* agree that the redemption will be treated for Federal income tax purposes as a redemption distribution to *A*." The divorce instrument further provides that it "supersedes all other instruments or agreements concerning the purchase, sale, redemption, or other disposition of the stock that is the subject of the redemption." By virtue of the special rule for the transferor spouse and under the tax consequences for redemptions not resulting in a constructive distribution, the tax consequences of the redemption are determined in accordance with its form as a redemption of *A*'s shares by

114. Treas. Reg. § 1.1041-2(e).

Corporation X and are not treated as resulting in a constructive distribution to *B*.[115]

Example 3. Assume the same facts as Example 1, except that the divorce instrument requires *A* to sell *A*'s shares to Corporation X in exchange for a note. *B* guarantees Corporation X's payment of the note. Assume that, under applicable tax law, *B* does not have a primary and unconditional obligation to purchase *A*'s stock and therefore the stock redemption does not result in a constructive distribution to *B*, because *B* does not have a primary and unconditional obligation to purchase *A*'s stock. Treas. Reg. § 1.1041-2 does not apply to the transfers of stock and redemption proceeds in connection with the redemption transaction. Accordingly, under Treas. Reg § 1.1041-2(a)(1) and (b)(1), the tax consequences of the redemption are determined in accordance with its form as a redemption of *A*'s shares by Corporation X.[116]

Example 4. Assume the same facts as Example 3, except that the divorce instrument provides as follows: *A* and *B* agree that the redemption shall be treated for Federal income tax purposes as resulting in a constructive distribution to B. The divorce instrument further provides that "it supersedes any other instrument or agreement concerning the purchase, sale, redemption or other disposition of the stock that is the subject of the redemption." By virtue of the special rule of Treas. Reg. § 1.1041-2(c), the redemption is treated as resulting in a constructive distribution to *B*.[117] Accordingly, under Treas. Reg. § 1.1041-2(a)(2) and (b)(2), *A* is treated as transferring *A*'s stock of Corporation X to *B* in a transfer to which I.R.C. § 1041 applies (assuming the requirements of I.R.C. § 1041 are otherwise satisfied). *B* is treated as transferring the Corporation X stock *B* is deemed to have received from *A* to Corporation X in exchange for a note in an exchange to which I.R.C. § 1041 does not apply and I.R.C. §§ 302(d) and 301 apply, and *B* is treated as transferring the note to *A* in a transfer to which I.R.C. § 1041 applies."

f. Sale to Third Party

A sale to a third party may be necessary to sell property, yet the parties may seek the protection of Section 1041 to avoid gain on the sale of the property. In *Ingham v. United States*,[118] the Court held that a sale of property to a third person was not "on behalf of a former spouse" since the former spouse was to share in half the sales proceeds and no obligation of the former spouse was

115. *See* I.R.C. § 302.
116. *Id.*
117. See Treas. Reg. § 1.1041-2(a)(2).
118. 167 F.3d 1240 (9th Cir. 1999).

being satisfied by the sale to the third party. This was a non-redemption of stock case.

In 1974, *H* & *W* purchased four lots, two of which were lakefront and two of which were road front. They built their house on one of the lakefront lots. In 1991, the four lots, including the house, had a fair market value of $4 million. In February 1991, *H* & *W* divorced. *W* received the two lakefront lots and the house, and *H* received the two road front lots. *W* also agreed to pay *H* $400,000 for his interest in the residence when the residence was sold. In May 1991, *H* & *W* sold all four lots to the same buyer for $4,250,000. The lakefront properties were sold for $3.1 million and the road front properties were sold for $1,150,000. *W* then paid *H* the $400,000.

W reported the sales on her return and paid Federal income taxes of nearly $400,000. *W* then filed an amended return seeking a refund of the taxes paid. Her argument was that the sale of the lakefront properties by her was on behalf of her former spouse, and, therefore, the gain realized from the sale of the lakefront properties was entitled to tax-free treatment. Essentially, *W* argued that although she sold the lakefront properties to a third person and not to her spouse, the sale should be treated as a constructive sale to her husband who then sold the property to the third-party purchase, because she sold the lakefront properties to satisfy her financial obligation to her husband. In effect, she attempted to shift the tax burden to *H* by arguing that the transaction should be treated as a sale by *W* to *H*, who then sold the property to a third person. *W*'s argument was based on Treas. Reg. § 1.1041-1T(c)(A-9), which exempts from taxation transfers to a third party on behalf of a former spouse.

The Ninth Circuit held that *W*'s sale of the lakefront properties was not a constructive sale on behalf of *H*, because *H* owed no liability to *W* or to a third party and, therefore, *W*'s sale of the lakefront properties to a third party did not relieve *H* of any obligation or liability he owed *W* or a third party. Rather, the sale allowed *W* to satisfy her debt to *H*. Since the sale by *W* did not relieve *H* of a specific legal obligation or liability, the sale did not qualify as a transfer to a former spouse incident to a divorce or on behalf of a former spouse. Compare *Arnes v. United States*, *supra*, where a transfer is considered to have been made on behalf of a former spouse if it satisfied an obligation or liability of the former spouse.

W should have transferred a one-half interest in the residence to *H*, and then they should have jointly sold it to a third party. The transfer from *W* to *H* would have been protected by I.R.C. § 1041, and they could have both split the sales proceeds and the tax liability. As structured, however, *W* bore the entire tax liability and *H* made out substantially better than *W* after taxes. This should have been part of the settlement agreement between them.

g. Assignment of Income and Losses

According to the IRS, the assignment of income doctrine takes precedence over I.R.C. § 1041. In Rev. Rul. 87-112,[119] *H*, a cash basis taxpayer, held Series E and EE bonds with maturity dates after 1985. The bonds were registered in *H*'s name and purchased with *H*'s funds. *H* did not elect, under I.R.C. § 454, to include in income any interest accrued on the bonds. As part of a property settlement, *H* transferred the bonds to *W*, his former spouse. The following year, *W* redeemed the bonds.

The IRS first held that the deferred, accrued interest on the bonds is includible in *H*'s gross income in the taxable year in which *H* transferred the bonds to *W* in a transfer described in I.R.C. § 1041. The deferred, accrued interest from the date of original issuance of the bonds to the date of transfer of the bonds to *W* is includible in *H*'s gross income. The amount includible in *W*'s gross income is the deferred, accrued interest from the date of the transfer of the bonds to the date of redemption. The reasoning of the IRS was that although I.R.C. § 1041(a) shields from recognition gain that would ordinarily be recognized on a sale or exchange of property, it does not shield from recognition income that is ordinarily recognized upon the assignment of that income to another taxpayer. Because the income at issue here is accrued but unrecognized interest, rather than gain, I.R.C. § 1041(a) does not shield that income from recognition. The transferred bonds in the present situation contain an interest element that has not been included in income. Accordingly, the specific rule of Treas. Reg. § 1.4541(a) for dispositions of interestdeferred obligations applies to require that the transferor include the accrued interest in income. The IRS then held that the transferee's basis in the bonds immediately after the transfer is equal to the transferor's basis in the bonds increased by the interest income includible by the transferor as a result of the transfer of the bonds.

See, however, Rev. Rul. 2002-22,[120] discussed later, which appears to have overruled Rev. Rul. 87-112.

In Priv. Ltr. Rul. 8813023, *W* agreed to relinquish her claims on *H*'s military retirement plan in exchange for payments by *H* of $42,000 over three years. Because the divorce occurred in a community property state, the military retirement pay was community property, a portion of which *W* was entitled to receive (and which would have been taxable to *W* as ordinary income when received). The IRS held that the $42,000 paid to *W* in exchange for her community property interest in *H*'s military pension represented payments for a right to future income rather than gain and, therefore, the payments are not tax free under I.R.C. § 1041, but rather are includible as ordinary income in *W*'s gross income under I.R.C. § 61. The reasoning of the IRS was that *W* assigned

119. 1987-2 C.B. 207.
120. 2002-1 C.B. 849.

to *H* her right to receive payments over her lifetime in exchange for payments from *H* over three years. The IRS thus refused to allow *W* to escape taxation of ordinary income by recharacterizing her assignment of income as a nontaxable transfer of property under I.R.C. § 1041.[121]

But see *Balding v. Commissioner*,[122] where the Court held that the wife's release of her community property interest in the military retirement benefits of her husband in exchange for payments of $15,000, $14,000, and $13,000 per year over three years from her husband was protected by I.R.C. § 1041 and did not constitute an assignment of income. Accordingly, the payments received by the wife were not income but were gifts which were nontaxable pursuant to I.R.C. §§ 1041 and 102.

If the transferor spouse does not transfer an ownership interest in the underlying asset to the transferee spouse, but merely agrees to pay to the transferee spouse a percentage of income received from the asset, the transferor has not assigned the income to the transferee spouse and is taxable on the receipt of the income.[123] In the ruling, the taxpayer obtained a patent in his name. The taxpayer filed numerous lawsuits for infringement of patent rights. In a decree of divorce, the Court ordered the taxpayer to divide any proceeds from the lawsuits with his wife by distributing to her a percentage of any net proceeds he received from the lawsuits. The proceeds were paid into an escrow account established by the spouses and the escrow agent disbursed the wife's percentage to her and the balance to the taxpayer. The IRS ruled that each payment to the wife was payment in a property settlement and was nontaxable to the husband under I.R.C. § 1041.

A transfer of a portion of a taxpayer's IRA to his spouse's IRA is considered a taxable distribution from the transferor's IRA, subject to inclusion in the gross estate of the transferor, even if "incident to a divorce."[124] The IRS rejected the transferor's argument that I.R.C. § 1041 applies to transfers and distributions and overrides the provisions of I.R.C. § 408.[125]

In Priv. Ltr. Rul. 200442003[126] the IRS held that the assignment of income doctrine did not apply where the husband paid a lump sum to his former wife in exchange for her community property interest in a nonqualified deferred compensation plan payable to the husband by his company. The IRS ruled that the payment of the lump sum was controlled by *Balding v. Commissioner*. In *Balding*, the Court held that the wife was not taxed on the lump sum to be received from the husband. According to the IRS, however, *Balding* focused

121. *See*, however, Rev. Rul. 2002-22, 2002-1 C.B. 849.
122. 98 T.C. 368 (1992).
123. Priv. Ltr. Rul. 9143050.
124. Priv. Ltr. Rul. 9422060.
125. *See also* Hawkins v. Comm'r, 102 T.C. 61 (1994).
126. For a detailed discussion of this PLR, see the text at Chapter 6, C.4.b.(2)(a)(ii).

on the amounts paid for the transfer of the spouse's interest in certain retirement benefits, not on which party is taxable when the retirement benefits are made. The IRS then looked to Rev. Rul. 2002-22, which rejected the application of the assignment of income doctrine to certain transfers of property incident to a divorce. Pursuant to Rev. Rul. 2002-22 and *Balding*, the IRS concluded that the assignment of income doctrine did not apply to the transfer by husband to the wife of the lump sum payments, or to the wife's transfer to the husband of her interest in the SERP, with the result that neither the husband nor the wife would be required to include any amount gross in income with respect to these transfers. Therefore, the assignment of income doctrine did not cause the wife to be taxable on any part of the SERP deferred compensation payments received by the husband from the company. In accordance with the representations set forth in the ruling, the husband was taxable on the full amount of SERP deferred compensation payments made to him by the company.

In *Pfister v. Commissioner*,[127] the Court held that the payee spouse was required to include in her income amounts she received from her former spouse's military retirement pay. The separation agreement between the parties provided that the wife "shall be owner of, and receive, one-half of husband's disposable, retirement pay, i.e., during the joint lives of the parties, the husband and wife shall each receive one-half of the husband's disposable retired or retirement pay."[128] The wife did not include any of the payments she received in income. The Court held that the wife was the owner of one-half of her former husband's retirement pay, and she should have reported that amount in income. Thus, the Court concluded that military retirement payments are gross income to the party who owns the right to those payments pursuant to the division of property in a divorce, and that income is taxable to the legal owner of the property producing the income.

5. Stock Option

In Rev. Rul. 2002-22,[129] the IRS ruled that a taxpayer who transferred an interest in nonstatutory stock options and nonqualified deferred compensation to the taxpayer's former spouse incident to a divorce did not have to have to include an amount in gross income on the transfer. And, the former spouse, not the taxpayer, is required to include an amount in gross income when the former spouse exercises the stock options or when the deferred compensation is paid or made available to the former spouse.

In Rev. Rul. 2002-22, prior to the divorce the husband received nonstatutory stock options as part of his compensation. Since the options had no readily

127. 359 F.2d 352 (4th Cir. 2004, *aff'g* T.C. Memo. 2002-198.
128. 359 F.2d 352, 353 (C.A.4,. 2004).
129. 2002-1 C.B. 849.

ascertainable fair market value when granted, no amount was included in the husband's gross income at the time of the grant. In addition, the husband participated in two unfunded, nonqualified deferred compensation plans under which he earned the right to receive post-employment payments from the corporation.

Under one of the plans, participants were entitled to payments based on the balance of the individual accounts of the kind described in Section 31.3121(v)(2)-(1)(c)(1)(ii) of the Employment Tax Regulations. Under the second plan maintained by the husband's corporate employer, participants were entitled to receive a lump sum or periodic payments following separation from service based on a formula regulating years of service and compensation history with the corporation. At the time of the divorce, the husband had accrued the right to receive a single lump sum payment under the plan following termination of employment. The husband's right to benefits under the plan was not contingent on his performance of future services.

According to state law, the stock options and unfunded deferred compensation rights earned by the husband during the marriage constituted marital property subject to equitable division between the spouses in the event of divorce. Pursuant to a separation agreement incorporated into the decree, the husband transferred to the wife one-third of the nonstatutory stock options issued to the husband, and the right to receive payments under the deferred compensation plans. Four years after the divorce, the wife exercised the stock options and received stock in the corporation with a fair market value in excess of the exercise price of the options. Nine years after the divorce, the husband terminated employment with the corporation and received a single sum payment under each of the deferred compensation plans.

The IRS, relying upon *Balding v. Commissioner*,[130] first held that stock options and rights in unfunded deferred compensation plans constitute "property" within the meaning of I.R.C. § 1041. The IRS next held that the transfer by the husband to the wife of his rights in the stock option plan and unfunded deferred compensation plans were not taxable to the husband per I.R.C. § 1041. Finally, the IRS held that the assignment of income doctrine did not apply to these transfers. Thus, the wife, not the husband, was required to include in gross income any income resulting from her exercise of the stock options or the payment of deferred compensation. When the wife exercises the stock options, she must include in income an amount determined under I.R.C. § 83(a) as if she were the person who performed the services. In addition, the wife must include the amount realized from payments of deferred compensation in income in the year such payments are paid or made available to the wife. The Service's reasoning was that applying the assignment of income doctrine in divorce cases

130. 98 T.C. 368 (1992).

to the transferor spouse when the transferee spouse ultimately receives the income from the property transferred in the divorce would frustrate the purpose of Section 1041 with respect to divorcing spouses. To conclude otherwise would thwart the purpose of allowing divorcing spouses to sever their ownership interests in property with as little tax intrusion as possible.

The IRS was careful to point out that the ruling only applied to transfers of property between spouses in connection with a divorce. The ruling does not apply to transfers of nonstatutory stock options, unfunded deferred compensation rights, or other future income rights to the extent such options or rights are unvested at the time of transfer or to the extent the transferor's rights to such income are subject to substantial contingencies at the time of the transfer. In addition, transfers of certain types of property incident to divorce, the tax consequences of which are governed by specific Code provisions, such as Sections 402, 408, 414, 424, or 453B, are not affected by the ruling.

Finally, the Service ruled that the same conclusions would apply if the spouses resided in a community property state and all or some of the income rights constituted community property that was divided between them as part of their divorce.

Rev. Rul. 2002-22 represents a 180-degree change in the IRS's earlier position on this issue.[131] Notwithstanding the conclusions of Rev. Rul. 2002-22, the Service ruled that it would apply prospectively Section 7805(b) and the assignment of income principles to treat income as gross income of the transferor and not of the transferee if (i) the income is attributable to an interest in a nonstatutory stock option or unfunded deferred compensation rights, or other similar intangible property rights; (ii) the options or rights were transferred from one party to a divorce to the other party to the divorce; (iii) the transfer was required by a provision of an agreement or court order; (iv) the provision was contained in the agreement or order before November 9, 2002 (the date of the ruling); and (v) the agreement or order specifically provides that the transferor must report gross income attributable to the transferred interest, or if it can be established to the satisfaction of the Service that the transferor has reported the gross income for Federal income tax purposes.

For the impact of the Federal Insurance Contributions Act (FICA) and the Federal Unemployment Tax Act (FUTA) taxes, see Rev. Rul. 2004-60.[132] Where the IRS held that the transfer of interests in nonstatutory stock options and nonqualified deferred compensation plans from an employee spouse to a

131. *See* FSA 200005006 (Nov. 1, 1999); PLR 9340032 (July 6, 1993) (An award to the wife of a percentage of the husband's nonqualified deferred compensation account is taxable to the husband-transferor and not to the wife-transferee under the assignment of income doctrine. Thus, when the payments were made by husband's employer to the wife from the husband's nonqualified compensation account, the payments are taxed to the husband.).

132. I.R.B. 2004-24; Rev. Rul. 2004-60 adopted and revised Notice 2002-31, 2002-19 I.R.B. 908.

nonemployee former spouse incident to a divorce does not result in a payment of wages for FICA and FUTA tax purposes to the transferor spouse. The facts in Rev. Rul. 2004-60 were the same as the facts in Rev. Rul. 2002-22.

Nonstatutory stock options are subject to FICA and FUTA taxes at the time of exercise by the nonemployee spouse to the same extent as if the options had been retained by the employee spouse and exercised by the employee spouse. The nonqualified deferred compensation also remains subject to FICA and FUTA taxes to the same extent as if the rights to the compensation had been retained by the employee spouse. To the extent FICA and FUTA taxation apply, the wages are the wages of the employee spouse. The employee portion of the FICA taxes is deducted from the wages as and when the wages are taken into account for FICA tax purposes. The employee portion of the FICA taxes is deducted from the payment to the nonemployee spouse.

The income recognized by the nonemployee spouse with respect to the exercise of the nonqualified stock options is subject to withholding under I.R.C. § 3402. The amounts distributed to the nonemployee spouse from the nonqualified deferred compensation plans are also subject to withholding under I.R.C. § 3402. The amounts to be withheld for income tax purposes are deducted from the payments to the nonemployee spouse. Pursuant to I.R.C. § 31, the nonemployee spouse is entitled to the credit allowable for the income tax withheld at the source on these wages.

The Social Security wages, Medicare wages, Social Security taxes withheld, and Medicare taxes withheld, if applicable, are reportable on a Form W-2 with the name, address, and Social Security number of the employee spouse. However, no amount is includible in Box 1 and Box 2 of the employee's Form W-2 with respect to these payments. The income with respect to the exercise of the nonqualified stock option by the nonemployee spouse and the distributions from the nonqualified deferred compensation plans to the nonemployee spouse are reportable in Box 3 as other income on a Form 1099-MISC with the name, address, and Social Security number of the nonemployee spouse. Income tax withholding with respect to these payments of wages is included in Box 4, Federal income tax withheld.

Income tax withholding on payments to the nonemployee spouse is included on a Form 945 filed by the corporation. The Social Security tax and Medicare tax is reported on the corporation's Form 941, and the FUTA tax is reported on the corporation's Form 940.

According to the American Payroll Association, there are many complex issues with regard to the ruling: First, why is the employer to withhold FICA tax from the nonemployee spouse when there was never an employment relationship with the nonemployee spouse? Furthermore, if the FICA tax is withheld from the nonemployee spouse, it is unfair to credit the wages and taxes to the employee spouse because the employee spouse is not really receiving these earnings. Further, it seems unfair to tax the nonemployee spouse on the full amount of the stock option or deferred compensation payout when FICA tax was taken off the top of it and not even credited to the nonemployee spouse.

Also, the income realized upon the exercise of a nonqualified stock option does not represent actual cash from which to withhold either the Federal income tax or FICA. And since this is required to be withheld from the nonemployee spouse, there are no other wages from which to withhold these amounts. One way to take the taxes would be to bill the transferee spouse for the taxes and wait to receive the money before recording the option to the earnings history of the employee and the nonemployee. Alternatively, the employer could require the transfer agent to retain enough of the stock from the option to be immediately sold in order to generate cash for the taxes. Either way, a great deal of coordination will be required between the employer and the transfer agent, assuming the employer even learns of the exercise. The employer will have to obtain information as to the number of options exercised, the option price, and the fair market value of each share in order to calculate the wages and taxes.

If the employee-spouse is no longer employed at the time of the exercise by or payout to the transferee-spouse, a W-2 will still have to be issued, reflecting only the FICA wages resulting from the benefit received by the nonemployee spouse. It may be difficult for the employer to keep up with address changes of an individual with whom it has no employment relationship. More importantly, it will be difficult to know if the former employee-spouse has had a name change, i.e., a change that will result in a name-number mismatch on the Form W-2, subjecting the employer to a penalty.

In the case of stock options, the employer will have to spend time and resources explaining to the spouse why he or she has to pay taxes that will not appear anywhere on his or her Form 1099. In the case of a deferred compensation payout, the employer will have to spend time and resources explaining to the transferee-spouse the reason why Form 1099 Box 3 less Box 4 does not equal the net amount of the payout—the difference being FICA taxes that the nonemployee-spouse paid on behalf of his or her ex-spouse.

If the IRS persists with its plan to require withholding on nonqualified stock options after divorce, query whether the IRS should allow them to be treated as noncash fringe benefits as outlined in Announcement 85-113.[133] Under that guidance, an employer may deem noncash fringe benefits as paid on a pay period, quarterly semiannually, annual, or other basis, provided the benefits are treated as paid at least annually. The announcement also allows employers to use a special fiscal year rule for withholding and reporting on noncash fringe benefits. Under this rule, employers may treat the value of benefits provided in

133. 1985-13 I.R.B. 31.

the last two months of the calendar year (or any shorter period) as paid during the following year.

The exercise of an option by a spouse is not protected by Section 1041. In *Davis v. Commissioner*,[134] the husband was granted a stock option in connection with the performance of his services. The exercise of the option generated ordinary income under Section 83.[135] In connection with the divorce, the taxpayer transferred 188.86 shares of stock in the family S corporation to his wife. He was then given an option to repurchase those shares from her. Shortly thereafter, the ex-wife sold her shares to the S corporation, which assumed her obligation under the option and granted the taxpayer the right to purchase the 188.86 shares from the corporation. Two years later the husband exercised his option. The corporation deducted the issuance of the shares under Section 83(h), which permits a deduction for the payment of reasonable compensation for services rendered. Since the corporation was an S corporation, the deduction flowed through to the stockholders who claimed the deduction on their returns. The husband did not report the value of the shares as income.

The Court first determined that the corporation granted the option to the husband who exercised it from the corporation, thus triggering the application of Section 83.

The taxpayer then argued that because his former spouse granted him the option that the corporation later assumed, his exercise of the option was shielded by Section 1041. The Court disagreed. It found that Section 1041 applied only to transfers of property between spouses or former spouses incident to a divorce, not to subsequent dispositions of the property by the recipient spouses or former spouse. Thus, the Court found that when the wife transferred the option to the husband pursuant to their divorce settlement, Section 1041 applied. But when the wife transferred the option to the corporation, which assumed her obligations, and the husband then exercised the option from the corporation, Section 1041 no longer applied. Thus, the exercise of the option was not protected by Section 1041.

6. Transferee

a. General Rule

Generally, the transferee does not recognize gain on the receipt of appreciated property from the transferor in exchange for the release of the transferee's

134. 716 F.3d 560 (C.A. 11, 2013), *aff'g* T.C. Memo. 2011-286.

135. Note that the grant of an option to purchase property does not constitute a transfer of property; rather, the transfer occurs when the option is exercised. Prop. Treas. Reg. §§ 1.83-3(a)(2) and 1.83-3(g).

marital rights.[136] In addition, the transferee spouse does not recognize gain on the release of the transferee's marital rights.[137]

b. Gift Treatment

The property is treated as acquired by the transferee spouse by gift.[138] As a result, whether property or cash is received, it is excluded from the gross income of the transferee. But the basis of the property in the hands of the transferee is not determined by the basis rules for gifts under I.R.C. § 1015(e), but by the basis rules set forth in Section 1041, as discussed immediately following.

c. Basis

The basis of the transferred property in the hands of the transferee is the adjusted basis of the property in the hands of the transferor immediately before the transfer.[139] This is known as carryover basis.[140] Thus, even though the transfer is treated as a gift, the basis of the property is not determined under the rules for gifts which provide different basis for gain and loss property.[141] Moreover, the carryover basis rules apply even if the transfer is a bona fide sale, and even if the adjusted basis of the property is less than, equal to, or greater than its fair market value at the time of the transfer.[142] Thus, the transferee does not acquire a basis in the transferred property equal to the transferee's cost (i.e., the fair market value of the property). The carryover basis rule applies for purposes of determining loss as well as gain upon the subsequent disposition of the property by the transferee.

In *Godlewski v. Commissioner*,[143] the husband and wife purchased a residence in 1973 for $32,200. In July 1984, the wife transferred her interest in the residence to the husband in exchange for $18,000 in cash. In October 1984, husband sold the house for $64,000 and purchased a replacement residence in December

136. I.R.C. § 1041(b); Temp. Prop. Treas. Reg. § 1.10411T(d)(A11); I.R.C. § 2501.
137. United States v. Davis, 370 U.S. 65 (1962), discussed at Chapter 6, B.1.a.
138. I.R.C. § 1041(b)(l).
139. I.R.C. § 1041(b)(2); Temp. Prop. Treas. Reg. § 1.10411T(d)(A11).
140. *See also* Rev. Rul. 67221, 19672 C.B. 63.
141. I.R.C. § 1015(e). The basis rules for gifts is that the basis of the property in the hands of the donee is the lesser of the adjusted basis of the property or the fair market value of the property at the time of transfer. Thus, the basis of appreciated property is its carryover basis, whereas the basis of depreciated property is its fair market value. In addition, the basis of property acquired by gift is increased by gift tax paid in connection with the gift to the extent the value of the property at the time of the gift exceeds the basis of the property in the hands of the donor immediately before the gift. This provision will not apply, however, because no gift tax is imposed on transfers to a spouse or former spouse incident to a divorce. *See* I.R.C. § 2523. Thus, I.R.C. § 1041 trumps § 1015.
142. Temp. Prop. Treas. Reg. § 1.10411T(d)(A11).
143. 90 T.C. 200 (1988).

1984 for $75,000. The IRS determined that the husband's basis in the residence sold was $32,200 and that he had gain realized of $31,800. He argued that his basis in the property should be increased by the $18,000 he paid the wife, thus decreasing his gain realized by $18,000. The Court, relying upon Temp. Treas. Reg. § 1.10411T(d)(A11), agreed with the IRS and held that the husband could not increase his basis by the $18,000 he paid to the wife. It should be noted that the husband could not avail himself of prior I.R.C. § 1034[144] treatment (pertaining to the rollover of gain into a new principal residence) because the husband moved out of the residence in 1981 and never returned. See also *Yonadi v. Commissioner*,[145] where the Court held that the transferee was liable for capital gains tax upon the sale of appreciated property because she acquired her interest in the property as a result of a property transfer, which, under I.R.C. § 1041, requires the basis in the property to be a carryover basis. The burden to establish basis is on the taxpayer.[146]

In *Jackson v. Commissioner*,[147] the husband transferred various securities to an irrevocable trust, which provided that the former wife was to receive all the income from the trust during her lifetime, and upon her death the remaining principal was to be paid to their children. The wife claimed a deduction for the amortization of her life interest in the trust. The IRS disallowed the deduction under Section 273, which disallows deductions for amortization of a life estate acquired by gift, bequest, or inheritance, contending that because the wife acquired her life interest in the trust incident to a divorce, Section 1041 requires that the life interest in the trust be treated as if the wife acquired her interest by gift. The Court agreed with the Service holding that the wife is treated for Federal income tax purposes as acquiring her life interest in the trust by gift. Thus, she was not entitled to an amortization deduction for the value of her life estate in the trust.

d. Holding Period

The holding period for property acquired pursuant to Section 1041 includes the time the property was held by the transferor. This is known as tacking of holding period.[148]

---

144. Prior § 1034 was replaced by current § 121 by the Tax Relief Act of 1997. See the discussion at Chapter 7, B.4.

145. 21 F.3d 1292 (3d Cir. 1994), *rev'g* T.C. Memo. 1992-602 (1992).

146. Lausterer v. Comm'r, T.C. Memo. 1995-130 (1995) (taxpayer disallowed depreciation deduction on property acquired from spouse in property settlement, since taxpayer failed to prove spouse's basis in property). *See also* Young v. Comm'r, 240 F.3d 369 (4th Cir. 2001), *aff'g* 113 T.C. 152 (1999), discussed at Chapter 6, C.4.b.(2(a)(i)).

147. T.C. Memo 1996-481.

148. I.R.C. § 1223(2).

e. Example

For example, in the preceding hypothetical, the transferee spouse would not realize or recognize gain on receipt of the vacant land. The transferee's basis in the vacant real estate received from the transferor pursuant to a property settlement would be $50,000. Thus, if the transferee were immediately to resell the property for $200,000, the transferee would realize and recognize gain of $150,000.[149]

f. Nonresident Alien

I.R.C. § 1041 does not apply to a transfer between spouses if the transferee spouse is a nonresident alien.[150] On the other hand, the transfer of property to a spouse who is a U.S. citizen or a resident alien would appear to be protected by Section 1041.

g. Property Subject to a Tax Lien

Caution is advised to the transferee spouse to accept property subject to a tax lien. In *Craft v. United States,*[151] the Supreme Court of the United States held that a Federal tax lien arising under I.R.C. § 6321 on property and rights to property of a delinquent taxpayer attaches to the taxpayer's rights in property held by the taxpayers as tenants by the entireties, even though state law insulates such property from creditors' claims against only one spouse. The case was decided under Michigan law, which is very similar to Maryland law. The Court stated that while state law determines what rights a taxpayer has in property, Federal law determines whether the state-defined rights are "property" or "rights to property" for purposes of I.R.C. § 6321.

In Notice 2003-60,[152] the IRS stated that a spouse of the taxpayer who obtained entireties property in a divorce acquires the property subject to the Federal tax lien. In the context of a divorce, a spouse is not in the class of persons protected by I.R.C. § 6323(a). Consequently, if the assessment giving rise to the Federal tax lien under I.R.C. § 6321 had occurred prior to the divorce, then the lien also attached to the taxpayer's rights in the entireties property. As a general rule, if the transfer occurred before *Craft,* then the IRS will treat the transfer as one for value and will not assert its lien against the property in the hands of the ex-spouse of the taxpayer. This will not apply if the IRS determines that, notwithstanding the divorce, the transfer was fraudulent. Since a divorce or transfer to a third party terminates the entireties estate (and, with it, the spouses' rights of survivorship), if the property is transferred to a third

149. Yonadi v. Comm'r, 21 F.3d 1292 (3d Cir. 1994), *rev'g* T.C. Memo. 1992-602 .
150. I.R.C. § 1041(d); Temp. Prop. Treas. Reg. § 1.10411T(a)(A3).
151. 533 U.S. 274 (2002).
152. 2003-2 C.B. 643.

party or to either spouse as a result of a divorce, then the Federal tax lien generally will have priority with respect to a one-half interest in the property over the bank's subsequent security interest.

In *Struble v. Internal Revenue Service*,[153] the Court held that a transfer of real property under a divorce settlement was subject to a Federal tax lien that attached while the parties were married. In *Struble*, the property was transferred subject to a tax lien based upon an assessment against the husband for unpaid income taxes. The husband was to remove the lien against the property within 30 months from the date of the settlement. When he did not act, the wife filed an action to clear the title and remove the lien. The Court held that the lien survived the transfer, that it related back to the time of the assessment and remains valid until satisfied or is unenforceable due to lapse of time.

7. Excludable Transactions

In addition to the protection provided by Section 1041 for transfers between spouses or former spouses incident to a divorce, the Code specifically excludes from recognition other transactions that would otherwise result in recognition, except that they occurred between spouses or former spouses incident to a divorce. Some of those transactions are (as discussed earlier):

(i) Assumption of liability in excess of basis.[154] This exception does not apply to transfers of property in trust where liabilities exceed basis.[155] The rules described previously apply even if the transferred property is subject to liabilities that exceed the adjusted basis of the property. Thus, no gain or loss is recognized by the transferor, and the basis of the property in the hands of the transferor is carried over to the transferee. Assume A owns property having a fair market value of $10,000 and an adjusted basis of $1,000. In contemplation of making a transfer of this property incident to a divorce from B, A borrows $5,000 from a bank, using the property as security for the borrowing. A then transfers the property to B and B assumes, or takes the property subject to, the liability to pay the $5,000 debt. Under I.R.C. § 1041, A recognizes no gain or loss upon the transfer of the property, and the adjusted basis of the property in the hands of B is $1,000. If, however, A makes a gift of the property to C, a non-spouse, A would recognize gain of $4,000. C would then have a basis in the property of $5,000 (the lesser of fair market value of the property at the time of the gift or the property's adjusted basis). But if property with liabilities in excess of basis is transferred to an alimony trust, gain is recognized by the transferor

153. 2003 U.S. Dist. LEXIS 17016 (D. N.J. 2003).

154. H. Rep. No. 98432, 98th Cong., 2d Sess. (1984), at 1492.

155. *See* I.R.C. § 1041(e).

on the excess and the basis to the transferee is the carryover basis plus gain recognized by the transferor. Thus, in the preceding example, if the transfer were to a trust, A would recognize gain of $4,000 and the basis of the property in the hands of the trust would be $5,000 (basis of property to A, plus gain recognized by A). The foregoing rules do not apply to transfers to a grantor trust since the grantor still owns the property after the transfer. Thus, I.R.C. § 1041(e) does not apply to transfers to a grantor trust where liabilities exceed basis.

(ii) Disposition of installment obligations.[156]

(iii) Depreciation recapture.[157]

(iv) Investment tax credit recapture.[158] A transfer under I.R.C. § 1041 generally does not result in a recapture of investment tax credits with respect to property transferred. Property transferred under I.R.C. § 1041 will not be treated as being disposed of by, or ceasing to be I.R.C. § 38 property with respect to, the transferor. However, the transferee will be subject to investment tax credit recapture if, upon or after the transfer, the property is disposed of by, or ceases to be I.R.C. § 38 property with respect to, the transferee. For example, as part of a divorce property settlement, *B* receives a car from *A* that has been used in *A*'s business for two years and for which an investment tax credit was taken by *A*. No part of *A*'s business is transferred to *B* and *B*'s use of the car is solely personal. *B* is subject to recapture of the investment tax credit previously taken by *A*.[159]

8. Summary of Tax Consequences of Transfers Subject to I.R.C. § 1041

a. Transferor

The transferor of property under I.R.C. § 1041 recognizes no gain or loss on the transfer even if the transfer was in exchange for the release of marital rights or other consideration.[160] This rule applies regardless of whether the transfer is of property separately owned by the transferor or is a division (equal or unequal) of community property.[161] Thus, the result under I.R.C. § 1041 differs from the result in *United States v. Davis*,[162] which is overruled.[163]

156. I.R.C. § 453B(g).
157. I.R.C. §§ 1245 and 1250.
158. I.R.C. § 47(e).
159. Temp. Prop. Treas. Reg. § 1.10411T(d)(A13).
160. Temp. Prop. Treas. Reg. § 1.10411T(d)(A10).
161. Temp. Prop. Treas. Reg. § 1.10411T(d)(A11).
162. 370 U.S. 65 (1962).
163. Temp. Prop. Treas. Reg. § 1.10411T(d)(A11).

b. Transferee

The transferee of property under I.R.C. § 1041 recognizes no gain or loss upon receipt of the transferred property.[164] In all cases, the basis of the transferred property in the hands of the transferee is the adjusted basis of such property in the hands of the transferor immediately before the transfer. Even if the transfer is a bona fide sale, the transferee does not acquire a basis in the transferred property equal to the transferee's cost (the fair market value). This carryover basis rule applies whether the adjusted basis of the transferred property is less than, equal to, or greater than its fair market value at the time of transfer (or the value of any consideration provided by the transferee) and applies for purposes of determining loss as well as gain upon the subsequent disposition of the property by the transferee. Thus, this rule is different from the rule applied in I.R.C. § 1015(a) for determining the basis of property acquired by gift.[165]

Where property is to be sold shortly before or after the transfer, the transferor would prefer to transfer low basis property and retain high basis property, whereas the transferee would prefer to receive high basis property in lieu of low basis property. On the other hand, where the transferor is elderly, the transferor may retain low basis assets in order to receive a stepup in basis upon death. These are obviously issues to be negotiated by the parties. Also, the parties should determine the basis of property at time of transfer.[166]

c. Conclusion

If the transferor spouse transfers income producing property, such as rental property, that produces rental income, or stocks or bonds that produce dividends or interest, the transferor reports such rental income, or dividends or interest, which is earned from the property on his or her return for the year in which the property is transferred, up until the time the property is transferred. The transferor spouse must report such rental income, dividend income, or interest income on his or her return for the year in which the property is transferred, after the time the property is transferred.

If the transferor spouse transfers an interest in a passive activity with unused passive activity losses, that transferor cannot deduct the unused losses, which are transferred to the transferee spouse who can increase the adjusted basis of the transferred property by the amount of the unused losses.

The transferor spouse does not have to recapture investment credit property. Such recapture passes to the transferee spouse, who may have to recapture the credit when he or she sells the property or changes its use before the end of the recapture period.

---

164. *Id.*

165. Temp. Prop. Treas. Reg. § 1.10411T(d)(A11). *See* Yonadi v. Comm'r.

166. *See* Lausterer v. Comm'r, T.C. Memo. 1995-130 (1995).

Finally, the transferor spouse does not include in income interests in nonstatutory stock options or nonqualified deferred compensation arrangements when such interests are transferred. Rather, the tax burden falls on the transferee spouse who includes such amounts in income when the transferee spouse exercises the stock option or when the deferred compensation is paid or made available to the transferee spouse.

9. Notice and Record Keeping Requirements with Respect to Transactions under I.R.C. § 1041

A transferor of property under I.R.C. § 1041 must, at the time of the transfer, supply the transferee with records sufficient to determine the adjusted basis and holding period of the property as of the date of the transfer.

In addition, in the case of a transfer of property which carries with it a potential liability for investment tax credit recapture, the transferor must, at the time of the transfer, supply the transferee with records sufficient to determine the amount and period of such potential liability. Such records must be preserved and kept accessible by the transferee.[167]

For a chart that summarizes the tax treatment of items of property transferred between spouses or former spouses pursuant to divorce, see I.R.S. Publication 504, Divorce or Separated Individuals, Table 5, page 21 (2021).

167. Temp. Prop. Treas. Reg. § 1.10411T(e)(A14).

7 The Residence

A. Introduction

To many married couples, a residence is their most valuable and important asset. Since it is likely to be the focal point of any property settlement, the tax consequences attendant to its transfer are extremely important.

This chapter first discusses the tax consequences of the sale of a principal residence, and then discusses the tax aspects of the payment of expenses of a principal residence incident to a divorce.

B. Transfer

1. Title in Transferor; Transfer of Entire Interest to Transferee

If title to the property is solely in the transferor's spouse's name and the transferor spouse passes his or her entire interest to the transferee in exchange for the release of the transferee's marital rights, the transferor will recognize no gain or loss on the transfer of the property to a spouse or former spouse (as long as the transfer is incident to the divorce).[1]

The transferee will then take a basis in the property equal to the adjusted basis of the property in the hands of the transferor.[2] This is known as carryover basis.

If the transfer does not fit within I.R.C. § 1041, it will be governed by the general exchanging rules of I.R.C. § 1001, and the basis rules of I.R.C. § 1012.

2. Transferor Remains as Sole Owner with Transferee in Possession

If the transferor spouse remains sole owner of the property, but the transferee spouse alone continues to reside in the residence, there are no tax consequences because the property has not been transferred.

The same result follows if the spouses retain title as joint tenants or tenants in common with the transferee in possession.

1. I.R.C. § 1041(a). See Chapter 6.
2. I.R.C. § 1041(b)(2).

In *Suhr v. Commissioner*,[3] the Court held that gain from the sale of the residence was taxable to the spouse who owned it. During the marriage, the wife purchased a home that was titled in her name alone. Several years later the husband and the wife took out a mortgage on which they were both liable. The husband made all the payments on the mortgage. The decree of divorce provided that the house, which was titled in the wife's name alone, "shall remain in the names of husband and wife," but granted the wife exclusive possession of the house. The decree required the house to be sold within eight years after the divorce. It then provided that the husband and the wife would each receive one half of the net equity form the sale of the house. The wife sold the house seven years after the divorce. Only she signed the contract of sale and the deed. The IRS contended that the husband was subject to gain on one half the proceeds from the sale of the house on the grounds the house was marital property. Under this theory, the IRS contended the husband had an ownership interest in the house. The Tax Court held for the husband. Its position was that the house was not marital property and was owned solely by the wife. Thus, the gain from the sale was solely taxable to the wife.

3. Transferor Transfers His or Her Joint Tenancy or Tenancy in Common Interest to Transferee

If the transferor and transferee spouses own the property as joint tenants or tenants in common, and the transferor transfers his or her joint tenant or tenant in common interest in the property to the transferee in exchange for the release of his or her marital rights, the transferor will not recognize gain or loss on the transfer if made to the transferor's spouse or former spouse (if incident to the divorce).[4] The transferee's basis in the property is the carryover basis of the property.[5] If the transfer does not fit within I.R.C. § 1041, it will be governed by the general exchanging rules of I.R.C. § 1001, and the basis rules of I.R.C. § 1012.[6]

4. Sales and Exchanges of Principal Residence to a Non-Spouse[7]

Gain from the sale of a principal residence can be excluded from gross income in one of two ways. First, gain realized from the sale or exchange of a principal residence will not be recognized if the property is transferred from an individual to a spouse or former spouse if the transfer is incident to a divorce under

3. T.C. Memo. 2001-28 (2001).
4. I.R.C. § 1041(a).
5. I.R.C. § 1041(b)(2).
6. *See* Robert A. Rombro & Theodore W. Hirsh, Federal Tax Aspects of the Acquisition, Ownership and Sale of a Taxpayer's Personal Residence, Residential Real Estate Transactions (MICPEL 5th ed., 2009).
7. *Id.*

Section 1041 discussed previously. Section 1041 protects gain from taxation whether the sale is during the marriage, before the divorce, or after the divorce. Second, gain realized from the sale of a principal residence is not included in gross income if the tests of Section 121, discussed below, are met. The following discusses the requirements of Section 121 that must be met to exclude from gross income gain realized from the sale of a principal residence.

a. Exclusion of Gain from Sale of Principal Residence

I.R.C. § 121(a) excludes from gross income the gain realized from the sale or exchange of property if, during the five-year period ending on the date of the sale or exchange, the property has been *owned* and *used* by the taxpayer as the taxpayer's principal residence for periods aggregating two years or more. If the tests of Section 121 are met, Section 121 mandatorily applies. No election to have Section 121 apply is necessary. On the other hand, a taxpayer can elect not to have Section 121 apply as discussed at 7.B.4.e of this chapter.

(1) Maximum Exclusion

Under I.R.C. § 121(b) the maximum amount of gain that may be excluded may not exceed —

- (a) $250,000 for a taxpayer who is single, married filing separate, or head of household; or
- (b) $500,000 for a husband and wife if:
  - i. they file a joint return for the year of the sale or exchange;
  - ii. *either* spouse meets the two-year ownership requirements of I.R.C. § 121(a);
  - iii. *both* spouses meet the two-year use requirements of I.R.C. § 121(a);
  - iv. *neither* spouse is ineligible for the benefits of I.R.C. § 121(a) by reason of I.R.C. § 121(b)(3) (restricting the exclusion of gain to one sale or exchange every two years).[8]

If the spouses do not meet all four tests, the amount of the exclusion that they may claim is the sum of the amounts each could claim if they had not been married. For purposes of this provision, each spouse is treated as owning the property during the period that either spouse owned the property.[9]

The exclusion does not apply to any sale or exchange by the taxpayer if during the two-year period ending on the date of the sale or exchange there was any other sale or exchange by the taxpayer to which the exclusion applied.

8. I.R.C. § 121(b)(2)(A); Treas. Reg. § 1.121-2(b)(1).
9. I.R.C. § 121(b)(2); Treas. Reg. § 1.21-2(a)(3)(ii).

Thus, the exclusion is allowed for sales or exchanges once every two years.[10] For example, assume the taxpayer owns Property A which he owns and uses as his principal residence for two full calendar years. In calendar year 3 the taxpayer purchases Property B which he owns and uses as his principal residence. The taxpayer sells Property A in calendar year 5 and excludes the gain realized from such sale. In calendar year 6 the taxpayer sells Property B. The taxpayer may not exclude the gain realized from the sale of Property B, even though the two-year ownership and use tests were met with respect to Property B, because the taxpayer excluded the gain realized from the sale of Property A within two years from the sale of Property B.

A married couple who does not qualify for the $500,000 exclusion of gain realized may still be able to exclude more than $250,000. For example, assume *H* owned and used a residence as his principal residence for five years. *W* owned and used the residence as her principal residence for one year. They sold the residence and realized a gain of $500,000. The amount of gain excludible by each is computed separately, since all four tests set forth above were not met (*W* did not meet the use test). Since *H* meets all four tests, *H* can exclude $250,000 of gain realized. *W*, however, does not meet the use test. Thus, *W* is entitled to the reduced maximum exclusion described in I.R.C. § 121(c)(1) discussed later. *W*'s exclusion is $125,000 (one year of use/two years of use = 50% × $250,000 = $125,000). Thus, *H* and *W* combined can exclude $375,000 of gain realized from the sale of the residence.[11]

(2) Reduced Maximum Exclusion

Special rules are provided for taxpayers who fail to meet the joint return test, the use and ownership test or the one-sale-every-two-years test for specific statutory purposes. A taxpayer who fails to meet the two out of five year use and ownership test or the limit of one-sale-every-two-years test may still exclude the gain from gross income if the sale or exchange is by reason of a change in place of employment, health, or, to the extent provided in regulations, unforeseen circumstances.[12] If the rules of I.R.C. § 121(c) apply, the amount of gain excluded is (i) the amount which bears the same ratio to the amount which would be so excluded if the ownership and use requirements had been met, as (ii) the shorter of (a) the aggregate periods during the five year period ending on the date of such sale or exchange, such property has been owned and used by the taxpayer as the taxpayer's principal residence, or (b) the period after the date of the most recent prior sale or exchange by the taxpayer to which I.R.C. § 121(a) applied and before the date of such sale or

10. I.R.C. § 121(b)(3).
11. I.R.C. § 121(b)(2)(B).
12. I.R.C. § 121(c)(2), Treas, Reg. § 1.121-3(a).

exchange, (c) bears to two years.[13] To illustrate, if a taxpayer sells his or her house within 18 months after use or ownership instead of the 24 month period because of a change in his or her place of employment, health, or unforeseen circumstances as set forth in the regulations, the amount excludible is 18/24th. If the taxpayer files as individual, the amount excludible is $187,500 (18/24 × $250,000). If the taxpayer files as married filing joint, the amount excludible is $375,000 (18/24 × $500,000).

The effect of the foregoing is to produce a reduced maximum exclusion for a qualified taxpayer whose sale or exchange is primarily caused by reason of a change in place of employment, health, or unforeseen circumstances.[14] Six factors that the Service will consider to determine if the taxpayer's primary reason for the sale or exchange is due to a change in the place of employment, health, or unforeseen circumstances are: (i) the sale or exchange and the circumstances giving rise to the sale or exchange are proximate in time; (ii) the suitability of the property as the taxpayer's principal residence materially changes; (iii) the taxpayer's financial ability to maintain the property is materially impaired; (iv) the taxpayer uses the property as the taxpayer's residence during the period of the taxpayer's ownership of the property; (v) the circumstances giving rise to the sale or exchange are not reasonably foreseeable when the taxpayer begins using the property as the taxpayer's principal residence; and (vi) the circumstances giving rise to the sale or exchange occur during the period of the taxpayer's ownership and use of the property as the taxpayer's principal residence.[15]

(a) Change in Place of Employment

A sale or exchange is by reason of a change in place of employment if the primary reason for the sale or exchange is a change in the location of the qualified individual's employment.[16] A sale or exchange is deemed to be by reason of a change in place of employment if the change in the place of employment occurs during the period of the qualified individual's (as defined later) ownership and use of the property as the qualified individual's principal residence; and the qualified individual's new place of employment is at least 50 miles farther from the residence sold or exchanged than was the former place of employment or, if there were no former place of employment, the distance between the qualified individual's new place of employment and the residence sold or exchanged is at least 50 miles.[17] Employment includes the commencement of

13. I.R.C. § 121(c)(1).
14. Treas. Reg. § 121-3(b).
15. *Id.*
16. Treas. Reg. § 121-3(c)(1).
17. Treas. Reg. § 121-3(c)(2).

employment with a new employer, the continuation of employment with the same employer, and the commencement or continuation of self-employment.[18]

Treas. Reg. § 1.121-3(c)(4) provides four examples that illustrate the availability of a reduced maximum exclusion where the sale or exchange is by reason of a change in place of employment.

(b) Health

A sale or exchange is deemed to be by reason of health if the primary reason for the sale or exchange is to obtain, provide, or facilitate the diagnosis, cure, mitigation, or treatment of disease, illness, or injury of a qualified individual, or to obtain or provide medical or personal care for a qualified individual suffering from a disease, illness, or injury.[19] In addition, a sale or exchange is deemed to be by reason of health if a physician, as defined in Section 213(d)(4), recommends a change of residence for reasons of health set forth in the preceding sentence.[20] A sale or exchange that is merely beneficial to the general heath or well-being of an individual is not a sale or exchange by reason of health.[21]

Treas. Reg. § 1.121-3(d)(3) provides five examples that illustrate the availability of a reduced maximum exclusion where the primary purpose for the sale or exchange is due to the health of a qualified individual.

(c) Unforeseen Circumstances

A sale or exchange is by reason of unforeseen circumstances if the primary reason for the sale or exchange is the occurrence of an event that the taxpayer could not reasonably have anticipated before purchasing and occupying the residence. A sale or exchange by reason of unforeseen circumstances (other than those described later) does not qualify for the reduced maximum exclusion if the primary reason for the sale or exchange is a preference for a different residence or an improvement in financial circumstances.[22]

---

18. Treas. Reg. § 1.121-3(c)(3).
19. Treas. Reg. § 1.121-3(d)(1).
20. Treas. Reg. § 1.121-3(d)(2). The taxpayer must establish that the sale or exchange was due to changes in the taxpayer's health, but if not, the Tax Court may give the taxpayer a second chance. In *Webert v. Commissioner*, T.C. Memo 2022-32, the taxpayers moved from their home in 2009 and rented the property intermittingly through 2015 when they sold it realizing a gain of nearly $200,000, which they excluded from income on the grounds that they moved because of the wife's health. The Tax Court first granted the Service's motion for partial summary payment because it established that the taxpayers did not use the house as their principal residence for at least two of the five years preceding the date of sale. The Court, however, graciously denied full summary judgment by requesting additional findings from the parties to determine whether the taxpayers' absence from the property and the sale were due to the taxpayers' health.
21. Treas. Reg. § 1.121-3(d)(1).
22. Treas. Reg. § 1.121-3(e)(1).

The sale or exchange is considered to be by reason of unforeseen circumstances if any of the following seven events occur during the period of the taxpayer's ownership and use of the residence as the taxpayer's principal residence: (i) the involuntary conversion of the residence; (ii) natural or man-made disasters or acts of war or terrorism resulting in a casualty to the residence (without regard to deductibility under Section 165(h)); (iii) the death of the qualified individual; (iv) the cessation of employment as a result of which the qualified individual is eligible for unemployment compensation (as defined in Section 85(b)); (v) a change in employment or self-employment status that results in the taxpayer's inability to pay housing costs and reasonable basic living expenses for the taxpayer's household (including amounts for food, clothing, medical expenses, taxes, transportation, court-ordered payments, and expenses reasonably necessary to the production of income, but not for the maintenance of an affluent or luxurious standard of living); (vi) a divorce or legal separation under a decree of divorce or separate maintenance; or (vii) multiple births resulting from the same pregnancy.[23]

The list of factors is not exclusive. In *United States v. Forte*,[24] the taxpayer sold a second house within two years of the sale of the first house. The taxpayer argued the second sale was caused by financial hardship from the sale of the first house which the taxpayer sold with seller financing which became uncollectible due to fraud by the buyer. The Court determined that there was a genuine dispute of a material fact as to whether the taxpayer's could have reasonably anticipated that they could not collect the full seller financing which forced them to sell the second house and denied the Service's motion for summary judgment. Thus, the Court looked to the financial hardship of the taxpayer to determine if the reduced maximum exclusion was available, a factor not specifically listed in the regulations.

Treas. Reg. § 1.121-3(e)(4) provides ten examples that illustrate the availability of the reduced maximum exclusion where the primary purpose for the sale or exchange is due to unforeseen circumstances.

(d) Qualified Individual

For purposes of applying the reduced maximum exclusion, the term "qualified individual" referred to above means the taxpayer; the taxpayer's spouse; a co-owner of the residence; a person whose principal place of abode is in the same household as the taxpayer; or a person bearing a relationship specified in Sections 152(a)(1) through 152(a)(8) (without regard to qualification as a dependent) to a qualified individual, or a descendant of the taxpayers' grandparent.[25]

23. Treas. Reg. § 1.121-3(e)2).
24. 544 F. Supp. 3d 1211 (D. Utah 2021).
25. Treas. Reg. § 1.121-3(f).

(e) Computation

The reduced maximum exclusion is computed by multiplying the maximum dollar limitation of $250,000 ($500,000 for certain joint filers) by a fraction. The numerator of the fraction is the shortest of: (i) the period of time that the taxpayer owned the property during the five-year period ending on the date of the sale or exchange; (ii) the period of time that the taxpayer used the property as the taxpayer's principal residence during the five-year period ending on the date of the sale or exchange; or (iii) the period of time between that date of a prior sale or exchange of property for which the taxpayer excluded gain under Section 121 and the date of the current sale or exchange. The numerator of the fraction may be expressed in days or months. The denominator of the fraction is 730 days or 24 months (depending on the measure of time used in the numerator).[26]

The computation of the reduced maximum exclusion is illustrated by the following two examples:

Example 1. Taxpayer A purchases a house that she uses as her principal residence. Twelve months after the purchase, A sells the house due to a change in place of her employment. A has not excluded gain under Section 121 on a prior sale or exchange of property within the last two years. A is eligible to exclude up to $125,000 of the gain from the sale of her house (12/24 × $250,000).

Example 2. Taxpayer H owns a house that he has used as his principal residence since 1996. On January 15, 1999, H and W marry and W begins to use H's house as her principal residence. On January 15, 2000, H sells the house due to a change in W's place of employment. Neither H nor W has excluded gain under Section 121 on a prior sale or exchange of property within the last two years. Because H and W have not each used the house as their principal residence for at least two years during the five-year period preceding its sale, the maximum dollar limitation amount that may be claimed by H and W will not be $500,000, but the sum of each spouse's limitation amount determined on a separate basis as if they had not been married. (See Treas. Reg. § 1.121-2(a)(3)(ii).) H is eligible to exclude up to $250,000 of gain because he meets the requirements of Section 121. W is not eligible to exclude the maximum dollar limitation amount. Instead, because the sale of the house is due to a change in place of employment, W is eligible to claim a reduced maximum exclusion of up to $125,000 of the gain (365/730 × $250,000). Therefore, H and W are eligible to exclude up to $375,000 of gain ($250,000 + $125,000) from the sale of the house.[27]

Some planning is available depending upon whether the sale takes place in the year before or after the divorce. If the sale occurs and the parties are

26. Treas. Reg. § 1.121-3(g)(1).
27. Treas. Reg. § 1.121-3(g)(2).

still married at the end of the year, the spouses can exclude up to $500,000 of gain realized on the sale of the residence in two ways. First, they can file a joint return for the year because they are still married. If they meet the four tests of Section 121(b)(2)(A)–(D) they can exclude up to the $500,000 exclusion available to joint filers. Before taking this step, however, it is recommended that the parties determine how they will divide the proceeds between them, whether equally or unequally. (Note that if the split is unequal, Section 1041 protects any transfer of an appreciated interest in the property from one spouse to the other from recognition of gain if the spouses are married or incident to a divorce, and Section 2516 protects any transfer of cash from Federal gift tax.)

Second, the parties can file as married filing separate for the year in which the sale takes place. Each spouse can then exclude up to $250,000 of gain realized as long as each spouse has owned and used the property as his/her principal residence for two years or more during the five-year period ending on the date of the sale. As discussed later, if one spouse acquires his or her interest in the residence and the transfer is protected by Section 1041, the transferor spouse can include the time the transferee spouse owned the property for purposes of the two out of five-year ownership test. No attribution is available, however, for the use tests. Attribution applies only to the ownership test.

b. Residence

Whether property is used by the taxpayer as the taxpayer's residence depends upon all the facts and circumstances. A property used by the taxpayer as the taxpayer's residence may include a houseboat, a house trailer, or the house or apartment that the taxpayer is entitled to occupy as a tenant-stockholder in a cooperative housing corporation (as those terms are defined in Section 216(b)(1) and (2)). Property used by the taxpayer as the taxpayer's residence does not include personal property that is not a fixture under local law.[28]

In the case of a taxpayer using more than one property as a residence, whether the property is used by the taxpayer as the taxpayer's principal residence depends upon all the facts and circumstances.[29] If a taxpayer alternates between two properties, using each as a residence for successive periods of time, the property that the taxpayer uses a majority of the time during the year ordinarily will be considered the taxpayer's principal residence. In addition to the taxpayer's use of the property, six relevant factors in determining a taxpayer's principal residence include, but are not limited to (i) the taxpayer's

28. Treas. Reg. § 1.121-1(b)(1).

29. *See also* Malat v. Riddell, 383 U.S. 569, 86 S. Ct. 1030 (1966), in which the Court, in a per curiam opinion, held that "primarily" in Section 1221, means "principally or of first importance." Thus, a principal residence could be the one of first importance, or the one that is primarily used as the residence.

place of employment; (ii) the principal place of abode of the taxpayer's family members; (iii) the address listed on the taxpayer's Federal and State tax returns, driver's license, automobile registration, and voter registration card; (iv) the taxpayer's mailing address for bills and correspondence; (v) the location of the taxpayer's banks; and (vi) the location of religious organizations and recreational clubs with which the taxpayer is affiliated.[30]

The sale or exchange of vacant land is not a sale or exchange of the taxpayer's principal residence unless (i) the vacant land is adjacent to land containing the dwelling unit of the taxpayer's principal residence; (ii) the taxpayer owned and used the vacant land as part of the taxpayer's principal residence; (iii) the taxpayer sells or exchanges the dwelling unit in a sale or exchange that meets the requirements of Section 121 within two years before or two years after the date of the sale or exchange of the vacant land; and (iv) the requirements of Section 121 have otherwise been met with respect to the vacant land.[31]

For purposes of Section 121(b)(1) and (2) (relating to the maximum limitation amount of the Section 121 exclusion), the sale or exchange of the dwelling unit and the vacant land are treated as one sale or exchange. Therefore, only one maximum limitation amount of $250,000 ($500,000 for certain joint returns) applies to the combined sales or exchanges of vacant land and the dwelling unit. In applying the maximum limitation amount to sales or exchanges that occur in different taxable years, gain from the sale or exchange of the dwelling unit, up to the maximum limitation amount under Section 121(b)(1) or (2), is excluded first and each spouse is treated as excluding one-half of the gain from a sale or exchange to which Section 121(b)(2)(A) and Treas. Reg. § 1.121-2(a)(3)(i) (relating to the limitation for certain joint returns) apply.[32]

If a dwelling unit and vacant land are sold or exchanged in separate transactions that qualify for Section 121 exclusionary treatment, each of the transactions is disregarded in applying Section 121(b)(3) (restricting the application to Section 121 to only one sale or exchange every two years) to the other transactions, but is taken into account as a sale or exchange of a principal residence on the date of the transaction in applying Section 121(b)(3) to that transaction and the sale or exchange of any other principal residence.[33]

If the sale or exchange of the dwelling unit occurs in a taxable year later than the sale or exchange of the vacant land and after the date prescribed by law (including extensions) for the filing of the return for the taxable year of the sale or exchange of the vacant land, any gain from the sale or exchange of the vacant land must be treated as taxable on the taxpayer's return for the taxable

30. Treas. Reg. § 1.121-1(b)(2).
31. Treas. Reg. § 1.121-1(b)(3)(i).
32. Treas. Reg. § 1.121-1(b)(3)(ii)(A).
33. Treas. Reg. § 1.121-1(b)(3)(ii)(B).

year of the sale or exchange of the vacant land. If the taxpayer has reported gain from the sale or exchange of the vacant land as taxable, after satisfying the requirements of Treas. Reg. § 1.121-1(b)(3), the taxpayer may claim the Section 121 exclusion with regard to the sale or exchange or the vacant land (for any period for which the period of limitation under Section 6511 has not expired) by filing an amended return.[34]

The following four examples illustrate the rules regarding the sale of a residence, principal residence, and vacant land.

Example 1. Taxpayer A owns two residences, one in New York and one in Florida. From 1999 through 2004, A lives in the New York residence for seven months and the Florida residence for five months of each year. In the absence of facts and circumstances indicating otherwise, the New York residence is A's principal residence. A would be eligible for the Section 121 exclusion of gain from the sale or exchange of the New York residence, but not the Florida residence.

Example 2. Taxpayer B owns two residences, one in Virginia and one in Maine. During 1999 and 2000, B lives in the Virginia residence. During 2001 and 2002, B lives in the Maine residence. During 2003, B lives in the Virginia residence. B's principal residence during 1999, 2000, and 2003 is the Virginia residence. B's principal residence during 2001 and 2002 is the Maine residence. B would be eligible for the Section 121 exclusion of gain from the sale or exchange of either residence (but not both) during 2003.

Example 3. In 1991 Taxpayer C buys property consisting of a house and ten acres that C uses as her principal residence. In May 2006 C sells eight acres of the land and realizes a gain of $110,000. C does not sell the dwelling unit before the due date for filing C's 2005 income tax returns. Therefore, C is not eligible to exclude the $110,000 of gain. In March 2007 C sells the house and remaining two acres realizing a gain of $180,000 from the sale of the house. C may exclude the $180,000 of gain. Because the sale of the eight acres occurred within two years from the date of the sale of the dwelling unit, the sale of the eight acres is treated as a sale of the taxpayer's principal residence. C may file an amended return for 2005 to claim an exclusion for $70,000 ($250,000–$180,000 gain previously excluded) of the $110,000 gain from the sale of the eight acres.

Example 4. In 1998 Taxpayer D buys a house and one acre that D uses as D's principal residence. In 1999 D buys 29 acres adjacent to D's house and uses the vacant land as part of D's principal residence. In 2003 D sells the house and one acre and the 29 acres in two separate transactions. D sells the house and one acre at a loss of $25,000. D realizes $270,000 of gain from the sale of the 29 acres. D may exclude the $245,000 gain from the two sales.[35]

---

34. Treas. Reg. § 1.121-1(b)(3)(ii)(C).
35. Treas. Reg. § 1.121-1(b)(4) Examples 1–4.

c. Use and Ownership Requirements

The requirements of ownership and use for periods aggregating two years or more may be satisfied by establishing ownership and use for 24 full months or for 730 days (365 × 2). The requirements of ownership and use may be satisfied during nonconcurrent periods if both the ownership and use tests are met during the five-year period ending on the date of the sale or exchange.[36]

(1) Use

In establishing whether a taxpayer has satisfied the two-year use requirement, occupancy of the residence is required. However, short temporary absences, such as for vacation or other seasonal absence (although accompanied with rental of the residence), are counted as periods of use.[37]

If a taxpayer has become physically or mentally incapable of self-care and the taxpayer sells or exchanges property that the taxpayer owned and used as the taxpayer's principal residence for periods aggregating at least one year during the five year period preceding the sale or exchange, the taxpayer is treated as using the property as the taxpayer's principal residence for any period of time during the five year period in which the taxpayer owns the property and resides in any facility (including a nursing home) licensed by a State or political subdivision to care for an individual in the taxpayer's condition.[38]

(2) Ownership

If a residence is owned by a trust for the period that a taxpayer is treated under Sections 671 through 679 (relating to the treatment of grantors and others as substantial owners) as the owner of the trust or the portion of the trust that includes the residence, the taxpayer will be treated as owning the residence for purposes of satisfying the two-year ownership requirement of Section 121, and the sale or exchange by the trust will be treated as if made by the taxpayer.[39] If a residence is owned by a single member LLC that is treated as a disregarded entity, the owner will be treated as owning the residence for purposes of satisfying the two-year ownership requirement of Section 121, and the sale or exchange by the entity will be treated as if made by the owner.[40]

If a residence is owned by a single member LLC that is treated as a disregarded entity, the owner will be treated as owning the residence for purposes of satisfying the two-year ownership requirement of Section 121, and the sale or exchange by the entity will be treated as if made by the owner.[41]

---

36. Treas. Reg. § 1.121-1(c)(1).
37. Treas. Reg. § 1.121-1(c)(2)(i).
38. Treas. Reg. § 1.121-1(c)(2)(ii).
39. Treas. Reg. § 1.121-1(c)(3)(i).
40. Treas. Reg. § 1.121-1(c)(3)(ii).
41. Treas. Reg. § 1.121-1(c)(4), Examples 1–5.

(3) Examples

The ownership and use provisions discussed above are illustrated by the following five examples. The examples assume that Treas. Reg. § 1.121-3 (relating to the reduced maximum exclusion) does not apply to the sale of the property.[42]

Example 1. Taxpayer E has owned and used E's house as E's principal residence since 1986. On January 31, 1998, E moves to another state. E rents E's house to tenants from that date until April 18, 2000, when E sells it. E is eligible for the Section 121 exclusion because E has owned and used the house as E's principal residence for at least two of the five years preceding the sale.

Example 2. Taxpayer F owns and uses a house as F's principal residence from 1986 to the end of 1997. On January 4, 1998, F moves to another state and ceases to use the house. F's son moves into the house in March 1999 and uses the residence until it is sold on July 1, 2001. F may not exclude gain from the sale under Section 121 because F did not use the property as F's principal residence for at least two years out of the five years preceding the sale.

Example 3. Taxpayer G lives in a townhouse that G rents from 1993 through 1996. On January 18, 1997, G purchases the townhouse. On February 1, 1998, G moves into G's daughter's home. On May 25, 2000, while still living in G's daughter's house, G sells his townhouse. The Section 121 exclusion will apply to gain from the sale because G owned the townhouse for at least two years out of the five years preceding the sale (from January 19, 1997, until May 25, 2000), and G used the townhouse as his principal residence for at least two years during the five-year period preceding the sale (from May 25, 1995 until February 1, 1998).

Example 4. Taxpayer H, a college professor, purchases and moves into a house on May 1, 1997. H uses the house as his principal residence continuously until September 1, 1998, when H goes abroad for a one-year sabbatical leave. On October 1, 1999, one month after returning from the leave, H sells the house. Because H's leave is not considered to be a short temporary absence, the period of the sabbatical leave may not be included in determining whether H used the house for periods aggregating two years during the five-year period ending on the date of the sale. Consequently, H is not entitled to exclude gain under Section 121 because H did not use the residence for the requisite period.[43]

Example 5. Taxpayer I purchases a house on February 1, 1998, that I uses as I's principal residence. During 1998 and 1999, I leaves I's residence for a two month summer vacation. I sells the house on March 1, 2000. Although, in the five-year period preceding the date of sale, the total time I used I's residence

42. Treas. Reg. § *1.121*-1(e)(1)

43. Although a sabbatical would appear to be a short temporary absence, it would appear that the Service concluded that such was not the case because the taxpayer sold the property one month after returning from sabbatical. Compare with Example 5.

is less than two years (21 months), the Section 121 exclusion will apply to gain from the sale of the residence because the two-month vacations are short temporary absences and are counted as periods of use in determining whether I used the residence for the requisite period.[44]

Section 121 does not apply to the gain allocable to any portion (separate from the dwelling unit) of property sold or exchanged with respect to which a taxpayer does not satisfy the use requirement. Thus, if a portion of the property was used for residential purposes and a portion of the property (separate from the dwelling unit) was used for nonresidential purposes, only the gain allocable to the residential portion is excludible under Section 121. No allocation is required if both the residential and nonresidential portions of the property are within the same dwelling unit. However, Section 121 does not apply to the gain allocable to the residential portion of the property.[45]

For purposes of determining the amount of gain allocable to the residential and nonresidential portions of the property, the taxpayer must allocate the basis and the amount realized between the residential and the nonresidential portions of the property using the same method of allocation that the taxpayer used to determine depreciation adjustments (as defined in Section 1250(b)(3)), if applicable.[46]

d. Special Rules

Special rules apply for the following 15 special situations:

(1) Joint Return

If a husband and wife make a joint return for the year in which the sale or exchange occurs, the exclusion rules of I.R.C. § 121(a) or the reduced exclusion rules of I.R.C. § 121(c), whichever are applicable, apply if *either* spouse meets the ownership and use requirements of I.R.C. § 121(a).[47]

If both spouses meet the use test, $500,000 can be excluded from gross income.[48] If only one spouse meets the use tax, only $250,000 can be excluded from gross income.[49]

---

44. Although a sabbatical would appear to be a short temporary absence, it would appear that the Service concluded that such was not the case because the taxpayer sold the property one month after returning from sabbatical. Compare with Example 5.
45. Treas. Reg. § 1.121-1(e)(1).
46. Treas. Reg. § 1.121-1(e)(3).
47. I.R.C. § 121(d)(1).
48. I.R.C. § 121(a) and (d).
49. I.R.C. § 121(a) and (b).

(2) Property Owned by a Spouse or Former Spouse

If property was transferred to an individual by that individual's spouse or former spouse in a transaction described in I.R.C. § 1041(a) as a transfer between spouses, or former spouses incident to a divorce, the period the transferee owns the property for purposes of I.R.C. § 121 includes the period the transferor owned the property.[50] For example if H were the sole owner of the residence and, as part of a divorce related transfer, H transfers his interest in the residence to W, W can include H's period of ownership for the two out of five year ownership test when W subsequently sells the property. W, however, may only exclude up to $250,000 of gain realized since W was not married at the time of the sale.

Use of a residence as a principal residence by an individual's spouse or former spouse pursuant to a divorce or separation instrument as defined in I.R.C. § 71(b)(2) constitutes use by the transferee solely for purposes of I.R.C. § 121.[51] A divorce or separation instrument means (i) a decree of divorce or separate maintenance or a written instrument incident to such a decree, (ii) a written separation agreement, or (iii) a decree not described in (i) requiring a spouse to make payments for the support or maintenance of the other spouse.[52] Thus, a taxpayer is treated as using property as his or her principal residence for any period that the taxpayer has an ownership interest in the property, and the taxpayer's spouse or former spouse is granted use of the property under a divorce or separation instrument, provided the spouse or former spouse uses the property as his or her principal residence.[53] This materially changes prior law, since under prior law once a taxpayer left the residence, the residence lost its character as the taxpayer's "principal" residence. Now, if one spouse continues to own the house after a divorce and the former spouse continues to use the house, the spouse who owns the house can exclude gain realized (within limits) from gross income.

For example, oftentimes one of the spouses will depart from the residence, no longer using it as his or her principal residence, while the other spouse continues to reside in the house for some period of time, often until the children have graduated high school. If the residence is sold more than three years after the departing spouse has left the residence, the departing spouse will fail to meet the two out of five-year use test and the gain realized attributable to the departing spouse will be taxable. To avoid this result, the departing spouse can

50. I.R.C. § 121(d)(3)(A), Treas. Reg. § 1.121-4(b)(1).
51. I.R.C. § 121(d)(3)(B), Treas. Reg. § 1.121-4(b)(2).
52. I.R.C. § 121(d)(3)(C).
53. Treas. Reg. § 1.121-4(b)(2).

still qualify for the benefits of Section 121 if the departing spouse continues to own the house and the divorce or separation instrument provides that the non-departing spouse can continue to reside in the residence for an agreed period of time, after which it will be sold. The result of this is that the non-departing spouse's use of the residence is attributed to the departing spouse, thus allowing the departing spouse to meet the ownership and use tests and thus qualify for exclusion of gain up to $250,000. In addition, the non-departing spouse will also qualify for exclusionary treatment up to $250,000 because he or she will have owned and used the residence for two out of five years preceding the year in which the sale occurred. Thus, for planning purposes, the spouses should provide in the divorce or separation instrument that the non-departing spouse can continue to occupy the principal residence for a period of time or until a certain event occurs, after which time, as part of the divorce or separation, the parties will agree to sell the residence.

(3) Deceased Spouse

In the case of an unmarried person whose spouse is deceased on the date of the sale or exchange, the period the unmarried person owned and used the property includes the period the deceased spouse owned and used the property before death.[54] In other words, to meet the use and ownership tests where one spouse is deceased, a taxpayer is treated as owning and using the property as the taxpayer's principal residence during any period that the taxpayer's deceased spouse owned and used the property as his or her principal residence before his or her death if: (i) the deceased spouse is deceased on the date of the sale or exchange of the residence, and (ii) the taxpayer has not remarried as of the date of the sale or exchange of the residence.[55] To illustrate, assume H has owned and used a house as his principal residence since 1987, that he married W in 1999, and that they used the house as their principal residence since then. The next year H dies and bequeaths the property to W who sells it two months later. Although W owned and used the house for less than two years, W will be deemed to have met the use and ownership requirements of Section 121 because the period that H owned and used the property is attributed to W, and W's use and ownership period will include the period H owned and used the property before death.[56]

(4) Involuntary Conversions

An involuntary conversion by destruction, theft, seizure, requisition or condemnation, or threat or imminence of condemnation is treated as a sale of

54. I.R.C. § 121(d)(2).
55. Treas. Reg. § 1.121-4(a)(1).
56. Treas. Reg. § 1.121-4(a)(2).

property for purposes of I.R.C. § 121.[57] In applying the involuntary conversion rules of Section 1033, the amount realized from the sale or exchange of the property is the amount determined without regard to the application of Section 121, reduced by the amount of gain included in gross income pursuant to Section 121.[58] If the basis of the property sold or exchanged is determined, in whole or in part, under Section 1033(b), the holding and use by the taxpayer of the converted property is treated as holding and use by the taxpayer of the property sold or exchanged.[59]

The regulations offer the following example: On February 18, 1999, fire destroys Taxpayer A's house, which has an adjusted basis of $80,000. A had owned and used this property as her principal residence for 20 years prior to its destruction. A's insurance company pays A $400,000 for the house. A realizes a gain of $320,000 ($400,000 – $80,000). On August 27, 1999, A purchases a new house at a cost of $100,000. Because the destruction of the house is treated as a sale for purposes of Section 121, A will exclude $250,000 of the realized gain from A's gross income. For purposes of Section 1033, the amount realized is $150,000 ($400,000 – $250,000) and the gain realized is $70,000 ($150,000 amount realized – $80,000 basis). A elects under Section 1033 to recognize only $50,000 of the gain ($150,000 amount realized less $100,000 cost of new house). The remaining $20,000 of gain realized is deferred and A's basis in the new house is $80,000 ($100,000 cost – $20,000 gain not recognized). A will be treated as owning and using the new house as A's principal residence during the 20-year period that A owned and used the destroyed house.[60]

(5) Like-Kind Exchange

If a taxpayer acquires property in a like-kind exchange under Section 1031, and then converts the property to her principal residence, Section 121 does not apply to the sale or exchange of such property by the taxpayer (or by any person whose basis in such property is determined in whole or in part by reference to the basis of the property in the hands of the taxpayer) during the five-year period beginning with the date of such acquisition.[61]

(6) Expatriates

The I.R.C. § 121 exclusion is not available to expatriates subject to I.R.C. § 877(a)(1).[62]

57. I.R.C. § 121(d)(5)(A); Treas. Reg. § 1.121-4(d)(1).
58. I.R.C. § 121(d)(5)(B); Treas. Reg. § 1.121-4(d)(2).
59. I.R.C. § 121(d)(5)(C); Treas. Reg. § 1.121-4(d)(3).
60. Treas. Reg. § 1.121-4(d)(4).
61. I.R.C. § 121(d)(10).
62. I.R.C. § 121(e), Treas. Reg. *§ 1.121-4(f)*.

(7) Depreciation

The Section 121 exclusion does not apply to the amount of the gain from the sale of the property which represents depreciation adjustments subject to recapture to the extent the deduction exceeds the straight line depreciation deduction attributable to periods after May 6, 1997, in respect of such property.[63] Thus, a taxpayer may recognize gain to the extent of any depreciation allowable with respect to rental or business use of the residence for periods after May 6, 1997.

(8) Out-of-Residence Care

If a taxpayer becomes physically or mentally incapable of self-care, and the taxpayer owns and uses the property as the taxpayer's principal residence at least one year during the five-year period ending on the date of the sale or exchange, then the taxpayer is treated as using the property as the taxpayer's principal residence during any time during the five-year period in which the taxpayer owns the property and resides in any facility (including a nursing home) licensed by a state or political subdivision to care for an individual in the taxpayer's condition.[64]

(9) Partial or Remainder Interests

A taxpayer may apply the Section 121 exclusion to gain from the sale or exchange of an interest in the taxpayer's principal residence that is less than the taxpayer's entire interest if the interest sold or exchanged includes an interest in the dwelling unit.[65] For purposes of the maximum excludible amount, sales or exchanges of partial interests in the same principal residence are treated as one sale or exchange. Thus, only one maximum limitation amount of $250,000 ($500,000 in the case of a joint return) applies to the combined sales or exchanges of the partial interest. If partial interests are sold or exchanged in different taxable years, in applying the $250,000/$500,000 exclusion the taxpayer may exclude gain from the first sale or exchange of a partial interest up to the taxpayer's full maximum limitation amount (i.e., $250,000 or $500,000) and may exclude gain from the sale or exchange of any other partial interest in the same principal residence to the extent of any remaining maximum limitation amount, and each spouse is treated as excluding one-half of the gain from the sale or exchange to which the $500,000 maximum limits for joint returns applies.[66]

For purposes of applying Section 121(b)(3) which restricts the application of Section 121 to only one sale or exchange every two years, each sale or exchange

63. I.R.C. § 121(d)(6).
64. I.R.C. § 121(d)(7).
65. Treas. Reg. § 1.121-4(e)(1)(i).
66. Treas. Reg. § 121-4(e)(1)(ii)(A).

of a partial sale is disregarded with respect to other sales or exchanges in the same principal residence, but is taken into account as of the date of the sale or exchange in applying Section 121(b)(3) to that sale or exchange and this sale or exchange of any other principal residence.[67]

The taxpayer may elect to have the exclusionary rule of Section 121 apply to the sale or exchange of a remainder interest in a principal residence.[68] If the election is made, the exclusion will not apply to the sale or exchange of any other interest in the residence which is sold or exchanged separately.[69] The election to exclude gain realized from the sale of a remainder interest does not apply if the sale is to a party related to the taxpayer as defined in Sections 267(b) or 707(b).[70] The election is made on the tax return filed for the year of the sale or exchange that does not include gain from the sale or exchange of the remainder interest in the taxpayer's gross income.[71] The taxpayer may make or revoke the election at any time before the expiration of the three year period beginning on the last day for the filing of the return for the taxable year in which the sale or exchange occurred, including extensions.[72]

The regulations offer the following example for this provision. In 1991 Taxpayer A buys a house that A uses as his principal residence. In 2004 A's friend B moves into A's house and A sells B a fifty (50) percent interest in the house, realizing gain of $136,000. A may exclude the $136,000 of gain realized. In 2005, A sells his remaining fifty (50) percent interest in the house to B realizing a gain of $138,000. A may exclude $114,000 ($250,000 – $136,000 gain previously excluded) of the $138,000 gain realized from the sale of the remaining interest.[73]

(10) Cooperative Housing Corporation

A taxpayer who holds stock as a tenant-stockholder in a cooperative housing corporation (see I.R.C. *§ 216(b)(1) and (2)*) may be eligible to exclude gain realized on the sale or exchange of the stock using Section 121. To determine whether the taxpayer meets the ownership and use tests of Section 121, the ownership test is applied to the time the taxpayer owned and held the stock, and the use test is applied to the time the house or apartment that the taxpayer is entitled to occupy by reason of the taxpayer's ownership of the stock.[74]

---

67. Treas. Reg. § 121-4(e)(1)(ii)(B)
68. Treas. Reg. § 121-4(e)(2)(i).
69. I.R.C. § 121(d)(8), Treas. Reg. §1.121-4(e)(2)(ii)(A).
70. I.R.C. § 121(d)(8)(B); Treas. Reg. § 1.121-4(e)(2)(ii)(B).
71. Treas. Reg. § 1.121-4(e)(2)(iii).
72. *Id.*
73. Treas. Reg. *§ 1.121-4(d)(3).*
74. I.R.C. § 121(d)(4); Treas. Reg. § 1.121-4(c).

(11) Conversion

Oftentimes taxpayers may desire to convert their principal residence to a rental property or convert their rental property to their principal residence, and after some period of time sell the property. These conversions may have positive or negative income tax consequences.

(a) To Rental Property

The immediate impact of converting a principal residence to rental property is to derive income before the property is sold. If the taxpayers convert the property to rental property they can still claim the benefits of Section 121 if they have occupied the property as their principal residence for at least two of the last five years before the date of the sale or exchange. Moreover, they do not have to allocate any of the gain between the periods of rental and personal use. It is recommended, however, that the taxpayers do not claim a depreciation deduction for the tax years during the short period in which the property is rented, because depreciation recapture will be required to be reported upon the sale as already noted. If, however, the taxpayers rent the property so that at the time of sale they have not used the property as their principal residence for at least two of the five years preceding the sale, they will not qualify for the Section 121 exclusion and the full amount of the gain realized will be recognized.

(b) From Rental Property

On the other hand, the conversion of rental property to residential property prior to a sale or exchange is subject to be nonqualified use exclusion of Section 121(b)(5). This provision provides that a portion of the gain from selling the residence is ineligible for exclusion from gain realized. The amount of gain that is allocated to the "period of nonqualified use" is based on a ratio the numerator of which is the aggregate "periods of nonqualified use" during the period the property was owned by the taxpayer, and the denominator of which is the period the property was owned by the taxpayer.[75] The result is the gain not eligible for the exclusion. For example, assume an individual taxpayer purchases a piece of property which she uses for business purposes for three years, after which she converts it to her primary residence which she uses as such for two years. At the end of the two-year period she sells the property and realizes a gain of $300,000. In this example, the taxpayer used the property sixty (60) percent of the time for nonqualified use and forty (40) percent of the time for qualified use. Thus, the taxpayer can exclude from gross income only forty (40) percent of the allowable exclusion of $250,000, or $120,000 ($300,000 × 40%). The remainder would be subject to capital gains tax. The "period of nonqualified use" is the period during which the property is not used as the principal

75. I.R.C. § 121(b(5)(B).

residence of the taxpayer or the taxpayer's spouse or former spouse.[76] However, "periods of nonqualified use" do not include (i) any portion of the five-year period which is after the last date that the property is used as the principal residence of the taxpayer or the taxpayer's spouse; (ii) any period of time not to exceed ten years in the aggregate during which the taxpayer or the taxpayer's spouse is serving in the armed forces, foreign service, or intelligence community; or (iii) any other period of temporary absence not to exceed two years in the aggregate due to a change of employment, health condition, or other unforeseen circumstances as specified by the IRS.[77]

(12) Reporting

If the total gain realized is less than $250,000 for an individual return or less than $500,000for a joint return, none of the gain realized even has to be reported on the tax returns of the sellers for the year in which the sale occurred.[78]

(13) Miscellaneous

Special rules also apply members of the uniformed service, foreign service and intelligence service,[79] and the peace corps.[80]

(14) Limited Liability Company

If the residence is owned by a single member limited liability company, the LLC will be deemed to be a disregarded entity and the single member owner will be treated as owning the residence for purposes of the ownership test,[81] for the period the LLC owns the property for the two-year ownership requirement.

(15) Grantor Trust

If a residence is owned by a grantor trust, the grantor is deemed the owner of the property for purposes of satisfying the two year ownership test for the period that the trust owns the property for the two-year ownership requirement.[82]

e. Election Out

Section 121 is mandatory. If its tests are met, it applies. Taxpayers may, however, *elect not* to have I.R.C. § 121 apply to the sale or exchange of a principal residence.[83] This may result where the taxpayer owns and uses two residences

76. I.R.C. § 121(b(5)(C)(i).
77. I.R.C. § 121(b)(5)(C)(ii)(I)-(III).
78. Section 121(a). IRS Publication 523 (2022) Selling Your Home.
79. I.R.C. § 121(d)(9).
80. I.R.C. § 121(d)(12).
81. Treas. Reg. § 1.121-1(c)(3)(ii).
82. Treas. Reg. § 1.121-1(c)(3)(i).
83. I.R.C. § 121(f).

as his or her principal residence and the taxpayer intends to sell both residences within two years of each other. The taxpayer should elect out of the sale of the residence which will produce the smaller gain and have the exclusion apply to the sale of the residence which will produce the larger gain. The taxpayer may also consider electing out if the sale of a second residence will produce a larger gain than the sale of the first residence because, as already noted, the taxpayer can only use the provisions of Section 121 once every two years.[84]

The election is made by filing a return for the taxable year of the sale or exchange that includes the gain from the sale or exchange of the taxpayer's principal residence. A taxpayer may make an election to have Section 121 not apply, or to revoke an election to have Section 121 not apply, at any time before the expiration of the three-year period beginning on the last day for the filing of the return for the taxable year in which the sale or exchange occurred, determined without regard to extensions.[85]

f. Gain in Excess of Allowable Exclusion

If the taxpayer sells a principal residence that meets the ownership and use tests, and if the gain exceeds the $250,000/$500,000 exclusionary amount, the gain in excess of the amount that can be excluded from gross income under Section 121 is subject to tax at the capital gains tax rate.

g. Reporting

If a husband and wife realize a gain from the sale of their principal residence that is less than $500,000, they do not have to report the gain. If the gain is in excess of $500,000, they must report the gain. The first $500,000 of gain will be excluded from gross income and the excess will be reported as long-term capital gain. If the home is owned individually or married filing separate, $250,000 is subtracted from $500,000 for reporting purposes.

C. Payment of Expenses

Generally, the tax aspects of household payments attributable to divorced or separated spouses may depend on which spouse owns the residence, which spouse occupies the residence, and which spouse pays the expenses. Payment of interest expenses is governed by Section 163; payment of taxes is governed by Section 164; and payment of other expenses such as mortgage principal, insurance, and utilities is governed by Sections 215 and 71 if the payments are characterized as alimony.

---

84. Section 121(b)(3).
85. Treas. Reg. § 1.121-4(g).

1. Transferor Transfers Entire Interest and Possession to Transferee

If the property is transferred to the transferee and the transferor pays mortgage principal, interest, taxes, insurance, rent, and utilities, such payments may be treated as alimony, and hence taxable to the transferee spouse and deductible by the transferor spouse, if all the alimony requirements of Section 71 are met,[86] and the payments are made pursuant to a divorce and separation instrument that was executed on or before December 31, 2018. Grandfathered instruments modified after December 31, 2018, are also grandfathered unless the modification expressly provides that the modified agreement is governed by the new law. If the divorce and separation instrument is executed after December 31, 2018, no alimony deduction is available because the alimony rules under Section 71 are no longer in effect. The transferee spouse may be entitled to deduct the mortgage interest under I.R.C. § 163(h) if the transferee spouse is liable on the debt and the residence is a qualified residence (as discussed later), and the transferee spouse may be able to deduct the real estate taxes under I.R.C. § 164 since the transferee spouse owns the property.

If, however, the payments are not deemed alimony because the tests of Section 71 are not met with respect to divorce or separation instruments entered into before 2018, or the payments are made during 2018–2025 pursuant to a post 2018 divorce or separation instrument, the transferor spouse may not deduct mortgage principal payments as alimony.[87] The transferor spouse may still be able to deduct the interest payments under I.R.C. § 163 if he or she remains personally liable on the mortgage and the other requirements for deductibility are met.

However, even though the transferor spouse remains liable on the mortgage, this does not automatically mean he or she can deduct the interest payments. A deduction with respect to interest arising out of a joint obligation of a taxpayer and another party is only allowable to the taxpayer to the extent he or she makes payment of the interest from his or her own funds.[88] Thus, where the transferor spouse pays alimony to the transferee spouse under a grandfathered instrument and the transferee spouse then uses the funds to pay mortgage interest, the transferor spouse cannot claim a deduction for the mortgage interest even if the agreement provides that he or she can.

The interest may be characterized as personal interest and hence be nondeductible unless a dependent of the taxpayer resides in the residence, in which

86. Section 71 (b)(1)(A); Temp. Prop. Treas. Reg. § 1.711T(A6). *See also* Mace v. United States, 1964 U.S. Dist. LEXIS 8536 (S.D. Cal. 1964).

87. Sydnes v. Comm'r, 68 T.C. 170 (1977), *aff'd on this issue*, 577 F.2d 60 (8th Cir. 1978) (mortgage payments made on duplex awarded the payee spouse in a divorce decree were made pursuant to a property settlement; accordingly, such payments are not deductible).

88. I.R.C § 163; Finney v. Comm'r, T.C. Memo. 1976-329 (1976); Rev. Rul. 71268, 19711 C.B. 58.

case the residence may be deemed a second residence; and, hence, the interest may be deductible as qualified residence interest under I.R.C. § 163(h)(3).[89]

Generally, for interest on a home mortgage to be deductible, the residence encumbered by the mortgage must be (i) the principal residence (within the meaning of I.R.C. § 121) of the taxpayer, or (ii) one other residence which is selected by the taxpayer to serve as a qualified residence and which is used by the taxpayer as a residence within the meaning of I.R.C. § 280A(d)(1).[90]

Thus, at first blush it would appear that the taxpayer cannot deduct the interest on the mortgage because the residence is neither his or her principal residence nor another residence which he or she uses.

I.R.C. § 280A(d)(1) provides that a dwelling unit is used as a residence for personal purposes for a number of days which exceeds the greater of (i) 14 days, or (ii) ten (10) percent of the number of days during the year for which the unit is rented at a fair rental. I.R.C. § 280A(d)(2) provides that a taxpayer is deemed to use a dwelling unit for personal purposes for a day if for any part of the day the unit is used for personal purposes by the taxpayer or any other person who has an interest in the unit or by any member of the taxpayer's family or such other person's which includes brothers, sisters, spouse, ancestors, and descendants, or by an individual who uses the unit under an arrangement which enables the taxpayer to use some other dwelling unit (such as a time share), or by any other individual unless for such day the dwelling unit is used for a rental which is a fair rental. Thus, it would appear that if a family member of the taxpayer resides in the residence or if the spouse or ex-spouse resides in the residence, and if the taxpayer is personally liable on the debt and if the taxpayer pays the debt from his or her funds, the interest will not be deemed "personal interest" and the taxpayer may deduct the interest on mortgage indebtedness.

In addition, the transferor spouse may not deduct payments of the real estate taxes under I.R.C. § 164, since such taxes are deductible only by the owner of the property. Accordingly, if the transferee, as owner of the property, pays the real estate taxes, he or she may deduct such payments under I.R.C. § 164.

2. Payor Spouse Remains as Sole Owner with Payee Spouse in Possession

If the payor spouse remains as the sole owner of the property, with possession in the payee spouse, payment of mortgage principal is not deductible as alimony because the sum is deemed paid by the payor spouse as a property

89. *See* I.R.C. §§ 163(h), 280A(d).
90. I.R.C. § 163(h)(4)(A)(i)(I) and (II).

owner.[91] Although I.R.C. § 71 (b)(1)(A) provides that payments made by the payor spouse on behalf of the payee spouse constitute alimony, Treas. Reg. § 1.71-1T (A-6) provides that "any payments to maintain property owned by the payor spouse and used by the payee spouse (including mortgage payments, real estate taxes, and insurance premium) are not payments on behalf of a spouse even if those payments are made pursuant to the terms of the divorce or separation instrument." The foregoing rules apply only to a divorce or separation instrument that was executed on or before December 31, 2018; that is, a grandfathered instrument to which the law in effect prior to the Tax Acts and Job Act of 2017 continues to apply. Grandfathered instruments modified after December 31, 2018, are also grandfathered unless the modification expressly provides that the modified agreement is governed by the new law. Otherwise, Section 71 is repealed effective for divorce or separation instruments executed after December 31, 2018. On the other hand, since the payor spouse owns the residence he/she may deduct the real estate taxes under I.R.C. § 164 if the residence is the taxpayer's qualified residence.[92]

The interest on the mortgage and the taxes on the residence may still be deductible by the payor spouse under I.R.C. §§ 163 and 164, respectively. The interest, however, may be characterized as personal interest and hence be non-deductible unless the interest is characterized as "acquisition indebtedness" or "home equity indebtedness" for a "qualified residence," all of which are discussed later in the chapter.[93]

Thus, no deduction is allowed for personal interest, which means any interest other than six categories of interest, one of which is qualified residence interest.[94] "Qualified residence interest" is any interest that is paid or accrued during the taxable year on acquisition indebtedness with respect to any qualified residence of the taxpayer, or home equity indebtedness with respect to any qualified residence of the taxpayer.[95] The determination of whether any property is a qualified residence of a taxpayer is made as of the time the interest is accrued.[96]

---

91. Bradley v. Comm'r, 30 T.C. 701 (1958).

92. Note that for taxable years 2018 through 2025 the aggregate amount of state and local taxes for any taxable year may not exceed $10,000 ($5,000 in the case of a taxpayer who files a married filing separate return). I.R.C. § 164(b)(6)(B).

93. I.R.C. § 163(h)(3).

94. I.R.C. § 163(h)(2). The six categories are: (i) interest paid or accrued on indebtedness allocable to a trade or business, (ii) investment interest, (iii) interest taken into account in computing income from a passive activity, (iv) qualified residence interest, (v) interest relating to educational loans, and (vi) interest payable on underpayment, non-payment or extension of time to pay estate taxes on the value of reversionary or remainder interests in property. I.R.C. § 163(h)(2)(A)–(F).

95. I.R.C. § 163(h)(3)(A)(i) and (ii).

96. I.R.C. § 163(h)(3)(A) [Flush language].

a. Acquisition Debt

Acquisition indebtedness is indebtedness which is incurred to acquire, construct, or substantially improve a qualified residence of the taxpayer and is secured by the residence.[97] Acquisition indebtedness also includes any indebtedness secured by a qualified residence of the taxpayer resulting from the refinancing of indebtedness that is incurred in acquiring constructing or substantially improving any qualified residence of the taxpayer.[98] The aggregate amount of the acquisition indebtedness cannot exceed $1 million for taxpayers filing joint returns and for unmarried taxpayers, and $500,000 for married taxpayers filing separate.[99] As a result of the Tax Cuts and Jobs Act of 2017, special rules exist for taxable years 2018 through 2025. First, the $1,000,000 cap is reduced to $750,000, and the $500,000 cap is reduced to $375,000 for tax years beginning after December 31, 2017, and before January 1, 2026.[100] Second, these new caps, however do not apply to any indebtedness incurred on or before December 15, 2017,[101] or pursuant to a binding written agreement entered into prior to December 15, 2017, which is required to close before January 1, 2018, though the purchase of the residence had to close before April 1, 2018.[102]

Finally, for taxable years beginning after December 31, 2025, the $1,000,000/$500,000 limit under Section 163(h)(3)(B)(ii) is to be applied to the aggregate amount of any acquisition indebtedness of the taxpayer described in Section 163(h)(3)(B)(i) without regard to the taxable year in which the indebtedness was incurred.[103] Thus, there is a return to the $1,000,000/$500,000 cap even if the indebtedness was incurred during the years 2018 through 2025.

b. Home Equity Indebtedness

Home equity indebtedness is indebtedness other than acquisition indebtedness secured by a qualified residence.[104] The amount of the indebtedness cannot exceed the fair market value of the qualified residence less the acquisition indebtedness with respect to the indebtedness.[105] This provision was repealed for calendar years 2018 through 2025 by the Tax Cuts and Jobs Act of 2017.[106]

97. I.R.C. § 163(h)(3)(B)(i)(I) and (II).
98. I.R.C. § 163(h)(3)(B)[Flush language].
99. I.R.C. § 163(h)(3)(B).
100. I.R.C. § 163(h)(3)(F)(i)(II).
101. I.R.C. § 163(h)(3)(F)(i)(III).
102. I.R.C. § 163(h)(3)(F)(i)(IV).
103. I.R.C. § 163(h)(3)(F)(ii).
104. I.R.C. § 163(h)(3)(C)(i).
105. I.R.C. § 163(h)(3)(C)(ii).
106. I.R.C. § 163(h)(3)(F)(i)I(I).

c. Qualified Residence

Generally, for interest on a home mortgage to be deductible, the residence encumbered by the mortgage must be a "qualified residence" which means: (i) the principal residence (within the meaning of I.R.C. § 121) of the taxpayer, or (ii) one other residence which is selected by the taxpayer to serve as a qualified residence and which is used by the taxpayer as a residence within the meaning of I.R.C. § 280A(d)(1).[107]

If a married couple does not file a joint return for the taxable year, the couple is treated as one taxpayer for purposes of the qualified residence test, and each spouse is entitled to take into account one residence unless both individuals consent in writing to one individual taking into account the principal residence and one other residence.[108] For this purpose, if the taxpayer does not rent a dwelling unit at any time during a taxable year, the unit may be treated as a residence for such taxable year, notwithstanding Section 280A(d)(1).[109]

I.R.C. § 280A(d)(1) provides that a dwelling unit is used as a residence during the taxable year if the taxpayer uses the dwelling unit (or a portion of it) for personal purposes for a number of days which exceeds the greater of (i) 14 days, or (ii) ten (10) percent of the number of days during the year for which the unit is rented at a fair rental. This provision was repealed for calendar years 2018 through 2025 by the Tax Cuts and Jobs Act of 2017.[110] I.R.C. § 280A(d)(2) provides that a taxpayer is deemed to use a dwelling unit for personal purposes for a day, if for any part of the day the unit is used for (i) personal purposes by the taxpayer or any person who has an interest in the unit, or by any member of the taxpayer's family[111] which includes brothers, sisters, spouse, ancestors, and lineal descendants,[112] or (ii) an arrangement which enables the taxpayer to use some other dwelling unit (whether or not a rental is charged for the use of such other unit),[113] or (iii) by any other individual, other than certain employees who use the residence of the employer under Section 119, unless for such a day the dwelling unit is rented at fair rental.[114] Thus, it would appear that if a family member of the taxpayer resides in the residence or if the spouse or exspouse resides in the residence, and if the taxpayer is personally liable on the debt and if the taxpayer pays the debt from his or her funds, the

107. I.R.C. § 163(h)(4)(A)(i)(I) and (II).
108. I.R.C. § 163(h)(4)(A)(ii)(I) and (II).
109. I.R.C. § 163(h)(4)(A)(iii).
110. I.R.C. § 163(h)(3)(F)(i)I(I).
111. I.R.C. § 267 (c)(4).
112. I.R.C. § 280A (d)(2)(A).
113. I.R.C. § 280A (d)(2)(B).
114. I.R.C. § 280A (d)(2)(C).

interest will not be deemed "personal interest" and the taxpayer may deduct the interest on mortgage indebtedness.

Payment for utilities such as gas and electric may be deductible as alimony if they meet the alimony payment tests and if paid pursuant to a pre-2019 divorce or separation instrument. But that the payor spouse is not entitled to an alimony deduction for the fair rental value of the residence occupied rent free by the taxpayer's former spouse, nor is depreciation allowable as an alimony deduction since Section 167 only allows a deduction for depreciation for property used in a trade or business or held for the production of income.[115] Notwithstanding the preceding, any payments to maintain property owned by the payor spouse and used by the payee spouse (including mortgage payments, real estate taxes and insurance premiums) are not considered payments of alimony, and so are not deductible by the payor spouse, even if made pursuant to a pre-2019 divorce or separation instrument.[116]

3. Property Titled Jointly with Payee Spouse in Possession

Finally, where the spouses jointly own the residence as tenants in common or as joint tenants or tenants by the entireties with the payee spouse in possession, payment by payor spouse of mortgage principal, interest, insurance, and taxes may be deemed alimony to the extent of the payee spouse's interest in the property.[117] Thus, only one-half the mortgage principal and interest, and real estate taxes, may be deductible by the payor spouse as alimony if all the alimony tests are met and if the payments are made pursuant to a divorce or separation instrument that is executed before January 1, 2019, or the pre-2019 divorce or separation instrument is modified after 2018 and the parties do not expressly provide in the modified agreement that the rules of the Tax Cuts and Jobs Act of 2017 apply. Concomitantly, the payee spouse must include one-half of the payments in income if made pursuant to a pre-2019 divorce or separation instrument, but the payee may deduct one half the real estate taxes and one-half the mortgage interest of the residence is the qualified residence of the payee spouse. See *Zinsmeister v. Commissioner*,[118] where the Court held that one-half the mortgage payments for which the spouses are jointly liable are includable in the gross income of the payee spouse as payment in discharge of indebtedness of the personal obligation of the payee spouse, and deductible by the payor spouse as alimony (if the tests of alimony are met). Thus, the payor

115. Bradley v. Comm'r, 30 T.C. 701(1958).

116. Temp. Prop. Treas. Reg. § 1.71-1T (A-6).

117. Cothran v. Comm'r, 57 T.C. 296 (1971); Rev. Rul. 67420, 19672 C.B. 63. *See* I.R.C. § 71(b)(1)(A); Temp. Prop. Treas. Reg. § 1.711T(A6).

118. T.C. Memo. 2000-64 (2000).

can deduct, as alimony, one-half of the mortgage payments, real estate taxes, and home insurance premiums as alimony. Where, however, only the payor spouse is liable on the mortgage, payment of mortgage principle is not deductible as alimony. The balance of the mortgage principal is not deductible by the payor spouse since it represents his or her share of the mortgage obligation.[119]

But the payments for interest and real estate taxes attributable to the payor spouse's interest in the property may be deductible under I.R.C. §§ 163 and 164, respectively, notwithstanding the changes in the alimony rules enacted by TCJA 2017.[120] Generally, real estate taxes are deductible by the owner of the property since that is the person who is personally liable for payment of the taxes. Taxpayers who are married but who file separate returns, and divorced taxpayers who own the property as joint tenants or as tenants by the entireties, may deduct the real estate taxes which he or she pays.[121] The interest, however, may be characterized as personal interest and hence be nondeductible unless the interest is characterized as "acquisition indebtedness" or "home equity indebtedness" for a "qualified residence."

If a married couple does not file a joint return for the taxable year, the couple is treated as one taxpayer for purposes of the qualified residence test, and each spouse is entitled to take into account one residence unless both individuals consent in writing to one individual taking into account the principal residence and one other residence.[122] For this purpose, if the taxpayer does not rent a dwelling unit at any time during a taxable year, the unit may be treated as a residence for such taxable year, notwithstanding Section 280A(d)(1).[123]

I.R.C. § 280A(d)(1) provides that a dwelling unit is used as a residence during the taxable year if the taxpayer uses the dwelling unit (or a portion of it) for personal purposes for a number of days which exceeds the greater of (i) 14 days, or (ii) ten (10) percent of the number of days during the year for which the unit is rented at a fair rental. For purposes of the ten (10) percent test, a unit is not treated as rented at a fair rental for any day for that it is used for personal purposes.[124] I.R.C. § 280A(d)(2) provides that a taxpayer is deemed to use a dwelling unit for personal purposes for a day, if for any part of the day the unit is used for: (i) personal purposes by the taxpayer or any person who

119. Temp. Prop. Treas. Reg. § 1.711T(A-6).

120. Higgins v. Comm'r, 16 T.C. 140 (1951).

121. Finney v. Comm'r, T.C. Memo. 1976-329 (1976); Rev. Rul. 71-268, 1971-1 C.B.8. For a chart regarding the treatment of expenses for a jointly owned home, see IRS Publication 504, Divorced or Separated Individuals, Table 4, p.12 (2021).

122. I.R.C. § 163(h)(4)(A)(ii).

123. I.R.C. § 163(h)(4)(A)(iii).

124. I.R.C. § 280A(d)(1) [Flush Language].

has an interest in the unit, or by any member of the taxpayer's family[125] which includes brothers, sisters, spouse, ancestors, and lineal descendants,[126] or (ii) if the unit is used under an arrangement that enables the taxpayer to use some other dwelling unit (whether or not a rental is charged for the use of such other unit),[127] or (iii) by any other individual, other than certain employees who use the residence of the employer under Section 119, unless for such a day the dwelling unit is rented at fair rental.[128] Thus, it would appear that if a family member of the taxpayer resides in the residence or if the spouse or exspouse resides in the residence, and if the taxpayer is personally liable on the debt and if the taxpayer pays the debt from his or her funds, the interest will not be deemed "personal interest" and the taxpayer may deduct the interest on mortgage indebtedness.

4. Rental Property

For payments made under a pre-2019 divorce or separation instrument, if the payee spouse lives in rental property and the payor spouse pays the rent, such rental payments on behalf of payee spouse may be deemed alimony if all the tests of alimony under I.R.C. § 71 are met, and the payments are made pursuant to a pre-2019 divorce or separation instrument per the Tax Cuts and Jobs Act of 2017.[129]

Payments by the payor spouse of the payee spouse's utility bills and homeowner's insurance may also constitute alimony if all the tests of alimony under I.R.C. § 71 are met, and the payments are made pursuant to a pre-2019 divorce or separation instrument per the Tax Cuts and Jobs Act of 2017.

Use the following chart as a summary to find how much of a payment is alimony and how much can be claimed as an itemized deduction.[130]

125. I.R.C. § 267 (c)(4).
126. I.R.C. § 163 (d)(2)(A).
127. I.R.C. § 163 (d)(2)(B).
128. I.R.C. § 163 (d)(2)(C).
129. Treas. Reg. § 1.71-1T (A-6).
130. See IRS Publication 504, Table 4, p. 14 (2022).

IF you must pay all of the . . .	**AND** your home is . . .	**THEN** you can deduct and your spouse (or former spouse) must include as alimony ...	**AND** you can claim as an itemized deduction . . .
Mortgage payments (principal and interest).	Jointly owned	One-half of the total payments.	One-half of the interest as interest expense (if the home is a qualified residence).[131]
Real estate taxes and home insurance.	Held as tenants in common.	One-half of the total payments.	One-half of the real estate taxes[132] and none of the home insurance.
	Held as tenants by the entirety or in joint tenancy.	None of the payments.	All of the real estate taxes and none of the home insurance.

131. The spouse or former spouse can deduct the other one-half of the interest if the home is a qualified residence.

132. The spouse or former spouse can deduct the other one-half of the real estate taxes.

8 Trusts

A. Section 682 Trusts as a Result of the Tax Cuts and Jobs Act of 2017

Section 682 was repealed by the Tax Cuts and Jobs Act of 2017. The repeal applies to (i) any divorce or separation instrument (as defined in Section 71(b)(2)) executed after December 31, 2018, and (ii) any divorce or separation instrument executed on or before December 31, 2018, and modified after such date if the modification expressly provides that the amendments made by such Section apply to such modification.[1]

B. Trusts Not Affected by the Tax Cuts and Jobs Act of 2017

Section 682, however, will continue to apply to trust income payable to a former spouse who was divorced or legally separated under a divorce or separation instrument executed on or before December 31, 2019, unless such instrument is modified after that date and the modification provides that the changes made by the Tax Cuts and Jobs Act of 2017 apply to the modification. Thus, the discussion that follows applies to those pre-2019 divorce or separation instruments in which payments are made from an alimony trust.[2]

1. Use and Purpose for Alimony Trust

An alimony trust is a trust established pursuant to a decree of divorce or separate maintenance into which a divorced spouse transfers property for the benefit of the other spouse. The Agreement generally provides that the spouse for whose benefit the trust is established will receive the income generated from the trust, or may invade the principal for the purposes stated therein. The trust is managed by a trustee which can be an individual or corporate trustee. The trust takes legal title to the assets transferred to it. The trust terminates when

1. Pub L. 115-97, Title I, § 11051(b)(1)(C), 131 Stat. 2089 (12-22-17). *See also* Notice 2018-37.
2. See Notice 2018-37.

the obligation to pay alimony to the former spouse terminates. Upon termination, the trust generally reverts to the grantor.

An alimony trust may be best used if the payor spouse has substantial assets, but the payee spouse is concerned that the payor spouse will not make his/her required alimony payments to the payee spouse. The payee spouse can assure protection of payments by having the payor spouse deposit in the trust the expected future value of the alimony payments to the payee spouse. For example, if the payor spouse is engaged in risky or speculative ventures or may be preparing for bankruptcy or other asset diminished events, the parties may desire to use an alimony trust to ensure payments.

On the other hand, the payor spouse may not want to make payments over a period of time. To avoid this, the payor spouse would deposit in the trust the expected future value of the alimony payments to the payee spouse.

An alimony trust may also be of benefit if the parties are concerned that either may be a spendthrift and may squander the funds.

The term "alimony trust" is a misnomer, utilized because of the heading to Section 682, since in essence it is a property settlement vehicle. When funds are transferred to the trust, the transferor does not receive an alimony deduction. Rather, the tax aspects to the transferor are governed by the general tax rules governing the transfer of property to a trust. Moreover, if structured properly the assets transferred to the trust will be removed from the gross estate of the transferor for Federal estate tax purposes.

2. Payee Spouse

Payments from a trust established under I.R.C. § 682 are taxable to the payee spouse under I.R.C. § 682 not as alimony payments under I.R.C. § 71 but as payments to a beneficiary of the trust. I.R.C. § 682(b), as amended by the 1984 Tax Reform Act, treats the payee spouse as the beneficiary of a trust for purposes of an alimony trust. Thus, there is included in the gross income of the payee spouse, who is divorced or legally separated from the payor spouse under a decree of divorce or separate maintenance, or under a written separation agreement, the amount of the income of any trust that the payee spouse is entitled to receive and that, but for I.R.C. § 682(a), would be included in the gross income of the payor spouse (because, for example, the grantor retained control over the assets of the trust).

Thus, the payee spouse is taxed on the distributable net income of the trust, which is paid and required to be distributed or credited to the beneficiary in the year required per the general trust rules of I.R.C. §§ 652 and 662. The character of the income in the hands of the payee spouse is the same as the character of the income in the hands of the trust, thus observing the conduit trust rules. For example, if the trust has tax exempt income, such income is tax free to the beneficiary even though it may qualify as alimony for nontax purposes.

The principal of the trust distributed to the payee spouse in excess of the income of the trust is not taxable to the beneficiary, and it is not deductible by the trust.

3. Payor Spouse

The payor spouse cannot deduct the payments made to the payee spouse from the trust, but neither are the payments includible in his or her gross income.[3] In some instances, however, it may be advisable for the trust income to be taxable to the grantor if the grantor is in a lower tax bracket than the trust beneficiary or has losses that can offset the trust income. If that is the desired result, a Section 682 trust should not be used.

In CCA 200923027, the Court ordered the husband to liquidate his IRA and to transfer the proceeds to a trust for the benefit of his wife and child. The trustee of the trust was ordered to make periodic payments to the wife pursuant to their divorce decree. The husband claimed the payments from the trust to the former spouse constituted alimony and deducted the payments from his gross income. The Service held that Section 682 did not apply to the transfer of funds to the trust because those funds were taxable to the husband on distribution from his IRA and, therefore, the amounts transferred to the trust constituted corpus, not income, of the trust.

The Service went on to say that the weekly payments from the trust to the wife might fit within Section 682 if the trust were a grantor trust and the corpus earned income on behalf of the wife. This would be the case if the wife was entitled to receive the income and the husband was required to include the income of the trust in his gross income if the husband were treated as the owner of the trust under the grantor trust rules even though the wife was the beneficiary of the trust. The Service begged off this issue, however, requesting more information before determining if the trust were a grantor trust. Therefore, the Service refused to rule on whether the payments from the trust to the wife were deductible by the husband as alimony under I.R.C. § 71 until it could determine whether the trust was a grantor trust.

4. Child Support

The gross income of the payee spouse does not include any income of the trust that the terms of the decree, written separation agreement, or trust instrument fix as payments for support of the minor children of the payor spouse.[4] Rather, the income of the trust will be taxed to the grantor of the trust, if the terms of the divorce or separation instrument or trust agreement so provide.

---

3. I.R.C. § 682(a).
4. *Id.*

5. Transfers to Trust

Except for transfers of property where liabilities exceed basis (see paragraph 7, below), transfers of property are not subject to income tax pursuant to I.R.C. § 1041 and are not subject to gift tax if the provisions of I.R.C. § 2516 apply. The property transferred may be excluded from the transferor's gross estate unless the transferor retains any interest in the trust (or the transfer is for adequate consideration). See Chapter 13, Estate Tax Aspects.

6. Example

Assume *H* transfers income-producing assets to a trust created in 2017 for the benefit of *W*. During the term of the trust, the income is to be paid to *W*, *H*'s former spouse. The income is not fixed by the divorce decree or instrument or by the terms of the trust agreement. Upon termination of the trust, the principal will revert to *H*. Although the trust is a grantor trust, since *H* has a reversionary interest in the income and corpus (if, as of the inception of that portion of the trust, the value of such interest exceeds 5 percent of the value of the portion[5]), I.R.C. § 682 provides that the income is not includible in *H*'s gross income. And, under I.R.C. § 61, the income of the trust is includible in the gross income of *W*. On the other hand, if the decree of divorce or written separation agreement provided for the income to be paid to the *W*, then the income of the trust would be includible in the gross income of the *W* under I.R.C. § 71.

7. Liabilities in Excess of Basis

Where property is transferred in trust, the transferor recognizes gain or loss to the extent that the sum of the amount of liabilities assumed, plus the amount of liabilities to which the property is subject, exceeds the adjusted basis of the property transferred.[6]

The basis of the property in the hands of the transferee trust is the same as the basis of the property in the hands of the transferor, increased by the gain recognized by the transferor.[7]

One difference between transferring property to a spouse or former spouse incident to a divorce and transferring property to a trust is that in a transfer to a spouse or former spouse incident to a divorce, the transfer of property with liabilities in excess of basis does not trigger recognition of gain to the transferor, whereas the transfer of such property to a trust does trigger recognition of gain to the transferor.[8]

5. I.R.C. § 673(a).
6. *Id.* § 1041(e).
7. *Id.*
8. I.R.C. § 1041(e).

C. Planning

As noted earlier, alimony trusts may continue to apply to pre-2019 divorce or separation instruments. In those limited situations, alimony trusts offer some limited planning opportunities.

The use of a trust can assure the payee spouse that alimony will be available, since the funds are set aside in trust for that purpose.

To assure the availability of funds, the trust should be irrevocable during the period of payment of alimony. Once the alimony payments cease, the trust principal can be returned to the payor spouse (in which case the trust will be included in the grantor's gross estate) or otherwise paid as directed by the terms of the trust.

Generally, the income from the trust is used to fund the payor spouse's alimony obligation, but the principal can be used for this purpose as well. Consideration should be given to characterizing the trust as a unitrust pursuant to which the payee spouse will be paid annually a fixed percentage of the value of the trust determined as of the last day of the prior taxable year.

Since the income received by the payee spouse-beneficiary from the trust is not characterized as alimony, but is characterized according to its character, the frontend loading alimony rules may be avoided. Thus, if a trust earns interest of $15,000, which is payable to the beneficiary, the beneficiary receives $15,000 of income, which is characterized as interest and not as alimony.

PRACTICE POINTER: A spendthrift provision should be included in the trust to protect against claims by creditors. The advisor should check the party's State's version of the Uniform Trust Code to determine if the former spouse and/or children can attach the assets of the trust if alimony or child support payments are not made by the grantor.

9 Certain Expenses

A. Introduction

This chapter discusses the tax aspects of the payment of certain expenses divorced or separated spouses may incur, such as medical expenses, life insurance premiums, and attorneys' fees. The taxation of other expenses such as the payment of mortgage principal and interest, real property taxes, rent, repair and maintenance, disability insurance, and education expenses, to name a few, are discussed in Chapter 1 and Chapter 7.

B. Medical Expenses

1. Payor and Payee Spouse

If the payor spouse and payee spouse are married when the medical services are rendered or when the medical expenses are paid, the medical expenses are deductible under Section 213 as an itemized expense to the extent such medical expenses exceed ten percent of adjusted gross income.[1]

If the spouses are divorced or separated under a decree of divorce or written instrument executed after December 31, 2018, the payments of medical expenses by each spouse are not deductible as alimony, since Section 71 has been repealed for payments under such instruments.

If the payor spouse and payee spouse are divorced or separated under a decree of divorce or written instrument executed before January 1, 2019, and if the payor spouse makes payments for medical and dental expenses of the payee spouse, including premiums for medical insurance, such expenses

1. *See* I.R.C. § 213(a). For taxable years 2013 through 2016 if the taxpayer or the taxpayer's spouse has attained age 65 before the close of the taxable year, or for taxable years beginning after 2016 and ending before 2019 in the case of any taxpayer, the medical expense was deductible to the extent such expenses exceeded 7.5 percent of adjusted gross income. I.R.C. § 213(f); Pub. L. 115-97, Title I, §§ 11002(d)(7), 11027(a), Dec. 22, 2017, 131 Stat. 2061, 2077.

may be includible in the gross income of the payee spouse and deductible by the payor spouse if all the tests for alimony contained in I.R.C. § 71 are met unless the parties elect to treat the payments as nonalimony under I.R.C. § 71(b)(1)(B). This is because payments made to or on behalf of the payee spouse qualify as alimony if made pursuant to a pre-2019 divorce or separation instrument and all the other tests for characterizing the payments as alimony are met,[2] unless the parties elect to treat the payments as non-alimony under I.R.C. § 71(b)(1)(B).[3] If the medical expense payments are considered alimony under a pre-2019 divorce or separation instrument and are included in the payee spouse's gross income, the payment of the medical expenses by the payee spouse may be taken into account by the payee in arriving at the allowable deduction for medical expenses under I.R.C. § 213.[4] Such expenses are deductible as medical expenses if the payee spouse pays the expenses, itemizes deductions, and meets the deductible floor. If deductible, the payee spouse must be careful that his or her itemized deductions are not phased out. Thus, even though the medical expenses may be deductible by the payee spouse, he or she must be aware of the deductible floor and the phaseout rules. These results follow regardless of whether the payments are made directly to the provider of the services or to the payee.[5] If the spouses file married/filing separate returns and if the medical expenses are paid from separate accounts, the spouse from whose account the expenses are paid may claim the medical expense deduction. If, however, the funds are paid from a joint account, each spouse can deduct half the medical expenses unless either spouse can establish that he or she paid the full expenses, in which case he or she may be entitled to claim the full medical expense deduction.

2. Child

a. General Rule

I.R.C. § 213(d)(5) provides that any child to whom I.R.C. § 152(e) applies (i.e., who as between the custodial and noncustodial parent is entitled to the dependency exemption in the case of a child of separated or divorced parents) is treated as a dependent of both parents for purposes of the medical expense deduction. For divorce or separation instruments entered into before 2019 in the absence of a qualified pre-1985 instrument,[6] a child may be treated as the dependent of the noncustodial parent only if the custodial parent releases the

2. *Id.*
3. *See* Chapter 1, B.3.d, No Non-alimony Statement (Alimony Test 4).
4. *See* Rev. Rul. 62106, 19612 C.B. 21. Note the ten percent floor.
5. I.R.C. § 71(b)(1)(A); Temp. Prop. Treas. Reg. § 1.711T(A6) and (A7).
6. *See* I.R.C. § 152(e)(3).

claim to the exemption.[7] If the custodial parent does not release the claim, the right to the exemption is determined under the general rules of I.R.C. § 152(c) or (d). Thus, the preamble to Treas. Reg. § 1.152-4(f) explains that if a custodial parent does not release the claim to the exemption, only the taxpayer who is entitled to claim the child as a dependent under I.R.C. § 152(c) or (d) may treat the child as a dependent for purposes of I.R.C. § 213(d)(5).

b. Exception

Rev. Proc. 2008-48[8] provides an exception to the general rule for divorce or separation instruments entered into before 2019. Where the tests of Rev. Proc. 2008-48 are met, the child of parents who are divorced, separated, or living apart is deemed the dependent of both parents for purposes of I.R.C. §§ 105(b) (exclusion from gross income for medical expense reimbursements), 106(a) (exclusion from gross income for employer provided accident or health plan), 132(h)(2)(B) (exclusion from gross income for no-additional cost services and qualified employee discounts), 213(d)(5) (deduction for medical expenses), 220(d)(2) (exclusion from gross income for distributions from Archer Medical Savings Accounts), and 223(d)(2) (exclusion from gross income for distributions from Health Savings Accounts) whether the custodial parent has not released the claim to the exemption under I.R.C. § 152(e)(2).

In order for this revenue procedure to apply, the following four tests must apply:

(1) The taxpayers are divorced or legally separated under a decree of divorce or separate maintenance or written separation agreement executed before 2019, or live apart at all times for the last six months of the calendar year.
(2) The taxpayers are the parents of a child who receives over one-half of the child's support during the calendar year from the child's parents.
(3) The taxpayers are the parents of a child who is in the custody of one or both parents for more than one-half of the calendar year.
(4) The taxpayers are the parents of a child who qualifies under I.R.C. § 152(c) or (d) as a qualifying child or qualifying relative of one of the child's parents.

Where these four tests are met, the child will be treated as the dependent of both parents, in which case both parents may claim the medical expense deduction for medical expense each pays for the child regardless of which

7. *See* Chapter 3, C.3.c. for a discussion of the release of the dependency exemption by the custodial parent in favor of the noncustodial parent.

8. 2008-36 I.R.B. 586.

parent claims the child as a dependent. As a result of test (2), however, this exception does not apply if the dependency exemption for the child is claimed under a multiple support agreement.

c. Planning

If the payor spouse has substantial adjusted gross income, all or part of the medical care expense deduction may be lost because such expenses are deductible only to the extent such expenses exceed ten percent of the payor spouse's adjusted gross income.[9] In such case, for payments made under a decree of divorce or separate maintenance executed before January 1, 2019, if the payee spouse has minimal income, the parties should consider having the payor spouse pay the medical expenses under the guise of alimony, and they would then be fully deductible by the payor spouse, and the payee spouse could then pay the medical expenses directly and receive a deduction therefor to the extent such expenses exceed ten percent of the payee spouse's adjusted gross income, which, if low in relation to the medical expenses paid, would mean that the payee spouse could deduct most of the medical expenses. To illustrate, assume that the parties are separated or divorced under a decree or written instrument executed before January 1, 2019, that the payor spouse has adjusted gross income of $100,000, and the payee spouse has adjusted gross income of $5,000. Assume medical care expenses for the minor child are $5,000. If the payor spouse pays the child's medical care expenses, none of such expenses are deductible by the payor spouse because they do not exceed ten percent of the payor spouse's adjusted gross income. If, however, the payee spouse pays the medical care expenses with money paid him or her as alimony (so that the payee spouse's adjusted gross income is $10,000), the payee spouse would have additional alimony income of $5,000, but in addition would be entitled to deduct $4,000 of the medical care expenses (the amount in excess of ten percent of adjusted gross income; i.e., $1,000).

Each parent should determine the amount of medical expenses each will pay to make sure that most medical expenses are deductible in light of the ten percent floor. For divorce or separation instruments executed before 2019, this can be accomplished easily by use of the "no nonalimony" statement under I.R.C. § 71(b)(1)(B). Since the medical deduction, alimony deduction and alimony income all tie into adjusted gross income, the use of the "no nonalimony" statement can vary adjusted gross income to maximize all deductions. And, as noted earlier, the election can be made as late as the filing of the tax return.

---

9. I.R.C. § 213(a); 7.5 percent for taxable years beginning after December 31, 2016, and ending before January 1, 2019.

C. Life Insurance

1. Payment of Premiums

For payments made under a divorce or separation instrument executed before January 1, 2019, premiums paid for term or whole life insurance on the payor's life made under the terms of the divorce or separation instrument qualify as payments on behalf of the payee spouse to the extent the payee spouse is the owner of the policy.[10] Where, however, the payor's borrowing against the policy exceeds the policy's cash surrender value, payment of the premiums may not be deductible.[11]

Thus, for payment of premiums to be taxable to the payee spouse and deductible by the payor spouse, it would appear that they must confer a presently ascertainable economic benefit on the payee spouse.[12] In *Wright* no such benefit was found because the term policy the husband maintained on his life was found to give the wife only limited rights so that she could not have constructively received an economic benefit from the payment of the premiums. In *Wright*, the wife lost her right to policy proceeds if she predeceased her husband, attained age 65, or remarried. Compare *Lane v. Commissioner*,[13] which involved a whole life policy that built up substantial cash surrender value. The policy was immediately assignable by the wife and she was entitled to the proceeds if she remarried or after she turned age 65. The wife was also the owner and irrevocable beneficiary of the policy, and the policy was immediately assignable by her. The Court concluded that the wife received a presently ascertainable economic benefit under the policy and therefore constructively received the premium payments.

The foregoing rules do not apply to divorce or separation instruments executed after December 31, 2018.

2. Transfer of Ownership of Policy

The transfer of ownership of a life insurance policy to the transferee spouse will not trigger a taxable event to the transferor spouse.[14] The basis of the policy in the hands of the transferee spouse is the same as the basis of the policy in the hands of the transferor spouse.[15]

---

10. Temp. Prop. Treas. Reg. § 1.711T(A6); *see* Chapter 1, B.3.b. Direct or Indirect Payment (Alimony Test 2).

11. Wright v. Comm'r, 62 T.C. 377 (1974), *aff'd*, 543 F.2d 593 (7th Cir. 1976); Ostrov v. Comm'r, 53 T.C. 361 (1969).

12. Wright v. Comm'r, 62 T.C. 377 (1974), *aff'd*, 543 F.2d 593 (7th Cir. 1976).

13. T.C. Memo. 2000-185, following Marten v. Comm'r, T.C. Memo. 1999-340.

14. I.R.C. § 1041(a).

15. *Id.* § 1041(b).

3. Receipt of Proceeds under the Policy

Generally, amounts received under a life insurance contract are excluded from the gross income of the recipient, under I.R.C. § 101(a), if they are paid by reason of the death of the insured. The transfer for valuable consideration rule of I.R.C. § 101(a)(2) does not apply to the transfer of a life insurance policy to a spouse incident to a separation or divorce as a result of the implementation of the carryover basis rules for the transfer of property between spouses or former spouses (if incident to a divorce).[16] Thus, the proceeds of a life insurance policy payable upon the death of the transferor is fully excludable from the gross income of the beneficiary.

D. Attorney Fees

NOTE: As a result of the Tax Cuts and Jobs Act of 2017, miscellaneous itemized deductions are not allowed for taxable years beginning after December 31, 2017, and before January 1, 2026. Thus, attorney's fees paid during this period will not be allowed, even if for tax advice under Section 212(3).[17]

1. Payee Spouse

Generally, attorney fees incurred by a party to a domestic relations case are nondeductible, personal expenses.[18] Under I.R.C. § 212(1), however, the payee spouse may deduct attorney fees allocable to the production or collection of taxable income such as alimony,[19] legal fees incurred to recover arrearage or increased payments,[20] and attorney fees allocable to tax advice.[21]

Although such attorney fees are deductible under Section 212 as a miscellaneous itemized deduction, subject to the two percent floor under Section 67, the Tax Cuts and Jobs Act of 2017 repealed Section 67 for taxable years beginning after December 31, 2017, and before January 1, 2026. Thus, attorney fees incurred by the payee spouse are not deductible unless they can fit under I.R.C. § 212(1) (production or collection of taxable income) or I.R.C. § 212(3) (tax advice) because of the repeal of miscellaneous itemized deductions for taxable years beginning after December 31, 2017, and before January 1, 2026.

16. *See* I.R.C. § 1041.
17. *Id.* § 67(g).
18. *Id.* § 262.
19. *See* Hesse v. Comm'r, 60 T.C. 685 (1973), *aff'd without op.*, 511 F.2d 1393 (3d Cir. 1975) (legal expenses paid by the payee spouse to secure alimony were deductible, where she had agreed to pay her attorney ten percent of the amount collected from the payor spouse in settlement of a divorce matter, because the amounts she received were includible in her gross income).
20. *See* Elliott v. Comm'r, 40 T.C. 304 (1963); Dalton v. Comm'r, 34 T.C. 879 (1960).
21. I.R.C. § 212(3). *See* Carpenter v. United States, 338 F.2d 366 (Ct. Cl. 1964); Rev. Rul. 72545, 19722 C.B. 179.

Alternatively, nondeductible attorney fees attributable to property transferred may be added to the basis of property transferred.[22]

2. Payor Spouse

Attorney fees paid by the payor spouse in defending a divorce action, as well as fees incurred in connection with a property settlement, are not deductible under I.R.C. § 212(2) as ordinary and necessary expenses incurred for the management, conservation, or maintenance of property held for the production of income.[23] This rule is based upon the Supreme Court's decisions in *United States v. Patrick*[24] and *United States v. Gilmore*,[25] in which the Court held that deductibility is determined by the origin and character of the claim with respect to which an expense is incurred, rather than its potential consequences upon the fortunes of the taxpayer. Thus, since the origin and character of attorney fees paid for defending a divorce suit emanate from a personal matter (marital dispute), payment of the fee is a nondeductible personal expense.

The payor spouse, however, could deduct attorney fees attributable to tax advice under I.R.C. § 212(3) for tax years prior to 2018.[26] But legal fees incurred to reduce alimony payments are not deductible.[27] Thus, attorney fees incurred by the payor spouse are not deductible unless attributable to tax advice under I.R.C. § 212(3). But since these payments were deductible as miscellaneous itemized deduction, and since TCJA 2017 repealed Section 67, which allowed miscellaneous itemized deductions, attorneys fees allocable to tax advice under I.R.C. § 212 (3) are no longer deductible for taxable years beginning after December 31, 2017, and before January 1, 2026.

To be deductible under Section 212(3), the legal fees must be payable for the taxpayer or the taxpayer's spouse if reported on a joint return. In *United States v. Davis*,[28] the Court held that the wife's legal fees paid by the husband were not deductible by the husband under I.R.C. § 212(3) because I.R.C. § 212(3) included only the expenses of the taxpayer himself and not those of his former wife. Thus, the fees he paid to her attorney were not "in connection with the determination, collection or refund of any tax of the taxpayer."[29]

Although such attorney fees attributable to tax advice under Section 212(3) were deductible as a miscellaneous itemized deduction, subject to the two

---

22. I.R.C. § 67(g); Pub. L. 115-97, Title I, § 11045(a), Dec. 22, 2017, 131 Stat. 2088.
23. Hesse v. Comm'r, 60 T.C. 685, 694 (1973), *aff'd without op.*, 511 F.2d 1393 (3d Cir. 1975); Prop. Treas. Reg. § 1.2621(b)(7).
24. 372 U.S. 53 (1963).
25. 372 U.S. 39 (1963).
26. Carpenter v. United States, 338 F.2d 366 (Cl. Ct. 1964); Rev. Rul. 72545, 19722 C.B. 179.
27. Sunderland v. Comm'r, T.C. Memo. 1977-116 (1977).
28. 370 U.S. 65 (1962).
29. *Id.* at 74.

percent floor under Section 67, the Tax Cuts and Jobs Act of 2017 repealed Section 67 for taxable years beginning after December 31, 2017, and before January 1, 2026, essentially repealing Section 212(3).[30]

3. Payee Spouse's Fees Paid by Payor Spouse

Generally, payment of the payee's legal expenses by the payor spouse is not deductible, regardless of whether the legal fees of the payee spouse are for the production of income under I.R.C. § 212(1) or for tax advice under I.R.C. § 212(3).[31] Again, because the Tax Cuts and Jobs Act of 2017 repealed the miscellaneous itemized deduction provision under Section 67 for taxable years beginning after December 31, 2017, and before January 1, 2026, the deductions under Sections 212(1) and 212(3) are effectively repealed.[32]

For payments made under pre-2019 divorce or separation instruments, however, because I.R.C. § 71(b)(1)(A) permits payment to be made "on behalf of a spouse," payment of the payee spouse's legal fees, whether directly to the payee spouse or to the payee spouse's attorney on behalf of the payee spouse, would appear to deductible if all the tests for alimony are met.[33]

30. Section 67(g); Pub. L. 115-97, Title I, § 11045(a), Dec. 22, 2017, 113 Stat. 2088.
31. Martin v. Comm'r, 73 T.C. 255 (1979).
32. Section § 67(g); Pub. L. 115-97, Title I, § 11045(a), Dec. 22, 2017, 131 Stat. 2088.
33. Treas. Reg §1.71-1T(A-7).

10 Filing Status

A. Introduction

1. Determination of Marital Status

The marital status of the parties determines the type of tax return they must file. As discussed in this chapter, the marital status of the parties is determined on the last day of the taxable year (Dec. 31 for most taxpayers).[1] If a spouse dies during the year, marital status is then determined on the date of death instead of the close of the taxable year.[2] But the surviving spouse may file a joint return with the deceased spouse for the year of death, unless the surviving spouse has remarried.[3] Spouses are deemed married unless they are legally separated under a decree of divorce or separate maintenance, or the deserted spouse rule applies.[4] A decree of support, alimony pendente lite, or temporary alimony is not a decree of separate maintenance, since these are merely support decrees and not decrees that separate or divorce the parties.[5] Spouses who are married during taxable year 1 and who file a joint return for that year, and whose

1. I.R.C. § 7703(a)(1); Prop. Treas. Reg. § 1.7703-1(a).
2. I.R.C. § 7703(a)(1); Prop. Treas. Reg. § 1.7703-1(a).
3. A surviving spouse is one whose spouse died during either of the two taxable years immediately preceding the taxable year, and who maintains as his/her home a household that constitutes for the taxable year the principal place of abode of a dependent who (i) (within the meaning of Section 152, determined without regard for subsections (b)(1), (b)(2), and (d)(1)(B) thereof), or a child or stepchild of the taxpayer, and (ii) with respect to whom the taxpayer is entitled to a deduction for the taxable year under Section 151. An individual is considered as maintaining a household only if more than half the cost of maintaining the household during the taxable year is furnished by the taxpayer. A taxpayer is not considered a surviving spouse, however, if the taxpayer remarries at any time before the end of the taxable year, or unless, for the taxpayer's taxable year during which the spouse died, a joint return could have been made under the provision of Section 6013 determined without regard to Section 6013 (a)(3), which pertains to the death of one or both spouses, I.R.C. § 2(a)(2).
4. I.R.C. §§ 7703(a)(2), 6013(d)(2).
5. See (3) Decree of support at Chapter 1.

marriage is annulled in year 2 are deemed single in year 1 and must file amended returns for year 1. The couple is treated as if never married.[6] A similar result arises where the marriage is invalid ab initio (where the ceremony was flawed or a marriage license was not obtained).[7] If parties are divorced under a final decree on or before December 31 of a year, the parties are considered unmarried for the entire year.

The filing status of the parties determines the tax rate schedule or tax table to be applied against the taxable income of the parties to determine their tax liability.

2. Compliance

For decrees of divorce or written separation instruments executed before January 1, 2019, the payee spouse must provide the payor spouse with his or her Social Security number. The payor spouse must provide the IRS with the name and Social Security number of the payee spouse on the first income tax return on which the payor spouse claims an alimony deduction.[8]

3. Withholding

For decrees of divorce or written separation instruments executed before January 1, 2019, the payor spouse does not have to withhold taxes on the payment of alimony, unless the payee spouse is a nonresident alien, in which case the payor spouse must withhold 30 percent of each payment.[9] The payor is personally liable for taxes, interest, and penalty for failing to withhold.[10] If, however, the payee spouse is a resident of a country that has a treaty with the United States exempting such payment from the 30 percent withholding tax, no withholding may be required if the payee spouse provides the payor spouse with IRS Form W-8 BEN.[11]

Where the payee spouse is a nonresident alien, the treaties of the United States with the country of the payee spouse should be reviewed. For decrees of divorce or written separation instruments executed before January 1, 2019, if the payor properly fails to withhold tax, then the nonresident payee spouse should file a Form 1040 NR and attach a Form 8833. On this Form the nonresident payee spouse should explain why no tax is due under the respective

6. Rev. Rul. 76-255, 1976-2 C.B. 40. *See also* Wilson v. Comm'r, T.C. Memo. 1976-285 (Following an annulment, taxpayers may amend prior year joint return and refile as single.).

7. Priv. Ltr. Rul. 200201001.

8. Temp. Prop. Treas. Reg. § 1.2151T(A1). Since under post-2018 decrees or written instruments alimony is not included in the gross income of the payee spouse, there is no tax to withhold.

9. I.R.C. §§ 1441(a), I.R.C. § 871(a)(1).

10. *Id.*

11. *Id.*

treaty. If, however, the payor spouse improperly fails to withhold, the nonresident payee spouse must file Form 1040 NR and pay the tax due. The withholding and payment of tax should be negotiated at the time of the written separation agreement or decree of divorce. If the payor spouse withheld 30 percent, but the tax should have been withheld at a lower rate pursuant to a treaty, the nonresident payee spouse should file Form 1040NR, attaching Form 8833, and claim a refund.

Since taxes are not required to be withheld by the payor spouse unless the payee spouse is a nonresident alien, the obligation of paying income taxes on alimony received falls on the payee spouse. Thus, the payee spouse should be advised to pay estimated taxes, as discussed later, and to be made aware that all the alimony received is not spendable income, but some of it should be set aside to pay income tax. Or, if the payee spouse is employed, the payee spouse should consider filing a Form W-4, Employee's Withholding Certificate, to adjust his/her withholding.

As a result of the Tax Cuts and Jobs Act of 2017, for decrees or written instruments executed after December 31, 2018, the preceding withholding rules do not apply because payments by the payor spouse to the payee spouse are not alimony, and therefore such payments are not included in the gross income of the payee spouse.

B. Filing Categories for Divorced or Separated Spouses

There are four filing categories for separated or divorced spouses—unmarried, married filing a joint return, married filing separate returns, and head of household. A married taxpayer may file a joint return or a married filing separate return, except in the limited case described in Section 7703, in which case the taxpayer may file as an individual or head of household. An unmarried taxpayer may file as a single individual or as head of household. These different filing categories are discussed following.

1. In General

If the parties are separated, they are considered married for the entire taxable year if, on or before the last day of their taxable year, they have not obtained a final decree of divorce or separate maintenance.[12] In other words, spouses legally separated under a decree of divorce or separate maintenance are not considered married and therefore cannot file a joint tax return.[13] As discussed later, a separated spouse may be treated as single and thus be eligible to file as head of household if the spouse qualifies as a "deserted spouse."

12. I.R.C. § 6013(d); Prop. Treas. Reg. § 1.60134(a). *See also* I.R.C. § 7703(a).
13. Treas. Reg. § 1.6013-4(a).

An interlocutory decree is not considered a final decree of divorce or separate maintenance, and the spouses retain the marital relationship and can file a joint return until the decree becomes final.[14] But a divorce a mensa et thoro (i.e., a decree from bed and board, more akin to a separation, where the marriage is not dissolved but the parties no longer cohabitate) is a decree of divorce or separate maintenance.[15] In addition, temporary alimony or alimony pendente lite are not decrees of divorce or separate maintenance.[16] Under any of these orders or decrees, except a divorce a mensa et thoro, the parties are still deemed married. A voluntary separation agreement is not a decree of divorce or separate maintenance, and thus the parties are deemed married, unless one of the spouses qualifies under Section 7703(b), which would permit such spouse to file for single status as discussed later in this chapter. Individuals who have entered into a civil union, domestic partnership, or similar arrangement are not considered married for Federal income tax purposes, unless such an arrangement is considered a marriage under State law.

2. Joint Return versus Separate Returns

If the parties are separated, they may file either a joint return or separate returns (ordinarily, married filing separately).[17] As noted later in this chapter, a separated spouse may be treated as single and thus be eligible to file as head of household if the spouse qualifies as a "deserted spouse."[18] A joint return may not be filed if one of the spouses is a nonresident alien at any time during the taxable year, unless the spouses agree to treat the nonresident spouse as a U.S. resident, in which case the world-wide income of both spouses must be reported for purposes of Federal income taxation.[19] In that case, the taxpayer will have to file as married filing separate.

In deciding under which category to file, the tax return preparer should be aware of any conflicts of interest that may arise in making that decision. Section 10.29 of IRS Circular 230 provides that a practitioner (which includes attorneys, certified public accountants, and enrolled agents) may not represent a client before the Service if such representation involves a conflict of interest. Preparing both spouses' returns or giving conflicting advice to the spouses

14. *Id.*; Rev. Rul. 57368, 19572 C.B. 896; *cf.* prior Prop. Treas. Reg. § 1.711(b)(3).

15. Rev. Rul. 67442, 19672 C.B. 65. *Cf. Boyer v. Comm'r*, 79 T.C. 143 (1982) (complaint for separate support under Mass. Ann. Laws, ch. 209, § 32, which provides a cause of action separate and distinct from the state's divorce statutes where a payee spouse has justifiable cause for living apart from her payor spouse).

16. *See* Chapter 1, B.3, Nine Tests for Qualification as Alimony.

17. I.R.C. § 6013.

18. *See* Chapter 10, B.2; I.R.C. § 7703(b).

19. I.R.C. § 6013(a); Prop. Treas. Reg. § 1.6013-1(b); Bhagava v. Comm'r, T.C. Memo. 1978-197; Schinasi v. Comm'r, 53 T.C. 982 (1969).

on the tax aspects of filing a return constitutes a conflict of interest which the practitioner should avoid absent a waiver of the conflict from both spouses. Conflicts generally arise where the practitioner represents both spouses without informing them of a conflict and the spouses each believe the practitioner represents him or her, or the practitioner prepares both spouses' returns without informing them of potential conflicts of interest. Finally, the practitioner should remember the privileged communication that one spouse tells the practitioner that the practitioner could use against the other spouse. In any case, be aware of the conflicts of interest rule and the privileged communication rule and, when in doubt, the practitioner should decline to represent both spouses unless a waiver is received from both spouses.

Four factors that a separated couple should consider in deciding whether to file a joint return or separate returns are (i) liability, (ii) switching from a joint return to a separate return or a separate return to a joint return, (iii) tax liability, and (iv) items reported on the return. Each of these factors is discussed in more detail in the following sections.

a. Liability

A joint return imposes joint and several liability on the spouses for any tax interest and penalty due and owing for the taxable year for which a joint return is filed.[20] Thus, a spouse may be liable for the entire tax due even though the income was earned by the other spouse. Compare Rev. Rul. 74611,[21] which holds that spouses who file a joint return do not have a joint interest in a refund, since the refund is the property of the spouse who paid the tax. In such case, each spouse has a separate interest in the jointly reported income and a separate interest in any overpayment. If separate returns are filed, however, each spouse is liable only for any tax and penalty due and owing with regard to his or her separate return. Accordingly, if the parties are married, and if one spouse suspects that the other spouse is understating income or overstating deductions, the suspecting spouse should not file a joint return.

If, however, the spouses file a joint return and a tax deficiency is assessed against the husband and wife, the spouse who did not understate income or overstate deductions should consider filing for innocent spouse treatment, which is discussed in Chapter 11.

---

20. I.R.C. § 6013(d)(3); Prop. Treas. Reg. § 1.60134(b).

21. 1974 – 2 C.B. 399. (H & W filed joint return. All tax paid by W. IRS held that the refund could not be credited against the tax liability of H for prior years and W, having paid the entire tax, is entitled to the entire refund.). Amplified by Rev. Rul. 85-70, 1985-1 C.B.361 (provides proper method to compute amount of overpayment shown on joint return that may be credited to one spouse's unpaid tax liability in a community property state) and Rev. Rul. 87-52, 1987-1 C.B. 347.

b. Switching

If the spouses file a joint return, they may not elect, after the due date of the return (including extensions), to switch and file separate returns for that year.[22] If the spouses did not file a timely return, they may file a joint return or a married filing separate return when they do file.[23]

On the other hand, if separate returns are filed, the spouses may later elect to switch to file a joint return.[24] The election to switch from separate to joint status may be made (i) anytime within three years from the due date of the return for the year (determined without regard to extensions);[25] (ii) before a deficiency notice is mailed to either spouse, if the spouse to whom notice is mailed files a timely petition with U.S. Tax Court;[26] (iii) before either spouse commences a suit for refund for such taxable year; and (iv) before either spouse enters into a closing agreement for the taxable year, or before any civil or criminal case arising against either spouse with regard to such taxable year has been compromised under Section 7122 (pertaining to compromises by the IRS on any civil or criminal case).[27]

Where the parties are undecided which filing status to elect by the due date of the return, it would appear to be advisable to file separate returns, thereby preserving the election to file a joint return should that filing status later be determined to be more advantageous than separate returns. The parties should sign an agreement to do this, in case one of them later changes his or her mind.

c. Tax Liability

The tax liability may be lower if the parties file a joint return, because the rate of tax is lower for a joint return than for separate returns.[28] For example, assume a separated couple has combined taxable income of $100,000 in 2022, all of which is earned by the payor spouse. If they file a joint return, their tax liability would be $23,528. If they file married filing separate returns, their tax liability would be $28,764. Thus, by filing a joint return, the separate couple can save $5,236 in taxes in which they can both share. Where, however, the incomes of the payor spouse and payee spouse are substantially equal, the disparity in tax

22. Prop. Treas. Reg. § 1.6013-1(a)(1), Laden v. Comm'r, 38 T.C. 520 (1962). A personal representative for a decedent's estate may change from a joint return elected by the surviving spouse to a separate return for the decedent. The change must be made within one year from the due date of the returns.

23. Rev. Rul. 72-539, 1972-2 C.B. 634, Phillips v. Comm'r. 86 T.C. 433 (1986).

24. I.R.C. § 6013(b)(1); Treas. Reg. § 1.60132(a)(1).

25. I.R.C. § 6013(b)(2)(A).

26. *See* Currie v. Comm'r, T.C. Memo. 1986-71 (1986); Swonder v. Comm'r, T.C. Memo. 1994-430 (1994).

27. I.R.C. § 6013(b)(2)(A)–(D); Treas. Reg. § 160132(b)(2)–(5).

28. I.R.C. § 1.

that results between filing a joint return and married filing separate returns is eliminated or substantially lessened.

There are other disadvantages for filing married filing separate rather than as joint, five of which are (i) the child tax credit may not be claimed, unless the spouses are living apart and are legally separated;[29] (ii) no credit is allowed under Section 21 for taxpayers who are married unless they file a joint return for the taxable year;[30] (iii) if one spouse itemizes, both spouses must itemize (One spouse cannot claim the standard deduction if the other spouse itemizes deductions.);[31] (iv) each spouse is entitled to a capital loss deduction of one-half of that which could be claimed on a joint return ($1,500 instead of $3,000);[32] (v) certain tests must be met to claim the earned income credit and adoption expense credit;[33] (vi) the filing threshold for a joint return for 2022 is $25,900 if both spouses are less than 65, $27,300 if one spouse is over 65 and the other is under 65 years of age, and a $28,700 if both spouses are over 65 years of age, whereas the filing threshold in 2022 for married filing separate is $5,000;[34] (vii) the standard deduction for married filing separate is one-half the joint return ($27,700 v. $13,800);[35] (viii) the State and local tax deduction for years 2018–2025 is $10,000 for a joint return and $5,000 for married filing separate;[36] and (ix) the marginal tax rate for married filing separate is twice the rate for a joint return.[37]

d. Reported Items

If a joint return is filed, both spouses must include all their income, exemptions, and deductions on that return.[38] If, however, separate returns are filed, each spouse reports only his or her income, exemptions, and deductions on his or her return. Moreover, if separate returns are filed and one spouse itemizes deductions, the other spouse must also itemize deductions, unless the other spouse files as single or unmarried head of household, as discussed later.[39]

If the taxpayer pays medical expenses with funds deposited into a joint account in which the taxpayer and his or her spouse have an equal interest, one-half of the medical expenses are deductible on a separate return unless

29. I.R.C. §§ 24 and 151.
30. Treas. Reg. § 1.21-3(a).
31. I.R.C. § 63(c)(6)(A).
32. I.R.C. § 1211 (b)(1).
33. I.R.C. § 32(b)(2)(A), I.R.C. § 23(f)(1).
34. IRS FS 2023-2 (Jan. 2023).
35. I.R.C. § 63(c)(2).
36. I.R.C. § 164(b)(6)(B).
37. Compare I.R.C. § 1(a) with I.R.C. § 1(d).
38. I.R.C. § 6013(b)(l).
39. I.R.C. § 63(c)(6)(A).

the taxpayer can establish that he or she alone paid the medical expenses.[40] If the spouses intend to file separate returns and each will pay his or her medical expenses, the parties should pay the expenses from separate checking accounts. If property is held as tenants by the entireties, a spouse can deduct on his or her separate returns the amount of property tax that the spouse alone actually paid.[41]

Mortgage interest paid on property held as tenants by the entireties is deductible on a separate return to the extent of the amount of mortgage interest that the taxpayer alone actually paid. If the home is owned as tenants by the entireties, one half the casualty loss is deductible by each spouse on a separate return. The preceding expenses can be claimed by each spouse on a separate return whether the spouse paid the expenses separately with his or her funds or jointly with his or her funds.[42]

e. Signature

Ordinarily, a joint return must be signed by both spouses.[43] However, a return may be signed for either or both spouses by an agent, or one spouse can act as the agent for the other.[44] To act as an agent in such case, a power of attorney executed for the purpose must be filed with the return. It is recommended that IRS Form 2848, Power of Attorney, be used and filed with the returns. However, oral authorization for one spouse to act as an agent for the other may be permissible where the spouse is physically unable to sign the return or a power of attorney.[45]

The requirement in a separation agreement that the payee spouse sign a joint return if requested by the payor spouse is not sufficient for the payor spouse to sign the payee spouse's name as his or her agent, since the intent to file a joint return is determined when the return is filed. To qualify, the agent spouse should give the other spouse an executed IRS Form 2848, Power of Attorney, authorizing the other spouse to sign the granting spouse's signature on a joint return. Although a suit in equity for specific performance may give remedial relief, this is an expensive and time-consuming procedure.

If a spouse dies before signing the returns, the executor or personal representative of the deceased spouse's estate should sign for the deceased spouse. If no executor or personal representative has been appointed, the surviving

---

40. IRS Publication 502, Medical and Dental Expenses (2022).
41. *Id.*
42. IRS Publication 936, Home Mortgage Interest Deduction (2022).
43. Treas. Reg. § 1.60131(a)(2).
44. *Id.*; I.R.C. § 1.60121(a)(5).
45. *Id.*; Rev. Rul. 70-216, 1970-1 C.B. 265. There are numerous cases that have held that a return was joint even though it was signed by only one spouse. E.g., Heim v. U.S., 251 F.2d 44 (C.A. 8, 1958) *aff'g*, 27 T.C. 270 (1956).

spouse should sign for the deceased spouse and note that he or she is filing as a surviving spouse.[46]

One practice tip to consider is that when the separation agreement is executed, the payor spouse should attempt to obtain a power of attorney (preferably IRS Form 2848) from the payee spouse, which authorizes the payor spouse to act as agent for the payee spouse if joint return status is desired. A separate IRS Form 2848 for each year should be executed. The power of attorney should be made irrevocable, or if revocable, and if the payee spouse revokes the power of attorney, then the agreement should impose sanctions against the payee spouse. On the other hand, the payee spouse should not give the payor spouse a "carte blanche" power of attorney, but rather should insist on reviewing the proposed joint return before it is signed. A compromise position may be to have the power of attorney held in escrow by the tax preparers for each spouse, or for the payee spouse to give the power of attorney to his or her attorney or tax return preparer.

But see *Riportella v. Commissioner*,[47] where the Tax Court held that a joint return signed by neither the payor spouse nor the payee spouse (only their names were typed in), who were in the process of divorce, was a joint return. The Court found that the payee spouse "intended" to file a joint return, even though she refused to sign the return, because her refusal was the use of her signature as a bargaining chip in the divorce process. As evidence of her intent, the Court noted that the payee spouse had no taxable income, was supported by the payor spouse, had signed joint returns for all other years of the marriage, and she was willing to "sell her signature." In so holding, the Court looked to the "particular factual scenario of this case." Thus, reliance upon this case is dependent upon whether the facts of your case can fit within the "particular facts" of this case.

f. Tacit Agreement

The Tax Court has adopted a tacit consent rule which holds that intent to file a joint return may be inferred from acquiescence or tacit approval from the non-signing spouse.[48] Among the factors the Court considers is whether the non-signing spouse filed a separate return, objected to the filing of a joint return, the prior filing history indicates an intent to file jointly, and relying on the other spouse to handle the family's financial matters, including the preparation of

46. IRS Tax Tip 2022-96(6.23.2022), I.R.C. § 6013(a)(3); Treas. Reg. § 1.6013-1(d)(3).

47. T.C. Memo. 1981-463 (1981). *See also* Park v. Comm'r, T.C. Memo 1978-23. *But see* Garland v. Comm'r, T.C. Memo. 1977-373 where husband signed separated wife's name on a joint return. When she discovered this, she notified the IRS. The Court held the wife did not intend to file a joint return.

48. Estate of Campbell v. Comm'r, 56 T.C. 1 (1971).

the family's tax returns. In *Soni v. Commissioner*,[49] in which the Court found that throughout the marriage the husband handled the financial matters, that the wife chose not to be involved in her family's finances or tax preparation, that she believed it was her role to trust her husband in financial matters and tax preparation, that for the year in issue and the following tax years the parties filed a joint return, and the standard of practice was for the husband to sign his name and his wife's name on the tax returns. Thus, the Court adopting the "ostrich in the sand theory" held that based on the above factors, the wife tacitly consented to the filing of a joint return.

Note, however, that the failure of one spouse to sign a return is not fatal to the finding of a joint return. The determinative factor is whether the spouses *intended* to file a joint return. This can only be gleaned from all the facts and circumstances of each case. For example, where the spouses have filed joint returns for many years, but one of the spouses failed to sign the return for the years in issue, the Tax Court has held that the returns were joint.[50]

3. Married Taxpayers Living Apart May File as Head of Household or Single

A married taxpayer living apart from his or her spouse may file a joint return, if the parties agree, or may file married filing separate.[51] In addition, a married taxpayer who lives apart from his or her spouse may be treated as single (i.e., unmarried) and be eligible to file as single or head of household if the following five tests of Section 7703(b) are met.

First, the individual is married.[52] The determination of whether an individual is married is made as of the close of his or her taxable year, except that if the spouse dies during the taxable year, such determination is made as of the time of such death.[53] An individual who is legally separated from his or her spouse under a decree of divorce or separate maintenance is not considered

49. T.C. Memo. 2021-17.

50. *See* Tuchman v. Comm'r, T.C. Memo 1981 – 731 (H and W filed joint returns for 20 years, lived together at the same address after the years in issue, W signed a refund claim for the years in issue, and the income of both H and W was reported on the returns. The Court held that the returns were joint returns). Crew v. Comm'r, T.C. Memo. 1982-535 (H and W filed joint returns for nearly 37 years. In year 38 they separated, and W filed separately. In the next two years, W did not file separately, but H had joint returns prepared which he signed in one of those years and the return preparer signed in the other year. The Court held that the filing of a separate return by W demonstrated that she was aware of the requirement to file a separate return if she so desired. Her failure to file separately for the next two years (the years in issue) inferred that she acquiesced to return to her prior custom of filing jointly. The history of filing joint returns and that she relied upon H to prepare and file the returns was evidence that the returns filed as joint returns were intended as such.).

51. I.R.C. § 6013.

52. I.R.C. § 7703(b)(1); Treas. Reg. § 1.7703-1(b).

53. I.R.C. § 7703(a)(1). Treas. Reg. § 1.7703-1(a).

married.[54] The Courts are instructed to look to the State of marital domicile to determine if the parties are married. A decree of support or alimony pendente lite, or a written separation agreement, is not a decree of divorce or separate maintenance for purposes of I.R.C. § 7703.[55]

The determination of whether a taxpayer is single is made under I.R.C. § 7703 and not I.R.C. § 71. In *Freyre v. United States*,[56] the taxpayer and his wife were married but resided in separate locations. On his 1996 federal income tax return, the husband filed as a "single" taxpayer. In reviewing the taxpayer's deduction, the IRS determined that the taxpayer should have filed as a "married individual." The Sixth Circuit agreed with the IRS. The Court looked to I.R.C. § 7703(a)(2), which provides that "an individual legally separated from his spouse under a decree of divorce or separate maintenance shall not be considered as married." According to State law, neither the taxpayer nor his spouse had filed for a legal separation and the divorce decree was not final during the year in issue. Accordingly, the taxpayer was not entitled to file as a "single" individual. Nevertheless, the taxpayer argued that prior I.R.C. § 71 determines whether a taxpayer is single or married, and if the parties live apart, do not file a joint tax return, and one spouse receives payment from the other under a decree of alimony pendente lite requiring the husband to make payments for her support, then the parties are "legally separated," and, thus, the taxpayer is entitled to file as a "single" taxpayer. The Court rejected this argument and found that the use of the term "legally separated" in prior I.R.C. § 71 makes no reference to the requirement of I.R.C. § 7703(a)(2) that a married individual must be "legally separated" to file a tax return as a single person.[57]

Second, the spouses file separate returns.[58]

Third, the spouse maintains as his or her home a household which constitutes, for more than one-half the taxable year, the principal place of abode of a child as defined in Section 152(f)(1)[59] with respect to whom the spouse is entitled to claim a dependency exemption for the taxable year (or would be so entitled but for Section 152(e), pertaining to who can claim the dependency exemption as between divorced or separated spouse as described in Section

54. I.R.C. § 7703(a)(2).

55. Dunn v. Comm'r, 70 T.C. 361 (1978); Johnson v. Comm'r, T.C. Memo. 1980-9 (1980); *see also* prior I.R.C. § 71.

56. 135 Fed. Appx. 863 (6th Cir. 2005).

57. *See* IRS Publication 501, Table 4, p. 10 (2021), Who Is a Qualifying Person Qualifying You to File as Head of Household?, for a chart describing who is a qualifying person for filing as head of household.

58. I.R.C. § 7703(b)(1); Treas. Reg. § 1.7703-1(b)(1)(ii).

59. "Child" is defined I.R.C. § 152(f)(1) as a son, daughter, stepson, stepdaughter, adopted child, or eligible foster child. An eligible foster child is an individual who is placed with the taxpayer by an authorized placement agency or by judgment, decree, or other order of any Court of competent jurisdiction. I.R.C. § 152(f)(1)(C).

152(e).[60] The household must actually constitute the home of the individual for more than one-half the taxable year. A physical change in location of the home is permissible, but the home must be occupied by the taxpayer and the qualifying child for the required period of time. Temporary absence due to special circumstances such as illness, education, business, vacation, military service, or a custody agreement under which a child is absent for less than six months in the taxable year is considered a temporary absence and will not prevent the house from qualifying as the principal place of abode provided it is reasonable to assume that the taxpayer or child will return to the household and the taxpayer continues to maintain the household or a substantially equivalent household in anticipation of such return.[61] The spouse is entitled to claim a dependency exemption for such child for the taxable year, even if the dependency exemption is claimed by the other spouse (such as by release of the exemption).

Fourth, the spouse furnishes more than half of the cost of maintaining the household during the taxable year.[62] The cost of maintaining a household includes expenses incurred for the mutual benefit of the occupants of the house, such as property taxes, mortgage interest, rent, utility charges, upkeep and repairs, property insurance, and food consumed on the premises.[63] The "cost of maintaining the household" differs from the cost of support. Support expenses, such as the cost of clothing, education, medical treatment, vacations, life insurance, and transportation, the value of services performed in the household by the taxpayer or any other person qualifying as a head of household or surviving spouse, or as expenses paid or reimbursed by any other person, are not considered expenses of maintaining a household.[64]

Fifth, the other spouse is not a member of the household during the last six months of the taxable year.[65] This test applies if it is not the spouse's place of abode during such time.[66] In other words, the spouses must live separate and apart, in separate residences, for the last six months of the taxable year. According to the U.S. Tax Court, the parties must live in separate residences.[67] In *Sydnes v. Commissioner*,[68] the Eighth Circuit Court of Appeals held that the parties did not have to live separate and apart. This reversed the Tax Court's holding[69] that the parties had to live separate and apart.

---

60. *Id.* § 7703(b)(1).
61. Treas. Reg. § 1.7703-1(b)(3). Attendance at college is a temporary absence. Blair v. Comm'r, 63 T.C. 214 (1974).
62. I.R.C. § 7703(b)(2); Prop. Treas. Reg. § 1.7703-1(b)(1)(iii) and (b)(4).
63. Treas. Reg. § 1.7703-1(b)(4).
64. Treas. Reg. § 1.7703-1(b)(4).
65. I.R.C. §§ 7703(b), 7703(b)(3).
66. Treas. Reg. § 1.7703-1(b)(5).
67. Hopkins v. Comm'r, T.C. Memo. 1992-326 (1992).
68. 577 F.2d 60 (8th Cir. 1978).
69. 68 T.C. 170 (1977).

Thus, if a married taxpayer meets the tests of I.R.C. § 7703(b), the taxpayer may be deemed unmarried for purposes of unmarried filing status and head of household filing status. To then file as head of household, the "married deemed unmarried" taxpayer must meet the head of household test discussed in Chapter 10, B.4.b.

4. Filing Categories for Divorced Spouses

Spouses who are divorced may file as single or head of household.

a. Single Returns

If the parties have obtained a final decree of divorce or separate maintenance on or before the last day of the taxable year, they are considered unmarried for the entire year.[70] In addition, if the parties obtain a decree of annulment, which provides that no valid marriage ever existed, they are considered unmarried for that tax year.[71] In either case, the parties must file as single, unless they meet the tests for unmarried head of household discussed below.

In *Boyter v. Commissioner*,[72] the Court was asked to determine whether spouses are married or divorced where the parties divorce at the end of the year and remarry at the beginning of the next year solely to be able to file single returns. The Court looked to state law to determine marital status and found that Maryland has no statute or judicial decision that addresses the validity of a migratory divorce obtained in a foreign country by a Maryland domiciliary where both parties remain domiciled in Maryland during the divorce proceeding. Therefore, the Tax Court adopted the rule it believed the Maryland Court of Appeals would adopt; that is, Maryland would not recognize a Haitian or Dominican divorce as valid for the following reasons: (i) the Court looked to principles of comity, (ii) comity provides that a foreign decree rendered by a Court having jurisdiction to do so will be given full force and effect in another county, (iii) comity has exceptions, however. A decree of divorce will not be recognized under the principle of comity, where it was obtained by a procedure that denies due process of the law in the real sense of the term, or where it has been obtained by fraud, or where the divorce offends the public policy of the state in which recognition is sought, or where the foreign Court lacked jurisdiction.

The Court found that throughout the foreign divorce proceeding, the taxpayers resided and were domiciled in Maryland. The Court believed that the Maryland Court of Appeals would require domicile of one of the parties in that country for a judgment of divorce by a foreign tribunal to be recognized as

70. I.R.C. § 6013(d)(2).

71. E.g., Rev. Rul. 76-255, 1976-2 C.B. 240.

72. 74 T.C. 989 (1980).

valid under principles of comity. The Tax Court distinguished decrees awarded by a sister state under the Full Faith and Credit Clause of the Constitution from decrees awarded by a foreign country under principles of comity. Thus, even if both parties participate in the foreign divorce, Maryland will not recognize the termination of the marriage, because if neither party was domiciled in the foreign country, jurisdiction was lacking and comity will not apply.

b. Head of Household

The advantages of filing as head of household are lower marginal tax rates and a larger standard deduction as compared to married filing separate rates or single rates.[73] In addition, a taxpayer who files as head of household may claim the standard deduction even if the other spouse itemizes deductions on his or her return.[74]

To qualify for head of household status, the taxpayer must file a separate return and meet the following *three tests*:

First, the taxpayer must not be married or considered as unmarried on the last day of his or her tax year.[75] As noted earlier,[76] this means that the spouses must be legally separated under a decree of divorce or separate maintenance.[77] A taxpayer is also not considered married for head of household purposes if at any time during the taxable year the spouse to whom the taxpayer is married at the close of the taxpayer's taxable year was/is a nonresident alien,[78] or the taxpayer's spouse was a nonresident alien and died during the taxable year.[79] On the other hand, a taxpayer is considered as married at the close of the taxable year if the taxpayer's spouse died during the taxable year, provided the deceased spouse was not a nonresident alien.[80]

Second, the taxpayer cannot be a surviving spouse.[81] A surviving spouse is one (i) whose spouse died during either of the two taxable years immediately preceding the taxable year, and (ii) who maintains as his or her home a household that constitutes for the taxable year the principal place of abode (as a member of such household) of a dependent (a) who is a son, stepson, daughter, or stepdaughter of the taxpayer, and (b) with respect to whom the taxpayer is

73. Compare I.R.C. § 1(b) with I.R.C. §§ 1(c) and (d).
74. *See* I.R.C. § 63.
75. I.R.C. § 2(b)(1); Prop. Treas. Reg. § 1.22(b)(1) (1.19.2017). Head of household status denied where parties were married at end of tax year. Harless v. Comm'r, T.C. Memo, 1999-58; Keith v. Comm'r, T.C. Memo. 2000-117.
76. *See* Chapter 10, A.1.
77. I.R.C. § 2(b)(2)(A).
78. I.R.C. § 2(b)(2)(B); Prop. Treas. Reg. 1.2-2(b)(6) (1.19.2017).
79. I.R.C. § 2(b)(2)(C); Prop. Treas. Reg. § 1.22(b)(5) (1.19.2017).
80. I.R.C. § 2(b)(2)(C).
81. I.R.C. § 2(b)(1); Prop. Treas. Reg. § 1.22(b)(1) (1.19.2017).

entitled to a dependency exemption for the taxable year under Section 151.[82] An individual is considered as maintaining a household only if over half the cost of maintaining the household during the taxable year is furnished by such individual.[83] On the other hand, a taxpayer is not considered to be a surviving spouse of the taxpayer if the taxpayer has remarried before the close of the taxable year, or for the taxpayer's taxable year during which the taxpayer's spouse died, a joint return could have been filed under Section 6013.[84]

Third, the taxpayer must meet one of two household maintenance tests. The taxpayer must maintain as his or her home a household which constitutes for more than one-half of such taxable year the principal place of abode, as a member of such household, of (i) a "qualifying child" of the individual (as defined in I.R.C. § 152(c), determined without regard to I.R.C. § 152(e)), but not if the child (a) is married at the close of the taxpayer's taxable year,[85] and (b) is not a dependent of such individual by reason of I.R.C. §§ 152(b)(2), 152(b)(3), or both, or (ii) any other person who is a dependent of the taxpayer, if the taxpayer is entitled to a dependency deduction for the taxable year for the person under Section 151.[86] Alternatively, the taxpayer must maintain a household which constitutes for the taxable year the principal place of abode of the parent of the taxpayer, if the taxpayer is entitled to claim the dependency deduction for the taxable year for his/her father or mother.[87] For purposes of the maintenance of household test, the taxpayer is considered as maintaining a household only if over half the cost of maintaining the household during the taxable year is paid by the taxpayer.[88] These expenses include property taxes, mortgage interest, rent, utility charges, upkeep and repairs, property insurance, and food consumed on the premises. A taxpayer may treat a home's fair rental value as a cost of maintaining a household instead of the sum of the foregoing payments. Expense of maintaining a household does not include the cost of clothing, education, medical treatment, vacations, life insurance, and transportation; the value of services performed in the household; or an expense paid or reimbursed by any other person.[89]

---

82. I.R.C. § 2(a)(1)(A) and (B); Prop. Treas. Reg. § 1.22(a)(i) (1.19.2017). The statute also includes any other person who may be claimed as a dependent under I.R.C. § 151, such as a parent.

83. I.R.C. § 2(a); Flush language; I.R.C. § 2(a)(2)(A) and (B).

84. I.R.C. § 2(a)(2)(A) and (B); Prop. Treas. Reg. § 1.2-2(a)(1) (1.19.2017).

85. I.R.C. § 2(b)(1)(A)(i)(I); Prop. Treas. Reg. § 1.2-2(b)(2)(i) (1.19.2017).

86. I.R.C. § 2(b)(1)(A)(i) and (ii). Notice 2018-70. Even though the exempt amount is zero under Section 151(d) for purposes of the dependency exemption, it is deemed to be $4,1250 for tax year 2018 adjusted for inflation, so that for tax year 2022 it is $4,400 for purposes of defining a qualifying relative of a taxpayer for the dependency exemption.

87. I.R.C. § 2(b)(1)(B); Prop. Treas. Reg. §§ 1.2-1(b)(2)(ii), 1.2(b)(2)(iii) (1.19.2017).

88. I.R.C. § 2(b)(1)(B), [Flush language].

89. Prop. Treas. Reg. § 1.2-2(d)(1) (1.19.2017).

The term "principal place of abode" means a person's main home or dwelling where a person resides. To constitute a child's principal place of abode for more than half the year, and thus meet the third test just described, the child must actually occupy the parent's residence for over half the year.[90] In effect, an individual is a member of the taxpayer's household if the individual and the taxpayer reside in the same living quarters and the taxpayer maintains the household, in part, for the benefit of the individual.[91] Temporary absences for less than six months are permitted for reasons such as education, vacation, military service, or custody agreement.[92] Such absences are counted toward the "more than half the year" rule. The key to such temporary absences is a showing that the absence is temporary and the parent continues to maintain the home in anticipation of the child's return.[93]

Certain parents may not qualify as head of household. Only the custodial parent can qualify for head of household. If there are two children and each parent is the custodial parent for one of the children, each parent may qualify as head of household. Even if the dependency exemption is released by the custodial parent to the noncustodial parent under I.R.C. § 152(e)(2)(A), the noncustodial parent may not claim head of household status.[94] In addition, a taxpayer who is a nonresident alien may not qualify as a head of household.[95] The same person may not be used to qualify more than one taxpayer as the head of a household for the same taxable year.[96] A taxpayer who claims the dependency exemption under the multiple support provisions of I.R.C. § 152(d)(3) may not claim head of household status.[97]

A taxpayer is not considered to be a head of household by reason of an individual who would not be a dependent for the taxable year but for the individual being an individual (other than an individual who at any time during the taxable year of the spouse, determined without regard to I.R.C. § 7703, of the taxpayer) who, for the taxable year of the taxpayer, has the same principal place of abode as of the taxpayer and is a member of the taxpayer's household.[98]

To summarize who is a qualifying child to enable the taxpayer to file as head of household: (i) If the child is the taxpayer's unmarried qualifying child, then the child is deemed a qualifying child to enable the taxpayer to file as

---

90. Prop. Treas. Reg. § 1.22(c) (1.19.2017) Head of household denied where the child allegedly lived with the father in a one-bedroom home which had neither a room nor a bed for the child. Chappell v. Comm'r, T.C. Memo. 2001-146.

91. Prop. Treas. Reg. § 1.22(c) (1.19.2017).

92. *Id.*

93. *Id.*

94. I.R.C. § 2(b)(1)(A).

95. I.R.C. § 2(b)(3)(A); Prop. Treas. Reg. § 1.22(b)(6) (1.19.2017).

96. Prop. Treas. Reg. § 1.22(b)(4) (1.19.2017).

97. I.R.C. § 2(b)(3)(B)(ii); Prop. Treas. Reg. § 1.2-2(b)(4) (1.19.2017).

98. I.R.C. §§ 2(b)(3)(A), 2(b)(3)(B)(i), 152(d)(2)(H);.

head of household. (ii) If the child is the taxpayer's qualifying child who is married and who can nonetheless be claimed as the taxpayer's dependent, the child is deemed a qualifying child to enable the taxpayer to file as head of household, but if the taxpayer cannot claim the child as the taxpayer's dependent, then the child is not a qualifying child to enable the taxpayer to file as head of household. (iii) If the person is the taxpayer's qualifying relative who is the taxpayer's parent, and if the taxpayer can claim the parent as a dependent, then the parent is a qualifying relative to enable the taxpayer to qualify for head of household status, but if the parent cannot be claimed as a dependent, the parent is not a qualifying relative who could enable the taxpayer to file as head of household. (iv) If the person is a qualifying relative other than the taxpayer's parent: (a) if the qualifying relative lived with the taxpayer for more than half the year and the person is a relative who does not have to live with the taxpayer, and the taxpayer can claim the person as a dependent, then the person is a qualifying relative who can enable the taxpayer to file as head of household, but such a qualifying relative is not a qualifying person and does not enable the taxpayer to file as head of household, if (b) the person did not live with the taxpayer for more than half the year, (c) the person was not related to the taxpayer as a relative who did not have to live with the taxpayer, and if a qualifying relative only because the person lived with the taxpayer for the entire year as a member of the taxpayer's household; or (d) the taxpayer cannot claim the person as a dependent.[99]

5. Estimated Taxes

Any individual subject to tax not covered by withholding must make installment payments of estimated tax. No estimated tax payments are required where the amounts of income tax withheld at the source substantially covers a taxpayer's tax liability. Thus, a payee spouse whose only income is alimony must make installment payments of estimated tax. Failure to do so will subject the payee spouse to a variety of penalties.[100] This will apply to pre-2019 decrees of divorce and written instruments, or for pre-2019 instruments modified after 2018 where the modification does not expressly provide for Section 71 repeal provisions.

If a husband and wife make joint payments of estimated tax[101] but do not file a joint return, the payments may be treated entirely as payments of either spouse or may be allocated between them in such manner as they agree.[102] If

99. IRS Publication 501 (2022), Dependents, Standard Deductions and Filing Information, Table 4, Who Is a Qualifying Person Qualifying You to File as Head of Household.

100. *E.g.*, I.R.C. § 6654.

101. Even if the spouses make joint estimated payments, they can still file separate returns. Treas. Reg. § 1.6654-2(e)(5)(ii)(A).

102. Treas. Reg. § 1.6654-2(e)(5)(ii)(A.

they fail to agree to a division of the estimated payments, the estimated payments should be allocated in that proportion of the aggregate amount of all payments of income tax and self-employment tax reported on their separate returns that bears to the sum of the income and self-employment taxes shown on the separate returns of the spouses.[103] The source of the funds for payment of estimated tax is irrelevant in determining which spouse is entitled to claim credit for the estimated tax. Thus, spouses should attempt to negotiate how much of each estimated payment each is entitled to receive.

The following example illustrates the above rule. Assume that H and W make a joint payment of estimated tax of $19,500. H and W subsequently file separate returns for the taxable year showing income tax in the amount of $11,500 and $8,000, respectively. In addition, H's return shows an employment tax imposed in the amount of $500. H and W fail to agree to a division of the estimated tax paid. The amount of the aggregate estimated tax payments allocated to H is computed as follows:

(1) Amount of income tax shown on H's return	$11,500
(2) Plus: Amount of employment tax shown on H's return	500
(3) Total income and employment taxes shown on H's return	12,000
(4) Amount of income tax shown on W's return	8,000
(5) Total income and employment taxes shown on both H's and W's returns	20,000
(6) Proportion of such taxes shown on H's return to total amount of such taxes shown on both H's and W's returns ($12,000/20,000)	60%
(7) Amount of estimated tax payments allocated to H (60% of $19,500)	$11,700

Accordingly, H's return would show remaining tax liability in the amount of $300 ($12,000 taxes shown less $11,700 estimated tax allocated).[104]

An individual who is divorced during the year and claims any portion of a joint estimated tax payment made with the former spouse should enter the former spouse's Social Security number on the front of his or her tax return and write "DIV" (which alerts the Service that the parties are divorced) in the upper righthand corner of the return. This should be done even if the taxpayer

103. Treas. Reg. § 1.6654-2(e)(5)(ii)(B).
104. Treas. Reg. § 1.6654-2(e)(6).

remarries during the year. A statement of the amount claimed should be attached to the return.[105]

If an individual makes payments under one name but files a return under another name, the individual should attach a statement to the return listing when the payments were made, the amount of each payment, and the IRS Center where the payment was made.[106]

6. Refunds

a. Entitlement

An overpayment on a joint return belongs to the spouse who paid the tax liability and the IRS is authorized to refund any balance to such person.[107] Where an overpayment on a joint return filed by husband and wife for tax liability is paid entirely by the wife, the overpayment is the property of the wife and she is entitled to the entire overpayment. The IRS may not credit the overpayment on the joint return against the separate tax liability of the husband for a prior year.[108] The IRS's reasoning is that a joint income tax return does not create new property interests for either spouse in each other's income tax overpayment.[109] Thus, spouses who file a joint return do not have a joint interest in the refund, but they are jointly liable for any deficiency, unless one spouse is deemed to be an "innocent spouse."[110]

Rev. Rul. 80-7 [111] and Rev. Rul. 85-70[112] pertain to the amounts that may be applied by the IRS against the separate property of one of the spouses who resides in a community property state and who files a joint return in which an overpayment is reported. Rev. Rul. 80-7, Rev. Rul. 80-7, and Rev. Rul. 85-70 were amplified and clarified in Rev. Rul. 2004-71[113] (pertaining to overpayments from a joint return that the IRS may offset against a spouse's separate

105. IRS Publication 504, *Tax Information for Divorced or Separated Individuals (2022).*

106. *Id.*

107. I.R.C. § 6402(a); Rev. Rul. 74611, 19742 C.B. 399, *amplified by* Rev. Rul. 8570, 19851 C.B. 361 and Rev. Rul. 8752, 19871 C.B. 347; *United States v. Anthony*, 1999 U.S. Dist. LEXIS 7256 (D. Ariz. 1999) (wife filed head of household return seeking a refund of one half of the estimated tax payments credited to the tax account of the husband and the wife for a prior year in which they filed a joint return. The estimated tax payments were from the income of the husband's sole and separate business. Held: The husband is entitled to the full refund since he paid the tax.).

108. I.R.C. § 6402(b).

109. Rev. Rul. 74611, 19742 C.B. 399, *amplified by* Rev. Rul. 8570, 19851 C.B. 361 and Rev. Rul. 8752, 19871 C.B. 347.

110. See Chapter 11, Innocent Spouse Rules, for a discussion of the innocent spouse rules.

111. 1980-1 C.B. 296.

112. 1985-1 C.B. 36.

113. 2004-2 C.B. 76.

tax liability for taxpayers domiciled in Arizona or Wisconsin); Rev. Rul. 2004-72[114] (pertaining to overpayments from a joint return that the IRS may offset against a spouse's separate tax liability for taxpayers domiciled in California, Idaho, and Louisiana); Rev. Rul. 2004-73[115] (pertaining to overpayments from a joint return that the IRS may offset against a spouse's separate tax liability for taxpayers domiciled in Nevada, New Mexico, and Washington), and Rev. Rul. 2004-74[116] (pertaining to overpayments from a joint return that the IRS may offset against a spouse's separate tax liability for taxpayers domiciled in Texas). The Service has combined some states, such as Arizona and Wisconsin; or California, Idaho, or Louisiana; or Nevada, New Mexico, or Washington because in the view of the Service those states have similar community property laws. Because the rulings are fact specific, the IRS urges taxpayers to check the current law of each jurisdiction and apply it to their particular facts.

b. Allocation between Spouses

Where each spouse pays some of the tax liability, so that each spouse is entitled to a portion of the refund, Rev. Rul. 85-70, *supra*, provides a formula to determine each spouse's share of the refund. Thus, where the spouses file a joint income tax return showing an overpayment, the amount that may be credited to one spouse's income tax liability is computed by subtracting that spouse's share of the joint income tax liability, determined in accordance with the separate tax formula, from the spouse's actual contribution toward the payment of the joint income tax liability. The separate tax formula is:

$$\frac{\text{spouse's separate tax}}{\text{total spouse's separate taxes}} \times \text{joint tax liability shown on return}$$

A spouse's share of actual contributions toward payment of the joint income tax liability depends upon whether the payments are made by estimated tax payments or by withholding.

If the payments are made solely by estimated tax payments, Treas. Reg. § 1.6015(b)1(b) provides that if the spouses cannot agree on the allocation of the estimated tax payments, the estimated tax payments will be allocated between the spouses according to the following formula:

$$\frac{\text{separate tax liability}}{\text{both spouses separate tax liabilities}} \times \text{estimated tax liability}$$

114. 2004-2 C.B. 77.
115. 2004-2 C.B. 80.
116. 2004-2 C.B. 84.

If, on the other hand, the payments are made solely by withholding, each spouse's contribution toward the joint income tax liability is equal to the withholding tax credits attributable to the spouse.[117] If the spouses have income subject to withholding and they file a joint declaration of estimated tax and/or make a payment with their joint return, each spouse's contribution is determined by combining the two contribution methods. Each spouse's contribution includes the withholding tax credits reported by the spouse on the joint return and the formula for estimated tax payments set forth earlier.

Rev. Rul. 80-7, *supra*, offers the following example to illustrate the foregoing rules. H and W are married. Their joint federal income tax return reflects a tax liability of $13,004. H reports wages of $20,000, from which $6,000 is withheld, and H has other income of $10,000. W reports wages of $10,000, from which $2,000 is withheld, and W has other income of $5,000. They file a joint estimated tax declaration and pay $8,000 in estimated tax payments. H has an unpaid separate liability of $5,000 from a prior year.

The first step is to determine the tax liability of the spouses as if each had filed a separate return. If the spouses filed separate returns, H's income tax liability would have been $10,302 and W's income tax liability would have been $3,334.

The second step is to determine each spouse's deemed portion of the estimated tax payments. H's deemed portion of the estimated tax payments is $6,044, determined as follows:

$$\frac{\$10{,}302}{\$10{,}302 + \$3{,}334} \times \$8{,}000 = \$6{,}044$$

W's deemed portion of the estimated tax payments is $1,956, determined as follows:

$$\frac{\$3{,}334}{\$10{,}302 + \$3{,}334} \times \$8{,}000 = \$1{,}956$$

Thus, H's total contribution is $6,044 and W's total contribution is $1,944.

The third step is to determine each spouse's withholding tax credits. According to the facts, H had $6,000 withheld and W had $2,000 withheld.

The fourth step is to determine the total contribution of H and W. This is a combination of the estimated tax payments attributable to each and the withholding tax credits attributable to each. Thus:

(i) H's total contribution is $12,044 ($6,044 + $6,000), and
(ii) W's total contribution is $3,956 ($1,956 + $2,000).

117. Prop. Treas. Reg. § 1.31-1.

The fifth step is to determine each spouse's share of the joint tax liability. Having thus determined each spouse's contribution, each spouse's share of a joint overpayment is the difference between each spouse's liability and each spouse's contribution. Thus:

H's share of the joint liability is $9,825, determined as follows:

$$\frac{\$10{,}302}{\$10{,}302 + \$3{,}334} \times \$13{,}004 = \$9{,}825$$

W's share of the joint liability is $3,179, determined as follows:

$$\frac{\$3{,}334}{\$10{,}302 + \$3{,}334} \times \$13{,}004 = \$3{,}179$$

The sixth and final step is to determine each spouse's share of the refund.

(i) H's refund is $2,219 ($12,044 – $9,825)
(ii) W's refund is $777 ($3,956 – $3,179)

The overpayment credited to a spouse cannot, however, exceed the joint overpayment.

c. Overpayment Credited to Next Year

In Priv. Ltr. Rul. 200130036, the issue raised was the apportionment between spouses of an overpayment from one year credited to estimated tax payments for the next year. In 1998, the husband and wife filed a joint return and requested that the overpayment be credited to their 1999 estimated tax. For 1999, however, the parties filed separate returns. The husband claimed the entire overpayment on his 1999 return, and the wife claimed none of the overpayment. The wife later sought to have a portion of the credit allocated to her.

The IRS first said that the proper method to allocate the overpayment depends on whether it is treated as a joint estimated tax payment for 1999, or an overpayment for 1998. If it is an estimated tax payment, then it must be determined whether the parties agreed to the allocation. The IRS looked to prior Treas. Reg. § 1.6015(b)-1(b) (now Treas. Reg. §1.6654-2(e)(5)), which provides that joint estimated tax payments may be treated as payments on account of the tax liability of either spouse or may be divided between them in such manner as they agree. If the parties fail to agree, the IRS will allocate the payments in proportion to the spouses' separate tax for the year per a formula contained in the regulations. Thus, if the amount in dispute is an estimated tax payment for 1999, the regulations will be followed, unless the parties agree otherwise. If, however, the amount in dispute arises from an overpayment of the 1998 tax liability, I.R.C. § 6402(a) provides that the amount of any overpayment may be credited against the liability of the person who made the overpayment or be refunded to such person.

The issue before the IRS was whether to apply the provisions of Rev. Rul. 80-7, *supra*, to determine each spouse's separate interest in the 1998 overpayment that was applied to their 1999 estimated tax payments, or whether to treat the 1998 overpayment as a joint estimated tax payment. If the apportionment is based on Rev. Rul. 80-7, the IRS must determine each spouse's portion of the refund by determining each individual's contribution to the 1998 overpayment and individual liability for the 1998 tax. If the 1998 overpayment is a joint estimated tax payment in 1999, then the allocation will be made, in the absence of an agreement between the spouses, in proportion to the separate tax liabilities of the spouses for 1998.

The IRS relied on Rev. Rul. 76-140, 1976-1 C.B. 376 in which the IRS ruled, under similar facts, that the amount of the joint overpayment, which was credited to the following year's estimated tax, should be allocated between them pursuant to the allocation set forth in the Regulations under I.R.C. § 6015,[118] absent an agreement between the parties. Once the spouses elect to credit the amount of the overpayment to next year's estimated tax payments, it ceases to be an overpayment, and becomes an estimated tax payment. Thus, the allocation formula using the separate tax liabilities of the spouses in 1999 is the correct method to be applied in this case, unless there is an agreement to the contrary, which the IRS found did not exist.

d. Amended Return

The IRS will accept a claim for refund filed by a divorced taxpayer on a Form 1040X with respect to a jointly filed individual income tax return if Form 1040X is signed by only one of the taxpayers, and the IRS will issue a refund check in the name of the taxpayer that filed Form 1040X. The amount of the refund is determined by recomputing the taxpayer's share of the joint liability and subtracting that amount from the taxpayer's contribution toward the joint liability. The amount of the overpayment to the taxpayer is limited to the amount of the joint overpayment.[119]

For example, assume H and W file a joint federal income tax return reporting a tax liability of $6,668. H reports $20,000 of wages and withholding credits of $5,028. W erroneously reports a $10,000 tax-free stipend and withholding credits of $1,640. In the next year, H and W are divorced. After the divorce, W files a Form 1040X for the prior year showing a tax liability of $3,484, thus

118. *See* Treas. Reg. § 1.6654-2(e)(5) for the current regulation on this issue.
119. Rev. Rul. 808, 19801 C.B. 298.

correctly reporting the taxfree stipend as taxable income. Only W signs the Form 1040X and requests the refund check be issued in W's name alone.

In order to be consistent with Rev. Rul. 80-7 the Service will apply the separate tax method of allocation in order to determine a spouse's share of a joint overpayment that results from the filing of a separate claim for refund. Therefore, the taxpayer's individual refund will be calculated by determining the taxpayer's individual liability according to the separate tax formula.

(i) Since Rev. Rul. 807, 19801 C.B. 296, applies, the individual refund is calculated by determining the taxpayer's individual liability per the separate tax formula:

$$\frac{\text{taxpayer's recomputed separate tax liability}}{\text{both spouses recomputed separate tax liability}} \times \text{recomputed joint tax liability—Form 1040X}$$

and subtracting the taxpayer's individual tax liability from the taxpayer's contribution determined in accordance with Rev. Rul. 807.

(ii) H and W's joint income tax liability as originally reported is $6,668, and their joint liability as reported on the Form 1040X filed by W is $3,484. The total joint refund is $3,184 ($6,668 – $3,484).

(iii) H's recomputed separate tax liability is $5,350 and W's recomputed separate tax liability is zero.

(iv) H's recomputed individual liability is $3,484.

$$\frac{\$5{,}350}{\$0 + \$5{,}350} \times \$3{,}484 = \$3{,}484$$

W's recomputed individual liability is zero.

$$\frac{\$0}{\$0 + \$5{,}350} \times \$3{,}484 = \$3{,}484$$

(v) H's refund is $1,544 ($5,028 – $3,484). W's refund is $1,640 ($1,640 – $0).

(vi) The total of H's and W's individual refunds equals the amount of the joint refund. The IRS will issue W a refund of $1,640 upon the filing of a Form 1040X with only W's signature. Upon the filing of a Form 1040X by H, the IRS will issue a refund to H of $1,544.[120]

120. *See* Rev. Rul. 808, 19801 C.B. 298.

e. Agreement

If the parties file a joint return and expect to receive a refund, the agreement should specify how the refund will be allocated between the payor spouse and the payee spouse.

f. Refund Check

Because the refund check will be made payable to both spouses, consideration should be given to how to cash the check if one spouse subsequently refuses to endorse the check. In this instance, IRS Form 2848 should be used. For example, if a joint return is filed and a refund is due that is to be allocated entirely to the payor spouse, the payee spouse should execute Form 2848 authorizing the payor spouse to endorse the refund check on his or her behalf. Where the refund is to be allocated equally between the spouses, but neither will execute a Form 2848 in favor of the other, one spouse should consider "buying" the refund from the other. For example, if a joint return is filed and a $1,000 refund is due, which is to be split equally between the payor spouse and the payee spouse, the payor spouse should pay the payee spouse $500 (his or her share of the refund) in exchange for the payee spouse's execution of the Form 2848 in favor of the payor spouse. Alternatively, the spouses may have the refund deposited in their attorneys' escrow account and disbursed from such account pursuant to an agreement between the parties.

g. Net Operating Loss

When a spouse incurs a net operating loss (NOL) in a separate return year that is carried back or forward, Rev. Rul. 806, 19801 C.B. 296, modifying Rev. Rul. 75368, 19752 C.B. 480, provides the following formula to determine the amount of the spouse's individual refund.

(1) The NOL is carried back and forward only to the income that would have been reported by the taxpayer had a separate return been filed.
(2) Joint rates are applied to the reduced joint taxable income.
(3) The amount of the individual refund is calculated by determining the taxpayer's recomputed share of the joint tax liability according to the following separate tax formula.

$$\frac{\text{taxpayer's recomputed separate tax liability}}{\text{both spouses' recomputed separate tax liability}} \times \text{recomputed joint tax liability}$$

(4) The amount determined in (3) is then subtracted from the taxpayer's contribution, determined in accordance with Rev. Rul. 807, 19801 C.B. 296.

(5) The amount of the refund is limited to the amount of the joint overpayment.
(6) In computing each taxpayer's separate tax liability, the tax rates for married filing separate returns is used.

h. Deficiency

If the parties file a joint return and after they are divorced a deficiency is determined on the joint return, both parties are liable for the deficiency.[121] This differs from the rule set forth in Rev. Rul. 74611, 19742 C.B. 399, which holds that tax refunds are not the joint property of the spouses but belong to the spouse whose payments created the refund. The ruling then proceeds to give an illustration and analysis of a net operating loss from a single filing tax year to a joint tax year.

If, however, each has agreed to be responsible for his or her share of deficiency, the separate share formula discussed earlier with respect to refunds could be used to determine each parties' liability for the deficiency.

For an example of problems that may arise here, see Priv. Ltr. Rul. 8911015.

121. I.R.C. § 6013(d)(3).

11 Innocent Spouse Rules

A. Introduction

One of the benefits of married couples filing a joint return is that the income tax brackets are lower than if they filed married filing separately, unless the income of each spouse is equal to the income of the other spouse. On the other hand, one of the detriments of a married couple filing a joint return is that they are subject to joint and several liability for any income tax reported on the joint returns; i.e., each spouse is responsible for payment of the entire tax (plus interest and penalty) reported on the joint return regardless of who earned the income. To protect a spouse whose only contribution, or at least major contribution, to the return was to sign it and thus expose herself/himself to tax liability, Congress enacted the innocent spouse rules, which are designed to relieve an innocent spouse from any liability reported on the return. This chapter discusses the innocent spouse rules and the requirement the spouse seeking innocent spouse treatment must meet to be relieved of joint and several liability.

Congress first adopted innocent spouse tax treatment to relieve an innocent spouse from joint and several liability in 1971 when it enacted Section 6013(e)[1] in 1984. Congress expanded the innocent spouse provisions to include more terms that may have resulted in an understatement of tax in order to offer more protections to an innocent spouse,[2] in 1998. The Department of Treasury sent to the Commission on Ways and Means of the U.S. House of Representatives a Report to the Congress on Joint Liability and Innocent Spouse Issues in which it recommended a reform of the innocent spouse provisions under prior Section 6013(e).[3]

---

1. Pub. L. No. 91-67, 84 Stat.2063(1971).
2. Pub. L. No. 98-369, 98 Stat. 494 (1984).
3. Report to the Congress on Joint Liability and Innocent Spouse Issues from the Department of Treasury, February 9, 1990.

The result of the Report was the Restructuring and Reform Act of 1998, which repealed prior I.R.C. § 6013(e) and added new I.R.C. § 6015. The purpose for the new provision was to make innocent spouse relief more accessible to taxpayers than had been the case under prior Section 6013(e).[4]

B. Types of Relief

The 1998 Act bifurcates innocent spouse treatment between two groups of taxpayers. I.R.C. § 6015(b) (Treas. Reg. § 1.6015-2) (sometimes referred to as "(b) relief") sets forth the procedures for relief from liability applicable to all joint filers. This provision allows a spouse to escape full or apportioned joint and several liability for an understatement of tax attributable to erroneous items of the nonrequesting spouse if the requesting spouse did not have actual or constructive knowledge of the understatement and it is inequitable to hold the requesting spouse liable for the tax. I.R.C. § 6015(c) (Treas. Reg. § 1.6015-3) (sometimes referred to as "(c) relief") sets forth the procedures for proportionate relief from joint and several liability for taxpayers who are divorced, separated, widowed, or not living together for 12 months to allocate his or her tax deficiency between the spouses as if separate returns had been filed if the requesting spouse did not have actual or constructive knowledge of the understatement. This provision allows a spouse to request limited relief from a portion of the understatement or deficiency. Claims for (b) and (c) relief must be made within two years of the first collection activity taken by the IRS against the requesting spouse as discussed later in this chapter.

Section 66 provides relief for a spouse who did not file a joint return in a community property state and who did not include in gross income an item of community income that would be attributable solely to the nonrequesting spouse but for the operation of state community property law.

If relief is not available under I.R.C. § 6015(b) and (c), I.R.C. § 6015(f) (Treas. Reg. § 1.6015-4) (sometimes referred to as "(f) relief") authorizes the IRS to grant relief if it is inequitable to hold a taxpayer liable for any unpaid tax or deficiency.

Table 11.1 summarizes the rules for innocent spouse relief.

4. Pub. L. 105-206, § 3201, 112 Stat. 734, H. Conf. Rep. 105-599 at 249 (1998).

Table 11.1 Innocent Spouse Relief

Factors	Rules for Innocent Spouse Relief for all Joint Filers (b) Relief	Rules for Separation of Liability for Taxpayers No Longer Married or Taxpayers Legally Separated or Not Living Together (c) Relief	Rules for Equitable Relief (f) Relief
Type of Return	The requesting spouse must have filed a joint return that has an understatement of tax due to an erroneous item of the nonrequesting spouse.	The requesting spouse must have filed a joint return that has an understatement of tax due, in part, to an item of the nonrequesting spouse.	The requesting spouse must have filed a return that has either an understatement or an underpayment of tax. The income tax liability from which the requesting spouse seeks relief is due to (i) an item of the nonrequesting spouse with whom the requesting spouse filed the joint return, or (ii) an unpaid tax resulting from the nonrequesting spouse's income.
Marital Status	Married	The requesting spouse must be no longer be married, to, or is legally separated from, or has not been a member of the nonrequesting spouse's household for an entire year before the requesting spouse files for relief.	
Knowledge	The requesting spouse must establish that at the time he/she signed the joint return the requesting spouse did not know, and had no reason to know, that there was an understatement of tax.	If the IRS establishes that the requesting spouse actually knew at the time of the signing of the return of the item giving rise to the deficiency, then the requesting spouse is not entitled to relief to the extent of the actual knowledge. The foregoing does not apply if the requesting spouse establishes that he/she signed the return under duress.	The requesting spouse must not have knowingly participated in the filing of a fraudulent return. The requesting spouse and the nonrequesting spouse must not have transferred property to each other as part of a fraudulent scheme. The nonrequesting spouse did not transfer property to the requesting spouse for the main purpose of avoiding tax or the payment of tax.

Table 11.1 Innocent Spouse Relief *(continued)*

Factors	**Rules for Innocent Spouse Relief for all Joint Filers (b) Relief**	**Rules for Separation of Liability for Taxpayers No Longer Married or Taxpayers Legally Separated or Not Living Together (c) Relief**	**Rules for Equitable Relief (f) Relief**
Other Qualifications		Liability of requesting spouse is increased by the value of disqualified assets transferred to avoid tax.	The requesting spouse does not qualify for innocent spouse relief or separation of liability.
Inequitable	It would be inequitable to hold the requesting spouse liable for the understatement of tax taking into account all the facts and circumstances.		It must be inequitable to hold the requesting spouse liable for the underpayment or understatement of tax taking into account all the facts and circumstances.
Refunds	The requesting spouse can generate a refund.	The requesting spouse cannot generate a refund.	
Filing	File Form 8857 no later than two years after the IRS has begun collection activities from the requesting spouse.	File Form 8857 no later than two years after the IRS has begun collection activities from the requesting spouse.	File Form 8857 no later than two years after the IRS has begun collection activities from the requesting spouse.

A requesting spouse may submit a single claim electing relief under both or either (b) or (c) relief, and requesting relief under (f) relief. However, equitable relief under I.R.C. § 6015(f) is available only to a requesting spouse who fails to qualify for (b) or (c) relief. If a requesting spouse elects the application of either (b) or (c) relief, the Service will consider whether relief is appropriate under either elective provision and, to the extent relief is unavailable under either (b) or (c), then whether it is available under (f). If a requesting spouse seeks (f) relief the IRS may not grant (b) or (c) relief in the absence of an affirmative election made by the requesting spouse under either of those sections. If in the course of reviewing a request for (f) relief only the IRS determines that the requesting spouse may qualify for relief under (b) relief or (c) relief instead of (f) relief, the Service is required to correspond with the requesting spouse to see if the requesting spouse would like to amend his or her request to elect the application of (b) relief or (c) relief. If the requesting spouse chooses to amend the claim for relief, the requesting spouse must submit an affirmative election under (b) relief or (c) relief. The amended claim for relief will relate back to the original claim for purposes of determining the timelines of the claims.[5]

An executor of a decedent's estate may not only pursue a request for relief from joint and several liability under Section 6015 made during the decedent's lifetime, but also may file a request for (b), (c), or (f) relief from joint and several liability on behalf of the decedent.[6]

Relief is not available for liabilities that are required to be reported on a joint Federal income tax return but are not income taxes imposed under Subtitle A of the Internal Revenue Code (e.g., domestic service employment taxes under Section 3510).[7]

1. Definition of Requesting Spouse

A requesting spouse is an individual who files a joint return and elects (b) or (c) relief or requests (f) relief from Federal income tax liability arising from that return.[8] On the other hand, a nonrequesting spouse is the individual with whom the requesting spouse filed the joint return for the year for which relief from liability is sought.[9]

2. Procedure for Relief from Liability Applicable to All Joint Filers—I.R.C. § 6015(b) ("b Relief")

a. Tests for (b) Relief

Section 6015(b) provides for full or apportioned relief from joint and several liability if its tests are met to the extent such liability is attributable to an understatement of tax caused by the nonrequesting spouse. To qualify for complete innocent spouse treatment applicable to all joint filers, i.e., to qualify for (b) relief, *five tests* must be met:

First, a joint return must have been filed for the taxable year in issue.[10] See *Raymond v. Commissioner*,[11] where the Court held that to be eligible for relief under I.R.C. §§ 6015(b), (c), and (f), the taxpayer must file a joint return. In *Raymond*, the taxpayer filed "married filing separate."[12] The Court denied (b)

5. Treas. Reg. § 1.6015-1(a)(2). *See also* Prop. Treas. Reg. § 1.6015-1(a)(2)(12.07.15)
6. Rev. Rul. 2003-36, 2003-1 C.B. 849.
7. Treas. Reg. § 1.6015-1(a)(3).
8. Prop. Treas. Reg. § 1.6015-1(h)(1) (11.20.2015) which changes "elects" to "requests."
9. Treas. Reg. § 1.6015-1(h)(2).
10. I.R.C. § 6015(b)(1)(A); Treas. Reg. § 1.6015-2(a)(1). *See also* Chapter 11, B.2 for a discussion of what constitutes a joint return, and I.R.C. § 6013 for the basic rules for joint returns.
11. 119 T.C. 191 (2002).
12. *See also* Rev. Proc. 2013-34, 2013-2 C.B. 397, discussed at Chapter 11, B.4.b. Where the taxpayer's liability arises under Section 6672, trust fund recovery penalty, which is not shown on and did not arise from the filing of a joint Federal income tax return, the taxpayer is not eligible for innocent spouse relief from the trust fund recovery penalty under I.R.C. § 6015(b), (c) or (f)). Chavis v. Comm'r, 158 T.C. No. 8 (6.15.22).

and (c) relief because a joint return was not filed. Generally, to constitute a joint return the return must be filed by the spouses who are married on the last day of the taxable year.[13] Where the parties are divorced but nonetheless file a joint return, the requesting spouse is not eligible for innocent spouse relief because the parties did not file a valid joint return.[14] But if only one spouse signs the return based upon authorization of the other spouse, a joint return will be found to have been filed.[15] Where a husband files a joint return without objection of the wife, who fails to file a separate return, it may be presumed a joint return was filed with the tacit consent of the wife.[16] But where the parties are estranged, lived separate and apart, the wife earned no income and the husband, being unable to obtain the wife's signature on the return, signs the wife's name, a joint return will not be presumed.[17] Although a taxpayer may not physically sign a return, the taxpayer may be deemed to have tacitly consented to the electronic filing of a return where the requesting spouse gave the nonrequesting spouse his tax information which she then gave to a paid preparer who prepared the return and filed it electronically.[18] The key fact is the intent of both parties—did they intend to file a joint return?[19] For example, if one spouse files a return under duress, or if the spouse's signature is signed by the other without his or her consent, intent cannot be established.[20] Where a spouse disapproves of the signing of a joint return, the spouse must show both (1) that he or she was unable to resist demands to sign the return, and (2) that he or she would not have signed the return except for the constraint applied to his or her will.[21] Thus, to qualify for innocent spouse treatment the parties must establish that a joint return was filed freely, willingly, and intentionally. If the parties can establish that a joint return was not filed, then the parties should contest the Service's contention of joint and several liability.

Second, on the return there is an understatement of tax attributable to erroneous items of the nonrequesting spouse who filed the joint return.[22] The

---

13. I.R.C. § 6013(a), (d)(1)(A).
14. James v. Comm'r, T.C. Memo. 2021-7.
15. Moran v. Comm'r, T.C. Memo. 2005-66.
16. Carroro v. Comm'r, 29 B.T.A. 646 (1933).
17. Hennen v. Comm'r, 35 T.C. 747 (1961).
18. Jacobsen v. Comm'r, T.C. Memo. 2018-115.
19. Lane v. Comm'r, 26 T.C. 405 (1956); Stone v. Comm'r, 22 T.C. 893 (1954); Hennen v. Comm'r, *supra*.
20. Treas. Reg. § 1.6013-4(d).
21. Stanley v. Comm'r, 81 T.C. 634 (1983).
22. I.R.C. § 6015(b)(1)(B); Treas. Reg. § 1.6015-2(a)(2). "Understatement" is defined in Treas. Reg. § 1.6015-2(b) by reference to I.R.C. § 6662(d)(2)(A) and the regulations thereunder which defines an understatement to mean the excess of the amount of tax required to be shown on a return for the taxable year over the amount of tax imposed which is shown on the return. Essentially, an understatement is a proposed assessment or deficiency.

unreported income can occur in unexpected ways, such as where misappropriated funds of an S corporation is not reported as income on the stockholder's income.[23]

Third, the requesting spouse establishes that in signing the joint return he or she did not know, and had no reason to know,[24] that there was an understatement.[25] A requesting spouse has knowledge or reason to know of an understatement if he or she actually knew of the understatement, or if a reasonable person in similar circumstances would have known of the understatement[26].

A taxpayer who signs a return is charged with constructive knowledge of its contents. To establish that a taxpayer had no reason to know of an understatement on a return, the taxpayer must show that he or she was not aware of the circumstances that gave rise to the error and not merely unaware of the tax consequences. The taxpayer may not turn a blind eye to readily available facts.[27] An individual has reason to know of the understatement if a reasonably prudent taxpayer in a similar position when the return was signed could be expected to know that the return contained an understatement.[28] In applying the reasonably prudent standard, the Courts consider four factors: (1) the requesting spouse's level of education;[29] (2) the requesting spouse's

23. Where income of a medical practice was misappropriated by the nonrequesting spouse who worked at the medical practice, the medical practice was required to report the fees as its income, and since the medical practice of which the reporting spouse was the sole stockholder was an S corporation, the requesting spouse as the stockholder was required to include the misappropriated fees in income. Thus, the unreported fees that should have been reported on the joint return gave rise to understatement of tax on the couple's joint return. Hence, the second test for (b) relief was not met. Francel v. Comm'r, T.C. Memo. 2019-35. *But see* Blappert v. Comm'r, (Docket No. 10417-8), a bench opinion issued December 9, 2021, in which the Court granted the requesting spouse innocent spouse relief because the requesting spouse did not participate in her husband's bookkeeping, that the business's account was separate from their personal accounts, that she had no access to the business accounts, and did not know about the source, receipt, or amount of the omitted income. Accordingly, the Court held that the requesting spouse did not know and had no reason to know about the omitted income. [Note: A bench opinion is a summary opinion and may not be cited as precedent.]

24. In Charlton v. Comm'r, 114 T.C. 333 (2000), the Court held that since the requesting spouse had unfettered access to the financial records of the nonrequesting spouse's business in preparing their income tax returns, he had reason to know of the understatement of income by the business.

25. I.R.C. § 6015(b)(1)(C); Treas. Reg. § 1.6015-2(a)(3). Where a spouse seeking innocent spouse relief has actual knowledge of the underlying transaction that produced the income, innocent spouse relief is denied. Cheshire v. Comm'r, 113 T.C. 183 (2000), *aff'd.* 282 F.3d 326 (C.A. 5, 206). According to the Court, this standard applies to both (b) and (c) relief provisions.

26. Treas. Reg. § 1. 6015—2(c).

27. Porter v. Comm'r, 132 T.C. 203, 211-212 (2009).

28. Hopkins v. Comm'r, 121 T.C. 73, 77 (2003).

29. The education referred to here is a financial education and not an education in general. Financial education includes a formal education in business, accounting, or finance. Jacobsen v. Comm'r, T.C. Memo. 2018-115 at 16.

involvement in the family's financial and business activities; (3) any substantial unexplained increase in the family's standard of living; and (4) the nonrequesting spouse's evasiveness or deceitfulness about the family's finances.[30] Thus, the requesting spouse has a duty of inquiry with respect to the return in issue.[31]

All of the facts and circumstances are considered in determining whether a requesting spouse had reason to know of an understatement.[32] The facts and circumstances that the income tax regulations identify include, but are not limited to the following eight non-exhaustive factors: (i) the nature of the erroneous item and the amount of the erroneous item[33] relative to other items; (ii) the couple's financial situation; (iii) the requesting spouse's educational background and business experience;[34] (iv) the extent of the requesting spouse's participation in the activity that resulted in the erroneous item; (v) whether the requesting spouse failed to inquire, at or before the time the return was signed, about items on the return or omitted from the return that a reasonable person would question; (vi) any lavish or unusual expenditures compared

---

30. Price v. Comm'r, 887. F.2d 959, 965 (C.A. 9, 1989) (Even though this case was decided before the enactment of Section 6015, its factors are still applicable.) *See also* Jacobsen v. Comm'r, T.C. Memo. 2018 for a discussion and application of each of these factors. *See also* Schorse v. Comm'r, T.C. Memo. 2018-176 at 10–11 where the requesting spouse had a college degree, owned his own business, was involved in the family's financial activities, was aware of the financial affairs of the nonrequesting spouse, was involved in the preparation of their joint return, maintained a high standard of living from which he benefited, and the nonrequesting spouse did not try to hide or deceive anything from the requesting spouse, the court held that a reasonably prudent person could be expected to know the returns contained understatements when signed. Thus, (b) relief was denied. Embezzlement by nonrequesting spouse, who was also an accountant, was evasive and deceitful. Jacobsen v. Comm'r; Rogers v. Comm'r. T.C. Memo. 2018-53 (Taxpayer was highly educated, had multiple advanced degrees, including a JD and MBA, understood complex financial, accounting, and tax concepts, was actively involved in the household finances and family business, maintained a high standard of living, and there was no evidence of deceit by the nonrequesting spouse. Thus, requesting spouse knew or had reason to know of the understatements and therefore (b) relief was denied.).

31. Butler v. Comm'r, 114 T.C. 276, 283-284 (2000).

32. Treas. Reg. §1.6015-2(c). See text at Chapter 11, B.2.c., for rules relating to a requesting spouse's actual knowledge. The rules for actual knowledge for (b) relief and (c) relief are substantially the same.

33. An erroneous item is any item that results in an understatement or deficiency in tax to the extent the item is omitted from or improperly reported (including an improper characterization) on a tax return. Treas. Reg. § 1.6015-1(h)(4). According to this regulation, an example of an erroneous item is unreported income from an investment asset which results in an understatement or deficiency in tax. Similarly, ordinary income that is improperly reported as capital gain resulting in an understatement or deficiency in tax is also an erroneous item.

34. Where wife was college educated and a cursory review of the return would have realized large negative income and thus caused a reasonably prudent person to question the accuracy of negative income reported on the return, the taxpayer was held to have had reason to know of the understatement of tax on her joint income tax return. Briley v. Comm'r, T.C. Memo. 2019-55.

with past spending levels;[35] and (vii) whether the erroneous item represented a departure from a recurring pattern reflected in prior years' returns (e.g., omitted income from an investment regularly reported on prior years' returns), and (viii) any deceit or evasiveness of the nonrequesting spouse.[36] A requesting spouse has knowledge or reason to know of the portion of an understatement related to an item attributable to the nonrequesting spouse under Treas. Reg. § 1.6015-1(n) if the requesting spouse knows or has reason to know of the nonrequesting spouse's erroneous item or items that resulted in the increase to adjusted gross income. Depending on the facts and circumstances, if the requesting spouse was abused by the nonrequesting spouse (as described in Treas. Reg. § 1.6015-1(o)), discussed later, or the nonrequesting spouse maintained control of the household finances by restricting the requesting spouse's access to financial information, and because of the abuse or financial control, the requesting spouse was not able to challenge the treatment of any items on the joint return for fear of the nonrequesting spouse's retaliation, the requesting spouse will be treated as not having knowledge or reason to know of the items giving rise to the understatement. If, however, the requesting involuntarily executed the return, the requesting spouse may choose to establish that the return was signed under duress. In such a case, Treas. Reg. § 1.6013-4(d) applies.[37]

According to the U.S. Tax Court in *Greer v. Commissioner*,[38] there are two lines of cases interpreting "knowledge." On the one hand is the case of *Bokum v. Commissioner*,[39] where the Court held that knowledge of a transaction is sufficient knowledge of an understatement to bar innocent spouse relief. On the other hand, in *Price v. Commissioner*,[40] the Ninth Circuit Court of Appeals held

35. Engaging in a high standard of living and sending children to private school indicates that the requesting spouse had knowledge of the family's finances from which he benefited. Schorse v. Comm'r, T.C. Memo. 2018-176.

36. Treas. Reg. § 1.6015-2(b). Schorse v. Comm'r, T.C. Memo. 2018-176. In *Riley-Casey v. Comm'r*, T.C. Memo. 2013-92, the Court denied innocent spouse treatment to the wife reasoning that as a sophisticated real estate agent who also managed her husband's properties, she should have known if that income was unreported and deductions were overrated, and she had a duty of inquiry that would have lead a reasonably prudent person to inquire further. *See also* Rev. Proc. 2013-34, 2013-2 C.B. 397 (discussed at Chapter 11, B.4.b.).

37. Prop. Treas. Reg. § 106015-2(b) (11.20.2015).

38. T.C. Memo. 2009-20, *aff'd*, 595 F.3d 338 (C.A. 6, 2010).

39. 94 T.C. 126 (1990), *aff'd* 992 F.2d 1132 (C.A. 11, 1993).

40. 887 F.2d 959 (C.A. 9, 1989). In *Price*, the Ninth Circuit Court of Appeals held that in erroneous deduction cases, the requesting spouse's mere knowledge of the existence of the transaction underlying the deduction is not enough to deny relief. In order to be denied relief, the requesting spouse must know or have reason to know that the deduction would give rise to a substantial understatement. The requesting spouse, however, has a duty to inquire and question an erroneous deduction. Failure to inquire about a $90,000 deduction taken against total income of $103,000 was sufficient to deny innocent spouse relief. In *Mora v. Comm'r*, 117 T.C. 279 (2001),

that a taxpayer meets the standard for relief if the taxpayer did not know or did not have reason to know that an erroneous deduction or credit would give rise to an understatement despite the presence of the deduction on the returns. In other words, if a spouse has reason to know of a possible understatement, the spouse incurs a duty of inquiry. A spouse has constructive knowledge of an understatement if such a duty arises and is not discharged.[41] The *Price* Court listed four factors to determine whether a taxpayer had reason to know of an understatement: (i) the education of the requesting spouse, (ii) the involvement of the taxpayer in the financial affairs of the transaction that caused the understatement, (iii) whether the requesting spouse directly benefitted from the reported tax treatment of the transaction through a change in the standard of living, and (iv) whether the nonrequesting spouse was evasive and deceitful with the requesting spouse, or misled the requesting spouse regarding the transaction in issue. In *Greer*, the deficiency arose from the disallowance of investment credits and partnership losses. According to the Court, knowledge of the transaction creating the understatement is sufficient knowledge of the understatement to bar (b) relief. In reaching this conclusion, the *Greer* Court relied upon the four factors in *Price* and determined that the requesting spouse should have made further inquiry about the tax benefits the taxpayers claimed on the return.

It is important to note that *Bokum* and *Price* were decided under the pre-1998 Act. In *Jonson v. Commissioner*,[42] *Doyel v. Commissioner*,[43] and *Greer v. Commissioner*, the Court held that because the pre- and post-1998 standards are substantially similar, pre-1998 cases interpreting former 6013(e) "remain instructive in analyzing the issue presented by [current] Section 6015(b)(1)(C)."

Fourth, taking into account all the facts and circumstances, it would be inequitable to hold the requesting spouse liable for the deficiency in tax attributable to the understatement.[44] One relevant factor for this purpose is whether the requesting spouse significantly benefited, directly or indirectly, from the understatement.[45] A significant benefit is any benefit in excess of normal sup-

---

the Court held that where the deductions were between 2/3 and 3/4 of wages, a reasonably prudent taxpayer should have questioned a deduction of that size in relation to their income. Where the requesting taxpayer failed to question the deductions, the taxpayer has failed to meet her burden that a reasonable person would not have reason to know of an understatement. Thus, (b) relief was denied.

41. Jacobsen v. Comm'r, T.C. Memo. 2018-115 at 14–15.
42. 118 T.C. 106 (2002).
43. T.C. Memo. 2004-35.
44. I.R.C. § 6015(b)(1)(D); Treas. Reg. § 1.6015-2(a)(4).
45. Treas. Reg. § 1.6015-2d. *See Varela v. Comm'r*, T.C. Memo 2014-222, where the Court held that where the requesting spouse used the understated funds to pay household expenses for the family, the requesting spouse did not receive a benefit traceable to the funds beyond ordinary support. In *Francel v. Comm'r*, T.C. Memo. 2019-35, the requesting spouse was deemed to have

port. Evidence of direct or indirect benefit may consist of transfers of property or rights to property, including transfers that may be received several years after the year of the understatement. Thus, for example, if a requesting spouse receives property (including life insurance proceeds) from the nonrequesting spouse that is beyond normal support and traceable to items omitted from gross income that are attributable to the nonrequesting spouse, the requesting spouse will be considered to have received significant benefit from those items. Other factors that may also be taken into account, if the situation warrants, include the fact that the requesting spouse has been deserted by the nonrequesting spouse; that the spouses have been divorced or separated; and that the requesting spouse received a benefit on the return from the understatement.[46]

In *Alt v. Commissioner*,[47] the Court considered other factors such as whether the requesting spouse would experience economic hardship if relief from liability was not granted given her level of income, whether the requesting spouse was deserted, divorced, or separated, and whether the failure to report the correct tax liability on a joint return results from concealment, overreaching or any other wrongdoing on the part of the other spouse.

Fifth, the party seeking innocent spouse treatment elects the benefits of innocent spouse treatment under I.R.C. § 6015(b) not later than two years after the IRS has started collection activities with respect to the individual making the election.[48] Generally, a "collection activity" is a Notice of Intent to Levy with Collection Due Process Rights, or refund offsets due on subsequent year tax returns with notice of appeal rights. *See also* Rev. Proc. 2000-15.[49] A qualifying election for (b) or (c) relief, or a request for (f) relief is the first timely claim for relief from joint and several liability for the tax year for which relief is sought. A qualifying election also includes a requesting spouse's second election to seek (c) relief from joint and several liability for the same tax year when the following two additional qualifications are met: (i) the requesting spouse did not

---

benefited from the unreported cash fees because his wife spent some of the cash on the house and car of the requesting spouse. Thus, he significantly benefited from the unreported income because the requesting spouse still lived in the house that was improved by unreported cash fees and still owned the car that was restored with the unreported cash fees. His accumulated wealth was attributable in part to the unreported cash fees. Thus, the fourth test was not met.

46. Treas. Reg. § 1.6015-2(d). *See also* Rev. Proc. 2013-34, 2013-2 C.B. 397 (discussed at Chapter 11, B.14). Rev. Proc. 2013-34 sets forth factors that Court will examine to determine whether it would be inequitable to hold a requesting spouse liable under Section 6015(f). In *Jacobsen v. Comm'r*, however, the Court also applied these factors to determine if it would be inequitable to hold a requesting spouse liable under Section 6015(b). Thus, the taxpayer should consider the factors if the taxpayer is seeking (b) relief and definitely (f) relief as discussed later.

47. 119 T.C. 306 (2002). The Court first held that the requirements of I.R.C. § 6015(b)(1)(D) are virtually identical as the same requirement of former I.R.C. § 6013(e)(1)(D).

48. I.R.C. § 6015(b)(1)(E).

49. 2000-1 C.B. 447 at § 2.03.

qualify for (c) relief when the IRS considered the first election solely because the divorce or separation requirements were not satisfied; and (ii) at the time of the second election, the qualifications for (c) relief are satisfied.[50]

b. Partial Relief

In addition, an individual may qualify for partial innocent spouse treatment under I.R.C. § 6015(b)(2).[51] That section provides that an individual who meets tests one, two, four, and five above, but who fails to meet test three and who establishes that in signing the return the individual did not know, and had no reason to know, the extent of such understatement, then the requesting spouse may be relieved of liability for tax (including interest and penalty) for the taxable year to the extent that the liability is attributable to the portion of such understatement of which such individual did not know and had no reason to know.[52] In general, if a requesting spouse had no knowledge or reason to know of only a portion of an erroneous item, the requesting spouse may be relieved of the liability attributable to that portion of that item, if all other requirements are met with respect to that portion.[53]

For example, assume H and W are married and file their 2004 joint income tax return in March 2005. In April 2006, H is convicted of embezzling $2 million from his employer during 2004. H kept all of his embezzlement income in an individual bank account, and he used most of the funds to support his gambling habit. H and W had a joint bank account into which H and W deposited all of their reported income. Each month during 2004, H transferred an additional $10,000 from the individual account to H and W's joint bank account. W paid the household expenses using this joint account, and regularly received the bank statements relating to the account. W had no knowledge or reason to know of H's embezzling activities. However, W did have knowledge and reason to know of $120,000 of the $2 million of H's embezzlement income at the time she signed the joint return because that amount passed through the couple's joint bank account. Therefore, W may be relieved of the liability arising from $1,880,000 of the unreported embezzlement income, but she may not be relieved of the liability for the deficiency arising from $120,000 of the unreported embezzlement income of which she knew and had reason to know.[54]

For purposes of I.R.C. § 6015(b), "understatement" means the excess of the amount of tax required to be shown on the return over the amount of tax

50. Treas. Reg. § 1.6015-1(h)(5).
51. *See* I.R.C. § 6015(a)(2).
52. I.R.C. § 6015(b)(2); Treas. Reg. § 1.6015-1(e)(1).
53. Treas. Reg. § 1.6015-2(e)(1).
54. Treas. Reg. § 1.6015-2(e)(2).

imposed which is shown on the return.[55] For example, if the correct amount of tax due is $60,000, and the amount shown on the return is $20,000, the understatement is $40,000.

3. Procedures to Limit Liability for Taxpayers Who Are No Longer Married or Who Are Legally Separated or Not Living Together—IRC §6015 (c) ("(c) Relief")[56]

a. Tests for (c) Relief

Section 6015(c) allows proportionate tax relief through allocation of the deficiency to those who meet its tests. An individual who qualifies for (c) relief is only entitled to relief from unpaid liabilities resulting from understatements of liability; the individual is not entitled to a refund under Section 6015(c).[57] To qualify for (c) relief and to be eligible to elect the application of the limitation of liability rule, the following four tests must be met: First, the deficiencies in tax must be attributable to the requesting spouse under Section 6015(d).[58] Unreported cash fees received by a medical practice which were misappropriated from the requesting spouse by the nonrequesting spouse, and where the requesting spouse was the sole stockholder of the medical practice which was an S corporation, the unreported fees should have been reported as income by the S corporation and allocable to the requesting spouse as the sole stockholder of the S corporation. Accordingly, deficiencies resulting from the unreported cash fees are allocable to the requesting spouse.[59]

Second, the requesting spouse must have filed a joint return.[60] See *Raymond v. Commissioner*,[61] where the Court held that to be eligible for relief under I.R.C. §§ 6015(b), (c), and (f), the taxpayer must file a joint return. In *Raymond*, the taxpayer filed "married filing separate." *See also* Rev. Proc. 2013-34.[62] Whether a return is joint is a question of fact. The key fact is the intent of both parties—did they intend to file a joint return?[63] For example, if one spouse files a return under duress, or if the spouse's signature is signed by the other without his or her consent, intent cannot be established.[64] Thus, before filing a request for

---

55. I.R.C. § 6015(b)(3), which refers to I.R.C. § 6662(d)(2)(A) for the definition of "understatement." An understatement is a proposed assessment or deficiency. See footnote 22 of this chapter.
56. I.R.C. § 6015(c).
57. Treas. Reg. § 1.6015-3(c)(1) (11-20-15).
58. I.R.C. § 6015(c)(1).
59. Francel v. Comm'r, T.C. Memo. 2019-55.
60. I.R.C. § 6015(c)(1).
61. 119 T.C. 191 (2002) discussed in the text at footnote 11.
62. 2013-2 C.B. 397, discussed at Chapter 11, B.4.b.
63. Lane v. Comm'r, 26 T.C. 405 (1956).
64. Treas. Reg. § 1.6015-4(d) (11-20-15).

innocent spouse status, it must first be determined if the return was a joint return.[65]

Third, a requesting spouse may allocate a deficiency if, at the time the election is filed, the requesting spouse is no longer married to, or is legally separated from, or is widowed or widowered from, the individual with whom the requesting spouse filed the joint return to which the election relates, or the requesting spouse has not been a member of the same household as the nonrequesting spouse at any time during the 12-month period ending on the date the election is filed.[66] An election cannot be made by either spouse who files a joint return if the IRS demonstrates that assets were transferred between them as part of a fraudulent scheme by them.[67] The marital status of a deceased requesting spouse is determined on the earlier of the date of the election or the date of death.[68] A determination of whether a requesting spouse is divorced or legally separated is made in accordance with Section 7703 and the regulations thereunder. Section 7703(a)(1) provides that the determination of whether an individual is married is made as of the close of the taxable year. Such determination is made as of the date the election is filed.[69] A determination of whether a requesting spouse is legally separated is made in accordance with Section 7703 and the regulations thereunder. Section 7703(a)(2) provides that an individual who is legally separated from his or her spouse under a decree of divorce or separate maintenance is not considered married. Such determination is made as of the date the election is filed.[70] A requesting spouse and a nonrequesting spouse are considered members of the same household during either spouse's temporary absences from the household if it is reasonable to assume that the absent spouse will return to the household, and the household or a substantially equivalent household is maintained in anticipation of such return. Examples of temporary absences may include, but are not limited to, absence due to incarceration, illness, business, vacation, military service, or education.[71]

65. Where the taxpayer's liability arises under Section 6672, trust fund recovery penalty, which is not shown on and did not arise from the filing of a joint Federal income tax return, the taxpayer is not eligible for innocent spouse relief from the trust fund recovery penalty under I.R.C. § 6015(c). Chavis v. Comm'r, 158 T.C. 8 (6.15.2022).

66. I.R.C. § 6015(c)(3)(A)(i)(I) and (II); Treas. Reg. § 1.6015-3(a). Taxpayer eligible to request (c) relief because she was not married to the nonrequesting spouse when she filed her request for relief from joint and several liability. Mora v. Comm'r, 117 T.C. 297 (2001).

67. I.R.C. § 6015(e)(3)(A)(ii).

68. Treas. Reg. § 1.6015-3(a). *See* I.R.C. § 7703(a)(1), which provides that for purposes of I.R.C. §§ 151–153 pertaining to the dependency exemption, and any other provisions that refer to those sections, the determination of whether an individual is married is made as of the close of the taxable year, except that if the spouse dies during the taxable year, the determination of whether an individual is married is made as of the time of such death.

69. Treas. Reg. § 1.6015-3(b)(1).

70. Treas. Reg. § 1.6015-3(b)(2).

71. Treas. Reg. § 1.6015-3(b)(3)(i).

A husband and wife who reside in the same dwelling are considered members of the same household. In addition, a husband and wife who reside in two separate dwellings are considered members of the same household if the spouses are not estranged or one spouse is temporarily absent from the other's household as noted earlier.[72]

Fourth, the election may be made at any time after a deficiency for such year is asserted but not later than two years after the date on which the IRS has begun collection activities with respect to the individual making the election.[73] "Collection activities," as noted earlier with respect to (b) relief, mean a Notice of Intent to Levy with Collection Due Process Rights, or offset of refund due on subsequent tax returns with notice of hearing rights. If the IRS demonstrates that a requesting spouse making the election had actual knowledge at the time the requesting spouse signed the return in issue of any item giving rise to a deficiency (or position thereof) which is not allocable to the requesting spouse under Section 6015(d), the election will not apply to such deficiency or provision thereof.[74] The foregoing rule, however, will not apply where the individual with actual knowledge establishes that he or she signed the return under duress.[75]

An individual who qualifies and who elects (c) relief may be able to limit his or her liability for any deficiency that is assessed with respect to the return to the portion of the deficiency properly allocable to the individual under I.R.C. § 6015(d).[76]

b. Burden of Proof

Each individual who elects (c) relief has the burden of proof to establish the portion of any deficiency allocable to such individual, except that[77] the burden of proof shifts to the IRS in two instances. First, the burden of proof is on the IRS to demonstrate that assets were transferred between individuals filing a joint return as part of a fraudulent scheme by such individuals.[78] If the Service carries its burden, an election by either individual for (c) relief is deemed invalid.[79]

Second, the burden of production and the burden of persuasion both shift to the IRS to demonstrate by the preponderance of the evidence that an individual making an election for (c) relief (i.e., the requesting spouse) had actual

72. Treas. Reg. § 1.6015-3(b)(3)(ii).
73. I.R.C. § 6015(c)(3)(B).
74. I.R.C. § 6015(c)(3)(C).
75. *Id.*
76. I.R.C. § 6015(c)(1).
77. I.R.C. § 6015(c)(2), Treas. Reg. § 1.6015-3(d)(3).
78. I.R.C. § 6015(c)(3)(A)(ii).
79. *Id.*

knowledge at the time the requesting spouse signed the returns for the year in issue of any item giving rise to a deficiency (or portion thereof) which is not allocable to the individual.[80] Thus, if the IRS demonstrates that at the time the return was signed the requesting spouse had actual knowledge of an erroneous item that was allocable to the nonrequesting spouse, the election to allocate the deficiency attributable to that item is invalid, and the requesting spouse remains liable for the portion of the deficiency attributable to that item. Notwithstanding the foregoing, however, the individual can rebut the IRS if the individual with actual knowledge establishes that he or she signed the return under duress.[81]

c. Knowledge

The standard under the (c) relief provision is "actual knowledge." "Actual knowledge" for purposes of Section 6015(c)(3)(C) is an actual and clear awareness (as opposed to reason to know) of the existence of an item which gives rise to the deficiency.[82] It is not what a reasonably prudent person would be expected to know.[83] In an omitted income situation "item" refers to the item of income that should have been reported on the return.[84] Knowledge of an item includes both omitted income and erroneous deductions, both of which are discussed next.

(1) Omitted Income

In the case of omitted income, knowledge of the item includes knowledge of the receipt of the income. For example, assume W received $5,000 of dividend income from her investment in X Co. but did not report it on the joint return. H knew that W received $5,000 of dividend income from X Co. that year. H had actual knowledge of the erroneous item (i.e., $5,000 of unreported dividend income from X Co.), and (c) relief is not available for the deficiency attributable

---

80. I.R.C. § 6015(c)(3)(C); Treas. Reg. § 1.6015-3(b)(2)(i). *See, e.g.,* Martin v. Comm'r, T.C. Memo. 2000-346, and Mitchell v. Comm'r, T.C. Memo. 2000-332; Culver v. Comm'r, 116 T.C. 189 (2001). (IRS held and failed to carry the burden of proving by a preponderance of the credible evidence that the requesting spouse had actual knowledge of embezzlement income of the nonrequesting spouse).

81. I.R.C. § 6015(c)(3)(C). Only items that are not attributable to the requesting spouse under I.R.C. § 6015(d) are subject to the actual knowledge exception of § 6015(c)(3)(C). King v. Comm'r. The "actual knowledge" test of § 6015(c)(3)(C) is an exception to the general rule under which items resulting in the deficiency are allocated as if the spouses had filed separate returns.

82. Cheshire v. Comm'r, 115 T.C. 183 (2000), *aff'd.* 282 F.3d 326 (C.A. 5, 2002); Culver v. Comm'r, 116 T.C. 189 (2001). Charlton v. Comm'r (IRS has burden to show that the requesting spouse had actual knowledge of the income causing the deficiency. Since the IRS could not prove this by preponderance of the evidence, the requesting spouse was granted innocent spouse relief.).

83. Culver v. Comm'r.

84. Cheshire v. Comm'r, 115 T.C. 183 (2000), *aff'd.* 282 F.3d 326 (C.A. 5, 2002).

to the dividend income from X Co. This rule applies equally in situations where the other spouse has unreported income although the spouse does not have an actual receipt of cash (e.g., dividend reinvestment or a distributive share from a flow-through entity shown on Schedule K-1, "Partner's Share of Income, Credits, Deductions, etc.").[85]

(2) Erroneous Deduction

In the case of an erroneous deduction or credit, knowledge of the item means knowledge of the facts that made the item not allowable as a deduction or credit. If a deduction is fictitious or inflated, the IRS must establish that the requesting spouse actually knew that the expenditure was not incurred, or not incurred to that extent.[86]

(3) Partial Knowledge

If a requesting spouse had actual partial knowledge of an erroneous item, then relief is not available for that portion of the erroneous item.[87] For example, if H knew that W received $1,000 of dividend income and did not know that W received an additional $4,000 of dividend income, relief would not be available for the portion of the deficiency attributable to the $1,000 of dividend income of which H had actual knowledge. A requesting spouse's actual knowledge of the proper tax treatment of an item is not relevant for purposes of demonstrating that the requesting spouse had actual knowledge of an erroneous item. For example, assume H did not know W's dividend income from X Co. was taxable, but knew that W received the dividend income. Relief is not available under I.R.C. § 6015(c). In addition, a requesting spouse's knowledge of how an erroneous item was treated on the tax return is not relevant to a determination of whether the requesting spouse had actual knowledge of the item. For example, assume that H knew of W's dividend income, but H failed to review the completed return and did not know that W omitted the dividend income from the return. Relief is not available under I.R.C. § 6015(c).[88]

Knowledge of the source of an erroneous item is not sufficient to establish actual knowledge. For example, assume H knew that W owned X Co. stock, but H did not know that X Co. paid dividends to W that year. H's knowledge of W's ownership in X Co. is not sufficient to establish that H had actual knowledge

85. Treas. Reg. § 1.6015-3(c)(2)(i)(A).

86. Treas. Reg. § 1.6015-3(c)(2)(i)(B)(1) and (2). In *King v. Comm'r*, 116 T.C. 198 (2001), the court considered the standard for "actual knowledge" giving rise to "erroneous deductions." The Court held that the taxpayer was entitled to (c) relief even though she was aware of the activities giving rise to the erroneous deduction because she did not know the predicate facts causing the loss to be nondeductible.

87. Treas. Reg. § 1.6015-3(c)(2)(ii).

88. Treas. Reg. § 1.6015-3(c)(2)(ii).

of the dividend income from X Co. In addition, a requesting spouse's actual knowledge may not be inferred when the requesting spouse merely had reason to know of the erroneous item. Even if H's knowledge of W's ownership interest in X Co. indicates a reason to know of the dividend income, actual knowledge of such dividend income cannot be inferred from H's reason to know. Similarly, the IRS need not establish that a requesting spouse knew of the source of an erroneous item in order to establish that the requesting spouse had actual knowledge of the item itself. For example, assume H knew that W received $1,000, but he did not know the source of the $1,000. W and H omit the $1,000 from their joint return. H has actual knowledge of the item giving rise to the deficiency ($1,000), and relief is not available.[89]

There are a number of factors upon which the IRS may rely to demonstrate that the requesting spouse had actual knowledge of an erroneous item at the time the return was signed. One factor that may be relied upon in demonstrating that a requesting spouse had actual knowledge of an erroneous item is whether the requesting spouse made a deliberate effort to avoid learning about the item in order to be shielded from liability; whether the erroneous item would have been allocable to the requesting but for the tax benefit rule discussed herein. This factor, together with all other facts and circumstances, may demonstrate that the requesting spouse had actual knowledge of the item, and the requesting spouse's election would be invalid with respect to that entire item. Another factor that may be relied upon in demonstrating that a requesting spouse had actual knowledge of an erroneous item is whether the requesting spouse and the nonrequesting spouse jointly owned the property that resulted in the erroneous item. Joint ownership is a factor supporting a finding that the requesting spouse had actual knowledge of an erroneous item. If the requesting spouse has actual knowledge of an erroneous item, the portion of the deficiency with respect to that item will not be allocated to the nonrequesting spouse.[90]

A requesting spouse is not considered to have had an ownership interest in an item based solely on the operation of community property law. Rather, a requesting spouse who resided in a community property state at the time the return was signed is considered to have had an ownership interest in an item only if the requesting spouse's name appeared on the ownership documents, or there otherwise is an indication that the requesting spouse asserted dominion and control over the item. For example, assume H and W live in State A, a community property state. After their marriage, H opens a bank account in his name. Under the operation of the community property laws of State A, W owns one-half (½) of the bank account. Assuming that there is no other

89. Treas. Reg. § 1.6015-3(c)(2)(iii).
90. Treas. Reg. § 1.6015-3(c)(2)(iv).

indication that she asserted dominion and control over the item, however, W does not have an ownership interest in the account because the account is not held in her name and there is no other indication that she asserted dominion and control over the item.[91] Proposed Treas. Reg. § 1.6015-3(c)(3)(iv) (11-20-15) provides factors to support actual knowledge. To demonstrate that a requesting spouse had actual knowledge of an erroneous item at the time the return was signed, the Internal Revenue Service will consider all the facts and circumstances, including but not limited to, whether the requesting spouse made a deliberate effort to avoid learning about the item to be shielded from liability; whether the erroneous item would have been allocable to the requesting spouse but for the tax benefit rule; and whether the requesting spouse and the nonrequesting spouse jointly owned the property that resulted in the erroneous item. These factors, together with all other facts and circumstances, may demonstrate that the requesting spouse had actual knowledge of the item. If the requesting spouse had actual knowledge of an erroneous item, the portion of the deficiency with respect to that item will not be allocated to the nonrequesting spouse.

(4) Abuse

The Proposed Regulations provide a special exception from actual knowledge where the requesting spouse has been abused or has been restricted from access to financial information. Depending on the facts and circumstances, if the requesting spouse was abused by the nonrequesting spouse (as described in Prop. Treas. Reg. § 1.6015-1 (o)), *supra*, or the nonrequesting spouse maintained control of the household finances by restricting the requesting spouse's access to financial information, and because of the abuse or financial control, the requesting spouse was not able to challenge the treatment of any items on the joint return for fear of the nonrequesting spouse's retaliation, the limitation on the requesting spouse's ability to allocate the deficiency because of actual knowledge will not apply. The requesting spouse will be treated as not having knowledge of the items giving rise to the deficiency. If, however, the requesting spouse involuntarily executed the return, the requesting spouse may choose to establish that the return was signed under duress. In such a case, Treas. Reg. § 1.6013-4(d) applies.[92]

d. Disqualified Assets

The portion of the deficiency for which the requesting spouse electing (c) relief is liable is increased (up to the entire amount of the deficiency) by the value of

---

91. *Id.*
92. Treas. Reg. § 1.6015-3(c)(2)(v).

any "disqualified asset" transferred to the requesting spouse.[93] In other words, relief is only available to the extent that the liability exceeds the value of any "disqualified assets" transferred to the requesting spouse by the nonrequesting spouse. Thus, a transfer of "disqualified assets" to the requesting spouse increases the liability of the requesting spouse. The value of a disqualified asset is the fair market value of the asset on the date of transfer.[94]

A "disqualified asset" is any property or the right to property that is transferred from a nonrequesting spouse to the requesting spouse if the principal purpose of the transfer is the avoidance of tax or payment of tax (including penalty and interest).[95] For this purpose, any transfer which is made by the nonrequesting spouse to the requesting spouse during the 12-month period before the mailing date of the first letter of proposed deficiency which allows the taxpayer an opportunity for administrative review in the Appeals Office of the IRS is sent (generally, the 30-day letter or the 90-day letter) is presumed to have as its principal purpose the avoidance of tax or payment of tax, i.e., is presumed to be a disqualified asset.[96] A marital home constitutes a disqualified asset when the husband transferred the property to the wife by quitclaim deed well after the IRS issued a notice of deficiency in the underlying matter.[97]

The foregoing presumption does not apply to any transfer pursuant to a decree of divorce or separate maintenance or a written instrument incident to such a decree (see I.R.C. § 71 for definitions) or to any transfer which an individual establishes did not have as its principal purpose the avoidance of tax or the payment of tax.[98] If the presumption does not apply, but the Internal Revenue Service can establish that the purpose of the transfer was the avoidance of tax or payment of tax, the asset will be disqualified, and its value will be added to the amount of the deficiency for which the requesting spouse remains liable. If the presumption applies, a requesting spouse may still rebut the presumption by establishing that the principal purpose of the transfer was not the avoidance of tax or payment of tax.[99]

e. Examples

The following eight examples from Treas. Reg. § 1.6015-3(c)(4) illustrate the foregoing rules:

93. I.R.C. § 6015(c)(4)(A); Treas. Reg. § 1.6015-3(c)(3)(i). *See* Briley v. Comm'r, T.C. Memo. 2019-55.
94. Treas. Reg. § 1.6015-3(c)(3)(i).
95. I.R.C. § 6015(c)(4)(B)(i); Treas. Reg. § 1.6015-3(c)(3)(ii).
96. I.R.C. § 6015(c)(4)(B)(ii)(I); Treas. Reg. § 1.6015-3(c)(3)(iii).
97. Briley v. Comm'r, T.C. Memo. 2019-55.
98. I.R.C. § 6015(c)(4)(B)(i)(II); Treas. Reg. § 1.6015-3(c)(3)(iii).
99. Treas. Reg. § 1.6015-3(c)(3)(iii).

Example 1. Actual knowledge of an erroneous item. (i) H and W file their 2001 joint Federal income tax return on April 15, 2002. On the return, H and W report W's self-employment income, but they do not report W's self-employment tax on that income. H and W divorce in July 2003. In August 2003, H and W receive a 30-day letter from the Internal Revenue Service proposing a deficiency with respect to W's unreported self-employment tax on the 2001 return. On November 4, 2003, H files an election to allocate the deficiency to W. The erroneous, item is the self-employment income, and it is allocable to W. H knows that W earned income in 2001 as a self-employed musician, but he does not know that self-employment tax must be reported on and paid with a joint return.

(ii) H's election to allocate the deficiency to W is invalid because, at the time H signed the joint return, H had actual knowledge of W's self-employment income. The fact that H was unaware of the tax consequences of that income (i.e., that an individual is required to pay self-employment tax on that income) is not relevant.

Example 2. Actual knowledge not inferred from a requesting spouse's reason to know. (i) H has long been an avid gambler. H supports his gambling habit and keeps all of his gambling winnings in an individual bank account, held solely in his name. W knows about H's gambling habit and that he keeps a separate bank account, but she does not know whether he has any winnings because H does not tell her, and she does not otherwise know of H's bank account transactions. H and W file their 2001 joint Federal income tax return on April 15, 2002. On October 31, 2003, H and W receive a 30-day letter proposing a $100,000 deficiency relating to H's unreported gambling income. In February 2003, H and W divorce, and in March 2004, W files an election under Section 6015(c) to allocate the $100,000 deficiency to H.

(ii) While W may have had reason to know of the gambling income because she knew of H's gambling habit and separate account, W did not have actual knowledge of the erroneous item (i.e., the gambling winnings). The Internal Revenue Service may not infer actual knowledge from W's reason to know of the income. Therefore, W's election to allocate the $100,000 deficiency to H is valid.

Example 3. Actual knowledge and failure to review return. (i) H and W are legally separated. In February 1999, W signs a blank joint Federal income tax return for 1998 and gives it to H to fill out. The return was timely filed on April 15, 1999. In September 2001, H and W receive a 30-day letter proposing a deficiency relating to $100,000 of unreported dividend income received by H with respect to stock of ABC Co. owned by H. W knew that H received the $100,000 dividend payment in August 1998, but she did not know whether H reported that payment on the joint return.

(ii) On January 30, 2002, W files an election to allocate the deficiency from the 1998 return to H. W claims she did not review the completed joint return, and therefore, she had no actual knowledge that there was an understatement of the dividend income. W's election to allocate the deficiency to H is invalid because she had actual knowledge of the erroneous item (dividend income from ABC Co.) at the time she signed the return. The fact that W signed a blank return is irrelevant. The result would be the same if W had not reviewed the completed return or if W had reviewed the completed return and had not noticed that the item was omitted.

Example 4. Actual knowledge of an erroneous item of income. (i) H and W are legally separated. In June 2004, a deficiency is proposed with respect to H's and W's 2002 joint Federal income tax return that is attributable to $30,000 of unreported income from H's plumbing business that should have been reported on a Schedule C. No Schedule C was attached to the return. At the time W signed the return, W knew that H had a plumbing business but did not know whether H received any income from the business. W's election to allocate to H the deficiency attributable to the $30,000 of unreported plumbing income is valid.

(ii) Assume the same facts as in paragraph (i) of this Example 4 except that, at the time W signed the return, W knew that H received $20,000 of plumbing income. W's election to allocate to H the deficiency attributable to the $20,000 of unreported plumbing income (of which W had actual knowledge) is invalid. W's election to allocate to H the deficiency attributable to the $10,000 of unreported plumbing income (of which W did not have actual knowledge) is valid.

(iii) Assume the same facts as in paragraph (i) of this Example 4 except that, at the time W signed the return, W did not know the exact amount of H's plumbing income. W did know, however, that H received at least $8,000 of plumbing income. W's election to allocate to H the deficiency attributable to $8,000 of unreported plumbing income (of which W had actual knowledge) is invalid. W's election to allocate to H the deficiency attributable to the remaining $22,000 of unreported plumbing income (of which W did not have actual knowledge) is valid.

(iv) Assume the same facts as in paragraph (i) of this Example 4 except that H reported $26,000 of plumbing income on the return and omitted $4,000 of plumbing income from the return. At the time W signed the return, W knew that H was a plumber, but she did not know that H earned more than $26,000 that year. W's election to allocate to H the deficiency attributable to the $4,000 of unreported plumbing income is valid because she did not have actual knowledge that H received plumbing income in excess of $26,000.

(v) Assume the same facts as in paragraph (i) of this Example 4 except that H reported only $20,000 of plumbing income on the return and omitted $10,000 of plumbing income from the return. At the time W signed the return, W knew that H earned at least $26,000 that year as a plumber. However, W did not know that, in reality, H earned $30,000 that year as a plumber. W's election to allocate to H the deficiency attributable to the $6,000 of unreported plumbing income (of which W had actual knowledge) is invalid. W's election to allocate to H the deficiency attributable to the $4,000 of unreported plumbing income (of which W did not have actual knowledge) is valid.

Example 5. Actual knowledge of a deduction that is an erroneous item. (i) H and W are legally separated. In February 2005, a deficiency is asserted with respect to their 2002 joint Federal income tax return. The deficiency is attributable to a disallowed $1,000 deduction for medical expenses H claimed he incurred. At the time W signed the return, W knew that H had not incurred any medical expenses. W's election to allocate to H the deficiency attributable to the disallowed medical expense deduction is invalid because W had actual knowledge that H had not incurred any medical expenses.

(ii) Assume the same facts as in paragraph (i) of this Example 5 except that, at the time W signed the return, W did not know whether H had incurred any medical expenses. W's election to allocate to H the deficiency attributable to the disallowed medical expense deduction is valid because she did not have actual knowledge that H had not incurred any medical expenses.

(iii) Assume the same facts as in paragraph (i) of this Example 5 except that the Internal Revenue Service disallowed $400 of the $1,000 medical expense deduction. At the time W signed the return, W knew that H had incurred some medical expenses but did not know the exact amount. W's election to allocate to H the deficiency attributable to the disallowed medical expense deduction is valid because she did not have actual knowledge that H had not incurred medical expenses (in excess of the floor amount under section 213(a)) of more than $600.

(iv) Assume the same facts as in paragraph (i) of this Example 5 except that H claims a medical expense deduction of $10,000 and the Internal Revenue Service disallows $9,600. At the time W signed the return, W knew H had incurred some medical expenses but did not know the exact amount. W also knew that H incurred medical expenses (in excess of the floor amount under section 213(a)) of no more than $1,000. W's election to allocate to H the deficiency attributable to the portion of the overstated deduction of which she had actual knowledge ($9,000) is invalid. W's election to allocate the deficiency attributable to the portion of the overstated deduction of which she had no knowledge ($600) is valid.

Example 6. Disqualified asset presumption. (i) H and W are divorced. In May 1999, W transfers $20,000 to H, and in April 2000, H and W receive a 30-day letter proposing a $40,000 deficiency on their 1998 joint Federal income tax return. The liability remains unpaid, and in October 2000, H elects to allocate the deficiency under this section. Seventy-five percent of the net amount of erroneous items are allocable to W, and 25 percent of the net amount of erroneous items are allocable to H.

(ii) In accordance with the proportionate allocation method, H proposes that $30,000 of the deficiency be allocated to W and $10,000 be allocated to himself. H submits a signed statement providing that the principal purpose of the $20,000 transfer was not the avoidance of tax or payment of tax, but he does not submit any documentation indicating the reason for the transfer. H has not overcome the presumption that the $20,000 was a disqualified asset. Therefore, the portion of the deficiency for which H is liable ($10,000) is increased by the value of the disqualified asset ($20,000). H is relieved of liability for $10,000 of the $30,000 deficiency allocated to W and remains jointly and severally liable for the remaining $30,000 of the deficiency (assuming that H does not qualify for relief under any other provision).

Example 7. Disqualified asset presumption inapplicable. On May 1, 2001, H and W receive a 30-day letter regarding a proposed deficiency on their 1999 joint Federal income tax return relating to unreported capital gain from H's sale of his investment in Z stock. W had no actual knowledge of the stock sale. The deficiency is assessed in November 2001, and in December 2001, H and W divorce. According to a decree of divorce, H must transfer one-half of his interest in mutual fund A to W. The transfer takes place in February 2002. In August 2002, W elects to allocate the deficiency to H. Although the transfer of one-half H's interest in mutual fund A took place after the 30-day letter was mailed, the mutual fund interest is not presumed to be a disqualified asset because the transfer of H's interest in the fund was made pursuant to a decree of divorce.

Example 8. Overcoming the disqualified asset presumption. (i) H and W are married for 25 years. Every September, on W's birthday, H gives W a gift of $500. On February 28, 2002, H and W receive a 30-day letter from the Internal Revenue Service relating to their 1998 joint individual Federal income tax return. The deficiency relates to H's Schedule C business, and W had no knowledge of the items giving rise to the deficiency. H and W are legally separated in June 2003, and, despite the separation, H continues to give W $500 each year for her birthday. H is not required to give such amounts pursuant to a decree of divorce or separate maintenance.

(ii) On January 27, 2004, W files an election to allocate the deficiency to H. The $1,500 transferred from H to W from February 28, 2001 (a year before the 30-day letter was mailed) to the present is presumed disqualified. However, W may overcome the presumption that such amounts were disqualified by establishing that such amounts were birthday gifts from H and that she has received such gifts during their entire marriage. Such facts would show that the amounts were not transferred for the purpose of avoidance of tax or payment of tax.

f. Determination of Amount of Deficiency

An eligible electing spouse who elects (c) relief may be relieved of joint and several liability for the portion of any deficiency that is allocated to the nonrequesting spouse pursuant to the following allocation methods.[100] Relief may be available to both spouses filing the joint return if each spouse is eligible for (c) relief and each elects (c) relief.[101] The amount of the deficiency allocated to the requesting spouse is determined under I.R.C. § 6015(d) as follows: The portion of any deficiency on a joint return allocated to the requesting spouse is an amount which bears the same ratio to such deficiency as the net amount of items taken into account in computing the deficiency and allocable to the requesting spouse bears to the net amount of all items taken into account in computing the deficiency.[102] If a deficiency (or portion thereof) is attributable to the disallowance of a credit, or any tax (other than the income tax imposed under I.R.C. § 1 or the alternative minimum tax imposed under I.R.C. § 55) required to be included on a joint return, and such item is allocated to one individual, such deficiency, or portion thereof, is allocated to the individual. Any such item is not taken into account in computing the ratio under I.R.C. § 6015(d)(1).[103]

g. Allocation of Items Giving Rise to the Deficiency

A request to allocate a deficiency limits the requesting spouse's liability to that portion of the deficiency allocated to the requesting spouse as discussed later. Only a requesting spouse may receive (c) relief. A nonrequesting spouse who does not also elect (e) relief remains liable for the entire amount of the deficiency. Even if both spouses elect to allocate a deficiency, there may be a portion of the deficiency that is not allocable, for which both spouses remain jointly and severally liable.[104]

The general rule for allocating items giving rise to the deficiency provides that except with respect to the disregard of limitations on separate returns and the liability of a child under I.R.C. § 6015(d)(4) and (5) (discussed later), any item giving rise to a deficiency on a joint return is allocated to the individuals filing the return in the same manner as it would have been allocated if the individuals had filed separate returns for the taxable year.[105]

---

100. Prop. Treas. Reg. § 1.6015-3(a).
101. *Id.*
102. I.R.C. § 6015(d)(1).
103. *Id.* § 6015(d)(2).
104. Treas. Reg. § 1.6015-3(d)(1)(i) and (ii).
105. I.R.C. § 6015(d)(3)(A); Treas. Reg. § 1.6015-3(d)(2).

There are four exceptions to the general rule.[106] The first exception is where the requesting spouse received a tax benefit on the joint returns.[107] Thus, an erroneous item otherwise allocable to one spouse is allocated to the second spouse to the extent that the requesting spouse received a tax benefit on the joint return and the nonrequesting spouse did not receive a tax benefit.[108] An erroneous item can be allocated to a requesting spouse or a nonrequesting spouse, but only a spouse who requests innocent spouse relief may allocate the deficiency. A spouse who does not request innocent relief remains fully liable for the deficiency. An allocation from a requesting spouse to a nonrequesting spouse reduces the amount for which a requesting spouse remains liable while an allocation from a nonrequesting spouse to a requesting spouse increases the amount for which a requesting spouse remains liable.[109] Under Section 6015(d)(3)(A), the items giving rise to the deficiency on a joint return must be allocated to each spouse filing the joint return in the same manner as the items would have been allocated if the spouses had filed separate returns. In determining whether a spouse received a tax benefit from the item, each spouse's hypothetical separate return taxable income should be calculated, determined without regard to the erroneous items.

The second exception is where the return is fraudulent. In that case, the IRS may allocate any item between the spouses if it establishes that such allocation is appropriate due to fraud by one or both spouses.[110]

The third exception is where an erroneous item of income is allocated to the spouse who was the source of the income. Wage income is allocated to the spouse who performed the services producing such wages. Items of business or investment income are allocated to the spouse who owned the business or investment. If both spouses owned an interest in the business or investment, the erroneous item of income is generally allocated between the spouses in proportion to each spouse's ownership interest in the business or investment, subject to the limitations of Treas. Reg. § 1.6015-3(c) discussed earlier. In the absence of clear and convincing evidence supporting a different allocation, an erroneous deduction item relating to an asset that the spouses owned jointly is generally allocated 50 percent to each spouse, subject to the limitations in Treas. Reg. § 1.6015-3(c) discussed earlier and the fourth exception discussed

106. Treas. Reg. § 1.6015-3(d)(2).

107. Treas. Reg. § 1.6015-3(d)(2)(i).

108. *See Mora v. Comm'r*, 117 T.C. 279 (2001) for an example of the application of a tax benefit exception where the court found the requesting spouse received a tax benefit from the erroneous deduction of the nonrequesting spouse because she did not pay tax on her separate return share of the income.

109. Prop. Treas. Reg. § 1.6015-3(d)(2)(1)(A) (11.20.2015).

110. I.R.C. § 6015(d)(3)(C); Treas. Reg. § 1.6015-3(d)(2)(ii).

later. For rules regarding the effect of community property laws, see Treas. Reg. § 1.6015-1(f) and (c)(2)(iv).[111]

The fourth exception pertains to erroneous deductions related to a business or investment are allocated to the spouse who owned the business or investment. If both spouses owned an interest in the business or investment, an erroneous deduction item is generally allocated between the spouses in proportion to each spouse's ownership interest in the business or investment. In the absence of clear and convincing evidence supporting a different allocation, an erroneous deduction item relating to an asset that the spouses owned jointly is generally allocated 50 percent to each spouse, subject to the limitations in Treas. Reg. § 1.6015-3(c) and Treas. Reg. § 1.6015-3(d)(4). Deduction items unrelated to a business or investment are also generally allocated 50 percent to each spouse, unless the evidence shows that a different allocation is appropriate.[112]

Except for establishing actual knowledge, the requesting spouse must prove that all of the qualifications for making an election under this section are satisfied and that none of the limitations (including the limitation relating to transfers of disqualified assets) apply. The requesting spouse must also establish the proper allocation of the erroneous items.[113]

If an item of deduction or credit is disallowed in its entirety solely because a separate return is filed, such disallowance is disregarded and the item is computed as if a joint return had been filed and then allocated between the spouses appropriately.[114]

If the liability of a child of the taxpayer is included on a joint return, such liability is disregarded in computing the separate liability of either spouse and such liability is allocated appropriately between the spouses.[115]

h. Allocating the Deficiency between Spouses

There are four methods of allocating the deficiency between the spouses: (i) the proportionate allocation method, (ii) the separate treatment of items method, (iii) the child's liability method, and (iv) the allocation of certain items method. The choice of which method to elect to use depends upon which method the taxpayer can utilize. Each of these methods is discussed as follows:

Under the first method, the proportionate allocation method, the portion of a deficiency allocable to a spouse is the amount that bears the same ratio to the deficiency as the net amount of erroneous items allocable to the spouse bears

111. Treas. Reg. § 1.6015-3(d)(2)(iii).
112. Treas. Reg. § 1.6015-3(d)(2)(iv).
113. Treas. Reg. § 1.6015-3(d)(3).
114. I.R.C. § 6015(d)(4).
115. *Id.* § 6015(d)(5).

to the net amount of all erroneous items. This calculation may be expressed as follows:

$$X = (\text{deficiency}) \times \frac{\text{net amount of erroneous items allocable to the spouse}}{\text{net amount of all erroneous items}}$$

where X = the portion of the deficiency allocable to the requesting spouse.[116]

This method applies to any portion of the deficiency other than the following six items:

(1) Any portion of the deficiency attributable to erroneous items allocable to the nonrequesting spouse of which the requesting spouse had actual knowledge;
(2) Any portion of the deficiency attributable to separate treatment items (as defined in Treas. Reg. § 1.6015-4(d)(ii));
(3) Any portion of the deficiency relating to the liability of a child (as defined in Treas. Reg. § 1.6015-3(d)(4)(iii)) of the requesting spouse or nonrequesting spouse;
(4) Any portion of the deficiency attributable to alternative minimum tax under Section 55;
(5) Any portion of the deficiency attributable to accuracy-related or fraud penalties;
(6) Any portion of the deficiency allocated pursuant to alternative allocation methods authorized under Treas. Reg. § 1.6015-3(d)(6).[117]

Notwithstanding the foregoing exceptions, an item allocable to a spouse under the second method is allocated to the other spouse filing the joint return to the extent the item gave rise to a tax benefit on the joint return of the other spouse.[118]

The second method, the separate treatment of items method, provides that any portion of a deficiency that is attributable to an item allocable solely to one spouse and that results from the disallowance of a credit, or a tax or an addition to tax (i.e., a penalty) (other than tax imposed by Section 1 (the general tax rate section of the Code) or Section 55 (alternative minimum tax)) that is required to be included with a joint return (a "separate treatment item") is allocated separately to that spouse. If such credit or tax is attributable in whole or in part to both spouses, then the IRS will determine on a case-by-case basis how such item will be allocated. Once the proportionate allocation is made, the

116. I.R.C. § 6015-(d)(1); Treas. Reg. § 1.6015-3(d)(4)(i)(A).
117. Treas. Reg. § 1.6015-3(d)(4)(i)(B)(1)–(6).
118. I.R.C. § 6015(d)(3)(B).

liability for the requesting spouse's separate treatment items is added to the requesting spouse's share of the liability.[119]

Third, under the child's liability method, if the liability of a child of a taxpayer is included on a joint return, such liability is disregarded in computing the separate liability of either spouse and such liability is allocated appropriately between the spouses.[120] Thus, any portion of a deficiency relating to the liability of a child of the requesting and nonrequesting spouse is allocated jointly to both spouses. For purposes of this method, a child does not include the taxpayer's stepson or stepdaughter, unless such child was legally adopted by the taxpayer. If the child is the child of only one of the spouses, and the other spouse had not legally adopted such child, any portion of a deficiency relating to the liability of such child is allocated solely to the parent spouse.[121]

Finally, under the allocation of certain items method, any portion of a deficiency relating to the alternative minimum tax under Section 55 is allocated appropriately, and any accuracy-related or fraud penalties under Sections 6662 or 6663 are allocated to the spouse whose item generated the penalty.[122]

i. Examples of Allocation Rules

The regulation provides the following six examples to illustrate the allocation rules. In each example, assume the regulations assume the requesting spouse or spouses qualify to elect to allocate the deficiency, that any election is timely made, and that the deficiency remains unpaid. In addition, unless otherwise stated, the regulations assume that neither spouse has actual knowledge of the erroneous items allocable to the other spouse. The examples are as follows:[123]

The first example pertains to the allocation of erroneous items. H and W file a 2003 joint Federal income tax return on April 15, 2004. On April 28, 2006, a deficiency is assessed with respect to their 2003 return. Three erroneous items give rise to the deficiency: (i) unreported interest income, of which W had actual knowledge, from H's and W's joint bank account; (ii) a disallowed business expense deduction on H's Schedule C; and (iii) a disallowed Lifetime Learning Credit for W's post-secondary education, paid for by W. H and W divorce in May 2006, and in September 2006, W timely elects to allocate the deficiency. The erroneous items are allocable as follows: The interest income would be allocated ½ to H and ½ to W, except that W has actual knowledge of it. Therefore, W's election to allocate the portion of the deficiency attributable to this item is invalid, and W remains jointly and severally liable for it. The

119. I.R.C. § 6015(d)(2); Treas. Reg. § 1.6015-3(d)(4)(ii).
120. I.R.C. § 6015(d)(5); Treas. Reg. § 1.6015-3(d)(4)(iii).
121. I.R.C. § 6015(d)(5); Treas. Reg. § 1.6015-3(d)(4)(i)(B)(iii)(iv)(A) and (B).
122. Treas. Reg. § 1.6015-3(d)(4)(a) and)(B).
123. Prop. Treas. Reg. § 1.6015-3(d)(5), Examples (1)–(6).

business expense deduction is allocable to H. The Lifetime Learning Credit is allocable to W.

The second example pertains to proportionate allocation. W and H timely file their 2001 joint Federal income tax return on April 15, 2002. On August 16, 2004, a $54,000 deficiency is assessed with respect to their 2001 joint return. H and W divorce on October 14, 2004, and W timely elects to allocate the deficiency. Five erroneous items give rise to the deficiency—(i) a disallowed $15,000 business deduction allocable to H; (ii) $20,000 of unreported income allocable to H; (iii) a disallowed $5,000 deduction for educational expense allocable to H; (iv) a disallowed $40,000 charitable contribution deduction allocable to W; and (v) a disallowed $40,000 interest deduction allocable to W.

In total, there are $120,000 worth of erroneous items, of which $80,000 are attributable to W and $40,000 are attributable to H.

W's Items	H's Items
$40,000 charitable deduction	$15,000 business deduction
$40,000 interest deduction	$20,000 unreported income
$80,000	$5,000 education deduction
	$40,000

The ratio of erroneous items allocable to W to the total erroneous items is 2/3 ($80,000/$120,000). W's liability is limited to $36,000 of the deficiency (2/3 of $54,000). The Internal Revenue Service may collect up to $36,000 from W and up to $54,000 from H (the total amount collected, however, may not exceed $54,000). If H also made an election, there would be no remaining joint and several liability, and the Internal Revenue Service would be permitted to collect $36,000 from W and $18,000 from H.

The third example pertains to proportionate allocation with joint erroneous items. On September 4, 2001, W elects to allocate a $3,000 deficiency for the 1998 tax year to H. Three erroneous items give rise to the deficiency—(i) unreported interest in the amount of $4,000 from a joint bank account, (ii) a disallowed deduction for business expenses in the amount of $2,000 attributable to H's business; and (iii) unreported wage income in the amount of $6,000 attributable to W's second job.

The erroneous items total $12,000. Generally, income, deductions, or credits from jointly held property that are erroneous items are allocable 50 percent to each spouse. However, in this case, both spouses had actual knowledge of the unreported interest income. Therefore, W's election to allocate the portion of the deficiency attributable to this item is invalid, and W and H remain jointly and severally liable for this portion. Assume that this portion is $1,000. W may allocate the remaining $2,000 of the deficiency.

H's Items	W's Items
$2,000 business deduction	$6,000 wage income

The total allocable items is $8,000.

The ratio of erroneous items allocable to W to the total erroneous items is 3/4 ($6,000/ $8,000). W's liability is limited to $1,500 of the deficiency (3/4 of $2,000) allocated to her. The Internal Revenue Service may collect up to $2,500 from W (3/4 of the total allocated deficiency plus $1,000 of the deficiency attributable to the joint bank account interest) and up to $3,000 from H (the total amount collected, however, cannot exceed $3,000).

Assume H also elects to allocate the 1998 deficiency. H is relieved of liability for 3/4 of the deficiency, which is allocated to W. H's relief totals $1,500 (3/4 of $2,000). H remains liable for $1,500 of the deficiency (1/4 of the allocated deficiency plus $1,000 of the deficiency attributable to the joint bank account interest).

The fourth example pertains to separate treatment items (STIs). On September 1, 2006, a $28,000 deficiency is assessed with respect to H's and W's 2003 joint return. The deficiency is the result of four erroneous items—(i) a disallowed Lifetime Learning Credit of $2,000 attributable to H, (ii) a disallowed business expense deduction of $8,000 attributable to H, (iii) unreported income of $24,000 attributable to W, and (iv) unreported self-employment tax of $14,000 attributable to W.

H and W both elect to allocate the deficiency.

The $2,000 Lifetime Learning Credit and the $14,000 self-employment tax are STIs totaling $16,000. The amount of erroneous items included in computing the proportionate allocation ratio is $32,000 ($24,000 unreported income and $8,000 disallowed business expense deduction). The amount of the deficiency subject to proportionate allocation, is reduced by the amount of STIs ($28,000 – $16,000 = $12,000).

Of the $32,000 of proportionate allocation items, $24,000 is allocable to W, and $8,000 is allocable to H.

W's share of allocable items	H's share of allocable items
¾ ($24,000/$32,000)	¼ ($8,000/$32,000)

W's liability for the portion of the deficiency subject to proportionate allocation is limited to $9,000 (3/4 of $12,000) and H's liability for such portion is limited to $3,000 (3/4 of $12,000).

After the proportionate allocation is completed, the amount of the STIs is added to each spouse's allocated share of the deficiency.

W's share of total deficiency	H's share of total deficiency
$ 9,000 allocated deficiency	$3,000 allocated deficiency
$14,000 self-employment	$2,000 Lifetime Learning Credit
$23,000	$5,000

Therefore, W's liability is limited to $23,000 and H's liability is limited to $5,000.

The fifth example illustrates the requesting spouse receiving a benefit on the joint return from the nonrequesting spouse's erroneous item. In 2001, H reports gross income of $4,000 from his business on Schedule C, and W reports $50,000 of wage income. On their 2001 joint Federal income tax return, H deducts $20,000 of business expenses resulting in a net loss from his business of $16,000. H and W divorce in September 2002, and on May 22, 2003, a $5,200 deficiency is assessed with respect to their 2001 joint return. W elects to allocate the deficiency. The deficiency on the joint return results from a disallowance of all of H's $20,000 of deductions.

Since H used only $4,000 of the disallowed deductions to offset gross income from his business, W benefitted from the other $16,000 of the disallowed deductions used to offset her wage income. Therefore, $4,000 of the disallowed deductions are allocable to H and $16,000 of the disallowed deductions are allocable to W. W's liability is limited to $4,160 (4/5 of $5,200). If H also elected to allocate the deficiency, H's election to allocate the $4,160 of the deficiency to W would be invalid because H had actual knowledge of the erroneous items.

The sixth example illustrates the calculation of a requesting spouse's benefit on the joint return when the nonrequesting spouse's erroneous item is partially disallowed. Assume the same facts as in Example 5, except that H deducts $18,000 for business expenses on the joint return, of which $16,000 are disallowed. Since H used only $2,000 of the $16,000 disallowed deductions to offset gross income from his business, W received a benefit on the return from the other $14,000 of the disallowed deductions used to offset her wage income. Therefore, $2,000 of the disallowed deductions are allocable to H and $14,000 of the disallowed deductions are allocable to W. W's liability is limited to $4,550 (7/8 of $5,200).

The Proposed Regulations provide the following five examples to illustrate the allocation rules.[124]

The first example (Example 7 of the proposed regulations) provides for the calculation of tax benefit based on taxable income. On their joint Federal income tax return for tax year 2009, H reports $60,000 of wage income; W reports $25,000 of wage income; and H and W report joint interest income of

124. Prop. Treas. Reg. § 1.6015-3(d)(5) (11.20.2015) (Examples 7–11).

$2,000 and joint ordinary income from investments of $6,000. In addition, H and W properly deduct $30,000 for their two personal exemptions and itemized deductions, and W erroneously reports a loss from her separate investment in a partnership in the amount of $20,000. On May 3, 2012, a $5,000 deficiency is assessed with respect to their 2009 joint return. W dies in November 2012. H requests innocent spouse relief. The deficiency on the joint return results from a disallowance of all of W's $20,000 loss (which is initially allocable to W).

After taking all sources of income and all allowable deductions into consideration, H's separate taxable income is $49,000 and W's separate taxable income is $14,000, calculated as follows:

	Husband	**Wife**
Wages	$60,000	$25,000
Interest Income	$1,000	$1,000
Investment Income	$3,000	$3,000
Adjusted Gross Income	$64,000	$29,000
Exemptions & Deductions	($15,000)	($15,000)
Taxable Income	$49,000	$14,000
Wife's Disallowed Loss	($20,000)	$14,000
Tax Benefit Not Used by Wife		($6,000)
Tax Benefit to Wife		($14,000)
Tax Benefit to Husband	($6,000)	

As W only used $14,000 of her $20,000 loss from her separate investment in a partnership to offset her separate taxable income, H benefited from the other $6,000 of the disallowed loss used to offset his separate taxable income. Therefore, $14,000 of the disallowed $20,000 loss is allocable to W (7/10) and $6,000 of the disallowed loss is allocable to H (3/10). H's liability is limited to $1,500 (3/10 of the $5,000 deficiency).

The second example (Example 8 of the proposed regulations) illustrates the situation where the nonrequesting spouse receives a benefit on the joint return from the requesting spouse's erroneous item. (i) On their joint Federal income tax return for tax year 2008, W reports $40,000 of wage income and H reports $12,000 of wage income. In addition, H and W properly deduct $20,000 for their two personal exemptions and itemized deductions, H erroneously deducts a casualty loss in the amount of $5,000 related to a loss on his separately held property, and W erroneously takes a loss in the amount of $7,000 from an investment in a tax shelter. H and W legally separate in 2010, and on October 21, 2011, a $2,400 deficiency is assessed with respect to their 2008 joint return. H requests innocent spouse relief. The deficiency on the joint return results from a disallowance of all of H's $5,000 loss and all of W's $7,000 loss (which is allocable to W and for which H did not have actual knowledge).

The $5,000 casualty loss is initially allocated to H. As H's separate taxable income is only $2,000 ($12,000 wage income less $10,000 – 50 percent of the exemptions and itemized deductions), H only used $2,000 of his $5,000 casualty loss to offset his separate tax, and W benefited from the other $3,000 of the disallowed loss, which offset a portion of her separate taxable income. Therefore, $3,000 of the disallowed loss is allocable to W even though the loss is H's item, and $2,000 of the loss is allocable to H. The $7,000 tax shelter loss is also allocable to W as H did not have knowledge of the facts that made the tax shelter item unallowable as a loss. H's allocation percentage is 1/6 ($2,000/$12,000) and H's liability is limited to $400 (1/6 of $2,400 deficiency). The IRS may collect up to $400 from H and up to $2,400 from W (although the total amount collected may not exceed $2,400).

If the IRS could establish that H had knowledge of the facts that made the deduction for his casualty loss unallowable, the entire $5,000 casualty loss would be allocable to H. H's allocation percentage would be 5/12 ($5,000/$12,000) and H's liability would be limited to $1,000 (5/12 of $2,400 deficiency).

If W also requested innocent spouse relief (and H did not have knowledge of the facts that made his loss unallowable), there would be no remaining joint and several liability, and the IRS would be permitted to collect $400 from H ((1/6 ($2,000/$12,000)) of the $2,400 deficiency) and $2,000 ((5/6 $10,000/$12,000)) of $2,400 deficiency) from W. If the IRS could establish that W had knowledge of the facts that made the deduction for the casualty loss unallowable, W would then be liable for the entire $2,400 deficiency, while H would remain liable for up to $400.

The third example (Example 9 of the proposed regulations) allocates the liability based on joint erroneous loss item. On their joint Federal income tax return for tax year 2009, H reports $100,000 of wage income and W reports $50,000 of wage income. In addition, H and W properly deduct $40,000 for their two personal exemptions and itemized deductions, and erroneously report a loss in the amount of $50,000 from a jointly held investment in a tax shelter. H and W divorce in 2011, and on August 14, 2012, a $12,000 deficiency is assessed with respect to their 2009 joint return. W requests innocent spouse relief. The deficiency on the joint return results from a disallowance of all of the $50,000 loss.

In the absence of clear and convincing evidence supporting a different allocation, an erroneous deduction item related to a jointly owned investment is generally allocated 50 percent to each spouse. Thus $25,000 of the loss is allocated to each spouse. In determining the effect, if any, of the tax benefit rule of Treas. Reg. § 1.6015-1(d)(2)(i), H's separate taxable income is $80,000: $100,000 wage income minus $20,000, or 50 percent of the exemptions and itemized deductions, and W's separate taxable income is $30,000: $50,000 minus $20,000. As both H's and W's separate taxable income exceeds their allocated share of the disallowed loss, no additional amount is allocated between the spouses. W's allocation percentage is 1/2 ($25,000/$50,000) and W's liability is limited to $6,000 (1/2 of $12,000 deficiency). The IRS may collect up to $6,000 from W and up to $12,000 from H (although the total amount collected may not exceed $12,000).

If the IRS could establish that W had knowledge of the facts that made the loss unallowable, both H and W would then remain jointly and severally liable for the $12,000 deficiency.

The fourth example (Example 10 of the proposed regulations) calculates the tax benefit based on joint erroneous item. Assume the same facts as in the prior example, except that W's wage income is only $40,000 W's separate taxable income would then be only $20,000 ($40,000 wage income minus $20,000 – 50 percent of the exemptions and itemized deductions). W would only be able to use $20,000 of the $25,000 loss from the tax shelter to offset her separate taxable income. Accordingly, H benefited from the other $5,000 of the disallowed loss, which was used to offset a portion of his separate taxable income. Therefore $20,000 of the disallowed loss is allocable to W, and $30,000 is allocable to H: $25,000 (H's 50 percent of the disallowed loss) plus $5,000 (the portion of W's 50 percent that is allocable to H because H received a tax benefit). W's allocation percentage is 2/5 ($20,000/$50,000) and W's liability is limited to $4,800 (2/5 of $12,000 deficiency). The IRS may collect up to $4,800 from W and up to $12,000 from H (although the total amount collected may not exceed $12,000).

Finally, the fifth example (Example 11 of the proposed regulations) illustrates the allocation of erroneous item based on fraud of the nonrequesting spouse. During 2009, W fraudulently accesses H's brokerage account to sell stock that H had separately received from an inheritance. W deposits the funds from the sale in a separate bank account to which H did not have access. H and W file a joint federal income tax return for tax year 2009. The return did not include the income from the sale of the stock. H and W divorce in November 2010. The divorce decree states that W committed forgery and defrauded H with respect to his brokerage account. The IRS commences an audit in March 2011 and determines a deficiency based on the omission of the income from the sale of the stock. H requests innocent spouse relief. Items of investment income are generally allocated to the spouse who owned the investment, which in this case would be H. However, the IRS may allocate any item between the spouses if the IRS determines that the allocation is appropriate due to fraud by one or both spouses. The IRS determines that W committed fraud with respect to H and as a result it is appropriate to allocate the deficiency to W under rules of Treas. Reg. § 1.6015-3(d)(ii).

j. Alternative Allocation Method

There is an alternative allocation method available to the spouses, which is based on applicable tax rates. If a deficiency arises from two or more erroneous items that are subject to tax at different rates (e.g., ordinary income and capital gain items), the deficiency will be allocated after first separating the erroneous items into categories according to their applicable tax rate. After all erroneous items are categorized, a separate allocation is made with respect to each tax rate category using the proportionate allocation method described earlier. The Service, in its regulations, allows itself wiggle room to provide additional alternative methods for allocating erroneous items under section 6015(c). Those additional alternative methods may be prescribed by the Treasury and IRS in subsequent revenue rulings, revenue procedures, or other appropriate guidance.[125]

The following example illustrates the alternative allocation method based on applicable tax rates. H and W timely file their 1998 (joint federal income tax return). H and W divorce in 1999. On July 13, 2001, a $5,100 deficiency is assessed with respect to H's and W's 1998 return. Of this deficiency, $2,000 results from unreported capital gain of $6,000 that is attributable to W and $4,000 of capital gain that is attributable to H (both gains being subject to tax at the 20 percent marginal rate). The remaining $3,100 of the deficiency is attributable to $10,000 of unreported dividend income of H that is subject to tax at a marginal rate of 31 percent. H and W both timely elect to allocate; the deficiency and qualify under this section to do so. There are erroneous items subject to different tax rates; thus, the alternative allocation method of this paragraph (d)(6) applies. The three erroneous items are first categorized according to their applicable tax rates, then allocated. Of the total amount of 20 percent tax rate items ($10,000), 60 percent is allocable to W and 40 percent is allocable to H. Therefore, 60 percent of the $2,000 deficiency attributable to these items (or $1,200) is allocated to W. The remaining 40 percent of this portion of the deficiency ($800) is allocated to H. The only 31 percent tax rate item is allocable to H. Accordingly, H is liable for $3,900 of the deficiency ($800 + $3,100), and W is liable for the remaining $1,200.[126]

4. I.R.C. § 6015(f) ("(f) Relief")

The third form of innocent spouse relief available to a taxpayer is equitable relief, also known as (f) relief.

A requesting spouse who files a joint return for which an understatement or deficiency (as defined by Treas. Reg. § 1.6015-1 (h)(7) and (8)) was determined or for which there was unpaid tax (as defined by Treas. Reg. § 1.6015-1

125. Treas. Reg. § 1.6015-3(d)(6)(i) and (ii) (11-20-15).
126. Treas. Reg. § 1.6015-3(d)(6)(iii).

(h)(6)), and who does not qualify for full relief under Treas. Reg. § 1.6015-2 or § 1.6015-3, may be entitled to equitable relief. The Internal Revenue Service (IRS) has the discretion to grant equitable relief from joint and several liability to a requesting spouse when, considering all of the facts and circumstances, it would be inequitable to hold the requesting spouse jointly and severally liable.[127]

Relief under Section 6015(f) may not be used to circumvent the limitation of Treas. Reg. § 1.6015-3(c)(1). Therefore, (f) relief is not available to obtain a refund of liabilities already paid, for which the requesting spouse would otherwise qualify for relief under Treas. Reg. § 1.6015-3 (i.e., (c) relief). If the requesting spouse is only eligible for (c) relief under § 1.6015-3 (i.e., some portion of the deficiency is allocable to the requesting spouse), then the requesting spouse may be considered for relief under this section with respect to the portion of the deficiency for which the requesting spouse was not entitled to relief.[128]

For guidance concerning the criteria to be used in determining whether it is inequitable to hold a requesting spouse jointly and severally liable under this section, see Rev. Proc. 2013-34 (2013-2 C.B. 397), or other guidance published by the Treasury and IRS (see § 601.601(d)(2)).[129]

Unpaid tax and underpayment for purposes of Treas. Reg. § 1.6015-4 ((f) relief) means the balance due shown on the joint return, reduced by the tax paid with the joint return. The balance due shown on the joint return is determined after application of the credits for tax withheld under Section 31, any amounts paid as estimated income tax, any amounts paid with an extension of time to file, or any other credits applied against the total tax reported on the return. Tax paid with the joint return includes a check or money order remitted with the return or Form 1040-V, "Payment Voucher," or payment by direct debit, credit card, or other commercially acceptable means under Section 6311. If the joint return is filed on or before the last day prescribed for filing under Section 6072 (determined without regard to any extension of time to file under Section 6081), the tax paid with the joint return includes any tax paid on or before the last day prescribed for payment under Section 6151. If the joint return is filed after the last day prescribed for filing, the tax paid with the joint return includes any tax paid on or before the date the joint return is filed. A requesting spouse is not entitled to be considered for equitable relief for any tax paid with the joint return. If the tax paid with the joint return completely satisfies the balance due shown on the return, then there is no unpaid tax for purposes of equitable relief.[130]

---

127. I.R.C. § 1.6015 (f); Prop. Treas. Reg. § 1.6015-4(a) (11.20.2015).
128. Prop. Treas. Reg. § 1.6015-4(b) (11.20.2015).
129. Prop. Treas. Reg. § 1.6015-4(c) (11.20.2015)
130. Prop. Treas. Reg. § 1.6015-1(h)(6) (11.20.2015).

The term "understatement" means the excess of the amount of tax required to be shown on the return for the taxable year over the amount of the tax imposed which is shown on the return, reduced by any rebate (within the meaning of Section 6211(b)(2)).[131] The term "deficiency" has the same meaning given to that term in Section 6211 and Treas. Reg. § 301.6211-1.[132]

a. Tests for (f) Relief

The IRS may relieve a taxpayer from liability if the following two tests are met:

First, taking into account all the facts and circumstances, it would be inequitable to hold the individual liable for all or part of any unpaid tax or any deficiency arising from a joint return, or any portion of either; and, second, relief is not available to such individual under the innocent spouse rules of I.R.C. § 6015(b) or the divorce/separated spouse rule of I.R.C. § 6015(c), that is, (b) relief or (c) relief, respectively.[133] According to the proposed income tax regulations, equitable relief may be requested if (i) a joint return has been filed, (ii) there is an understatement or deficiency, (iii) all or some of the liability remains unpaid, and (iv) the requesting taxpayer does not qualify for full relief under the (b) relief provisions or the (c) relief provisions.[134] Thus, (b) relief and (c) relief apply only in the case of an understatement of tax or any deficiency in tax. When the liability arises from an underpayment of tax reported on a joint relief, relief is available only under Section 6015(f).[135] According to Prop. Treas. Reg. § 1.6015-4(a), the IRS has the discretion to grant equitable relief from joint and several liability to a requesting spouse when, considering all the facts and circumstances, it would be inequitable to hold the requesting spouse jointly and severally liable. Equitable relief is not available to spouses in community property states under Section 6015(f) but is available to spouses in community property states under Section 66. For guidance concerning the criteria to be used in determining whether it is inequitable to hold a requesting spouse jointly and severally liable under this regulation, see Rev. Proc. 2013-34, 2013-1 I.R.B. 397, discussed later.

According to the legislative history of I.R.C. § 6015(f), Congress intended that equitable relief be granted when a spouse "does not know, and had no

131. Prop. Treas. Reg. § 1.6015-1(h)(7) (11.20.2015)

132. Prop. Treas. Reg. § 1.6015-1(h)(8)(11.20.2015).

133. I.R.C. § 6015(f). Taxpayer First Act of 2019, Pub. L. No. 116-25, §§ 1001(b)(1)(A), 1203(a) (7.1.19).

134. Prop. Treas. Reg. § 1.6015-4(a) (11.20.2015). To prevail under I.R.C. § 6015(f), the taxpayer must prove that the Service's denial of equitable relief from joint liability was an abuse of discretion. Washington v. Comm'r, 120 T.C. 137 (2003).

135. Rev. Prop. 213-34, 2013-2 C.B. 397 (Section 2.04).

reason to know, that funds intended for payment of tax were instead taken by the other spouse for such other spouse's benefit."[136]

b. Rev. Proc. 2013-34

The IRS issued Rev. Proc. 2013-34[137] to provide guidance to taxpayers seeking equitable relief from joint and several liability under I.R.C. § 6015(f) or equitable relief under I.R.C. § 66(c) from income tax liability resulting from the operation of community property law.[138] Although the courts are not bound by IRS Revenue Procedures, the Court considers them in reviewing the Service's determination.[139] Thus, if the practitioner is of the opinion that (f) relief is available, the practitioner should follow the mandates of Rev. Proc. 2013-34 in preparing an innocent spouse relief under Section 6015(f).

The Revenue Procedure provides guidance in three areas. The first area provides the threshold requirements for any request for equitable relief. The second area sets forth the conditions under which the Service will make streamlined relief determinations granting equitable relief under I.R.C. § 6015(f) from an understatement of income tax or an underpayment of income tax reported on a joint return, or the operation of community property law under Section 66 (c). The third area provides a nonexclusive list of factors for consideration in determining whether relief should be granted under Section 6015(f) because it would be inequitable to hold a requesting spouse jointly and severally liable when the conditions set forth therein are not met. Thus, if the requesting spouse meets all of the threshold requirements[140], the Service will grant equitable relief if the requesting spouse meets the streamlined requirements. If, however, the streamlined elements are not met, the Service will look to the equitable factors to determine if equitable relief is appropriate. The factors will also apply in determining whether to relieve a spouse from income tax liability resulting from the operation of community property law under the equitable relief provisions of Section 66(c). Those three areas (threshold conditions, streamlining relief, and equitable relief) are discussed next.

---

136. H.R. Conf. Regs. No. 599, 105th Cong., 2d Sess. 254 (1998).

137. 2013-2 C.B. 397. The Rev. Proc. supercedes Notice 2012-8, 2012-4 I.R.B. 308; Rev. Proc. 2003-61, 2003-2 C.B. 296, and Rev. Proc. 2000-15, 2000-1 C.B. 447. It should be noted that Proposed Regulations issued November 15, 2015 incorporates by reference the general provisions of Rev. Proc. 2013-34. Prop. Treas. Reg. § 1.6015-4(c).

138. Although the Revenue Procedure expressly applies to a requesting spouse who requests relief under Section 6015(f), the Tax Court has applied these factors to a taxpayer who requests relief under Section 6015(b) in *Jacobsen v. Comm'r*, T.C. Memo. 2018-115 discussed at Chapter 11 B.2.a.

139. Pullins v. Comm'r, 136 T.C. 432, 438–39 (2011).

140. If all the threshold requirements are not met, the Court will not address whether relief is available under the streamline determination or the equitable factors. Heydon-Grauss v. Comm'r, T.C. Memo. 2018-209 (p. 15, n.1).

(1) Threshold Conditions

The first area provides seven threshold conditions all of which must be satisfied for a requesting spouse to be considered for equitable relief under Section 6015(f).[141] A requesting spouse must satisfy threshold conditions one (1) through seven (7) to be eligible to submit a request for equitable relief under I.R.C. § 6015(f), and must satisfy threshold conditions three (3) through seven (7) to be eligible to submit a request for equitable relief under I.R.C. § 66(c) pertaining to community property. If a requesting spouse meets all seven threshold conditions to be eligible to submit a request for equitable relief under Section 6015(f) or the last five threshold conditions to be eligible to submit a request for equitable relief under Section 66(c), the individual may be granted equitable relief if, taking into account all the facts and circumstances, the Service determines it is inequitable to hold the individual liable for all or any of the tax liability. The seven threshold conditions set forth in Section 4.01 of Rev. Proc. 2013-34 are as follows:

(1) The requesting spouse filed a *valid* joint return for the taxable year for which relief is available.[142] In *Sutherland v. Commissioner,*[143] the wife signed joint returns on prior years tax returns in the courthouse less than an hour before her husband was to be sentenced. She did not review the returns before signing them. The wife testified that she believed that signing the returns would help her husband avoid prison time. The returns were prepared by an accountant hired by the husband's defense attorney. The Court held that the wife knew, or should have known when she signed the returns, that the taxes reported on the returns would not then be paid by her husband at the time of filing nor shortly thereafter. According to the Court, the wife knew the 2005 and 2006 income tax liabilities were not paid in 2011 when the returns were filed because if the husband would be sentenced to jail time she would not be able to pay taxes which she felt was his responsibility because it resulted from his business. By signing the return, the wife is deemed to have constructive knowledge of its contents.[144] The tax liability must arise under a joint return. Where the taxpayer's liability arises under the trust fund recovery penalty under Section 6672, such liability is not reflected on and does not arise from the filing of a joint

141. See Sapp v. Comm'r, T.C. Memo. 2015-143; Hilloman v. Comm'r, T.C. Memo 2015-157.

142. James v. Comm'r, T.C. Memo. 2021-7 (A joint return filed by divorced spouses is not a *valid* joint return.). *See also* Raymond v. Comm'r, 119 T.C. 191 (2002).

143. T.C. Memo. 2021-110.

144. *See* Porter v. Comm'r, 130 T.C. 213 (2005).

return. Accordingly, the taxpayer is not entitled to innocent spouse relief under I.R.C. § 6015(f) for the trust fund recovery penalty.[145]

(2) Relief is not available to the requesting spouse under I.R.C. § 6015(b) and (c).

(3) The claim for equitable relief is timely filed. If the requesting spouse is applying for relief from a liability or a portion of a liability that remains unpaid, the request for relief must be made on or before the collection expiration date. This is the date the period of limitations on collection of the income tax liability expires as provided in Section 6502. Generally, that period is ten years after assessment of the tax, but it may be extended by other provisions of the Code. Claims for credit or refund of amounts paid must be made before the expiration of the period of limitation on the credit or refund as provided in Section 6511. Generally, that period expires three years from the time the return was filed or two years from when the tax was paid, whichever is later.

(4) No assets were transferred between the spouses filing the joint return as part of a fraudulent scheme by such spouses.[146] A fraudulent scheme may be found where the spouses transfer property with the intent to hide the transfers.[147] But where the nonrequesting spouse deeded property to the requesting spouse which was recorded in the public records, writes a check to the requesting spouse for $140,000, and transfers title to a truck to the requesting spouse, the court found that such transfers were not part of a fraudulent scheme to hide assets.[148]

(5) There were no "disqualified assets" (defined earlier) transferred to the requesting spouse by the nonrequesting spouse. If disqualified assets were transferred to the requesting spouse by the nonrequesting spouse, relief is available only to the extent that the income tax liability exceeds the value of the disqualified asset. Even if there were a transfer of disqualified assets, the requesting spouse may be eligible for relief if the nonrequesting spouse abused the requesting spouse or maintained control over the household finances by restricting the requesting spouse's access to financial information, or the requesting

145. Chavis v. Comm'r, 158 T.C. No. 8 (6.15.22).

146. Where a transfer of property between spouses to satisfy a judicial foreclosure due to the nonrequesting spouse's failure to pay the requesting spouse money pursuant to a divorce decree, and the transfer was made with the assistance and guidance of the requesting spouse's divorce attorney and was recorded on the public record, the Court found that there was no intent to misrepresent, conceal, or hide the transaction from the Service. Contreras v. Comm'r, T.C. Memo. 2019-12.

147. Chen v. Comm'r, T.C. Memo. 2006-160.

148. Pocock v. Comm'r, T.C. Memo. 2022-55.

spouse did not have actual knowledge that disqualified assets were transferred. As noted earlier, a disqualified asset is defined in I.R.C. § 6015 (c)(4)(B) as any property or right to property transferred to the requesting spouse by the nonrequesting spouse who filed a joint return together if the principal purpose of the transfer was the avoidance of tax or the payment of tax.

(6) The requesting spouse did not knowingly participate in the filing of a fraudulent joint return. The issue here is whether the requesting spouse was aware of excess deductions or omitted income when the requesting spouse filed the return. In *Durland v. Commissioner*,[149] the Court held that the requesting spouse knowingly participated in the filing of a fraudulent joint return by signing them with knowledge of omitted substantial amounts of income. On the other hand, in *Pocock v. Commissioner*, the Court held that the requesting spouse did not knowingly participate in the filing of a fraudulent joint return where she provided her tax information to her husband who had the returns prepared, she did not review the returns before they were filed, and the returns did not look fraudulent on their face. Furthermore, awareness of large refund checks was not evidence of participation in filing false joint returns where the requesting spouse was unable to question the nonrequesting spouse about the checks because when she did so, he verbally and physically intimidated her, and he was extremely secretive about his business dealings.

(7) The income tax liability from which the requesting spouse seeks relief is attributable (either in full or in part) to an item of the nonrequesting spouse or an underpayment resulting from the nonrequesting spouse's income.[150] If the liability is partially attributable to the requesting spouse, then relief can only be considered for the portion of the liability attributable to the nonrequesting spouse. Generally, the Court will attribute the items to the spouse who wrongfully reported or claimed them[151] Nonetheless, the Service will consider granting relief to the requesting spouse regardless of whether the understatement, deficiency, or underpayment is attributable (in full or in part) to the requesting spouse if any of the following five exceptions applies:
   (i) *Community property*. If an item is attributable or partially attributable to the requesting spouse solely due to the operation of community property law, then for purposes of Rev. Proc. 2013-34, that

149. T.C. Memo. 2016-133.
150. Raymond v. Comm'r.
151. Pocock v. Comm'r, and the cases cited therein.

item (or portion thereof) is considered to be attributable to the nonrequesting spouse.

(ii) *Nominal ownership*. If the item is titled in the name of the requesting spouse, the item is presumptively attributable to the requesting spouse. This presumption is rebuttable. For example, H opens an individual retirement account (IRA) in W's name and forges W's signature on the IRA in 2006. Thereafter, H makes contributions to the IRA and in 2008 takes a taxable distribution from the IRA. H and W file a joint return for the 2008 taxable year, but do not report the taxable distribution on their joint return. The Service later determines a deficiency relating to the taxable IRA distribution. W requests relief from joint and several liability under section 6015. W establishes that W did not contribute to the IRA, sign paperwork relating to the IRA, or otherwise act as if W were the owner of the IRA. W, thereby, rebuts the presumption that the IRA is attributable to W.

(iii) *Misappropriation of funds*. If the requesting spouse did not know, and had no reason to know, that funds intended for the payment of tax were misappropriated by the nonrequesting spouse for the nonrequesting spouse's benefit, the Service will consider granting equitable relief although the underpayment may be attributable in part or in full to an item of the requesting spouse. The Service will consider granting relief in this case only to the extent that the funds intended for the payment of tax were taken by the nonrequesting spouse.

(iv) *Abuse*. If the requesting spouse establishes that he or she was the victim of abuse prior to the time the return was filed, and that, as a result of the prior abuse, the requesting spouse was not able to challenge the treatment of any items on the return, or was not able to question the payment of any balance due reported on the return, for fear of the nonrequesting spouse's retaliation, the Service will consider granting equitable relief even though the deficiency or underpayment may be attributable in part or in full to an item of the requesting spouse.[152]

---

152. Abuse includes efforts to control, isolate, humiliate, and intimidate the requesting spouse or to undermine his or her ability to reason independently. Heyon-Grauss v. Comm'r., T.C. Memo. 2018-209 (Testimony that there was alcohol, drugs, gambling, sexual affairs, mismanagement of money, risky investments, and yelling in the household did not substantiate an allegation of abuse.) *See Sapp v. Comm'r*, T.C. Memo. 2015-143 where the Court held that because Mrs. Sapp established that she was physically and emotionally abused, this exception applied and she met all seven of the threshold tests. As a result, the Court looked to see if streamlined relief (discussed later in (B)) applied. *But see Agudelo v. Comm'r*, T.C. Memo. 2015-124 where the

(v) *Fraud*. The Service will consider granting relief notwithstanding that the item giving rise to the understatement or deficiency is attributable to the requesting spouse, if the requesting spouse establishes that the nonrequesting spouse's fraud is the reason for the erroneous item. For example, W fraudulently accesses H's brokerage account to sell stock that H had separately received from an inheritance. W deposits the funds from the sale in a separate bank account to which H does not have access. H and W file a joint Federal income tax return for the year, which does not report the income from the sale of the stock. The Service determines a deficiency based on the omission of the income from the sale of the stock. H requests relief from the deficiency under section 6015(f). The income from the sale of the stock normally would be attributable to H. Because W committed fraud with respect to H, however, and because this fraud was the reason for the erroneous item, the liability is properly attributable to W.

(2) Streamlined Relief

The second area, found in Section 4.02 of the Rev. Proc., sets forth the conditions under which the Service will make streamlined relief determinations granting equitable relief from an understatement of income tax or an underpayment of income tax reported on a joint return, or the operation of community property law under section 66(c).

If a requesting spouse who filed a joint return, or a requesting spouse who did not file a joint return in a community property state, satisfies the threshold conditions of Section 4.01 of Rev. Proc. 2013-34 set forth earlier, the Service will consider whether the requesting spouse is entitled to a streamlined determination of equitable relief under section 66(c) or section 6015(f). If a requesting spouse is not entitled to a streamlined determination because the requesting spouse does not satisfy all the following three elements, the requesting spouse is still entitled to be considered for relief under the equitable factors discussed later. The Service will make streamlined determinations granting equitable relief under section 66(c) or section 6015(f), in cases in which the requesting spouse establishes that the requesting spouse meets each of the following three tests:

Court denied the husband equitable relief, finding that the husband was not an abused spouse. *See also* Contreras v. Comm'r, T.C. Memo. 2019-12 where the Court found the wife was an abused spouse where the husband threw items at her, kicked-in-the bedroom door, damaged property, threw her possessions outside, and broke mirrors among other physical acts, and Hilliman v. Comm'r, T.C.2015-157 where the Court found that the wife was a victim of abuse because she was afraid to question her husband for fear of retaliation.

(i) The requesting spouse is no longer married to the nonrequesting spouse or is separated from the nonrequesting spouse at the time the Service makes its determination as set forth here;

(a) The requesting spouse would suffer economic hardship if relief is not granted as set forth in the factors discussed below at (3) Non-exclusive List of Factors.[153] The requesting spouse suffers an economic hardship if the following two tests are met: First, either the requesting spouse's income is below 250 percent of the Federal poverty level, or if the requesting spouse's monthly[154] income exceeds his or her reasonable basic monthly living expenses by $300 or less. Second, the requesting spouse does not have assets from which the requesting spouse can make payments toward the tax liability and still meet reasonable basic living expenses.[155] If the two tests are not met, the Service will consider all the facts and circumstances to determine whether the requesting spouse will suffer economic hardship if relief is not granted. Based on the many court decisions discussing this factor, requesting spouse's current income, expenses, assets, age, employment status or history, and ability to earn are considered to determine whether the requesting spouse will suffer an economic hardship; and

(b) For Section 6015(f) cases, the requesting spouse did not know or had reason to know that there was an understatement or

153. Hilloman v. Comm'r, T.C. Memo. 2015-157 where the requesting spouse failed to meet the economic hardship test and thus was not entitled to streamlined relief. The Court, however, looked at the seven threshold conditions nonexclusive list of factors discussed later. Gino v. Commissioner, T.C. Summary Op. 2121-14 (wife would not suffer economic hardship if she had to pay the tax liability because she was fully supported by her second husband). Although the *Gino* case is a Summary Opinion and therefore has no precedential value, it is included here to give the reader some idea of the factors the Tax Court will consider in weighing the economic hardship test.

154. *See* Contreras v. Comm'r, T.C. Memo. 2019-12 for a discussion of this test. In *Contreras*, the taxpayer relied on child support and government assistance to meet her basic living expenses. Even so, her monthly expenses exceeded her monthly income by $1,300. The taxpayer had some education, was unemployed during her marriage, had part-time employment for a brief period after the divorce, and was behind in her property taxes and other personal liabilities. Her income was below 250 percent of the Federal poverty guidelines. Thus, the Court held that the taxpayer met the poverty level test. On the other hand, *see* Benson v. Comm'r., T.C. Memo. 2018-15 where the Court held that the first test was not met because the taxpayer's income was far in excess of 250 percent of the Federal poverty level.

155. Contreras v. Comm'r, T.C. Memo 2019-12 where the wife's liabilities exceeded her assets. If the taxpayer were not afforded tax relief, the Court found she would be homeless and without income to provide for her basic living needs. *See* Pocock v. Comm'r, T.C. Memo. 2022-55 where the Court found that because the requesting spouse's liabilities exceeded her assets, she did not have sufficient assets to pay the tax liability and still meet reasonable basic living expenses. Also, for the years in issue, her annual income of $22,260 was lower than 250 percent of the Federal poverty level.

deficiency on the joint income tax return, as set forth in the third factor below, or did not know or have reason to know that the nonrequesting spouse would not or could not pay the underpayment of tax reported on the joint income tax return.[156] Factors to consider in determining whether the requesting spouse knew or should have known of an understatement or reason to know whether the nonrequesting spouse would or could not pay the tax liability include: (i) the requesting spouse's level of education, (ii) any deceit or evasiveness of the nonrequesting spouse, (iii) the requesting spouse's degree of involvement in the activity generating the tax liability or the household or business finances, (iv) the requesting spouse's business or financial expertise, and (v) the presence of lavish or unusual expenditures relative to past spending levels. If the nonrequesting spouse abused the requesting spouse or maintained control over the household finances by restricting the requesting spouse's access to financial information, and because of the abuse or financial control, the requesting spouse was not able to challenge the treatment of any items on the joint return, or to question the payment of the taxes reported as due on the joint return or challenge the nonrequesting spouse's assurance regarding payment of the taxes, for fear of the nonrequesting spouse's retaliation, then the abuse or financial control will result in this factor being satisfied even if the requesting spouse knew or had reason to know of the items giving rise to the understatement or deficiency or knew or had reason to know that the nonrequesting spouse would not pay the tax liability.[157]

156. *See* Benson v. Comm'r, T.C. Memo. 2018-157 for an excellent analysis of this test and the economic hardship test.

157. *See* Sapp v. Comm'r, where the Court held that even though the wife had reason to know of the understatement, and therefore failed this third test, the abuse exception applied, thus entitling her to equitable relief under section 6015(f). *See also* Contreras v. Comm'r T.C. Memo. 2019-12. In *Pocock v. Comm'r*, the Court found that the requesting spouse did not have actual knowledge of overstated withholdings, but did have constructive knowledge of overstated withholdings that the Court refused to hold because it found the requesting spouse was a victim of spousal abuse. The Court found that the nonrequesting spouse physically intimidated the requesting spouse by throwing a glass vase at her head when she asked him for information about a business dispute he had with her brother. In later years, he kicked her and threw household objects at her when she inquired about his business or finances. In addition, he restricted her access to financial information, was evasive about the nature of his business, and kept tight control of the mail. Medical records of the nonrequesting spouse's therapist describing abusive behavior toward family members and the testimony of his son that he was physically abused by his father was further evidence of abuse. Thus, the court held that the abusive behavior of the nonrequesting spouse prevented the requesting spouse from questioning the accuracy of the joint return or the payment of tax liabilities and she therefore satisfied the lack of knowledge requirement.

The requesting spouse in Section 66(c) cases did not know or have reason to know of an item of community income properly includible in gross income, which, under the rules contained in section 879(a), would be treated as the income of the nonrequesting spouse.

The requesting spouse must establish each of the three tests to receive streamlined relief determination. If the requesting spouse does not meet the three tests, the Service will look to the non-exclusive list of factors discussed following to determine if (f) relief is available.

(3) Nonexclusive List of Factors

The third area, found in Section 4.03 of the Rev. Proc., provides a nonexclusive list of seven factors to be considered in determining whether (f) relief should be granted because it would be inequitable to hold the requesting spouse jointly and severally liable when the conditions under which the Service will make streamlined determinations granted equitable relief under Section 66(c) (pertaining to equitable relief from income tax liability under community property law) or Section 6015(f).

This non-exclusive list of factors applies to a requesting spouse who requests relief under section 66(c) or section 6015(f), and who satisfies the threshold conditions, but does not qualify for streamlined determinations granting relief.

In determining whether it is inequitable to hold the requesting spouse liable for all or part of the unpaid income tax liability or deficiency, and whether full or partial equitable relief under section 66(c) or section 6015(f) should be granted, all the facts and circumstances of the case are to be taken into account. The factors listed here are designed as guides and not intended to comprise an exclusive list. Other factors relevant to a specific claim for relief may also be taken into account in making the determination. In evaluating a claim for relief, no one factor or a majority of factors necessarily determines the outcome. The degree of importance of each factor varies depending on the requesting spouse's facts and circumstances. Abuse or the exercise of financial control by the nonrequesting spouse is a factor that may impact the other factors, as described later.

The Service listed seven factors to consider whether to grant (f) relief or Section 66 (c) relief—marital status, economic hardship, knowledge or reason to know, legal obligation, significant benefit, compliance with income tax laws, and mental or physical health. Each of these seven factors is discussed next.[158] No single factor is determinative and all factors are considered and weighed

158. Hilloman v. Comm'r, where the requesting spouse was found to have met five of the seven threshold factors (the other two were neutral) and was therefore found to be entitled to equitable relief under section 6015(f). Hale v. Comm'r, T.C. Memo. 2018-93 gives a good analysis of each of these factors.

appropriately.[159] Not all factors bear equal weight. The Courts can apply more weight to any of the factors than to others.[160]

(1) *Marital status*. Whether the requesting spouse is no longer married to the nonrequesting spouse as of the date the Service makes its determination. If the requesting spouse is still married to the nonrequesting spouse, this factor is neutral. If the requesting spouse is no longer married to the nonrequesting spouse, this factor will weigh in favor of relief. For purposes of these factors, a requesting spouse will be treated as being no longer married to the nonrequesting spouse only in the following four situations: (i) the requesting spouse is divorced from the nonrequesting spouse, (ii) the requesting spouse is legally separated from the nonrequesting spouse under applicable state law, (iii) the requesting spouse is a widow or widower and is not an heir to the nonrequesting spouse's estate that would have sufficient assets to pay the tax liability,[161] or (iv) the requesting spouse has not been a member of the same household as the nonrequesting spouse at any time during the 12-month period ending on the date the Service makes its determination. For these purposes, a temporary absence (e.g., due to incarceration, illness, business, military service, or education) is not considered separation if the absent spouse is expected to return to the household. A requesting spouse is a member of the same household as the nonrequesting spouse for any period in which the spouses maintain the same residence.

(2) *Economic hardship*. Whether the requesting spouse will suffer economic hardship if relief is not granted. For purposes of this factor, an economic hardship exists if satisfaction of the tax liability in whole or in part will cause the requesting spouse to be unable to pay reasonable basic living expenses, such as food, clothing, housing, utilities, medical expenses, transportation, child care, or child support.[162] Whether the requesting spouse will suffer economic hardship is determined based on rules similar to those provided in Treas. Reg. § 301.6343-1 (b)(4), and the Service will take into consideration a requesting spouse's current income and expenses and the requesting spouse's assets. In determining the requesting spouse's reasonable basic living expenses, the Service will consider whether the requesting spouse shares expenses or has expenses paid by another individual (such as a family member, including a

159. Kellman v. Comm'r., T.C. Memo. 2013-186, where the court found two factors weighing against relief and the remaining factors are neutral.

160. Sleeth v. Comm'r, 991 F.3d 1201(C.A. 11, 2021); Jacobsen v. Comm'r, 950 F.3d 414 (C.A. 7, 2021).

161. The requesting spouse is deemed an heir of the estate of the nonrequesting spouse where she receives life insurance proceeds from the nonrequesting spouse upon his death. Hale v. Comm'r.

162. Rogers v. Comm'r, T.C. Memo. 2018-53 at 114.

current spouse).[163] If denying relief from the joint and several liability will cause the requesting spouse to suffer economic hardship, this factor will weigh in favor of relief.[164] If denying relief from the joint and several liability will not cause the requesting spouse to suffer economic hardship, this factor will be neutral.[165]

In determining whether the requesting spouse would suffer economic hardship if relief is not granted, the Service will compare the requesting spouse's income to the Federal poverty guidelines (as updated periodically in the Federal Register by the U.S. Department of Health and Human Services under the authority of 42 U.S.C. § 9902(2)) for the requesting spouse's family size and will determine by how much, if at all, the requesting spouse's monthly income exceeds the spouse's reasonable basic monthly living expenses. This factor will weigh in favor of relief if the requesting spouse's income is below 250 percent of the Federal poverty guidelines unless the requesting spouse has assets out of which the requesting spouse can make payments towards the tax liability and still adequately meet the requesting spouse's reasonable basic living expenses. If the requesting spouse's income exceeds 250 percent of the Federal poverty guidelines, this factor will still weigh in favor of relief if the requesting spouse's monthly income exceeds the requesting spouse's reasonable basic monthly living expenses by $300 or less, unless the requesting spouse has assets out of which the requesting spouse can make payments towards the tax liability and still adequately meet the requesting spouse's reasonable basic living expenses. If the requesting spouse's income exceeds 250 percent of the Federal poverty guidelines and monthly income exceeds monthly expenses by more than $300, or if the requesting spouse qualifies under either standard but has sufficient

163. Gino v. Comm'r, T.C. Summary Op. 2021-14 (wife would not suffer economic hardship if she had to pay the tax liability because she was fully supported by her second husband). Although the case is a Summary Opinion and therefore has no precedential value, it is included here to give the reader some idea of the factors the Tax Court will consider in weighing the economic hardship test.

164. Carcio v. Comm'r, T.C. Summary Op. 2021-31, a non-precedential case, the taxpayer had significant debt (credit cards, unpaid property taxes, loans, and unpaid legal fees) and her monthly expenses exceeded her monthly income. Her employment prospects were bleak and the Court determined she could not improve her financial condition in any meaningful way. Thus, requiring the taxpayer to pay the taxes due for the year in issue would impose an economic hardship on her which would leave her unable to pay reasonable living expenses for herself and her children, even though she had substantial equity in the home (The Court did not say, but it appears that the court was of the view that if she borrowed against the home it would put her deeper in debt and more unable to pay her daily living expenses, thus, excluding the home equity from consideration.) Note that this case is a Summary Opinion and may not be cited as precedent, but it is included here to give the reader some idea of the court's thinking and reasoning on this factor.

165. The burden of proof is on the taxpayer to establish that it would be an economic hardship if innocent spouse is not granted. Comm'r v. Neal, 557 F.3d 1262, 1269 (C.A. 11, 2009).

assets to make payments towards the tax liability and still adequately meet the requesting spouse's reasonable basic living expenses, the Service will consider all facts and circumstances (including the size of the requesting spouse's household) in determining whether the requesting spouse would suffer economic hardship if relief is not granted. If the requesting spouse is deceased, this factor is neutral.[166]

(3) *Knowledge or reason to know.*

(a) *Understatement cases – Section 6015(f).* Whether the requesting spouse knew or had reason to know of the item giving rise to the understatement or deficiency as of the date the joint return (including a joint amended return) was filed, or the date the requesting spouse reasonably believed the joint return was filed. If the requesting spouse did not know and had no reason to know of the item giving rise to the understatement, this factor will weigh in favor of relief. If the requesting spouse knew or had reason to know of the item giving rise to the understatement, this factor will weigh against relief. Actual knowledge of the item giving rise to the understatement or deficiency will not be weighed more heavily than any other factor. Depending on the facts and circumstances, if the requesting spouse was abused by the nonrequesting spouse, or the nonrequesting spouse maintained control of the household finances by restricting the requesting spouse's access to financial information, and because of the abuse or financial control, the requesting spouse was not able to challenge the treatment of any items on the joint return for fear of the nonrequesting spouse's retaliation, this factor will weigh in favor of relief even if the requesting spouse knew or had reason to know of the items giving rise to the understatement or deficiency.

(b) *Understatement cases – Section 66(c).* Whether the requesting spouse knew or had reason to know of an item of community income properly includible in gross income, which, under the rules contained in Section 879(a), would be treated as the income of the nonrequesting spouse.

(c) *Underpayment cases.* In the case of an income tax liability that was properly reported but not paid, whether, as of the date the return was filed or the date the requesting spouse reasonably believed the return was filed, the requesting spouse knew or had reason to know that the nonrequesting spouse would not or could not pay the tax liability at that time or within a reasonable period of time after the filing of the return. This factor will weigh in favor of relief if the requesting spouse reasonably expected the nonrequesting spouse to pay the tax liability reported on the return. A reasonable expectation of payment will be presumed if the spouses submitted a request for an installment agreement

166. In Sleeth v. Comm'r, 991 F.3d 1201 (C.A. 11, 2021) the Court held that although the requesting spouse's income fell below the poverty line, she had equity in her townhouse and could at least make some partial payments on her tax liabilities.

to pay the tax reported as due on the return. To benefit from the presumption, the request for an installment agreement must be filed by the later of 90 days after the due date for payment of the tax, or 90 days after the return was filed. The request must detail the plan for paying the tax, interest, and penalties, satisfy the liability within a reasonable time, and it must not be unreasonable for the requesting spouse to believe that the nonrequesting spouse will be able to make the payments contemplated in the requested installment agreement.

This factor will weigh against relief if, based on the facts and circumstances of the case, it was not reasonable for the requesting spouse to believe that the nonrequesting spouse would or could pay the tax liability shown on the return. For example, if prior to the return being filed, or the date the requesting spouse reasonably believed the return was filed, the requesting spouse knew of the nonrequesting spouse's prior bankruptcies, financial difficulties, or other issues with the Service or other creditors, or was otherwise aware of difficulties in timely paying bills, then this factor will generally weigh against relief.[167]

Depending on the facts and circumstances, if the requesting spouse was abused by the nonrequesting spouse, or the nonrequesting spouse maintained control of the household finances by restricting the requesting spouse's access to financial information, and because of the abuse or financial control, the requesting spouse was not able to question the payment of the taxes reported as due on the return or challenge the nonrequesting spouse's assurance regarding payment of the taxes for fear of the nonrequesting spouse's retaliation, this factor will weigh in favor of relief even if the requesting spouse knew or had reason to know about the nonrequesting spouse's intent or ability to pay the taxes due.

With respect to an underpayment of tax on an amended return that reports a liability based on items not properly reported on the original return, the initial inquiry is whether, as of the date the amended return was filed, or the date the requesting spouse reasonably believed the amended return was filed, the requesting spouse reasonably expected that the nonrequesting spouse would pay the tax within a reasonable period of time. If so, this factor will weigh in favor of relief. However, if it was not reasonable for the requesting spouse to expect that the nonrequesting spouse would pay the tax, the requesting spouse's knowledge or reason to know of the understatement on the original return will also be considered. If the requesting spouse knew or had reason to know of the item giving rise to the understatement on the original return, then this factor will weigh against relief. If the requesting spouse did not know or have reason to know of the item, then this factor will weigh in favor of relief.

---

167. *See* Sleeth v. Comm'r, where the Court found that since the requesting spouse signed the returns, it presumed she had constructive knowledge of the information reported on them.

(d) *Reason to know.* The facts and circumstances that are considered in determining whether the requesting spouse had reason to know of an understatement, or reason to know whether the nonrequesting spouse could or would pay the reported tax liability, include, but are not limited to, the requesting spouse's level of education, any deceit or evasiveness of the nonrequesting spouse, the requesting spouse's degree of involvement in the activity generating the income tax liability, the requesting spouse's involvement in business or household financial matters, the requesting spouse's business or financial expertise, and any lavish or unusual expenditures compared with past spending levels.[168]

(e) *Abuse by the nonrequesting spouse.* If the requesting spouse establishes that he or she was the victim of abuse (not amounting to duress, see Treas. Reg. § 1.6015-1 (b) discussed earlier), then depending on the facts and circumstances of the requesting spouse's situation, the abuse may result in certain factors weighing in favor of relief when otherwise the factor may have weighed against relief. Abuse comes in many forms and can include physical, psychological, sexual, or emotional abuse, including efforts to control, isolate, humiliate, and intimidate the requesting spouse, or to undermine the requesting spouse's ability to reason independently and be able to do what is required under the tax laws. All the facts and circumstances are considered in determining whether a requesting spouse was abused. The impact of a nonrequesting spouse's alcohol or drug abuse is also considered in determining whether a requesting spouse was abused. Depending on the facts and circumstances, abuse of the requesting spouse's child or other family member living in the household may constitute abuse of the requesting spouse. This factor is neutral.[169]

(4) *Legal obligation.* Whether the requesting spouse or the nonrequesting spouse has a legal obligation to pay the outstanding federal income tax liability. For purposes of this factor, a legal obligation is an obligation arising from

---

168. In Sleeth v. Comm'r, the Court held that since the requesting spouse signed the returns, was aware of their shared financial troubles, and knew of their prior problems with the IRS, the knowledge or reason to know factor would weigh against relief.

169. *See* Contreras v. Comm'r, T.C. Memo. 2019-12, where the Court found the requesting spouse had been abused by the nonrequesting spouse. In reaching this conclusion, the Court found that the nonrequesting spouse's controlling and abusive behavior hindered the taxpayer's ability to question the underpayment and to participate meaningfully in the returns; numerous police reports documented a volatile home environment; the couple's daughter testified that the nonrequesting spouse's abuse caused them to leave the home; the divorce decree included a protective order for the requesting spouse and her children; the requesting spouse was not a willing participant in filing the joint return; she signed the returns in issue "as to form only" indicating she did not understand the contents of the returns; the abusive and controlling behavior of the nonrequesting spouse prevented the taxpayer from questioning his ability to pay and to participate meaningfully in filing the joint returns; and the nonrequesting spouse controlled the records and finances of his business which was his only source of income during the years in issue.

a divorce decree or other legally binding agreement. This factor will weigh in favor of relief if the nonrequesting spouse has the sole legal obligation to pay the outstanding income tax liability pursuant to a divorce decree or agreement. This factor, however, will be neutral if the requesting spouse knew or had reason to know, when entering into the divorce decree or agreement, that the nonrequesting spouse would not pay the income tax liability. This factor will weigh against relief if the requesting spouse has the sole legal obligation. The fact that the nonrequesting spouse has been relieved of liability for the taxes at issue as a result of a discharge in bankruptcy is disregarded in determining whether the requesting spouse has the sole legal obligation. This factor will be neutral if, based on an agreement or consent order, both spouses have a legal obligation to pay the outstanding income tax liability, the spouses are not separated or divorced, or the divorce decree or agreement is silent as to any obligation to pay the outstanding income tax liability.

(5) *Significant benefit*. Whether the requesting spouse significantly benefited from the unpaid income tax liability or understatement. A significant benefit is any benefit in excess of normal support. For example, if the requesting spouse enjoyed the benefits of a lavish lifestyle, such as owning luxury assets and taking expensive vacations, this factor will weigh against relief.[170] If, however, the nonrequesting spouse controlled the household and business finances or there was abuse such that the nonrequesting spouse made the decision on spending funds for a lavish lifestyle, then this mitigates this factor so that it is neutral. If only the nonrequesting spouse significantly benefitted from the unpaid tax or understatement, and the requesting spouse had little or no benefit, or the nonrequesting spouse enjoyed the benefit to the requesting spouse's detriment, this factor will weigh in favor of relief. If the amount of unpaid tax or understatement was small such that neither spouse received a significant benefit, then this factor is neutral. Whether the amount of unpaid tax or understatement is small such that neither spouse received a significant benefit will vary depending on the facts and circumstances of each case.

(6) *Compliance with income tax laws*. Whether the requesting spouse has made a good faith effort to comply with the income tax laws in the taxable years following the taxable year or years to which the request for relief relates. If the requesting spouse is compliant for taxable years after being divorced from the nonrequesting spouse, then this factor will weigh in favor of relief.[171]

---

170. The burden to prove exorbitant spending appears to be on the Service. Where the Service presents no evidence of exorbitant spending, and the taxpayer presents no evidence of non-exorbitant spending, the Court will view this factor as neutral. Briley v. Comm'r, T.C. Memo. 2019-55.

171. Briley v. Comm'r. The failure of the requesting spouse to mention her interests in life insurance proceeds on Form 8857 mitigates against a finding that she complied with the income tax laws. Halle v. Comm'r, T.C. Memo. 2018-93 at 32–37.

If the requesting spouse is not compliant, then this factor will weigh against relief. If the requesting spouse made a good faith effort to comply with the tax laws but was unable to fully comply, then this factor will be neutral. For example, if the requesting spouse timely filed an income tax return but was unable to fully pay the tax liability due to the requesting spouse's poor financial or economic situation after the divorce, then this factor will be neutral. If the requesting spouse remains married to the nonrequesting spouse, whether or not legally separated or living apart, and continues to file joint returns with the nonrequesting spouse after requesting relief, then this factor will be neutral if the joint returns are compliant with the tax laws but will weigh against relief if the returns are not compliant. If the requesting spouse remains married to the nonrequesting spouse but files separate returns, this factor will weigh in favor of relief if the requesting spouse is compliant with the tax laws and will weigh against relief if the requesting spouse is not compliant with the tax laws. If the requesting spouse made a good faith effort to comply with the tax laws but was unable to fully comply, then this factor will be neutral. For example, if the requesting spouse timely filed an income tax return but was unable to fully pay the tax liability due to the requesting spouse's poor financial or economic situation as a result of being separated or living apart from the nonrequesting spouse, then this factor will be neutral.

(7) *Mental or physical health*. Whether the requesting spouse was in poor physical or mental health. This factor will weigh in favor of relief if the requesting spouse was in poor mental or physical health at the time the return or returns for which the request for relief relates were filed (or at the time the requesting spouse reasonably believed the return or returns were filed), or at the time the requesting spouse requested relief. The Service will consider the nature, extent, and duration of the condition, including the ongoing economic impact of the illness. If the requesting spouse was in neither poor physical nor poor mental health, this factor is neutral.

(8) *Additional factors*. In *Sutherland v. Commissioner*,[172] the Court noted that the Revenue Procedure was "not intended to comprise an exclusive list" and that "other factors relevant to the specific claim for relief may be taken into account." And that is just what the Court did. It found that when the requesting spouse signed the returns she knew she would receive a sizeable inheritance from her mother's estate, and that when she submitted the Form 8857 Innocent Spouse Request she had more than $400,000 in her bank account which she could have used to pay off her joint liability which totaled only 10 percent of the amount in her bank account. This was an additional factor to mitigate

172. T.C. Memo. 2021-110.

against relief.[173] Also in *Sutherland*, the Court found that the wife's testimony about her knowledge of the family's finances were "untrue or misleading at best," and lacked the "ring of truth."

Thus, taxpayers should be aware that although most of the time the Court will look to the seven factors in the ruling, on occasion it may look to additional factors. But this applies to taxpayers too. So, if a taxpayer believes he or she has additional factors to support his or her position, the taxpayer should present them to the Court or the Service.

c. Refunds

In both understatement and underpayment cases, a requesting spouse is eligible for a refund of separate payments made by the requesting spouse after July 22, 1998, if the requesting spouse establishes that the funds used to make the payment for which a refund is sought were provided by the requesting spouse. A requesting spouse is not eligible for refunds of payments made with the joint return, joint payments, or payments that the nonrequesting spouse made. A requesting spouse, however, may be eligible for a refund of the requesting spouse's portion of the requesting and nonrequesting spouse's joint overpayment from another tax year that was applied to the joint income tax liability to the extent that the requesting spouse can establish that the requesting spouse provided the funds for the overpayment. The availability of refunds is subject to the refund limitations of Section 6511.

d. File Form 8857

A requesting spouse seeking equitable relief under I.R.C. §§ 6015(f) or 66(c) must file Form 8857, Request for Innocent Spouse Relief (and Separation of Liability, and Equitable Relief), or other similar statement signed under penalties of perjury, within two years of the first collection activity against the requesting spouse.[174] If a requesting spouse has already filed an application for relief under I.R.C. § 6015(b) or I.R.C. § 6015(c), the IRS will consider whether equitable relief under I.R.C. § 6015(f) is appropriate for the portion of the liability for which relief under I.R.C. § 6015(f) is not necessary.

5. Time to File

a. General Rule

To elect (b) relief or (c) relief, or to request equitable relief ((f) relief), a requesting spouse must file Form 8857, "Request for Innocent Spouse Relief" (or other

173. *See* Torrisi v. Comm'r, T.C. Memo. 2011-3 (Depletion of life insurance proceeds while an outstanding Federal income tax liability exists is another factor weighing against relief.).

174. See FAQ "Innocent Spouse Questions and Answers" issued September 14, 2022.

specified form); submit a written statement containing the same information required on Form 8857, which is signed under penalties of perjury; or submit information in the manner prescribed by the Treasury and IRS in forms, relevant revenue rulings, revenue procedures.[175]

The Form 8857 or other similar statement must be filed with the Internal Revenue Service no later than two years from the date of the first "collection activity" against the requesting spouse, with respect to the joint tax liability.[176] Collection activity means any of the following four collection activities: (i) a section 6330 notice; (ii) an offset of an overpayment of the requesting spouse against a liability under section 6402; (iii) the filing of a suit by the United States against the requesting spouse for the collection of the joint tax liability; or (iv) the filing of a claim by the United States in a court proceeding in which the requesting spouse is a party or which involves property of the requesting spouse. Collection activity does not include the following three activities: (i) a notice of deficiency; (ii) the filing of a Notice of Federal Tax lien; or (iii) a demand for payment of tax. The term "property of the requesting spouse" means property in which the requesting spouse has an ownership interest (other than solely through the operation of community property laws), including property owned jointly with the nonrequesting spouse.[177] A section 6330 notice refers to the notice sent, pursuant to section 6330, providing taxpayers notice of the Service's intent to levy and of their right to a collection due process (CDP) hearing.[178]

According to the Instructions for Form 8857 (06/2022), there are three exceptions for the time to request equitable relief. The amount of time to request equitable relief depends on whether the taxpayer is seeking a credit or refund, or both. Generally, if there is a balance due, the taxpayer must file his/her request within the time period the IRS has to collect the tax. Generally, the IRS has 10 years from the date the tax liability was assessed to collect the tax. In certain cases, the 10-year period is suspended. The amount of time the suspension is in effect will extend the time the IRS has to collect the tax. See IRS Pub. 594, The IRS Collection Process, for details. Generally, if the taxpayer is seeking a credit or refund, the taxpayer must file his/her request within 3 years after the date the original return was filed or within 2 years after the date the tax was paid, whichever is later. But the taxpayer may have more time to file if the taxpayer lives in a Federally declared disaster area or is physically or mentally unable to manage his/her financial affairs. See IRS Pub. 556, Examination of Returns, Appeal Rights, and Claims for Refund, for details. Finally, if the taxpayer is seeking a refund of amounts paid and relief from a balance due over and above what the taxpayer has paid, the time period for credit or

175. Treas. Reg. § 1.6015-5(a).
176. *Id.* § 1.6015-5(b)(1).
177. *Id.* § 1.6015-5(b)(2)(i).
178. *Id.* § 1.6015-5(b)(2)(ii).

refund will apply to any payments the taxpayer has made, and the time period for collection of a balance due amount will apply to any unpaid liability

If the requesting spouse seeks relief based on community property laws, Form 8857 must be filed no later than six months before the expiration of the period of limitations on an assessment (including extensions) against the non-requesting spouse for the tax year in which relief is sought. If, however, the IRS begins an examination of the requesting spouse's return during the six-month period, the latest time for requesting relief is 30 days after the date of the IRS's initial contact letter to the requesting spouse.

An election for (b), (c), or a request for (f) relief may be made before collection activity has commenced. For example, an election or request for relief may be made in connection with an audit or examination of the joint Federal income tax return or a demand for payment, or pursuant to the CDP hearing procedures under sections 6320 in connection with the filing of a Notice of Federal Tax Lien. However, no request for relief may be made before the date specified in Treas. Reg. § 1.6015-5(b)(5).[179] That regulation provides that a claim for relief is premature if it is filed for a tax year prior to the receipt of notice of an audit or a letter or notice from the IRS indicating there may be an outstanding liability for that year. Such letters or notices, however, do not include notices issued pursuant to TEFRA notices.

The Service will not consider a premature election or request for (b), (c) or (f) relief. A premature claim is not considered an election or request under Treas. Reg. §1.6015-1(h)(5)[180]

Form 8857 may be filed several ways. If filed by U.S. Postal Service, the form should be mailed to: Internal Revenue Service, P.O. Box 120053, Covington, NY 41012. If filed by postal delivery or private delivery service, the form should be addressed to: Internal Revenue Service, 7940 Kentucky Drive, Stop 840F, Florence, KY 41042. Or the Form may be faxed to 855-233-8558. The request should not be filed with the taxpayer's tax return or the United States Tax Court, but only with the IRS by mail, private delivery or fax. The practitioner should check with the Instructions to IRS Form 8857 to verify the place of filing.

When the IRS receives a request for (b), (c) or (f) relief, it must notify the nonrequesting spouse that the requesting spouse has filed Form 8857.[181] It must also permit the nonrequesting spouse to participate in the process, and notify the nonrequesting spouse of the Service's preliminary and final determinations regarding the request for relief.[182] The IRS will not, however, disclose personal information of the requesting spouse to the nonrequesting spouse. If

179. *Id.* § 1.6015-5(b)(iii).
180. Treas. Reg. § 1.6015-5(b)(5).
181. I.R.C. § 6015(h)(1), Treas. Reg. § 1.6015-6(a).
182. I.R.C. § 6015(h)(2), Treas. Reg. § 1.6015-6(a) and (b).

the nonrequesting spouse participates in the process and files a rebuttal to the Form 8857 filed by the requesting spouse, this rebuttal will be made available to the requesting spouse. Upon the request of either spouse, the IRS will share with the one spouse the information submitted by the other spouse.[183]

b. Examples

The following five examples from the regulations illustrate the rules regarding the time and manner for requesting relief:[184]

Example 1. On January 11, 2000, a section 6330 notice is mailed to H and W regarding their 1997 joint Federal income tax liability. The Internal Revenue Service levies on W's employer on June 5, 2000. The Internal Revenue Service levies on H's employer on July 10, 2000. An election or request for relief must be made by January 11, 2002, which is two years after the Internal Revenue Service sent the section 6330 notice.

Example 2. The Internal Revenue Service offsets an overpayment against a joint liability for 1995 on January 12, 1998. The offset only partially satisfies the liability. The Internal Revenue Service takes no other collection actions. On July 24, 2001, W elects relief with respect to the unpaid portion of the 1995 liability. W's election is timely because the Internal Revenue Service has not taken any collection activity after July 22, 1998; therefore, the two-year period has not commenced.

Example 3. Assume the same facts as in Example 2, except that the Internal Revenue Service sends a Section 6330 notice on January 22, 1999. W's election is untimely because it is filed more than two years after the first collection activity after July 22, 1998.

Example 4. H and W do not remit full payment with their timely filed joint federal income tax return for the 1989 tax year. No collection activity is taken after July 22, 1998, until the United States files a suit against both H and W to reduce the tax assessment to judgment and to foreclose the tax lien on their jointly held business property on July 1, 1999. H elects relief on October 2, 2000. The election is timely because it is made within two years of the filing of a collection suit by the United States against H.

Example 5. W files a Chapter 7 bankruptcy petition on July 10, 2000. On September 5, 2000, the United States files a proof of claim for her joint 1998 income tax liability. W elects relief with respect to the 1998 liability on August 20, 2002. The election is timely because it is made within two years of the date the United States filed the proof of claim in W's bankruptcy case.

183. Treas. Reg. § 1.6015-6(a).
184. Prop. Treas. Reg. § 1.6015-5(b)(4).

6. Relief from Penalties and Interest

The Proposed Regulations provide the requesting spouse with relief from penalties and interest. Generally, a spouse who is entitled to (b), (c), or (f) relief is also entitled to relief from related penalties, additions to tax, additional amounts, and interest (collectively, "penalties and interest"). Penalties and interest, however, are not separate erroneous items from which a requesting spouse can be relieved separate from the tax. Thus, unless the taxpayer is granted relief from tax, the taxpayer cannot be granted relief from penalties and interest. Rather relief from penalties and interest related to an understatement or deficiency will generally be determined based on the proportion of the total erroneous items from which the requesting spouse is relieved. Penalties and interest on an underpayment are also not separate items from which a requesting spouse may obtain (f) relief. Relief from penalties and interest on the underpayment is determined based on the amount of relief from the underpayment to which the requesting spouse is entitled. If the underlying tax liability (whether an assessed deficiency or an underpayment) was paid in full after the joint return was filed but penalties and interest remain unpaid, the requesting spouse may be relieved from the penalties and interest if the requesting spouse is entitled to relief from the underlying tax. The fact that the requesting spouse is entitled to relief from the underlying tax but is not entitled to a credit or refund because Treas. Reg. § 1.6015-1(k) does not prevent the requesting spouse from being relieved from liability for the penalties and interest.[185]

7. Abuse by Nonrequesting Spouse

Abuse comes in many forms and can include physical, psychological, sexual, or emotional abuse, including efforts to control, isolate, humiliate, and intimidate the requesting spouse, or to undermine the requesting spouse's ability to reason independently and be able to do what is required under the tax laws. All the facts and circumstances are considered in determining whether a requesting spouse was abused. The impact of a nonrequesting spouse's alcohol or drug abuse is also considered in determining whether a requesting spouse was abused. Depending on the facts and circumstances, abuse of the requesting spouse's child or other family member living in the household may constitute abuse of the requesting spouse.[186]

8. Erroneous Item

An "item" is that which is required to be separately listed on an individual income tax return or any required attachments. Items include, but are

185. Prop. Treas. Reg. § 1.6015-1(m) (11-20-2015).
186. Prop. Treas. Reg. § 1.6015-1(o)11-20-2015).

not limited to, gross, income, deductions, credits, and basis.[187] An "erroneous item," on the other hand, is any item resulting in an understatement or deficiency in tax to the extent that such item is omitted from, or improperly reported (including improperly characterized) on an individual income tax return. For example, unreported income from an investment asset resulting in an understatement or deficiency in tax is an erroneous item. Similarly, ordinary income that is improperly reported as capital gain resulting in an understatement or deficiency in tax is also an erroneous item. In addition, a deduction for an expense that is personal in nature that results in an understatement or deficiency in tax is an erroneous item of deduction. An erroneous item is also an improperly reported item that affects the liability on other returns (e.g., an improper net operating loss that is carried back to a prior year's return). Penalties and interest are not erroneous items. Rather, relief from penalties and interest will generally be determined based on the proportion of the total erroneous items from which the requesting spouse is relieved.[188]

9. Qualify Election

A qualifying election for (b), (c), or request for (f) relief is the first timely request for relief from joint and several liability for the tax year for which relief is sought. A qualifying request also includes a requesting spouse's second request to seek relief from joint and several liability for the same tax year under Treas. Reg. § 1.6015-3 (i.e., (c) relief) when the following two qualifications are met: (i) the requesting spouse did not qualify for (c) relief when the Internal Revenue Service considered the first request solely because the qualifications of Treas. Reg. § 1.6015-3(a) were not satisfied; and (ii) at the time of the second request, the qualifications for relief under Treas. Reg. § 1.6015-3(a) are satisfied.[189]

The relief provisions of Section 6015 do not negate liability that arises under the operation of other laws. Therefore, a requesting spouse who is relieved of joint and several liability under (b), (c), or (f) relief may nevertheless remain liable for the unpaid tax (including additions to tax, penalties, and interest) to the extent provided by Federal or State transferee liability or property laws. For the rules regarding the liability of transferees, see Sections 6901 through 6904 and the regulations thereunder. In addition, the requesting spouse's property may be subject to collection under Federal or State property laws.[190]

The following example illustrates the transferee liability rule. H and W timely file their 1998 joint income tax return on April 15, 1999. H dies in March

187. Treas. Reg. § 1.6015-1(h)(4) (12-20-2015).
188. Prop. Treas. Reg. § 1.6015-1(h)(4).
189. *Prop. Treas. Re.* § 1.6015-1(h)(5). Note that Prop. Treas. Reg. § 1.60151(h)(5) (12-20-15) changes the word "election" to "request."
190. Treas. Reg. § 1.6015-1(j)(1).

2000, and the executor of H's will transfers all of the estate's assets to W. In July 2001, the Internal Revenue Service assesses a deficiency for the 1998 return. The items giving rise to the deficiency are attributable to H. W is relieved of the liability under Section 6015, and H's estate remains solely liable. The Internal Revenue Service may seek to collect the deficiency from W to the extent permitted under Federal or State transferee liability or property laws.[191]

10. Closing Agreements

A requesting spouse is not entitled to (b), (c), or (f) relief from joint and several liability for any tax year for which the requesting spouse has entered into a closing agreement with the IRS that disposes of the same liability that is the subject of the claim for relief. In addition, a requesting spouse is not entitled to (b), (c), or (f) relief from joint and several liability for any tax year for which the requesting spouse has entered into an offer in compromise with the IRS.[192] To clarify, if the taxpayer signed a Form 866, Agreement as to Final Determination of Tax Liability, the tax year is deemed closed and the taxpayer cannot apply for innocent spouse relief except for the two items noted on the form. If, however, the taxpayer signed a Form 906, Closing Agreement On Final Determination Covering Specific Matters, only those matters covered in the closing agreement are closed (except for the two items noted on the form), and innocent spouse relief may be requested for matters not covered in the closing agreement. It thus becomes important, as it always is when signing a form provided by the Service, to be sure it is the correct form that you or your client intend to sign, and that it is the most recent form (unless, of course, an earlier form is more favorable to the taxpayer).

Special rules apply to closing agreements with respect to TEFRA partnership proceedings for partnership proceedings for partnership items.[193]

If the IRS establishes that a spouse transferred assets to the other spouse as part of a fraudulent scheme, relief is not available under Section 6015, and Section 6013(d)(3) applies to the return. A fraudulent scheme includes a scheme to defraud the Service or another third party, including, but not limited to, creditors, ex-spouses, and business partners.[194]

191. Treas. Reg. §1.6015-1(j)(2).

192. Treas. Reg. § 1.6015-1(c)(1). See I.R.C. §§ 7121 and 7122 for rules relating to closing agreements and offers in compromise.

193. Treas. Reg. § 1.6015-1(c)(2).

194. Treas. Reg. § 1.6015-1(d). Section 6013 (d)(3) provides that if a joint return is made, the tax is computed on the aggregate joint income of the spouses and the liability with respect to the tax is joint and several.

11. Res Judicata

A requesting spouse is barred from relief from joint and several liability under Section 6015 by res judicata for any tax year for which a court of competent jurisdiction has rendered a final decision on the requesting spouse's tax liability if relief under Section 6015 was at issue in the prior proceeding, or if the requesting spouse meaningfully participated in that proceeding and could have raised relief under Section 6015.[195] A requesting spouse is deemed to have not meaningfully participated in a prior proceeding if, due to the effective date of Section 6015, relief under Section 6015 was not available in that proceeding.[196] In other words, Section 6015(g)(2) modifies the common law doctrine of res judicata for taxpayers seeking (b), (c), or (f) relief by not barring relief if relief under Section 6015 was not an issue in the prior proceeding, and the requesting spouse did not participate meaningfully in the prior proceeding.[197]

The proposed regulations substantially enhance the definition of "meaningful participation" and offer guidance on the meaningful participation exception to res judicata provided by I.R.C. § 6015(g)(2).[198] According to the proposed regulations, a requesting spouse meaningfully participated in the prior proceeding if the requesting spouse was involved in the proceeding so that the requesting spouse could have raised the issue of relief under Section 6015 in that proceeding. Meaningful participation is a facts and circumstances determination. The proposed regulations provide a non-exclusive list of acts be considered in determining the facts and circumstances. The factors listed in the proposed regulations are: whether the requesting spouse participated in the IRS Appeals process while the prior proceeding was docketed; whether the requesting spouse participated in pretrial meetings; whether the requesting spouse participated in discovery; whether the requesting spouse participated in settlement negotiations; whether the requesting spouse signed court documents, such as a petition, a stipulation of facts, motions, briefs, or any other documents; whether the requesting spouse participated at trial (for example, the requesting spouse was present or testified at the prior proceeding); and whether the requesting spouse was represented by counsel in the prior proceeding. No one act necessarily determines the outcome. The degree of importance

---

195. I.R.C. § 6015(g)(2); Prop. Treas. Reg. § 1.6015-1(e)(1) (11-20-15). According to the proposed regulation, (b), relief will not be considered to have been at issue in a prior proceeding if the requesting spouse only raised the issue of relief under Section 6015 in general and did not specify under which subsection relief was being requested, and the requesting spouse was not eligible for relief under Prop. Treas. Reg. § 1.6015-3 during the prior proceeding because the requesting spouse was not divorced, widowed, or legally separated, or had been a member of the same household as the nonrequesting spouse during the prior 12 months. Prop. Treas. Reg. 1.6015-1(e)(2).

196. *See* Diehl v. Comm'r, 134 T.C. 156 (2010) and cases cited therein.

197. Rogers v. Comm'r, T.C. Memo 2018-53 at 97.

198. Prop. Treas. Reg. § 1.6015-1(e)(3) (11-20-15).

of each act varies depending on the requesting spouse's facts and circumstances. These provisions incorporate factors from *Diehl v. Commissioner,*[199] *Thurner v. Commissioner,*[200] and *Monsove v. Commissioner.*[201]

Notwithstanding the fact that a requesting spouse performed any of the acts listed in the preceding paragraph, the requesting spouse will not be considered to have meaningfully participated in the prior proceeding if the requesting spouse establishes that the requesting souse performed any of the foregoing acts because the nonrequesting spouse abused[202] or maintained control over the requesting spouse, and the requesting spouse did not challenge the nonrequesting spouse for fear of the nonrequesting spouse's retaliation.[203] A requesting spouse is not considered to have meaningfully participated in a prior proceeding if, due to the effective date of Section 6015, relief under section 6015 was not available in that proceeding.[204]

In a case petitioned from a statutory notice of deficiency under Section 6213, the fact that the requesting spouse did not have the ability to effectively contest the underlying deficiency is irrelevant for purposes of determining whether the requesting spouse meaningfully participated in the court proceeding.[205]

In *Harbin v. Commissioner,*[206] the Court held that the taxpayer participated in the prior deficiency case in that he prepared the tax returns for the years in issue and started negotiation with the IRS when the audit began. Based on this, the IRS argued that res judicata barred the taxpayer's claim for relief under Section 6015. The Tax Court concluded that Mr. Harbin did not meaningfully participate in the prior deficiency case within the meaning of Section 6015(g)(2) in part because he could not effectively contest the part of the deficiency related to his ex-wife's gambling losses without her. The Tax Court found that Mr. Harbin could not effectively contest this part of the deficiency without his ex-wife because she "was the one with personal knowledge of the winnings and losses from the gambling activities" and was the one "who maintained and provided all of the documentation relating to the gambling activities." The Tax Court concluded that this knowledge and control of the documentation resulted in Mr. Harbin's ex-wife effectively exercising "exclusive control" of the case.[207] Therefore, the taxpayer was not barred from requesting innocent spouse relief. The parties agreed that if Section 6015(g)(2) did not apply, the

199. 134 T.C. 156 (2010) discussed later.

200. 123 T.C. 43 (2003).

201. T.C. Memo. 2004-190.

202. *See* Prop. Treas. Reg. § 1.6015-1(o) for a discussion of abuse, discussed at Chapter 11, Section 7.

203. Prop. Treas. Reg. § 1.6015-1(e)(3)(i) (11-20-15).

204. *Id.* Prop. Treas. Reg. § 1.6015-1(e)(3)(ii) (11-20-15).

205. Prop. Treas. Reg. § 1.6015-1(e)(3)(iii) (11.20.2015).

206. 137 T.C. 93 (2011).

207. *Id.* at 98.

taxpayer met the requirements of Section 6015(b)(1)(A), (B) and (E). The Court found that the taxpayer did not know or have reason to know there was an understatement of tax attributable to his wife's gambling losses at the time he signed the returns for the years in issue. Accordingly, the Court held that the husband qualified for (b) relief.

In *Diehl v. Commissioner*,[208] the Court again was asked to decide whether the taxpayer was precluded by the doctrine of res judicata set forth in Section 6015(g)(2) from claiming innocent spouse treatment. In *Diehl*, the taxpayer was a litigant in three consolidated cases before the Tax Court concerning the substation of business expense deductions claimed by the taxpayer and her husband. According to the Court, Section 6015(g)(2) creates an exception to the rule of res judicata which bars a taxpayer who was a party in a prior proceeding from claiming joint and several liability whether or not the innocent spouse claim had been raised in the prior proceeding. Section 6015(g)(2), however, created an exception to the rule of res judicata where the claim for relief was not an issue in the prior proceeding. But the exception does not apply if the Court determines that the taxpayer meaningfully participated in the prior proceeding. Thus, res judicata does not bar a taxpayer from requesting (b), (c), or (f) relief if relief from joint and several liability under Section 6015(b), (c) or (f) was not in issue in the prior proceeding, and the Court determines that the taxpayer did not participate materially in the prior proceeding. In other words, if a final decision was entered in a prior proceeding for a tax year and relief from joint and several liability was an issue in the prior proceeding, then Section 6015(g)(2) will bar the taxpayer from subsequently requesting the same relief for that year. Alternatively, if a final decision was entered in a prior proceeding for a tax year and the taxpayer materially participated in the prior proceeding, Section 6015(g)(2) will bar the taxpayer from subsequently requesting relief from joint and several liability that was or could have been an issue in the prior proceeding.

The Court looked at the following facts in determining that the taxpayer did not participate meaningfully in the prior proceeding: the taxpayer was not an attorney, had not completed high school, did not sign any court documents,[209] did not review the petition or stipulations of fact, did not agree to the stipulations of fact, did not discuss any court documents with her attorneys (who also represented her husband), did not meet with any IRS personnel,[210] did

208. 134 T.C. 156 (2010).

209. Thurner v. Comm'r, 121 T.C. 43 (2003) (Taxpayer deemed to have materially participated where he signed the Court documents, fully engaged in the prior proceeding, and maintained exclusive control over the prior proceedings.).

210. Huynh v. Comm'r, T.C. Memo. 2006-180 (Taxpayer deemed to have materially participated where the requesting spouse read and signed petitions filed with the Tax Court,

not participate in settlement negations with the IRS, did not attend meetings between the IRS and her attorneys, and her husband controlled the litigation.

Proposed Treas. Reg. § 1.6015-1(e)(4) sets forth nine examples which illustrate the res judicial and collateral estoppel rules.

Also, any final decisions rendered by a court of competent jurisdiction regarding issues relevant to Section 6015 are conclusive and the requesting spouse may be collaterally estopped from relitigating those issues.[211]

12. Collateral Estoppel

The proposed regulations provide for the application of collateral estoppel. According to those regulations, any final decision rendered by a Court of competent jurisdiction regarding issues relevant to the innocent spouse rules is conclusive, and the requesting spouse may be collaterally estopped from relitigating those issues.[212]

13. Attribution

The Proposed Regulations provide for attribution of an understatement or deficiency to a nonrequesting spouse which results from an increase to the adjusted gross income of such spouse. Any portion of an understatement or deficiency relating to the disallowance of an item (or increase to an amount of tax) separately listed on an individual income tax return solely due to the increase of adjusted gross income (or modified adjusted gross income or other similar phaseout thresholds) as a result of an erroneous item being solely attributable to the nonrequesting spouse will also be attributable to the nonrequesting spouse unless the evidence shows that a different result is appropriate. If the increase to adjusted gross income is the result of an erroneous item(s) of both the requesting and nonrequesting spouses, the item disallowed (or increased tax) due to the increase to adjusted gross income will be attributable to the requesting spouse in the same ratio as the amount of the item or items attributable to the requesting spouse over the total amount of the items that resulted in the increase to adjusted gross income.[213] The Proposed Regulations set forth four examples to illustrate the attribution rules.[214]

---

participated at pre-trial meetings with IRS personnel, signed stipulations of fact, testified at trial, signed trial brief and reply brief, and prepared the joint Federal income tax returns for the years in issue.) *See also Moore v. Comm'r*, T.C. Memo. 2007-156 (Material participation found where taxpayer participated in meetings with IRS personnel, and voluntarily entered into a settlement.).

211. Prop. Treas. Reg. § 1.6015-1(e) (11-20-15).
212. Prop. Treas. Reg. § 1.6015-1(e)(5) (11.20.2015).
213. Prop. Treas. Reg. § 1.6015-1(n)(1) (12-07-2015).
214. Prop. Treas. Reg. § 1.6015-1(n)(2) Examples 1–4 (12-20-2015).

14. Administrative Rights

A requesting spouse is entitled to only one final administrative determination for innocent spouse relief for a given assessment, unless the requesting spouse submits a second request for innocent spouse relief.[215]

As required by I.R.C. § 6015(h)(2) and Treas. Reg. § 1.6015-6, the IRS must notify the nonrequesting spouse of the requesting spouse's claim for (b), (c), or (f) relief and provide the nonrequesting spouse with an opportunity to participate in any administrative proceeding with respect to any such election for (b) or (c) relief or request for (f) relief to submit information to be considered by the IRS in determining whether the requesting spouse should be granted relief from joint and several liability.[216] The nonrequesting spouse is not required to submit information. The IRS will consider all relevant information submitted by the requesting spouse and the nonrequesting spouse in determining whether to grant or deny relief. Upon the request of either spouse, the IRS will share with one spouse the information submitted by the other spouse, unless such information would impair tax administration.[217] This provides a balancing act for the IRS in reviewing the information submitted by one spouse.

The IRS must notify the nonrequesting spouse of the Service's preliminary and final determinations with respect to the requesting spouse's claim for relief under Section 6015.

The IRS will consider all of the information (as relevant to each particular relief provision) that the nonrequesting spouse submits in determining whether relief from joint and several liability is appropriate, including information relating to the following ten factors: (1) the legal status of the requesting and nonrequesting spouses' marriage; (2) the extent of the requesting spouse's knowledge of the erroneous items or underpayment; (3) the extent of the requesting spouse's knowledge or participation in the family business or financial affairs; (4) the requesting spouse's education level; (5) the extent to which the requesting spouse benefitted from the erroneous items; (6) any asset transfers between the spouses; (7) any indication of fraud on the part of either spouse; (8) whether it would be inequitable, within the meaning of Treas. Reg. §§1.6015-2(d) and 1.6015-4, to hold the requesting spouse jointly and severally liable for the outstanding liability; (9) the allocation or ownership of items giving rise to the deficiency; and (10) anything else that may be relevant to the determination of whether relief from joint and several liability should be granted.[218]

---

215. Prop. Treas. Reg. § 1.6015-5(c)(1). *See* Treas. Reg. § 1.6015-5(c)(2) for an example which illustrates this rule. *See* Prop. Treas. Reg. § 1.6015-1(h)(5) for making the election or request.

216. *See also* Treas. Reg. § 1.6015-6(a)(1).

217. *Id.*

218. Treas. Reg. § 1.6015-6(b).

The failure of the nonrequesting spouse to submit information does not affect the nonrequesting spouse's ability to seek relief from joint and several liability for the same tax year. However, information that the nonrequesting spouse submits is relevant in determining whether relief from joint and several liability is appropriate for the nonrequesting spouse should the nonrequesting spouse also submit an application for relief.[219]

Once the IRS notifies the requesting spouse and the nonrequesting spouse of the preliminary determination regarding the requesting spouse's claim for relief, the requesting spouse, the nonrequesting spouse, or both spouses may file a protest and receive an Appeals conference as discussed below.

I.R.C. § 6015(e)(1)(A) allows the requesting spouse to petition the Tax Court from a notice of final determination. There are no provisions in I.R.C. § 6015 that allow the nonrequesting spouse to petition the Tax Court absent a notice of final determination.[220] If, however, the requesting spouse petitions the Tax Court, I.R.C. § 6015(e)(4) and the Tax Court's rules allow the nonrequesting spouse to become a party to the proceeding.

Revenue Proc. 2003-19[221] applies to a nonrequesting spouse who appeals the preliminary determination granting full or partial relief from joint and several liability to a requesting spouse. The ruling first sets forth the procedures the IRS will follow after mailing a preliminary determination regarding a claim for relief from joint and several liability, and then discusses the procedures for cases forwarded to Appeals.

The Service will first issue a preliminary determination letter to the requesting spouse based on the merits of the claim. In the event the preliminary determination grants full or partial relief, the Service will suspend processing of the claim for 45 calendar days, pending an appeal by the nonrequesting spouse. The Service will notify the requesting spouse that the nonrequesting spouse has the right to separately protest the Service's preliminary determination. The Service will notify the nonrequesting spouse of the preliminary determination at the same time the Service notifies the requesting spouse. The nonrequesting spouse has the right to file a written protest and request an Appeals conference to protest the preliminary determination to grant partial or full relief. To be eligible for an Appeals conference, the nonrequesting spouse must request an Appeals conference, in writing, within 30 calendar days of the mailing date of the notification letter. If the nonrequesting spouse appeals, the Service will suspend further processing of the requesting spouse's claim for relief pending the outcome of the nonrequesting spouse's appeal.

---

219. Treas. Reg. § 1.6015-6(c).

220. *See* Maier v. Comm'r, 119 T.C. 267 (2002).

221. 2003-1 C.B. 371.

The following procedures apply to Appeals conferences for I.R.C. § 6015 claims for relief:

If, after the Service issues a preliminary determination letter to the requesting spouse, only the nonrequesting spouse files a written protest requesting an Appeals conference, the Service must notify the requesting spouse of the nonrequesting spouse's request for an Appeals conference. The Service must hold an Appeals conference with the nonrequesting spouse. If Appeals proposes to change the preliminary determination, the requesting spouse will have an opportunity to request an Appeals conference to present his or her position including any relevant information before the final determination.

If, after the Service issues a preliminary determination letter to the requesting spouse, only the requesting spouse files a written protest requesting an Appeals conference, the Service must notify the nonrequesting spouse of the requesting spouse's request for a conference. The Service must hold an Appeals conference with the requesting spouse. If Appeals proposes to increase the relief recommended in the preliminary determination letter, the nonrequesting spouse will have an opportunity to request an Appeals conference to present his or her position including any relevant information before the final determination.

If, after the Service issues a preliminary determination letter to the requesting spouse, both spouses file written protest requesting Appeals conferences, the Service must notify each spouse of the other spouse's request for an Appeals conference. The Service must hold separate Appeals conferences with each spouse, with both spouses permitted to submit information. The Service, in its discretion, may hold a joint Appeals conference instead of separate Appeals conferences. Appeals conferences may be conducted by telephone, correspondence, face-to-face meetings or by a combination of these methods.

Upon reaching a final decision, Appeals must issue the notice of final determination to the requesting spouse, unless the requesting spouse executes a waiver pursuant to I.R.C. § 6015(e)(5); and notify the nonrequesting spouse of the final determination.

15. Petition to United States Tax Court

a. Jurisdiction

An individual against whom a deficiency has been issued by the IRS and who elects (b) or (c) relief or requests (f) relief may petition the United States Tax Court to determine if relief is available.[222] According to the Tax Court in *Francel v. Commissioner*,[223] there are three jurisdictional bases for the Court to review a taxpayer's claim for innocent spouse relief. First, a spouse can file a petition

222. I.R.C. § 6015(e)(1).
223. T.C. Memo. 2019-35.

pursuant to Section 6015(e)(1). This is known as a "stand-alone" petition. Such a petition seeks a review of the Service's denial of claim for relief from joint and several liability and is not a petition for redetermination of a deficiency. In such case, the Court's jurisdiction is limited to a determination of whether a taxpayer is entitled to relief under Section 6015, not whether the taxpayer is liable for the tax.[224] Second, the Court can review the claim in the context of a collection-due-process case under Section 6330(d)(1). Third, the claim can be asserted by a spouse as an affirmative defense in a proceeding to redetermine a deficiency pursuant to Section 6213(a). In *Block v. Commissioner*,[225] the Court held that where the taxpayer has filed a petition requesting relief to the IRS's denial of innocent spouse relief or has petitioned the IRS to make a timely determination of a request for such relief pursuant to I.R.C. § 6015(e), the Court's jurisdiction is limited to reviewing the IRS's denial of relief from an existing joint and several tax liability under I.R.C. § 6015(d), (c), and (f).

The Taxpayer First Act of 2019 codified the common law regarding the standard and scope of review. Section 6015(e)(7) provides that innocent spouse relief by the Tax Court is to be reviewed de novo by the Court and is to be based on the administrative record established at the time of the determination and any additional newly discovered or previously unavailable evidence. This allows the Tax Court to take a fresh look at the case without taking previous decisions into account.[226]

---

224. Abdelhadi v. Comm'r, T.C. Memo. 2018-183 (Petitioner filed a stand-alone petition because for the years in issue she was not married to the nonrequesting spouse and did not file a joint Federal income tax return. Thus, because a joint return was not filed, innocent spouse relief could not be granted.).

225. 120 T.C. 62 (2003).

226. Pub. L. 116-25, Title 1, §§ 1001(b)(1)(A), 1203(a)(7.1.19); 133 Stat. 985, 988. This provision is quite generous to both sides because newly discovered evidence is not always admissible under the rules of the various courts throughout the nation.

In *Thomas v. Comm'r*, 160 T.C. No. 4 (2023), the IRS denied the wife's request for innocent spouse treatment. The wife appealed to the Tax Court seeking a determination under Section 6015(e). The case centered around the admissibility of a series of blogs posted by the wife over a six-year period which contained information about her lifestyle, assets, and business, as well as her relationship with her husband (who deceased before the blogs were posted). The blog posts were not part of the administrative record, and the wife did not want the blogs admitted as evidence in the Tax Court proceeding. She maintained the blogs were publicly available during the administrative hearing and the IRS could have found them through an internet search of the petitioner's name. The IRS disagreed and maintained that the blogs were newly discovered evidence after the administrative hearing.

The Court, after analyzing the words "newly discovered," concluded that it should be given its ordinary meaning of "recently obtained sight or knowledge if for the first time." The Court then concluded that the blogs, discovered by the IRS after the administrative hearing and after the taxpayer filed the petition for relief with the Tax Court, should be admitted as "newly discovered evidence."

The moral to this story is that one must be careful what one posts on the internet since such information becomes available to the public and can be used against the poster long after it has

b. Time to File

In the case of an individual against whom a deficiency is asserted and who requests (b), (c), or (f) relief, such requesting spouse may, in addition to any other remedy provided by law, petition the U.S. Tax Court to determine the appropriate relief available to the individual under I.R.C. § 6015 or for review of denial of relief.[227] The petition must be filed by the requesting spouse within the earlier of (i) 90 days after the date the IRS mails by certified or registered mail a notice to such individual of the IRS's final determination of relief, or lack thereof, available to the individual (i.e., a notice of deficiency)[228] or (ii) if the IRS does not mail the requesting spouse a notice of deficiency within six months of the date the requesting spouse files a request under Section 6015, the requesting spouse may petition the Tax Court to review the request at any time after the expiration of the six month period and before expiration of the 90-day period. The Tax Court may also review a request for relief if the Tax Court has jurisdiction under another Section of the Code, such as Section 6213 pertaining to filing of a petition with the Tax Court and restrictions on assessments and Section 6330(d) pertaining to notice and opportunity for a hearing before a levy is made,[229] the date which is six months after the date the election for (b) or (c) relief is filed, or the request for (f) relief is made with the IRS and before expiration of the 90-day period.[230] Thus, rather than wait for any such notice, because, perhaps the Service does not mail such final notice to the requesting spouse, the requesting spouse may file such petition at any time after the date which is six months after the date such election is filed with the IRS and before

---

been posted. Furthermore, it is recommended that when meeting with a client and reviewing documents in the client's possession, the attorney should inquire whether the client has posted any matters on social media that could adversely impact the matter for which the attorney has been retained.

227. I.R.C. § 6015(e)(1), Treas. Reg. § 1.6015-7(a). Before petitioning the U.S. Tax Court, however, the taxpayer must file a request for innocent spouse relief with the IRS. Andrews v. U.S., 69 F. Supp. 2d 972 (N.D. Ohio 1999).

228. I.R.C. § 6015(e)(1)(A); Prop. Treas. Reg. § 1.6015-7(b) (11-20-15). Where taxpayer filed petition one day late based on erroneous advice she allegedly received from two IRS employees, the Court, although sympathetic to the taxpayer's circumstances, observed that such erroneous advice was irrelevant under the plain language of the statute. Nauflett v. Comm'r., 892 F. 3d. 649 (C.A. 4, 2018). Thus, counsel should make certain that the petition is timely filed as required by statute and should mail the petition by certified mail, return receipt requested, postage prepaid. See Sanders v. Comm'r, 160 T.C. 16 (2023) where a petition filed electronically 11 seconds late (i.e., 12:00:11 a.m. on the morning after it was due), was dismissed as untimely. Rule 22(d) of the Tax Court's Rules of Procedure provide that an electronically filed petition is considered timely filed if it is electronically filed at or before 11:59 pm eastern time on the last day of the applicable period for filing.

229. Prop. Treas. Reg. § 1.6015-7(b) (11.20.2015).

230. Prop. Treas. Reg. § 1.6015-7(b) (11.20.2015).

the close of the 90-day period.[231] This is substantially analogous to claims for refunds and suits for refunds.[232]

Nothing in 6015(e) appears to prohibit the Service from issuing more than one final determination letter for any given year. It is unclear, however, whether it is one final determination per request for innocent spouse or one final determination per tax year. Treas. Reg. § 1.6015-1(a)(2) limits claimants to a single qualified request for a given year. A qualified request is the first timely claim for relief, Treas. Reg. § 1.6015-1(h)(5). And the requesting spouse is entitled to only one final administrative determination for relief. Treas. Reg. §1.6015-5(c)(1). But a second spousal claim may be made resulting in a second final determination if, for example, there is a change in marital status. And the Internal Revenue Manual provides that a second final determination can be issued under these circumstances and that a second determination issued under the circumstances listed in the Internal Revenue Manual grants the requesting spouse the right to petition the Tax Court.[233]

In *Vera v. Commissioner*,[234] the taxpayer submitted a request for innocent spouse for 2013 which IRS denied as a final determination. The taxpayer later submitted a request for innocent spouse for tax years 2010 and 2013. The IRS issued a letter, the header of which referred to 2013, but the body of the letter referred to tax years 2010 and 2013. The letter denied relief for both years. The Court found that the second letter was a letter of final determination and therefore held it had jurisdiction to determine the appropriate relief available for tax years 2010 and 2013, even though the IRS had previously denied relief for both years. According to the Court, although the final determination unambiguously denied innocent spouse relief for both years, the Court has jurisdiction over both years. The IRS argument that 2013 was included in error was rejected on grounds that the letter was unambiguous and pertained to 2010 and 2013.

c. Restrictions on Collection

No levy or court proceedings may be made, started or prosecuted against a requesting spouse requesting (b), (c) or (f) relief for collection of any assessment to which the election or request relates until expiration of the 90-day period (if no petition is filed in the Tax Court) or until a decision of the United States

---

231. *Id.*

232. *See* I.R.C. §§ 6532 and 7422. Ewing v. Comm'r, 118 T.C. 494 (2002); Fernandez v. Comm'r, 114 T.C. 324 (2000); Butler v. Comm'r, 114 T.C. 276 (2000). For other cases involving the jurisdiction of the U.S. Tax Court to hear Section 6015 cases, *see* Kollar v. Comm'r, 131 T.C. No. 12 (2008); Washington v. Comm'r, 120 T.C. 137 (2003); Alt v. Comm'r, 119 T.C. 267 (2002); and Estate of Wenner v. Comm'r, 116 T.C. 284 (2001).

233. Internal Revenue Manual 25.15.17.7.

234. 157 T.C. No. 6 (2021).

Tax Court has become final (if a petition is filed in the Tax Court).[235] These restrictions do not apply if the IRS determines collection will be jeopardized by delay.[236] If a levy or court proceeding is implemented during the aforesaid periods of time, such action may be enjoined in a "proper court," including the Tax Court. The Tax Court has no jurisdiction to enjoin any action or proceeding unless a timely petition has been filed with the Tax Court to determine the appropriate relief available to the individual under I.R.C. § 6015(e)(1)(A) and then only in respect of the amount of the assessment to which the election for (b) or (c) relief relates or to which the request for (f) relief relates.[237] The U.S. Tax Court has determined that its jurisdiction in cases brought under Section 6015(e) encompasses a review of all of the Service's determinations with respect to all relief afforded by Section 6015. This would include (b), (c) and (f) relief. The restrictions on collection begin on the date the request is filed.[238]

If the requesting spouse appeals the Tax Court's decision, the IRS may resume collection of the liability from the requesting spouse on the date the requesting spouse files the notice of appeal, unless the requesting spouse files an appeal bond pursuant to the rules of Section 7485.[239]

d. Running of Limitations

At the same time, the running of the period of limitations on collection against the requesting spouse of the assessment to which a request for (b), (c), or (f) relief is made is suspended for the period during which the IRS is prohibited from collecting by levy or court proceeding, and for 60 days thereafter as discussed earlier.[240] If a waiver of the restrictions on collection under I.R.C. § 6015(e)(5) (discussed later) is made by the requesting spouse, the suspension of the running of the period of limitations is suspended from the date the claim for relief is filed and until (60) days after the waiver is filed by the IRS.[241]

If a suit for refund is started by either individual who filed the joint return, the Tax Court loses jurisdiction of the individual's action under I.R.C. § 6015 to the extent jurisdiction is acquired by the District Court or U.S. Court of Federal Claims over the taxable years that are the subject of the suit for refund, and the court acquiring jurisdiction has jurisdiction over the petition filed.[242]

235. I.R.C. § 6015(e)(1)(B)(i); Prop. Treas. Reg. § 1.6015-7(c)(1)(i) (11.20.2015).
236. Prop. Treas. Reg. § 1.6015-7(c)(1)(i) (11.20.2015).
237. I.R.C. § 6015(e)(1)(B)(ii)
238. Prop. Treas. Reg. § 1.6015-7I(1)(i) (11.20.2015).
239. . Treas. Reg. § 1.6015-1(c)(1)(iii) (11-20-15).
240. I.R.C. § 6015(e)(2)(A), Prop. Treas. Reg. § 1.6015-7(c)(3) (11-20-15).
241. I.R.C. § 6015(e)(2)(B), Prop. Treas. Reg. § 1.6015-7(c)(3) (11-20-15).
242. I.R.C. § 6015(e)(3).

The Tax Court is authorized to establish rules which provide the individual filing a joint return but not making the election for (b) or (c) relief, or the request for (f) relief with adequate notice and any opportunity to become a party to the proceeding.[243] Relief under this section is only available for unpaid liabilities resulting from understatements of liability. Refunds are not authorized under this section. Thus, the practitioner should be familiar with the Tax Court's Rules and Procedures before filing a petition.

An individual who elects (b) or (c) relief or who requests (f) relief (and who agrees with the Service's determination of relief) may waive in writing at any time the restrictions applicable to the collection of assessments under IRC § 6015(e)(1)(B) with respect to collection of the outstanding assessment (whether or not a notice of the Service's final determination of relief has been mailed).[244] For purposes of the restrictions on collection and suspension of the running of the period of limitations, the assessment to which the request for relief relates is the entire assessment of the understatement or balance shown on the return to which the request relates, even if the request is made to only part of the understatement or balance due.[245]

16. Community Property

a. Introduction

The purpose of Section 66(c) is to provide relief from unreported community income which, pursuant to Section 879(a), is attributable to the other spouse. If all of the tests of Section 66(c) are met, then the item of unreported income is includible solely in the income of the nonrequesting spouse.[246] In community property states Section 6015 may apply if the spouses file a joint return, and Section 66 applies if the spouses do not file a joint return.

There are two provisions for relief available to community property spouses under Section 66.[247] The first relief provision, known as "traditional relief," applies only to deficiencies arising out of omitted income.[248] The second relief provision, known as "equitable relief," applies to relieve a taxpayer of any deficiency or unpaid tax.[249] Each is discussed next.

243. I.R.C. § 6015(e)(4).

244. I.R.C. § 6015(e)(5).

245. Prop. Treas. Reg. § 1.6015-7(d)(4)(iii)(11.20.2015)

246. *Roberts v. Comm'r*, T.C. Memo. 1987-391, *aff'd*. 860 F.2d 1235 (C.A. 5, 1989).

247. *See* Rev. Proc. 2013-34, 2013-43 I.R.B. 399, discussed earlier, which provides guidance for a taxpayer seeking equitable relief from income tax liability under Sections 66(c) and 6015(f).

248. I.R.C. § 66(c)(1)–(4); Treas. Reg. § 1.66-4(c).

249. I.R.C. § 66(c) Flush language; Treas. Reg. § 1.66-4(c).

b. Traditional Relief

To qualify for "traditional relief" an item of community income is included in the gross income of the nonrequesting spouse, and not in the gross income of the requesting spouse, if the following four tests of Section 66(c) are met:

First, a joint return was not filed by the requesting spouse with the nonrequesting spouse for the taxable year for which relief is sought.[250]

Second, the requesting spouse did not include in gross income for the taxable year an item of community property income which, under Section 879 (which pertains to the tax treatment of certain community income in the case of nonresident aliens), would be treated as income of the nonrequesting spouse.[251]

Third, the requesting spouse establishes that he or she did not know and had no reason to know of the item of community income.[252] According to the income tax regulations, a requesting spouse had knowledge or reason to know of an item of community income if he or she either actually knew of the item of community income, or if a reasonable person in similar circumstances would have known of the item of community income. All of the facts and circumstances are considered in determining whether a requesting spouse had reason to know of an item of community income. The relevant facts and circumstances include, but are not limited to, the nature of the item of community income, the amount of the item of community income relative to other income items, the couple's financial situation, the requesting spouse's educational background and business experience, and whether the item of community income was reflected on prior years' returns (e.g., investment income omitted that was regularly reported on prior years' returns).[253]

If the requesting spouse is aware of the source of community income or the income producing activity but is unaware of the specific amount of the nonrequesting spouse's community income, the requesting spouse is considered to have knowledge or reason to know of the item of community income. The requesting spouse's lack of knowledge of the specific amount of community

250. I.R.C. § 66(c)(1); Treas. Reg. § 1.66-4(a)(1)(i). Where one spouse signs a return under duress, it is not a joint return for purposes of Section 6015, and the spouse who signed the joint return under duress will not be held jointly and severally liable for any tax deficiency assess by the IRS. Stanley v. Comm'r, 81 T.C. 634 (1983); Brown v. Comm'r, 51 T.C. 116 (1968). Prop. Treas. Reg. § 1.6013-4(d). According to the court in *Stanley*, to prove that a joint return was signed under duress the taxpayer must show that the taxpayer was unable to resist the demands of the taxpayer's spouse to sign the joint return, and that the taxpayer would not have signed the joint returns absent the constraint the taxpayer's spouse applied to the taxpayer's will. A return signed under duress is not a joint return.

251. I.R.C. § 66(c)(2); Treas. Reg. § 1.66-4(a)(1)(ii).

252. I.R.C. § 66(c)(3); Treas. Reg. § 1.66-4(a)(1)(iii).

253. Treas. Reg. § 1.66-4(a)(2)(i).

income does not provide a basis for relief under Section 66.[254] Whether a taxpayer has knowledge of an item of community income is determined by

254. Treas. Reg. § 1.66-4(a)(2)(ii). The "knowledge" requirement of the "traditional" relief test requires an item by item analysis.

The following are some of the cases where the court found that the requesting spouse had knowledge of the community income. In *Felt v. Comm'r*, T.C. Memo. 2009-245,) the Court held that if the requesting spouse is aware of the source of the income but is not aware of the amount, the requesting spouse is considered to have knowledge of the item. In *Hiramanek v. Comm'r*, T.C. Memo. 2011-280, the Court held that the requesting spouse did not qualify for traditional relief because she failed to establish that she did not know and had no reason to know of an item of community income where she knew her spouse was employed and used his wages to pay household expenses.

In *Roberts v. Comm'r*, T.C. Memo. 1987-391, *aff'd.* 860 F.2d 1235 (C.A. 5, 1989), the Court held that where the requesting spouse was aware of the business activities of the nonrequesting spouse, that she knew that such activities generated income though she did not know how much, the Court held that the requesting spouse knew of or had reason to know of the unreported income received by the nonrequesting spouse and thus failed to meet the third test of Section 66(c). Innocent spouse treatment denied.

Where the requesting spouse knew that the nonrequesting spouse was employed full time and earned substantial income commensurate with their life style, the Court held that the requesting spouse failed to meet the test of Section 66(c)(3) because she should have known, or had reason to know, of the income producing activity of the nonrequesting spouse. Horner v. Comm'r, T.C. Memo. 1994-44T. And in *Felt v. Comm'r, supra,* the taxpayer was denied traditional relief under Section 66(c) where funds were deposited into a bank account over which the requesting spouse had sole signatory authority, because she is deemed to have actual knowledge of that money and when the nonrequesting spouse deposited funds in her account that had the name of the business of the nonrequesting spouse on the checks, she is deemed to know the source of the funds giving rise to the deficiency, thus, denying her Section 66(c) traditional relief.

The test to be applied in determining whether a spouse "has reason to know" of an item of community income is what a reasonably prudent person would or should know under the circumstances, keeping in mind the person's level of intelligence, education and experience. Where the requesting spouse believed the business of the nonrequesting spouse was in financial difficulty, but knew it was the sole source of income of the nonrequesting spouse, yet knew nonrequesting spouse was able to provide support to the requesting spouse and make mortgage payments on property of the requesting spouse, the knowledge test of Section 66(c)(3) is not met. Moreover, the requesting spouse has a duty to attempt obtain from nonrequesting spouse or his or her accountant financial information about the business to determine if it is producing income. Lythe v. Comm'r, T.C. Memo 1992-185.

See also Butler v. Comm'r, T.C. Memo 1991-40 (requesting spouse knew of unreported income and benefited from same); Beck v. Comm'r, T.C. Memo 2001-198 (requesting spouse denied innocent spouse treatment where she was involved in husband's dental practice and knew its income. Also, she benefited from the income because she used dental practice income to make deposits to her separate bank account and to acquire more than 100 acres of land). The requesting spouse did not meet the test of I.R.C. § 66(c)(3) because she actively participated in two businesses which generated part of the unreported income, and she knew of, and wrote checks on account of, the business which generated the income. Rimple v. Comm'r, T.C. Memo. 1985-245.

Where the requesting spouse is directly and substantially involved with business operations of the nonrequesting spouse, the requesting spouse cannot satisfy the test of I.R.C. § 66(c)(3) that the requesting spouse did not know, or have reason to know, that the nonrequesting spouse had community income for which the requesting spouse is liable. Nelson v. Comm'r, T.C. Memo. 1987-369.

reference to knowledge of a particular income producing activity and not the exact amount of community income.[255]

Fourth, taking into account all of the facts and circumstances, it would be inequitable to include such item of community income in the gross income of the requesting spouse.[256] One relevant factor for this purpose is whether the requesting spouse benefitted, directly or indirectly, from the omitted item of community income.[257] A benefit includes normal support but does not include de minimis amounts. Evidence of direct or indirect benefit may consist of transfers of property or rights to property, including transfers received several years after the filing of the return. Thus, for example, if a requesting spouse receives from the nonrequesting spouse property (including life insurance proceeds) that is traceable to items of community income attributable to the nonrequesting spouse, the requesting spouse will have benefitted from those items of community income. Other factors may include, if the situation warrants, desertion, divorce or separation. Factors relevant to whether it would be inequitable to hold a requesting spouse liable, such as under Rev. Proc. 2013-34[258] or other applicable guidance published by the Internal Revenue Service, are to be considered in making a determination of inequitability.[259] The Internal Rev-

---

On the other hand, for cases in which the Court held that the requesting spouse did not know of, and had no reason to know of, community income, *see* Hilton v. Comm'r, T.C. Memo 1990-379; Berenbein v. Comm'r, T.C. Memo 1992-372; Costa v. Comm'r, T.C. Memo 1990-572 (Wife lived separate from nonrequesting spouse. She had no reason to know of illegal income of the nonrequesting space and did not benefit from same.); Dooley v. Comm'r, T.C. Memo 1992-39 (requesting spouse not liable on checking cashier, fees, since she was unaware of the income. But she was liable for taxes on commissions earned by nonrequesting spouse because she was aware of these.); Ollestad v. Comm'r, T.C. Memo 1996-139 (requesting spouse granted innocent spouse relief. Husband had unreported income of which wife was unaware. She completed 9th grade, married at 16 and was not involved in business of nonrequesting spouse. Moreover, she did not specifically benefit from unreported income of nonrequesting spouse.).

255. McGee v. Comm'r, 979 F.2d 66 (C.A.5, 1992), *aff'g*, T.C. Memo. 1991-510; Roberts v. Comm'r; Beck v. Comm'r, T.C. Memo. 2001-98 (Requesting spouse was aware of the income producing activity of the nonrequesting spouse because she occasionally worked in his office, often called the office to determine the amount the nonrequesting spouse made on a given day, and made deposits from the dental practice of the nonrequesting spouse into her separate bank account and their joint bank account).

256. I.R.C. § 66(c)(4); Prop. Treas. Reg. § 1.66-4(a)(3).

257. See Beck v. Comm'r, where the Court found that the requesting spouse benefited from the community income because she made significant deposits of the dental practice of the nonrequesting spouse into her separate bank account and used dental practice income to purchase more than 100 acres of property.

258. 2013-2 C.B. 397.

259. Treas. Reg. § 1.66-4(a)(3). *See* Felt v. Comm'r, T.C. Memo. 2009-245, where the taxpayer requested traditional relief, but not equitable relief. The Court looked to this regulation and concluded whether the requesting spouse's lifestyle was or was not lavish is a test for equitable relief and not for traditional relief. The taxpayer failed to establish that her standard of living fell below "normal support." *See also* Homer v. Comm'r, T.C. Memo 1994-447, where the requesting spouse's community income in issue was used to pay expenses of the requesting spouse and

enue Manual, which provides technical guidance to IRS employees who are working cases involving married taxpayers domiciled in community property states who filed separate returns or are non-filers,[260] provides that IRC § 66(c) relief is not available if the requesting spouse: (i) filed a joint return, (ii) transferred assets of the non-requesting as part of a fraudulent scheme, (iii) entered into a closing agreement that disposes of the same liability, or (iv) entered into an offer in compromise for the liability.[261]

c. Equitable Relief

A second form of "equitable relief," added by the Tax Reform Act of 1998, is available, if, taking into account all the facts and circumstances, it would be inequitable to hold the requesting spouse liable for any unpaid tax or deficiency attributable to any item for which relief is not available under the preceding traditional relief rules the IRS may relieve the requesting spouse of such liability.[262] This relief provision applies where the requesting spouse did not know and had no reason to know of the community income of the nonrequesting spouse. Equitable relief may be available when the four requirements of Section 66 (c) and Treas. Reg. § 1.66-4(a) applicable to "traditional relief," discussed earlier, are not satisfied, but it would be inequitable to hold the requesting spouse liable for the unpaid tax or deficiency. Factors relevant to whether it would be inequitable to hold a requesting spouse liable, more specifically described under the applicable administrative procedure issued under Section 66(c) (Revenue Procedure 2013-34, 2013-2 C.B. 397, discussed earlier, or other applicable guidance published by the IRS), are

---

her family, and the nonrequesting spouse was the primary source of financial support of the requesting spouse, the fourth test of section 66(c)(4) is not met because the requesting spouse benefitted from the untaxed income. *See* Roberts v. Comm'r, T.C. Memo 1987-391, *aff'd.* 860 F.2d 1235 (C.A. 5, 1987) where the Court held that the requesting spouse had no reason to know of interest income earned on certificates of deposit held by the nonrequesting spouse because the requesting spouse was unaware of the certificates of deposit. Therefore, it would be inequitable to include such item of income in the income of the requesting spouse.

260. IRM Section 25.15.5.1(1) (7.24.2017).

261. IRM Section 25.15.5.1.1(3) (7.24.2017).

262. I.R.C. § 66(c) flush language; Treas. Reg. § 1.66-4(b). Relying upon the tests set forth in Rev. Proc. 2003-61, 2003-2 C.B. 296, the Court in *Hiramanek v. Comm'r*, T.C. Memo. 2011-280, granted the taxpayer innocent spouse treatment. The Court found the requesting spouse was divorced from the nonrequesting spouse; that the requesting spouse would suffer economic hardship if the relief were denied; that she received no gifts or other benefits beyond normal support and thus did not receive significant benefit from the community income; she made a good faith effort to comply with the income tax laws in subsequent years; and was abused by the nonrequesting spouse. Whereas the traditional test asks whether it would be inequitable to include a specific item in one spouse's past income, the equitable relief test looks to the present—would it be inequitable to make that spouse pay the liability today? Felt v. Comm'r, T.C. Memo. 2009-45

to be considered in making a determination for equitable relief.[263] The standard for review of equitable relief under Section 6015(f) and the standard for review of equitable relief under Section 66(c) are the same.[264]

It should be noted that traditional relief applies only to deficiencies arising out of items of omitted income, whereas equitable relief applies to any deficiency (whether caused by omitted income or overstated deductions) or any unpaid tax.[265]

When the requesting spouse qualifies for relief under either the traditional relief provision or the equitable relief provision, the IRS must assess any deficiency of the nonrequesting spouse arising from the granting of relief to the requesting spouse in accordance with Section 6212.[266]

The following two examples illustrate the preceding rules.[267] The first example provides an item-by-item approach. H and W are married, living together, and domiciled in State A (a community property state). H and W file separate returns for taxable year 2002 on April 15, 2003. H earns $56,000 in wages, and W earns $46,000 in wages, in 2002. H reports half of his wage income as shown on his Form W-2, in the amount of $28,000, and half of W's wage income as shown on her Form W-2, in the amount of $23,000. W reports half of her wage income as shown on her W-2, in the amount of $23,000, and half of H's wage income as shown on his Form W-2, in the amount of $28,000. Neither H nor W reports W's income from her sole proprietorship of $34,000 or W's investment income of $5,000 for taxable year 2002. The Internal Revenue Service proposes deficiencies with respect to H's and W's taxable year 2002 returns due to the omission of W's income from her sole proprietorship and investments. H timely requests relief under Section 66(c). Because the IRS determines that H satisfies the four requirements of the traditional relief provision of Section 66(c) with respect to W's omitted investment income, the IRS grants H's request for relief as to the omitted investment income. The IRS determines that H does not satisfy the four requirements of the traditional relief provision of Section 66(c) as to W's sole proprietorship income. The IRS further determines that, under the equitable relief provision of Section 66(c), it is not inequitable to hold H liable for the sole proprietorship income. Relief is applicable on an item-by-item basis. Thus, H is liable for the tax on half of his wage income in the amount of $28,000, half of W's wage income in the amount of $23,000, half of W's sole

---

263. Treas. Reg. § 1.66-4(b), Prop. Treas. Reg. § 1.66-4(a)(3) and (b) (11.20.15).

264. Beck v. Comm'r, T.C. Memo. 2001-98 (Equitable relief denied because the nonrequesting spouse benefited from the income of the dental practice, failed to establish she would suffer economic hardship if the relief were denied, failed to comply with orders of the Tax Court, and failed to cooperate with the IRS in preparing for trial).

265. *Id.* § 1.66-4(c).

266. *Id.* § 1.66-4(d).

267. *Id.* § 1.66-4(e).

proprietorship income in the amount of $17,000, but none of W's investment income, for which H obtained relief under Section 66(c). W is liable for the tax on half of H's wage income in the amount of $28,000, half of W's wage income in the amount of $23,000, half of W's sole proprietorship income in the amount of $17,000, and all of W's investment income in the amount of $5,000, because H obtained relief under Section 66(c).

The second example provides a benefit approach. H and W are married, living together, and domiciled in State B (a community property state). Neither H nor W files a return for taxable year 2000. H earns $60,000 in 2000, which he deposits in a joint account. H and W pay the mortgage payment, household bills, and other family expenses out of the joint account. W earns $20,000 in 2000. W uses a portion of the $20,000 to make monthly loan payments on the family cars but loses the remainder at the local racetrack. In 2002, the IRS audits H and W. H requests relief under Section 66(c), stating that he did not know or have reason to know of W's additional income, as H travels extensively while W handles the family finances. Regardless of whether H had knowledge or reason to know of the source of W's income, H is not eligible for traditional relief under Section 66(c) because H benefitted from W's income. H's benefit, the portion of W's income used to make monthly payments on the car loans, was more than a de minimis amount. While this benefit was not in excess of normal support, it is enough to preclude relief under the traditional relief provision of Section 66(c). H may still qualify for equitable relief under Section 66(c), depending on all of the facts and circumstances.

d. Miscellaneous

If the IRS establishes that a spouse transferred assets to his or her spouse as part of a fraudulent scheme, neither traditional relief nor equitable relief is available. A fraudulent scheme includes a scheme to defraud the IRS or another third party, such as a creditor, ex-spouse, or business partner.[268]

A requesting spouse is not entitled to relief from the Federal income tax liability resulting from the operation of community property law under Section 66 for any taxable year for which the requesting spouse has entered into a closing agreement (other than an agreement pursuant to Section 6224(c) relating to partnership items) with the IRS that disposes of the same liability that is the subject of the request for relief or has entered into an offer in compromise.[269]

A taxpayer has three opportunities to request relief from the Federal income tax liability resulting from the operation of community property law under Section 66. First, the requesting spouse must file, within the time period prescribed below, Form 8857, "Request for Innocent Spouse Relief" (or other

268. Treas. Reg. § 1.66-4(f), *See also* Felt v. Comm'r, T.C. Memo. 2009-245.

269. Treas. Reg. § 1.66-4(h).

specified form), or other written request, signed under penalties of perjury, stating why relief is appropriate. The requesting spouse must include the nonrequesting spouse's name and taxpayer identification number in the written request. The requesting spouse must also comply with the IRS's reasonable requests for information that will assist the IRS in identifying and locating the nonrequesting spouse.[270] Second, if the taxpayer contests a notice of deficiency by filing a petition with the United States Tax Court, the taxpayer should raise the innocent spouse request in the petition as an affirmative defense. Finally, the taxpayer may still raise Section 66(c) equitable defense relief as a defense in any collection hearing under Section 6330. This gives the taxpayer three bites at the apple of innocent spouse equitable relief.[271]

The earliest time for submitting a request for traditional relief from the Federal income tax liability for an amount under reported on, or omitted from, the requesting spouse's separate return, is the date the requesting spouse receives notification of an audit or a letter or notice from the IRS stating that there may be an outstanding liability with regard to that year. The latest time for requesting traditional relief is 6 months before the expiration of the period of limitations on assessment, including extensions, against the nonrequesting spouse for the taxable year that is the subject of the request for relief, unless the examination of the requesting spouse's return commences during that 6-month period, in which case the latest time for requesting traditional relief is 30 days after the commencement of the examination.[272]

The earliest time for submitting a request for equitable relief from the Federal income tax liability is the date the requesting spouse receives notification of an audit or a letter or notice from the IRS stating that there may be an outstanding liability with regard to that year. A request for equitable relief from the Federal income tax liability resulting from the operation of community property law for a liability that is properly reported but unpaid is properly submitted with the requesting spouse's individual Federal income tax return, or after the requesting spouse's individual Federal income tax return is filed.[273]

The IRS will not consider a premature request for relief under Section 66(c). The notices or letters referenced earlier do not include notices issued pursuant to Section 6223 relating to TEFRA partnership proceedings. These notices or letters include notices of computational adjustment to a partner or partner's spouse (Notice of Income Tax Examination Changes) that reflect a computation

270. Treas. Reg. § 1.66-4(j)(1).

271. Felt v. Comm'r, T.C. Memo. 2009-245 (equitable relief denied where taxpayer failed to file Form 8857 and failed to request equitable relief in the petition).

272. Treas. Reg. § 1.66-4(j)(2)(i); *See* Felt v. Comm'r.

273. Treas. Reg. § 1.66-4(j)(2)(ii).

of the liability attributable to partnership items of the partner or the partner's spouse.[274]

When the IRS receives a request for traditional or equitable relief from the Federal income tax liability resulting from the operation of community property law, the IRS must send a notice to the nonrequesting spouse's last known address that informs the nonrequesting spouse of the requesting spouse's request for relief. The notice must provide the nonrequesting spouse with an opportunity to submit any information for consideration in determining whether to grant the requesting spouse relief from the Federal income tax liability resulting from the operation of community property law. The IRS must share with each spouse the information submitted by the other spouse, unless the IRS determines that the sharing of this information will impair tax administration.[275] The IRS will consider all of the information (as relevant to the particular relief provision) that the nonrequesting spouse submits in determining whether to grant relief from the Federal income tax liability resulting from the operation of community property law under this Section.[276]

17. Credit or Refund

Notwithstanding any other law or rule of law (except as provided in Section 6511 (pertaining to limitations on credits or refunds), Section 6512(b) (pertaining to overpayments determined by the U.S. Tax Court), Section 7121 (pertaining to closing agreements), and Section 7122 (pertaining to compromises), credit or refund shall be allowed or made to the extent attributable to the application of Section 6015.[277] Notwithstanding the foregoing, in the case of a request for (b), (c), or (f) relief, if a decision of a Court in any prior proceeding for the same taxable year has become final, the decision shall be conclusive, except with respect to the qualification of the individual for relief which was not an issue in the prior proceeding.[278] No refund or credit is allowed for a request for (c) relief.[279]

The Proposed Regulations adopt new standard for a requesting spouse to receive a credit or refund of tax liability. A requesting spouse who is eligible for relief can receive a credit or refund of payments made to satisfy the joint income tax liability, whether the liability resulted from an understatement or an underpayment.[280]

274. Treas. Reg. § 1.66-4(j)(2)(iii).
275. Treas. Reg. § 1.66-4(k)(1).
276. Treas. Reg. § 1.66-4(k)(2).
277. Section 6015(g)(1).
278. Section 6015(g)(2).
279. Section 6015(g)(3); Rivera v. Comm'r, T.C. Memo. 2005-33.
280. Prop. Treas. Reg. § 1.6015-1(k)(1) (12-20-2015).

There are, however four situations in which the Proposed Regulations disallow a requesting spouse a credit or refund, or limit the credit or refund. First, a requesting spouse is not entitled to a credit or refund of any payments made on the joint income tax liability as a result of allocating the deficiency under Treas. Reg. § 1.6015-3.[281] In other words, no credit or refund is allowed as a result of an election under Section 6015(c).[282]

Second, a request for (f) relief may not be used to circumvent the limitation of no refunds as a result of a (c) election. Therefore, relief is not available to obtain a credit or refund of liabilities already paid, for which the requesting spouse would otherwise qualify for (c) relief under Treas. Reg. § 1.6015-3. For purposes of determining whether the requesting spouse qualifies for (c) relief, the fact that a refund is barred by Section 6015(g)(3) and Prop. Treas. Reg. § 1.6015-1(k)(2) does not mean that the requesting spouse did not receive full relief. A requesting spouse is entitled to full relief under Treas. Reg. § 1.6015-3 if the requesting spouse is eligible to allocate the deficiency in full to the nonrequesting spouse.[283]

Third, the availability of a credit or refund is subject to the limitations provided by Sections 6511[284] and 6512(b).[285] Generally, the filing of Form 8857, "Request for Innocent Spouse Relief," is treated as the filing of a claim for credit or refund even if the requesting spouse does not specifically request a credit or refund. The amount allowable as a credit or refund, assuming the requesting spouse is eligible for relief, includes payments made after the filing of the Form 8857, as well as payments made within the applicable look-back period provided by Section 6511 (b).[286]

Finally, a requesting spouse is only eligible for a credit or refund of payments to the extent the requesting spouse establishes that he or she provided the funds used to make the payment for which he or she seeks a credit or refund. Thus, a requesting spouse is not eligible for a credit or refund of payments made by the nonrequesting spouse. A requesting spouse is also generally not eligible for a credit or refund of joint payments made with the nonrequesting spouse. A requesting spouse, however, may be eligible for a credit or refund of the requesting spouse's portion of an overpayment from a joint return filed with the nonrequesting spouse that was offset under Section 6402 to the

281. Prop. Treas. Reg. § 1.6015-1(k)(2) (12-20-2015).

282. I.R.C. § 6015(g)(3).

283. Prop. Treas. Reg. § 1.6015-1(k)(3) (12-20-2015).

284. Section 6511 limits the allowance of credits or refunds if the claim for credit or refund is not filed within the period of limitations for filing a claim.

285. Section 6512(b) grants the Tax Court the jurisdiction to determine the amount of an overpayment which, when the decision becomes final, may be credited or refunded to the taxpayer.

286. Prop. Treas. Reg. § 1.6015-1(k)(4) (12-20-2015).

spouses' joint income tax liability, to the extent that the requesting spouse can establish his or her contribution to the overpayment.[287]

18. Injured Spouse

Although his chapter has focused on the concept of "innocent spouse" under Section 6015, there is also a concept known as "injured spouse" under Section 6402. Generally, "innocent spouse" status provides that the requesting spouse will not be responsible for the payment of taxes that may be due as a result of the understatement of tax liability by the nonrequesting spouse. On the other hand, "injured spouse" status permits the injured spouse to receive a refund of his or her interest in a joint refund that the IRS has retained to offset a debt of the nonrequesting spouse, such as a debt owed for Federal or State income taxes, student loans, child or spousal support owed to a State, or State unemployment compensation debts.

To qualify for an injured spouse claim, six tests must be met. First, the requesting spouse must have filed a joint return with the nonrequesting spouse.[288] Second, the requesting spouse must not have been responsible for a legally enforceable debt of the nonrequesting spouse.[289] For example, such a debt may be a debt for a student loan incurred by the nonrequesting spouse before the parties married. Third, the requesting spouse must have reported income on the joint return filed with the nonrequesting spouse on which he or she reported income from wages, self-employment income or investment income and some of the refund is attributable to this reported income. Fourth, the requesting spouse must have paid taxes on that income. Fifth, all or part of the requesting spouse's overpayment must have been applied against the debt of the nonrequesting spouse. Finally, the reporting spouse must be entitled to all or a portion of the tax refund or be entitled to a refundable tax credit, such as the earned income credit or the child tax credit.

An injured spouse claim is made by filing IRS Form 8379. The form may be filed by the spouse on a jointly filed income tax return when the joint overpayment was applied or offset against a past due obligation of the other spouse. The purpose is for the injured spouse to get back his or her share of the refund. The Form 8379 must be filed for each year for which the injured spouse wants his or her portion of any offset refunded.

---

287. Prop. Treas. Reg. § 1.6015-1(k)(5) (122-7-2015).

288. See Chapter 10 where the existence of a joint return is discussed.

289. The debt must be one described in section 6402. These include offset of past due support against overpayments, collection of past-due legally enforceable state income tax obligations, and collection of unemployment compensation debts (I.R.C. § 6402(c)–(f)).

Form 8379 should be filed as soon as the injured spouse becomes aware that his or her share of any refund is being applied against his or her spouse's legally enforceable past due obligation. Generally, the injured spouse becomes aware that his or her share of any refund is being applied against his or her spouse's legally enforceable past due obligation when the injured spouse receives a Notice of Offset from the IRS. Thus, the injured spouse may attach Form 8379 to the original return, to an amended return, or by itself if the taxpayer receives a Notice of Offset. If the Form 8379 is filed by itself, it must list both spouse's Social Security numbers and be signed by the requesting spouse.

12 Gift Tax Aspects

A. General Rule

I.R.C. §§ 2501 and 2512 impose a gift tax on a donor of property for transfers of property for "less than full and adequate consideration in money or money's worth." The amount of the gift is the excess of the value of the property transferred over the consideration received. Treas. Reg. § 25.25128 provides that the relinquishment or promised relinquishment of dower, curtesy, or other marital rights in a spouse's property or estate does not constitute consideration.[1] Thus, a transfer of property by one spouse to another in exchange for the release of the marital rights of the other spouse constitutes a taxable gift, unless any of the six exceptions discussed in this Chapter apply.

In Rev. Rul. 79312,[2] the signature of the payee spouse was required to sell property in the payor spouse's name alone. The payee spouse agreed to sign if she received one-half of the proceeds. The transaction occurred before the divorce and the agreement made no mention of the property sold. Under state law the payee spouse was deemed to have an inchoate interest in the property. The Service held that the entire gain on the sale was taxable to the payor spouse for income tax purposes, and the transfer of proceeds to the payee spouse was a gift, taxable to the payor spouse for gift tax purposes. One solution to the problem presented in Rev. Rul. 79312, is for the payor spouse to have a property settlement agreement with the payee spouse and to have transferred the property to him or her pursuant to such agreement. Such a transfer may be deemed a property settlement covered by Section 1041. Another solution is through use of the unlimited Federal gift tax marital deduction discussed below.

1. *See also* Merrill v. Fahs, 324 U.S. 308 (1945); Comm'r v. Wemyss, 324 U.S. 303 (1945).
2. 1979-2 C.B. 29.

B. Exceptions

1. Transfers Pursuant to a Court Decree

The first exception is where the transfer is pursuant to a court decree. A transfer of property in exchange for the release of marital rights, made pursuant to a court decree, does not constitute a gift. The Court's reasoning in *Harris v. Commissioner*[3] was that an agreement adopted by a court imposed an obligation to transfer, which, therefore, could not constitute a gift. Thus, to be excepted from the gift tax, not only must the payments be made pursuant to a court decree, but also the payments must be made for the release of marital rights.

If, however, the transfer is pursuant to an agreement between the parties, this exception does not apply, unless the agreement is incorporated in the decree and the court issuing the decree has the power to alter or modify the agreement,[4] or unless the tests of I.R.C. § 2516, discussed next, are met.[5]

Unlike I.R.C. § 2516, the decree does not have to be a final decree of divorce, but may be a decree of support or separate maintenance, or an interlocutory decree. Also unlike I.R.C. § 2516, payments for the support of an adult child may be treated as a nontaxable gift under this exception, whereas payments for the support of an adult child under I.R.C. § 2516 are treated as taxable gifts. Payments for the support of a minor child may fall within either this exception or the next exception.

2. Transfers Pursuant to a Separation Agreement — I.R.C. § 2516

a. Tests

The second exception is where the transfer is pursuant to a written separation agreement and the divorce takes place within a fixed period of time after the written separation agreement is entered into. I.R.C. § 2516 provides that transfers of property or interests in property pursuant to a written separation agreement[6] do not constitute a gift if the following three tests are met:

3. 340 U.S. 106 (1950).

4. McMurtry v. Comm'r, 203 F.2d 659 (1st Cir. 1953).

5. *Compare* Rev. Rul. 60-160, 1960-1 C.B. 374 (not only must the agreement be incorporated into the decree, but also the Court must have the power, under state law, to settle all property rights of the parties or to modify the terms of the agreement) *with* Natchez v. United States, 705 F.2d 671 (2d Cir. N.Y. 1983) (an agreement incorporated into the decree is sufficient if the Court had the power to approve the agreement. Thus, an estate tax deduction was allowed for a bequest made pursuant to a separation agreement.).

6. *See* Chapter 1, B.2.c.1 for a discussion of a written separation agreement in the context of alimony payments under I.R.C. § 71. Neither Section 2516 nor the regulations promulgated thereunder define "written agreement" for purposes of Section 2516.

First, the payor spouse and payee spouse enter into a written separation agreement relative to their marital and property rights. An oral agreement will not suffice.[7]

Second, the parties are divorced within the three-year period beginning on the date one year before the agreement is entered into and ending on the date two years after the agreement is entered into, whether or not such agreement is approved by the divorce decree. Thus, the parties must enter into a written separation agreement within two years before and one year after the divorce.

The divorce must be a "final decree of divorce."[8] Thus, the divorce must be a vinculo and not a mensa et thoro. A divorce a mensa et thoro is not a final divorce but a temporary divorce where the parties are separated from bed and board but are still married. A decree of support or separate maintenance does not satisfy this requirement. The agreement does not have to be incorporated into the decree.

The three-year period is inflexible. Modifications of the agreement must also take place within the three-year period.[9] Thus, if the modification occurs more than two years before or more than one year after the divorce, payments made pursuant to the modification will be treated as gifts. The two-year period refers only to the time within which a divorce must occur after the agreement has been executed. It does not refer to the time within which the property must be transferred. Thus, it would appear that the property can be transferred at any time before, during, or after the divorce.

Third, any transfers of property or interests in property pursuant to the agreement are in settlement of a spouse's marital or property rights or provide a reasonable allowance for the support of minor children of the marriage. This includes transfers to adopted and natural children.[10] Transfers to an adult child are not covered by I.R.C. § 2516 and thus are deemed gifts. Transfers to an adult child, however, may fit within the decree exception just discussed. Neither Section 2516 nor the regulations promulgated thereunder define "minority." Although one cannot state with certainty, the age of minority would appear to be based on local law, which varies from jurisdiction to jurisdiction.

Query whether the written separation agreement has to be legally enforceable. For purposes of the alimony provisions of Section 71 requiring the payments to be made pursuant to a decree of divorce or separate maintenance,

---

7. *See* Priv. Ltr. Rul. 200519011 where the IRS held that I.R.C. § 2516 did not apply to the determination of the taxability of the transfer of options between a spouse and former spouse incident to a divorce since the parties did not enter into any agreement relative to their marital and property rights in the options within the three-year period prescribed in I.R.C. § 2516.

8. Treas. Reg. § 25.25161(a).

9. Rev. Rul. 79118, 19791 C.B. 315. The three-year period was extended by the 1984 TRA, effective for transfers made after July 18, 1984. Before the 1984 TRA, the parties had to be divorced within two years after the date of the agreement.

10. Treas. Reg. § 25.2516-2.

the Service has ruled that the written separation agreement does not have to be legally enforceable.[11] Thus, it would appear that the same informalities for written separation agreements for alimony purposes should apply to written separation agreements for gift tax purposes.

b. Incorporation

If an I.R.C. § 2516 agreement is incorporated into the decree, both the first exception and this exception would seem to apply, whereas if the agreement is merged into the decree, the first exception would seem to control.[12]

c. Transfer to Trust

A transfer to a trust for the benefit of the payee spouse or minor child qualifies for nongift treatment.[13] If the payee spouse or minor child is to receive only income from the trust, only the value of his or her income interest qualifies for I.R.C. § 2516 nongift tax treatment.[14]

d. Prenuptial Agreement

Unless monetary consideration passes to the donor, a transfer of property pursuant to a prenuptial agreement is not protected by I.R.C. § 2516 and, therefore, constitutes a gift.[15]

e. Release of Rights

Release of support rights in exchange for the transfer of an income interest is exempt from federal gift tax.[16]

In Priv. Ltr. Rul. 200442003, the IRS held that the payment of a lump sum of money by the husband to the wife in exchange for the wife's community property interest in a nonqualified deferred compensation plan payable to the husband by his company was a transfer "for full and adequate consideration in money or money's worth" under I.R.C. § 2516 that will not result in a taxable gift by either the husband or the wife to the other. The transfer of the lump sum payment by the husband to the wife was made pursuant to a Judgement of Dissolution. The transfer was in full satisfaction of the wife's interest in the SERP. Accordingly, the IRS concluded that, to the extent of the wife's interest in the nonqualified deferred compensation plan, the transfer of a lump sum will be deemed made for full and adequate consideration in money or money's worth

11. *See* Chapter 1, B.2.c.(1)(b).
12. See the discussion at Chapter 1.B.2.c.(2)(g) regarding the doctrine of incorporation and the doctrine of merger.
13. Rev. Rul. 7573, 19751 C.B. 313; Rev. Rul. 57506, 19572 C.B. 616.
14. Rev. Rul. 79363, 19792 C.B. 345.
15. Comm'r v. Wemyss, 324 U.S. 303 (1945).
16. Spruance v. Comm'r, 60 T.C. 141 (1973).

under I.R.C. § 2516, and therefore the exchange will not result in a taxable gift by the husband or the wife to the other.

3. Transfers for Support

The third exception is where the transfer is made pursuant to a legal obligation of support. A transfer of property made by one spouse for the legal obligation of support of the other, or for the legal obligation for the support of their minor children, does not constitute a gift, provided the value of the property transferred does not exceed the reasonable value of such rights of support.[17] But if the value of the property transferred exceeds the reasonable value of the rights of support, the excess may constitute a gift, unless the other exceptions apply.[18] The value of support can also be fixed by agreement.[19]

4. Gift Tax Marital Deduction

The fourth exception involves the unlimited Federal gift tax marital deduction. A transfer made between spouses before the divorce is not a taxable gift because of the unlimited gift tax marital deduction.[20] As a result of this provision, a gift of property between separated (not divorced) spouses is not subject to the Federal gift tax.

Thus, to avoid the gift tax, assuming none of the other exceptions apply, it is recommended that the transfer be made while the spouses are married in order to take advantage of the unlimited Federal gift tax marital deduction. Since the transfer is not deemed a gift, the basis of the property in the hands of the donee will be determined by reference to the basis of the property in the hands of the donor (i.e., carryover basis).[21]

The unlimited Federal gift tax marital deduction is allowed for transfers of qualified terminable interest property[22] as described in Section 2523(f)(2). Terminable interests described in Section 2523(b)(2) do not qualify as qualified terminable interest property. Section 2523(f)(2) provides that qualified terminable interest property is property that is transferred by the donor spouse to the donee spouse, the donee spouse has a qualifying income interest for life, and an election to treat the property as qualified terminable interest property is made by filing a gift tax return with respect to the transfer.

---

17. Rev. Rul. 77314, 19772 C.B. 349; Rev. Rul. 68379, 19682 C.B. 414. Treas. Reg. § 25-2516-2.

18. *Id.*; Rev. Rul. 7167, 19711 C.B. 271. (Look to income, worth of payor, and standard of living to determine the reasonable value of the right of support.) *See also* Fenton v. Comm'r, 70 T.C. 263 (1978) (Look to husband's annual income, extent of his assets, relative ages of parties, and probability of wife's remarriage).

19. Harding v. Comm'r, 11 T.C. 1051 (1948).

20. I.R.C. § 2523.

21. I.R.C. § 1041(b)(2).

22. I.R.C. § 2523; Prop. Treas. Reg. 25.2523(f)-1(a)(i).

5. Annual Exclusion

The fifth exception to the gift tax is the gift tax annual exclusion. This exclusion allows the donor to make an unlimited number of gifts to an unlimited number of donees, provided the amount of the gift does not exceed the annual exclusion. The annual exclusion for 2022 is $16,000 per donee. The $16,000 (adjusted for inflation in 2022) per donee annual gift tax exclusion for gifts of present interests in property applies whether the transfer occurs during or after the marriage.[23] The annual exclusion applies to gifts of a present interest (i.e., where the donee has the unrestricted right to the immediate use, possession, and enjoyment of the property or the income from the property).

No part of the value of a gift of a future interest may be excluded in determining the total amount of gifts made during the "calendar period." "Future interest" is a legal term, and includes reversions, remainders, and other interests or estates, whether vested or contingent, and whether or not comported by a particular interest or estate, which are limited to commence in use, possession, or enjoyment at some future date or time. The term has no reference to such contractual rights as exist in a bond, note (though bearing no interest until maturity), or in a policy of life insurance, the obligations of which are to be discharged by payments in the future. But a future interest or interests in such contractual obligations may be created by the limitations contained in a trust or other instrument of transfer used in effecting a gift.[24]

An unrestricted right to the immediate use, possession, or enjoyment of property or the income from property (such as a life estate or term certain) is a present interest in property. An exclusion is allowable with respect to a gift of such an interest (but not in excess of the value of the interest). If a donee has received a present interest in property, the possibility that such interest may be diminished by the transfer of a greater interest in the same property to the donee through the exercise of a power is disregarded in computing the value

23. I.R.C. § 2503(b); Rev. Proc. 2021-45, IRB 2021-48 (11.29.21). Specifically, the statute provides that the first $10,000 of gifts of present interests per donee per year, *adjusted for inflation*, will not be subject to federal gift tax. As a result of inflation, the annual exclusion for 2004 through 2023 is as follows:

Tax Years	Annual Exclusion
2004–2005	$11,000
2006–2008	$12,000
2009–2012	$13,000
2013–2017	$14,000
2018–2021	$15,000
2021–2022	$16,000
2022–2023	$17,000

I.R.C. § 2503(b)(2).

24. Treas. Reg. § 25-2503-3(a).

of the present interest, to the extent that no part of such interest will at any time pass to any other person.[25]

6. Tuition and Medical Expenses

The final exception applies to payments of tuition and medical expenses. Direct payments of tuition to an educational institution described in Section 170(b)(1)(A)(ii)[26] for the education or training of the intended donee or to any person for who provides medical care (as defined in Section 213(d)) with respect to such individual as payment for such medical care (including insurance premiums) are excluded from gift tax.[27] These include voluntary payments, payments made pursuant to an agreement or court order, and payments made directly to the educational institution or medical provider.[28]

a. Qualifying Educational Expenses

Only payments of tuition are excluded from gift tax. Payment for books, supplies, dormitory fees, room, and board or other similar expenses are not excluded from gift tax.[29] The tuition may be for a full-time or part-time student paid directly to the qualifying educational institution.[30] The payments must be made to an educational institution that normally maintains a regular faculty and curriculum and normally has a regularly enrolled body of pupils or students in attendance at the place where its educational activities are regularly carried on.[31]

b. Direct Payments

The payment must be made *directly* to the educational institution or medical provider.[32] Reimbursements to the student or person who requires medical treatment, or to a trust who then uses the funds to pay school tuition or the medical provider, do not qualify for the exclusion.[33]

---

25. Treas. Reg. § 25-2503-3(b).
26. These are educational organizations that normally maintain a regular faculty and curriculum and normally have a regularly enrolled body of pupils or students in attendance at the place where its educational activities are regularly carried on. Prop. Treas. Reg. § 25-2503-6(b)(2).
27. I.R.C. § 2503(e).
28. Treas. Reg. § 25.2503-6.
29. Treas. Reg. § 25.25036(b)(2) & (3).
30. Treas. Reg. § 25.25036(b)(2).
31. Treas. Reg§ 170(b)(1)(A)(ii).
32. Treas. Reg. § 25.25036(b)(1).
33. I.R.C. § 2503(e)(2); Treas. Reg. §§ 25.25036(b)(2)and 25.25036(c), examples 3 and 4.

c. Qualifying Medical Expenses

Qualifying medical expenses include only those defined in I.R.C. § 213(d) and include expenses incurred for the diagnosis, cure, mitigation, treatment, or prevention of disease, or for the purpose of affecting any structure or function of the body or for transportation primarily for and essential to medical care.[34] Also included are amounts paid for medical insurance on behalf of any individual.[35] The exclusion does not apply, however, to amounts paid for medical care that are reimbursed by the donee's insurance.[36] The payments must be made directly to the medical provider.

d. Amount Excludable

The exclusion of tuition and medical expenses from gift tax treatment is available in addition to the applicability of the $17,000 annual exclusion.[37] Thus, if a payment of tuition and/or medical expenses is not excluded from gift tax treatment under this special rule, it may still be excludable under the $17,000 annual exclusion. For example, if a divorced parent pays $17,000 directly to a university for a child's tuition and also pays $16,000 for books, room, and board, the tuition payment is excluded from gift tax, as is $17,000 for books, room, and board.

e. Relationship

The exclusion is permitted without regard to the relationship between the donor and the donee.[38]

f. Examples

Treas. Reg. § 25.2503-6(c) provides the following four examples, which illustrate the preceding rules (modified to the current year):

(1) In 2022, *A* made a tuition payment directly to a foreign university on behalf of *B*. *A* had no legal obligation to make this payment. The foreign university is described in I.R.C. § 170(b)(1)(A)(ii). *A*'s tuition payments are exempt from the gift tax under I.R.C. § 2503(e).

(2) *A* transfers $100,000 to a trust, the provisions of which state that the funds are to be used for tuition expenses incurred by *A*'s grandchildren. *A*'s transfer to the trust is a completed gift for Federal gift tax

34. Treas. Reg. § 25.25036(b)(3).
35. *Id.*
36. *Id.*
37. Treas. Reg. § 25.25036(a).
38. Treas. Reg. § 25.25036(a). See note 23 in this chapter for the gift tax annual exclusion for tax years 2004–2023. This amount will likely increase in the future since it is adjusted annually for inflation.

purposes and is not a direct transfer to an educational organization and does not qualify for the unlimited exclusion from gift tax under I.R.C. § 2503(e).

(3) *C* was seriously injured in an automobile accident in 2022. *D*, who is unrelated to *C*, paid *C*'s various medical expenses by checks made payable to the physician. *D* also paid the hospital for *C*'s hospital bills. These medical and hospital expenses were of the type described in I.R.C. § 213 and were not reimbursed by insurance or otherwise. Because the medical and hospital bills paid in 2022 for *C* were medical expenses within the meaning of I.R.C. § 213 of the Code, and since they were paid directly by *D* to the person rendering the medical care, they are not treated as transfers subject to the gift tax.

(4) Assume the same facts as in example (3) except that instead of making the payments directly to the medical service provider, *D* reimbursed *C* for the medical expenses that *C* had previously paid. The payments made by *D* to *C* do not qualify for the exclusion under I.R.C. § 2503 and are subject to the gift tax on the date the reimbursement is received by *C*, to the extent the reimbursement and all other gifts from *D* to *C* during the year of the reimbursement exceed the $17,000 annual exclusion provided in I.R.C. § 2503(b).

7. Transfers of Interests in Trust or Other Property Special Valuation Rules—I.R.C. § 2702[39]

a. General Rule

When a person creates a trust or makes another transfer of property that provides a beneficial interest (e.g., an income interest for life) to his or her spouse (or former spouse) and the remainder interest to a member of his or her family, the special valuation rules set forth in I.R.C. § 2702 must be considered. These rules may apply not only to a transfer in trust but to any transfer of an interest in property in which there is a temporary interest and a remainder interest, such as a transfer to a spouse or former spouse of a life estate in a residence owned by transferor where the remainder is to pass to the children at the end of the term interest. For purposes of the following discussion, these rules will be described in terms of a transfer to a trust.

I.R.C. § 2702 applies to transfers of interests in a trust for the benefit of a "member of the family" (as defined in I.R.C. § 2704(c)(2) to mean transferor's spouse, any ancestor or lineal descendant of the transferor or transferor's spouse, any sibling of the transferor, and the spouse of any such person) when the transferor or "applicable family member" (as defined in I.R.C. § 2701(e)(2)

39. The author wishes to thank Marcia C. Fidis, Esq. of Pasternak & Fidis, P.C. for preparing this section on Gift Tax Aspects.

to mean the transferor's spouse, an ancestor of the transferor or the transferor's spouse, and the spouse of any such ancestor) retains or is provided an interest in the same trust.

With a few exceptions, I.R.C. § 2702 provides that if a taxpayer transfers assets to a trust and grants a member of his or her family an interest in the trust, then the value of any interest the taxpayer or an "applicable family member" of the taxpayer has in the trust shall be valued at zero. As a result, the value of the gift of remaining interest in the trust (e.g., a remainder interest granted to the taxpayer's children) for gift tax purposes shall equal the total value of the property the taxpayer transferred to the trust without reduction for the retained interest.

Even though a transfer of property in trust to a spouse (or former spouse) of a beneficial interest pursuant to a marital agreement may be excluded from gift tax if the agreement falls within the "window" of I.R.C. § 2516 (since such transfers are deemed to be for full and adequate consideration, as discussed), such transfer may nevertheless be subject to the special valuation rules of I.R.C. § 2702 if a member of the transferorspouse's family also is given a beneficial interest in the trust.

There is an exception to these special valuation rules in the case of a transfer of a beneficial interest in a trust to a spouse if the transferorspouse retains the remainder interest in the trust.[40] For example, if, pursuant to an agreement that is described in I.R.C. § 2516 (discussed earlier), a taxpayer transfers property to a trust that is required to pay all of the income to his or her spouse (or former spouse) for a ten-year period (or for life) and if the taxpayer retains the remainder interest in the trust (i.e., the principal reverts to the taxpayer at the end of his or her spouse's interest), then the special valuation rules set forth in I.R.C. § 2702 do not apply. However, if the remainder interest in the trust passes to a member of the taxpayer's family (e.g., his or her children or siblings) at the end of the spouse's interest, then according to the regulations, the special valuation rules do apply for purposes of determining of the value of the gift of the remainder interest for gift tax purpose.

If the foregoing exception does not apply because the remainder interest in the trust does not revert to the taxpayer, then the "joint purchase" regulations may apply.[41] These regulations treat the transferee-spouse (i.e., the spouse who acquired the beneficial interest in the trust) as if he or she had acquired (or purchased) all of the property transferred the trust and then had transferred the remainder to the beneficiaries who are to receive the property at the end of the transferee-spouse's interest. Because I.R.C. § 2702 values the interest "retained" by the transferee-spouse at zero, that spouse is treated as having

40. Treas. Reg. § 25.27021(c)(7).
41. Treas. Reg. § 25.27024(c).

made a gift of the entire property transferred to the trust (less the value of any consideration paid by the beneficiaries receiving the remainder interest). Thus, under the "joint purchase" regulations of I.R.C. § 2702, if pursuant to an agreement described in I.R.C. § 2516, a husband transfers $2,000,000 to a trust that provides his wife with a lifetime income interest and provides that the remainder interest passes to their children upon the wife's death, the wife is treated as having made a gift to the children. However, the value of the gift to the children is limited to the consideration the wife paid to obtain the interests in the trust. If the value of the consideration paid by the wife (i.e., the value of the rights the wife relinquished) was equal to her income interest ($1,300,000) then the deemed taxable gift by the wife is equal to $1,300,000, the consideration paid by the wife for all interests in the property. The remainder interest of $700,000 would be deemed a gift by the husband.

b. Exceptions

As mentioned earlier, if the transferor-spouse retains the remainder interest in the property gifted pursuant to an agreement described in I.R.C. § 2516, I.R.C. § 2702 does not apply.[42]

If the transfer of the remainder to a person other than the transferor is not a completed gift (for instance because the transferor has retained certain powers to change the beneficiaries) then I.R.C. § 2702 does not apply.[43]

If the interest given to the transferee-spouse is a "qualified interest," such interest will not have a zero value under I.R.C. § 2702. A "qualified interest" includes (1) a fixed amount payable at least annually, or (2) a fixed percentage of the fair market value of the property in trust determined and paid at least annually. The value of the qualified interest as well as the gift of the remainder interest is then determined under the valuation rules and tables of IRC I.R.C. § 7520. Please note that a life income interest to spouse that will meet the requirements of the Qualified Terminable Interest Property rules of I.R.C. § 2057(b) to qualify the transfer to the spouse for the unlimited marital deduction from estate and gift tax does not constitute a "qualified interest" for purposes of avoiding I.R.C. § 2702.

If the transferor transfers a residence to a Qualified Personal Residence Trust that meets the rules applicable to this kind of trust, then the special valuation rules of I.R.C. § 2702 do not apply.[44]

42. Treas. Reg. § 25.27021(c)(7).
43. I.R.C. § 2702 (a)(3)(B).
44. I.R.C. 2702 (a)(3)(A)(ii); Treas. Reg. § 25.2702-5(c).

8. Gift Tax Return

A gift tax return must set forth each gift made during the calendar year that under Sections 2511 through 2515 is to be included in computing taxable gifts; the deductions claimed and allowable under Sections 2521 through 2524; and the taxable gifts made for each of the preceding reporting periods.[45] Section 2516 provides that certain transfers of property pursuant to written property settlements between husband and wife are deemed to be transfers for full and adequate consideration in money or money's worth if divorce occurs within two years. In any case where a husband and wife enter into a written agreement of the type contemplated by Section 2516 and the final decree of divorce is not granted on or before the due date for the filing of a gift tax return for the calendar year in which the agreement became effective (see Treas. Reg Section 25.6075-1), then, except to the extent Treas. Reg. Section 25.6019-1 provides otherwise, the transfer must be disclosed by the transferor upon a gift tax return filed for the calendar year in which the agreement becomes effective, and a copy of the agreement must be attached to the return. In addition, a certified copy of the final divorce decree must be furnished to the internal revenue officer with whom the return was filed not later than 60 days after the divorce is granted. Pending receipt of evidence that the final decree of divorce has been granted (but in no event for a period of more than two years from the effective date of the agreement), the transfer will tentatively be treated as made for a full and adequate consideration in money or money's worth.[46]

45. Treas. Reg. § 25.6019-3(a).
46. *Id.* Treas. Reg. § 25.6019-3(b).

13 Estate Tax Aspects

A. Deduction of Payments

1. Introduction

If the payor spouse is required to make payments beyond his or her death, are the payments deductible by the estate? For example, if a divorce or separation instrument requires the payor spouse to pay the payee spouse $5,000 per year for five years as a property settlement, and the payor spouse dies after year two, and the payor's estate is obligated to make the remaining three payments, is the estate entitled to deduct the obligation?

2. General Rule

a. Court Decree

An obligation imposed on an estate as a result of a court decree is deductible by the estate. I.R.C. § 2053(c)(1)(A) also allows a deduction for claims made against the estate founded on a promise or agreement to the extent such claims were contracted bona fide and for adequate and full consideration in money or money's worth.[1] Transfers of property pursuant to I.R.C. § 2043(b)(2) and I.R.C. § 2516 are deemed to be for adequate consideration.

b. Support Rights

The release of support rights or an obligation to support a minor child are considered adequate consideration and, therefore, are deductible as a claim against the estate.[2] On the other hand, the release of support rights for an adult child is not deductible.[3]

1. Harris v. Comm'r, 340 U.S. 106 (1950).
2. Rev. Rul. 71-67,1971-1 C.B. 271. *See also* Estate of Kosow v. Comm'r, discussed in the text at note 6 in this chapter.
3. Estate of Keller v. Comm'r, 44 T.C. 851 (1965).

3. Property Rights

I.R.C. § 2043(b)(1) provides that a relinquishment or promised relinquishment of dower or curtesy, or of a statutory share created in lieu of dower or curtesy, or of other marital rights in the decedent's property or estate, are not considered to be consideration "in money or money's worth." Thus, a transfer of property by the estate of one spouse to another for the release of the marital property rights of the other spouse are not deductible under I.R.C. § 2053, unless any of the following *exceptions* apply.

In *Estate of Herrmann v. Commissioner*,[4] the Court denied an estate tax deduction for property left to a spouse pursuant to a prenuptial agreement on the grounds that the wife's waiver of any testamentary rights she might acquire on account of her marriage to the decedent did not qualify as consideration in money or money's worth pursuant to I.R.C. § 2043(b)(1).

In *Estate of Waters, Jr. v. Commissioner*,[5] the Court allowed an estate tax deduction for property transferred to a former spouse under a property settlement agreement. The Court held that I.R.C. § 2043(b) did not apply because the rights covered in the agreement did not fall within I.R.C. § 2043(b). Rather the Court determined that the agreement was more akin to an exchange of property amounting to an equitable nontaxable division of commonly owned property.

In *Estate of Kosow v. Commissioner*,[6] the Court allowed an estate a deduction for payments made to decedent's children pursuant to a separation agreement. The Court found that the decedent's promise to make bequests to his children was supported by full and adequate consideration from the decedent's former wife. The "adequate consideration" was the ex-wife's acceptance of monthly support payments that were substantially less than amounts necessary to maintain the lifestyle she had during the marriage; the ex-wife waived her rights to increased support; and decedent could have afforded to pay her more support than she agreed to receive under the agreement.

4. Deductible Payments

Payments from a decedent's estate to a surviving exspouse are deductible as a claim against the estate if any of the following four tests apply:

First, the payments are made pursuant to a decree of divorce entered by a court of competent jurisdiction.[7] To illustrate, if the obligation arises from a decree of divorce entered by a court of competent jurisdiction, the estate may deduct the remaining payments.

---

4. T.C. Memo. 1995-90 (1995), *aff'd*, 85 F.3.d 1032 (C.A. 2, 1996).
5. 48 F.3d 838 (4th Cir. 1995), *rev'g and remanding* T.C. Memo. 1994-194 (1994).
6. 45 F.3d 1524 (11th Cir. 1995), *vacating and remanding* T.C. Memo. 1992-539 (1992).
7. Treas. Reg. § 20.20534.

Second, the payments are made pursuant to a separation agreement that is incorporated in a decree of divorce issued by a court that has the power to alter or modify the decree or agreement.[8]

Third, the payments are made for the support of a spouse or their minor child or children.[9]

Fourth, the payments are made pursuant to an obligation created under a written separation agreement that qualifies under I.R.C. § 2516 (discussed earlier in Chapter 12.B.2). I.R.C. § 2043(b)(2) provides that a transfer of property that satisfies the requirements of I.R.C. § 2516(1) is considered to be made for full and adequate consideration in money or money's worth. Thus, I.R.C. § 2043(b)(2) allows an estate a deduction for transfers pursuant to claims arising under a written agreement of marital or property rights where the agreement would have qualified those transfers as nontaxable for gift tax purposes under I.R.C. § 2516. Thus, where the transferor dies prior to completing the transfer under the written agreement, the property transferred is deductible from the gross estate so that no estate tax will be imposed with respect to the property transferred by the estate. In essence, this exception conforms the estate tax treatment with respect to transfers of property to a former spouse under a written agreement with the tax treatment that allows a gift tax exemption for such transfers.

These exceptions incorporate the decree and support exceptions of the gift tax aspects discussed earlier.

5. Life Insurance

Where a payee spouse sued a payor spouse under the separation agreement for failure to name her as beneficiary of certain life insurance policies, a deduction under I.R.C. § 2053 was disallowed because the claim was founded on the separation agreement and not on the divorce decree. Thus, the divorce decree exception noted earlier was inapplicable, because there was no consideration as required under I.R.C. § 2053(c)(1)(A) where the claim is founded on the agreement.[10] See also Rev. Rul. 78379, 19782 C.B. 238, in which the IRS held that where a spouse was required to maintain a life insurance policy on his life naming his minor children as the beneficiaries, the spouse died and the policies were included in his gross estate, the payment of the proceeds to his children were not deductible. The IRS's reasoning was that the spouse's obligation to support his children ceased upon his death and, therefore, the support exception did not apply.

8. *See* Harris v. Comm'r, 340 U.S. 106 (1950); Rev. Rul. 75395, 19752 C.B. 370; Rev. Rul. 60160, 19601 C.B. 374.

9. Rev. Rul. 68379, 19682 C.B. 414; Rev. Rul. 7167, 19711 C.B. 271.

10. Estate of Satz v. Comm'r, 78 T.C. 1172 (1982).

6. Income Tax Deduction

The preceding applies to deductions from the gross estate for Federal estate tax purposes. On the other hand, an estate may not claim an income tax deduction under I.R.C. § 215 on its income tax return (Form 1041) for alimony payments. Such payments of alimony are treated as distributions to a beneficiary of an estate and, applying the conduit theory, are includible in the gross income of the beneficiary and deductible by the estate under the fiduciary income tax rules of I.R.C. § 682. The amount deductible is the present value of the obligation.[11] But see *Kitch v. Commissioner*,[12] in which the Tax Court rejected the petitioners' contention that the payee spouse must include in income alimony received from the payor spouse's estate only to the extent of the estate's distributable net income as computed under the conduit rules of part I, subchapter J. Instead, the court held that the full amount of the alimony paid was includible as income in respect of a decedent under I.R.C. § 691, which was alimony in character.

B. Transfers

If a payment is deductible under any of the aforementioned rules, a transfer of property under any of these rules will be excluded from the gross estate of the transferor.

For example, a transfer pursuant to a court decree, or a transfer pursuant to an agreement that is incorporated in the decree where the Court has the power to alter or modify the decree or agreement, is excluded from the gross estate of the transferor.

11. Estate of Van Horne v. Comm'r, 720 F.2d 1114 (9th Cir. 1983); Estate of Nesselrodt v. Comm'r, T.C. Memo. 1986-286 (1986).
12. 104 T.C. 1 (1995).

Index